C000304229

Town and Country Walks Guide

HOLIDAY WHICH?
Town and Country Walks Guide

Edited by Tim Locke

Published by Consumers' Association
and Hodder & Stoughton

Which? Books are commissioned and researched by
The Association for Consumer Research
and published by Consumers' Association Ltd
2 Marylebone Road, London NW1 4DX and Hodder & Stoughton Ltd
47 Bedford Square, London WC1B 3DP

Typographic design by Paul Saunders
Cover design by Dick Vine
Cover photograph, from Zefa, of Dunster in Somerset: see Walk 101
Walk maps by Tim Locke. County maps by David Perrott Cartographics
Special thanks to Humphrey Southall and Stephen Locke

British Library Cataloguing in Publication Data
Holiday Which? town and country walks guide. – (Which? books).
    1. Great Britain – Visitors' guides
    2. Locke, II. Series 914.104859

ISBN 0-340-51440-X

Typeset by Barbican Print & Marketing Limited, London
Printed and bound in The Netherlands
by Rotatie Boekendruk B.V., Krommenie

CONTENTS

Scotland

Wales

INTRODUCTION

Much has been written on the gentle art of putting one foot in front of the other. There's a good deal to be said about this ever-more-popular activity. As well as being a straightforward and excellent method of exercise, walking is undoubtedly one of the best ways to explore Britain. With 125,000 miles of public paths in England and Wales, and informally free access to much of Scotland, the choice for walkers seems endless.

This guide to over 180 town and country walks, covering much of Britain, is a highly selective anthology: every walk included has been chosen carefully, on the basis that it has a special appeal, for which it is worth going out of your way. Compiling the *Holiday Which? Good Walks Guide*, an earlier collection of walks to which this is a companion volume, we got to know both the British landscape and the subtleties of putting a walk together in such a way that it reveals the best of a locality – whether exceptional views, wild flowers or bird life, interesting villages, scenic splendour or historic buildings. As with the *Good Walks Guide*, the litmus test for inclusion of any walk has been whether we would do it again, purely for enjoyment.

Wherever possible, the walk forms a circuit. This can pose a problem, for example if half a route follows a scenic path along a cliff-top or attractive valley, and the other half is rather dull. We admit to including a few there-and-back walks, among them a walk near Snowdon and one at Kinlochleven. Occasionally you have to complete a route by public transport; this is particularly the case with our walks on the east coast of Scotland, where good bus services enable rambles along the coast between some very attractive fishing villages and towns, thereby avoiding a comparatively dull inland return.

A town and country theme

While most of the routes in this book are unmistakably rural in character, we have mapped out some complementary walks in small towns and even large cities. Some among these are comprehensive tours of fine historic centres, such as York, Edinburgh, Winchester and Bath; but rather more combine town and country elements, such as walk 125, which follows the River Swale away from the hill-top town of Richmond in the Yorkshire Dales, or walk 77, a stroll in ancient woodland deep in the South London suburbs.

We have not included trails in towns so small that a special guide would be superfluous: medieval England had a very small population and so the historic areas of many ancient towns and cities are extremely compact. We would have had to compensate for the brevity of the routes by detailing minutiae of local history – something local guide-books often do admirably. So we make no apologies for omitting some favourite small towns (particular gems being Bradford-on-Avon, Ludlow, Wells, Stamford and Warwick).

Country walks are mostly between four and seven miles long and of two to three-and-a-half hours' duration. We are delighted to have found good walks in areas not covered in the *Good Walks Guide*: there are routes in this volume in Northamptonshire, Bedfordshire, Lancashire, Dumfries and Galloway, the Yorkshire Wolds and County Durham. The Lake District, which yielded fourteen routes in the *Good Walks Guide* and a further twenty-one in the *Holiday Which? Guide to the Lake District*, has provided a few more of vintage quality. We apologise to readers in Nottinghamshire, Tyneside, the Isles of Man and Wight, Orkney and Shetland – we drew a blank in these places this time round.

What makes a good walk: our house rules

Finding a series of connecting paths in a scenic area is not enough. The walk must follow a pleasing sequence, so finding the most appropriate starting point is important.

The walk must be legal and physically manageable

To the best of our knowledge, none of the walks in the *Guide* involves trespass: they are all along public paths, bridleways, roads or permitted paths (see pages 17-18).

Although it's possible to turn an ankle on the gentlest stroll, none of these rambles should present an unacceptabe degree of danger, so we have excluded any route requiring climbing and scrambling, such as the bridgeless ravines and slithery scree slopes of the great high-level routes on the Scottish munroes, Snowdonia and among high Lakeland fells. One walk in the Torridons in the Scottish Highlands does necessitate crossing a gushing brook, but this merely means taking off shoes and socks and drying your feet afterwards.

A general snag is that stiles may go missing and paths become overgrown. There is a legal duty (see page 17), in England and Wales for local authorities to ensure that paths are not blocked. None of these routes was obstructed at the time of checking: if you find a path that is blocked, write to the local County Council (see How to complain, below). The start should be easy to find. If it is not, directions are given. We assume readers have a standard road atlas. There must be some car parking near the start, although this may simply be by the roadside.

The sequence of the walk should make the outing memorable

Opening stages should get you into the right mood straight away, and not be along a noisy main road or crunching over flat ploughed fields fringed by housing estates.

There should, ideally, be a pub or café halfway along the walk so that you can continue your walk feeling refreshed. The climax of the walk should not be too early: in this way, interest should be sustained throughout. Walk 164 on the isle of Lismore, Strathclyde, reaches a dramatically situated ruined castle after the toughest part of the walk, then towards the end offers views to the mainland from an ancient stone tower. Walk 27 in the Peak District has a splendid finale high up on Froggatt Edge, and walk 36 in South Devon ends with a charming riverside path along Bow Creek. The very end of the walk should not be too demanding on the feet or too difficult to follow.

Road walking should generally be avoided

This particularly applies to busy roads. Quiet lanes are often pleasant for a distance, but can become monotonous after a while. Nevertheless, some lanes are actually preferable to fiddly routes across fields or through forests. Road walking should never be more than a about a third of the total length (or time) of the route.

There should be plenty of attractions to sustain interest

These might include ridge walks, castles, stately homes, viewpoints, nature reserves, rivers, cliff-tops and attractive villages. The terrain should be as varied as possible: some of the best walks derive distinction from continuous changes of landscape, such as walk 107 in Surrey which leads through a complex landscape, around a wooded valley to emerge into hilly farmland with views suddenly opening out, then, right at the end, an impressive view from a heathy hill-top. Fortunately the British landscape lends itself admirably to varied short walks. Above all, the walk should have a sense of purpose, and give the walker a feeling of achievement.

The walk shouldn't demand great feats of navigation

We have been at pains to ensure that route-finding problems are kept to a minimum. Compass reading is not necessary for any of the walks in this book (although it is sensible to carry a compass to guide you through mist on upland walks, and we often refer to compass directions when describing views). Ways through forests and over moorland often pose difficulties, and we have spent many hours re-walking sections to make sure you have some landmark or a good path to guide you.

Obvious walks are excluded
Waymarked circuits, organised trails and there-and-back walks up
mountains or along long-distance paths may be splendid in their
own right but hardly need a guide to locate them; we have, however,
incorporated parts of ready-made walks into our own routes.

The walker should be walking into the view, not away from it
A gradual descent can be a glorious way of savouring views. At
Rhossili Down (walk 171) in Glamorgan, a sharp haul up to the
summit is rewarded by a marvellous stroll along a gently descending
moorland track with the whole of the Gower peninsula stretched
out ahead.

Holiday Which! Town and Country Walks Guide **cross references**
At the start of each county section, where the walks in that county
are listed and mapped, we also list the walks that appeared
in *Holiday Which! Good Walks Guide*, first published by
Consumers' Association in 1987 and available in bookshops or
direct from Consumers' Association, Castlemead, Gascoyne Way,
Hertford SG14 1LH.

Tim Locke

August 1990

How the walks are presented

Each walk is introduced by a summary telling you what to expect, including what the terrain is like, the ascent (if relevant), any potential problems of access (for instance, closure of an area during the shooting season), and how easy the route is to find. Next comes some basic information. **Length** and **time** (at an average walking pace, excluding stops) are stated for the full walk and any variants. **Difficulty** is graded from 1 to 5; for an explanation see the inside front cover. For the **start**, we assume readers have a standard road atlas and give further directions where needed. We have inserted a grid reference where helpful. The key on all Ordnance Survey maps explains how to use a grid reference, which will locate a point within 100 metres. Railway stations are stated, where relevant, but because of the uncertainties following the deregulation of bus services, it hasn't been possible to say which bus to take (enquire at the relevant bus station or Tourist Information Centre). **Ordnance Survey (OS) map numbers** are given, for those who want them, at 1:50,000 (*Landranger* maps, about 1 1/4 in to the mile) and 1:25,000 (*Pathfinder* maps, about 2 1/2 in to a mile) scales. Some of the latter are covered by Outdoor Leisure sheets which cover a larger area than the Pathfinder sheets. At present, Pathfinder maps have two sets of numbers, those based on the national grid e.g. TF 46/56, plus a Pathfinder number e.g. 784; eventually the latter will replace the former. We give both numbers in this guide. **Refreshments** covers pubs, cafés, restaurants and tea-rooms on the route, though it is possible that one or two have slipped through the net (please tell us if you find any more, or if any of those listed have closed). As it has not been possible to inspect the refreshment places, we do not make specific recommendations. Where no refreshments are listed, we found none.

The feedback we have had from checkers encouraged us to make the **walk directions** very detailed. We have broken up the text into numbered sections which refer to the map. If you feel confident of finding the way for one section, skip the text for a bit and pick it up later. As well as telling you where to turn right, left, and so on, we have peppered the text with 'confirmers' – features confirming that you're on the right path or helping you identify certain points on the route. Though we've always tried to use the most obvious confirmer, often the only way of identifying the route is by the tedious use of distances: this typically happens in woodland criss-crossed by paths and tracks, with few or no landmarks. We've paced these out carefully, and they should be followed carefully; the number of yards given is based on paces. Some otherwise useful 'confirmers' were thought likely to disappear: we have avoided the less permanent features such as dead trees, paths across arable fields and colours of houses. Particularly susceptible to disappearance are signposts, waymarks, gates and stiles and field boundaries: sometimes we mention several confirmers in one breath, for instance 'after 100 yards, immediately after shed, cross stile on right (signposted Exton), and proceed along left edge of field making for prominent barn'. If you come across a landmark noted in the text, which has changed or even disappeared, so making the directions hard to follow, please tell us about it (write to Dept CD, Association for Consumer Research, 2 Marylebone Road, London NW1 4DX).

On the route lists points of interest and occasionally references to other paths we tried, including unsuccessful ones, so that readers do not waste time. Although the directions do not include compass bearings, a compass can be useful to pick out landmarks from viewpoints.

Clothing

It might be worth your while investing in some of the following items of clothing (essential for the more taxing walks in this guide): which should make walking more comfortable.

Footwear Comfortable walking boots are essential for walks graded 3 – 4 and higher, and make the going noticeably easier on less demanding routes. Even if you plan to do walks only three or four times a year, it might be worthwhile to invest in a pair of walking boots. Providing they are cleaned after use, and treated with dubbin, they should last for years.

Some advantages are:

Ankle support. Rough ground is not confined to scree and boulders; it is quite possible to turn an ankle walking across a ploughed field.

Protection. If boots are well-dubbined, they should keep out most water. Boots also protect you against mud, branches, scree, wire and rough terrain.

Comfort. Boots that fit you properly will make walking far less tiring than will ordinary shoes. Wellington boots are quite good for wet, level walks of up to about four miles, but thereafter can begin to be uncomfortable. Stout shoes are generally fine for short lowland strolls, though the suction effect of mud can prise off shoes completely.

Socks Wear a thin pair next to the skin, then a thicker woollen pair (ideally, knee-length loopstitch type) over the top. Take a spare pair of each in case the others get soaked.

Trousers Corduroy or woollen trousers (or, even better, breeches) are the best; jeans restrict knee movement too much when wet and are not advisable. Overtrousers keep out the wind effectively; some brands are waterproof without causing the wearer to sweat. They are also a good means of keeping the mud off your trousers.

Jackets There is a wide range of anoraks, cagoules (nylon or 'breathable' man-made materials), and waxed cotton jackets on the market, and which you use is largely a matter of taste. For hill walks take two woollen sweaters – one thick and one thin – to help maintain your body heat in case the weather changes rapidly.

Gloves Take a pair that won't get soaked through in the rain; waxed wool or leather is best.

Hat A substantial amount of body heat is lost through the head: a woollen hat or balaclava, coupled with the hood of your jacket (in case of rain) should prove effective.

Other equipment Essential for hill and mountain expeditions (can be useful on less ambitious outings, too):

Compass Many of the upland routes in this book are easy to find in reasonably clear weather, but in thick mist all the landmarks can vanish and if you have no compass, you will have to rely on your sense of direction. This can quickly fail even experienced walkers.

Whistle For emergency use only; the distress signal is six blasts, repeated every minute.

Torch Useful for all types of walks in case you are benighted; can also be used for signalling. Take spare batteries.

Food and drink Water purifying tablets will enable you to drink spring water safely. Otherwise, emergency rations should include chocolate, mint cake or anything with plenty of sugar, to give you quick energy. Take some food with you for long lowland walks, too (especially those where no pubs or tea-rooms are listed in the text).

Survival bag To get into to avoid exposure.

Rucksack Even the cheapest day sack will be much more satisfactory (and safer, as it's easier to balance yourself) than a bag slung over your shoulder or carried in your hand.

OS maps Our sketch-maps and painstaking directions should (we hope) make it difficult for you to get lost on lowland routes, but in accordance with what we have said about the need to take a compass, an OS map for hill and mountain walks is essential in case of mist, or if you have to stray off the route (for example in an emergency).

First-aid kit Include plasters and a needle (which can be sterilised by passing it through a flame) for blisters; antiseptic cream; massage cream for cramp or other muscular discomfort.

Optional extras
Map-cases protect your map or this book from the elements. They are available at most camping and outdoor equipment shops and map shops, though it is quite possible to make one of your own with some thick, clear plastic and zip, stud or velcro fastening. A *folding pocket lens* (about 8x or 10x magnification; available at some optical shops) can add greatly to the enjoyment of wild flowers. A pair of *lightweight binoculars* is useful for bird-watching. The contents of a *vacuum flask* can warm you up on a cold hill-top.

Sense and safety on foot

Although we have not included in this guide walks that require great feats of navigation or an unacceptably high degree of physical danger, some of the hill and mountain walks could cause problems for anyone who isn't sensibly prepared. Even on the most innocuous-looking day, the weather on high ground can surprise you with a sudden change for the worse – mist, gale-force winds, blizzards or driving rain, for instance. Also, while serious risks on a lowland walk are fairly unlikely, suitable clothing will make the outing more comfortable and you should be able to cover greater distances without getting tired. Occasionally we refer in the text of the walks to areas of possible danger: a disused mine-shaft, or an eroded cliff path, for example. In researching the walks, we do not claim to have pinpointed every possible hazard, so you should generally take care.

Walking safely on the hills

Allow plenty of time and attempt only walks that are well within your capability. The grading system for standard of difficulty and rough timings are designed to help you choose the walks that suit you.

Time yourself carefully

The timings are rough ones, based on an average rate; you will need to add on estimated stoppage time for refreshments and looking at features of interest. Generally, two miles per hour is an average speed for lowland walking; quite a lot of time is spent crossing stiles and reading directions. Types of terrain that can easily be crossed include downland tracks, gentle descending mountain tracks, firm sandy beaches and old railway lines, where an average speed of three miles per hour is likely. Much slower are shingle beaches, mountain ascents, steep mountain descents, scree, boulders and boggy moorland, where you should reckon on an average speed of one mile per hour.

Slow and steady wins the mountain race

A useful rule for mountain ascents is to walk at a slow but rhythmic plod, a rate so gentle that you won't need to stop too often on the way and so can gain some momentum. A brisk pace can be exhausting and, except for the fittest and most experienced fell-walkers, is nearly always slower than the rhythmic plod over a long distance.

It is safest to walk in a group of at least four: if one member gets injured or ill, one can stay with him or her while the other two go off to find help. Learn some elementary first-aid. If bad weather conditions suddenly develop, huddle against a wall, boulder or anything else at hand, put on all the clothes in your rucksack and improvise a shelter with a survival bag or whatever is available. Do not rub to keep warm, or take alcohol, as both encourage blood to the surface of the body, which reduces the core body temperature.

Look after your feet
If your boot is rubbing unpleasantly, take it off immediately and put a plaster over the sore part before it develops into a blister. Blisters should be lanced with a sterilised needle, squeezed with a tissue and then covered with a cushioned plaster trimmed of its medicated gauze surround, which can otherwise aggravate the blister further.

Check the weather
Before setting out, check the local weather forecast. In National Parks, information centres should be able to help you; otherwise pre-recorded weather forecasts are provided by weather centres over the telephone. One way of telling what the weather will do in the next few hours is to stand with your back to the surface wind: if the clouds come from the right-hand side, it will probably improve; if the clouds come from the left-hand side, it will probably deteriorate; and if the clouds are moving in parallel, then there is unlikely to be a change.

Leave messages
Leave a note of where you are going with a hotel, youth hostel, tourist office or on a car windscreen. Be sure to tell them when you get back, otherwise a search party may be sent out.

Take the right equipment
See page 13.

Walking in the countryside: law and practice

To the best of our knowledge, none of the walks in this book involves trespassing or following obstructed footpaths. But if you're walking in the countryside it's useful to have an understanding of the rights and duties of visitors to it. The countryside isn't an open playground through which we can wander at will, but the law in England and Wales (see below for Scotland) gives you specific rights of access to parts of it. And even where there are no such rights, many landowners are happy to allow you on part of their property.

Paths for the walker

Public rights of way On these, you have a legal right of passage, and no one can stop you using it. Most rights of way are marked on Ordnance Survey (OS) maps. You can walk along a public right of way, whether it's a public footpath, a public bridleway (where you can also ride or cycle) or a byway (or 'road used as a public path', which you can often drive along). Such paths should, by law, be signposted where they leave a road, but in practice signs may be missing. On the way, a landowner, local authority, local footpath group or private individual may have waymarked the route, but waymarkings are far from universal. A recent change in the law as we went to press now makes it compulsory for landowners to waymark the way over private land and we hope this will make life much easier for the walker. The conventional symbols are yellow arrows for public rights of way, blue ones for bridleways and acorn motifs for Countryside Commission Long-Distance Paths.

Forestry Commission tracks and paths i.e. those that are not public rights of way. You have permissive access – which means you're generally welcome, but you cannot insist on any legal rights of access, so that tracks can be closed off, notably during tree-felling.

Canal towpaths Unless there is a sign to the contrary, you can usually use them.

Other paths and tracks If you find a well-trodden path or track but an OS map doesn't show it as a right of way, it isn't safe to assume you can use it. However, some landowners, including some private ones as well as, for example, local councils and water authorities, give permissive access to parts of their land (signposts or waymarks will confirm if this is so), and occasionally a new public right of way may have been created.

Land you are allowed on

Some commons A common is simply an area of land over which local people have various rights, for example, to graze cattle. There is not necessarily any legal right for the public to walk or picnic. But some privately owned common land is open to the public, and any local authority-owned common will have been set aside for public use.

Areas where 'access agreements' have been made Occasionally, a local authority will have made a formal agreement with a landowner to allow public access (except in some cases in the lambing or shooting seasons). These have occurred in some National Parks, but otherwise are rather uncommon. Notices will usually be displayed where public access is permitted.

Moorland Much moorland is owned privately, often for the purpose of raising game birds, and you should not assume you have access to it. But out of the shooting season the public is permitted access to many moorland paths and tracks.

Country parks and picnic sites The public has access if they are owned by a local authority.

Beaches Access is allowed if owned by a local authority, and usually if privately owned, too.

National Trust land including open land, beaches and woodland, often marked by signs and shown on OS maps. The public is allowed access unless there are notices to the contrary.

How to complain

If you want to complain about missing or broken stiles, ploughed-out paths, impenetrable vegetation, bulls, fierce dogs, missing signposts or other problems hindering your use of a public right of way, contact the rights of way section of the County Council, which may refer you to the District Council. The District Council holds the *County Definitive Map*, a record of rights of way, including the latest footpath diversions, closures and creations. It also has a legal duty to see that public rights of way are usable: it should provide signposts where a public right of way leaves a public road and is responsible for maintaining the surface of the right of way. Where necessary, it has a duty to put pressure on landowners to erect stiles and remove obstructions. Do report problems (we do), because otherwise the path may deteriorate further and fall into disuse. Local authorities will welcome reports (and may even rely on them) and though they may not have the resources to act immediately, they should look into it in due course. A quick telephone call should be enough.

Some questions answered

The path I want to use has a sign saying 'Trespassers will be prosecuted' and there's an irate landowner pacing towards me. What should I do?
If you are on a public right of way, legally there is nothing he can do to stop you. But if you are somewhere you have no right to be, then he is entitled to feel irate: you are trespassing and he can order you off his land by showing you to the nearest public right of way or road. If necessary, he can use reasonable force to evict you. He can sue you for trespass, but he won't recover much unless he can show you have caused damage – for example, to his livestock, crops or fences. Whatever the notice might say, you can't normally be *prosecuted* for trespassing on private land because this isn't a criminal offence, except on land owned by the Ministry of Defence or British Rail, or as a public order offence. (Despite this, however, this meaningless sign is still widely used, as our researches for this book have revealed time and time again).

The Ordnance Survey map shows a public path crossing a field, but I can see no trace of it. Am I entitled to follow the route?
Usually, yes – but make sure you follow the precise route. By walking the route you are quite within your rights, and are doing a service to others by marking the line of the path, and making the landowner aware that people want to use it. A path might be obscured by crops: you have a right to follow the route through them, but if they are really impenetrable you are entitled to skirt the field. There's a chance that the path may have been closed or diverted; if so, you could expect signs to that effect. By law, within two weeks of ploughing farmers must make good the surface of a public path which crosses a field, and must not plough paths which skirt fields. Unfortunately this law is often flouted.

I can see where the path goes, but I can't get to it. What should I do?
It's all too common for a path to be obstructed by rubbish, thick vegetation, fallen trees or barbed wire. You may remove just enough of an obstruction to allow you to pass, but be sure not to cause any unnecessary damage and ensure that no livestock can stray as a result of your action. It may be more practical to find a way round the obstacle, but if this takes you on to someone else's land, you are trespassing. By law a landowner must not keep a fierce dog which deters people from using a right of way. On the other hand, a farmer

19

can quite legally put a bull in a field crossed by a right of way, provided the bull is either of a non-dairy breed and is accompanied by cows or heifers, or is less than 11 months old. If such a bull (or indeed any bull) charges you, the farmer would be liable for damages if the bull injures you and he knew that the bull was dangerous.

Can the dog come with us wherever we go?
Generally, yes, and certainly on rights of way, provided you keep it under close control at all times. It is best to put the dog on a lead if you are crossing a field with livestock in it. A farmer is quite within his rights to shoot a dog that is worrying livestock – and the dog-owner could face prosecution. A dog can do untold damage to birds during the nesting season, and to other wildlife, even if it is doing no more than hunting along a hedgerow. It may also be unwelcome on moorland: some moorland areas display notices expressly prohibiting dogs.

There's an unfenced field with a pretty view: may we have a picnic there?
Don't assume that an unfenced field is intended as an open invitation, but provided you take your litter with you, you can normally picnic anywhere to which you're allowed access (see above). But you don't have any legal rights to do so, and you may have to move on if a landowner asks you to.

May I pick wild flowers and wild fruit?
As a general rule, leave wild flowers well alone. Some species are protected, and picking them is a criminal offence. In many areas it is permissible by consent or custom, although not by legal right, to gather wild fruit (particularly blackberries), provided you do not stray from the public right of way or area to which you are allowed access.

Scotland
The law and practice differs in two main ways. First, you do not have legal rights of access to much of the countryside or along many of its paths. But there is a tradition of relatively free access to moorland and mountain areas (subject to closure at certain times, principally deer-stalking and shooting seasons). And if a path is defined on the ground you may usually assume that you may follow it. In fields, keep to the edges. Second, such public rights of way as exist are not distinguished from other paths on OS maps, although they are normally signposted. Black dashed lines on OS maps can be anything from a right of way to an unfollowable route across moorland, and plenty of clear paths (sometimes even signposted ones) do not appear on OS maps at all. For further information on rights of way, contact the Planning Department of the District or Regional Council.

England

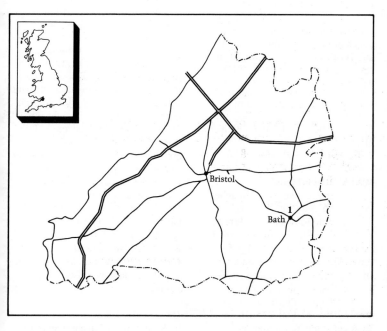

1 Bath

Holiday Which? Good Walks Guide

1 Burrington Combe and Dolebury Warren

Bath

Our finest Georgian city, Bath has been a tourist attraction since Roman times, and continues more than ever to attract visitors. So much of the 18th-century plan has survived that it is not difficult to imagine Bath in the days of Beau Brummel and Jane Austen.

Length 2 miles (3km), 3 hours
Difficulty 1
Start By abbey and Roman Baths in city centre
Refreshments Full range

WALK DIRECTIONS

(1) Go between west door of abbey [a] (on left) and Roman baths museum [b], to reach York Street, cross Abbey Street and take street opposite and slightly to right to enter Abbey Green [c], where immediately turn left into North Parade Passage [d].

At end, cross Pierrepont Street at traffic lights and take North Parade Road [e] opposite (signposted Warminster), cross river, then (2) immediately left down steps to river [f] where turn right towards Pulteney Bridge, where take steps up. Detour right (Great Pulteney Street [g]); continue left over the bridge [h] and at junction with High Street (abbey away to left) take Upper Borough Walls opposite and slightly to right. (3) Take first right into New Bond Street Place [i], turn left into New Bond Street which curves right and becomes Milsom Street [j].

Turn right at T-junction with George Street and first left into Bartlett Street (signposted Assembly Rooms). (4) Cross Alfred Street [k] and take Saville Row opposite, turn left along Bennett Street [l] to reach The Circus [m].

Exit right by Brock Street to reach Royal Crescent [n] and follow to far end of Crescent (5), then go left along Marlborough Buildings, then left (where railings on left end) on to tarmacked path running below Royal Crescent; after passing the Crescent, turn right at cross-junction, left along Royal Avenue.

(6) After road goes through ornamental gateway [o], turn left into Queens Parade Place [p], right into Gay Street [q] to enter left-hand side of Queen Square [r]. Take first left (Wood Street), turn right into Queen Street which becomes Trim Street [s] and continues after archway as Trim Bridge.

(7) Cross Upper Borough Walls, take Bridewell Lane opposite. At Westgate Street, take St Michael's Place opposite and slightly to right (signed to Little Theatre Cinema). (8) At Cross Bath [t], turn left into Bath Street; left at Stall Street and immediately right under colonnade to enter square by abbey and Bath House.

ON THE ROUTE

[a] Roman Bath Museum and Pump Room The Romans built the city of Aquae Sulis around these hot springs, where ¼ million gallons of hot water (120°F) gushes out daily, and dedicated a temple to goddess Sulis Minerva. In the 17th century, Queen Anne visited the baths and the city became a fashionable place to take the waters and indulge in romance; later, curative powers of the waters were claimed. The **Pump Room** was completed in 1791, and retains the opulence of the golden era of the city, a huge ballroom where you can sip tea by the Corinthian columns to the strains of the Pump Room trio while the statue of Beau Nash looks on. Up to 1939, visitors in attended Bath chairs would have been visible through the window outside. Adjacent is the **Roman Bath Museum**, where just 20 feet below street level you are taken straight back into 1st century Roman Britain and you encounter the famous bubbling sulphurous water; there is also a host of Roman finds from excavations. Edwardian statues of Roman emperors are lined along the edge of the great bath. Not to be missed, despite the crowds. (Open daily, 9-7 summer, 9-5 in winter.)

[b] **Bath abbey** The site is 1,200 years old – Edgar, first king of a united England, was crowned here in AD973 – but the church which survives from the abbey is largely 15th-century Perpendicular with 19th-century additions. Inspired by a dream of angels on a heavenly ladder, Bishop Oliver King rebuilt the Norman abbey; the **west front** depicts his dream. **Memorials** include those to William Oliver (creator of Bath Oliver biscuits), Isaac Pitman (who devised the phonetic alphabet and Pitman's shorthand) and Beau Nash (master of ceremonies in Bath, responsible for ensuring genteel behaviour of the citizens).

[c] **Abbey Green**   Once used by abbey monks as a bowling green, this small square shaded by a plane tree is a rare pre-Georgian survival in the city. Nelson reputedly stayed at the Crystal Palace tavern when it was a private house while he recovered from wounds received at the Battle of the Nile.

[d] **North Parade Passage**   (or Old Lilliput Alley) On left, **Sally Lunn's House**, dating from 1482, is the oldest residential building in Bath; its facade was originally on the abbey side. Here, 'Sally Lunns' (spongy tea-cakes) were first cooked. At the end of the passage, detour left and immediately left again for a slit-view of **Ralph Allen's Town House**, a fine baroque house at the end of a narrow alley. Ralph Allen, who was a patron of the arts and postal

reformer, bought stone quarries near Bath and played an important part in encouraging architect John Wood to adopt this material in the building of Bath in the 18th century.

[e] **North Parade Road** has attracted distinguished residents, including William Wilberforce and William Wordsworth (at No. 9), the Duke of York, brother of George III (at No. 10) and Oliver Goldsmith (No. 11).

[f] **River Avon** The abbey, parade gardens and city centre are in view, but it is primarily **Pulteney Bridge**, beyond the weir, that impresses. Robert Adam's design of 1774 features tollbooths at either end of the bridge and, like the Ponte Vecchio in Florence, shops built on the sides. It was constructed for William Pulteney, who had land in Bathwick, E of the river. On a hill in the far distance to the S stands **Prior Park**, built 1745 by Ralph Allen who wished to advertise the qualities of Bath stone.

[g] **Argyle Street**, to your right as you emerge on to the bridge, is, together with **Great Pulteney Street** (into which it merges), the longest and broadest of Bath's Georgian streets. The Holburne Museum at the far end is a fine arts museum with crafts centre. A 'Penfold hexagonal' post-box (1866) can be seen on left, just before the fountain.

[h] On left are the **Guildhall** (1776), with its fine banqueting room (open Mon-Fri 9-4.30) and the **Victoria Art Gallery** (open 10-6, 10-5 Sat, closed Sun and bank hols).

[i] On right at the end of New Bond Street Place, a plaque on right commemorates John Roebuck Rudge, co-inventor of the Biophantascope, the earliest form of moving pictures.

[j] **Royal Photographic Society** (on right halfway along the street). Early and contemporary photographs are exhibited together with antique

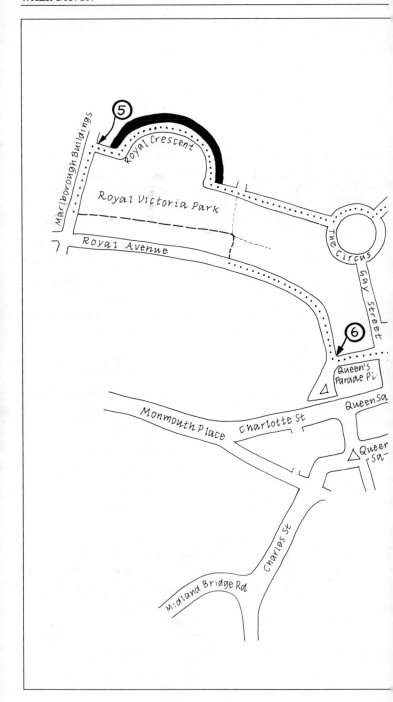

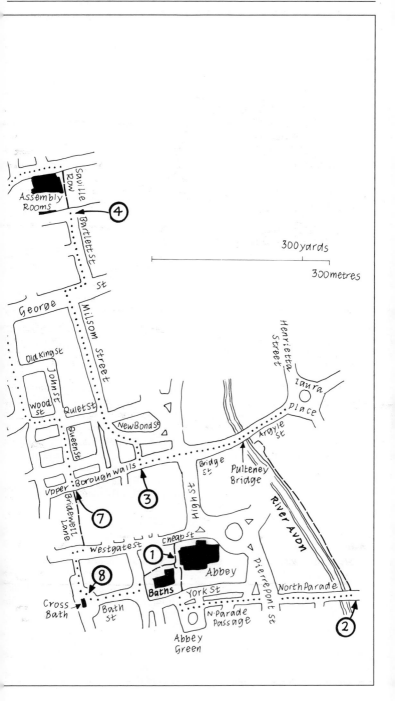

Assembly Rooms

Saville Row

Bartlett St

④

300 yards

300 metres

St

George

Milsom Street

Henrietta Street

Old King St

John St

Laura Place

wood St

Quiet St

New Bond St

Argyle St

Queen St

Bridge St

Pulteney Bridge

Upper Borough walls

③

High St

River Avon

Bridewell Lane

⑦

Cheap St

①

Westgate St

Abbey

Pierrepont St

⑧

Baths

York St

North Parade

Cross Bath

Bath St

N. Parade Passage

②

Abbey Green

photographic equipment. The building was originally the Octagon Chapel (1767); William Herschel, who in 1781 discovered the planet Uranus, was organist here.

[**k**] **Alfred Street** On left, **No. 14** has a bust of King Alfred over the porch and, by the entrance, conical snuffers for torches carried by 'link boys' to light the way for sedan-chairs. Above Alfred Street, the **Assembly Rooms** (1771), designed by John Wood the Younger, now houses a museum of costume, with a large collection of clothing and costume, toys and jewellery from the 16th century to the present.

[**l**] **Camden Works Museum** (Open 2-5 daily). *Turn right along Bennett Street, first left into Russell Street and turn right at the top).* An old tennis court converted to an industrial heritage centre, recreating a 19th-century brass foundry and a mineral water manufactory, together with a display on the extraction of Bath stone.

[**m**] **The Circus** An elegant circular Palladian composition of John Wood the elder, begun 1754. Among distinguished residents have been William Pitt the Elder (No. 7, 1755-67), Clive of India (No. 14, 1774), Thomas Gainsborough (No. 17, 1759), who was establishing himself as the fashionable portrait painter of the day, and David Livingstone (No. 13, 1864). All the way around this estate is a frieze of 528 motifs of art and science.

[**n**] **Royal Crescent** (1767-74) Not only the most famous street of its period in Bath, but one of the most noted in the world, the Crescent is the supreme masterpiece of John Wood the younger. Its grand sweep takes in 114 Ionic columns for its 30 houses. The site, high up, is exposed and Marlborough Buildings on the W side was added in 1790 as a windbreak; the 'ha-ha', or raised

bank, allowed an uninterrupted view of the grazing-land beyond. **No. 1**, open in summer (except Mon), gives a good idea of a typical town-house of the wealthy in Jane Austen's day. At **No. 11** lived Richard Brinsley Sheridan, who eloped with Elizabeth Linley in 1772.

[**o**] The lions on the **gateway** at the entrance to Victoria Park were installed in 1833.

[**p**] On right in Queens Parade Place are two booths, originally **sedan attendants'** houses, used by attendants while the passengers visited the houses in Queen Square.

[**q**] **No. 41 Gay Street** (on left; now offices). Home of John Wood the younger, and designed by his father. Through a ground floor window you can glimpse a round room, once used as the powder room.

[**r**] **Queen Square** (1729-36). This was the first major design of John Wood the elder (who made No. 24 his home), the **N side** being the finest – a complete composition rather than just a terrace of houses. In 1799, Jane Austen stayed with her brother Edward at **No. 13** (on the S side), where she probably revised *Northanger Abbey*, much of which is set in Bath. On the E side, **No. 4a** was the first to be built in the square.

[**s**] At **No. 5 Trim Street**, on left, General Wolfe lived with his parents. It is thought that it was here he heard he was to lead the expedition to Quebec in 1759.

[**t**] **Cross Bath** Standing in the centre of a small square, this structure encloses a bath where Mary of Modena, wife of James II, had a cross placed, in thanks for the birth of her child, (after she had bathed here). On right is the entrance to **St John's Hospital**, founded in 1174 for the benefit of the sick and poor. In the 18th century, the Duke of Chandos employed John Wood the elder to rebuild it.

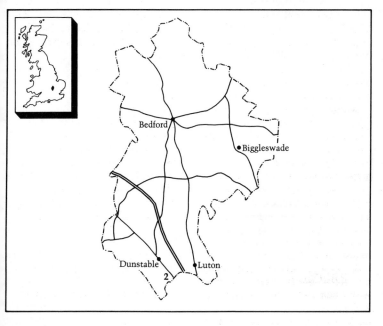

2 Dunstable Downs and the Tree Cathedral

Dunstable Downs and the Tree Cathedral

An excellent concentration of interesting features and varied scenery in a county not renowned for good walks. Route-finding a little complex at times but made easier by good waymarking.

Length 5 miles (8km), 2½ hours
Difficulty 2-3
Start Whipsnade Heath car park, at junction of B4540 and B4541 (S of Dunstable). Grid reference 016180
OS maps 1:50,000 166; 1:25,000 TL 01/11 (Pathfinder 1095)
Refreshments Pubs at Whipsnade

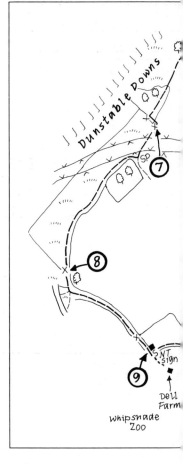

WALK DIRECTIONS

① Take path through barrier out of car park, immediately fork right and go forward at a cross-junction near bench 30 yards later [a]. Keep forward after 180 yards at next cross-junction, to reach barrier out of woods, where go forward with fence and field on left.

② Cross stile, go across field towards stile (with house beyond), and turn right on road. After 80 yards (just after barn on left) take signposted stile on left, and follow enclosed path until taking stile on left, on to track along which turn right. Soon, go over cattlegrid and keep along right edge of field as waymarked, leaving the track but rejoining it a little further down; ignore another track forking left, but follow main track which passes just to right of barn (gate in front of barn is hard to open: access is via concealed stile just to left of it) ③.

Beyond the barn, continue forward to enter field and go along its left edge. After 100 yards, take stile on left and head up diagonally towards stile by signpost and wooden power-post. Proceed along long field, keeping level and midway up the slope (the top of which is on your right).

④ At end, cross stile and follow woodland path to reach field where keep left [b] on track along edge of field. After 250 yards, leave track where it bends left, and enter field on right by waymark post, immediately keeping left along left edge of field (roughly towards mast).

⑤ 50 yards after passing under power-lines, take waymarked narrow path on left into woods, then soon keeping along right edge of field to road. Turn right on road. ⑥ At T-junction with main road, go forward, across grass until low scrubby trees (visitor centre nearby

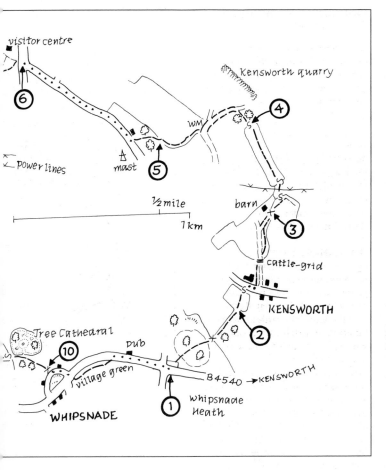

to right), in front of which turn left along the level, on path running closely to top of edge of Dunstable Downs escarpment, with view on right [**c**]. This is soon enclosed on both sides by scrub, and reaches gate by National Trust sign (leading into big field crossed by pylons): do not go through the gate but turn left uphill to take next gate ⑦.

Proceed along the top edge of this field. Just after passing under second set of power-lines ignore bridleway signpost pointing left. ⑧ At end of field, go through gate, keep alongside bushes at top of slope, past waymark post after 30 yards and 40 yards later bearing to left (again waymarked) into bushes to follow enclosed path for 1/4 mile [**d**] to reach signpost just beyond modern house ⑨.

Turn left to take stile by National Trust sign for Whipsnade. Follow right edge of field towards woods; go over stile into woods and immediately keep left to enter grassy area fringed by planted trees (Tree Cathedral [**e**]). Go forward as waymarked, with trees on your right for 150 yards, until broad gate gives access to track ⑩. Go forward to large green in Whipsnade village [**f**] and turn left along B4540 (or walk along green) to reach starting point.

ON THE ROUTE

[a] **Whipsnade Heath** A medieval clearing in the woods, with the trees now partly re-established; hollows here are chalk and flint excavations made by commoners in previous centuries. A circular path encompasses the heath.

[b] To the right, **Kensworth quarry** is worked by a cement company, but it is designated a Site of Special Scientific Interest because of the opportunities its exposed faces present for the study of chalk formations and fossils.

[c] **Dunstable Downs** Chalk downland, owned by the County Council, rising 800 feet above sea level with a view over Ivinghoe Beacon, Totternhoe Knolls and the SE Midlands. There may also be gliders to watch, from the nearby London Gliding Club. Diverse flora, birdlife and insect life.

[d] This **green lane**, or 'holloway', is part of an ancient route from Whipsnade to Eaton Bray, superseded after 1800 by the present road to the W.

[e] **Tree Cathedral** Created by Edmund Kell Blyth who planted a variety of species in the form of a cathedral, representing transepts, cloisters, chapels and nave. The dew pond commemorates two friends killed in the First World War. Blyth was inspired by the building of Liverpool's Anglican cathedral. Services are sometimes held, and explanatory maps are displayed. Now owned by the National Trust, but free access is always available.

[f] **Whipsnade** Attractive village with huge green; houses around it date from 17th century.

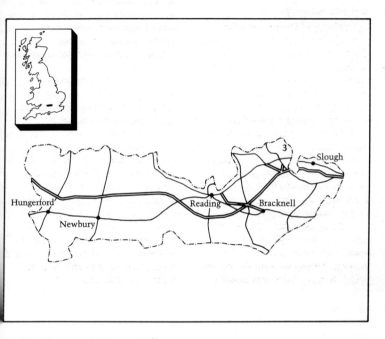

3 Cookham and Winter Hill

Holiday Which? Good Walks Guide

Cookham and Winter Hill

A Thames Valley route full of interest, beginning over fields and through beechwoods. The southern edge at Winter Hill adds drama, when the walk descends to join the Thames towpath into Cookham.

Length 6½ miles (10.5km), 3½ hours
Difficulty 2
Start Cookham Moor National Trust car park, just W of Cookham (N of Maidenhead), opposite small bridge (there is National Trust sign 'Footpath Cockmarsh' at car park). Grid reference 893854
By train Cookham (limited Sunday service in summer). Leave station on side by shops, follow road ahead then left just before The Gate Pub into Poundcroft Lane; proceed ahead along gravel track to reach road. Left then immediately right on to gravel track, 50 yards later cross signposted stile into golf course at ②.
OS maps 1: 50,000 175; 1:25,000 SU 88/98 (Pathfinder 1157)
Refreshments Pubs in Cookham Dean; pubs, café and tea-rooms in Cookham

WALK DIRECTIONS

① With your back to road, leave car park at far left-hand corner by footpath signpost to cross low footbridge over stagnant water, and crossing a stile to proceed along right edge of field (with tree-lined ditch on right).

When field narrows (50 yards before end) bear left up slope to stile then continue along narrow enclosed path. Emerge on to gravel track, turn right to stile 50 yards away (or left to return to station; left on road then immediately right along Poundcroft Lane), to enter golf course ②. Follow edge of golf course; where fence on left ends, keep forward across railway bridge.

On other side continue straight ahead, slowly climbing through middle of golf course, passing just to right of brown corrugated building, then soon with hedge on left. Where hedge ends, turn left on to fenced path shortly to reach road ③.

Cross road and take path opposite: proceed with fence on right, to reach road by stile beside gate, just to right of white buildings (with red roof) of Hillgrove Farm. Continue ahead down Alleyns Lane to road T-junction at bottom, where turn right along Dean Lane for 70 yards, then turn left steeply up Warners Hill, either by following the road or using short parallel path on right.

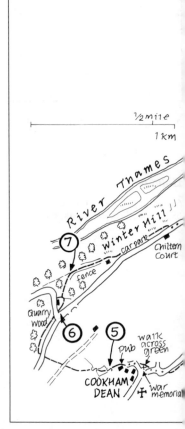

④ At T-junction at Uncle Tom's Cabin (pub), turn right (either along road or along grass of Hardings Green). After the green, road bends right; at junction just after this bend, keep left, then immediately turn right across middle of Cookham Dean village green in direction of pub sign for Hare and Hounds [a].

On reaching pub buildings turn right on narrow signposted path, through copse to reach stile ⑤, where continue slightly left in field ahead, soon with wire fence on right to find stile in far corner at edge of small valley. Maintain direction down through middle of next field to

reach track at valley bottom; proceed ahead up the other side to double power-post.

Emerge on road, take narrow woodland path opposite, then turn right after 25 yards on path that runs closely parallel to road. ⑥ At road junction cross Quarry Wood Road and take enclosed path opposite, just to right of house garden, and follow to T-junction of paths where turn left for 15 yards; then where iron fence on right ends, take path on right (*note* if path from Quarry Bank Road is too overgrown, turn left along that road, then after 100 yards, just after last house, turn right on

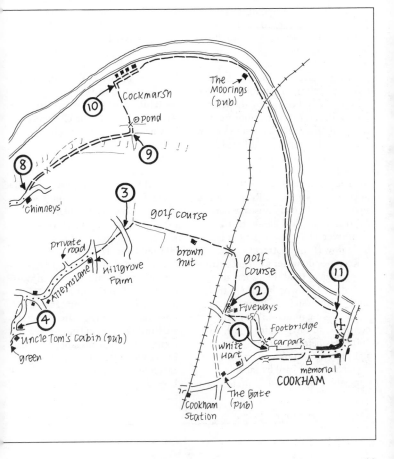

33

path then left 70 yards later, just where iron fence is about to begin on left). At this point there was a metal post (remains of signpost) at time of inspection.

Follow path through woods (there are white arrow-markers on trees); soon ⑦ reach top of edge, where path bends to right. Fence soon begins on right; ignore a sharp left turn. Join gravel drive for 20 yards, then just before road turn left along narrow path to emerge on top of Winter Hill [**b**].

Continue along top of hill, keeping off road on your right for as long as possible, but rejoining road near house called Chiltern Court; ignore left road turn (Gilbraltar Lane) soon after. ⑧ 30 yards beyond house called Chimneys, fork left down broad gravel track by National Trust sign for Cockmarsh [**c**].

30 yards after passing gate beside stile, ignore minor left fork (which descends) but keep along the level; 100 yards later ignore minor right fork (which ascends). Soon the main track gently drops. ⑨ At bottom of slope bear left to gate beside stile and signpost, and follow path across field across houses, to reach corner of concrete farm road. Keep forward towards the line of houses, where ⑩ turn right, still along the track join River Thames towpath at last bungalow (Ferry Cottage).

Keep beside water's edge, continue along edge of field then soon along well defined towpath close to the river, with houses on your right. After passing under railway bridge, continue on towpath for 1 mile. ⑪ 100 yards before next bridge, turn right to enter Cookham churchyard.

Leave churchyard by far side opposite house called Churchgate;

turn left and continue ahead to reach road; turn right then right again along length of Cookham High Street [**d**]. After war memorial, walk along surfaced path (raised causeway). Just before causeway crosses brick bridge, turn right down steps and cross road to return to car park.

ON THE ROUTE

[**a**] **Cookham Dean** Kenneth Grahame, author of *The Wind in the Willows*, used to stay here as a child with his grandmother. His uncle used to take him on the river, where he discovered the attractions of messing about in boats. In later life, when he became Secretary of the Bank of England, he came back to live at Mayfield, 1906–1910. *The Wind in the Willows* began as a series of bedtime stories for his son, Alastair, and was shaped into a book and published in 1908.

[**b**] **Winter Hill** Fine views across the Thames Valley to the Chilterns.

[**c**] **Cockmarsh** 130 acres of flat, marshy meadows and steep chalk slopes, preserved by the National Trust and designated as a Site of Special Scientific Interest. It had five ancient burial mounds, only one of which is now discernible. An excavation in the last century revealed two cremated bodies.

[**d**] **Cookham** The artist Stanley Spencer was born here in 1892; throughout his life, Cookham was an essential source of his inspiration. Such paintings as his *Resurrection* (in the Tate Gallery) are firmly rooted in the Cookham scene. The Spencer Gallery is open Easter-Oct, daily: 10.30-5.30; Nov-Easter Sat, Sun and Bank Hols, 11-1, 2-5.

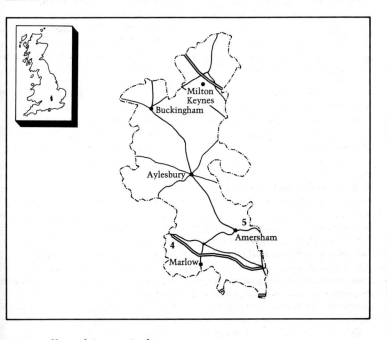

4 Turville and Stonor Park
5 The Chess Valley

Holiday Which? Good Walks Guide

70 Bradenham and West Wycombe
71 Hampden House and Coombe Hill

Turville and Stonor Park

A quiet corner of the Chilterns, offering an enjoyable blend of mixed woods and open farmland; route passes through the deer park of Stonor House. The rolling nature of the terrain gives changes of altitude, but there are no steep climbs.

Length 8½ miles (13.5 km), 4 hours
Difficulty 2-3
Start Turville, W of High Wycombe and S of M40. Grid reference 767912
OS maps 1:50,000 175; 1:25,000 SU 68/78 and SU 69/79 (Pathfinder 1156 and 1137)
Refreshments Pubs at Turville, Pishill and Stonor

WALK DIRECTIONS

① Start on the village green in Turville, between the Bull and Butcher pub and the church [**a**]. Walk down village street to left of church; at end of village, by Turville village sign, turn left down track marked by public bridleway sign. Follow track through belt of trees and for 300 yards along left hand edge of field, ignoring turn to left half way down side.

② At corner (which is not very clear-cut), turn left into wood on clear path, but after 10 yards turn sharp right and slightly uphill. After 20 yards, this path divides; take left hand fork, as indicated by arrow on tree, and go diagonally up hill on narrow but clear path.

At top of slope turn right along woodland track, which continues to ascend and then runs along just inside top edge of wood, with field on left. After 500 yards, just before end of wood, turn left at T-junction of tracks towards buildings of Turville Court. Turn right on surfaced farm road by house and continue down this to the road junction ③.

At the junction, go up bank to right

and over stile into field, following public footpath sign. Cross field to closest point on far hedge, then turn left following hedge towards Turville Grange. Shortly before house, go right over stile and then turn left towards house. Soon cross another stile into garden and maintain direction down track to left of house. At end of wall on left, go through gate out on to Turville Heath then bear slightly right and emerge in front of house [**b**].

Turn left on surfaced track,

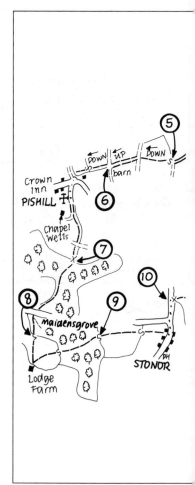

opposite wrought-iron gates to house, and follow to public road at junction. Turn right along road signposted to Northend and Watlington. ④ 70 yards later, at next road junction, continue forward on signposted footpath taking direction from sign to 'Saviours'. Path goes to left of gate to Saviours and immediately enters (first) field by gate. Keep to left of house keeping level and making for stile into second field. Continue forward to stile into third field, then

maintain direction (diagonally) to reach kissing-gate and turn right on to fenced track.

Track soon enters field (but continues with fence on right). Follow track into next field; ⑤ after 100 yards, track divides (with left fork leading towards Stonor village, visible in its valley): take right-hand fork, marked by white arrows. Soon cross stile and descend to bottom of valley on well-defined field path to open-sided barn. Keep right of barn and then ascend to ridge, ignoring

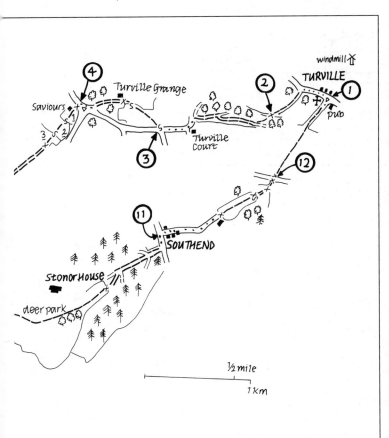

crossing path. Path becomes track.

⑥ At top of rise cross surfaced lane. Continue downhill alongside hedge on left to cross stile at corner of field and continue on broad path, (past house and garden on left), to further stile. Turn left on track, soon reaching road where turn right. After 50 yards on road, turn left on surfaced lane signed to Pishill church and marked as Oxfordshire Way (pub is 100 yards detour to the right along road).

Pass Pishill church on your right then, at end of the lane, take footpath to left of entrance to Chapel Wells, on footpath marked 'PS22, OW'. After 75 yards, take left-hand fork marked OW, then down left edge of field. At bottom, ignore cross-track and continue up edge of field to enter wood ⑦. Continue forward into woods on footpath going uphill, and at top of rise maintain direction keeping field visible on right.

¼ mile into the woods, fork left (the right fork goes towards nearby house), now descending gently towards road. Cross road, and take right-hand path opposite (the narrower of two paths): this ascends through woods with edge of woods close on right.

After 200 yards, and shortly before end of woods, ignore stile on right but 20 yards later ⑧ take stile ahead to emerge into field. Continue straight ahead across field towards farm buildings, but at end of field do not leave field; instead, turn sharp left on to path running diagonally across the field, keeping just to the left of a pylon, to stile.

Cross this stile into woods and continue forward downhill on woodland path marked by white arrows, ⑨ to enter field by stile: continue forward and make for village of Stonor clearly visible at the bottom of the slope (crossing

this and the next field, then following enclosed path into the village). Turn left on road (or detour 100 yards to right for pub).

⑩ After 300 yards, iron railings around Stonor Park start on right: here enter park through gate by sign 'Private Deer Park' and take grassy path heading uphill and away from fence towards a line of trees. Follow the line of trees as path becomes better defined and marked by white arrows [c].

After ½ mile, leave the deer park by a gate into wood. Ignore side turns (keep forward at first junction; ¼ mile later, near edge of woods, avoid left and right turns) and proceed up to road. Turn left along the road for 100 yards to minor junction at hamlet of Southend, where ⑪ turn right on surfaced track marked as public footpath, keeping small common on right. At end of common, keep to left of pair of brick houses and take farm road signed to Southend Farm.

Follow this concrete track to end of farm buildings, and when track swings right around buildings continue forward over stile beside gate marked by white arrows. Cross field keeping just to the right of pylons to gate beside stile in middle of far edge, then steeply down fenced track through wood. At end of wood, take gate beside stile directly ahead, (ignore gate to left), then descend down left hand edge of field to gate beside stile and road ⑫.

Cross road and enter field by gate beside stile, then forward across field; when inspected, this path was very well defined but if unclear take direction from windmill on hill ahead [d]. At end of field, enclosed path continues ahead, emerging after 200 yards on road by bungalows. Follow this down to main village street and starting point.

ON THE ROUTE

[a] **Turville** is a small village with a number of attractive half-timbered houses and a flint church of Norman origin with a 16th-century tower.

[b] **Turville Grange** 18th-century, with fine facade.

[c] View of **Stonor House**, its walled garden, and private chapel. Home of the Stonor family for 600 years, the original Tudor manor was extended in Tudor times, and a new roof and windows added in 1760. During the Elizabethan religious troubles, the Jesuit, Edmund Campion, had a secret printing-press here.

[d] **Cobston Windmill** 18th-century smock-mill (with rotating top portion).

The Chess Valley

The walk takes in three attractive villages and varied and unspoilt country in and around the Chess Valley: green hills, patched with woodland, and two imposing houses. Paths are well-walked but because of the intricate nature of the terrain the directions should be followed carefully.

Length *Full walk* 6½ miles (10.5km), 3 hours *Short walk omitting Sarratt* 3 miles (5km), 1½ hours
Difficulty 2-3
Start Car park (grid reference 005982), ¼ mile north of A404, 2½ miles NW of Chorleywood; turn off

A404 at E end of Little Chalfont into Stony Lane (signposted Latimer and Flaunden); car park is on left just where woods begin
By train Chalfont and Latimer. Leave by exit on London-bound platform, turn right outside station, left into Bedford Avenue, then right into Chenies Avenue, which follow to its end, ignoring side turns; where it becomes unsurfaced continue into woods, where pass to far side of fence 20 yards away and take right-hand of two paths which descend through the woods: start walk at ②.
OS maps 1:50,000 176, or 165 and 166; 1:25,000 SU 89/99 and TQ 09/19 (Pathfinder 1138 and 1139)

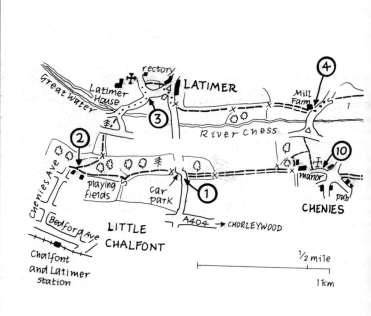

Refreshments Pubs at Church End and Chenies; pub and shop at Sarratt

WALK DIRECTIONS

① From car park follow road downhill 50 yards, then take bridleway on left, which follows top edge of woods. After ¼ mile, ignore stile on left into playing field, but continue inside edge of woods.

¼ mile later pass close to modern house, then 100 yards later turn sharp right to other side of fence (or to return to Chalfont and Latimer station, turn left through barrier into Chenies Avenue) on descending woodland path ②.

At bottom of woods, go through barrier (with Latimer House visible on hill ahead), follow right edge of field, then cross road and take signposted gate opposite, along left edge of small field to road junction, where continue forward, over bridge [**a**], along road.

③ At T-junction, turn left, then opposite path to church [**b**], take narrow path on right into field. Cross field diagonally, making down to houses, then follow path between hedges into main part of Latimer. Cross village green, turn right on road, then left 80 yards later by signpost, into field. Follow fence on left until it reaches a corner, then forward 80 yards to corner of next fence, walking parallel with River Chess away to right; proceed

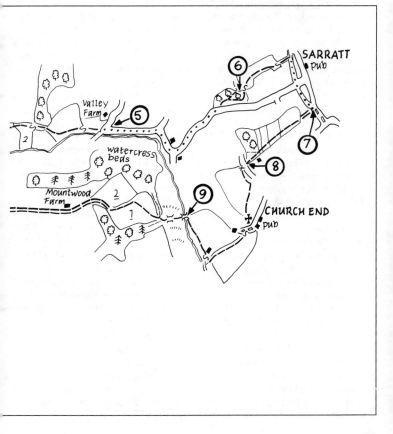

alongside this fence. After next field, continue on farm track, through farm, to reach road ④.

For short walk turn right and follow road over river, then bear right where road divides, to reach T-junction, where take path opposite into woodland. Immediately fork left and follow path up left edge of woods, then proceeding on path between hedges to reach Chenies church and manor house; this is point ⑩ (resume walk directions with church on right; route will now return to the woods you have just left).

For full walk turn left on road, then right after 100 yards to take signposted stile: route is along top of pronounced grassy bank (marking old field boundary). Follow left edge of second field, then through woods, on other side of which keep right, soon joining river; in next field continue alongside river to reach corner of farm road ⑤ (left leads past Valley Farm), where keep forward for ¼ mile [c], to join corner of another road. Turn right along this, then left at next junction (ahead is cul-de-sac), 50 yards after woods begin, take signposted footpath on left; keep left at fork, close to edge of woods.

⑥ Ignore gate beside stile on left (just after water hydrant) leading out of woods but continue forward to stile into field: follow right edge of field, then at end take path into Sarratt [d]. Turn right along village green. ⑦ Just after pillar-box and post office, take lane on right, signposted Church End; after last house, cross stile and follow left edge of four fields, enter woods and fork left 20 yards later; path runs along ramshackle fence then in same direction behind back gardens, before reaching lane ⑧.

Take kissing-gate opposite, turn left in field alongside woods, then

forward to church. Emerge by church gate on to lane [e], bear half right (over stile) towards signpost (for Chorleywood) 30 yards away, where cross driveway and take stile into field. Turn right in field, along edge, to bottom corner, then go forward on track; turn right a few yards later to pass below cottage and over stile. Walk close to river.

⑨ At end of field, turn left, over footbridge. Path then crosses another footbridge (over channel), immediately after which avoid right fork. On entering woods, fork right, enter bottom of field which cross diagonally (waymarked), uphill. On reaching opposite hedgerow, follow it uphill, and in next field proceed along left edge to pick up farm track leading past left-hand side of farm, then on ⅓ mile to Chenies [f].

Take gravel driveway on opposite side of village green, to church ⑩, just after which turn right on path between walls. Descend into woods, where turn left, along top edge. 120 yards later, fork left to continue along top edge. Soon emerge from woods, pass just to right of silos and barn, then 30 yards later take woodland track on right. Ignore side-turns; track soon leaves woods; proceed to reach road by car park.

ON THE ROUTE
[a] The first of a series of fine views over the **Chess Valley**; the Chess in this section has been dammed to create a landscaping effect for Latimer House, the grandiose 19th-century, Elizabethan-style mansion (now a National Defence College), on the hillside.
[b] **Latimer** A handsome early 18th-century rectory close to the church; the rest of the village surrounds a trim village green. Look out for the wooden sheep 'grazing' in the field crossed on the way from the church to the village.

[c] On the right are **watercress** beds.

[d] **Sarratt** has a half-mile-long village green flanked by mostly 18th- and 19th-century cottages.

[e] The Norman church, early 19th-century almshouses and pub at **Church End** make an appealing group. The next section is one of the walk's visual highlights, with views over the Chess Valley, and a descent to the river, which is marshy and remote-feeling.

[f] **Chenies** has a triangular village green flanked by estate cottages built in the 1850s by the Earl of Bedford. The church is heavily restored, but worth a look for the spectacular array of 16th-century and 17th-century monuments in the Bedford chapel. Adjacent is the step-gabled and brick-turreted Elizabethan manor house, with a shell of one wing at the rear open to the elements.

CAMBRIDGESHIRE

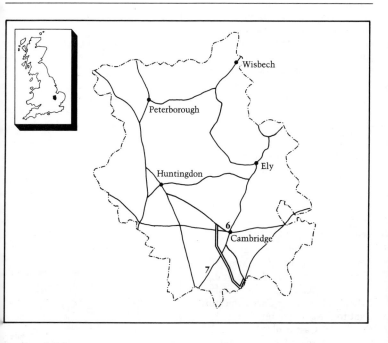

Holiday Which? Good Walks Guide
106 Wicken Fen

Cambridge

The Backs, with its immaculate gardens and pastures, provides some of the most famous views of the colleges; but less familiar are other parts of the riverside and the green swathes that almost encompass the historic city. The colleges are private, but you can walk through the courts (except at exam time).

Length 3 miles (5km), 4 hours
Difficulty 1
Start Market Hill (market-place)
Refreshments Full range

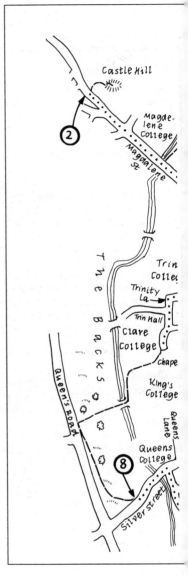

WALK DIRECTIONS

① From Market Hill with Great St Mary's church behind you, take Market Street (to left of Marks & Spencer). Turn left into Sidney Street [a] (becomes Bridge Street) [b], and cross river at Magdalene Bridge [c]; detour ahead up hill, pass traffic lights, and just after Castle Inn turn right to the grassy mound of Cambridge Castle [d] **②**.

Return across Magdalene Bridge, turning left on other side on to walkway by river, soon past Spade and Becket pub and on to Jesus Green. **③** At footbridge over river (do not cross), take the middle of three surfaced paths on your right (the other two are both along avenues of trees), leading to end of Lower Park Street, which you cross and take gate into Jesus College grounds (to left of end of house terrace; if pedestrian gate is locked, turn right along Lower Park Street, first left and left into Jesus Lane to reach college gate on other side).

Keep to right-hand side of college buildings, past a modern block, and leave by main gate by porter's lodge (detouring around college to see Cloister Court and chapel [e]) on to Jesus Lane opposite church **④**. Turn left and then right into Manor Street, then left along King Street.

Just after Champion of the Thames pub, turn right into Milton's Walk and after 20 yards (after bollards) turn left, past tennis courts on right and follow edge of park to main road. Cross road by pelican crossing to your right, and **⑤** proceed along grassy area of New Square [f]; leave

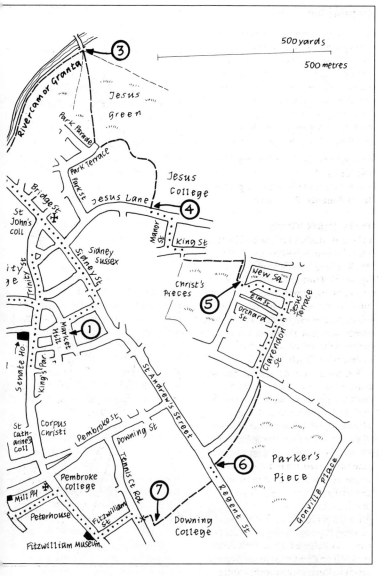

the square by its far right-hand corner bearing right into Jesus Terrace (which continues as Clarendon Street [**g**]).

Cross main road and follow right-hand side of large grass area (Parker's Piece) [**h**] to reach main road (Regent Street) by traffic lights and University Arms Hotel ⑥. Cross road, turn left and right after 30 yards through gates into Downing College. Follow main gravel track through college grounds.

⑦ Opposite Howard's Building (the last college building on left) turn right through small gateway

47

and immediately left to take gate
into Tennis Court Road. Turn right
and immediately go left into
Fitzwilliam Street. Reach main road
opposite Fitzwillam Museum [i],
turn right [j].

By church [k] turn left into Little
St Mary's Lane and turn right at end
of street by river, to reach bridge by
Mill pub (where you can divert over
the bridge and turn left to walk
around the grassy area of Coe Fen).
Pass the Mill pub, continue ahead
past bollards along alley (Laundress
Lane), past Anchor Inn to emerge on
to Silver Street, which you cross
(you can detour right and then left
into Queen's Lane for entrance to
Queen's College [l]).
Turn left to cross Silver Street
Bridge. ⑧ At end of college
buildings on right, by signpost for
Backs, fork right on to path skirting
area and veering to right until
emerging on Queens Road by traffic
lights. Immediately take gateway on
right to King's College [m].
⑨ Continue to left of the chapel
past Clare College [n] on your left
and proceed along Trinity Lane past
Trinity Hall, which bends right to
Trinity Street ⑩. Explore Trinity
Street to the left entering Trinity [o]
and St John's colleges [p] on your
left; return along Trinity Street to
King's Parade and Great St Mary's
Church.

ON THE ROUTE

[a] **Sidney Sussex College** One of the
smaller colleges, largely rebuilt in
the 1820s by Jeffry Wyatt who is
best known as the rebuilder of
Windsor Castle. Oliver Cromwell
was a student here.
[b] **The Church of the Holy
Sepulchre (the Round Church)** Dates
from about 1130, but much restored.
One of five medieval churches in
England with a circular nave.
[c] **Magdalene College** A college

which has often attracted the smart,
the fashionable and the sporting
fraternity. The diary of Samuel
Pepys is in the library.
[d] **Castle Hill** No castle remains,
but this is the highest point in
Cambridge, offering a view over the
city. St John's College chapel is the
most prominent building, but King's
College chapel and the University
Library are also in sight.
[e] **Jesus College** Its position a little
apart from the other colleges
inspired James I's remark that he
would like 'to pray at King's, dine at
Trinity, and study and sleep at
Jesus'. The chapel is a fine one:
medieval, with work by Pugin.
William Morris, Burne-Jones, Sterne
and Coleridge studied here.
[f] **New Square** This attractive square
has been rescued in recent years
from being a permanently clogged
car park – a reflection of the stern
efforts the City Council has made to
keep traffic out of the centre.
[g] **Orchard Street**, leading off to the
right is a demure little street,
carefully renovated, of single-
storeyed shuttered cottages with
unusually steep roofs.
[h] **Parker's Piece** The great Surrey
and England batsman Jack Hobbs
played much of his early cricket
here.
[i] **Fitzwilliam Museum** (Tue-Fri
lower galleries 10-2, upper galleries
2-5; Sat 10-5 (all departments); Sun
2.15-5 (all departments; closed Mon).
Time is needed to do any justice to
the magnificent collection of art and
antiquities, but a visit to the
entrance foyer is recommended for a
glimpse of the palatial interior.
[j] **Peterhouse** The oldest college,
founded 1284. Thomas Gray, author
of the celebrated *Elegy*, had rooms
facing Trumpington Street. He was
terrified of fire and had a bar built
into his window to facilitate the use
of a rope-ladder. The story runs that

a group of students hoaxed him by shouting 'Fire!' Gray made his escape to the pleasure of the crowd and subsequently decamped up the road to Pembroke College. The bar is still visible.

[k] Hobson's Conduit The deep gutter on both sides of the street was named after a local innkeeper who was the origin of the expression 'Hobson's choice': the traveller could choose any horse he wanted from the stable, providing it was the one next to the door.

[l] Queen's College Unlike the other colleges in character; the contrasts it offers between mellow red-brick and black and white give the buildings a quality of their own. The great Dutch 16th-century humanist Erasmus studied here: his rooms were in what is now called, Erasmus Tower in Pump Court.

[m] King's College Chapel The architectural high point of the university, built 1446-1515, it is one of the greatest examples of the Perpendicular style and has a magnificent fan-vaulted ceiling. Charles Darwin, whose college was Christ's, said of his time at Cambridge: 'I acquired a strong taste for music, and used very often to time my walks so as to hear on weekdays the anthem from King's College Chapel. This gave me intense pleasure, so that my backbone would sometimes shiver.' Today the service of lessons and carols on Christmas Eve has a worldwide audience. In the present century, Rupert Brooke and E.M. Forster were members of the college.

[n] Senate House (to the right) Designed 1722-30 by James Gibbs; graduation and other university functions are held here. **Clare College** (to the left), is a 14th-century foundation, but what we see now is a range of superb buildings of the 17th and 18th centuries.

Together with Kings, Clare forms a crucial part of one of the greatest architectural compositions in England. The next college on the left, Trinity Hall, was founded in the 14th century and is long celebrated for its connection with legal studies.

[o] Trinity College The largest college, founded by Henry VIII (1546) whose effigy dominates the great gate. His sceptre was replaced some years back by a chair planted by a student. The wood had swollen with the wet, and the leg was sawn through, gilded and left in place. Its successor is there still. The Great Court beyond is the largest in all the Oxbridge colleges, being slightly larger than Tom Quad at Christchurch, Oxford. A traditional but very testing challenge for college athletes is to run the perimeter of the court while the clock chimes twelve. Newton had first-floor rooms on the northern side of the gate; Thackeray occupied the rooms below next to the chapel; and Byron had rooms on the first-floor of the central staircase in Nevile's Court. In the right-hand arcade of the last-named court, Newton experimented to determine the speed of sound: stamping on the flagstone at one end produces what appears to be a knock on the door at the other end. The library is by Wren (1676-95), with limewood carvings by Grinling Gibbons on the bookcases. Display cases hold some of the library's cherished possessions.

[p] St John's College, That most famous and fortunate Nurse of all learning Saint John's in Cambridge .. 'an universitie within itself;' (Thomas Nashe, 1589). Nashe was the first of a number of poets connected with the college, including Herrick and Wordsworth, who later described his life in *The Prelude*. His rooms now form part of the kitchen.

Shepreth and Barrington

Nature reserves and thatched Cambridgeshire villages are the highlights of this level walk through pastoral countryside with a strong botanical interest.

Length 3¹/₂ miles (5.5km), 1¹/₂ hours
Difficulty 1
Start Shepreth station. Grid reference 392482. *Alternatively* at car park by sign for Shepreth Riverside Walk, grid reference 385490, beginning the walk at ⑦.
OS maps 1:25,000 TL 24/34
Refreshments Pubs at Shepreth and Barrington

WALK DIRECTIONS

① With Shepreth station on left walk along the road to the village, passing a sign pointing left to the Willers Mill Wildlife Park [a] and then the village hall. When road junction is reached bear left past telephone box.

② Road passes weatherboarded mill house [b]. Beyond the roadbridge in front of the mill, take Angle Lane bearing left and signposted Public Footpath to Barrington. This leads behind the Wildlife Park, and after 300 yards reaches railway at the gated crossing ③.

Beyond the crossing the route continues as a wide farm track with a stream on left. Just short of derelict farm buildings, ignore track to right and keep straight ahead for 200 yards to signpost Public Footpath signpost ④, indicating a route half right across field, directly under the line of electricity poles. On far side of field, path turns left.

300 yards later, path crosses small stream by footbridge and passes entrance on left to nature reserve maintained by Cambridgeshire Wildlife Trust and occupying the area between the stream and the

main river. The path continues with stream now on right for 60 yards to where it enters the River Rhee 100 yards below Barrington Mill ⑤.

Cross the river via the footbridge and follow the footpath for a further 300 yards, past an old cemetery, then along Boot Lane. Continue to T-junction at Barrington high street and continue left through village for ¹/₂ mile, using paths along the green to the left of the road [c]. The village cricket ground is passed away to the right [d], and then the Royal Oak on the near side.

⑥ At duckpond and junction with road to Orwell, continue straight on along the road in direction signposted to Shepreth, passing after 300 yards a modern bungalow on left incorporating the remains of a stone built tower windmill [e]. 200 yards later, the road turns sharply left, crossing the River Rhee and ⑦ reaches small car park on the right-hand side with sign for Shepreth Riverside Walk.

Leave the car park by kissing-gate in corner and take well-trodden path across pasture, with the river on the right and a narrow stream on the left-hand side of the field. After ¹/₂ mile, the path leaves the main river then later ⑧ crosses a stile and follows the small stream on the left into trees. Continue through the wood for ¹/₄ mile.

When it leaves the trees, notice the man-made lake with islands for water birds on the right-hand side. The path skirts on end of arable land reaching a road (Malton Lane) opposite a cottage. ⑨ Turn left to road junction where, turn left again at sign for North End, signposted Shepreth.

⑩ 150 yards past Stone Lane turning, cross footbridge with a stile (on right) leading into the Shepreth L-Moor Nature Reserve [f]. Take the path bearing left, faint at first but becoming clearer. It bears right, away from the road, to reach an area of disturbed ground. 10 yards later, fork right on to path leading towards clump of hawthorn trees with overhead wires of railway visible beyond. This leads to a stile beside gate with a low foot-tunnel under the line ⑪.

Go through the tunnel, then along path through field to another stile and on to a wide, grassy track. At T-junction with stonier path, turn left, passing Shepreth church [**g**] to emerge on to a road ⑫. Bear left along village street, passing pub, to the grass triangle opposite Docwra's Manor [**h**].

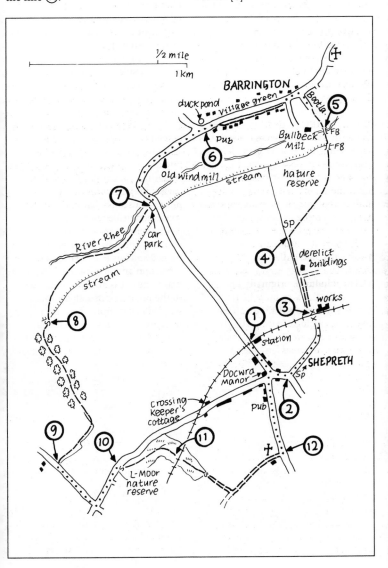

⑬ From here, Shepreth station is closely accessible, but a recommended diversion left for 400 yards will bring you to the former crossing-keeper's cottage [i].

ON THE ROUTE

[a] **Willers Mill Wildlife Park** has a collection of birds, animals and fish. Open throughout the year. Entrance free.

[b] **Shepreth Mill** is the last survivor of four mills and was in use until the 1950s.

[c] **Barrington** has a number of ancient thatched houses and one of the longest village greens in England. Barrington Mill, at the end of Mill Lane, was mentioned in the Domesday Book. In 1338 it passed to Michaelhouse, later Trinity College, Cambridge, and is now occupied by a company making scientific instruments.

[d] The U-shaped house at the rear of the green, to the left of the cricket pavilion, retains within its structure evidence that it was originally a medieval **aisled hall** of the 14th century.

[e] **The windmill**, originally known as Orwell Mill, was built in 1822 and was in use until 1890. An earlier mill existed on this site in 1604.

[f] **L-Moor Nature Reserve** consists of about 20 acres of fen (one of the best such areas in south Cambridgeshire) and is managed by the County Wildlife Trust. Birds found here include grasshopper warblers and kingfishers, and there is interesting flora. It is important that visitors do not stray from the rights of way and that great care is taken to avoid interference with plants and wildlife.

[g] **Shepreth church** is small, simple, early Gothic, with a Norman chancel arch and 18th-century memorials.

[h] **Docwra's Manor** Close inspection of what appears to be 18th-century brickwork reveals a sham facade, one brick thick, on an earlier timber-framed house. The garden (open Wed and Fri, Apr-Oct, 10-5) was created by celebrated botanist John Raven and is of remarkable quality: the walled garden between May and July presents a sea of silver and green spangled with colour.

[i] The former crossing keeper's **cottage garden** is exceptionally well-tended and has been featured on television and in national magazines. It is always freely open to the public, with a charmingly worded notice from the owner inviting one to enter it. There is a discreetly placed collection box in aid of the National Gardens Scheme.

CHESHIRE

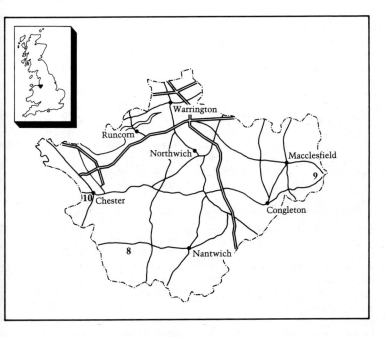

8 Maiden Castle and Raw Head
9 Three Shires Head and Shutlingsloe
10 Chester

Holiday Which? Good Walks Guide

72 Beeston Castle and the Peckforton Hills   73 Ingersley Vale and Kerridge
Hill   74 The River Bollin and Quarry Bank Mill   75 Lyme Park and the
Macclesfield Canal

Maiden Castle and Raw Head

This walk along and beneath the Central Cheshire Ridge, which divides the Cheshire Plain, is upland in character: heath and woods, with extensive views from the sandstone cliff. Easy route-finding, thanks to good waymarking throughout.

Length 5½ miles (9km), 2½ hours
Difficulty 2
Start Copper Mine Inn, Brown Knowl, on A534, between junctions with A49 and A41 (between Wrexham and Nantwich); car park at rear of inn. Grid reference 501522
OS maps 1:50,000 117; 1:25,000 SJ 45/55 (Pathfinder 790)
Refreshments Copper Mine Inn (at start)

WALK DIRECTIONS

(1) From main road, take minor road to right of pub, bearing left at next junction, through Brown Knowl village (ignore minor turns to right and then to left by telephone box). Past Methodist church, road bends right (ignore cul-de-sac ahead).

(2) 40 yards later turn left into another cul-de-sac. This enters woods and becomes track (there is a driveway to Tanglewood on your left); immediately after, keep left as waymarked (yellow arrow), where right fork ascends. Soon, reach National Trust sign for Larkton Hill: turn left, past children's football pitch on your left. (3) At end of the pitch, take path on right uphill, along power-lines.

At top of rise, turn left on well-defined path along ridge, heading towards big hill (which you soon reach). Path drops slightly before ascending to the top. (4) At top (by plaque about Maiden Castle) [a], bear left: you are now on the Sandstone Trail, waymarked with arrow and bootprint motifs marked with an 'S', contained within yellow circle.

Follow the trail along the top edge of the hill, with big drops on left [b] (the trail briefly leaves the edge at one point but returns to it after signpost pointing left to Raw Head where ahead is private). (5) At road, turn left (signposted) and go forward at crossroads to reach T-junction with A534 [c]. Take cul-de-sac opposite, to left of house. This lane rises past The Paddocks and a car park on your left, then (6) 50 yards later keep straight on (signposted Raw Head) where left goes to Chiflik (house).

The Sandstone Trail now proceeds as an enclosed track with woods on left and soon narrows to path along top of edge. Reach trig point (summit pillar) at Raw Head [d] and continue along edge for 200 yards to reach fork (7): left fork (waymarked with yellow arrow) is the continuation, leaving the top of the edge. Before descending however, continue along the edge 250 yards to see the Queen's Parlour [e]: immediately before path crosses stile into woods, take steep path on left to reach the cave.

Return to the fork mentioned above and descend through woods to tarmacked lane. Left on lane, then (8) right after 100 yards on waymarked path (opposite track signposted Gallantry Bank), through woods to stile. Follow right edge of field, past house, then over stile into woods, where follow well-defined path to reach stile into field (9). Turn left and follow left edge of field, heading towards Harthill village.

100 yards before house, take stile on left leading on to enclosed track into village. Cross to turning opposite and slightly to the right (signposted A534), into village square (with church on your right. (10) Keep to the left, leaving the square by far left-hand corner on

farm track which passes barns of Church Farm on your right. Track then runs along top of field with woods on left.

⑪ Where woods reach corner (near cattle trough), go forward, with fence on left. At bottom left-hand corner of field, cross stile and enter next field to follow bottom edge 50

yards (pub visible ahead), then take footbridge on right. Follow left edge of next field, then left along road to reach the Copper Mine Inn.

ON THE ROUTE
[a] Maiden Castle Two four-foot banks survive of this Iron Age hill-fort. **Views** throughout this high-

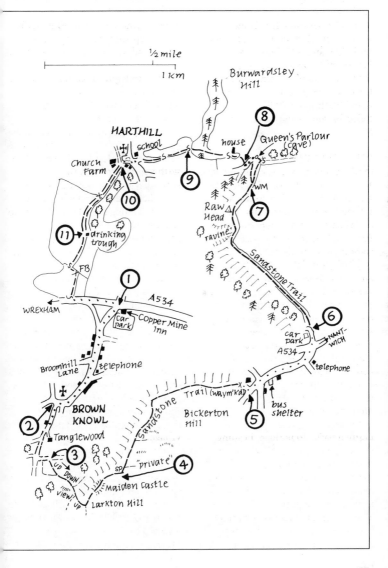

level section W to N Wales,
including the Clwydian Range.

[b] **Bickerton Hill** A plateau, where
heathland vegetation has grown up
since pasture was abandoned
the 1930s.

[c] The main road is an old **salt
route** between Nantwich and Wales.
$1/2$ mile NE, by the road, is a
pumping-house chimney from a
long-abandoned **copper mine**.

[d] **Raw Head** At 746ft, the highest
point on this range, made more
impressive by sheer sandstone cliffs
whose honeycomb patterns are the
result of weathering away of weaker
bands of rock. A small cave by the
trig point is said to have been the
haunt of brigands.

[e] **Queen's Parlour** Large cave,
excavated for sand (used locally for
cleaning cottage floors).

Three Shires Head and Shutlingsloe

The route mostly follows defined tracks up and along river valleys that dissect landscape of exposed grassy moors and hills. An optional but highly recommended ascent of Shutlingsloe is the climax.

Length 6 miles (9.5km), 3½ hours; 45 minutes less if avoiding ascent of Shutlingsloe

Difficulty 3-4 (with ascent of Shutlingsloe), 2 (without)

Start Clough House car park, Wildboarclough, N of A54 (Buxton-Congleton). Turn off A54 past Crag Inn in Wildboarclough; ¾ mile later pass prominent signpost for path to Langley via Shutlingsloe on your left: car park is just after, on right, but sign is not prominent. (There is also parking just S of Crag Inn.) Grid reference 987698

OS maps 1:50,000 118 and 119; 1:25,000 Outdoor Leisure 24

Refreshments Pub at Wildboarclough

WALK DIRECTIONS

① Follow surfaced track through car park, uphill, past Clough House Farm on your right, to reach road by grass triangle. Take track opposite, signposted Cat and Fiddle. This ascends valley, soon crossing stream where keep right on other side, up valley, soon with woods on right.

② After ¼ mile, keep close to stream, ignoring left fork to cottage. **③** Soon after, reach gate and turn right on track around top of waterfall. **④** Reach road ½ mile later. Cross crash barrier opposite and find stone stile in far left-hand corner of small field. Beyond, turn left alongside wall, downhill, to reach track: there is now a farm away to your left.

Turn right on the track; **⑤** at end of field, go through gate, and turn left, down hill alongside wall, towards bottom of valley. Soon wall on left bends right; keep alongside it (parallel with power-lines on right), soon on well-defined path along valley floor, with stream on left. Reach bridges at Three Shires Head [a]. Keep on right-hand side of stream, on level track. **⑥** After ⅓ mile, reach tarmacked lane: take stile opposite and slightly to the right, just to right of house. Cross small yard to enter field: path follows close to wall on left heading towards Shutlingsloe (the crescent-shaped hill-top just peering over the skyline, soon disappearing from view).

Where wall reaches a corner, path becomes poorly defined: continue towards Shutlingsloe. Wall on your right is a useful guide; keep parallel to it, veering left as it does the same. At top, wall becomes dilapidated and eventually ends at top of slightly pronounced valley. **⑦** Just before it ends, find narrow stile in it with clear path beyond, still heading for Shutlingsloe.

Reach road, cross to signposted stile opposite and follow well-defined path over moorland; beyond a stone hut, path becomes grassy and descends into wood to road **⑧**. Turn right along the road, bear left at junction by Crag Hall [b], then past church (ignore track forking right) to T-junction. Turn left, then after 70 yards **⑨** sharp right (or keep on a few yards for the pub) on rising farm road.

⑩ After ¼ mile reach cattle-grid: right, on track to Bank Top, is continuation; left is *detour* to summit of Shutlingsloe. Ascent route is straightforward (100 yards before reaching next farm, leave road as waymarked for path on left and ascend via stile visible ahead to summit [c]; descend same way). Follow track past Bank Top; at end

57

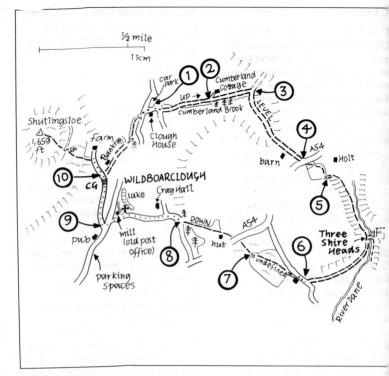

of next field, where wall on left ends, keep forward alongside woodland fence, ignoring track on left which rises between walls. Soon cross stile and proceed forward, now with wall on left, to follow well-defined path ¼ mile to road. Left on road and right soon after, into the car park.

ON THE ROUTE
[a] Three Shires Head Two stone bridges mark an attractive meeting point of three counties: Cheshire (near side), Derbyshire (over the first bridge) and Staffordshire (over the second).

[b] Wildboarclough Below Crag Hall on the right of the road, is the handsome **old post office**, previously Crag Mill; three storeys, fine clock and a densely fenestrated facade (627 panes of glass on the front, and more at the back).

[c] Shutlingsloe (1,659ft) Conical grassy hill makes an excellent viewpoint; a view-indicator points to landmarks, which include Mow Cop (SSW), Roach End (SE), Cat's Tor (NE), Croker Hill (with mast, SW), the Cloud (SW), the Cheshire plain and Macclesfield (W), Macclesfield Forest (NW) and Tittesworth Reservoir (S).

Chester

Founded by the Twentieth Norman Legion as Deva, Chester owed its early prosperity to the River Dee, and was the most important port in the north-west during the 13th and 14th centuries. Impoverishment followed with the later silting up of the river, but a change in fortunes brought wealth in the 18th century. Chester's most famous features are the virtually intact two-mile-long city walls and the famous medieval Rows, but there is much to discover in the Georgian and Victorian buildings that give the city such a rich sense of history.

Length 3 miles (5km), 3 hours
Difficulty 1
Start Little Roodee car park (long stay), on A483 just N of Grosvenor Bridge
Refreshments Full range

WALK DIRECTIONS

① [a] Join city wall (the path between the two parts of the car park), running eastwards, just above Castle Drive [b], [c]. On reaching road, go forward along it, then left under Bridgegate into Lower Bridge Street. ② Take first left (Shipgate Street), which bends round right up steps (St Mary's Hill) then bear right again where left goes to castle to reach Castle Street (with Golden Eagle public house ahead).

Turn right along Castle Street, then left up Lower Bridge Street [d] to the Cross ③. Explore Watergate Street and Eastgate Street before returning to the cross, then proceed along Northgate Street [e].
④ Detour right into St Werburgh Street to see cathedral.

Just after Pied Bull Hotel, take King Street on left [f]. ⑤ At main road, go up on to city wall (access round to the right via steps), which crosses bridge over main road (St Martin's Gate). Follow city wall over railway to point where it bends sharp left [g], then ⑥ return along the wall, over St Martin's Gate and Northgate [h].

Wall bends right at King Charles Tower [i]. Just before cathedral, take steps down on right to cobbled Abbey Street and into Abbey Square. Return to wall, proceed over Eastgate then over Newgate ⑦.
Recommended detour: just after Newgate, leave wall by steps: detour into Little St John Street (the main road to the left as seen from the wall) to see Roman amphitheatre [j], just after which turn right in front of St John's church, left through gate into gardens at rear of church, then right on path to reach river by Queen's Park Bridge. Turn right along the Groves (by the river) [k], then after bandstand take first road on right to reach Newgate.
Continue along wall [l], over Bridgegate. On reaching road, walls continue 100 yards later. At car park and by pelican crossing, detour right to Grosvenor Street to see museum [m], which is on right-hand side of the street.

ON THE ROUTE

[a] **Grosvenor Bridge** Graceful structure over the River Dee; the largest single span in the world when opened in 1832.
[b] **City walls** These are the best preserved city walls in Britain, offering a fascinating walk (much at high level) around the historic centre. The existing wall is mostly medieval, although there are vestiges of the original Roman structure.
[c] **Chester castle** A mound and tower from the inner bailey survive from the medieval castle, but most of what you see are 18th-century barracks, offices and court-rooms.
[d] **The Rows** A unique feature of

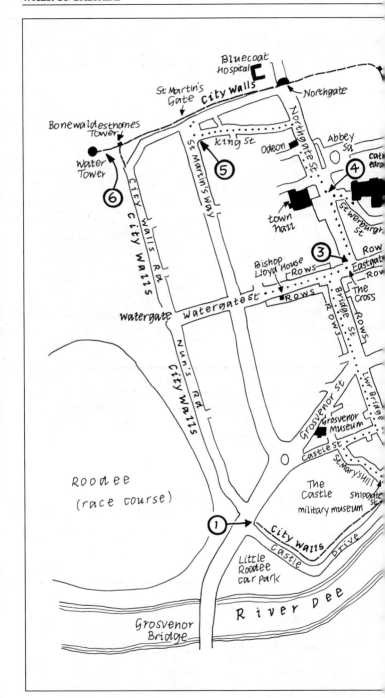

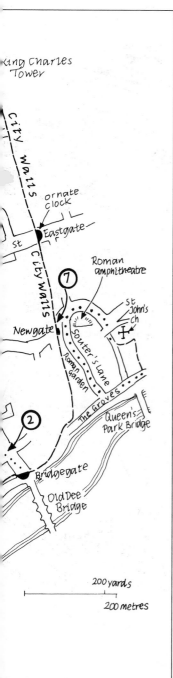

Chester are these first-floor shopping galleries. In the Middle Ages, shop-keepers built over their existing shops, making a continuous line of stalls with views down to the busy street below. The date of the Rows is unknown, but they may be part of a grand rebuilding scheme after a disastrous fire in 1278 destroyed much of the city. At the central crossroads a town-crier can often be heard, close by the much-photographed black-and-white Victorian mock-Tudor buildings. Genuine half-timbering can be seen along **Watergate Street**, notably Bishop Lloyd's House (on left, roughly opposite Crook Street).

[e] **Northgate Street** Some rather inconsequential modern building is offset by the bold Gothic town hall, which dominates the city skyline. To the right, and rather less prominent, lies the **cathedral**, noted for its superb choir stalls. It has Saxon origins as the Abbey of St Werburgh, and was extended over the centuries and much restored in Victorian times.

[f] **King Street** Curving, cobbled and narrow, with mostly three-storey houses; no single building stands out, but the composition of the whole is very pleasing.

[g] Two towers, **Water Tower** and **Bonewaldsthorne Tower**, guarded the Dee in medieval times when Chester was a port. There is a fine view into Wales, including Moel Fammau, the highest point on the Clwydian Range.

[h] **Bluecoat Hospital** A charitable foundation established in 1700; the present building was constructed in 1717. Adjacent is a sideless footbridge over the canal, built to give direct access to the chapel of St John (inside the present Bluecoat Hospital) for condemned felons from a nearby gaol; rebuilt in 1793 and known as the **Bridge of Sighs**.

[i] **King Charles Tower** (Open April-Oct, daily). In 1645 Charles I watched the defeat of his army by the Parliamentarians, on Rowton Heath. In the closing stages of the battle he allegedly took refuge in the cathedral tower, where a bullet missed him by inches, killing the captain by his side. The king retreated to Denbigh with 500 men, and the garrison and citizens held out under siege in Chester for four months, by which time they were eating rats. Close to the cathedral is **Abbey Square**, a handsome group of 18th-century houses around a grass oval; the N side is the earliest, dating from the 1750s. There is a close-up view from the wall of the modern belfry, an unusual design using slate and sandstone. The **Jubilee Clock** (1897) on Eastgate is a colourful landmark.

[j] **Roman amphitheatre** A section of Britain's largest known site of its kind, seating approximately 7,000.

[k] **River Dee** Boats for hire at the Groves. Opulent villas on the far bank enjoy some of the most pleasant views of the city.

[l] Visible from this section of the wall: on left, a small garden contains re-erected **Roman columns** and remains of a **Roman central-heating system**; on right a plaque indicates the six survivors of the Nine Houses; 17th-century brick and timber-framed, with shuttered ground floor windows; on right, **Albion Street** has particularly well-preserved artisans' cottages of the 19th century, complete with period street lamps.

[m] **Grosvenor Museum** (free, open 10.30-5, 2-5 Sun). Reconstructed period rooms; Roman artefacts, masonry and finds; natural history; local landscape pictures. **Cheshire Military Museum** (small fee, open 9-5) is in the castle site.

CORNWALL

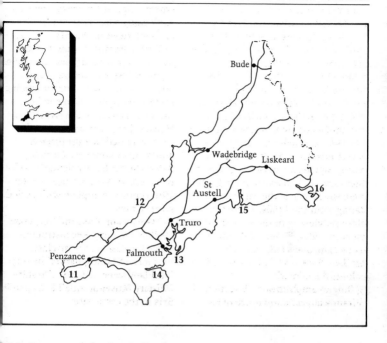

1 St Levan and the Logan Rock
2 Wheal Coates and St Agnes Beacon
3 St Anthony in Roseland
4 Gillan Creek and Helford River
5 Pont Pill and Lantic Bay
6 Mount Edgcumbe and Cawsand

Holiday Which! Good Walks Guide
2 Land's End and Nanjizal   3 Lamorna Cove and the Merry Maidens
4 Carnyorth Common and the Levant tin mines   5 Morvah Cliff and Chûn
Castle   6 St Ives and the coffin route   7 Pentire Point, the Rumps and St
Enodoc's church   8 The Luxulyan Valley and Treffry Viaduct   9 The West
Looe River, Talland Bay and Polperro   10 High Cliff and Cambeak

St Levan and the Logan Rock

The cliffs between Land's End and
Penberth Cove are generally
reckoned to be Cornwall's most
dramatic; after a mild start across
mostly level fields from Treen to St
Levan's church, this route takes in
some of the best coastal scenery,
culminating in a sensational
headland by the Logan Rock.
Undefined paths across fields, steep
sections along the coast.

Length 5 miles (8km), 3 hours
Difficulty 3-4
Start Treen, off B2383, ESE of Land's
End; car park at end of road in Treen
village. Grid reference 394230
OS maps 1:25,000 SW 32/42;
(Pathfinder 1368) 1:50,000 203
Refreshments Pub, shop and tea-
room in Treen

WALK DIRECTIONS

① Go back along road to village,
and 20 yards after telephone box,
fork left as road bends right, then
immediately fork right (thus keeping
to right of thatched cottage). This
leads to stone steps beside gate into
field. Proceed along left edge of this
and second field, and continue in
same direction in third field (close to
left edge) and in fourth field (along
right edge).

In the fifth field, bear half left to
find stile in front of farm. Follow
right edge of sixth field to emerge on
to surfaced track in front of farm **②**
Turn left on the track, and
immediately after end of farm
buildings on right, go through gate
and bear quarter right across field to
gateway. Go forward in second field
to gate leading into third field;

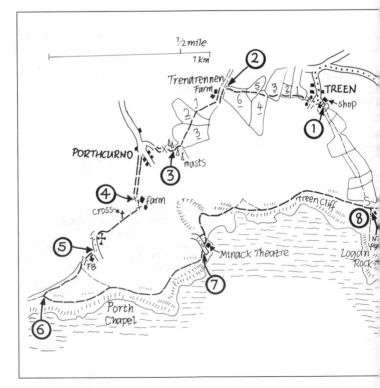

proceed towards masts entering rough land ③ (with two masts, to left and two masts to right).

Find path leading diagonally right to reach gate in bottom corner of the rough land, beyond which a track leads down to Porthcurno village. Turn right at bottom on road leading past garages on right to reach principal road in village. Cross the road to take rising track half left opposite (to left of Sea View House).

Track rises steadily to reach farm buildings ④, where turn left through kissing-gate into yard and keep to right-hand side of yard to take another kissing-gate on right at the end of the yard. Go forward (towards houses) along unploughed strip (a former field boundary; **NB** if this is ploughed out, which seems unlikely, the route is at 90° to the wall with

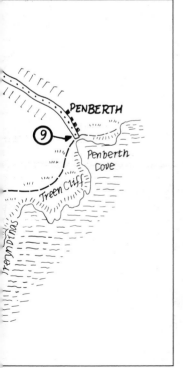

kissing-gate) and proceed along left edge of next field to reach St Levan's church [**a**], from which steps drop down to surfaced lane leading to left below the churchyard.

⑤ Just after end of churchyard, fork right on to track signed to Porthgwarra Cove beyond house on left, the path leads over stream; 50 yards later fork right, up through gorse and along right edge of field then soon reaching junction with coastal path ⑥. Turn sharp left and follow coastal path (3½ miles to Penberth Cove) [**b**].

⑦ On reaching road after 1 mile at Porth Curno Theatre car park, signs warn of a steep descent beyond the car park opposite: it takes rough steps, past the theatre [**c**] and is not a problem for those sensibly shod; the easier alternative is left along road, right at junction by sports ground on your left, then turn left by stone gate posts in front of house on to narrow path down to bottom.

Either way, the route at the bottom continues to left of diamond-shaped cable marker [**d**] then up on to cliffs; where path divides it is usually best to keep right. ⑧ Reach dramatic headland (Treryn Dinas, with Logan Rock), which you can divert onto, but be careful [**e**]. Continue along coast path (there is a path signposted to Treen which is a shorter alternative across fields back to start), along Treen Cliff and down to Penberth Cove ⑨ [**f**], where turn left on road inland. ⑩ After ½ mile, turn left at road junction and left again into Treen.

ON THE ROUTE

[**a**] The church at St Levan sits snug against the hillside. Its churchyard contains a Saxon cross and a communal grave of the grain ship *Khyber* which was wrecked at Porth Loe (to W) in 1905. The wealth of carving makes the church interior

memorable, with pew ends of varying ages displaying clowns, fish, eagles and faces, and there is a fine 16th-century rood screen adorned with Passion motifs; the simple font is Norman.

[b] The path passes a small stone structure, **St Levan's Well**, which still supplies water for baptism. Nearby, Porth Chapel beach is small but wonderfully sited beneath towering cliffs.

[c] On the right as you descend, **Minack Open-Air Theatre** has the Atlantic as a backdrop and its seats hewn out of the cliff to create a remarkable amphitheatre. It was the creation of Rowena Cade, who began the project here on her own estate in 1932 with a production of *The Tempest*.

[d] At **Porth Curno**, there is a transatlantic cable marker; up on the cliffs to the east, a pyramid marks the site of the first cable, laid in 1880, linking England to New York via Brest.

[e] **Treryn Dinas**, a superb headland, often reckoned to be the most dramatic feature of the Cornish coast, has a chaos of rocks providing an awesome profile. It is famous for its 84-ton logan (or rocking) stone, dislodged by a naval lieutenant in 1824. After a public outcry he was forced by the Admiralty to replace it. The rock survives, though it is much harder to budge. The headland is the site of an Iron Age cliff castle, whose ramparts are still visible. Although it is not quite as difficult to manage the walk along the headland as it first appears, care does need to be taken on the rocks.

[f] At **Penberth Cove**, navy-smocked fishermen and lobster pots provide an authentic atmosphere; this unspoilt hamlet is owned by the National Trust and let to local tenants.

Wheal Coates and St Agnes Beacon

From St Agnes the walk leads out along the side of a valley to the cliff-tops, then round St Agnes Head before climbing gently on to one of Cornwall's best-known viewpoints. Relics of tin and copper mining are evident in the rugged landscape of moorland cliffs. Route-finding generally easy, but a little complicated around the Beacon.

Length 5 miles (8km), 3 hours
Difficulty 3
Start St Agnes (on B3277 NW of Truro); start at car park which is signed in centre of village. Grid reference 720505
OS maps 1:50,000 203 and 204, 1:25,000; SW 75 (Pathfinder 1352); also tiny part of SW 74/84 (Pathfinder 1360)
Refreshments Pubs, cafés and shops in St Agnes; also hotel bar and café at ⑤.

WALK DIRECTIONS

① Turn right out of car park to main street in St Agnes, along which turn left [a], soon past St Agnes Hotel. After the church, fork right downhill (signposted Perranporth) down Town Hill. ② After 80 yards fork left on to steep path called Stippy Stappy, descending with terrace of cottages on left; at end of the terrace the path bends left and then immediately fork right.

The path drops to cross stream and rises to road. Turn right on road. ③ After 50 yards turn sharp left on to driveway signposted as footpath to the Cliffs. After 40 yards keep forward ignoring a turn to the right [b]. When path bends right by bench above the sea, ignore left turn (too steep for comfort) but continue to next junction by marker-post for coastal path where ④ turn left down to road and houses.

Turn right on road ⑤ and take first left, just after 30 mph speed derestriction sign and just before small car park. Beyond end of the road, continue for 2½ miles along cliff-path (keep to seaward side wherever path forks) [c]. ⑥ Reach spectacular mine ruins of Wheal Coates [d], and turn left in front of them on to stony track leading inland towards right end of St Agnes Beacon.

Turn left of road and immediately after first house on right (called Blue Hills) ⑦ turn right on driveway between walls. Ignore side-turns (keep right after 100 yards where left goes into small caravan site), to enter farmyard at end of driveway by gate. Keep to the right, between barns then soon into field with St Agnes Beacon up ahead. Head on up towards right end of Beacon; field walls taper outwards – leave left-hand wall and keep up across middle of field to stile and gateway 90 yards to right of top left-hand corner.

In second field, carry on up left edge to gate beside stile to emerge on to corner of path at edge of rough moorland ⑧. Keep forward and 50 yards later fork left up to trig point on summit [e]. From summit go forward, taking right fork ahead (not turning 90° right, which heads to outskirts of St Agnes).

When close to small covered reservoir on the right, and just before field ahead, fork left. ⑨ 50 yards later bear half left at four-way junction, initially close to field fence on right but soon diverging from it. 100 yards later, fork right (concrete platforms of old buildings are seen by path); path soon swings round to left and just as road comes into view a short distance below, turn sharp right at oblique path junction.

⑩ Emerge on to a road, cross and take stile opposite, follow left edge of (first) field to where field tapers in narrowly: here, take stile on right into second field, where proceed quarter left to stile. In third and fourth fields keep to left edge (partly on enclosed paths) then forward on enclosed track which soon bends to the right.

(11) Reach road (Beaconsfield Place) at edge of St Agnes. Cross to tarmacked path opposite (not grassy path just to right of it) leading into main street. Turn right to reach the car park.

ON THE ROUTE

[a] **St Agnes** A former tin and copper mining community, now a retirement town and resort. The mines have closed but the ruined mine buildings have survived. On the left as you go along main street, **St Agnes Miners' and Mechanics' Institute** (1893), was founded by John Passmore Edwards, a Victorian philanthropist who was responsible for the setting up of many colleges, orphanages and hospitals in England

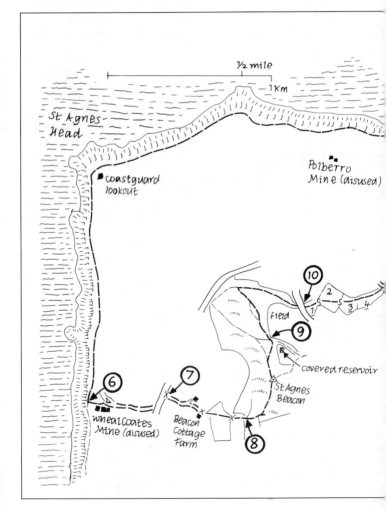

Stippy Stappy is the town's quaintest street name, and is thought to mean merely 'very steep'. [b] New buildings on the outskirts of St Agnes have recently changed this valley's appearance, but two abandoned mine buildings dominate the scene: to the left is **Wheal Friendly** and to the right **Wheal Kitty**: the latter was worked 1834-1930.
[c] The coast path passes close to **Polberro Mine**, which is briefly seen to the left as you gain the cliff-top; this was once the richest mine in Cornwall. **St Agnes Head** is a noted place for sea-birds with 900 pairs of kittiwakes representing the largest colony in the area, and there are also herring gulls, fulmars, and guillemots breeding here. Migrants include gannets, skuas, petrels and shearwaters; out to sea you may catch a glimpse of a grey seal or the (entirely harmless) basking shark. **View** of Bowden Rocks, sometimes called Man and His Man; as you round the Head, the coastline S to Godrevy Point (on E side of St Ives Bay) is revealed.
[d] **Wheal Coates** Perched on a cliff-top, this tin mine was worked for most of the 19th century and for a few years before the First World War, but was never especially productive. Its ruins are among the most evocative industrial relics in Cornwall, and have recently been restored by the National Trust.
[e] **St Agnes Beacon** (630ft). From this modest moorland summit a panorama extends over the whole of this walk and inland too. **St Michael's Mount** may be seen SW; S are the uplands beyond Redruth, while shipping may be observed in Falmouth harbour to the SE. The hill has man-made lumps on it, possibly ancient burial mounds and an enclosure which may be of Roman origin.

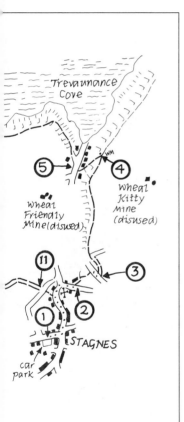

St Anthony in Roseland

**A round walk of considerable
distinction on a beautiful peninsula,
first along cliffs and then looking
over the harbour to Falmouth before
the final section along the wooded
Porthcuel river. No problems with
route-finding and the going is easy
all the way.**

Length 4½ miles (7km), 2½ hours
Difficulty 1–2

Start Towan Beach car park by
Porth Farm, on Roseland Peninsula
E of Falmouth; car park is on right
just after Porthcuel river appears on
right, and then Towan Beach villas
sign is seen on left; follow signs for
St Anthony from Gerrans. Grid
reference 868329
OS maps 1:50,000 204; 1:25,000 SW
83 (Pathfinder 1366)

WALK DIRECTIONS

① Cross road from car park and
take path opposite and slightly to
the left signed to the beach. ② Just
before beach, turn right on to cliff
path, past Porthmellin Head and
later emerging on to road after Zone
Point (near toilets) [a]. ③ When
level with end of cottages on right
(ex-Captain's and Lieutenant's
quarters) turn left on path signposted
to lighthouse, dropping abruptly.

At the bottom (before you reach
the lighthouse) turn sharp right at a
path junction. Path follows coast
until woods near Amsterdam Point
④ [b], where path turns right uphill
(waymarked) along field edge with
woods on left. Cross stile at top and
continue down to left of next
field and emerge on to track.
Turn right.

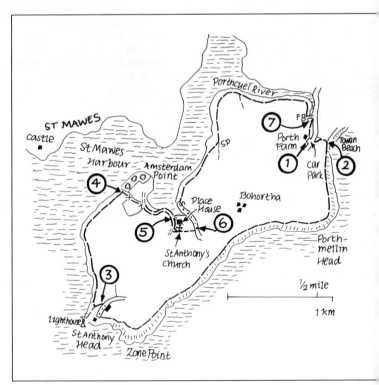

(5) Fork right at entrance to Place House (left goes into grounds which are private) [c]. When you are past church at back of the house, fork left and immediately left again as waymarked, down steps past church entrance, and go forward through churchyard to road (6).

Turn left on road, to reach quay where take signposted stile on right. The path follows riverside all the way, until crossing bridge at end of the creek (7). Turn right on the other side of bridge on path parallel to road then ꓳund right-hand side of field to farm building, where you emerge just below car park.

ON THE ROUTE

[a] **View** from Zone Point and St Anthony Head over Carrick Roads, a broad estuary providing superb natural anchorage for vessels of all sizes. Falmouth lies to the W, the town dominated on its seaward aspects by the impressive Pendennis Castle, one of the chain of forts built by Henry VIII against a possible French invasion. The castle's outer curtain wall was added in the 16th century; inside it lies a 16-sided rampart encompassing a circular keep. Falmouth was a particularly prosperous port after 1688 until the 19th century when it flourished as a base for Mail Packets which operated from here to Spain, Portugal, the West Indies and North and South America. The **lighthouse** at St Anthony Head is open to the public.

[b] Across the water is **St Mawes**, an old port which has expanded into a busy yachting centre. The castle 1540-43 was built by Henry VIII, and has a round tower and bastions on three sides; this allows guns to fire round a wide arc. Carrick Roads (see [a]) was never attacked and the guns are still in place in their original condition.

[c] **Place House** The manor house is on the site of a 13th-century monastery, and the church dates from then but has been substantially restored; inside the latter are memorials to the Spry family (who own Place House), including Admiral Thomas Spry and nautical Commander-in-Chief, Richard Spry.

Gillan Creek and Helford River

Wooded combes dotted with wild flowers, a complex landscape of estuaries and small boats in sheltered creeks contribute to what is possibly the best round walk on the Lizard Peninsula. Easy to find the way, and there are no steep gradients. Dogs not allowed in Bosahan Estate (between St Anthony and Helford).

Length 5 miles (8km), 3 hours
Difficulty 2
Start Manaccan (East of Helston); road-side parking opposite turn for Gweek. Grid reference 764250
OS maps 1:50,000 204; 1:25,000 SW 72/82 (Pathfinder 1370)
Refreshments Pub and shop in Manaccan; pub, shop and tea-room in Helford

WALK DIRECTIONS

① [a] With Gweek turning behind you, take path by restored well (passing to right of thatched cottage) leading beside row of cottages up to right side of church, reaching road by post office. Keep right on road and opposite church gate turn right on to unmade lane (signposted as a footpath); keep forward after 100 yards, ignoring path on right to Carne.

Track soon bends slightly right by barn, signposted St Anthony, and continues as concrete track to house (Roscaddon), where ② bear slightly left as signposted downhill on grassy path, initially between garden hedges and then entering woodland. Path proceeds to reach road ③. Turn left on road.

④ At church of St Anthony [b], road bends left uphill. Just after passing gate at the top of churchyard, fork right on to path up towards kissing-gate by signpost and Bosahan Estate sign, which briefly leads through woods. On emerging into open, fork left at signpost (right fork detours to Dennis Head and returns), proceeding uphill along edge of field.

At end of field turn left again through kissing-gate and follow coast path. ⑤ At next small bay (Ponsence Cove) cross stream and keep left on other side and almost immediately right as waymarked. ⑥ Join track by buildings, then proceed until reaching corner of road. Turn right downhill on the road.

⑦ Just before Treath Cottage, turn left up signposted steps. Path

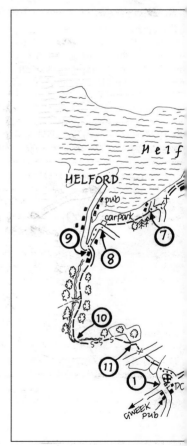

leads through woods, then along edge of field (ignore a kissing-gate on right when level with Sailing Club), to reach car park by road and former chapel **(8)**. Turn right downhill into Helford, past footbridge (do not cross except for detour to village and pub) [c]. **(9)** Where road is about to cross river, keep left steeply uphill on concrete driveway (signposted Manaccan).

By thatched house this proceeds as a broad path into woods [d]. Soon ignore a right fork (over footbridge), but continue with stream always to your right. **(10)** Path and stream make major left turn; 50 yards later

path crosses stream and soon continues as a sunken path with fields up on your right. Emerge into field by stone stile. Keep slightly right up across field to projecting corner of woodland **(11)**.

Keep forward with the woodland fence on your left, then after only 20 yards turn right up to top of field to find small gate in hedgerow which lines the top of the field. Turn left on road and immediately right by signpost over stile. Follow left edge of two fields and proceed on to road at edge of Manaccan, where turn to the right.

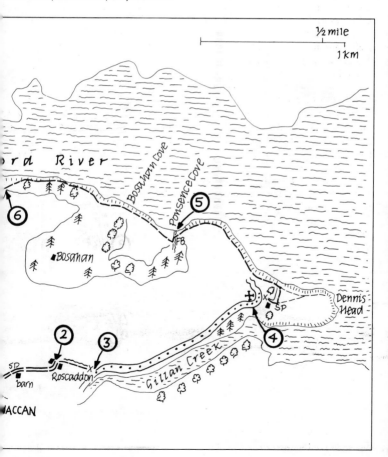

73

ON THE ROUTE

[a] **Manaccan** occupies a sloping site amid a green, unspoilt landscape of steep lanes, pastoral farmland, neatly rounded hills and secluded wooded combes. At the bottom of the village is a covered well and pub, while above, palms grow in the churchyard and a fig tree is set in the church's south wall.

[b] **St Anthony in Meneage** A beautifully sited church which overlooks Gillan Creek, with a handsome granite and sturdy 15th-century oak roof; look for a German carving in the east wall of the same period as the roof, depicting the Last Supper.

[c] **Helford** is a sheltered village of lush blooms and thatched cottages, set beside a wooded creek, with much boating activity in summer.

[d] The walk through these woods is a particular delight in early spring when daffodils and primroses give a blaze of colour.

Pont Pill and Lantic Bay

**From Polruan quay the route snakes
up narrow steps between
precariously stacked-up terraced
cottages, then follows two
contrasting scenic sections – first
along the Pont Pill (a deep river
valley) then along the coast from
Lantic Bay. Easy route-finding; some
brief steep sections.**

Length 5½ miles (9km), 3 hours
Difficulty 2-3
Start Polruan (E of and across river
from Fowey). Grid reference 126510.
Start by Polruan quay. Parking at top
of town or at top of Fowey,
passenger ferry from Fowey every 15
mins, all year (note last ferry times
as you leave)
OS maps 1:50,000 200; 1:25,000 SX

05/15 (Pathfinder 1354)
Refreshments Full range in Polruan

WALK DIRECTIONS

① [a] From quay follow road past
Lugger Inn, after which road soon
bends right. Immediately turn left
into East Street, following signposts
for The Hills: at end of the street
keep right up steps (signposted); at
top of steps **②** fork left (signposted).
This becomes an earthy path and is
generally level.

③ After ½ mile fork right, passing
National Trust sign for North
Downs 30 yards later. **④** Join and
keep forward on track coming in
sharply from left, but 20 yards later
fork left on to waymarked path (still
keeping level). **⑤** On reaching gate
on to road, do not pass through the

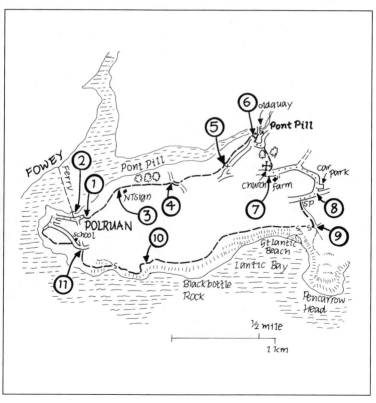

gate but keep left (signposted to Pont and Hall Walk) over stile and following path closely parallel to road which is beyond the hedge; the path drops abruptly.

⑥ At T-junction with track at bottom of steps, turn right up to road (or left for detour to Pont Quay [**b**]). Turn left on road and immediately right at hairpin bend on to grassy track just to right of entrance to Pont Poultry Farm: follow this up to Llanteglos-by-Fowey churchyard [**c**] and on to surfaced lane ⑦.

Turn left on lane (immediately ignore minor track forking to right by farmhouse) and follow lane down and then up (ignoring left fork to Carne Farm). ⑧ At T-junction with road, turn right towards Polruan. After 150 yards take gate beside stile on left by National Trust sign for Pencarrow Head. Follow left edge of field towards the sea and where field boundary on left bends left follow it around to gate giving on to Pencarrow Head ⑨: cross stile immediately on right to continue along the cliff-top coast path (the next stile on left can be taken for detour on to Great Lantic Beach) [**d**].

Pass Blackbottle Rock National Trust sign; later ⑩ path drops into undercliff; ignore a later right fork (which peters out). ⑪ Path reaches gate and goes on to road at edge of Polruan. Turn left on road past primary school then fork left on to signposted track on to cliff again and later reaching narrow road, which follow down to Polruan Quay.

ON THE ROUTE
[**a**] **Polruan** Connected to its twin

port Fowey by passenger ferry; both towns cling to their respective hillsides. Blockhouse forts guard the harbour mouth and there are mazes of double-yellow-lined streets, old inns, narrow steps between huddled terraces, and spectacular views across the harbour. Ships from nearby china clay works, $1/2$ mile up the river, wend their way past the small boats in the harbour. Fowey was Sea Rat's little grey town' in *The Wind in the Willows*. The town received its charter in 1245 to supply ships to the Navy; in the 15th century the Fowey Gallants attacked the French coast so persistently that Edward IV agreed to stop them, and when they refused, he organised his Dartmouth men to steal the Fowey ships.

[**b**] **Pont Pill** The quay has been restored by the National Trust. A notice dated 1894 posted on the farmhouse gives dues for discharging and shipping.

[**c**] **Llanteglos-by-Fowey** The tower dominates the scene for miles around; just outside the porch a 12-ft lantern cross, lichen-covered, is of great antiquity. The Perpendicular church is, despite some restoration, one of Cornwall's finest and the endearingly drunken angles of the arches and the roofs have not been straightened out.

[**d**] **Great Lantic Beach** A sandy beach at the foot of rugged cliffs in a crescent-shaped bay. The cliffs have been degraded into rounded slopes by the forces of erosion to create the profile seen today. Views inland of the strange moonscape uplands of the china clay country over near St Austell.

Mount Edgcumbe and Cawsand

A walk of three differing moods: first naval Plymouth, then the lush woodland and parkland landscape of Mount Edgcumbe, and finally a quintessential Cornish bay with an enchanting coastal village. Route-finding is straightforward most of the way.

Length 6 miles (9.5km), 3 hours
Difficulty 2
Start Maker car park, Mount Edgcumbe Country Park, S of Plymouth; follow B3247 E from Millbrook to turn off by War Memorial for Maker Church (lone and prominent); the car park is behind church. Grid reference 447520. *Alternative start* from main car park for Country Park by bus terminal at Cremyll ferry (Grid reference 454534) at [5]
OS maps 1:50,000 201; 1:25,000 SX 45/55 (Pathfinder 1356)
Refreshments Café in Country Park; pubs, shops and fish and chip shop in Cawsand; tea gardens at Friary Manor at ⑩

WALK DIRECTIONS

① Return from car park, past lodge and turn right just after end of Maker church [a], signposted Empacombe and Cremyll Ferry, walking across the grass to find gate, and cross the road. Take signposted path opposite into woods, descending and ② keeping forward at first path crossing. The path bends right, left and right again and at end of field appearing on left, take stile into the field.

Proceed initially along right edge of field then drop to track down on your right and turn left along the track to reach gate on to road ③. Cross the road and take stile opposite along edge of field, walking close to the estuary [b] [c] and later

emerging by houses at Empacombe ④.

Keep to the water's edge and pick up surfaced driveway to left of the houses; but immediately keep forward on unmade track where the driveway bends right. Soon this track enters woods and later passes houses (ignore side forks, one to the right then one to the left), to reach road at Cremyll ferry ⑤.

Take signposted coastal path into country park directly opposite (mansion is seen up the hill) [d]. As soon as you enter park gate, bear left to go under archway, past orangery in ornamental garden, then immediately after the orangery keep left to regain coastal views at blockhouse fort.

Pass around the bay and follow the coast-path signposts; route is easy to find, through woods, past the mock temple by pond and later reaching gate into field, where path passes close to folly ruin, re-enters woods and after view opens towards Cawsand, reaches stile on to road ⑥. Turn right on road, then left at road corner after 40 yards over signposted stile for easy path to Kingsand and Cawsand.

⑦ As soon as you reach road at village [e], the route continues immediately right, steeply up Devonport Hill: the road soon ends and the route continues forward along path (signposted Maker Church) up to path junction ⑧, where turn right. Just after blockhouse fort, path bends left to reach road. Turn right on road and ⑨ after 40 yards take signposted stile on left for Maker Church. Turn right to follow right edge of field, initially parallel to road but bending left in field corner still along right edge of field.

Follow the field edge until kissing-gate on right gives on to road. Turn right on road and keep left at next

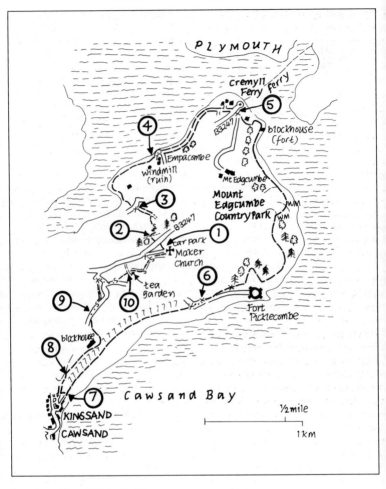

junction. After 100 yards take signposted stile on left by telegraph pole and proceed towards Maker church, alongside telegraph poles in this field; in second field continue to stile just to left of house (Friary Manor) ⑩.

Take enclosed path opposite, to left of the house, soon into and along left edge of field (towards church) and shortly crossing stile on left and continue to turn right in next field, still towards the church, along right edge of the field. Reach stile giving on to grass in front of Maker church.

ON THE ROUTE

[a] **Maker church** Commands a huge view over Plymouth. Among the numerous gravestones to sailors and soldiers killed in the vicinity is that of a naval gunner (1819), with the epitaph 'What I am this humble stone ensures, What I was is no affair of yours'. Look inside the church for its fine sculptured Norman font. The church tower was used for many years as a naval signalling station.

[b] Extensive views of **Plymouth**

tower-blocks, shipping, the city centre and the Tamar Bridge, with the uplands of Dartmoor in the distance. Although much of the city was obliterated in a bombing raid in the last war, Plymouth is nevertheless one of the most spectacularly sited of British cities, in a huge and complex natural harbour at a meeting of drowned river valleys. Blockhouse forts guard the harbour entrance; three are passed on this walk, and together with the grey barrack buildings are all indicators of the city's naval importance.

[**c**] On the right, is a ruin of a **Tower Windmill**, long since derelict.

[**d**] **Mount Edgcumbe** (grounds open all year, house open April-Oct, Wed-Sun and bank hol Mons). The mansion stands in the earliest landscaped parkland in Cornwall (although this was part of Devon when the house was begun in 1740); it was the home of the Edgcumbe family from 1553 to 1987, and rebuilt in 1941 after bomb damage. The coast-path leads around the edge of the estate, past a temple-like pavilion by a pond, through fine ornamental woodlands and past a gothic 'ruined' folly. You can divert into the park to see the fallow deer herds, the mansion and the collection of camellias. At a blockhouse fort, there is another fine view over Plymouth together with Drake's Island, on which were installed a fort and prison.

[**e**] **Cawsand and Kingsand** Two villages in one, with precariously steep lanes and shuttered, colour-washed cottages crammed into a dip in the coastline. Venlee Narrow cottage, opposite the Rising Sun Tavern, has an almost comically narrow frontage. The village has a conspiratorial atmosphere, and it's not surprising that it was once busy with smugglers.

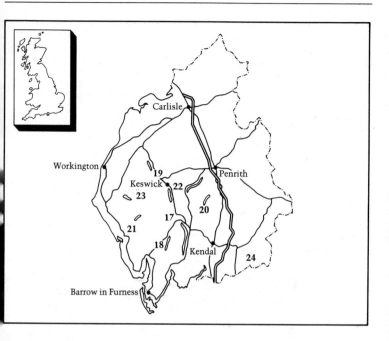

17 Around Langdale
18 Walna Scar Road and Coniston Water
19 Newlands Beck and Barrow
20 Mosedale and Swindale
21 Miterdale and Illgill Head
22 Walla Crag and Ashness Bridge
23 Haystacks
24 Dentdale

Holiday Which? Good Walks Guide

Around Langdale

Few places in Britain have such an enchanting mix of upland and lowland: this route encircles Lingmoor Fell and shows off the best of the dale at low level. Some moderate short ascents; route not always defined.

Length 8½ miles (13.5km), 4½ hours
Difficulty 3
Start Free National Trust car park, Dungeon Ghyll New Hotel, Langdale. Turn off A593 (Coniston to Ambleside) at Skelwith Bridge, and follow B5343 into Langdale; car park is on right just past sign for

Sticklebarn bar and café. Grid reference 295064. (Additional parking available at Elterwater and above Blea Tarn)
OS maps 1:50,000 90; 1:25,000 Outdoor Leisure 6
Refreshments Café at start; pub and shop at Elterwater and Chapel Stile

WALK DIRECTIONS

① Take gate at back of car park (by toilets), signposted Stickle Ghyll, leading on to enclosed path. After 50 yards this emerges into small meadow: keep forward on well-defined path, after 50 yards passing corner of fence on your left where

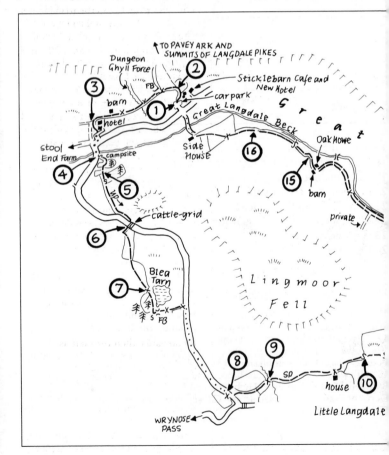

2 fork left on to level path alongside wall on left (right fork rises up Stickle Ghyll and then up to the Langdale Pikes) [a].

Continue along until **3** just past house on left, where wall on left ends: here turn left to take right-hand of two gates, and follow enclosed path down to road. Keep forward, over bridge, to reach main valley road. Turn right along road; keep left with principal road after 50 yards at cross-junction, then **4** after 150 yards (just after crossing stream) take signposted stile on left into wooded area (sometimes a campsite). Keep

alongside right-hand wall, bearing right after 50 yards as wall bends right; where wall ends, cross small grassy area to take stile into wood. Path leads through the wood, to emerge between stone gate-posts into field, where continue forward and slightly to the right (no path), heading for obvious gap in woodland wall 50 yards ahead **5**. Pick up woodland path and on leaving the wood, keep forward alongside wall on right, ascending steadily. Where road appears on other side of wall, do not cross stile to join it but continue uphill (closely parallel to road) until crossing next ladder-stile at cattle-grid over road. Cross the road (do not go over cattle-grid) and go forward alongside wall on left (Blea Tarn is down to your left), and after 20 yards **6** turn left on well-defined path down to Blea Tarn [b].

7 Fork left 20 yards into woods. At end of Blea Tarn, turn left over footbridge on path leading up to road along which turn right, downhill for ½ mile. **8** 150 yards after wall begins on right, fork left (opposite gate in the wall) on to rising grassy track: this joins a wall, where keep forward (with wall on left). Soon cross fence (via gap) and pick up a path which becomes well defined, with a wall gradually joining from the right (as wall on left leaves path and goes uphill) [c].

9 On crossing stream, turn sharp right on other side, on path (still with wall and fence close on right). Pass by gate on right (with house beyond), continue with wall on right for 50 yards, then turn left as signposted, steeply uphill, rejoining the wall at a corner. **10** After ladder-stile, keep forward on level to next ladder-stile, then path drops to reach stony track, along which turn to the left.

11 Keep to right fork on entering woods [d] and proceed to corner of

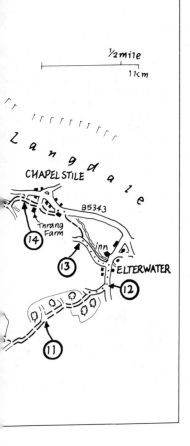

½ mile

1 km

L a n g d a l e

CHAPEL STILE

B5343

Thrang Farm

14

inn

13

ELTERWATER

12

11

tarmacked lane where keep forward.
⑫ At T-junction, turn left and
follow road towards Elterwater
village. Turn left immediately before
road crosses river (thus route does
not quite go into village [e]), on to
road. ⑬ After 350 yards, fork right
on to signposted path, which leads
down to river. Cross footbridge and
emerge on road at Chapel Stile
village. Left on road, past
Wainwright's Inn, 50 yards after
which turn left on to stony track (by
School road-sign), now with wall on
right. 250 yards later turn left on to
tarmacked lane, past houses
(including Thrang Farm); after 75
yards, lane ends; go forward on
signposted path between walls.
⑭ After 60 yards, where walls
open out, fork left (right goes to
road), on track which soon bends left
and crosses bridge over Great
Langdale Beck), and turn right on
other side (along the river) [f].
Eventually track bends left to leave
river; on rejoining it, ignore
footbridge, but follow the track to
reach house (Oak Howe). Turn right
immediately after the house to pass
between barn (left) and the house
itself and pick up level path with
dilapidated wall on left.
⑮ Where the wall bends left,
keep left alongside it; soon the path
is well defined and has wall on right.
⑯ Take gate with stile alongside
(avoid another stile just to the right
of these, which leads on to riverside
path), and follow path ahead, later
through kissing-gate and down to
farmhouse 300 yards ahead (Side
House). In farmyard, turn right on
tarmacked farm road, to reach road.
Take road turning opposite, signed
'free car park'.

ON THE ROUTE
[a] Views W along Langdale, with the
Langdale Pikes (2,415 feet) on the
right (perhaps the best-known
mountain shape in the Lake District,
with cliff feature of Pavey Ark on
top); the slopes are littered with
vestiges of a Neolithic stone axe
'factory', not discovered until this
century. The rock was worked with
granite hammers and shipped for
export. Ahead, **Crinkle Crags** (left,
2,816ft) and Bow Fell (2,960ft) seal
off the dale.
[b] **Blea Tarn** Memorably sited small
lake, beneath Wrynose Fell; a
plantation of mixed trees and
rhododendrons on its W side make a
small oasis of civilisation in an
otherwise wild place.
[c] **View** on your right is of **Fell Foot
Farm** (a nearby mound is a 'thing
mound', or ancient meeting place for
an annual Viking parliament). The
road beyond is the start of the
exciting **Wrynose Pass**, part of an
ancient route used by the Romans
into Eskdale and to the Cumbrian
coast. E of the farm lies **Little
Langdale Tarn.**
[d] **View** (to right) of Elter Water (the
smallest lake in the district,
according to some; but much
depends on what you classify as a
lake and what a tarn) and across to
Loughrigg Fell.
[e] **Elterwater** Has a tiny, informal
village green which almost doubles
as a garden to the rambling old
Britannia Inn. Its cottages were
mostly built for workers in nearby
gunpowder works, which grew up to
supply local quarries and mines; the
site of the works is now a timeshare
complex, but slate continues to be
quarried locally.
[f] Pretty section of **Great Langdale
Beck**, and along Great Langdale with
Bow Fell in the distance. The old
bridge is dated 1818, with the name
of the builder and his wife. The beck
features on some older maps as the
River Elter (hence Elter Water).

Walna Scar Road and Coniston Water

A gradual ascent through dry-stone-wall country and sheep pastures, followed by a level route contouring the slopes below the Old Man of Coniston, looking over to neighbouring Wetherlam and Furness Fells; strongly contrasting later section alongside Coniston Water. Most paths and tracks are well defined, and the route is quite easy to find.

Length 9 miles (14.5km), 4¹/₂ hours
Difficulty 3

Start Torver, at junction of A5084 and A593, SSW of Coniston (park in front of Wilsons Arms); grid reference 284942
Or start at Coniston; grid reference 303976 and start walk at ⑦
OS maps 1:50,000 96 or 97; 1:25,000 Outdoor Leisure 6
Refreshments Pubs at Torver; pubs, cafés and shops in Coniston

WALK DIRECTIONS

① Take signposted track immediately to right of Wilsons Arms, between walls. After ¹/₄ mile, fork right (left goes through gate and up to house). ② 180 yards later turn right at cross-junction (left goes through gate up to house) to reach corner of tarmacked lane by houses, along which bear left (signposted Walna Scar). Beyond the houses, the lane becomes an unsurfaced track, running level or gently uphill [**a**].

③ Track bends left at stone hut, through gate; 20 yards later, fork right (keeping on main track) as signposted (alongside wall on right). On crossing stream, keep forward at cross-junction (left goes to house), heading towards quarry spoil and the Old Man of Coniston, to reach gate into sheep-pen ④ where go forward to the next gate (found in a second, stone-walled sheep-pen).

Turn right (signposted Walna Scar) through gate, to cross footbridge over stream (Torver Beck), and turn left on other side (again signposted to Walna Scar), ascending with beck close by (but not always visible) down to left. After pool with waterfall on left [**b**], path rejoins the beck. ⑤ When you are level with a stone wall on other side of beck, (coming in at a right angle to the beck), take grassy path half right, slightly uphill (path straight ahead ascends to Goat's Water and on to top of the Old Man of Coniston).

After 200 yards, reach the Walna Scar 'Road' (a stony track) along which turn right [**c**]. ⑥ Keep straight on by gate by signpost, and follow tarmacked lane which descends to Coniston [**d**]. ⑦ From bridge by church in village centre, follow A593 towards Broughton and Ulverston, take next left just after filling station (this is Lake Road, signposted to Beck Yeat and Gondola Steam Yacht Pier).

⑧ Where road bends left in front of Lake Road Workshops, keep forward over stile by gate signposted Coniston Hall, and turn right on path along edge of field to reach gate at end where continue on track, forking left 100 yards later in front of trees; track soon merges into tarmacked drive and reaches Coniston Hall [**e**]. Keep to right of the hall, on driveway which becomes unsurfaced track just before reaching 10mph sign marking edge of campsite ⑨; here, track forks; keep left, then turn left by National Trust sign stating Stop: No Cars or Camping Beyond This Sign.

This brings you to lakeside where turn right, soon picking up well-defined path alongside Coniston Water for 2 miles (soon through woods, then into the open) [**f**]. ⑩ Path eventually leaves lake and goes uphill, with woods and wall on

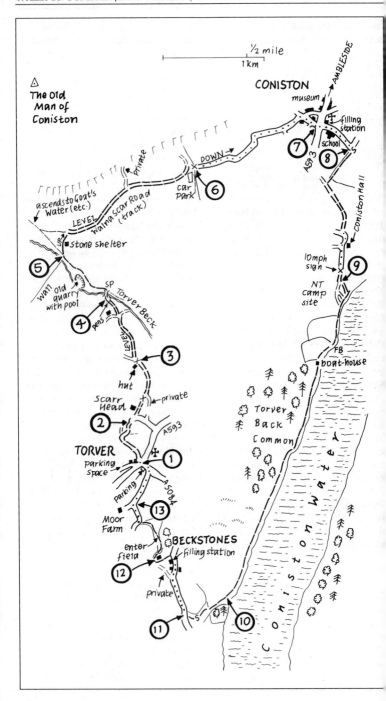

eft. 200 yards later, just before
woods end, fork half right on to
broad path (avoid sharper right fork)
and follow to reach road ⑪.

Turn right along the road, up to
hamlet of Beckstones. Immediately
after filling station (where road
bends right) take signposted
bridleway on left, descend to cross
bridge by house and ⑫ turn sharp
right on other side on path
signposted to Torver. This passes to
left of the house and into woods
(keep to left edge), then along left
edge of field to join surfaced lane.
Turn right along the lane, ⑬ bear
right at T-junction then left at main
road to reach Torver.

ON THE ROUTE

a] View of the **Old Man of Coniston**
2,635ft); the conical peak on the
right-hand side of the nearby range;
left of it is the jagged outline of **Dow
Crag**; further left, **Brown Pike**
appears as a rounded knob.

b] Abundant evidence of quarrying
once carried out on the slopes of
these fells; here, a waterfall
cascading into a former slate quarry
(now a large pool) has made an
unexpectedly attractive feature.

c] Easy walking along the level
track known as the **Walna Scar
Road**, a prehistoric routeway linking
Coniston with Seathwaite in
Dunnerdale, and providing a grand
viewing platform; the Fairfield and
Helvellyn range are NNE,
Morecambe Bay is to S, Pennines E

and Forest of Bowland to the SE.

[d] **Coniston** Former mining village
now geared to tourism. John Ruskin,
19th-century writer, essayist, critic
and artist, is buried in the
churchyard; his cross depicts his
major life's works. The Ruskin
Museum (open Easter-Oct, 10-5.30
daily) contains many of Ruskin's
sketches, mineral specimens and
personal effects, and there is also a
small display on Donald Campbell.

[e] **Coniston Hall** Built as a peel
tower in 1250 but much altered and
extended; its huge chimneys make it
one of the lake's landmarks.

[f] **Coniston Water** 5½ miles long,
and almost dead straight; the scene
of Donald Campbell's attempt in
1967 to break his water-speed record
of 260.35mph set eight years earlier.
His boat, *Bluebird*, crashed and his
body has never been recovered. On
the opposite side of the lake from
Coniston Hall is **Brantwood**,
Ruskin's home from 1872 until his
death in 1900. Seven lancet windows
at the side of the house are said to be
a reference to Ruskin's famous work
The Seven Lamps of Architecture.
From spring to autumn, the restored
steam yacht *Gondola*, built 1859
and disused by the 1950s, drifts
silently along the lake. It was
restored and reinstated by the
National Trust in 1980. **Peel Island**
at the S end of the lake was Wildcat
Island in Arthur Ransome's
children's book *Swallows and
Amazons.*

Newlands Beck and Barrow

A riverside walk in the Newlands Valley, followed by a gradual 1,250ft rise on to a low fell called Barrow, keeping the finest section down a long, turfy ridge, for the end. Most paths quite easy to find, though turn-off at ⑥ requires care.

Length 5½ miles (9km), 3½ hours
Difficulty 3–4
Start Braithwaite, on B5292 W of Keswick; roadside parking in village centre limited, may be easier to park by housing estates on N side of village. Grid reference 231236
OS maps 1:50,000 89 or 90; 1:25,000 Outdoor Leisure 4

Refreshments Hotel bar and shop in Braithwaite

WALK DIRECTIONS

① [a] Start at road-bridge at village centre (by village shop) and take signposted turn for 'Keswick 2 ½'. After 50 yards, take path on right signposted for Little Braithwaite, and keep alongside river (Newlands Beck), crossing it ② at next footbridge ¼ mile on [b]. Continue along riverside until reaching Little Braithwaite Farm, in front of which leave river, as waymarked, to pass above barn and below farmhouse.

Turn left on road, then after 100 yards (after crossing Newlands Beck)

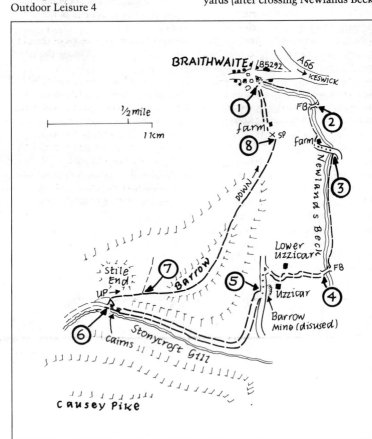

③ take riverside path on right signposted Stair. ④ After ¹/₂ mile, cross stone bridge over the river and pick up farm track, past Lower Uzzicar (on right) and turning right at Uzzicar Farm; track bends right just after to reach road. Turn left on road [c], then ⑤ after 200 yards fork right on to signposted stony track. Follow it up valley with stream (Stonycroft Gill) down on your left, later with distinctive pointed summit (Causey Pike) to the left.

⑥ After one mile from road, where valley and track are about to bend markedly left, turn right 40 yards after cairn (piled-up stones), to pick up rising narrow path (ignore minor right fork after a further 30 yards). This path soon levels out. ⑦ After hillock of Stile End on left, ignore left fork (which descends) but keep forward along path which soon reaches top of Barrow ridge [d] and then descends along the middle of it for its entire length. ⑧ At bottom, go forward to farm, where keep forward at crossing of tracks to return to Braithwaite.

ON THE ROUTE

[a] **Braithwaite** was the original site of the Cumberland Pencil Factory, established 1868; after a fire in 1898 the firm moved to Keswick.

[b] **Newlands Beck valley** The 'new lands' were reclaimed after the draining of Husaker Tarn. It is now a green and pastoral dale, but it teemed with mining activity from the time of Elizabeth I until this century. Copper was the first mineral to be mined, with lead, silver and barites worked later. Plunging grassy slopes surround the valley: Cat Bells and Maiden Moor are to the left; Barrow is close by on right and Causey Pike beyond; Dale Head is due S at the end of the valley.

[c] Vestiges of spoil heaps of the old **Barrow Mine** are visible on the left of the road.

[d] **View** from Barrow (1,494ft) NW over Braithwaite and Thornthwaite Forest; N is Bassenthwaite Lake (the only body of water in Lakeland actually called a lake; the lake inspired the scene for the death of Arthur in Tennyson's *Idylls of the King*); NE the huge mass of Skiddaw (3,054ft); ENE Keswick; ESE the distant Helvellyn range (3,116ft).

Mosedale and Swindale

A route in one of Lakeland's least known and emptiest areas, using passes to link a series of contrasting valleys. 1,900ft of ascent (none of it particularly steep); intermittently boggy ground (most of which can be avoided) in Mosedale. Paths undefined in places, but the route is not difficult to find.

Length 8 miles (13km), 4 hours
Difficulty 4
Start Car park at S end of Haweswater (end of road). Grid reference 469107
OS maps 1:50,000 90; 1:25,000 Outdoor Leisure 5 and 7

WALK DIRECTIONS

(1) From car park, pass through gate and end of reservoir road. After 50 yards, turn left (signposted Longsleddale); path (Gatesgarth Pass) rises immediately [a].

At top of pass, go through gate, ignoring right turn just before it (which rises up Harter Fell). Descend to next valley [b], and reach track by sheep-pens. (2) Just after pens turn left at signpost for Swindale Head: there is no path, so head up valley, aiming for crags at the lowest point of the skyline.

(3) Pass through gate at head of valley and descend into Mosedale [c] keeping to left-hand side of valley.

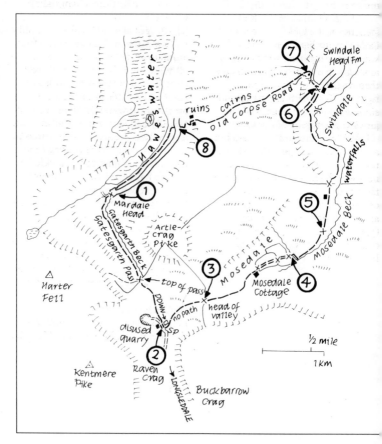

Soon, lone farmstead (Mosedale Cottage) comes into view – make towards it, and pick up track beyond it. Follow track through three gates. ④ Just after third gate, track crosses stream and becomes less distinct; 50 yards later keep on track as it swings to the left.

Where track peters out, keep to left-hand side of valley. ⑤ At head of valley, pass through gate, then immediately bear right to follow Swindale Beck and its waterfalls [d] down into Swindale. At bottom, ignore footbridge and keep on left-hand side of beck: soon pick up track and follow past two farmsteads to Swindale Head (a farm, where the road begins) ⑥.

Just before road, turn left by signpost for Old Corpse Road [e]. Path ascends between stone walls - where they taper outwards keep alongside the right-hand wall; pass through gate, continue along wall on right for 50 yards then fork left on to sunken path (with huge boulder providing natural waymarking).

⑦ 100 yards later turn sharp left at cairn (piled-up stones). Path heads up towards distant corner of wall, near which cross stream and follow faint path (easy to follow thanks to cairns), eventually reaching ruins [f] and dropping to Haweswater. ⑧ Cross reservoir road, take path opposite [g] signposted to head of lake and proceed to car park.

ON THE ROUTE

[a] **Gatesgarth Pass** climbs 1,000ft from Haweswater into Longsleddale, the 7-mile-long valley of the River Sprint. Close-up views on the ascent of Harter Fell, the summit to the right of the path.

[b] **Longsleddale** opens up suddenly ahead, framed majestically by Goat Scar to the right (S) and Great Howe to the left (SE).

[c] **Mosedale**, green and empty, offers a taste of the austere landscape making up most of the eastern flanks of the Lake District.

[d] The fine series of waterfalls are a prelude to the descent into **Swindale**, whose mellow character comes as a welcome change after Mosedale.

[e] **The Old Corpse Road** was used by coffin-bearers to bring the dead from Mardale over the moors to Shap, 8 miles to the E, before Mardale had a church-yard of its own. Mardale itself was abandoned to make way for the controversial enlargement of Haweswater into a reservoir in 1934, after which the graves were removed to a special graveyard at Shap. A picture of 17th-century Mardale church hangs in Bampton Grange church, NE of Haweswater.

[f] Excellent **view** over Haweswater from these ruins, making a fine climax to the walk, with High Street (2,719ft) towering to the W. The lake is a favourite with bird-watchers: among the species to be found is the golden eagle, re-introduced to this valley.

[g] Along the lakeside path are remains of stone walls, reminders of the now flooded pastures of Mardale.

Miterdale and Illgill Head

Tracks and paths in forested Miterdale and a long, 1,850ft ascent precede the walk's outstanding feature: two miles along the turfy Illgill Head ridge, high above Wasdale. Route not defined some of the way; compass essential in case of mist.

Length 9½ miles (15km), 6½ hours
Difficulty 5
Start Miterdale car park (not signposted); from Eskdale Green go W (towards Santon Bridge) and take unsigned right turn immediately after turn on left (which is signposted Irton Road Station); this turn is by lamp-post and concrete bench. Park at end of road by bridge. Grid reference 146011
OS maps 1:50,000 89; 1:25,000 Outdoor Leisure 6
Refreshments Pub and shop at Eskdale Green; Bower House Inn (all off the route)

WALK DIRECTIONS

①Cross bridge and follow track to reach farm (Low Place); keep right just after the farmhouse (signposted Wasdale), through gate and along track. At ford, keep left (do not cross stream) alongside wall; where wall bends left, keep forward on track, heading up

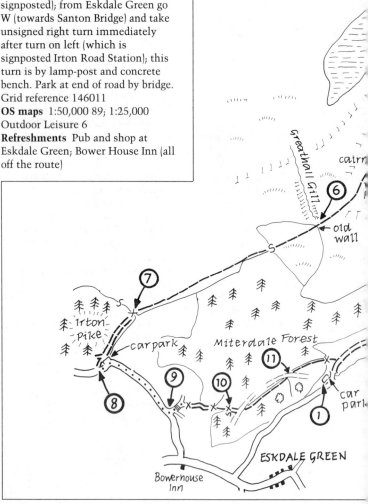

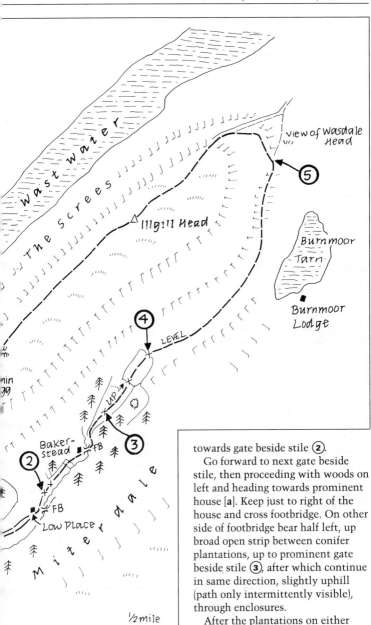

towards gate beside stile ②.

Go forward to next gate beside stile, then proceeding with woods on left and heading towards prominent house [**a**]. Keep just to right of the house and cross footbridge. On other side of footbridge bear half left, up broad open strip between conifer plantations, up to prominent gate beside stile ③, after which continue in same direction, slightly uphill (path only intermittently visible), through enclosures.

After the plantations on either side end, keep forward up to next gate beside stile, to emerge on to open land ④, where pick up faint path, ahead (still slightly uphill; path gets better defined). Path eventually curves round to left, as Burnmoor Tarn (a small lake) comes into view down to your right, and path levels out.

(5) ¼ mile after end of the tarn, fork left uphill (if you miss this fork, carry on to obvious traversing wall, where turn left steeply up to top of ridge) [b]. Continue to top of E end of the Illgill Head ridge, and follow path along the top for 2 miles [c], following cairns (piled-up stones). At minor summit of Whin Rigg, path descends, passing around to left of orange-coloured chasm (Greathall Gill) (6).

Cross ladder-stile over wall (Irton Pike, a wooded hill with a grassy crown is directly ahead) and follow path which runs close to wall on left. (7) Reach recessed corner of wall and take gate beside stile into woods, to follow woodland track down to road (keep left at fork three-quarters the way down). (8) Turn left on road, follow ½ mile.

(9) Turn left on track, signposted Miterdale and Wasdale Head; fork left 50 yards later, over cattlegrid. 100 yards later, fork right (signposted Bridleway), to follow track across pasture. Enter semi-wooded area by next gate; 50 yards later, ignore minor left turn, and soon proceed on track with wall on right and forest on left, to enter forest by gate beside stile (10).

The track leads to cross-junction with hard forestry track: here, take minor track opposite, leading half left (and proceeding with old wall on right). The track narrows, then after the old wall ends, it continues as a path. (11) Emerge on to hard forestry track: take track opposite, (with old wall on left) and follow until emerging into open by gate. Miterdale car park is a short distance to the right.

ON THE ROUTE

[a] As you ascend, views unfold gradually over **Great How**, with the sea to the right and behind. The route later passes **Burnmoor Tarn**, with its solitary lodge beneath green upland slopes.

[b] **View** ahead of Harter Fell, Scafell and Scafell Pike; from the latter, the highest peak in England (3,206ft), Samuel Taylor Coleridge wrote a letter on 5 August 1802 describing the view. Later, **Wasdale**, the cradle of British rock-climbing, which started here at the end of the 19th century, opens up; left to right ahead are **Yewbarrow**, **Kirk Fell** and **Great Gable** (the last-named appears on the National Park logo).

[c] A grand high-level section along the ridge, with a panorama of the Cumbrian coast, including the massive nuclear reprocessing works and power station at **Sellafield**.

Walla Crag and Ashness Bridge

A gentle woodland track, an exhilarating moorland edge and a brief stroll by Derwent Water form three sharply contrasting sections to this route. Reasonably straightforward route-finding; 1,000 ft of ascent.

Length 4½ miles (7km), 3½ hours

Difficulty 3

Start Great Wood National Trust car park, signed on E side of B5289 1 mile SSE of Keswick. Grid reference 271212

OS maps 1:50,000 89 or 90; 1:25,000 Outdoor Leisure 4

WALK DIRECTIONS

(1) Take gate out of car park (with sign for Ashness Bridge and Walla Crag just beyond). Keep right at junction after 50 yards, but 20 yards later turn left signposted Walla Crag via Rakefoot). Follow this woodland track [a], (2) forking right after ½ mile by signpost for Rakefoot and

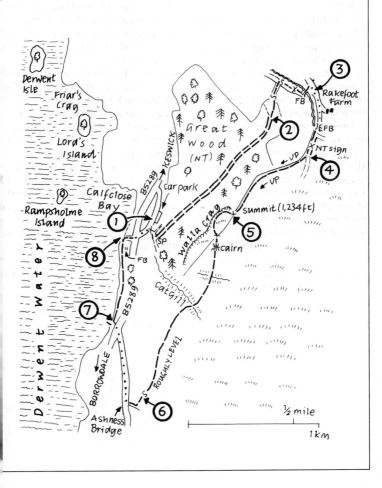

Walla Crag, to reach stile out of wood, and follow fenced path.

At path T-junction, turn right over stile, on path running on right-hand side of stream in wooded dingle. At end of wood, cross footbridge and follow path to small gate, emerging on to tarmac lane (just to left of the gate) ③. Turn right on lane, fork right after 100 yards (signposted Walla Crag). Where lane ends (100 yards later), cross footbridge, ascend track with wall on your immediate right; ④ where wall bends right, keep alongside it.

⑤ Reach cairn (piled-up stones) at top and take kissing-gate on right; follow path along top of Walla Crag [b]. After cairn on the last crag, path leads to stile: cross the stile, turn right alongside wall, but then immediately left at cairn on to broad grassy path leading across moorland and away from wall. Path is well-defined and curves around to the right, crossing two streams [c] and eventually dropping to cross ladder-stile ⑥ a short distance above surfaced lane: path now soon bends to the right to reach the lane at Ashness Bridge [d].

Turn right along the lane, and descend to B5289. Cross road to take wooden steps opposite, and ⑦ turn right along shore of Derwent Water [e]. Just after shore veers half left, there is a footbridge on your right: 150 yards later ⑧ leave shore to take track between fences and rejoin B5289. Cross to road opposite (No Entry sign refers to vehicles) and follow up to Great Wood car park.

ON THE ROUTE

[a] **Great Wood** A few oaks of the original wood remain but otherwise larches predominate; frequented by red squirrels.

[b] **Walla Crag** A series of precipitous crags high above Derwent Water, giving a grandeur of view belying its modest height (1,234ft). Across the lake are Cat Bells and Grisedale Pike; NW is Bassenthwaite Lake, breeding ground for over 70 bird species; SSW the entrance to Borrowdale; Skiddaw (3,053ft) towers to the N; Brandelhow Park in the SW corner of the lake is an area of woodland which in 1902 was the first Lake District property to be acquired by the National Trust.

[c] The deeply incised stream, **Cat Gill**, owes its name to wild cats which are thought to have lived here in the mid-18th century although half a century later they had disappeared from England. Cat Bells may be a corruption of 'cat bields' (cat shelters).

[d] **Ashness Bridge** The little packhorse bridge over the stream provides a much-photographed scene, with Derwent Water and Skiddaw beyond.

[e] **Derwent Water** Its site among the fells mentioned above is further enhanced by its islands, the four largest being at its N end: Rampsholme Island, St Herbert's Island (the southernmost; named after a hermitage established here in 685), Lord's Island (formerly the site of the Earl of Derwentwater's house) and Derwent Isle (which was home to a colony of German miners in the 16th century).

Haystacks

The fell has a barren and almost sinister aspect from its base, but once the 1,350ft ascent has been made, the path leads through a crater encompassed by small hillocks and passing several tarns (small lakes) before views suddenly open out in dramatic fashion. Ground is rough most of the way; boots essential.

Length 4 miles (6.5km), 3 hours
Difficulty 4
Start Gatesgarth car park on B5289 between Honister Pass and Buttermere, by 25% Honister Pass warning sign (if full, try other minor car park 200 yards or so along road towards Buttermere).
Grid reference 195150
OS maps 1:50,000 89 or 90; 1:25,000 Outdoor Leisure 4

WALK DIRECTIONS

① With car park on left, follow road towards Honister Pass; 100 yards later, just after house on right, take signposted bridleway on right. The track leads into Warnscale Bottom [**a**]. ② At beginning of ascent, take the path well-marked by cairns (piled-up stones) some way to the left of stream (Warnscale Beck): its

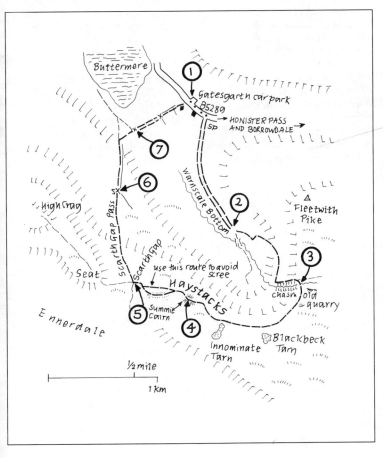

route up is visible from the bottom – it can be seen bending right half way up, towards the stream, where it turns left and follows the stream (which at this point cuts into a small chasm).

3 At top of chasm, cross the stream (easy natural stepping stones) and take well-defined path on other side. At top of main ascent, keep right and follow cairns, passing two big tarns (small lakes) [**b**], then climbing to summit cairn on Haystacks (by old metal fence posts) **4** [**c**].

Descend carefully: the most direct route is down via loose stones (scree), but it is easier to take a diagonal descent to prominent junction of paths at saddle of Scarth Gap **5** where turn right. Skirt the next summit (Seat) on your left and path soon descends.

After gate beside stile, wall joins on your right **6**; near bottom of slope where wall bends sharp right, fork right and follow the path alongside the wall to bottom **7**. Go through gate and follow farm track to Gatesgarth, turning right as signposted in the farm, on enclosed path, to reach road by car park.

ON THE ROUTE
[**a**] The **track** is an old road serving the now-vanished Dubs slate quarry once sited at the SE end of this valley. Straight ahead is the foreboding black jagged outline of Haystacks.
[**b**] The second major **tarn** to your left was once called Loaf Tarn, but seems to have lost its name when its loaf-shaped islets sank; it is now called Innominate Tarn (surely a contradiction in terms). Behind is Great Gable.
[**c**] The summit is satisfying for its sharply defined top as well as the magnificent **view** over Buttermere, Crummock Water and continuing along Lorton Vale, with Ennerdale the next valley to the left. Major peaks in sight include Pillar (2,927ft) to the SW (Pillar Rock is a rock-climbers' favourite), Grasmoor and Mellbreak (to right and left of Crummock Water, respectively) to NW, Skiddaw just in view to NE and Helvellyn to E.

Dentdale

A steep haul out of the village is rewarded by views of the dale, with easy walking along a stone-walled track. After dropping to the valley floor, a field route (care needed to find it) joins the river leading back towards Dent. Modern county boundaries place this walk in Cumbria, but there is no doubt that scenically it belongs to the Yorkshire Dales.

Length 5 miles (8km), 3 hours
Difficulty 2–3
Start Dent (car park in village) Grid reference 704871
OS maps 1:50,000 98; 1:25,000 Outdoor Leisure 2
Refreshments Pubs, cafés and shops in Dent

WALK DIRECTIONS

① [a] Take road to left of Dentdale Memorial Hall, opposite toilets and car park entrance. This rises past village green, is later signposted to Flinter Gill and Outrake, and bends right just after passing United Reform Church. **②** After last houses, the road becomes an unsurfaced track between walls, rising (with wooded ravine called Flinter Gill on your left).

Ignore minor side-turns. **③** Turn left at T-junction, and follow broad, level track between walls for one mile [b]. **④** At next junction, turn left downhill on enclosed track, to emerge on road after 3/4 mile **⑤**. Cross road to enclosed path opposite (signposted Mill Bridge), soon

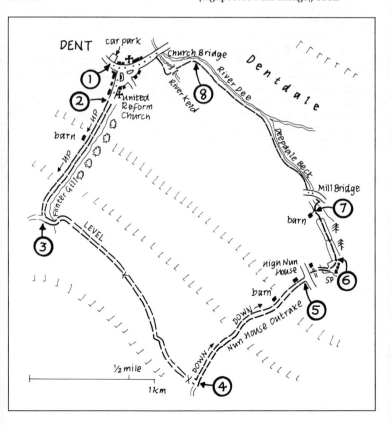

crossing farm track where take gate opposite, through small enclosure and then head downhill on track along right edge of field.

In far corner of the field, emerge by gate above three farm buildings, and turn left to take stile by the leftmost of these ⑥. Continue forward (slightly downhill) to far end of field (30 yards to left of fir trees which line bottom of field). Go forward in next (second) field, which is irregularly shaped, keeping close to bottom edge to find stile at far end.

In third field go forward, on the level, to right end of wall which is 50 yards ahead, at which point ⑦ bear quarter right down to trees, aiming for Footpath signpost, then descend to riverside path, where turn left to reach Mill Bridge. Turn left on lane and immediately right on path signposted Church Bridge. This proceeds alongside river (which may be dried up in places) and is easy to find. ⑧ After 1 mile (near Dent), path leaves river, passes ruin and goes over River Keld, then turns right beyond gate, along field edge to reach Church Bridge. Turn left into Dent.

ON THE ROUTE
[a] **Dent** (mostly seen at end of walk). Dentdale's main settlement is a gem – cobbled main street, sturdy colourwashed cottages, twisting lanes and a village green slightly away from the centre. The memorial in Shap granite commemorates Adam Sedgwick, geologist and Fellow at Trinity College, Cambridge, who was born in Dent in 1785. St Andrew's Church, has memorials to the Sedgwick family.
[b] Fine **views** over Dentdale; up to 1900 it was a marble-producing area. Whernside is straight ahead to SE: its 2,419ft summit is the highest point in the Yorkshire Dales National Park. Half left (E) is Widdale Fell, and the fells above Sedbergh are farther to W.

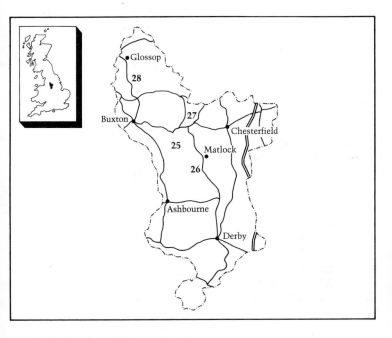

25 Bradford Dale and Lathkill Dale
26 Around Cromford, site of the early Industrial Revolution
27 The River Derwent and Froggatt Edge
28 Kinder Downfall

Holiday Which? Good Walks Guide

76 Ladybower Reservoir   77 Wolfscote Dale and Biggin Dale   78 High Tor
and the Heights of Abraham   79 Edensor and the Chatsworth Estate
80 The River Derwent and Padley Chapel   81 Lose Hill, Winnats Pass and
Castleton   82 Monsal Dale and Miller's Dale   83 Wool Packs, Fox Holes
and Edale   84 Dove Dale and Milldale   85 Calke Abbey Park and Staunton
Harold

Bradford Dale and Lathkill Dale

The dale becomes more dramatic and eventually rugged as it is followed westwards; the short route cuts off at Cales Dale. The link sections, across grassy fields and down a pleasant lane, provide views and contrast.

Length *Full walk* 9½ miles (15km), 4½ hours. *Short walk* 7 miles (11 km), 3½ hours
Difficulty 2-3
Start Youlgreave (roadside parking in village), on minor road S of Bakewell. Grid reference 210642
OS maps 1:50,000 119; 1:25,000 Outdoor Leisure 24
Refreshments Shops, pubs and tea-room in Youlgreave

WALK DIRECTIONS

① [a] With Youth Hostel on left and post office on right follow Main Street. Take first left into Holywell Lane, and descend past toilet to river Bradford. **②** Turn left by signpost for Limestone Way on near side of river and follow riverside path.

③ At cluster of houses, cross road and take track opposite still with river on right; track soon bends left (at crags), crossing river. Proceed now with river on left; by next bridge, which do not cross, continue on riverside path, soon picking up track again but leaving it 50 yards later for gap-stile – a deliberate gap in wall – giving on to riverside path.

④ Reach gate at edge of Alport and proceed to road by telephone box. Cross to track opposite, signposted Conksbury; route proceeds closely parallel to River Lathkill, with wall on right, for ½ mile [b], passing just below house to road, where take path opposite.

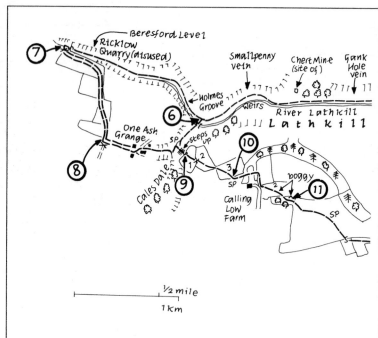

(5) ¹/₄ mile later, turn right on road; cross Bridge over river, then immediately take path on left along bottom of Lathkill Dale. At lane and houses, by next bridge, path continues opposite and slightly to right, through barrier [**c**]. **(6)** After 1 ³/₄ miles, (³/₄ mile after leaving woods), reach footbridge.
For short walk cross bridge and follow path up Cales Dale for 300 yards then left by nature reserve sign, up rough steps. This is point **(9)**.
For full walk do not cross footbridge but continue up Lathkill Dale – the terrain gets rougher and eventually the slopes diminish in size. **(7)** At end of dale (where barn is visible ahead in distance and where rugged terrain gives way to pasture) cross stile into pasture then 20 yards later turn sharp left through gate on to track which first initially doubles

back above the dale but soon turns right across fields.
(8) ¹/₃ mile later keep left on main track, now between walls and descending to farm. After first barn on left, turn left on track, fork right 40 yards later (waymarked) to find gap-stile into field. Go forward, along bottom edge of field, which becomes bottom of small valley, to reach stile into woods; path descends into Cales Dale, with Lathkill Dale visible to left. Turn right at signpost for Limestone Way, to stile by nature reserve sign, where go up rough steps.
(9) At top, beyond stile, cross first field to kissing-gate and go forward to follow right side of second field to leave at top right-hand corner, then head for farm. **(10)** In field before farm [**d**], turn left as signposted, through a series of kissing-gates taking you around the left side of the

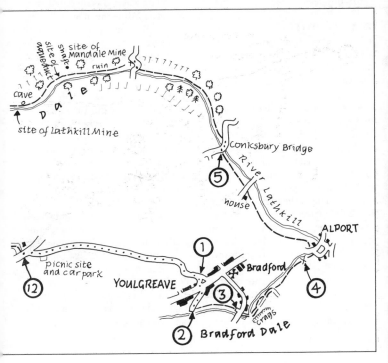

farm through small area of woodland, a narrow field and another small area of woodland.

Beyond farm, emerge into large field, turn right as signposted along edge to next gate. In second field (with farm track away to your right) bear half left diagonally across field (often boggy in the middle, but passable) to stile in far left-hand corner, into woods. Continue to next stile visible to left out of wood (can be rather boggy: best to keep left alongside wall as soon as you enter it.

(11) Emerge into large field, bear half right across field on broad path, which soon bends left, then right at signpost in middle of field. In next field, bear left a few yards to stile then go forward along wall towards building, leaving field by stile in far right-hand corner, on to road (12). Take minor road opposite, signposted to picnic site and follow [e] to Youlgreave.

ON THE ROUTE

[a] **Youlgreave** Sizable village with large church with 15th-century tomb to Thomas Cockayne; stained glass in the E and S windows by Burne-Jones.

[b] **River Lathkill** Charles Cotton, in the supplement to *The Compleat Angler* (1676) observed this river to be 'the purest, the most transparent stream that I ever saw either at home or abroad, and breeds, 'tis said, the reddest and best trout in England'. The Lathkill is unique in the Peak District as being a river whose catchment area is entirely in the limestone country. Weirs have been created along the river for the purpose of making trout hatcheries. Much of the dale is a **nature reserve**, of interest for its limestone flora and insect life; this is one of the best sites in England for the orange-tip

butterfly. The N bank was planted in the 1800s with a mixture of ash, beech, elm, sycamore and Scots pine; coppicing still plays an important role in woodland management.

[c] Relics of the once-flourishing **lead-mining industry** in Lathkill Dale are seen from here to the end of the dale (see map for locations). Mineral extraction here goes back probably to about the 11th century, but by the 1700s mining was well underground, and elaborate measures were needed to solve the problem of flooding. These included canalising the river and lining its bed with clay, and constructing soughs (brick tunnels) and leats (waterways; now dry) for draining water into the river; however, by the 1860s mining had become uneconomic and was abandoned. In 1848 a Cornish beam engine for pumping water was installed at **Mandale Mine**; the 'bob wall' still stands. Beyond are the pillars of the **aqueduct** (built 1840) carrying a leat (water channel) across the river. **Lathkill Mine** has a pit which once contained a 52-ft wheel, again for pumping water. **Gank Hole vein** is the site of ochre mining in the 1880s. Screes at Ricklow Quarry are of Eyam (or Cawdor) limestone, which was used as black marble; the quarry closed in 1900. Nearby **Ricklow Mine** has the initials of owner Isaac Beresford and the date 1787 by its entrance.

[d] **Calling Low Farm** (visible here) and **One Ash Grange Farm** (passed earlier on the full walk) were once both monastic granges of the Cistercians of Roche Abbey in South Yorkshire; at that time, sheep-farming supplied wool to Italy.

[e] Good views S over **Bradford Dale** and **Youlgreave**.

Around Cromford, site of the early Industrial Revolution

Takes in Arkwright's historic village and mills, the track of the vanished High Peak Railway and the Cromford Canal towpath. Easy route-finding once on the High Peak Trail.

Length 5 miles (8km), 2½ hours
Difficulty 1-2
Start Cromford village centre, at junction of A5012 and B5036, between Matlock and Wirksworth. Grid reference 296569 *By train* Cromford
OS maps 1:50,000 119; 1:25,000 Outdoor Leisure 24
Refreshments Cafés, pubs, shops in Cromford; café at Cromford Mill

WALK DIRECTIONS

① Make your way up the main street (B5036) towards Wirksworth. Opposite A5012 (Via Gellia) take narrow lane on left to see sluice [a] and follow path beyond it to the right, to reach road. Turn right to reach North Street (tall terraced houses on either side) [b] and turn right along it to rejoin main road.

② Turn left, uphill, [c] 100 yards to bus-stop, then left into Bedehouse Lane. Immediately fork right, then right again 30 yards later by 'no cycling' sign on path between walls (with houses on right and Black Rock, which you soon reach, visible on skyline ahead). By lamp-post [d], path bends right and immediately left to become lane. Follow up to T-junction with residential road **③**, where take enclosed path opposite and slightly to the right. Reach lane, turn left along it: lane bends right uphill after 50 yards. 150 yards later keep right at fork (left is signposted Black Rock and High Peak Trail).

④ Immediately before house, take small gate on right and walk alongside wall (heading towards distant quarry) along top of field. At end, enter woods, bear quarter right, slightly downhill, to fence 50 yards away; pick up clear path ascending through woods and soon leaving fence, passing car park away to your right. **⑤** Reach old railway track (enclosed by stone walls), at base of Black Rock. Turn left along the railway track (the High Peak Trail) to continue, or detour to the top of the rocks [e].

Follow the railway track for 1½ miles [f], down a long slope and under the A6 to reach canal **⑥** [g]. Cross to far side, turn left along towpath to continue route but first turn right along towpath to detour past pumphouse to aqueduct; then return and follow the towpath to Cromford, emerging opposite church **⑦** [h].

Left on road, past Cromford Mill on your right [i], them cross A632 (or turn right along it for ¼ mile to detour to Masson Mills [j], into village centre. Here you can detour to see two more mills: take first right (before reaching Greyhound Hotel) on narrow lane signposted to post office; at junction with main road, one mill is ahead and on left [k]. Return along main road, past mill pond and mill complete with water-wheel.

ON THE ROUTE

[a] The semi-circular **sluice**, constructed 1785, supplied water to local cotton-mills.
[b] **North Street** Model three-storey dwellings fronting directly on to a broad street. This was the first planned street of its kind in industrial Derbyshire, built by Richard Arkwright (see [i]) in 1776-77 to house mill-workers.
[c] More industrial revolution houses front Cromford's main street. **Nos. 9, 11, 31 and 37** (all on left as you go up the street) are good examples,

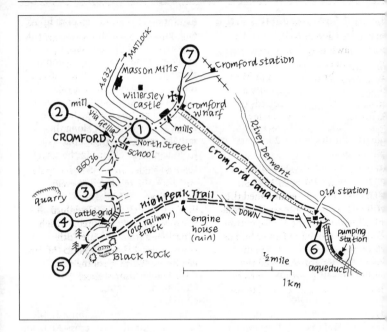

retaining their original small-pane windows.

[d] At the top of Bedehouse Lane, by the lamp-post, are the single-storey 17th-century **almshouses** that give the lane its name.

[e] **View** from Black Rock: on the other side of Cromford, the neat, symmetrical mansion in honey-coloured stone is **Willersley Castle**, built for Richard Arkwright but not completed until 1792, after his death. To the left of it are **Masson Mills** (to which you can detour later in walk). Beyond are the **Derwent Gorge**, **High Tor** (an inland cliff) and the cable-car line to **The Heights of Abraham**; **Riber Castle** is away to the right.

[f] **High Peak Trail** Follows an old railway track which operated 1831-1967, connecting the Cromford and Peak Forest canals. The 33-mile goods line rose 990 feet to a height of 1,264ft, making the sharp ascent at the Cromford Canal end via the **inclined plane** down which the walk

passes; haulage for trains was provided by an engine house at the top of the incline (now partly ruined, but with explanatory plaque). At the bottom, beyond a short tunnel with half a railway truck embedded in it, is a short section of reinstated track, with two old guards' vans, by the **old station**.

[g] **Cromford Canal** Completed 1793, it runs 14½ miles to join the Erewash Canal at Langley Mill, so linking Cromford with Manchester, Liverpool and other major industrial centres, and used to transport raw cotton, yarn and minerals. The canal leads to the right past the **Leawood Pumphouse**, built 1849 for pumping water into the canal (still with its original beam engine; occasionally open to the public), to the **Wigwell aqueduct**, triple-arched and 600ft long. Returning along the canal towards Cromford, the still-extant **railway** on the right was opened in 1849 as the Manchester, Buxton, Matlock and Midlands Junction

Railway. At **Cromford Wharf**, once a busy goods and passenger port, a horse-drawn barge for tourist traffic operates in summer.

[**h**] Arkwright is buried in **St Mary's church**, which was originally a private chapel in the grounds of Arkwright's home, Willersley Castle, but became the village church in 1797.

[**i**] **Cromford Mill** (open 10-4.30 Mon-Fri, 11-5 Sat and Sun; closes 3.30 in winter). Here in 1771 Sir Richard Arkwright established the world's first water-powered cotton-spinning-mill. In the 1840s, cotton production moved to Lancashire as water power gave way to steam power. Arkwright perfected the water frame in nearby Arkwright House in 1768, and decided to use water power from the Bonsall Brook and Cromford Sough for this mill. A second mill on the site was in production by 1777. Opposite the mill entrance is the **mill manager's house**, and on the hill is **Rock House**, Arkwright's home before he moved to Willersley Castle.

[**j**] **Masson Mills** (off route: follow A632 towards Matlock) Another Arkwright mill, built 1783. Its six storeys, Venetian windows, cupola and alien red brick tell of great prosperity.

[**k**] The mill ahead is **Cromford Corn-Mill** (being restored), which functioned from the late 18th-century until about 1930; to the left is a former paint-grinding mill retaining its water-wheel.

The River Derwent and Froggatt Edge

A route with splendid variety: mixed woodlands, river banks and pasture on the valley floor, before a steep rise up on to the gritstone edge for two miles of majestic views; finishes with an abrupt descent to Calver. Not all field-paths are defined.

Length 6½ miles (10.5km), 3½ hours

Difficulty 3

Start The Bridge pub, Calver, on A623 (NNE of Bakewell) at E end of village, by bridge and signpost for Froggatt and Curbar. Parking on minor road by pub and school. Grid reference 248744

OS maps 1:50,000 119; 1:25,000 Outdoor Leisure 24

Refreshments Pub at Calver; pub, tea-room and shop at Grindleford; Grouse Inn near ⑨

WALK DIRECTIONS

① With pub on left and church on right take road half right with speed derestriction sign and signpost for Froggatt and Sheffield. Road runs beside river, and mill is seen on other side [**a**]. 100 yards after mill, take signposted riverside path on left, later passing weir [**b**]. ② Cross road-bridge and turn right on other side, on riverside path. ③ Cross next road-bridge, then turn left at T-junction, ignoring an immediate right turn called The Green; follow through village.

④ At next junction keep straight on, signposted Grindleford Bridge, where right goes steeply uphill. This lane soon becomes unsurfaced, then wall on left ends. Where wall on right reaches corner (with barn up on right) bear half right across field to entrance in wall (ahead is signed as private) then ⑤ keep forward, with wall on left.

In next field, continue forward to stile into Froggatt Woods by National Trust sign. Path through woods may be muddy, but is easy to follow – running along wall on your left until slab bridge then proceeding ¼ mile to gap-stile into field ⑥. Go forward, with wall on left; 50 yards after the wall is replaced by a fence, take gate on left, head diagonally across field towards filling station (to right of bridge) at edge of Grindleford [**c**].

Turn right on road, then after 30 yards ⑦ take track on right. After houses on left end, track bends right 50 yards later, just before isolated group of cottages, take path on left (signposted Froggatt Edge and Grouse Inn) which climbs through woods towards top of slope (at first with wall on left; where wall reaches corner, continue up and slightly to right; keep forward after 200 yards at cross-junction by metal well-cover). ⑧ Close to top, turn right at path T junction, to reach stile by power-post ⑨. (*To detour to Grouse Inn, turn left, then left again by signpost, to cross stile; 50 yards later, take gate on right and cross fields diagonally to inn visible ahead – stile on to road is just to the right of the inn*).

Turn right to continue, soon reaching stile; path then drops to cross stream and rises to road. Turn right on road, and immediately ⑩ left through gate by sign for Eastern Moors Estate. Follow this broad path along Froggatt Edge for 2 miles [**d**]. ⑪ Beyond gate by next Eastern Moors sign, turn right, down towards Curbar, to reach road, and follow it until taking path on left by National Trust sign for Curbar Gap (continue down road back to start).

Path heads through old enclosures, reaching two stone posts after 50 yards, where continue down towards village, with wall on right, to National Trust sign (facing other

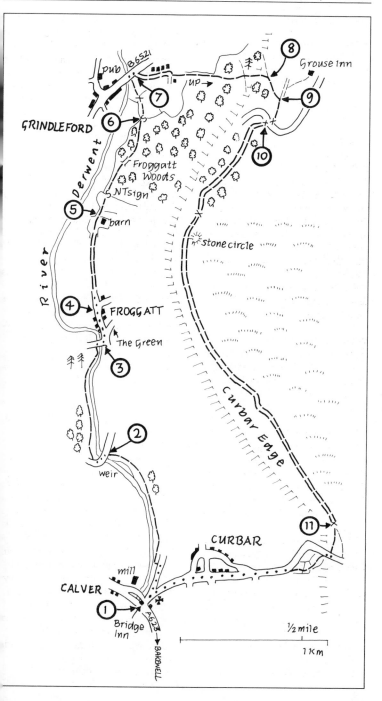

way), then forward 30 yards to squeeze-stile, and along left edge of fields to rejoin road. ⑫ Follow road down through Curbar and back to start (keep straight on at crossroads by telephone box).

ON THE ROUTE

[a] **Calver mill** across the river was built by Richard Arkwright in 1805 on the site of an 18th-century cotton-mill.

[b] In the 18th century Daniel Defoe observed the **River Derwent** to be 'a fury of a river . . . a frightful creature when the hills load her current.' Banking has now reduced the risk of flooding, but the weir, old bridges and fine broad-leafed woodlands still contribute to its romantic quality.

Wild geese are a common sight.

[c] An antique **footpath signpost** is dated 1908. Several of this vintage survive in the Peak District.

[d] **Froggatt Edge** Coppice gives way to boulders, tors and overhangs along the gritstone edge, which in its entirety can be followed for a 15-mile walk. Particularly dramatic at the south end, with an extensive view of the valley and an outcrop shaped like a lizard's head. Local **quarries** once provided many of the nation's millstones. 200 yards after the gate, just to left of path, look out for a **Bronze Age stone circle**, about 25ft in diameter, with some eight uprights (depending on what is included), three feet high.

Kinder Downfall

**A taste of the wilderness on a route
that belies its proximity to
Manchester; high up along the edge
of Kinder Scout with the Hayfield
valley far below. Care needed to find
route at ①, otherwise route is self-
evident in clear weather. *Ascent
1,000ft.***

Length 7 miles (11km), 4½ hours
Difficulty 3-4
Start Bowden Bridge car park
between Hayfield and Kinder
Reservoir. From Hayfield, take Bank
Street (by National Westminster
Bank); keep right after 100 yards at
junction. Car park is on left after

¾ mile). Grid reference 048869
OS maps 1:50,000 110; 1:25,000
Outdoor Leisure 1
Refreshments Shop at camp site
near car park; teas at Tunstead
House

WALK DIRECTIONS

① Turn left out of car park (away
from Hayfield) on road, initially
with stream on right (ignore minor
right fork after a few yards). Follow
to reservoir gates by sign for Kinder
Reservoir Treatment Works ②. Here
fork right (signposted) on road over
stream; 80 yards later fork left on to
signposted path which goes through
woods and over footbridge to rejoin

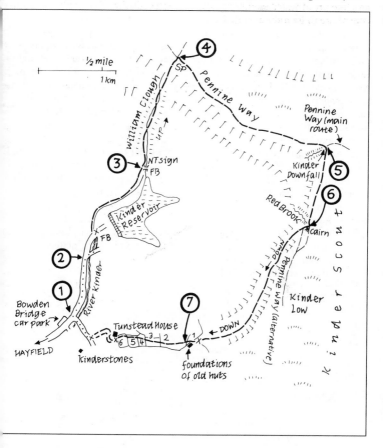

reservoir road, which cross to take path opposite.

Path rises initially, then levels out to run just above reservoir. **(3)** At end of reservoir do not cross footbridge on right but continue up William Clough (valley) by National Trust sign. **(4)** At top of pass turn right by signpost, ascending hill by well-defined path (Pennine Way) which keeps close to the edge, with Kinder valley on your immediate right [**a**].

(5) After 1 mile, reach top of Kinder Downfall (large boulder-strewn chasm) [**b**] after which keep right along top of edge (path still very well defined). **(6)** ½ mile later cross another, much smaller chasm (Red Brook), again with boulders; immediately after, keep to right fork (left goes past cairn, piled-up stones) and fork right again 60 yards later on narrow path which descends slightly from top of edge. This turn-off needs care in spotting, but the path becomes increasingly clear as soon as you are on it, as it levels out, contouring just below top of slope.

(7) After 1 mile, path is joined on right by wall, then goes through gate beside stile in fence, beyond which keep alongside wall. After 100 yards take gate beside stile on right (by foundations of ruined buildings) into enclosure. Bear left, immediately through gate into second field, where continue forward, always with wall close on left, to reach next

gate beside stile.

(8) In third field, continue forward down to next gate; in fourth field bear slightly right to next gate (by signpost) then in fifth field aim down to left-hand of two gates. Proceed in sixth field with wall on right down to Tunstead House, past which a winding track bends to the right to reach road by bridge and small weir **(9)**: keep forward (do not cross bridge) and follow to reach car park.

ON THE ROUTE

[**a**] **Kinder Scout** A 20-square mile plateau of grouse moors, scene of the famous mass trespass in the 1930s where walkers demonstrated against the lack of public access to the countryside. This protest was a milestone in the move towards National Parks and registered rights of way, which came into being in the next decade. The vast area of blanket bog is the first (and quite formidable) obstacle for walkers attempting the 270-mile Pennine Way, which starts from Edale.

[**b**] **Kinder Downfall** With an annual rainfall here of 63 inches, there is a good chance of finding the waterfall in spate. In winter the Downfall can be a magnificent show of icicles. Further along the edge is **Kinder Low**, no more than a slight rise, the highest point on the plateau at 2,088ft.

DEVON

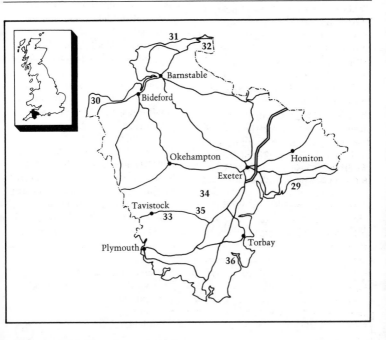

Holiday Which? Good Walks Guide

Hooken Cliffs and Branscombe

Takes the coast path out of Beer, passing Beer Head and descending into the undercliff to reach sea-level at Branscombe Mouth, then up West Cliff. Here the sea views soon disappear, but there is a panorama of the gentle green landscape around Branscombe. Beyond the village, there is one steep ascent on to Stockham's Hill before the leisurely drop on a green track down into Beer. A little care is needed with the directions in section ⑦, otherwise the route is easy to follow.

Length 5 miles (8km), 2½ hours
Difficulty 2–3
Start Cliff car park, Beer (1 mile W of Seaton). Follow main street to sea, keeping right behind The Anchor Inn, on Common Lane. Car park is ¼ mile up, on left.
Grid reference 229889
OS maps 1:50,000 192 ; 1:25,000 SY 08/18 and SY 29/39 (Pathfinder 1330 and 1316)
Refreshments Plenty in Beer; café at Branscombe Mouth; shop and pub in Branscombe.

WALK DIRECTIONS

①[a] Take Little Lane, signposted Coast Path to Branscombe Mouth, by car park. This soon becomes path, bending left in front of caravan site and crossing edge of field before running close to cliff (there is always a fence between you and the edge).

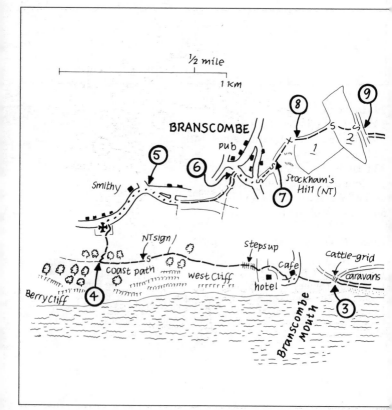

② After ¾ mile, take stile on left, signposted Coast Path, which descends into the undercliff [**b**]. Later, pick up track through caravan site, but **③** leave it at cattlegrid (signposted Coast Path), descending to Branscombe Mouth. Continue on coast path, keeping left (seaward side) of thatched café, then right immediately after it (signposted); path now ascends West Cliff. At top, path bends right and enters woodland, losing sight of the sea.

¼ mile later, keep straight on by stiles and National Trust sign for West Cliff (facing other way). **④** 350 yards later turn right by post with yellow arrow waymarkers leaving the coast path and descend to Branscombe church (first with fence

on right, then after doubling back beyond stile down steps then along edge of field). [**c**] Beyond church, turn right on road. **⑤** At road junction by houses, take cul-de-sac on right opposite bus stop (signposted Link to Public Footpath, Branscombe Mouth).

Where this lane ends, continue forward through gate by National Trust sign for Manor Mill and follow left edge of field, at end of which keep to left of seat. Go over footbridge and pick up enclosed path, then lane, into Branscombe village centre. **⑥** Emerge at small square, turn sharp right (signposted to beach) and follow to T-junction. Turn left on road then after 30 yards turn right on to enclosed path up

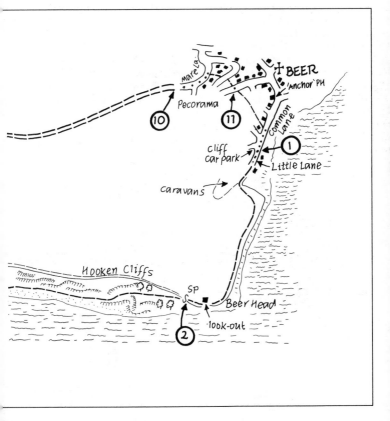

steps by National Trust sign for Stockham's Hill.

(7) On reaching stile into open ground, turn left, with fence and woodland on left (soon ignore stile on left), still ascending. 200 yards later, by another stile, fence veers half right: path turns right here, still uphill and now away from fence, and bends right a few yards later, up to stile into field (8). Turn left and go alongside hedge on left side of the field and leave field by stile at far end (near corner). Continue forward across second field to stile ahead, then (9) forward on track (which soon runs between hedges), eventually descending to pass car park on your left and Pecorama on your right (10); track has now become a road on outskirts of Beer.

At T-junction turn left, then where road bends left after 75 yards, take enclosed path on right (signposted). Descend to road and take path opposite to reach another road (11). Here either turn left (for centre of Beer) or take lane opposite (for cliff car park). Ignore Higher Meadow on your left, then ignore right turn, soon picking up another enclosed path to reach road where turn right to car park.

ON THE ROUTE

[a] **Beer** Small resort, joined on to larger Seaton, with fishing still important. Its past activities included smuggling, lace-making and quarrying; the latter dates back to Roman times. Stone quarried here was used in the building of Exeter cathedral.

[b] **Hooken undercliff** Spectacular rock towers and pinnacles, thick undergrowth, and a broken terrain caused by landslips; the white chalk contrasts with the orange sandstone cliffs in view W of Branscombe Mouth.

[c] **Branscombe** A village in two parts; in the 9th century it was owned by King Alfred, and it later belonged to the Benedictine Abbey in Exeter. Around the church is a single row of houses including Church Living Cottage, mostly 16th-century, but dating from the 13th century; the origins of its name are uncertain – 'living' may be a dialectal word for farm and the cottage owned by the Canons of Exeter, or it may simply have been a guest-house for visiting clerics. The **church** (mostly 11th- to 16th-century) has murals of the Seven Deadly Sins, a central tower and contains a rare priest's room and has vestiges of Saxon work. Also of note are an 18th-century triple-decker pulpit and an Elizabethan gallery. Further along the road, on the left, a still-functioning **smithy**, has a canopied thatched roof projecting over its cobbled forecourt. The walk continues into the detached portion of the village (called Vicarage on some maps), which is on various levels, with its centre tightly clustered around a picturesque pub.

Hartland Point and Quay

Remote, but worth the pilgrimage, not just for Stoke church but also for some of England's most exciting cliff scenery. The inland sections at the start are along easily managed green lanes dipping and rising between hedges; the coast is tough going and includes several quite tiring ascents; the wind can make it even more demanding. There should be no difficulty in finding the way. The walk can be extended along the coast south of Hartland Quay to take in the waterfalls at Speke's Mill Mouth.

Length 6 miles (9.5km), 3 hours
Difficulty 4
Start Stoke village (W of Hartland), by church; roadside parking in village. Grid reference 235247
OS maps 1:50,000 190; 1:25,000 SS 22/32 (Pathfinder 1253)
Refreshments Hotel at Hartland Quay

WALK DIRECTIONS

①[a] Facing the church lych-gate by toilets where the main road bends to left towards Hartland Quay, take the minor road to the right which is signed 'unsuitable for motors'. This drops to valley floor [b] and then rises. ② Past a farm, where road bends right, keep straight on taking a track between hedges, which drops and then rises.

③ Fork right in front of next farm; the track heads up to right of rightmost barn, to reach road along which turn right. ④ After 300 yards turn left on signposted bridleway (a track, narrowing to path, between hedges). This drops (ignore signposted stile on left at bottom) and crosses a footbridge, and then has stream on left for a few yards until reaching gate.

Just beyond this ⑤ turn right at track T-junction by signpost. Follow

to farm, at end of which the track bends left; 50 yards later ignore the track on your left and ⑥ keep forward another 50 yards later at track junction (by silo on left and with tollbooth away to right). You are now following surfaced track leading past car park; keep to the surfaced track, through a gate towards the look-out hut on Hartland Point [c], then ⑦ fork left 50 yards after the gate (just before pillars on either side of track) on to signposted coastal path which you follow to Hartland Quay along the cliff tops.

⑧ After 2 miles the coast path drops through valley by cottage; continuation is to the left of the cottage to regain cliff top, ⑨ Reach road (Hartland Quay [d] is reached by a detour down to right; use the path to right of road: path then crosses road and continues on other side). Turn left on road but immediately take signposted gate on left into field and turn right along field edge closely parallel to road leading to Stoke church. At edge of village, path still avoids road all the way to the churchyard which is then crossed.

ON THE ROUTE

[a] **Stoke** The highest church tower in the county soars 128 feet, and was built as a landmark for sailors. There is an extensive view from the top. This is one of the most absorbing country churches in Devon, with a notable delicate medieval screen (the oak tie-beam above it was taken from the wooden battleship *Revenge*), well-preserved wagon roofs and an intricately carved Norman font.
[b] View of **Hartland Abbey** on the right, a castellated mansion on the site of a 12th-century abbey.
[c] **Hartland Point** Among some of the most spectacular cliffs in the

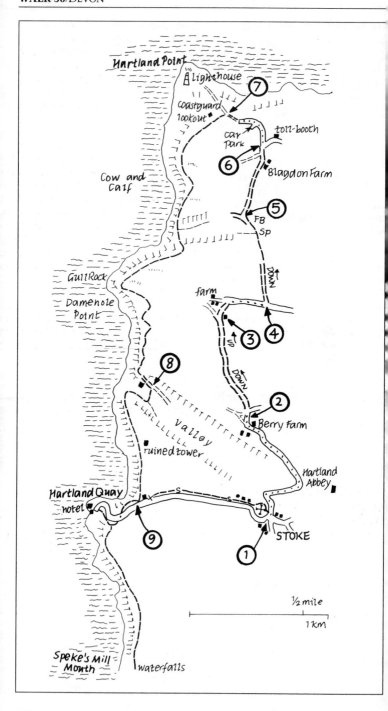

South-West. The Point has a view of
the isle of Lundy, 11 miles out to
sea, and the Glamorgan coast. A
coastguard look-out is perched high
on the cliff, with the lighthouse
(briefly glimpsed after you head
round the headland) far below. To
the S the view opens out along Bude
Bay. Vertical tilting and uplifting of
strata, combined with the forces of
the sea, have created some bizarre
coastal landforms.

d] Hartland Quay The hotel is
created from the former harbour
buildings, which included stables for
donkeys that carried cargo up the
hill from the quay; the quay
functioned for 400 years, dealing
with the movement of grain and
building materials before being
washed away in storms in the 19th
century. A small museum here has
displays about shipping and the
coastline. A mile S of the quay, the
coast path reaches a series of
waterfalls at **Speke's Mill Mouth**,
where a stream tumbles 160 feet to
the beach (return the same way to
resume the walk).

Holdstone Hill and the Ladies' Mile

Exmoor's famous varied landscape is neatly encapsulated in this stunningly beautiful walk, beginning on a gentle downhill track through moorland, with patchwork fields and green hills in the distance, then along the side of an incised combe. The finale is the coast path from above Heddon's Mouth to the 360-degree panorama on Holdstone Hill. The route is quite easy to find and ascents are gentle.

Length 6 miles (9.5km), 3 hours
Difficulty 2
Start Holdstone Hill car park, between Combe Martin and Hunter's Inn; turn off A399 opposite London Inn at S end of Combe Martin on road heading E (signposted Buzzacott Manor); at crossroads keep forward, signposted Trentishoe and Hunter's Inn; car park is on left by group of houses after 1 mile. Grid reference 624474
OS maps 1:50,000 180; 1:25,000 SS 64/74 (Pathfinder 1214)

WALK DIRECTIONS

①Turn left out of car park, along road. After 300 yards turn right, signposted Trentishoe Mill (site of), by metal posts. The track drops gently. ② 100 yards before reaching corner of wall keep straight on (ignoring right fork). The wall is then close by on your right; the track narrows to path width and soon bends left leaving the wall and dropping into trees.

③ At oblique path T-junction, turn left to cross a stile, on the level 'Ladies' Mile' path [**a**]. ④ Reach four-way signpost where valley is about to swing to right; keep to the level path, signposted Rhydda Bank Corner. ⑤ Emerge on to road, turn right then after 50 yards reach crossroads where turn left

signposted Trentishoe church.

Turn right at next T-junction, soon past Trentishoe church [**b**], where road bends to right. ⑥ One field after last house on left in Trentishoe, turn left by National Trust sign for Headon Valley Estate and signpost for coast path [**c**]. The path is soon joined by field boundary on left and leads to the sea, then bending left alongside the field boundary.

⑦ Path drops down six steps to signposted stile on left and leaves cliff to cross moorland, over another stile beside gate: follow main path (ignore left fork just after). ⑧ Reach signpost at four-way junction, keep straight on, soon through breach in

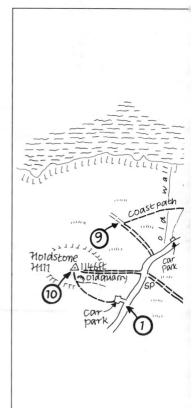

w over-grown wall, to reach
blique junction with broad track,
with bungalows visible to left ⑨.
Turn sharp left towards the
bungalows, at which turn right along
road. Either follow road back to car
park, or when past two bungalows
n right, turn right (opposite track
n which you started walk) to follow
ack to top of Holdstone Hill [**d**].
⑩ At summit turn sharp left,
escending past small abandoned
quarry on left; 50 yards later fork
ght and descend to car park.

N THE ROUTE

The Ladies' Mile A path specially
created to enjoy wonderful views
long a terrace halfway up the slope

of this deep and steep-sided valley,
which includes attractive woodlands
and moorland features.

[**b**] **Trentishoe** A tiny village with
diminutive church to match. Its
tower may well have been a hiding-
place for contraband. The church
contains a musicians' gallery of
1731; a chunk cut out of the parapet
enabled the double-bass player to
have enough room to bow!

[**c**] Views of **Heddon Mouth** and
(once a small port) **Heddon Valley**,
with the **Glamorgan coast** visible on
a clear day.

[**d**] The views from **Holdstone Hill**
(1,146ft) are not that different from
those already seen but the extra
height gives added exhilaration.

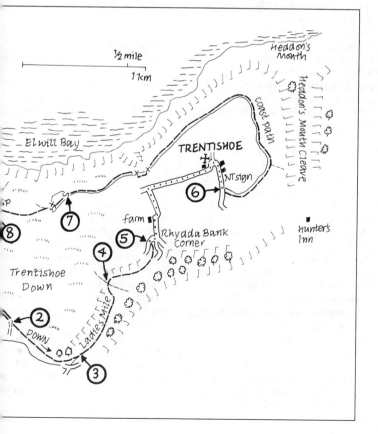

Doone country

Doone Valley is the scenic highlight, but the bracing moorland tracks that precede it are equally enjoyable, with high, uncluttered horizons graced with distant sea views. An exposed walk, it is perhaps best enjoyed on a sunny day. The route is not defined in section ⑩, and some care is needed, although finding your way should not be a great problem in clear weather. Easy-going underfoot, on hard tracks and stony paths, or over springy turf.

Length 5½ miles (9km), 3 hours
Difficulty 2
Start Malmsmead car park, on Devon-Somerset border S of A39. Follow minor road E from Brendon. Car park is on left.
Grid reference 791477
OS maps 1:50,000 180; 1:25,000 SS 64/74 (Pathfinder 1214)

WALK DIRECTIONS

① [a] Turn left out of car park, along road, and after 40 yards (just before road junction) turn very sharp right on rising track signposted Malmsmead Hill. This leads up into woods and levels out, then drops [b] to road ②. Turn left on road and immediately left on to rising woodland path signposted Brendon Common and Malmsmead Hill.

③ Keep forward on emerging from woods, following gently rising path (soon merging into track coming sharply from left), heading to right of nearby gentle moorland rise (Southern Ball). ④ Reach gate on to road, take hard track opposite (not lesser track half right) signposted Brendon Common and Doone Valley.

⑤ After ¼ mile fork right (left fork ascends Malmsmead Hill). ⑥ [c] ¼ mile later take path on left (signposted Doone Valley), where the track bends abruptly right as a

ford: this path bends immediately right too. ⑦ ¼ mile later keep forward at next signpost at crossing of tracks (valley of Lank Combe comes into view down to left). Turn left at next crossing of tracks, signposted Doone Valley. This lead down to cross Lank Combe and rise half left.

⑧ Where the track becomes indistinct, keep forward (roughly level for ¼ mile; Lank Combe is about 400 yards away to your left), to find gate in fence ⑨. Go forward (route initially indistinct but heads 90° from the fence), gently downhill path soon becomes better defined, fording a stream and later with wall on the left.

⑩ At signpost near footbridge, turn left, uphill in Malmsmead direction; 50 yards later turn right T-junction of path to follow path along Doone Valley [d]. ⑪ When close to Cloud Farm ignore footbridge but proceed through gate and follow cart track to reach road ⑫. Turn right to reach Malmsmea

ON THE ROUTE

[a] **Malmsmead** A two-arched packhorse bridge by the ford spans the county border of Devon and Somerset. The hamlet, nestling in sheltered valley in some of the mos attractive country in inland Exmoc is famous as the setting for R.D. Blackmore's novel *Lorna Doone*. It is matter of debate as to whether Lorna Doone Farm was the farm where Blackmore envisaged John Ridd to have brought his bride Lorna.
[b] **View** of the deep and sinuous East Lyn valley around Brendon.
[c] The high moorland plateau give a good idea of the empty expanses inland Exmoor. To the N, the sea a Lynmouth is glimpsed with, in cle weather, the South Wales coast visible beyond.

Bagworthy (pronounced Badgery) **Water** runs along Doone Valley, a mellow surprise after the open and windswept section of the walk that precedes it. At the point the river is joined, faintly discernible grassy humps mark the site of a medieval village. A memorial stone to Blackmore, erected in 1969 for the centenary of *Lorna Doone*'s publication, is passed mid-way along the valley.

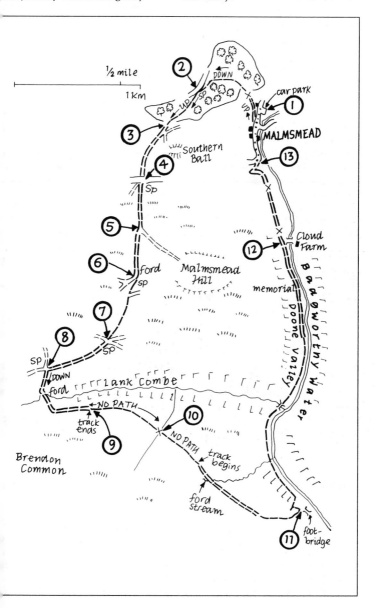

Leather Tor and the Dartmoor Railway

The going is gentle all the way, but the landscape wild and varied, peppered with tors, relics of mineral excavation and the occasional medieval waymarker. The route from Sharpitor is undefined for ½ mile and extra care needs to be taken in mist; otherwise the route is easy to find.

Length 8½ or 9½ miles (13.5 or 15km), 4½ or 5 hours
Difficulty 3
Start Princetown, on B3212 NE of Yelverton. Grid reference 591735. *Alternatively* start at car park at ⑤, at E end of Burrator Reservoir by Norsworthy Bridge (Grid reference 568694)
OS maps 1:50,000 191 and 202; 1:25,000 Outdoor Leisure 28
Refreshments Full range in Princetown

WALK DIRECTIONS

① [a] Standing at junction of B3212 and B3357, take turn opposite B3357 and to right of Devil's Elbow pub, leading past toilets and continuing as track on to moor. After short section between walls this continues alongside wall on left, past South Hessary Tor after ½ mile then ② when wall bends left, leave it and proceed forward.

Pass three boundary stones before reaching T-junction with well-defined track ③. Turn right and follow track gently down hill [b], with woods appearing on right after 1½ miles ④. Ignore right turns into the wood, and keep to main track to reach corner of road ⑤. Go forward along road, over Norsworthy Bridge, then fork right after 400 yards.

⑥ Where open land appears by stone cross on right, turn right and head up (no path) to rocks at summit of Leather Tor. Proceed to next tor

(Sharpitor), from where road is visible below. Head down to prominent car park by pond ⑦ and cross road. Proceed forward (no path down towards nearest house (½ mile ahead).

⑧ Before house is reached, turn right on meeting well-defined old railway track, which you follow al

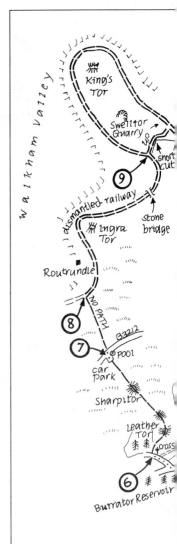

e way to Princetown [**c**], [**d**]. *For
ort walk* ⑨ after track passes
der a stone bridge you can fork
ght uphill alongside wall on right
cut out loop around King's Tor:
here wall bends right, track
lows it for a few yards before
nding left to rejoin old railway,
ong which turn right.

Both walks [**e**] ⑩ shortly before
Princetown, a plantation appears on
left: track here bends right to road.
Turn left on road into Princetown.

ON THE ROUTE
[**a**] **Princetown** Sited 1400 feet above
sea level, the village owes its
existence to Sir Thomas Tyrwhitt,

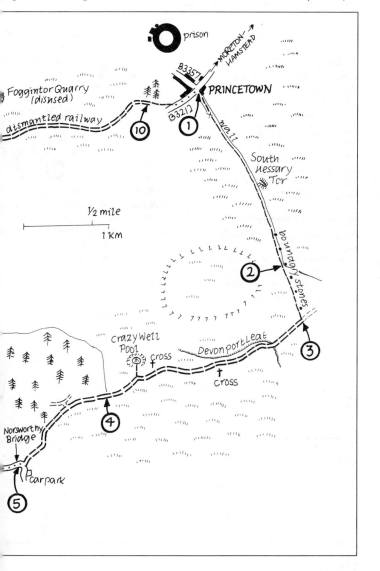

secretary to the eldest son of George III, who as Duke of Cornwall leased Tyrwhitt land here for flax growing and granite quarrying. The village was built to house labourers, but after struggling to entice them to stay here, Tyrwhitt had the idea in 1805 of building a prison to accommodate French prisoners of war. After 1814 the prison lay empty until, on Prince Albert's recommendation, it was brought back into service as a prison for long-term convicts.

[b] The track crosses **Devonport Leat**, a 15-mile long water-channel constructed in 1796 to supply water to Devonport in Plymouth, and fed by the West Dart river, the Lowsic and the Blackbrook. Later on the left, a medieval **stone cross** stands on a route across the moors between abbeys at Buckfast and Tavistock. 1/2 mile later, where a stream is crossed, detour right along artificial valley 300 yards to **Crazy Well Pool**, created by the tin mines, the evidence of whose former activity litter the hillsides. Just after the stream, in a sharp right direction another **stone cross** is visible. Fine **views** throughout this slow descent,

with Down Sheep's tors to the left and Leather Tor and Sharpitor to the right framing a view over Burrator Reservoir.

[c] **The Plymouth and Dartmoor Railway** The Great Western Railway operated this line from Yelverton and Princetown, 1881-1956, partly using the bed of an earlier horse-drawn tramway which served granite quarries. Remains of iron rail-chairs can be seen in one or two places. The railway track now makes splendid level walking, with panoramas over the Walkham valley, western Dartmoor (including the television mast on North Hessary Tor) and over the Tamar valley into east Cornwall; later, the working Merrivale quarry is seen across the valley. Had the railway survived the severe pruning of the rail network inflicted by Dr Beeching, the line would doubtless be a major tourist attraction.

[d] From **Swell Tor quarry**, on the right before King Tor, came the stone for Nelson's Column.

[e] **Foggin Tor quarry** away to the left, supplied the stone for Princetown Prison.

ound Tor and oneybag Tor

rs provide natural waymarking **d** splendid focal points for much the way. The walk starts by **imbing** on to one of Dartmoor's **ost** exciting features, Hound Tor, **en** follows a superb ridge route to **oneybag** Tor, via easy moorland **ths.**

ngth 5½ miles (9km), 3 hours

ifficulty 2

art Hound Tor car park, NE of **idecombe** in the Moor (signposted **W** Widecombe in the Moor-Bovey **acey** Road). Grid reference 739791

OS maps 1:50,000 191; 1:25,000 Outdoor Leisure 28

WALK DIRECTIONS

① Make your own way from car park up to summit of Hound Tor [**a**], then continue to left-hand side of next group of rocks (Greator Rocks). Just before the rocks are reached, you pass remains of a medieval village (which appears as a series of tiny stone enclosures).

② Do not take signposted gate at left end of Greator Rocks, but turn right along the rocky ridge. At end of ridge keep forward and roughly level (there is a wall down on left and the

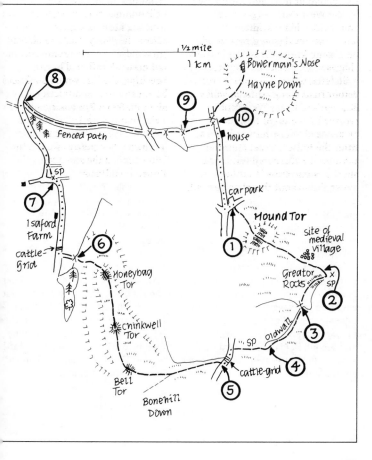

Becka Brook beyond it at the bottom of the valley) to find gate signposted Bonehill Down in the wall ahead) **③**.

Continue forward alongside wall on right (keeping alongside it as it bends slightly right) and just before wall ends at a corner **④** bear right to cross the wall and walk 100 yards to signpost from where proceed to stile beside gate giving on to road.

Turn left on road, over cattle-grid, then **⑤** turn right on to open land on rough path (which becomes well defined) with wall initially close away to right: you are heading for rocks on Bell Tor; where the wall away to right reaches a corner, fork right to Bell Tor. At the tor [b] continue right along dramatic ridge, past Chinkwell Tor, then dropping and rising to Honeybag Tor (where ridge ends).

Here turn left, descending carefully on uneven ground and aiming for gate just to right of woodland below **⑥**. Beyond the gate follow a track between walls down to reach surfaced lane. Turn right on lane, soon past Isaford Farm on left, then **⑦** when lane bends left you can cut off a small corner by continuing forward through signposted gate and walking along right-hand side field to re-emerge on to lane, which follow up past small wood.

⑧ Immediately after wood ends turn right through gate (signposted Hayne Down and Manaton), on enclosed track. Cross next road and take signposted gate opposite. Go forward, following left edge of first and second fields. **⑨** In third field proceed down to gate in far left-hand corner on to lane **⑩**.

From here it is a short walk back to Hound Tor along the lane to the right but first you can turn left along the lane for a few yards then ascend slope on the right to detour to the unmistakable Bowerman's Nose [c] and its adjacent rocks on Hayne Down.

ON THE ROUTE

[a] **Hound Tor** Without doubt one Dartmoor's most impressive rock groups, with resistant rocks surviving weathering to leave a complex jointed rock and pinnacle The **medieval village** between this and Greator Rocks comprises 11 buildings, including longhouses an outbuildings; entrances and fireplaces can be made out. The Black Death of 1348 probably ende the village's life. Fine **view** SE (ahe as you look towards Greator Rock to the pyramidal form of Haytor Rocks, E the deep wooded valley o the River Bovey in the vicinity of Lustleigh Cleave.

[b] **Bell Tor**, **Chinkwell Tor and Honeybag Tor** A trio of mini-summits with the last being the most dramatic. To the left (W) is t East Webburn valley, lined on its f side by the bulky form of Hamel Down, with Widecombe in the M on the valley floor; Hound Tor car be seen to the right.

[c] **Bowerman's Nose** The most prominent of a sizeable rock grou sprawling over Hayne Down. The should be no difficulty picking ou this much-photographed 30-foot high feature. It s name immortalis John Bowerman, a local man who died in 1663 and is buried in Nort Bovey. **View** N to Easdon Tor and NE to Manaton church.

The Webburn Valley and Dr Blackall's Drive

A pleasant riverside and field-path walk, with some sections along roads as far as Bell Tor Corner, but the drama begins in the second half, with grand views from Dr Blackall's Drive. Field-path sections need some care, otherwise the route is quite easily found.

Length 5½ miles (9km), 3 hours

Difficulty 2

Start New Bridge car park, on the Two Bridges-Ashburton road (B3357) do not confuse with Dartmeet Bridge which is 4 miles NW). Grid reference 711709

OS maps 1:50,000 191 and 202; 1:25,000 Outdoor Leisure 28

Refreshments Leusdon Lodge near Leusdon church after ⑥

WALK DIRECTIONS

① [a] From car park, walk to river, just to right of New Bridge and follow riverside path under the bridge; the path continues just above the river; where path nearly meets road, do not emerge on to road but continue down hill, still beside river, through woods and open ground.

② Path later emerges on to road, along which turn right. Ignore private driveway on left by lodge but ③ take next left, signposted Lowertown) leading uphill.

④ Where after 300 yards this road is about to bend right across stream, keep forward on track signposted Poundsgate. This track goes through double gates and enters woods proceeding with stream on right and later emerging into field by gate.

Keep forward, along right edge of field; then take left-hand of two gates and go forward with hedgerow on right in the second and third fields, to join road ⑤. Turn right along road. Just after red-brick bungalow on left, take signposted

gate on right and follow left edge of field for 100 yards, until taking narrow gate on left (ignore broad gate just before this).

Proceed along left edge of two more fields to reach houses at Lowertown, where a track takes you on to road ⑥. Turn left to follow road uphill. Past church on right, ignore a left turn, then ⑦ turn right at T-junction with more major road. ⑧ Just after Ponsworthy village sign, as road bends left, take signposted gate on left into Sweaton Farm.

In farmyard, take gate directly ahead and slightly uphill, leading on to rising track between walls. After ¼ mile, this reaches gate into field ahead where keep forward along left edge until ⑨ crossing stile on left near end of field. Immediately turn right along right edge of next field to cross stile and turn left on road next to road junction, where turn right (signposted Dartmeet).

⑩ After ⅓ mile, as soon as open land appears on left, turn left on to it, keeping alongside wall on left [b]. Where wall ends at a corner, continue to the left on track between walls [c]. ⑪ At end of section between walls, keep right at fork of tracks (or ascend Mel Tor on right for detour) and follow this spectacular and well-defined route for one mile until reaching road ⑫.

Turn right on road, immediately keeping left on major road towards Ashburton, to descend to New Bridge (it is best to walk along the open land on right-hand side of the road until road makes bend to left).

ON THE ROUTE

[a] **New Bridge** New in 1413, the granite bridge spans the Dart at a popular beauty spot on a very attractive wooded section of the river.

[b] **Bell Tor Corner** An impressive

viewpoint, looking W to the television mast on North Hessary Tor and Dartmoor prison, S to Venford Reservoir and E to Haytor Rocks.

[c] The track is **Dr Blackall's Drive**, specially created for Dr Joseph Blackall of Spitchwick Manor (the house just after ⑤) in the 1870s as a scenic carriage ride across the edge of the moorland, looking into the magnificent wooded Dart gorge. It is one of the finest high-level walks in the National Park, and yet is quite easily managed.

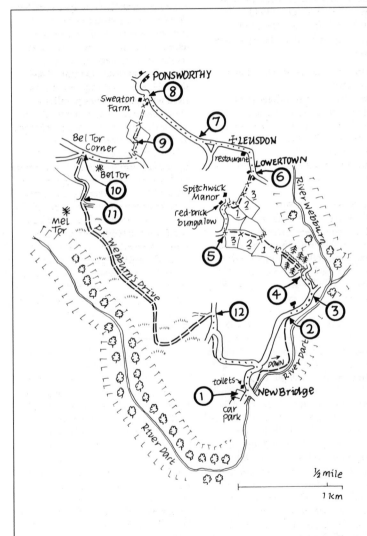

Tuckenhay and Bow Creek

Gentle, hidden landscape, dissected by plunging wooded valleys – perhaps the best inland scenery in Devon outside Dartmoor and Exmoor. Less walked than it deserves to be; although most stiles were in good repair when we were here, the routes across fields are not always obvious. The final section is along the estuary of Bow Creek.

Length 6 miles (9.5km), 3 hours

Difficulty 3

Start Cornworthy Village (S of Totnes), by church; roadside parking in village. Grid reference 829555

OS maps 1:50,000 202; 1:25,000 Outdoor Leisure 20

Refreshments Pubs in Cornworthy and Tuckenhay

WALK DIRECTIONS

①[a] From top of Cornworthy village street, near church, with parish hall on left, follow road out of village, immediately forking left towards East Cornworthy. At crossroads go forward, signposted Broadgates (you pass an ugly scrapyard; rest assured that the scenery soon improves!). This lane drops and becomes an unsurfaced track, crossing a bridge, and ¼ mile after reach T-junction of tracks ②.

Turn right, along the valley. ③ After ⅓ mile, where track is about to cross bridge, take signposted gate ahead; proceed along bottom edge of field to gate into woods, where follow path uphill and soon along the level (ignore minor path coming from the left where the level section begins), with valley floor down to right (there were some fallen trees when we were here, making progress rather difficult).

The path leaves wood by gate and continues as a semi-enclosed grassy track along the level (a fixed gate where the track becomes fully enclosed was on our visit hard to climb and required special care); down below is a house to your right. ④ The track finally drops to lane, where turn right and immediately keep left to take signposted gate leading to house garden.

Immediately beyond gate turn left down to small footbridge over stream; turn right on other side to narrow gate, after which the route continues into field on left but immediately keeps to right of old shed. Head straight up dip in (first) field with power-lines parallel a short distance away to your left, to find stile just to right of ruined stone barn at top of field.

In second field, head 100 yards to right of prominent gate on skyline to find stile into third field ⑤, where proceed to gate to farm (gate is just to right of leftmost barn). Beyond the farm cross a surfaced farm road and keep close to right edge of field (*not* along enclosed section actually along the right edge) to take gate ahead at end (ignore the right-hand gate).

Head diagonally left across the next two fields, heading for gates. ⑥ Emerge on to road, go forward on road signposted Totnes. Keep right at next junction for Totnes. ⑦ 100 yards later, just after Gitcombe Cottage on left, take signposted stile on left and head forward and slightly right across field [b] to find stile 50 yards to left of far right-hand corner.

Beyond the stile, head down towards Gitcombe House, emerging at bottom of field on to driveway, by gate just to right of the house. Turn right uphill on driveway. ⑧ 90 yards later, just as driveway is about to bend right and at end of first field on left, take path on left waymarked with yellow arrow, leading to enclosed section for reaching field (*note* this may be overgrown in

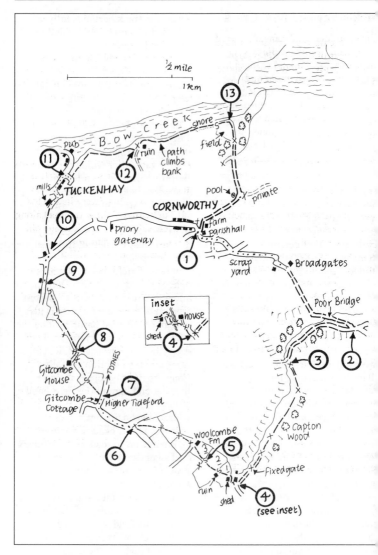

summer: if it is impenetrable you
may have to use the field to the left
of the path, keeping to top edge and
rejoining route via gate on right
at the end of the enclosed section
of path).

Keep forward on entering field,
along the left edge. At end of field
cross a stile and head down steep
field to find stile in bottom far

corner (house visible beyond), after
which a short path leads to road ⑨
Turn right on road, turn right at road
T-junction [c] then ⑩ after 80 yards
take track between hedges on left;
this narrows and goes through
woods before emerging on end of
road by mill buildings.

Proceed down into Tuckenhay
village, keeping right at T-junction

ist after you cross stream (left is
signposted Cornworthy). ⑪ Cross
next bridge on right (or detour ahead
for old part of village and pub) [d].
After 40 yards, where road is about
to bend right, take signposted stile
on left. This path follows close to
riverside. ⑫ After ¹/₃ mile, ignore
track on right (heading inland) but
take gate (marked 'Private Land') [e],
passing ruin on right and proceeding
by river at shore level in meadow.

At end of meadow keep close by
water's edge to find stile (semi-
concealed) leading up to top of bank.
Later the path follows shore before
entering field by stile beside gate.
⑬ At the end of the field, leave the
river (no entry into woods ahead) by
turning right alongside woodland
fence on left. Leave end of field by
gate and follow enclosed track back
to Cornworthy (at pool on right,
ignore left fork which is private)
emerging through farmyard where
you bear left to reach corner of road
by Cornworthy church.

ON THE ROUTE

[a] **Cornworthy** A climbing main
street rises to St Peter's church,
which has escaped Victorian
restoration; it contains a medieval
rood screen, box pews and 18th-
century clear-glass windows. The
bulk of the church is 14th-century,
its sandstone font surviving from a
Norman building.

[b] **View** ahead across the South
Hams, the name which is given to
the area S of Totnes ('ham' is an Old
English word for meadow-land). In
the distance can be seen Southern
Dartmoor, with several of its
towering tors.

[c] Further to the right, along the
road to Cornworthy and off the route
itself, a 14th-century **gatehouse** is a
remnant of an Augustinian priory,
and now stands solitary in a field.

[d] **Tuckenhay** Follow the road along
the left side of the creek to the old
village, a former port with its
warehouses, a water-mill (the old
wheel is still attached), cider-press
and recently converted former
bakehouse. The old corn- and paper-
mills at the top of the village have
recently been restored, and the mill
race (water channel) reconstructed.
The port was a busy place around
1850, but its days were over when
the harbour became silted up,
despite attempts to protect it with a
wall (remains of which are visible at
low tide).

[e] The riverside path passes remains
of a **lime kiln**, which once produced
lime for fertiliser; nearby are ruins of
a lime-worker's cottage.

DORSET

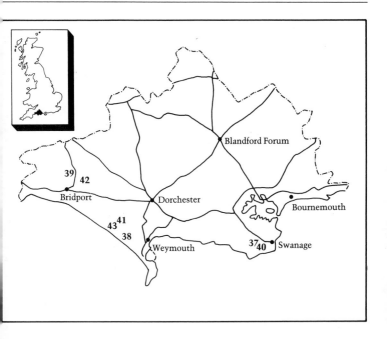

Holiday Which? Good Walks Guide

Purbeck Forest and Godlingston Hill

The main Purbeck ridge, a striking landscape feature, gives a particularly rewarding walk along its long, grassy top. Before you reach it, there are varied sections through Purbeck Forest and Godlingston Heath, the latter being part of Dorset's largest area of heathland. Directions need some care in the opening sections, across fields, but route-finding becomes increasingly easier as walk progresses.

Length 10 miles (16km), 5 hours
Difficulty 3
Start Corfe Castle, on A351 between Wareham and Swanage; car park in village. Grid reference 960821
OS maps 1:50,000 195; 1:25,000 Outdoor Leisure 15
Refreshments Pubs, tea-rooms and shops in Corfe Castle

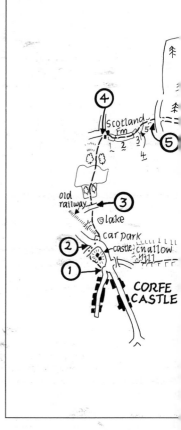

WALK DIRECTIONS

①[a] From the cross in the village square, facing Bankes Arms, take lane on left by National Trust tea-room and find footpath to right of house called Bartholomews. This skirts base of castle on your right.

② Reach road, turn right and cross main road, into car park by café. At back of car park, find stile at top of bank, and almost immediately cross old railway track on right (following yellow waymark arrows), on other side of which turn left, alongside railway track and soon over stile into woods.

Reach T-junction of paths when level with old railway bridge away to left, and turn right; path runs along edge of woods, with fence on left, reaching road ③. Cross to stile opposite, and go forward across field to enter woodland, on far side of which bear quarter right across field to stile in far right-hand corner, then passing into woods.

Soon path snakes through semi-open heathland, reaching stile giving onto corner of road just to left of prominent open-sided barn. Turn right, immediately leaving road, on track into farm. Turn right in front of stone barn in farmyard, then immediately left (waymarked) to leave farmyard, then right (waymarked) to enter large field ④.

Follow left edge of field and take second entrance on left (waymarked), just before bottom left-hand corner of field. In second field keep level and cross middle of field to reach waymarked gate at far end. Turn left in third field, to gate ahead. In fourth field, head for stile

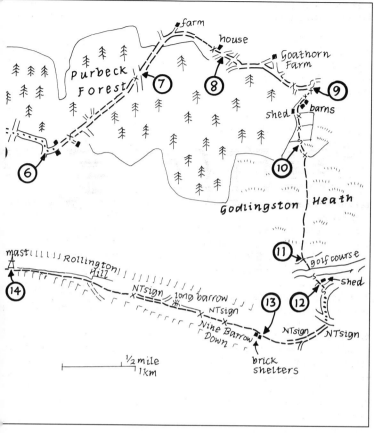

just to right of two power-posts.
In fifth field, path leads half left,
over bridge, to reach cattle-grid on
to road **(5)**.

Cross to track opposite and
slightly to left, and turn right after
100 yards, now with woods on left.
Reach road junction and take road
ahead signposted 'Bridleway'. After
1/4 mile, road bends right; **(6)** 80 yards
later turn left at junction. Beyond
houses, road becomes unsurfaced
track and enters forest. Immediately
pass through gate ahead (with 'Fire'
sign and fire-beaters), ignoring right
turns just in front of it, and follow
broad woodland track, ignoring
further right turn 200 yards later and

keeping to main track, avoiding any
side-turns.

(7) 1/2 mile later, reach barrier and
cross road to track opposite, along
power-lines. Just after leaving forest,
ignore left turn but take gate on
right 50 yards later, giving on to
track along left edge of field, soon
through area of gorse, with forest
away to your right [**b**]. Soon house
comes into view ahead: head for gate
on its right-hand side, then **(8)** keep
half left on main track in woods,
soon ignoring sharp right, where
power-lines cross overhead.

Where Goathorn Farm comes into
view ahead, fork right as waymarked
(left is private to farm). At next

T-junction, bear right over small bridge (left goes to the farm), immediately forking right again. 300 yards later, pass through barrier (right goes to house).

(9) 200 yards later, where track bends left, take gate on right signed 'Bridleway', into field and follow track along edge to two barns, taking signed gates ahead; at end of field after second barn reach shed and bear left through further signed gates, follow edges of fields until **(10)** taking stile onto Godlingston Heath [**c**]. Bear half left (waymarked), keeping close to fence on right (skirting round bogs as necessary) to reach gate, beyond which take broad path uphill for 3/4 mile across heath.

(11) Reach edge of golf course (clubhouse visible away to right) and turn left along track skirting golf course, signposted Agglestone and Studland. 100 yards later, by another signpost bollard, turn right across golf course, between hole 6 (left) and hole 4 (right), picking up enclosed path leading to road. Cross to stile opposite, head uphill, aiming just to right of derelict shed, then continue down to stile **(12)**, where drop down slightly right to stile on to road.

Turn right on road, soon ignore sharp right turn, but 75 yards after take track on right by National Trust sign for Godlingston Hill. Track winds gently uphill (ignore minor left fork after 200 yards). **(13)** At top, pass just to right of brick shelters, and walk along the ridge top for 2 1/2 miles [**d**]. **(14)** Reach mast, and head for Corfe Castle church

(quarter left), leaving ridge top and descending gradually on well-defined path. At bottom, turn right on road into village.

ON THE ROUTE

[**a**] **Corfe Castle** The ruined castle (National Trust, open daily, 10 – 6) is one of Dorset's most famous landmarks, built on a steep-sided hillock at the breach in the Purbeck ridge, and hence an ideal defensive site looking N and S. Built in the 12th to 16th centuries, it was beseiged by Parliamentarians in 1646. The church is dedicated to King Edward the Martyr who was murdered by his stepmother in AD978 so that her true son could succeed to the throne. The village is in the same grey stone (some of which was pilfered from the castle).

[**b**] View over **Poole Harbour** with oil derricks and 'nodding donkey' visible; the oilfield is as yet largely unexploited.

[**c**] **Godlingston Heath Nature Reserve** A huge, windswept expanse, part of the largest remnant of Dorset heathland.

[**d**] The main **Purbeck ridge**, has wide views on both sides; N across Poole Harbour (Brownsea Island is the birthplace of the Boy Scout Movement: it was to here in 1907 that Baden-Powell took 20 boys to camp in order to teach them woodcraft and discipline). The view includes Bournemouth, which provides a sedate contrast to the majesty of the Purbecks; S is Swanage and the coast.

The Fleet

An opportunity to get close-up views of the inland side of Chesil Beach, which encloses a huge seawater lagoon good for bird-watching. Easy link sections back to start via farm tracks and woodland tracks (the latter was rather muddy at time of inspection) ensure route-finding is reasonably straight-forward.

Length 5 miles (8km), 2½ hours
Difficulty 1-2
Start Langton Herring, 4 miles NW of Weymouth. Roadside parking in village (best by telephone box). Grid reference 615825
OS maps 1:50,000 194; 1:25,000 SY 67/77 and SY 68/78 (Pathfinder 1343 and 1332)
Refreshments Pub at Langton Herring; Moonfleet Hotel at ③

WALK DIRECTIONS

① Take road opposite telephone box into village, turn right by Elm Tree Inn and bear left just after church. At T-junction turn left, signposted 'Bridleway only, private road'. Follow ¾ mile to reach the water's edge ②.

Take stile on left signposted East Fleet and follow coast path along bottom edge of field, close to the water. Path is well signposted all the way to East Fleet and keeps to waterside apart from cutting off small headland (Herbury) after ½ mile [**a**]. ③ On passing close to Moonfleet Hotel on your left (with castellated top) [**b**], path goes over stile into field; coast path goes over next stile in bottom right-hand corner of field, close to the water, but the woodland path beyond is often very wet: easier is the stile just

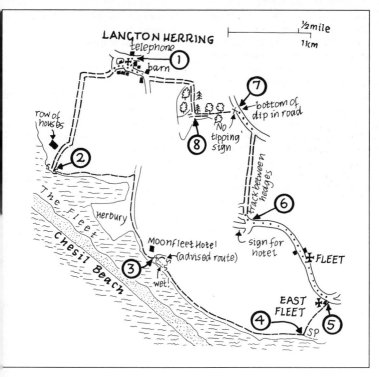

inland from here, leading to a path which rejoins the waterside coast path on the other side of this woodland.

④ Reach point level with houses (away to left) and turn left, leaving the coast path, on path signposted East Fleet, bearing right by first house and church [c]. Path passes cottages and reaches road junction ⑤. Turn left along road, soon passing East Fleet's 'new' church.

⑥ ¹/₃ mile later turn right on surfaced track by sign for West Fleet Holiday Park (ahead is driveway for Moonfleet Hotel); immediately fork right and 200 yards later keep right at track junction, now on unsurfaced track between hedges. Follow to road, along which turn left for 300 yards. At bottom of dip, and just after trees on left go through gate on the left ⑦.

Follow woodland path, which broadens to track. ⑧ ¹/₄ mile after, just before track enters field, take rising woodland track on right. Shortly after leaving woods, track bends left, heading towards farm. Go through the farm and reach Langton Herring.

ON THE ROUTE

[a] **The Fleet** A narrow tidal lake, 8 miles long, the second oldest nature reserve in Britain (Wicken Fen in Cambridgeshire is the oldest); noted for its **flora** and **marine life** including seaweed (150 species), eelgrass (harbouring eels and stickleback). Among the **bird-life** are mute swans, but there is also a sizable population of waders and diving birds (notably around the mudflats at Herbury), including dunlin, reed warbler and shelduck. The lagoon is hemmed in by the 18-mile long shingle bank, **Chesil Beach**, and a curving stretch of pastoral, undulating farmland on the landward side. The shallow stretch of water was the testing ground for the 'bouncing bomb' used by the famous dam-buster raid in the last war.

[b] **Moonfleet Hotel** Previously Fleet House, dates from the 17th century.

[c] **East Fleet** Little remains of the village, which suffered in a great storm in 1824 known as 'the Outrage'. A 30-foot tidal wave breached Chesil Beach and virtually destroyed the church, the chancel of which now survives as a tiny chapel; however, the 17th-century Mohun family brasses are still there. A new church, which you soon pass, was built in 1829 to replace it. The village has had real and fictitious connections with smuggling: the Mohun vault in the old church has a secret passage used by smugglers, and Mead Falkner's smuggling novel *Moonfleet*, published 1898, is set here (the hotel was named after the book, not the other way round).

Mapperton and Parnham

Two country mansions, in outstanding countryside, the finest scenery being between Loscombe and Parnham. A quiet valley leads to Mapperton Manor and there are views from Gold Hill. Mud can be a problem in sections (7) and (8); route-finding somewhat involved, and directions need to be followed with care. Crosses one ford, so boots or a towel useful.

Length 8 miles (13km), 4 hours
Difficulty 3
Start Half Moon Inn and church, Melplash (on A3066 3 miles NNE of Bridport). Grid reference 485975
OS maps 1:50,000 193 and 194; 1:25,000 ST 40/50 and SY 49/59 (Pathfinder 1298 and 1317)
Refreshments Pub at starting-point; buttery in Parnham House (when house is open). NB OS maps show a pub and shop in Netherbury, but these have closed down

WALK DIRECTIONS

(1) Take track opposite church and immediately take gate on left and cross field, finding stile just to left of where power-lines leave field. Proceed on path through orchard to surfaced lane (2). Turn right, immediately leaving the lane, for the right-hand of two gates and follow left (bottom) edge of field, with farms down to your left.

At end of field, gate leads on to lane (now unsurfaced): turn right, immediately fork left, then turn right 30 yards later by barns; by last barn (track you are on heads to road) (3) enter field on left and cross it diagonally, finding gate and follow path beyond through orchard, at end of which reach gate. Bear half left down to low footbridge and proceed with woods on left, heading towards distant farm. Path enters woods.

(4) 80 yards later cross stream at ford and continue half right past waymark post (with yellow arrow), to pick up path and to reach track, where turn right (left goes into farm). Turn right along road, then left at T-junction, on cul-de-sac. After 200 yards take farm track on left and reach Loscombe Farm 1/4 mile later. Bear left in middle of farmyard, then immediately right on to track.

(5) Just where track reaches woods on left, fork left, through gate on to woodland track which soon fords stream; then after passing ruined cottage on your right, path proceeds along valley bottom – keep forward on joining grassy track which comes in sharp right. (6) Where fence on left ends and Mapperton Manor (which you soon reach) is visible ahead, the gate you want is to the left of the one straight ahead. Reach it by keeping half left, uphill, on main track, then after 80 yards taking faint track on right leading to gate into manor grounds. Just before this path reaches archway by estate house, turn left and then right to reach end of driveway, with church and manor on right [a].

Follow driveway to road, along which turn left. (7) After 1/3 mile, fork right by 'posy tree' (on small grass triangle: the tree has a plaque identifying it) [b], on to track between hedges (can be muddy). 1/4 mile later [c] fork right, now on track along edge of field. Later, belt of trees appears on left.

(8) 200 yards after belt of trees ends, reach woodland (30 yards before this is a new plantation, just planted when walk was checked; we imagine it will take several years before it too resembles woodland). Turn left (ahead goes into woods), soon descending. Eventually reach farm and pass to right of farmhouse, on farm road. (9) At main road turn right then immediately left along

Parnham House driveway (open to pedestrians even if house is closed: No Entry signs refer to vehicles) [**d**].

Pass just to right of house, under bridge, then over footbridge across river. Follow woodland path to reach T-junction with track, where turn left. Where trees on left end, ignore sharp right turn; 100 yards later, track bends left and 50 yards after that take gate beside stile on right ⑩. Turn left in front of open-sided barn beside ruined farm, and ignore

right turn 50 yards later (which leads up to house). Soon path goes along left edge of field and into woods. Pass Netherbury churchyard [**e**] and ⑪ turn left on tarmacked lane opposite main church gate, into Netherbury.

Turn left at village centre, signposted Beaminster, along village street, then right at next crossroads, on unmade farm track. ⑫ After ½ mile, track ends: take left-hand of two gates, into field and follow right

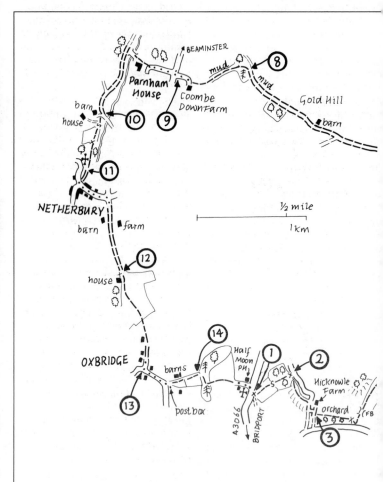

(bottom) edge. Soon farm comes into view ahead – make for left-hand side of it, finding track and proceed to road ⑬ [**f**]. Turn left, then where road bends right after 200 yards take stile to left of post-box. Turn left and follow left edge of field, past barns on your left, and leave by stile in top left-hand corner. Follow edge of next field to stile into woods ⑭.

New plantations here at time of writing made the path obscure, but church tower (your objective) was clearly visible ahead. It is best to turn right for 100 yards then left along broad unplanted area to reach field. Proceed across field to left of house which itself is to left of church, finding track leading to starting point.

ON THE ROUTE

[**a**] **Mapperton Manor** (house and gardens open 2 – 6 Sun – Fri) Dates from 1550, but is 17th- and 18th-century in character; originally owned by the Morgan family, who married into the Brodrepps (whose family crest is over the door). Inside are fine plaster ceilings and Jacobean overmantels. An immaculately kept terraced garden has box hedges and ponds.

[**b**] **Posy tree** The plaque records this as a landmark past which victims of the plague (by which Mapperton was hard hit) were carried to a common grave at nearby Warren Hill. Posies of herbs were used as a protection against the plague – local people used to meet here carrying them.

[**c**] Extensive **view** from Gold Hill over Beaminster and the Dorset Downs.

[**d**] **Parnham House** (open Apr–Oct, 10–5 Sun, Wed, bank hols) Another great Dorset house; 16th-century, with alterations in 1753 and then by Nash in 1810. A fibreglass marine-blue statue of Morecambe and Wise looks somewhat incongruous here.

[**e**] **Netherbury** Large village on River Brit, once a busy valley with flax-mills that supplied the Bridport fishing-net industry. The church at the top end of the village is 14th- and 15th-century, with a 17th-century pulpit and a monument to the Moore family of Melplash Court.

[**f**] **Oxbridge**, a tiny hamlet, has a house aptly called Camford.

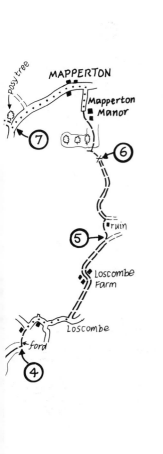

Swyre Head and Kimmeridge Ledges

A coastal walk at two levels, making it an absorbing route throughout: high along the grassy ridge past Swyre Head, following an easy farm-track skirting the top edge of the slope, then a cliff-top walk eventually ascending Hounstout Cliff. Easy route-finding.

Length 7 miles (11km), 3 hours
Difficulty 2-3

Start Kingston car park, 1½ miles S of Corfe Castle. Turn off B3069 at Kingston, by Scott Arms, fork right in front of church (with big tower); car park is ¼ mile down this lane, on left immediately after driveway on left to Encombe House (signposted path for Hounstout Cliff). Grid reference 954795

OS maps 1:50,000 195; 1:25,000 Outdoor Leisure 15

Refreshments Pub in Kingston; tea-room in Kimmeridge

WALK DIRECTIONS

(1) Turn left out of main car park entrance on lane by which you arrived from Kingston; soon lane leaves woods [**a**]. **(2)** ½ mile later, fork left by sign to Encombe Farm, taking track between gate pillars, but immediately leaving it for gate on right: follow the track across a field, soon forking right and reaching gate. Keep forward on track, with wall and belt of trees on right.

(3) Bear sharp right in front of stile (which leads to grassy mound and Swyre Head) [**b**], and follow track along top edge of hillside (signposted Kimmeridge), with fence on left. **(4)** After 1½ miles, track descends to road: turn left, then at road junction immediately after take signposted stile for Kimmeridge church. Path descends to churchyard.

Beyond, go forward on road through village **(5)**, and follow ¾ mile to sea. Fork left by houses, then **(6)** take track on right 50 yards later (signposted Toilets). Where track

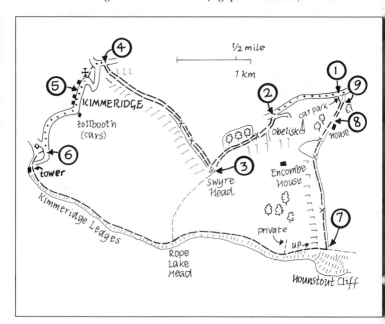

bends left, take path straight ahead, soon reaching coast and turn left on coast path, down steps, then up steps and past tower [**c**]. Walk along cliff top path. After 3 miles, coast path makes major ascent of Hounstout Cliff, with undercliff down to right [**d**]. ⑦ Turn left at top by stone seat, over stile, leaving coast path. Follow path by wall along top of ridge [**e**].

⑧ After one mile, enter woods, passing house on your right, then turn right at T-junction, avoiding immediate right turn (private) but, just after, taking right-hand of three tracks, signposted Kingston.

⑨ Opposite signpost to Hounstout you can turn left into car park.

ON THE ROUTE

[**a**] View of **Corfe Castle** and the **Purbeck Ridge** on right (N) at start.

[**b**] **Swyre Head** (666ft) gives an impressive view along the wildest part of the Purbeck coast looking W into the army training area around Worbarrow Tout. The **grassy mound** is a tumulus, on a site obviously chosen for its natural position.

[**c**] The cliffs here are formed of fossiliferous Kimmeridge clay, comprising alternate bands of crumbly dark shale and harder yellow limestone; the rock is almost horizontal here, forming the Kimmeridge ledges. A 'nodding donkey' on the W side of the bay was the first onshore oil well in Britain, installed by BP in 1959. Earlier schemes to exploit the shale were largely abortive: Sir William Clavell in the 17th century boiled seawater, using energy from the shale, to make salt, and also tried to set up an alum and glass industry here. An ambitious plan in 1847 to use the shale to provide (among other things) gas for street lighting in Paris, failed because of the strong sulphur odour that was created. A seven-foot dinosaur head found here is now in the museum in Dorchester. The **tower** was built in 1831 by Revd John Clavel as a garden feature for nearby Smedmore House and was later used as a coastguard look-out post.

[**d**] **Hounstout Cliff** towers 500 feet above the sea and has a tumbled undercliff.

[**e**] Ancient **field systems** (lynchets) are visible as faint terracing on the grassy hillside to your left. At the bottom of the valley nestles **Encombe House**, built *c* 1735; still the seat of the Earls of Eldon.

Hardy Monument and Bronkham Hill

One ascent through grassy fields and woodland at the start, then all the rest is effortless walking along grassy ridges, with views all round, and gorse providing colour.

Length 5 miles (8km), 2¹/₂ hours
Difficulty 2-3
Start Portesham, just N of B3157 and 5 miles NW of Weymouth. Roadside parking. Grid reference 603858
OS maps 1:50,000 194; 1:25,000 SY 68/78 (Pathfinder 1332)
Refreshments Pubs, tea-room and shop in Portesham

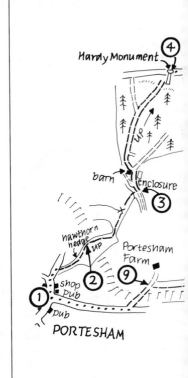

WALK DIRECTIONS

① From main street with Portesham church on left, take road uphill signposted Hardy Monument. 75 yards after village store, take bridleway on right (signposted Hardy Monument), rising and soon entering field, where keep left along hawthorn trees. **②** At field corner, turn right now with wall on left, to leave field by next corner on track which runs between walls. Where walls taper outwards after only 30 yards, keep along right-hand wall in this and the next field (Hardy Monument, which you soon reach, is visible ahead), at end of which **③** turn left on enclosed track. Fork right after 50 yards and descend to pass between barn (on your left) and walled enclosure (right), just after which fork left, again signposted to Hardy Monument. Follow this rising woodland path, **④** forking right after 400 yards by another signpost, to leave woods and reach Hardy Monument **⑤** [a].

Beyond monument, turn right (downhill) on road. Where woods on right end, take second track on right (first track goes into woods), signposted Corton Hill; follow this

along the ridge for 1¹/₄ miles [b], ignoring left turn signposted Martinstown after ³/₄ mile. **⑥** On reaching pylons, turn right on farm track (left is 'private road') and follow down to road **⑦**.

Turn right along road, and at next junction **⑧** take gate on right (actually just on the Portesham road). Ascend grassy ridge [c], and follow the top – soon over stile, then with wall on right. Soon, turn right on track for a few yards, but leave it where it goes through a gate, and continue along top of ridge with fence on right. **⑨** At end of field take left-hand of two gates, continue with fence on right to next gate where proceed still along top of ridge to reach farm track with farm away to right. Turn left and follow the

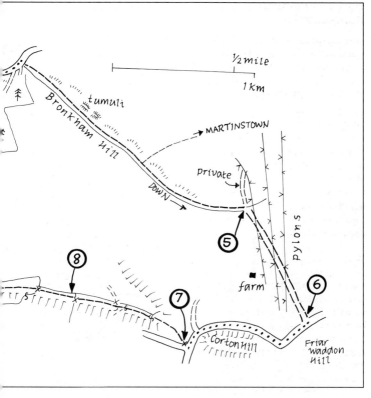

farm track down to road where turn to the right into Portesham.

ON THE ROUTE

[a] Hardy Monument
Commemorates not the writer but Admiral Sir Thomas Masterman Hardy, Nelson's flag captain at Trafalgar, who lived in Portesham. The monument itself, erected 1844, is a landmark for miles around. View of coast extends from White Nothe (near Lulworth) to the E as far as Golden Cap to the W, with the Isle of Portland in the middle. The adjacent heathland is a designated Site of Special Scientific Interest for its heath vegetation.

[b] Bronkham Hill is lined with ancient burial mounds. The gorse-clad ridge, with elevated views on both sides, offers some very enjoyable walking.

[c] This nameless ridge is covered with **strip lynchets** (remains of ancient field systems); more good **views** too, with the Hardy Monument to the N and over Waddon Vale to the coast to the S.

Two Dorset valleys near Powerstock

The route leads immediately into remote countryside, with charming local views followed by a deeper and even less spoilt valley beyond West Milton. The return from South Poorton is along the quietest of country lanes. Paths are not visible on the ground all the way, but route-finding is reasonably easy.

Length 3½ miles (5.5km), 2 hours
Difficulty 2
Start Powerstock, 5 miles NE of Bridport. Park by church. Grid reference 516963
OS maps 1:50,000 194; 1:25,000 SY 49/59 (Pathfinder 1317)
Refreshments Pub in Powerstock

WALK DIRECTIONS

① [a] Take lane with No Through Road sign, opposite church, just to right of seat and signpost. Follow it down to building on left with Gothic windows behind which turn left on path between hedges. This soon bends right and runs along side of valley, with stream always a short distance down to left. Keep level: West Milton soon comes into view ahead.

② After ½ mile pass house away to your left and keep forward, soon over footbridge, then bear uphill, just to left of prominent stone barn, finding gate into churchyard [b]. Emerge on road, turn right along it but after only 30 yards **③** take signposted track on right: keep to

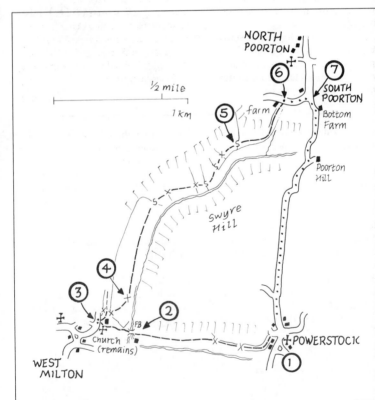

ft of houses to reach gate, then
llow track between hedges for 150
ards to a point where there are
ates on both sides. Take fixed gate
n right and cross field, keeping
vel and skirting hillside on your
ft, to reach gate ④.

Route now follows left side of
alley, with stream close down to
ght: there is a clear path nearly all
he way, crossing next stile just
bove level of woods [**c**]. After one
ile hedge is now on right; ⑤ 200
ards later, cross stile on right as
edge bends left up subsidiary
alley: keep forward in semi-wooded
rea, picking up clear path after 30
ards (with stream stile a short
stance away to right). Eventually
ath is enclosed on both sides by
edges and bends left up to farm (on
our left): just after, path reaches
ad ⑥.

Turn right, into hamlet of South
orton, then ⑦ sharp right
pposite house with post-box in
all, on surfaced lane. 20 minutes'
alking will take you back to

Powerstock: ignore left turns to
Poorton Hill and Poorton Hill Farm.

ON THE ROUTE
[**a**] **Powerstock** An appealing village,
occupying a sloping site. The church
has quaint 19th-century murals
with slogans and a highly
ornamented Norman chancel arch.
[**b**] **West Milton** The old church
tower stands by itself at the edge of a
field, looking over to Eggardon Hill,
capped by one of England's most
impressively sited ancient hill-forts.
The **church** was demolished in the
1840s, its stone used for building
Powerstock school (the building
with Gothic windows passed by at
the start of the walk), after which a
new church was built in the village.
[**c**] Much of the charm of this
nameless valley lies in its natural
state: hedgerows are retained, the
rough grassland is too steep for
ploughing and gorse thrives; there is
a profusion of wild flowers in spring
and early summer.

Abbotsbury

A figure-of-eight route round a much-visited village. The first circuit leads up to the downs north of Abbotsbury; this requires a little effort, but is recommended for the exhilarating views. The more leisurely, second circuit tours the village's famous sights – the church, tithe barn, Swannery, Chesil Beach and St Catherine's Chapel. Care is needed to find the way on first circuit, but route-finding on the second circuit is quite easy.

Length 6 miles (9.5km), 3 hours (can be split into two walks of 2$\frac{1}{2}$ and 3$\frac{1}{2}$ miles)

Difficulty 2

Start Abbotsbury village centre, on B3157 between Bridport and Weymouth. Grid reference 577853

OS maps 1:50,000 194; 1:25,000 SY 58 (Pathfinder 1331)

Refreshments Pubs, tea-room and shop in Abbotsbury

WALK DIRECTIONS

For first circuit ① Take Back Street, opposite Ilchester Arms and by 'Toilets' sign. After 150 yards, just after 30 mph sign, turn left on track (signpost bollard to White Hill was on verge of collapse at time of inspection, but may have been reinstated). Ignore right fork after 30 yards (leading into field) and ascend. Soon emerge into open and then pass signpost: ignore the half right direction it gives to Lime Kiln car park but continue uphill to gate ②.

Beyond this, proceed towards top of ridge, finding gate to right of open-sided barn and then bear half right as signposted over hummocky area to reach the top [a]. Follow ridge, soon reach signpost for Hardy Monument: here take the left-hand of two gates and walk along ridge with fence on right. ③ $\frac{1}{4}$ mile later reach another signpost by gate, with

woods beginning away to left: keep alongside fence on right for 80 yards, but where it veers half right keep straight on, walking parallel to woods away to your left.

④ Reach signpost in front of fence ahead, and turn sharp right (leaving fence immediately); Chapel Hill (with chapel on top) comes into view – head for it. Shortly, pick up defined track, through gate and descending, still heading for the chapel. Further down, near signpost, is a gate ⑤: beyond it follow right edge of two fields, then turn right on road into Abbotsbury.

For second circuit [b], start with Ilchester Arms on right and follow main street, then turn right into Church Street, turning left into churchyard and passing to right of church [c]. ⑥ Leave churchyard by far gate, turn right on road, through gateway, then left on road at T-junction. After passing tithe barn, fork right, signposted Swannery Pedestrians, No Cars Please.

⑦ After 200 yards take stile on right signposted St Catherine's Hill (or detour ahead to see Swannery [d]). Path follows right edge of small field, to emerge at base of Chapel Hill. Path proceeds to right for 50 yards to cross stream, where turn sharp left, signposted West Bexington (coast path). Path leads into woods, on far side of which keep forward, skirting base of hill without losing height, soon past signpost bollard ⑧ [e] and later past pill-box, eventually reaching gate in corner of fence. Go forward, still skirting hill, with fence on left until stile gives on to enclosed track ⑨.

Detour left to Chesil Beach [f]; right, to Abbotsbury, is the continuation. Fork right when level with farms on your left, and fork right again $\frac{1}{4}$ mile later. Just after passing stone barn on your right, detour right to St Catherine's

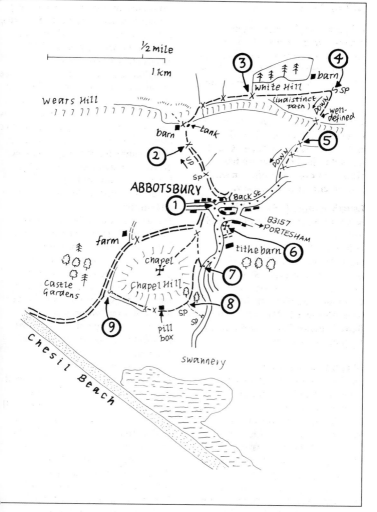

hapel (on hill-top) via gate [**g**]; left
to Abbotsbury is the continuation.

N THE ROUTE

] Superb **view** over Abbotsbury,
ith a great sweep of the Dorset
ast, including Chesil Beach,
rtland Bill (the island joined on to
e SE end of the Beach) and (to W)
s highest point at Golden Cap,
eyond which are the cliffs near
dmouth. The top of the ridge is

dotted with **prehistoric burial
mounds**, and one mile W is the
ancient earthwork of Abbotsbury
Castle.
[**b**] **Abbotsbury** Mellow orange stone
and a preponderance of thatch make
the main village street one of
Dorset's most memorable.
[**c**] **Church of St Nicholas** Mostly
15th-century, but with 17th- and
18th-century touches; plaster barrel
ceiling and a Jacobean pulpit (look

for the bullet holes in its canopy, made by the Parliamentarians in a Civil War attack). At the back of the churchyard is a labelled fragment of the wall of the Benedictine abbey (founded in the 11th century by Ore, a member of King Canute's household), which gives Abbotsbury its name. Below is the huge medieval **tithe barn**, 272ft long. One tenth of local produce was stored here, paid as tax to the abbey.

[d] The **Swannery** [open mid-May – mid-Sept, 9.30–4.30], at the W end of the lagoon enclosed by Chesil Beach (known as the Fleet), has existed since at least 1393 and was created by the abbey; over 500 swans, some wild geese and varieties of duck live here. If detouring ahead on the road to the Swannery you can either return to this point or leave the road a little further towards the Swannery, past the cluster of houses, where a plank footbridge is signposted to sub-tropical gardens: cross field to stile then turn left at signpost bollard, at point **⑧**.

[e] Grassy terraces on the steep-sided Chapel Hill are good examples of **medieval field systems**.

[f] **Chesil Beach** (or Chesil Bank) From here you can look down the length of this extraordinary natural feature, a 16-mile long shingle bank culminating at Portland Bill; the orange cliff of Golden Cap lies in the other direction. The pebbles get larger as you proceed towards Portland Bill. A unique place, sadly vulnerable to the whims of pirate gravel extractors who have recently removed chunks of it. Walking even a few hundred yards along the beach is a stiff challenge; swimming is dangerous, because of undercurrents

[g] The **chapel** belonged to the Benedictine abbey, dedicated (like several other such buildings on hill-top sites) to St Catherine, and built about 1400. It has not been used since the Reformation, but it still has an ornate ceiling (partly restored); the floor is of bare earth. (English Heritage, open mid-Mar – mid-Oct, 9.30-6.30 weekdays, 2-6.30 Sun; mid-Oct – mid-Mar, 9.30-4 weekdays; 2-4 Sun.)

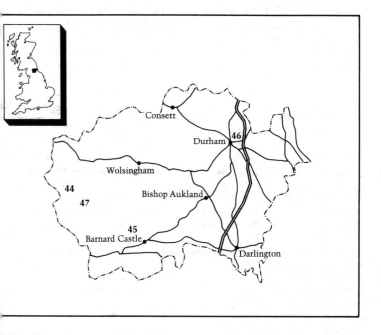

Cauldron Snout and Cow Green reservoir

A route showing Upper Teesdale at its most impressive, with remote countryside and a sinuous river valley. Leaves the Pennine Way at Cauldron Snout to skirt the reservoir and follow a quiet lane downhill, with wide views over the dale.

Length 8 miles (13km), 4 hours
Difficulty 2-3
Start Langdon Beck Hotel, Langdon Beck (on B6277 SE of Alston and NW of Middleton in Teesdale). Roadside parking opposite hotel or on road signposted to Cow Green Reservoir. Grid reference 853312
OS maps 1:50,000 91 or 92; 1:25,000 Outdoor Leisure 31
Refreshments Langdon Beck Hotel; teas and snacks at Widdy Bank Farm

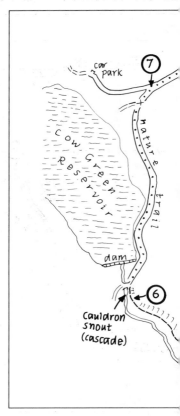

WALK DIRECTIONS

(1) Take road signposted to Cow Green reservoir and Harwood in Teesdale. (2) By sign for Intake Farm, cross bridge over river on left, keep left on other side alongside river, pass through yard of farm before rejoining riverside. (3) Reach footbridge (do not cross) and turn right on surfaced track (this is the Pennine Way, which you follow until Cauldron Snout) to Sayer Hill Farm.

Keep just to left of farm as signposted up rise to cross stile (in line with stone barn in distance); then bear half right to prominent nature reserve sign by stile [a]. Maintain direction towards and beyond next stile (4), making for right-hand end of hill (Cronkley Scar) ahead; Widdy Bank Farm, which you soon reach, is in view.

Soon reach river and walk beside it, through gate; near end of enclosure leave river for stile beside gate, to right of Widdy Bank Farm, to reach track (5) where turn left

through the farm. Track leaves farmyard by gate and soon rejoins river; eventually track ends and route along river becomes rougher (but still a well-defined path).

(6) At Cauldron Snout (waterfall) [b], path ascends rocky slope to reach reservoir road, along which turn right (leaving Pennine Way, which crosses bridge) up past dam and alongside reservoir [c]. Beyond gate, keep right on tarmacked road. (7) At T-junction turn right and follow road downhill 2¼ miles to starting place (ignore sharp left turn after 1 mile, just after cattle-grid).

ON THE ROUTE

[a] **Upper Teesdale Nature Reserve**
3,497 hectares (8,742 acres), mostly

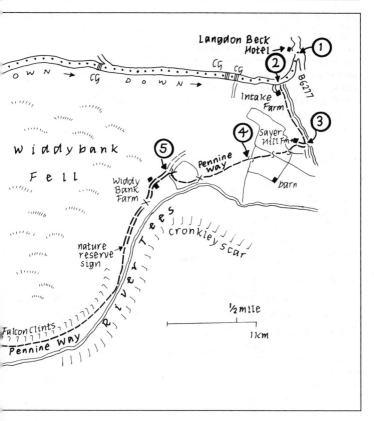

sheep pasture and grouse moor. Famous for its limestone flora, including rare arctic alpine species, which can be found on Widdybank Fell (which this walk encircles). The Teesdale violet is unique to this area.

Cauldron Snout Impressive cascade tumbling 600ft over the Whin sill. The foot of the fall is the boundary between Durham and Cumbria; before re-organisation in 1974 three counties met here –

Yorkshire, Durham and Westmorland.

[c] **Cow Green reservoir** A site of great value to botanists was lost in 1970 when this valley was flooded. Nevertheless, the scene has austere grandeur: the three summits to the left are (left to right) Great Dun Fell (with radio mast), Little Dun Fell and flat-topped Cross Fell (at 2,930ft the highest point in the Pennines). A **nature trail** leaflet is available from Cow Green reservoir car park.

155

Barnard Castle and Teesdale

Open farmland for the early
sections, with no hint of what is to
follow: at Barnard Castle the route
follows a dramatic stretch of the
wooded Tees until the River Balder
is crossed, near the end. Field-paths
near start not always clear (no
waymarks at time of inspection), but
route gets easier to follow later on.

Length 7 miles (11km), 3½ hours
Difficulty 2
Start Cotherstone (on B6277 NW of
Barnard Castle); roadside parking.
Grid reference 011198
OS maps 1:50,000 92; 1:25,000

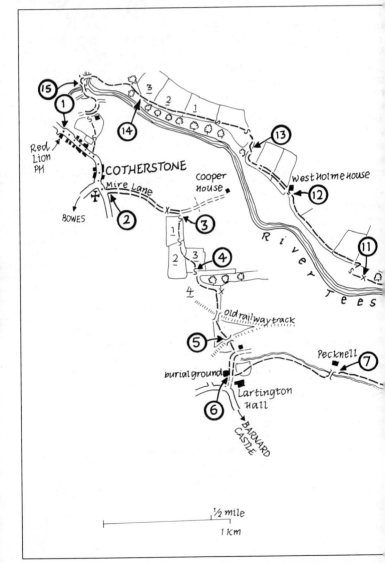

utdoor Leisure 31
efreshments Pub and shop in
otherstone; full range in Barnard
astle

ALK DIRECTIONS

) [a] With Red Lion Inn on right
llow main village street; near
urch, ignore minor right turn
gnposted Bowes; ② 50 yards later
mmediately after pillar-box in wall)
ke track on left, signposted Public
otpath.

After ¹/₃ mile track goes through
te and proceeds across field
wards house). ③ 50 yards later,
mediately before wall on right
ds, take stone steps on right over
all and proceed along edge of field
th wall on left. 120 yards into
cond field take stile on left and
rn right along edge of third field to

find stile 30 yards to the left of the
corner ④.

In fourth field, proceed as
waymarked, just to right of
projecting corner of woods ahead.
Keep alongside woods (on your left),
with power-lines parallel to your
right. At end of fourth field turn
right (avoiding gate ahead) towards
old railway bridge (prominent for its
grassy hump) [b].

Beyond the bridge bear half left to
go under archway under another old
railway line ⑤, cross small paddock
beyond, to emerge on to track with
entrance to Home Farm on left.
Turn right on the track, over stream
and avoiding minor turns. ⑥ Take
path on left signposted to Barnard
Castle, opposite gate into burial
ground; path leads through woods to
stile. Go forward across field to stile
near diagonally opposite corner, just
above stream [c].

Continue forward alongside
stream until reaching gate on to
track at stone bridge ⑦; turn left on
the track to cross bridge. 100 yards
later take stile on right and follow
woodland path; the stream is close
by on your right, but not in view.

⑧ After ¹/₃ mile, fork left at start
of conifer plantation, and emerge on
to broad path where turn right to

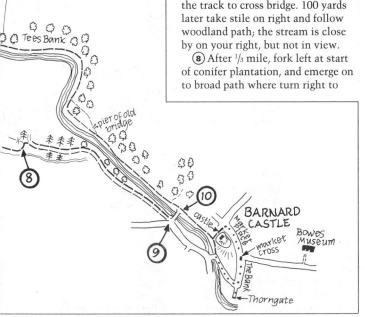

reach forest track 50 yards later; turn right along this track, later passing house, crossing bridge then going close to edge of field to reach road.

⑨ Turn left on road, then immediately take footbridge on left over River Tees ⑩ [d]. Left is the continuation; right is for *detour* into Barnard Castle (see On the Route [e] to [i]).

To continue Follow river path into woods [j], ignoring all turns to right; path later rises above level of river.

⑪ Reach gate into field; keep forward along right edge of field; 80 yards later take waymarked gate on right, ascend path steeply to stile into field [k].

Turn left along edge of fields (the route across these fields is clearly waymarked with yellow arrows; in case waymarks go missing, the following may be helpful). ⑫ Pass close by farm, keeping farmyard on right and small shed on left, and pick up farm track out of farm. Where track ends continue along left edge of field.

⑬ 100 yards after turning right at field corner, take stile on left into woods; path descends to footbridge, after which go uphill diagonally to gate. Go forward, aiming for right corner of woods ahead, then keep forward with wall on left to cross stile. Proceed along left edge of next two fields. ⑭ Halfway through third field (farm visible in next field) take steps next to gate on left, into woods.

Follow path which descends gently to river level, then go forward through field with river on left to cross footbridge over river Tees. Turn left and cross footbridge over River Balder; on other side take steeply rising path ahead up grassy slope.

⑮ After steps, at oblique T-junction near top of slope, keep left, to reach track. Turn right on the

track, then just after first house on left, take signposted stile on left. Cross field to stile in diagonally opposite corner; turn left then immediately right into next field to cross steps just to right of gate, into Cotherstone village.

ON THE ROUTE

[a] **Cotherstone** gives its name to a cheese still made locally.

[b] The first **old railway** ran from Barnard Castle to Middleton in Teesdale; the line closed in 1964; th one you soon cross was a trans-Pennine route to Kirkby Stephen.

[c] **Lartington Hall** comes into view on right: most of the house was rebuilt by the Victorian architect Joseph Hanson, but the Georgian chapel remains.

[d] Excellent view of **Barnard Castle** on a cliff above the Tees, with the town beyond, and County Bridge (1569, although a 19th-century plaque on it reads '1596') spanning the river. The **castle** (English Heritage, open 10-6 daily, Easter-Sept; entrance from town centre side) is named after Bernard de Balio who founded it in the 12th century. The Bishop of Durham seized it in 1296 and added the hall. The keep is 14th-century.

[e] – [i] *Barnard Castle town walk. Turn right alongside river, keeping right at path junction at castle; path then drops to road by bridge: keep forward on road in Darlington direction (do not cross bridge)*

[e] Detour right into **Thorngate**. Thorngate House on left is an imposing 18th-century town house; on the right further along are several former weavers' cottages, which had workshops on the top floor. At the end are several textile mills (now serving new functions) sited next to the river. *Proceed up The Bank towards the town centre.*

[f] On right, **Blagraves House** is the

ost distinctive house in town, ith stone architraves, flagged roof nd square bay windows. Here lived ie Blagrave family from 1672; Oliver Cromwell is thought to have ayed here on a visit to the town in 672. 19th-century musician figures re placed on the wall just above hall oor level.

each Market Cross [g] This ctagonal structure, originally a iarket hall, was built in 1747 and is ow the focal point of the town entre. Two bullet holes in the eather vane were made in 1804 by vo local men, a gamekeeper and a olunteer soldier, who were ontesting their marksmanship from ie nearby Turk's Head.

etour right to Bowes Museum i] **Bowes Museum** (open 10-5.30, Ion-Sat, 2-5 Sun; closes 4 Nov-Feb, Mar, Apr and Oct). Worth seeing om the outside at least, a vast iâteau-like edifice housing the ollection of John Bowes, a local coal iagnate who married a French oman. Fine art collections include aintings by Goya, Canaletto, iepolo, and El Greco, furniture, and eramics of the second Napoleonic Empire. In the entrance hall is the famous Silver Swan, an automaton which moves its head and takes a 'fish' from the water.

Return to Market Cross and turn right along Market Place.

[i] The main shopping street of town. Charles Dickens stayed at the King's Head Hotel on 2 February, 1838 and visited a watchmaker opposite the hotel, where he saw a clock that gave him the inspiration for the title of *Master Humphrey's Clock.* The shop has been demolished, but a plaque records the site.

Where main road bends right, turn left into Scar Top (signposted to castle). 100 yards after passing castle entrance, turn sharp right (rejoining the river path).

[j] Among these fine mature **woodlands** (oak, beech, ash, sycamore) are the piers of the old **railway bridge** over the river. Near Towler Hill on the opposite bank, Turner painted a view of Barnard Castle in 1816.

[k] Sudden change in scenery, with rolling pastures and views of the **Durham Pennines** of Upper Teesdale.

Durham

One of the great cathedral sites of the world, on a spur above a tight loop in the sandstone gorge of the River Wear. The main sights are close together, but this route explores the more rural parts around the river, offering a sequence of outstanding views of the city, before exploring the historic area around the cathedral and university.

Length 2 miles (3km), 3 hours
Difficulty 1
Start Market Place, by tourist information centre
Refreshments Full range

WALK DIRECTIONS

① [a] From Market Place take Saddler Street (to left of National Westminster Bank), signposted To Cathedral and Castle. Take the first left turn, Elvet Bridge. ② Just before river, take steps on left then turn right under bridge – [b] on riverside path [c]. ③ Cross the next major bridge - Prebends Bridge [d]; on other side turn right and immediately fork left on to rising path. At top emerge via a few steps into South Street ④. Turn right [e]. At end turn right and right again over Framwelgate Bridge. ⑤ On other side, take steps down on right; fork left 20 yards later (signposted Cathedral and Castle); follow path rising above river, then ⑥ take next left (Windy Gap) into Palace Green [f].

Turn right into cathedral [g] (if cathedral is closed, carry on into cobbled Duncow Lane, to right of Abbey House; then detour right along South Bailey to see College Green, which is entered by archway on right). Leave cathedral by door opposite to that by which you entered, signed Monk's Dormitory, Norman Undercroft (and others), to enter cloisters [h]. Leave by diagonally opposite corner and go through archway into College Green.

Go forward towards the green itself, then left down to archway under gatehouse ⑦. Enter South Bailey [i]: left is the continuation to return to Market Place, after detouring to right to Water Gate.

ON THE ROUTE

[a] **Market Place** Durham has held its market charter since the 12th century, but this square, where a Saturday market is still held, is mostly 19th-century in character. The Town Hall incorporates parts of the 17th- and 18th-century guildhall and has a 19th-century hammerbeam roof in imitation of Westminster Hall.

[b] **Elvet Bridge** The first bridge was built here c.1160 by Bishop Hugh of Le Puiset; a later bridge was broadened in 1805. The riverside path from here to Bow Lane (the next entrance to the S) is known as the Fearon Walk, named after the headmaster of Durham School, who constructed the path in the 1880s for the benefit of rowing enthusiasts.

[c] **River Wear** The key to Durham's site: the sandstone cliffs on three sides of the old centre are a splendid natural defence. Many of the slopes are densely wooded, giving a river walk of remarkable rurality, passing under **Kingsgate Bridge** (1963), designed by Sydney Opera House architect Ove Arup. Among the sandstone are seams of coal; a shaft on the opposite bank after Kingsgate Bridge is part of the disused **Elvet Colliery**. Just before Prebends Bridge **Count's House** is a Regency summerhouse built in Greek Doric style and once belonging to a house in South Bailey. The name refers to Count Boruwlaski, a dwarf violinist who lived in a house by the bridge and some of whose memorabilia can be seen in the Town Hall.

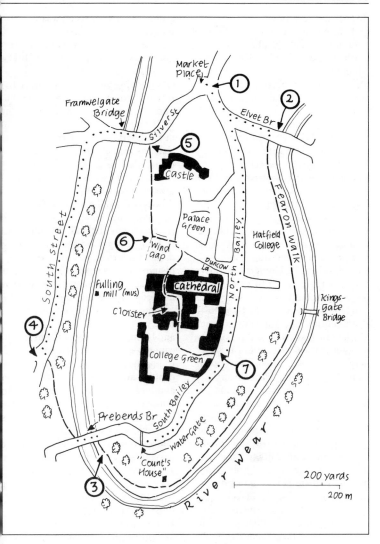

[d] **Prebends Bridge** (1778) provides glorious river views; the weir a little further on once powered fulling- and corn-mills that can still be seen on both sides of the river. The right-hand mill (not on route) houses the Museum of Archaeology (open daily 11-4 Apr-Oct, 1-3.30 Nov-Mar).

[e] **South Street** High up on a rise to the W side of the city peninsula, this was once a highway used by people

travelling a N-S route who wanted to avoid the river crossing into Durham. The **view** over the cathedral and castle, at its best when caught by the evening sun, was reckoned by architectural critic Sir Nikolaus Pevsner to be one of the finest in Europe. A handsome row of houses of mostly Georgian appearance lines its W side, with Abbey View (No. 42) an unusual

161

timber-frame survival.

[f] **Palace Green** The historic heart of Durham is a delightful tour de force: with the exception of the cathedral, all of what you see now belongs to the university (England's next oldest after Oxford and Cambridge), which is run on a collegiate system. Away to the left, the **castle** dates from the 1070s; the Earl of Northumberland ordered it to be built on the site of an earlier fort, to protect the cathedral against Scottish attacks. It was later enlarged into a Palace for the Prince Bishops of the Palatinate, which extended from Yorkshire to the Scottish Border, minted its own coinage and had its own army. After the powers of the Prime Bishops ended, it became University College in 1836; the 14th-century octagonal keep was rebuilt four years later as student accommodation. Despite 18th-century alterations to external walls, much survives on the site, including the Great Hall of 1284, a large inner courtyard of a variety of periods and styles, 15th-century kitchens, the Norman crypt and chapel, the famous 'Black Staircase' of 1662, and a 16th-century chapel with carved stalls. There are guided tours around the castle (Mon, Wed, Sat in term-time, daily in vacations). Across the green from Windy Gap, **Bishop's Hospital** was founded in 1666 as almshouses by Bishop Cosin, whose coat of arms is over the door; left of this, **Bishops Cosin's Hall**, formerly the Archdeacon's inn, is late 17th-century with an elaborately carved door.

[g] **Durham Cathedral** The crowning triumph of the Norman style in Britain, perhaps in the world. Its superb unity of design derives from the speed at which it was built, mostly over only 40 years from 1093. Rib-vaulting, whereby greater spaces could be made between structural columns so creating a stunning sense of scale, was pioneered here, its first use in NW Europe; the transverse pointed arcades were also probably the first of their kind in England.

Outstanding views can be enjoyed from the tower, but the walk up the narrow steps is not for the unfit. The cathedral was founded as a shrine for St Cuthbert of Lindisfarne, whose remains are here; this is also the burial place of the Venerable Bede, the historian, whose remains were moved here in 1020 from Jarrow.

[h] **Cloisters and precincts** The most complete survival of a Benedictine monastery in England. The **library** contains early manuscripts, some dating back to Bede's time; early bishops' graves are contained within the **chapterhouse**; and the **treasury** is housed in the former monks' common room. **College Green** was once part of the priory enclosure, and became property of the dean and canonry after the Reformation. Here the octagonal **Prior's kitchen** is 14th-century and is used for storing archives. Also octagonal is the **well house** (1751) at the top of the green. Beyond is **Durham Cloister School**, set back, with the castellated **Diocesan Registry** to the right of it. As you approach the arched gatehouse, the **deanery**, on left, was once the Prior's House and dates back to the 11th century although most of the present structure is 18th-century.

[i] **South and North Bailey** The narrow, cobbled street is one of the city's most attractive.
Detour right along South Bailey. Nos. 1 and 3, are both *c.*1730 and now part of St John's College. **No. 12** (St Cuthbert's Society) is 18th-century with a fine 19th-century scalloped door-piece. **Water Gate**, at the end of the street, is a stone arch built in 1778 to enable carriages to pass through the medieval city walls

and over Prebends Bridge.
Return along South Bailey (later becomes North Bailey, then Saddler St).
Opposite No. 22, a **horse mounting-block** by the wall recalls earlier days.
Next to it, a 19th-century **sewer gas destructor** is a curious survival.
Durham Heritage Centre, on right in a former church, gives a historic overview of the city. Just after Owengate, on left is the site of the Northgate, one of the city wall gateways, rebuilt 1420 (see plaque); also here approached by a doorway on left, is the old county gaol (1820), seen as a circular building at the end of a narrow yard.

High Force

Wild, rugged country with splendid waterfalls and views up the dale; of special interest for wild flowers. Route not defined throughout, and special care is needed from ⑥ to ⑩. Best to time arrival at High Force for late afternoon, when coach parties have left.

Length 7 miles (11km), 3½ hours
Difficulty 3
Start Car park at picnic site for Bowlees visitor centre (signposted just off N side of B6277 SE of Alston and NW of Middleton in Teesdale). Grid reference 908282
OS maps 1:50,000 91 or 92; 1:25,000 Outdoor Leisure 31

WALK DIRECTIONS

① From car park, cross bridge, following sign for visitor centre, where emerge on road. Keep right to reach main road by telephone box.

Take signposted path opposite and slightly to the right; this crosses field to gate ②, then goes across next field to stile into woods, where keep forward on broad path to cross Wynch Bridge [a].

Beyond it, take path half left (to left of life-belt), leaving river to enter field, crossing small bridge then going over stile. In next field, maintain same direction (keeping to right of barn) up to prominent gap in wall ③, then go forward to reach corner of tarmacked lane. Turn left on to lane.

④ At edge of hamlet of Holwick [b], turn right at T-junction, on lane which soon becomes an unsurfaced track. After house on left, ignore right fork, but keep forward (rising, past old quarry spoil). Keep on main track avoiding these four minor forks: at end of quarry spoil, keep right (left is signed as private); 50 yards later keep left, still ascending

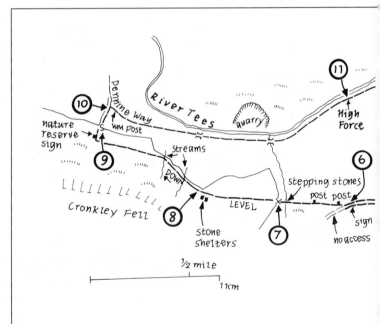

right is 'private road'); 150 yards later, ignore left fork (through gate); and 100 yards after wall on left ends, **⑤** ignore left fork. Track passes through gate by Upper Teesdale Nature Reserve sign [**c**].

⑥ ⅓ mile later, bear half right (track ahead is private) on to grassy path (marked by isolated post: path itself is not particularly well defined but heads for distant gate, keeping level). **⑦** Beyond gate keep forward in same direction: path is barely defined but occasionally marked by cairns (piled-up stones).

⑧ After passing stone shelters, a wall appears close on your right. Descend alongside the wall, crossing two streams (the first of these may be dry but is marked by loose stones of stream bed). After the second stream (crossed by stepping-stones), leave the wall for a broad grassy path (can be seen ahead ascending the hill, but don't take it that far).

⑨ Turn right by nature reserve sign to go through gate 100 yards away, then go forward with fence on left. **⑩** At top of rise, turn right along top of grassy ridge (joining Pennine Way at a waymarker post in centre of ridge), soon descending and proceeding along duckboards.

Path is mostly obvious from here as it follows close to river, later passing High Force **⑪** [**d**]; river then disappears from view for a while, but reappears shortly before farm, where head down to bridge **⑫**. Do not cross the bridge, but continue alongside river to Low Force, then re-cross Wynch Bridge and retrace steps through woods and across fields to visitor centre.

*Optional detour from car park to Gibson's Cave [**e**] (10-15 minutes' walk each way); from car park with river on left, take track past warden's hut, then fork left alongside river, past small waterfalls*

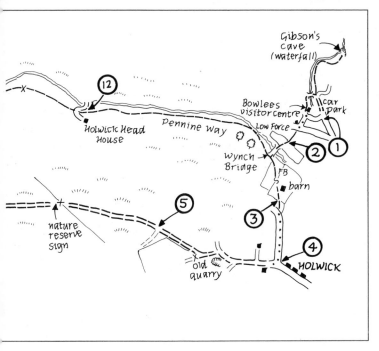

(do not cross footbridge) to end of
path at Gibson's Cave; return the
same way.

ON THE ROUTE

[a] **Wynch Bridge**, over the Tees, is
an 1830 replacement for what is
thought to have been the first
suspension bridge in Europe (built
1704 by Holwick lead-miners); the
original consisted of chains attached
to rocks on both sides of the river. In
1802 a villager was killed when one
chain snapped. On the right is **Low
Force**, where the river flows over
whinstone rocks, an extremely
popular beauty spot.

[b] **Holwick Scar**, the hill above
Holwick, is part of the Whin Sill (a
cliff composed of hard quartz
dolerite igneous rock), popular with
rock-climbers.

[c] **Upper Teesdale Nature Reserve**
These tracts of sheep pastures and
grouse moors have been recognised
as botanically important since the
late 18th century; unusual soil
conditions and a harsh climate have
encouraged rare arctic and alpine
species to survive from the time
when the ice-cap retreated. Rare
orchids and spring gentians can be
found.

[d] **High Force** The largest and
mightiest waterfall in England,
plunging 70ft and bearing a huge
volume of water.

[e] **Gibson's Cave** (nature trail leaflet
from visitor centre). A cave and
waterfall together, with resistant
limestone overhanging the partly
eroded weaker shale and sandstone.
This provided shelter for a
highwayman in the 1700s.

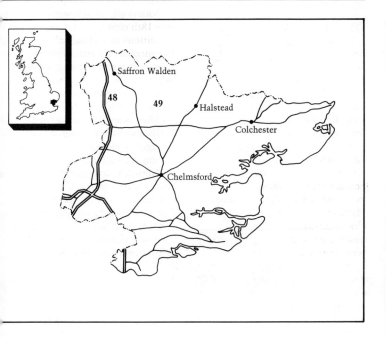

Widdington, Debden and Newport

Three distinctive East Anglian villages; rolling farmland with views all round and patches of woodland and parkland add variety to this walk. Mostly on defined tracks, but cross-field routes may be invisible.

Length *Full walk* 8 miles (13km), 4 hours
Difficulty 2-3
Length *Short walk omitting Newport* 4 miles (6.5km), 2 hours
Difficulty 2
Start *Full walk* Newport rail station (on B1383 SW of Saffron Walden; at south end of village). Grid reference 523336.
Short walk village green at Widdington (SE of Newport; grid reference TL 538317): take lane signposted to Widdington church, at which keep right, and begin walk at ④
OS maps 1:50,000 167; 1:25,000 TL 43/53 (Pathfinder 1050)
Refreshments Pub and shop in Newport and Debden; pub in Widdington

WALK DIRECTIONS

① Cross bridge over railway to London-bound platform, exit station, turn right on road. Just before chalk pits, take signposted path on left, between hedges, then later along left edge of field. ② Ignore sharp left turn (leading to trig point), continue forward to road, where turn left then keep straight on after 50 yards where road bends left, to take track past barns.

Track soon crosses field, with woods away to left. Just after joining woods reach junction of tracks by barn. Turn right, heading across field to right end of woods 200 yards away, ③ where continue forward alongside woods, then over ditch by plank; tower of Widdington church

(which you will soon reach) is visible half right. Path should be obvious as it heads quarter right across field, making towards leftmost house.

On far side of field, turn right along field edge, then at field corner near church bear left to reach lane by church lych-gate. Turn right for Widdington village [a], or left to continue route, which follows lane. ④ 300 yards later, pass driveway leading to triple-gabled house away to your left, then immediately after take stile on right into field (as lane proceeds to converted weather-boarded barn); turn left in field, along edge (continuing direction of lane, thus passing round to right of converted barn).

Where hedgerow on left reaches corner, continue same direction across this (large) field; in winter months, chimney stack of Swaynes Hall may be seen in trees ahead; make towards left end of trees ahead, where continue forward along right edge of second and third fields [b]. ⑤ At end of third field turn left on track enclosed on both sides by hedgerow trees.

After ¼ mile, track continues ahead along right edge of field, then left edge of next (large) field. ⑥ 100 yards after entering small woodland, pass through break in hedgerow on left to enter field, and descend left edge (Debden village visible on hillside ahead); soon continue forward on sunken path between hedges, and descend to road. Cross road to gates of sewage works (no entry), in front of which turn right on narrow path alongside fence; cross stile, turn left, still alongside sewage works fence, then proceed on track ahead leading 30 yards to field, where go forward along edge of field to woods.

Keep forward, with woods on left, then ⑦ forward along right edge of field ahead to Debden [**c**]. Turn left on road, then left again, signposted Debden church. Pass through churchyard (if the gates are locked, which seems unlikely, turn right to skirt churchyard), and proceed on path on other side. (**8**) Reach T-junction with track by lake [**d**]. *For short walk* turn left and follow track uphill (ignore signposted footpath on right after 50 yards), to and through woods, on other side of which reach barn and continue forward across field, heading for right edge of woods 200 yards ahead; this is point (**3**).

For full walk turn right on winding track (ignore minor side turns) and follow 1/2 mile to road. Cross road and take signposted track opposite, up to corner of wood where turn left (along power-lines), descending to

farm (**9**). Turn left, downhill, on surfaced farm track, then just before reaching road turn sharp right on driveway; after driveway ends, cross fence ahead (no stile at time of checking, but wooden fence is of a type that doubles as a stile), and proceed along bottom edge of field, at end of which turn left to enter second field, and follow right edge (which is slightly raised).

(**10**) In next field, shortly after fence bends markedly right, ignore left fork, but keep alongside fence until stream comes into view on left; now follow stream, soon entering woods by gate. Keep forward all the way to Newport; track enters field and finally goes under viaduct at edge of village. Left on main road through village [**e**], back to starting point.

ON THE ROUTE

[a] **Widdington** Triple-gabled hall, with older half-timbered portion at rear. The triangular village green is flanked by pleasant old cottages.

[b] **Swaynes Hall** and **Mole Hall** Both fine farmhouses; continue right in corner of third field for view over fence of Mole Hall, with duckpond and flamingoes. A splendid example of a moated Elizabethan house (with wildlife park attached: continue down road to T-junction where go left; entrance is soon on left).

[c] **Debden** Despite new development, the old centre with pond, pub and village pump retains its character. Debden Park has a semi-landscaped appearance. The artificial lake and estate church make a picturesque scene.

[d] Final sections of walk from Debden Hall Farm to Newport are the most attractive, with views over Debden Park and further, then small-scale charm of the partly wooded valley of Debden Water.

[e] **Newport** is an outstandingly preserved village, retaining early buildings, many plastered with decorative 'pargetting' (an East Anglian speciality); one fine street is on the right immediately before the viaduct, and the green close to the large Perpendicular church is worth taking in. The main concentration of buildings is the main street, including the exceptional brick and timber house, Monks Barn (with carved oriel window depicting the Virgin and Child) and the old toll house (with board showing charges).

Great Bardfield and Finchingfield

Two strikingly attractive villages, each with a village green, medieval church and wooden windmill. In between, the route follows brooks and tracks across gently rolling farmland, with wide skies and empty horizons lending an unmistakably East Anglian flavour. Stinging-nettles in summer make shorts or skirt unsuitable. There are some undefined routes across grassy and arable fields.

Length 4^1/$_2$ miles (7km), 2^1/$_2$ hours
Difficulty 2
Start War memorial cross in Great Bardfield village centre near Vine public house; on B1057, E of Thaxted. Grid reference 675305
OS maps 1:50,000 167; 1:25,000 TL 63/73 (Pathfinder 1051)
Refreshments Pubs, tea-rooms and shops in Great Bardfield and Finchingfield

WALK DIRECTIONS

① [a] Take signposted track to right of Vine pub, soon into (first) field. Go half left to find stile in double hedgerow, emerging into second field where find footbridge and stile in opposite hedgerow, but a little down the slope to your right.

Proceed in third field to gate beside stile, and turn half right in fourth field down to stile near brook. Keep right, along right edge of fifth field (with brook just to your right) **②** Cross footbridge over brook shortly before barns, and turn left on other side, now alongside brook on the left.

By a weir and brick hut, the path is now enclosed. Ignore a footbridge on your left, but just after **③** cross stile into field and turn right, up field edge to stile on to road. Left on road, and go forward at junction, signposted Pitley Farm. After 80

yards, take signposted gate on right and follow farm track in first field. After 100 yards, in middle of field (immediately after hedgerow away to left reaches a projecting corner), turn left and enter second field, proceeding along left edge alongside deep ditch.

After 250 yards, at end of field, enter the right-hand of two fields ahead via plank footbridge, to follow left edge of third field for 150 yards until taking plank footbridge on left in field corner **④**. Bear diagonally left across middle of fourth field (roughly in line with direction given by the footbridge itself) to far end of the left-hand hedgerow (at time of inspection, the field-path was obscured by crops, but you are entitled to cross the field and will be doing a service to others by treading the correct route).

Emerge at corner of well-defined farm track (leading ahead and to right), and turn right. The track immediately bends left, then right alongside ditch on left and heads for Finchingfield church, later with fence on right. Emerge into village, turn left on road to reach village green [b].

⑤ Take either bridge by pond and keep right. Take first turn on right (just after red-brick Georgian house and before Finch Inn). This lane runs between walls a short distance; 50 yards after left-hand wall ends, take signposted path on right. As soon as you cross footbridge, fork left and follow enclosed path, soon out of woods and into field. Continue always alongside Finchingfield Brook on your left.

After ^{1}/$_4$ mile, in field containing greenhouses, keep to left of outhouse, still beside brook and soon across end of private garden. **⑥** Emerge on to farm track and continue opposite and slightly to right, to enter field where keep along

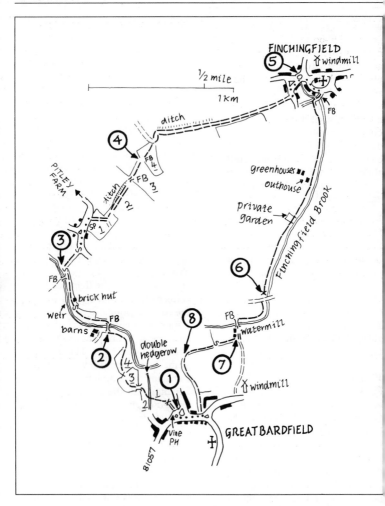

left edge, (still alongside brook which has however disappeared from view).

⑦ After field and the route bend right, cross footbridge on left and go forward over field past watermill and cottage, then immediately turn right. Enter field, with brook about 50 yards to your right: keep to left edge of fields until ⑧ ditch is reached ahead, where route continues to left, now along right edge of field with back gardens on right and windmill away to left.

Keep forward at end of field and join road at Great Bardfield. Turn right and keep right at next junction (or left to detour to church [c]), to reach war memorial.

ON THE ROUTE
[a] **Great Bardfield** The main street is wide and gently sloping, with village greens and a variety of medieval timber-framed and brick Georgian houses. Between the wars the village was home to several artists.
[b] **Finchingfield** The village centre

makes a beautiful composition, with green, duck-pond and colour-washed cottages (the pargetted walls, adorned with decorative plasterwork, are very much the local style) leading the eye to the weatherboarded windmill. Opposite a group of almshouses, the churchyard is entered under an overhanging building that was the hall of a Guild of the Holy Trinity up to the Reformation. The church is somewhat nonchalantly capped by a comically undersized bell-turret (the original tower collapsed in a storm in 1658), but has an impressively grand interior.

[c] **Great Bardfield church** Splendid 14th-century screen; tie-beams above the chancel dated 1618; Tudor brasses.

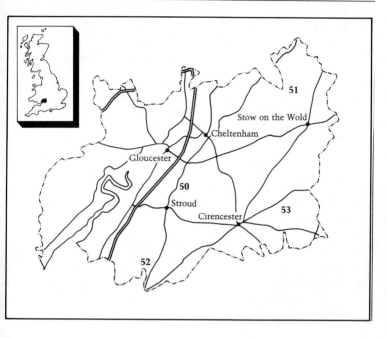

50 Painswick and Slad
51 Blockley
52 Lasborough Park and Ozleworth
53 Bibury and the Coln Valley

Holiday Which? Good Walks Guide

86 Chedworth Villa   87 Cleeve Common and Postlip Warren
88 Shenberrow Hill and Stanton   89 The Thames and Severn Canal and Sapperton

Painswick and Slad

A short walk in Laurie Lee country, with fine views of the old wool town of Painswick and many old Cotswold stone buildings. It makes an ideal family ramble. Some sections are muddy.

Length 4 miles (6.5km), 2–3 hours
Difficulty 2–3
Start Falcon Hotel, opposite the church in Painswick on the A46 Cheltenham-Stroud road (NB there is a large free car park about 200 yards on the left down the road towards Stroud)
OS maps 1:50,000 162 (Gloucester and Forest of Dean); 1:25,000 SO 80/90 Stroud (Pathfinder 1113)
Refreshments The Woolpack, Slad; pubs and tea-shops in Painswick

WALK DIRECTIONS

(1) [a] With your back to the Falcon Hotel, cross road and turn right for 20 yards then left into churchyard to left of bus shelter. Keep to left of spire, to pass church porch [b], then when level with end of church turn right under arch of yews to leave churchyard by Stocks Gate. Continue forward down Hale Lane [c], which narrows to an alley, then at end turn right on road.

When road forks by post-box, continue sharply downhill on Knapp Lane, and when this bends round to the right continue forward and downhill on footpath with stone wall on left. At bottom of hill, cross road and continue forward on access road to houses [d].

Once past the entrance to mill, follow road around to the right and uphill as it becomes track between fences, following public footpath sign. After 80 yards, turn right in front of field gate, and continue on path between fences. Follow this around corner of field and through squeeze-stile in barrier, then

(2) immediately fork to the left and continue uphill on the path between the fences.

When this ends, go over stile into next field and continue forward with hedge on right, then through gate beside stile to next field. At the far right corner of this field, exit through gate beside stile on to track between hedges coming in from right, and continue forward to road [e].

(3) Cross road, and go forward to left of barn to stile into field. At top left corner of field, go up bank to stile into wood. Ignore cross-track running just inside wood, and continue uphill on well-defined path. When path reaches complex junction of tracks, take track half left and uphill for 20 yards, then turn right on to path going directly uphill signed by blue waymarks.

(4) At top of rise, turn right on track, with wall and field on right, but after 20 yards turn half left on track running downhill into wood. Go down through wood on this track, following blue waymarks and ignoring cross-tracks; at bottom turn half right on to path running just within bottom edge of wood.

After 100 yards, fork left and after further 100 yards path drops down to left on to access road to houses. Go down this to main road at war memorial (5).
For Woolpack pub turn right along main road for 1/3 mile; pub is on left opposite parish church. On leaving pub, return same way along main road for 200 yards, but then fork right along Steanbridge Lane just before red-brick house. After another 200 yards, follow road around to the right, ignoring road uphill to the left.
For route omitting pub go straight across main road by the war memorial and continue downhill on minor road, which bends round to the right. At the bottom of the hill

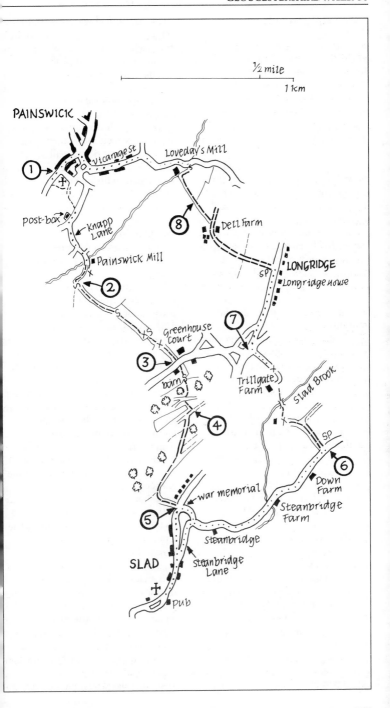

½ mile

1 km

PAINSWICK

① Vicarage St   Loveday's Mill

Post-box

Knapp Lane

⑧   Dell Farm

■ Painswick Mill

②

LONGRIDGE

SP   Longridge House

Greenhouse Court

③   ⑦

barn   Trillgate Farm   Slad Brook

④   SP

⑥

Down Farm

war memorial   Steanbridge Farm

⑤   Steanbridge

SLAD   Steanbridge Lane

Pub

turn sharp left at road junction. *Both routes* Continue down Steanbridge Lane to the bottom of the valley [f]. Pass Steanbridge Farm [g] on your right, go uphill, pass Down Farm also on right, then ⑥ when farm road bends slightly to right turn left into field on gravel track signposted to Trillgate. Follow track along edge of field, with wall on the left.

At end of field, bear left and downhill, ignoring track branching to right. After another 100 yards, turn right through gate into field, following signposted 'Public footpath to Bulls Cross'. Go down across field, making for buildings of Trillgate Farm on other side of small valley; at bottom of valley, cross stream by bridge and go through gate beside stile, then ahead up slope keeping to right of fence and farm buildings.

When level with right-hand end of buildings, go left through gate beside stile on to farm road and turn right. Follow farm road uphill through two gates to main road ⑦. Turn right on main road, but immediately left on to minor road signposted to Sheepscombe. The road crosses small common: ignore minor junction after 120 yards. Descend on road to group of houses, and just after passing Longridge House on right, turn left on track between hedges, following the public footpath sign.

Follow track down to Dell Farm and go through farmyard, passing house on right and main group of buildings on left [h]. Once through farmyard, when vehicle track ahead starts to climb slightly, turn half left towards marker-post with yellow arrow, and from there continue along left edge of field.

⑧ After another 100 yards, follow track through gap in hedge to left, again with marker-post. In next field, continue downhill with hedge on left. At bottom left corner of field turn right and continue along side of the same field for 40 yards, then go left over stile on to road.

Turn left on to road, across stream [i], and follow road for ¼ of a mile uphill into Painswick. Immediately after 30mph limit signs, road joins Vicarage Street, merging in from right. Follow it [j] to small square before Royal Oak public house, then turn right up Bisley Street [k]. At crossroads, turn left along New Street to return to start [l].

ON THE ROUTE
[a] **The Falcon Hotel** dates from 1711, and supposedly used to stage cockfights.

[b] The earliest parts of **St Mary's church** date from *c*.1378, and its most notable feature is the fine 17th- and 18th-century tombs, reflecting the wealth of the clothiers of Painswick; a guide to a 'Tomb Trail' around the churchyard is available in the church. The inscriptions on many of the tombs are now unreadable, but you may be able to find, near the east end of the church, a monument, with a metal plaque, to William Hogg who died in 1800: 'he was for fifty years a much esteemed gratuitous preacher of the gospel.' The churchyard also contains 99 yew trees, mostly about 200 years old.

[c] On your right at this point is the **Court House**, a traditional gabled Cotswold building, built *c*.1604.

[d] The mill-pond which served **Painswick Mill** is on your right. The mill was built in 1634 and made cloth until the mid-19th century.

[e] Look left along the road from here, to glimpse a fantastic **Gothic stable** which appears to have had one whole side demolished to make room for the road.

[f] **Steanbridge** The house on the right

at the bend is Elizabethan at the back. There was a cloth mill here until 1825, and the house figures in Laurie Lee's classic childhood novel/autobiography *Cider with Rosie* as the squire's house.

[g] **Steanbridge Farm** 17th-century, with a fine front with parapet.

[h] A sign announces the **Cotswold Minor Centre**, a large collection of aged Morris Minors.

[i] The house on your left was **Loveday's Mill**, named after one of the principal family of clothiers. The millhouse is 17th-century, the mill building early 19th-century.

[j] **The Friends' Meeting House** (down a path on the left) dates from 1706. Dover House, by the start of this path, is a perfect example of an early Georgian Cotswold house. Yew Tree House, shortly after this, was built *c*.1688 for Thomas Loveday and one of the yew trees in the garden is thought to have been planted in the reign of Elizabeth I.

[k] **Bisley Street** used to be the main street of the village. Friday Street, halfway up on the left, was the site of the Friday market, and the houses on the right, The Chur and the Little Fleece, date from the 14th century.

[l] **New Hall**, on the left at the junction of Bisley Street and New Street, was first mentioned as a Cloth Hall in 1429. The Post Office on the right in New Street is the town's only exposed timber-framed house and dates from the 1400s.

Blockley

An attractive, varied tour round one of the most handsome villages of the Cotswolds, tucked away in remote countryside.

Length 5 miles (8km), 2½ hours
Difficulty 2-3
Start Blockley village (SE of Chipping Campden on B4479, N of A44), by British Legion Hall (in front of the church). Grid reference 164349
OS maps 1:50,000 151; 1:25,000 SP 03/13 (Pathfinder 1043)
Refreshments Pub at Blockley

WALK DIRECTIONS

(1) [a] With front of British Legion hall behind you, turn left along village street, which you follow, ignoring side turnings. This soon takes you past the Crown Inn and, after 500 yards, to the end of the village where **(2)**, just beyond letter-box on right, turn right on stony track.

Fork right after 100 yards, soon passing house on your right, where you pass through gate and into wood. Follow track for ½ mile, ignoring two turnings to your left and bearing right to reach road **(3)**. Cross road and continue on path opposite, which swings left on entering the wood and then plunges downhill.

At bottom of rise, where main track swings away to left, take second track on your right, which soon rises along the valley floor. Ignore cross-track and reach a gate at corner of wood **(4)**. Take broad gate on the right, and turn half right in field, to continue uphill heading for the row of tall horse chestnut trees

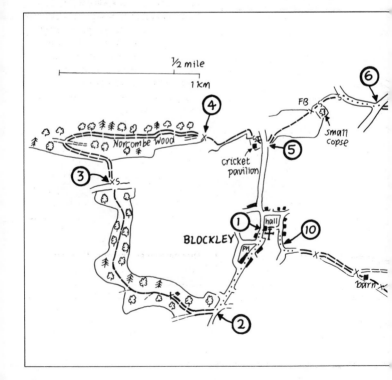

with fencing beyond.

Turn left on reaching fence, to continue with fence on your right. Make for stile which soon becomes visible on your right. Turn half left after crossing stile, to skirt cricket ground making for footpath sign in left corner and cottages beyond.

(**5**) Turn left on road, and after 10 yards turn half right through second of two gates. Continue forward into field, first with fence on your right. When fence bends away to right, turn half right to continue downhill [**b**]. Path is indistinct at this point but barrier soon becomes visible in hedge at bottom of field (yellow waymarker).

Cross over barrier and into wood, soon over small footbridge into second field. Continue around left side of this field, to find stile after 150 yards, leading to surfaced drive

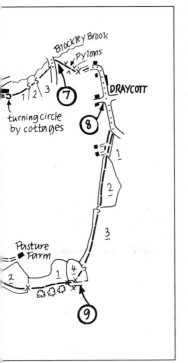

on other side. Turn right along this. (**6**) Cross over road and follow driveway on far side, soon passing a row of cottages on your left. Fork right after passing these to continue on gravel driveway which soon forms a loop. From the top of the loop, aim for stile and yellow marker-post ahead.

Turn half left over stile, bisecting angle between fence on your left and power-lines on your right. Cross stile and footbridge and bear quarter left in second field to find stile in far left corner. Continue forward into third field at first with hedge on your left, and head for metal gate.

(**7**) Turn left on road for 10 yards, and then immediately right to cross stile just before bridge. On emerging into field, bear half right heading for pylon at T-junction of power-lines. On reaching this, continue in same direction, soon walking with fence, trees and ditch to your left. Turn left through metal gate to follow clear track between fences. This brings you to a road which soon swings right to pass through hamlet [**c**].

(**8**) Continue forward over crossroads and after 200 yards fork right on track signposted 'Oldborough Farm'. Avoid second fork to right, and on reaching driveway to main house keep left along narrow path to left of outbuildings (yellow waymarks). Cross stile and continue along right side of three fields. In fourth field continue direction to gate in middle of far side (**9**).

Turn right after passing through this gate to go through first gate opposite (marked with blue arrow – avoid the second gate which has a yellow arrow). Continue forward across three fields, keeping fence to your left, and passing to the left of large barn in third field (with blue waymark). Track then merges from right: continue forward downhill to reach road ⑩. Turn right on road, and after 200 yards turn left on surfaced path between stone walls, later passing between metal posts to cross churchyard and return to the start.

ON THE ROUTE

[a] **Blockley** A surprisingly large village for such a remote location, its size due to its long-established silk industry (as late as 1884 there were six mills employing 600 people). Lack of 20th-century development has left it remarkably unspoilt, with many attractive town houses and cottages, especially in the High Street. St Peter and St Paul's church is late Norman, with gothic and later additions, and some fine brasses.

[b] The park on the far side of the wall belongs to **Northwick Park**, a part-17th-, part-18th-century house with Venetian features designed by Lord Burlington in the 1730s. There is an underground ice-house in the grounds.

[c] **Draycott** Pleasant hamlet with attractive cottages, all 17th- and 18th-century. The main farmhouse has a fine doorway dated 1704.

asborough Park and
zleworth

aried scenery on the edge of the
otswolds, including parkland,
oods, and two isolated churches.
lostly follows valley floors (where
ense vegetation may be a problem
 summer); route-finding can be
tricate.

ength 6¹/₂ miles (10.5km),
/₂ hours

ifficulty 3

tart Hunters' Hall Inn, on A4135
etbury–Dursley) 2 miles W of
tersection with A46 (Stroud–
ath). Grid reference 814960

S maps 1:50,000 162; 1:25,000 ST
9/79 and ST 89/99 (Pathfinder 1132
d 1133)

efreshments Hunters' Hall Inn at
art of walk

ALK DIRECTIONS

) Standing outside the Hunters'
all Inn, turn right along the main
ad for 50 yards, then immediately
ter crossing minor road signed to
agworth turn right into field
rough kissing-gate. Continue
rough field, alongside wall on
ght, until you join a defined track
hich continues ahead then
escends to a gate into next field.

Go through gate and continue
ightly downhill on grassy track
nning along top edge of field, with
lt of trees to left, until track starts
 run alongside stone wall on left.
Vhen this ends, go forward through
te ahead, then go half left to cut
ff corner of field while continuing
 descend.

② Meet and turn left along fence
head, but at end of field on right go
rough gate to right into corner of
ood, then forward on track running
ist inside right-hand edge of wood,
ith field on right. After 100 yards,
 through gate and immediately
in path joining from left, where

continue forward along the inside
edge of the wood.

Boundary on right becomes a
stone wall, and track eventually
runs out into field to right through
gate in wall. Maintain direction,
keeping stone wall on left, to emerge
through gate on to road, with
Newington Bagpath church directly
ahead ③ [a]. Turn left along road,
but when churchyard ends go right
through gate into field. Walk
alongside fence on right, but at
corner of field turn left, staying
within field, and continue with
stone wall on right.

At next corner, go forward through
gate into park [b]. Path ahead
descends slightly, but after 100 yards
ascend again to pass to right of
clump of trees ahead, coming within
20 yards of wall on right. Maintain
direction to pass to left of wood, and
descend towards Lasborough Park
(large house) [c].

As the house becomes visible, bear
slightly to the left, aiming for the
fork in the drive; one fork goes to
house and the other goes to the right
down the side of the house ④ .
Cross the driveway at this fork and
maintain direction across grass to
gate beside stile ahead, then
continue on clear track descending
slowly across field into valley to left.
Eventually proceed along valley
bottom, with wood on left [d].

Shortly after gate there is a very
muddy section crossing stream,
followed by a clear track with
stream to right, then you cross
stream again. ⑤ Shortly after this,
go up and through an old gate in a
tumbledown wall, then after 20
yards over another old wall and
descend again. Continue down
valley on clearest path ahead,
keeping close to stream.

⑥ Eventually come to vehicle
track running across valley; turn
right on this for 15 yards, then left

by metal footpath sign on to well-defined path running diagonally uphill marked by yellow arrows. This path rises and then runs at roughly the same level along the wooded slope.

(7) After 1/2 mile, path turns sharply right around hill, rises for 200 yards and comes close to edge of field on right, then descends for 50 yards to meet track coming uphill from left. Turn left here and descend track to gate into field, then continue forward and downhill, keeping edge of wood and then row of trees on left.

When field narrows to a point, continue ahead through gate then over footbridge (8). On far side of bridge, climb steep bank by steps cut into slope, then turn left along path at top. After 50 yards, turn right uphill on cross-path, then left after 40 yards on wide track through wood. Soon go through gate on to fenced path with wood on right and field on left.

When field ends, turn right around end of wood to continue on path running just inside wood, with second field on left. Path becomes track and runs more within wood but continues to ascend, passing through gate; ignore tracks merging in from right.

Leave wood and continue to rise, with hedge and then metal railings on left, until you pass buildings of Ozleworth Park on right and come to junction with surfaced drive (9). Turn right, follow drive, keeping hedge on left, around corner of house [e] until Ozleworth church becomes visible on right [f].

Continue under arch in stable block, with clock above, then straight ahead on track, passing through two gates, into field. Keep alongside fence on right and after 200 yards descend on track through gate into wood. When track forks

(100 yards after gate) take right-hand fork and continue to descend through field into the valley of the Marlees Brook, as track bends right and then left around wood on left.

(10) On reaching bottom of valley track passes through field-gate and then almost immediately turns right over a low bridge. Cross the bridge and continue forward for 15 yards, then turn left on footpath up valley which soon becomes indistinct but runs parallel with stream on left. After separate field begins on left bank of stream, the field you are in narrows to a point at which there is a gate. Go through the gate, and ahead on grass track between trees, initially with stone wall on right.

Follow grassy track up valley for 1/2 mile to fence with two gates (11), go through the left-hand gate then

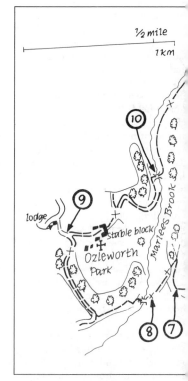

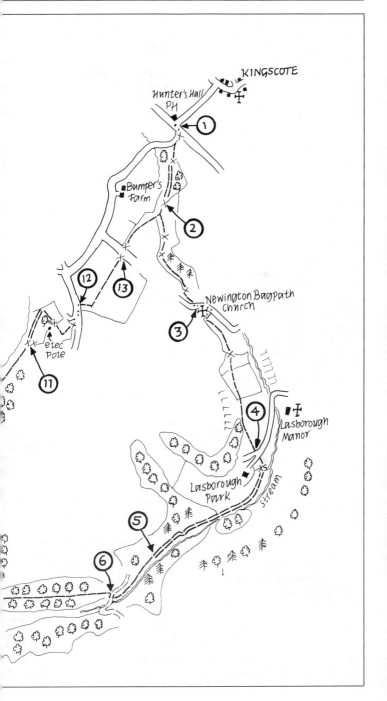

ahead on grassy track across field, climbing steeply and curving slightly to the right, then left, then right again. When track approaches wooden fence, turn sharp right around row of thorn trees then proceed slightly uphill on very indistinct path. Keep well to the right of all visible farm buildings, but avoid descending slight bank to right, aiming just to the left of trees visible ahead.

After 150 yards, go through gate just to the left of electricity pole and continue forward and slightly uphill, keeping to the right of a line of trees. As you approach the wooden fence at the end of the field, turn sharply left around the line of trees and then uphill on a much more clearly defined track to gate ahead. Go through the gate then continue forward and uphill on surfaced farm road which swings in from left (at this point ignore track to right).

⑫ At top of slope, turn right along slightly more major road and then, after 60 yards, half left up slope into field entry. This entry leads to two fields, the right-hand one through a wide entrance, the left-hand through a narrow gap in stone wall; enter the left-hand field, turn right to follow wall on right for 50 yards, but on reaching skyline turn left (roughly at 10 o'clock angle) to cross field to gate in middle of far side (if you have difficulty finding it, the direction you want is just to the right of farm visible beyond the next field) [g] ⑬.

Go through gate on to road and cross to gate into field immediately opposite, then continue ahead alongside hedge on left. Just before end of first field on left, when bottom of valley ahead becomes visible, turn quarter right away from hedge, making for section of wall at junction of field boundaries in valley bottom. Climb wall by stone steps

forming stile just to right of this junction, then cross wire fence immediately beyond by another stile.

Go forward up field, alongside fence on left and ignoring gate after 50 yards, then after 100 yards continue forward through gate when fence turns right across your route. Go uphill on clear track, initially with stone wall on right but increasingly diverging away. Track becomes less well defined, but continues to run along top edge of field with belt of trees on right, then becomes better defined again and runs up to gate to right of clump of trees.

Go through gate and continue through field ahead keeping stone wall on left to kissing-gate at far corner, then 50 yards left along road to return to the Hunters' Hall Inn.

ON THE ROUTE

[a] Newington Bagpath church
Completely restored in 1858, but now derelict and locked up. Just beyond the church is a motte (relic of an ancient castle) with a ditch about 150ft in diameter and 10ft deep.

[b] The large house visible to left is **Lasborough Manor**, built *c*.1610 for Sir Thomas Estcourt, and behind it Lasborough church.

[c] Lasborough Park was designed in 1794 by James Wyatt, again for the Estcourt family.

[d] On this section there is a **hydraulic ram**, where the pressure of water itself is used to pump a part of the flow uphill; this is clearly identifiable by the noise it makes, until track runs into wood through gate ahead.

[e] Ozleworth Park was built in the 18th century and extended in the early 19th century, and covers the site of the original very small settlement of Ozleworth.

[f] **Ozleworth church** is an interesting early Norman church, notable for its very rare hexagonal tower. It is built on a circular site, possibly of pre-Christian origin, and there seems never to have been a larger settlement in the vicinity. The original church, dating from the early 12th century, consisted of just the tower and a very short chancel to the east, the nave being added at a later date.

[g] As you cross the field, there is a fine **view** of the Cotswold plateau ahead, the wide expanses of which make a sharp contrast to the deep valleys through which much of this walk leads.

Bibury and the Coln Valley

An exploration of one of the most idyllic valleys in the Cotswolds, coupled with a visit to one of the area's finest villages. Easy walking, mostly on field-paths; the return route is straightforward and passes through quiet and unspoilt countryside.

Length 7 miles (11km), 3½ hours
Difficulty 2
Start Coln St Aldwyns village, 3 miles N of Fairford. Grid reference 146052
OS maps 1:50,000 163; 1:25,000 SP 00/10 (Pathfinder 1114)
Refreshments Swan Hotel and tea-shops in Bibury; hotel serving bar meals in Coln St Aldwyns

WALK DIRECTIONS

① [a] With Coln St Aldwyns post office behind you, take the road to your left, heading downhill between cottages, soon passing the New Inn on your left, and later a water-mill [b] on your right. Soon afterwards the road crosses over River Coln: turn immediately right in front of single-storey toll-house. Pass through gate and bear half right across field, keeping river well to your right. Pass through gate and into wood.

② On leaving wood, continue on clear path following left edge of field. Pass through gate into second field, soon walking with the river to your right. Go through gate and into small copse, soon emerging into

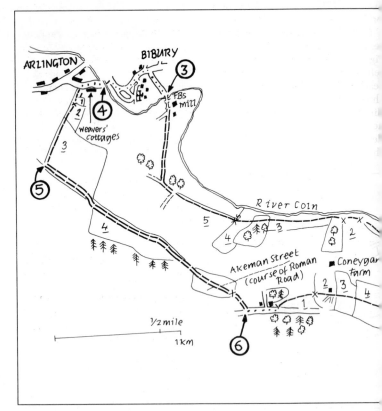

hird field. After passing through a urther copse, bear half left in fourth ield and head for gate (avoiding stile ust to the right of it going into voodland).

Continue along right edge of fifth ield. Avoiding all turnings to your eft, continue forward on what is now a clear track which passes etween trees, soon dropping lightly downhill. This later ecomes a road which twists round o the right past mill buildings to ross river at weir.

③ Continue uphill on the other ide [**c**] and turn left at T-junction nto Bibury village, soon joining nain road [**d**] which reaches river fter 250 yards. Turn left over ridge, and continue forward on urfaced path, soon crossing second ridge.

④ Continue with row of cottages ·] on your left and small stream on ight; path later rises steeply. Turn eft on to unmade driveway on eaching T-junction at top. Pass hrough metal gate and continue irection across small field, then cross two more keeping alongside egraded fence/dry-stone wall on he right.

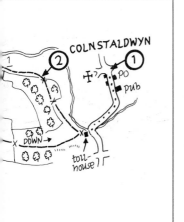

⑤ At end of third field, just before reaching metal gate, turn left on track with wall on your right, and continue direction in fourth field, now alongside hedge on left. Pass through gate at bottom of rise, and continue uphill on clear track [**f**]. After passing through gate in far corner of field, turn left on rough track with fence on your left and hedge on your right.

⑥ Turn left on reaching road. 20 yards after second of two cottages on your left, turn left through wooden gate on signposted bridleway. Turn half right, taking a course half-way between woodland to your left and power-lines to your right. Pass through metal gate on opposite side of field, which soon comes into view; there is an electric transformer just next to it.

Continue forward in second field, passing house to your left. Cross gravel driveway and continue forward across two more fields to pass into large irregularly shaped field dotted with trees and with a valley opening up to your left. Bear quarter left downhill in this field. The path is undefined at this point, but at the bottom of the slope you are joined by the track along the River Coln on which you started out. Turn right through gate into toll-house garden, and turn left on road to return to starting point.

ON THE ROUTE

[**a**] **Coln St Aldwyns** Attractive and peaceful Cotswold village clustered round a small green; numerous fine cottages, some 17th- and some 19th-century, built by the local estate. St John's church is heavily restored but has an ancient door and a fine part-Norman tower.

[**b**] **Corn-mill** 19th-century, just to your right.

[**c**] **Bibury Court** Visible to your left, is the striking gabled building, part-

189

Tudor, but hugely extended in the mid-17th century by the Sackville family. Now a hotel.

[d] **Bibury** The centre of the village is just off to your left here (well worth a detour), round a square. Some very fine 17th- and 18th-century cottages. St Mary's church has Saxon features, visible on the posts supporting the chancel; the font is Norman.

[e] **Arlington Row** This picturesque row of weavers' cottages was restored in 1929 by the Society for the Protection of Ancient Buildings, founded by the pioneer socialist William Morris. Bibury was one of Morris's favourite villages, and it was he who 'discovered' it and helped to protect it from development. The cottages have been dwellings since the early 1600s but the original building is clearly much older – possibly a monastic structure of the 14th century.

[f] If you look back from the corner of this field, you can see clearly the line of Akeman Street, which formed an important part of the Roman road network, linking Bicester with Cirencester and the Fosse Way.

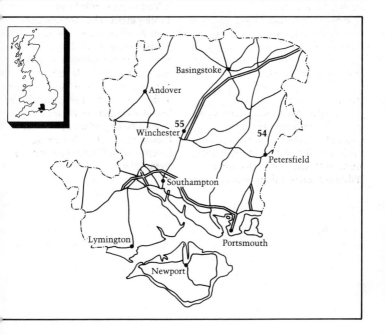

54 Selborne and Noar Hill
55 Winchester

Holiday Which? Good Walks Guide

Selborne and Noar Hill

**A ramble in the countryside of
naturalist Gilbert White (see [c]),
taking in much of the best landscape
in eastern Hampshire: grassy fields,
downland, orchards and deciduous
woodlands clinging to steep
escarpments. Beyond Selborne, route
ascends two hills, with good views
on the way. Route-finding involved
but not particularly difficult;
signposting and waymarking is quite
thorough.**

Length *Full walk* 10 miles (16km),
5 hours
Difficulty 3
Short walk, omitting Hawkley
5 miles (8km), 2¹/₂ hours
Difficulty 2
Start *Full walk* Hawkley village
green, 2¹/₂ miles W of Liss. Grid
reference 746291
Short walk Selborne, on B3006
between Alton and Liss. Start walk
at ⑩. Grid reference 741337
OS maps 1:50,000 186; 1:25,000 SU
62/72 and SU 63/73 (Pathfinder 1265
and 1244)
Refreshments Pub in Hawkley;
pubs, shop and tea-room in Selborne

WALK DIRECTIONS

① From village green take road
signposted West Liss, passing pub.
At T-junction, go straight on, on
signposted path between fences.
② At end turn left on road, past
Uplands, then where road bends left
take signposted path on right, enter
field and follow right edge.

③ At end take signposted Gate,
then turn right on surfaced lane. At
farm [a], take centre of three tracks,
initially level but soon descending
gently. Reach large field, which
cross in same direction to find gate
at far end ④. Continue on track
beyond, crossing a stream and
ascending gently to reach surfaced
lane. Turn right on lane (ignore an

immediate left turn), down to T-
junction where take signposted
woodland path opposite and slightly
to the right (do not confuse with a
broader track just to the left of this)
path skirts garden fence on your
right and soon reaches stile ⑤.

Cross field to next stiles and turn
left on lane (the driveway to 'Le
Court'), immediately ignoring
further left turn by grassy triangle.
100 yards later, turn left on
signposted track which skirts close
to Le Court (on your right) and
passes through an orchard. After Le
Court, it bends left as it enters
another orchard, soon passing brick
barn: keep on level (soon with fence
on left).

⑥ Reach signpost by water-tank
turn left then immediately left again
over stile into woods. Path climbs
for 40 yards, then turn right to enter
field, and follow left edge – soon
houses come into view, and you pick
up a track which leads to road. Left
on road [b], then after 300 yards
(opposite signpost and sign for
Wildwood Antiques) take track on
right to enter orchard ⑦.

Keep along fence on your right
until crossing a stile on right,
beyond which path doubles back to
another stile, then goes sharp left,
along left edge of field to reach stile
into woods and to lake. Go over stile
near lake, keep lake close to your
left and walk along edge of (often
boggy) field: soon further stiles
ahead indicate the route ahead – up
centre of small valley, at far end of
which ⑧ cross stile (slightly to left)
into woods, to reach orchard. Bear
half right, finding track between tall
hedge (right) and orchard (left). In
corner, waymark post indicates left
turn, soon after which take gate on
right on to road.

Left on road; after 300 yards when
roads bends left, take signposted
track on right (*not* the track

immediately after a farm : it's a little further on than this), to enter large field and follow right edge as signposted. In field corner turn left (signposted), still along field edge.

⑨ At end of field, route is ahead and slightly to left (signposted) with ditch and line of trees on right. Soon continue forward by signpost along right edge of recreation field until taking path on right. Reach road and turn left, then right at next junction through Selborne [**c**].

⑩ Pass Selborne Arms and museum on your left, then after church turn left into Gracious Street. Just after houses end and where road bends right, take gate ahead and follow left edge of field to reach stile into woods, where turn left on woodland path skirting base of wooded hill, with fence on left.

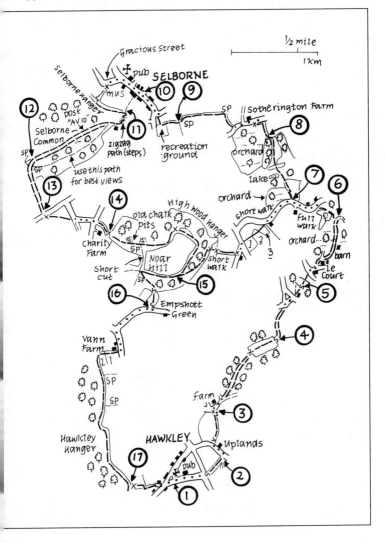

⑪ After ¹/₄ mile, at National Trust sign for Selborne Common, take path ahead which zigzags up steps [**d**]. At top turn right along house garden fence, keeping to left fork of broad woodland paths (right fork goes along top edge of slope; *note* there is a left fork you can take 70 yards later which gives views to the S – see map) [**e**]. Follow path through woods and semi-open areas. ⑫ After ³/₄ mile, do not take gate out of woods ahead (near National Trust sign which faces other way), but turn left just before it by four-way signpost, and go straight on at the next signpost a few yards later: track descends, leaving woods, soon to reach road.

⑬ Cross road to gate opposite and bear half left across field, leaving by signpost in diagonally opposite corner, keeping woods to your right and turn right on road (*note* if this field is ploughed or cropped, it is easier to omit it by turning left on the road then right at next junction). Follow road to T-junction, take signposted bridleway between hedges opposite and slightly to the left. This soon enters semi-wooded area by gate and sign for Noar Hill Nature Reserve ⑭ [**f**].

Follow track, keeping straight on at signpost after ¹/₄ mile (ignoring right turn used as a short cut). Track leads through woods and semi-open area and reaches gate: fork right keeping close to edge of woods, around top of hill. Track eventually narrows and goes further into woods. ⑮ Reach T-junction.

For short walk turn left and descend to bottom; take gate into field. Head to next gate then forward, with fence on right to reach road. Left on road and at main road take signposted path opposite (if ploughed or cropped it is easier to turn left along main road, then first right): head across first field to waymark post just to

left of corner of hedge then cut across second field corner to next signpost, where continue in third field towards house, emerging on road by signpost, and turn right on road. Ignore driveway on right to Le Court. ¹/₄ mile later, turn left on track opposite signpost and sign for Wildwood Antiques, to enter orchard. This is ⑦.

For full walk turn right at T-junction ⑮. After ¹/₄ mile, turn left at signpost for Hangers Way, descending through woods. At bottom take stile into field, cross to stile in bottom corner then forward (with fence on left) to surfaced lane. ⑯ Turn right on lane and left at T-junction. Pass Vann House and Vann Farm on your right, then take signposted stile on right, follow right edge of two fields towards wooded hill, and turn left (signposted) in corner of second field, still skirting field. Follow this path along bottom of hillside for one mile [**g**], ignoring signposted footpath and (later) bridleway to left. ⑰ When level with Hawkley away to left, gate on left gives access to field path back to village. Left at road T-junction to reach village green.

ON THE ROUTE
[**a**] **Mabbutts Farm** Half-timbered, with a thatched roof, in a traditional landscape.
[**b**] **View** over the Hampshire/Surrey borders.
[**c**] **Selborne** Gilbert White, naturalist and author of *The Natural History and Antiquities of Selborne* (published 1789), was born in 1720 in the Vicarage. His home and death place (1793), The Wakes, is now a museum to him and Captain Lawrence Oates, who accompanied Scott to the South Pole, 1911-12, and died on the return journey (open 11-5.30, last admission 5, Wed to Sun). A signpost in the churchyard points

to White's grave. White would have been no doubt gratififed to know that much of the surrounding countryside has been safeguarded and the importance of its natural history recognised: the National Trust owns 275 acres of nearby common, woodland, and meadows. Also in the village is a restorer of gipsy caravans and horse-drawn carts, whose workshop is sometimes open at weekends.

[d] In 1753 Gilbert White and his brother John cut this **zigzag path** to the top of Selborne Hanger.

[e] The beech woods clinging to these escarpments are known as hangers. On top of **Selborne Hill** is a plateau with an area of old common-land. This is a fine example of a woodland habitat on the clay-capped Hampshire chalk, supporting a rich variety of woodland species. **View** from the escarpment over Selborne; 1½ miles E of the village is a farm on the site of an Augustinian priory.

[f] **Noar Hill Nature Reserve** Chalk pits and scrub. The disturbed land is a good site for chalkland **flora** (including autumn gentian, kidney vetch, and yellow-wort), which attracts a variety of butterflies such as marbled white and Duke of Burgundy. Some bad damage from the 1987 storm, but fortunately most of the site is intact.

[g] This pleasant final section skirts the bottom of **Hawkley Hanger**, where there are more beech woods.

Winchester

An historic, religious and commercial centre, as well as a seat of learning, Winchester has Roman origins and became the fifth largest town in Roman Britain; the Roman wall has largely disappeared, but it defines the extent of the ancient city centre. Winchester has close associations with royalty – it was England's capital in Saxon times and staunchly Royalist in the Civil War – and was an important centre for wool and cloth during the Middle Ages.

Length 3 miles (5km), 4 hours
Difficulty 1
Start Westgate
Refreshments Plenty

WALK DIRECTIONS

① Looking down High Street from Westgate [a], detour right to see Great Hall [b], then go down High Street [c] to City Cross, where take alley on right [d] to cathedral close. ② Take path immediately right of cathedral [e], signposted Wolvesey Castle and water meadows.

Pass under buttresses on S side of cathedral, detour right to see the Deanery and Cheyney Court [f], then go through archway to continue along S side of cathedral, soon on path between walls.

Turn right into Colebrook Street, soon take gate on left into Abbey Gardens [g]. Keep to left edge of gardens to reach Broadway ③ [h]. Turn right, soon reaching river [i] with City Mill on left [j]; detour ahead to St Giles Hill viewpoint (signposted) [k] – where Bridge Street bends left take path on right, soon up steps and turn right at the top to reach St Giles Hill ④ [l].

Retrace steps to river (detouring right on the way, into St John's Street to see church [m]), and take riverside path [n] opposite City Mill.

Soon castle wall is followed, and you leave river. ⑤ Pass entrance to ruin of castle [o] on your right; opposite Wolvesey Palace (Bishop's House) detour left for St Cross (signposted into College Walk, taking next right turn (signposted) at end of lane turn left on path alongside brook (straight ahead is private, into college) and follow path along the water meadows [p]. ⑥

At road, path continues ahead and slightly to the right. At St Cross, turn right at nearest corner of wall then left through archway to see courtyard and chapel [q]. Return to Wolvesey Palace, turn left into College [r] then turn right ⑦ under Kingsgate [s],[t], then left along St Swithun's Street. Take second turn on right [u] (St Thomas' Street), halfway along which turn left up St Thomas' Passage. ⑧ Turn right along Southgate [v], then left up High Street to reach Westgate.

ON THE ROUTE

[a] **Westgate** One of two surviving city gates (there were originally five) probably on the site of the Roman gate. Retains gun ports, portcullis slot and five openings for dropping whatever on unwelcome visitors. A chamber above the gate was once a prison, and now contains a small museum with a painted 16th-century ceiling from the headmaster's study in Winchester College, the old city coffer and a drawing of Wren's proposed royal palace which was never built. Open 10-5 Mon-Sat, 2-5 Sun (2-4 winter; closed Mon in winter).

[b] **Great Hall** (free, 10-5 weekdays, 10-4 weekends) Outstanding example of a Norman hall, part of the castle built for Henry III 1222-36. On the wall is a painting of the famous 18-ft Round Table, executed for the visit of Charles V and Henry VIII in 1522 and depicting King

Arthur, with names of the knights of the Round Table around the edge. Also here is Gilbert's bronze statue of Queen Victoria, not looking at all amused, and a 19th-century mural emblazoned with the names of Hampshire's past knights. Outside, surrounded by municipal offices, are some excavated ruins of the round tower.

c] High Street This was the main street in Roman times; the rest of the city centre street pattern is primarily Saxon. **No. 57**, on right, double-fronted with Georgian bow windows, is a well-preserved shop-front, premises since 1813 of the Hampshire Chronicle, first established in Southampton in 1772. Opposite the projecting clock (above which a curfew bell has been rung since William I's time) **Godbegot House** is a timber-framed tenement dating from the 15th century. It stands on the site of the ancient manor of Godbegot, former property of Emma, wife of King Canute and then left to St Swithun's Priory. In a side-alley close by, the **Royal Oak** boasts the oldest bar in England. Public proclamations used to be read from the 15th-century **City Cross**; three of the four statues on this structure were replaced in a thorough restoration last century. Just beyond, on right, The Pentice is a row of shops behind columns supporting an overhang and stands on the site of the old city mint.

d] A plaque in this alley indicates a stone chimney-breast of **William I's palace**. To the left at the end of the alley, the **Eclipse Inn**, a former 16th-century rectory for St Lawrence, was named because of its rivalry to 'The Sun'; the latter has long since closed. The free **City museum** displays fine Roman mosaics and masonry; there are also reconstructed Victorian shops and an Edwardian bathroom.

e] Cathedral The world's longest medieval building. Begun 1079 by William I on the site of a 7th-century cathedral founded by King Cenwealh of Wessex. The Norman building, constructed on a raft of logs on marshy land, experienced great structural problems over many years, culminating in heroic work by William Waulker around the turn of the century, who worked for five years removing rotten timber for underpinning. Much of the rebuilding was 15th-century Perpendicular; the best windows of that period are in the N wall of the nave. Memorials here include those to Jane Austen (the slab in the N aisle is original; the tablet and window were added later), Izaak Walton (author of *The Compleat Angler*), and a statue to William Waulker. The marble font depicts a curious tale of an innkeeper who made his children into sausage-meat; despite this gruesome touch, Henry VII's son and Henry III were both baptised in it.

[f] The Cathedral Close is one of England's loveliest. At **No. 4** judges used to lodge during the Winchester Assizes; **No. 7** was the home of Izaak Walton; the **Pilgrim's Hall**, adjoining the preparatory school for cathedral choristers, has a remarkable hammer-shaped roof c 1290; on the far side of the green, **Cheyney Court**, the city's most-photographed half-timbered building, where the bishop held a court with jurisdiction over much of the city until dissolution by statute in 1835; adjacent is the **old deanery**, with three pointed 13th-century arches, used by Charles II as an audience chamber. Tulip trees in the close were planted by Thomas Garner, Dean and keen botanist (died 1872).

[g] Abbey Gardens Once the gardens of Abbey House (which is now the official Mayor's residence), with a classical garden temple c 1751.

[h] **King Arthur's statue** (1901), erected on a block of Cornish granite; the king of Wessex brought prosperity to southern England and was buried in Hyde Abbey near the city centre.

[i] Close by are **St John's Hospital**, a charitable foundation on both sides of the High Street, and the huge Gothic revival **Guildhall**, begun in 1871.

[j] **City Mill** (National Trust; open to visitors Apr-end Sept, daily except Mon and Fri, 1.45-4.45; Oct-end Mar by prior arrangement with YHA warden) An 18th-century mill on the site of a medieval mill, still with mill-race and mill-room.

[k] In Cheshil Street, **Old Cheshil Rectory**, now a restaurant, is a half-timbered structure built 1450.

[l] **St Giles Hill** Once a fairground when the city prospered as a cloth centre; retains a rural character to a

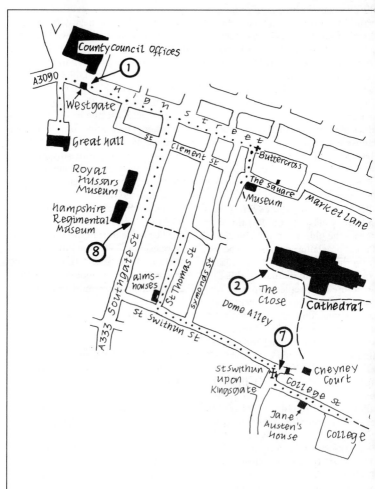

surprising degree. The impressive panorama of the whole city is described on a view-indicator. St Catherine's Hill away to the left was probably the first site to be settled here and has traces of an ancient hill-fort.

[**m**] **St John's Church** In St John's Street, on right; the city's oldest church, with its 15th-century rood-screen and remains of 13th-century wall-paintings.

[**n**] **The Weirs** Riverside walk looking on to backs of houses, the pantiled tower of St Peters, and passing a five-storey mill (1885) which once housed the terminal offices and warehouses of the Itchen Navigation.

[**o**] On right, **Wolvesey Castle** (English Heritage, open 10-1, 2-6 Easter-end Sept), the original Bishop's Palace, was started by Bishop Henri de Blois *c* 1130.

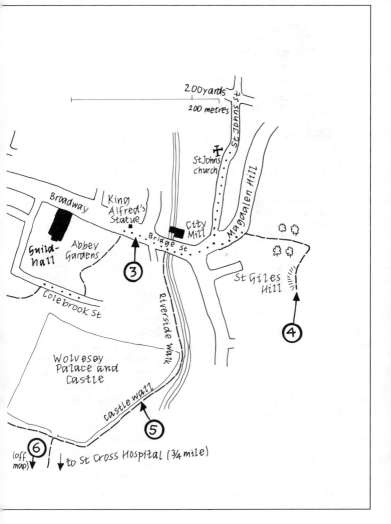

Parliamentarian forces destroyed it in the Civil War, but the ruins are still quite extensive, and include the West and East Halls, an enclosed courtyard and the fortified Wymond's Tower as well as remains of the kitchen block. The adjacent **Palace** (not open), built 1684 for Bishop Morley to the design of Sir Thomas Fitch, represents the city's finest example of architecture of the period.

[p] The **water meadows** by the mill stream remind us that Winchester was built on marshy land. These meadows were created as fertile farmland, fed by channels with enriching silt from the river, and irrigated in times of drought. Views of **St Catherine's Hill** and the 19th-century buildings of **Winchester College**.

[q] **St Cross Hospital** A charitable foundation dating from 1136, now effectively a retirement home. Its resident brothers still sport the gowns and hats whose colours signify the original bequests: red for Cardinal Beaufort's charter for 13 poor and infirm people and 35 men and three women of noble birth; black for Bishop Henry's charter for 100 men to be fed each day. 'Wayfarer's Dole', consisting of bread and ale, must be given at the porter's lodge free of charge (but you have to ask for it specifically). Most of the buildings fronting the courtyard date from 1446, when Cardinal Beaufort refounded the hospital; the chief exception is the church, an interesting transition in style, both round-arched Norman and Early English Gothic – just at the time when the latter started to take over. There is also a fascinating old kitchen with equipment, range and adjacent dining hall.

[r] **The College** (Guided tours Apr-Sept, at 11, 2 and 3.15; otherwise ask at the porter's lodge to have a quick look inside). The handsome courtyards, with chapel and hall, have strong similarities to Oxbridge colleges. Winchester College, one of the most celebrated English public schools, was founded by William of Wykeham, Bishop of Winchester, in 1382. Seventy scholars were taught, mainly in the classics, as preparation for going to Wykeham's New College, Oxford. Winchester College was used by Henry VI as a model when he founded Eton College. Also in College Street, on left, a plaque marks the house where **Jane Austen** died in 1817, aged 42. After falling ill, she had moved from Chawton to be near to her Kingsgate doctor.

[s] **Kingsgate Street**, on left, is of predominantly 18th-century character. Its completeness is its main delight. **No. 8** has an unusual fanlight incorporating a lantern; **No. 9a** has a plaque to church composer Samuel Sebastian Wesley.

[t] **Kingsgate** was added to four Roman gates in the city wall in 1148. The tiny church above the gate is dedicated to St Swithun; when the saint's remains were exhumed on 15th July AD971 and taken to the minster, it poured relentlessly all day, leading to the saying that if it rains on St Swithun's Day it will rain for 40 days.

[u] **Christ's Hospital** A foundation of 1607 for the maintenance of six old men, one matron and four boys; also 'for the assistance of one scholar in each of the two English universities'. Charming cottage gardens laced with roses and laburnum.

[v] On left, the **Royal Hampshire Regimental Museum** (open Mon-Fri 10-12.30, 2-4; in summer Sat, Sun and Bank holidays 12-4) is in Serles House (1730), and has a garden of remembrance.

HEREFORD & WORCESTER

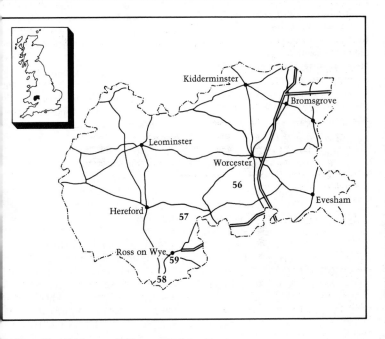

56 Storridge Ridge and Worcestershire Beacon
57 Woolhope and Ridge Hill
58 English Bicknor and Symonds Yat
59 Ross-on-Wye and Penyard Hill

Holiday Which? Good Walks Guide

90 Symonds Yat and the Chickenwire Bridge   91 The Malvern Hills and
Eastnor Castle   92 Witley Court and Abberley Hill   93 Old Radnor and
Hergest Ridge   94 Bircher Common, Croft Ambrey and Croft Castle
95 Lickey Hills and Bittell Reservoirs

Storridge Ridge and Worcestershire Beacon

By straddling the striking main ridge of the Malvern Hills, the walk takes in the differing scenery of the two old counties of Worcestershire and Herefordshire, the former on the Severn plain, to one side, the latter consisting largely of rolling hills, to the other. Note that part of route may be muddy.

Length 6½ miles (10.5km), 3½ hours; variant excluding New Inn at Storridge saves ½ mile
Difficulty 2–3
Start Northern end of Belvue Terrace, Great Malvern town centre, outside W.H.Smith. Parking limited in Malvern town centre. *Alternative start* at North Malvern quarry at ③
OS maps 1:50,000 Sheet 150; 1:25,000 Sheet SO 64/74
Refreshments Pub at Storridge; ice-cream, fruit and cider at Knight's Cider in Storridge; café at St Ann's Well; full range in Malvern town centre

WALK DIRECTIONS

① Standing with your back to W.H.Smith's, turn left along the pavement, then by the Unicorn pub turn left up St Ann's Road, following signs to 'Worcestershire Beacon' [a].

100 yards after the Red Lion pub, when road bends to left, continue forward and uphill on surfaced track marked by dead-end sign. Follow track to start of open hill, marked by signs 'Malvern Hills Conservators - No Wheeled Vehicles', where ② turn sharply right on level path running around and slightly uphill.

Soon come to junction of five paths, where continue forward and uphill. After 100 yards, keep right on joining gravel path merging in from left and soon pass Ivy Scar Rock on left [b]. Continue on well-defined gravel path ignoring side-turns, first

level with wood on right and then starting to drop.

As clock-tower becomes visible ahead, path becomes surfaced track with abandoned workings of North Malvern quarry to left; continue through car park ③ to road ahead. On reaching road, turn left, shortly passing clock-tower on left [c]. When the pavement ends, cross road and continue forward on opposite pavement.

After ¼ mile, the road makes a sharp left-hand bend and the footpath is protected by a railing; at the end of the railing, and opposite 51 West Malvern Road, go down steps to right on to footpath descending very steeply between houses.

④ At bottom, ignore footpath directly ahead and turn right on road for 100 yards, then left over stile on to path between fences. At bottom, descend to road by steps then turn left along road for 50 yards. After entrance to Cowleigh Park Farm, turn right on track running between field and farm buildings. Follow track as it curves to left and ascends minor ridge.

At the top of the rise [d], there are four gateways; go through the third from the left, marked by a 'Worcestershire Way' waymark. After 20 yards, turn right on footpath running within belt of trees between fields. Soon enter field over stile with waymark and continue on well-defined path, keeping hedge on right. At corner of field, cross stile and immediately turn left, keeping fence on left, and soon cross stream by footbridge ⑤.

For route avoiding New Inn (saves ½ mile) after bridge, continue forward across field and uphill towards wood. Maintain the direction given by bridge and make for old track visible on hillslope ahead, which bends to right as it reaches brow of the hill. Continue along this as it runs level for 100 yards and then through gate to short section of fenced track, used as sheep pens at time of inspection.

After 50 yards, continue forward and slightly uphill as second track merges in from right. Track passes through belt of trees then runs between fences, swinging to left at top of rise and then running slightly downhill towards Hill Farm. Follow track to left of farm buildings, but at end of buildings do not follow main track down to road. Instead, turn right along track beside buildings and then at end of buildings turn left down track with fence on left.

At bottom, turn half right for 20 yards, left through gap in hedge, then half right along track with hedge on right to farm shop and car park. Keep to right of building and emerge at road junction; resume directions at (7).

For route via New Inn at Storridge
After footbridge, turn half right and cross field keeping to right of hillock. At corner of field, cross stile marked by 'Worcestershire Way' sign, then continue forward on track through orchard. On reaching further hedge, turn left following waymark, then right after 20 yards over footbridge with stiles at either end.

Continue through next two fields, keeping alongside hedge on right, to emerge on minor road to right of cottage. Take left-hand of two field entrances immediately opposite and maintain direction keeping fence on right. (6) At end of field, ascend short track to main road [e] and turn left; the New Inn is almost immediately on your right.

About 100 yards beyond the pub, at a point where electricity lines cross the road, turn left on track into field. Once in field, by black corrugated-iron barn, follow track half right up hill towards buildings, keeping fence on right. At top of hill, enter garden of Crumpton Hill Cottage but turn left in front of house and follow track around to minor road. Turn right on road for $^1/_3$ mile, as it climbs slightly and then descends to join a more major road at a sharp bend.

(On your left at this point is Knight's Cider; this is the end of the short-cut avoiding the New Inn.)
Both routes (7) [f] Immediately cross the more major road and go through gate marked by 'Public Footpath' sign. Follow track uphill towards Whitman's Hill Farm, and at top continue forward over stile into field. Maintain direction steeply uphill to further stile and wood. On entering wood, path becomes sunken way, the Tinker's Path, and continues to ascend to ridge.

(8) At summit, turn left on slightly less well defined path. After 100 yards, take right-hand fork over stile into field but maintain direction, keeping woodland fence on left [g].

At corner of field, return to wood over stile. After another 200 yards, path emerges to run just inside wood with fence and field on right.
(9) Shortly after the field ends, join another path merging in from the right and turn left and slightly uphill to return to the ridge.

Path soon forks again; take right-hand fork to continue along the ridge and ignore all turns to left or right (the next section can be muddy). After $^1/_2$ mile, pass through gate [h], and after another 200 yards through a second gate (10) to emerge at the rear of Croft Farm. Descend to the left, through farmyard and, on reaching farm buildings, turn left on lane which soon becomes private road (to vehicles) between suburban houses and runs up hill to join public road.

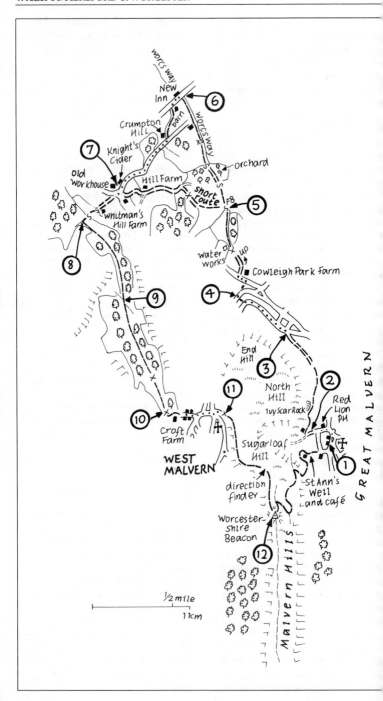

On reaching public road, cross to pavement then turn left and steeply up hill to crossroads, with main entrance to St James' and the Abbey girls' school on your right. Cross and continue forward up short section of road, following direction sign to Great Malvern, Worcestershire Beacon, etc., then through gate on to open hill ⑪. Road becomes track, and after 50 yards continue forward and slightly uphill at junction of paths [i].

The path climbs gently around the side of the Sugar Loaf to a pass on the summit ridge of the Malvern Hills, marked by a stone direction finder. Turn right on to the left-hand of two paths in the general direction marked as 'the Beacon', but after 20 yards, by a metal bench, this cuts through a clear ridge, or dyke, with a ditch on the far side: turn right and go uphill walking along the top of the dyke [j].

Follow the dyke to the summit of Worcestershire Beacon ⑫ [k]. Stand by the trig point (summit pillar) with the view-indicator to your left and walk straight ahead towards a nearby bench which is just visible beyond a rock. Cross a surfaced vehicle track and immediately before the bench turn half left on a grassy track.

Continue down this until another track comes in from the left; turn sharply right on this to continue downhill to a second sharp corner, with only a rough hill path continuing ahead, and here turn sharply left. Continue along this for some distance until you come to a third zig-zag ⑬, where turn sharp right to join another path coming in from the left and continuing to your right and downhill.

From this point you will be able to see the buildings of St Ann's Well and café downhill to your left, and after 50 yards turn left by a bench on to a rough path going steeply downhill. This soon reaches another constructed path running around the hill; turn left along this for 40 yards, then right down the slope to emerge on a vehicle track by the buildings. Cross the track and descend down steps, to the left of the buildings, to the entrance to St Ann's Well and cafe [l].

From the café, zigzag NE downhill by following a steep surfaced track which winds down through trees. At the bottom, turn right on road then almost immediately fork left. After 30 yards, as road becomes entrance to house, turn left down flight of steps. At bottom of steps, continue downhill with public lavatories on right, and turn left on to Belvue Terrace to return to beginning of walk.

ON THE ROUTE

[a] The houses in **St Ann's Road** are the oldest buildings in Malvern apart from the priory. Donkey carts used to take Victorian holidaymakers up to the Worcestershire Beacon from here.

[b] **Ivy Scar Rock** One of the largest natural rock faces on the Malvern Hills, used for climbing. There are good **views** over Malvern towards Worcester from this section.

[c] The **clock tower** was erected by Malvern council to commemorate the coronation of Edward VII in 1901.

[d] View of the antennae on the north site of the **Royal Signals and Radar Establishment** can be seen; one of the largest electronics research establishments in Europe and Malvern's principal employer.

[e] Here signs mark the **old county boundary** between Worcestershire and Herefordshire, which at this point corresponds very precisely with the edge of the Worcestershire plain.

[f] The house to your right at the bend is the former **Storridge workhouse**.

[g] The path follows the ridge for some 1½ miles, and wherever the trees open out there are fine **views** to the W across the valley of the Cradley Brook towards the Ledbury Hills, the Much Marcle Ridge (with a television transmitter on top), and the high, flat tops of the Black Mountains in Powys in the far distance.

[h] This section of the route is a permissive path running through a **nature reserve**, owned by the Hereford & Worcester Nature Trust; be sure not to stray from the path. The tops of old **lime kilns** are visible to the right of the path.

[i] Just to your left at this point is a **spring** which is regularly checked as safe to drink from.

[j] This is the **Shire Ditch** or **Red Earl's Dyke**, constructed in the Dark Ages to divide the lands of Leofric, Earl of Mercia, from those of the Bishop of Hereford; it runs the length of the Malvern Hills.

[k] **Worcestershire Beacon** At 1,381ft, the highest point of the Malvern Hills; there is nothing higher eastwards until the Urals in Russia. The summit offers excellent views in all directions; a view-indicator indicates features which range from the Shropshire Hills to the N, the Welsh Marches and Offa's Dyke country to the W, the fruit-growing area of the Vale of Evesham to the E, with the escarpment of the Cotswolds rising beyond it.

[l] On the café, which is open daily Mar-Oct and at winter weekends, a plaque honours **'Blind George' Pullen**, who played his harmonium here for over 50 years and died in 1936.

Woolhope and Ridge Hill

Takes you through varied countryside on the Woolhope Dome, one of the classic geological areas of Britain. Country churches, pubs and fine views westwards into Wales and east to the Malvern Hills and the Cotswolds are the principal features.

Length 5½ miles (9km), 2½ hours
Difficulty 2–3
Start Sollers Hope church, N of Ross-on-Wye and just off B4224. Coming from Hereford, turn left off B4224 at a bend about 2 miles beyond Fownhope village, and shortly after the Gurney's Oak pub. Grid reference 612331
OS maps 1:50,000 149; 1:25,000 SO 63/73 (Pathfinder 1041)
Refreshments Crown Inn at Woolhope; Butcher's Arms ⅓ mile E of Woolhope

WALK DIRECTIONS

(1) With your back to the entrance to the churchyard, go forward 20 yards then turn left into farmyard to pass between farmhouse on left and barn with dovecote in end gable on right [a]. Continue forward through gate into [first] field, bear slightly left, then forward again on clear path down middle of field. At end, go forward through gate into second field, and continue down centre of this long narrow field which swings slightly to right, staying close to right-hand edge.

At end of wood on right, field swings round to right, but continue forward through gate. In third field, maintain direction over rise, keeping edge of field on left. (2) At corner of this field, go over stile then immediately turn left down side of fourth field to footbridge at corner, with stiles at both ends.

After crossing bridge, continue forward in fifth field, keeping hedge on right for 100 yards then follow hedge round as it turns to right. Continue with hedge on right to corner of field, then exit through gate on to track between hedges; after 15 yards, track swings half left. Continue down track, which becomes a concrete farm road as it passes the entrance to Alford's Mill on the right, but when farm road swings left, 100 yards after mill, continue forward through gate into field following footpath sign.

Initially keep hedge on right, but when this turns away to right continue across field to stile 60 yards to left of prominent oak tree in middle of far hedge (3). Once over stile, take bearing slightly to right of Woolhope church [b], visible ahead, and to left of middle of row of three pear trees in middle of field, towards stile in far hedge.

Cross this stile to farm road, and immediately over second stile directly opposite. Turn half right, with hedge on right, towards footbridge with stiles at both ends. From footbridge, continue forward over next stile, then maintain direction up slight ridge in centre of next field.

Follow this ridge, marked by short row of trees, to gate on to road coming in from the right and follow this for ¼ mile to Woolhope village. (4) At road junction in Woolhope village, *detour left for Woolhope church and Crown Inn*, almost immediately on right, or *turn right to continue walk* following signpost to Putley and Ledbury.

Follow this road for ⅓ mile to the Butcher's Arms. Immediately before the pub car park, turn right up farm road. Pass barn on right and (5) after ¼ mile continue forward and uphill, ignoring left turn, as road becomes track between hedges.

Follow track as it swings slightly to left then sharply to the right, past cottage on right, then (6) at end of

207

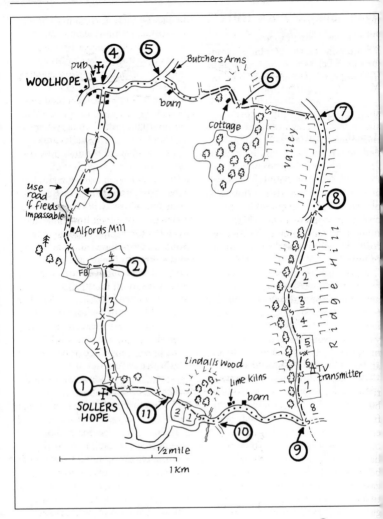

track continue forward through gate into field. Go directly ahead across field to stile at left-hand corner of wood, then downhill on clear path just inside wood with fence and field on the left.

At bottom of wood, go through gate beside stile into large field and follow left-hand edge into valley, then uphill ahead to gate at corner, leading to track between hedges, after 100 yards reaching road just below summit of ridge ⑦ [c]. Turn right on to the road, and follow this for half a mile along the crest of the ridge [d].

⑧ When the road turns left away from the ridge, continue forward up steps to stile marked by footpath sign, then follow path along crest of ridge through a succession of fields, always keeping close to right edge of field, with steeply sloping woodland beyond. Shortly before end of third field, note trig point marking summit of Ridge Hill with views to west; sixth field contains Ridge Hill aerial, the main television transmitter for the south-west Midlands.

(9) At end of eighth field, descend steps and cross stile by footpath sign, into track between hedges, then turn right down track. Follow track for half a mile, ignoring gates to left and right; pass barn and Lyndalls Wood on right [e], then (10) at end of wood turn right at junction of tracks. Track becomes farm road, crosses minor stream by bridge marked by railings on either side of road, then climbs slightly and turns to left.

By second telephone pole after bridge, turn right over stile into field and cross to gate at right-hand end of far side. In second field keep edge of field and stream on right, and 100 yards after gate descend slightly on minor track over small bridge to gate and road by Whittlebury Farm (11).

Turn left on road but immediately right through gate at end of farm building, and then half left across field, keeping parallel with left-hand edge, to gate at projecting corner opposite. In next field, follow left hand-edge until farm buildings become visible ahead, then make for gate at end of buildings. Follow track to left of farm buildings through two gates to emerge in front of Court Farm, then turn left to Sollers Hope church and start of walk.

ON THE ROUTE

[a] **Sollers Hope church** is a 14th-century restoration of a Saxon church, believed to have been financed by Robert Whittington, brother of Dick. It contains memorials to the Whittington family, as well as an early Norman font. Court Farm, next to the church, is an ancient half-timbered building.

[b] **Woolhope church** occupies an ancient circular site, and is notable for three early medieval tombstones inside the church, one of which appears to feature a witch preparing a potion.

[c] This section of the walk gives a particularly clear idea of the **geology** of the Woolhope area. The first ridge consists of Wenlock limestone and from the top there is a good view back over Woolhope and the centre of the dome, which consists of sandstone ringed by Woolhope limestone, with the Black Mountains far to the west. You then descend into a valley underlain by more easily eroded shales, and then climb up to the outermost and highest ridge made up of Aymestrey limestone.

[d] For the next $1^{1}/_{2}$ miles there are excellent **views** to the E. The town of Ledbury, with its steepled church, can be seen clearly with the wooded Ledbury hills and then the bare Malvern hills visible behind. Slightly to the south, the Cotswold escarpment can be seen in the far distance. As you approach the Ridge Hill television transmitter, May Hill, topped by a prominent clump of trees, can be seen ahead, and beyond is the wooded upland of the Forest of Dean.

[e] Shortly after the barn, two **lime kilns**, which produced fertiliser for agricultural use, are visible, set into the wooded slope to the right of the track.

English Bicknor and Symonds Yat

Involves some climbing, but rewarded by wonderful views of the romantic Wye Gorge. Route-finding intricate but not particularly difficult.

Length 7 miles (11km), 4 hours
Difficulty 3–4
Start Goodrich Castle car park; turn off the A40 at Pencraig, 4 miles SW of Ross-on-Wye, and turn left up access road in the centre of Goodrich; car park free, but entrance fee to castle. Grid reference 576196
OS maps 1:50,000 162; 1:25,000 Outdoor Leisure 14
Refreshments Pub and shop in Goodrich, café in Symonds Yat Rock car park

WALK DIRECTIONS

(1) Walk back down access road into Goodrich village, then turn left on road signed to Courtfield and Welsh Bicknor, taking road-bridge over another road below. Continue uphill on road until fork (2), where go forward up steps between the two forks. Follow multi-coloured waymarks on clear path going steeply up Coppet Hill, ignoring path coming up from right half-way up, to reach trig point (summit pillar) (3) [a].

Turn left on level path making for end of wood, where turn left: follow Wye Valley Walk waymarks downhill on clear path, with occasional constructed steps, keeping wall and wood always on right. (4) Eventually descend on to road, turn right along it and uphill, soon going over cattle-grid, then downhill. At first fork in road go left, then ignore the next two left forks following signs to Youth Hostel.

(5) Shortly after third fork, turn half right and steeply downhill on path signed to 'riverside, church, and youth hostel'. Descend to riverside path and turn right. Continue along river bank, ignoring fork to right, but just before bridge turn right up bank then turn left to cross river by the bridge [b].

(6) Once over the bridge, turn left down steps then right along track signed to Lydbrook. Follow track, which leads around the end of factory, then up bank to right of playing field and then reaches road by gate beside stile. (7) Turn right on road, passing entrance to the factory and sign for Lower Lydbrook, then immediately right down farm road to Stowfield Farm.

When level with farmhouse bear half left and uphill. Keep to left of all farm buildings and, when the surfaced farm road swings right to enter house, continue forward through gate on track between hedges. (8) When track ends by three field gates, go through leftmost gate and continue forward into first field with hedge on right, then after 100 yards turn right as the hedge does the same, and continue uphill with hedge on right (note: this hedge seemed to be being removed when walk was inspected and if there is no fence to replace it, look carefully for vestiges of hedge: however, track is likely to remain visible).

Maintain direction on track, passing through gate into second field, then in third field make for projecting corner of hedge ahead; do not go through gate to left of this corner, but remain in field past the corner, keeping close to hedge on left, then over stile at next corner. Continue forward, with hedge on left and English Bicknor church clearly visible ahead [c], through gate beside stile, (9) but on reaching gate on to road do *not* join road, instead turn 90 degrees right across field, making for stile halfway along wire

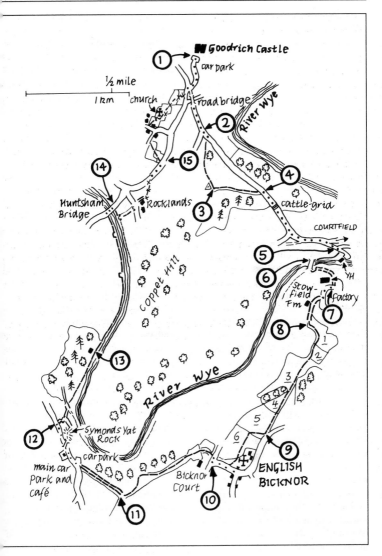

Goodrich Castle

car park

church

road bridge

River Wye

½ mile

1 km

Huntsham Bridge

Rocklands

cattle-grid

COURTFIELD

Coppet Hill

YH

Stow-field Fm

Factory

River Wye

Symonds Yat Rock

car park

main car Park and café

Bicknor Court

ENGLISH BICKNOR

fence ahead, approximately on brow of hill.

From this stile, make for right-hand end of wall to right of church, then continue with wall and schoolyard on left to stile at corner of field. Once over stile, turn half right down right-hand side of playground, then through gate to left of house and turn right down road.

Descend to T-junction ⑩ and turn right for 40 yards along road, then left on to path by sign, attached to telephone pole, to 'Coldwell Walks'.

Go up bank by steps, then at top go over stile and cross paddock, keeping close to fence on left to next stile. Go half left across next field, keeping to right of farm building and making initially for high stile visible

211

in middle of opposite fence. However, do not go over this stile, but instead cross lower stile 40 yards to right, at corner of field.

Once inside wood, continue forward keeping close to fence on left until you cross track coming up from right and exiting through gate on left, then bear half right on level path. Continue for $1/2$ mile as path winds along, roughly level and never too far from edge of wood on left [**d**].

(11) Go over stile just before crossing small stream, and continue slightly uphill on path to emerge in corner of Symonds Yat car park. Go through car park, then turn right along road; (for refreshment hut, turn left into main car park just after 'Low gear' sign; for Symonds Yat viewpoint, cross the footbridge); continue along road and under footbridge [**e**].

(12) Turn half right off road 200 yards after going under the bridge, just by two stone arches on right (the remains of an old lime kiln), following footpath sign to Welsh Bicknor and Ross. Go through pair of bollards to right of house, then curve round to the right and start to descend on very well defined path. Path bends sharp left in front of cottage, descends very steeply past stone building on right, then bends sharp right.

40 yards after this bend, turn left and downhill by signpost (path ahead is signed for Ross and Welsh Bicknor). Descend by short flight of steps to cross gravel track, then descend by further flight of steps and continue downhill on clear path, following Wye Valley Walk, to proceed along river bank. **(13)** After passing isolated cottage on left, and 50 yards after going through narrow gap between rocks, take right-hand fork by second large rock. Wood soon ends and path continues close to river through two large fields [**f**].

(14) At Huntsham bridge, turn left to join road then right over bridge.

Once over bridge, turn sharp right to return to river bank, then left along bank (thus doubling back from previous direction). When garden on left ends, go forward over stile but immediately turn left up side of field. At left-hand corner of field go through squeeze-stile, cross drive to house, and continue up track to left of farm buildings, passing through series of gates to reach road.

Turn right along road for 200 yards, then **(15)** left through kissing-gate opposite start of track on right. Go half right across (first) field to stile just to left of top right corner, and then half right across second field, again to top right corner. Proceed on track between hedges to road and turn left for 50 yards, then right on private road signed as public footpath, starting opposite prominent black and white building.

When road opens out on to area of grass, turn half right to enter churchyard by gate, and follow surfaced footpath around right-hand end of church, ignoring track entering churchyard to right, and exit by metal kissing-gate at far corner.

Continue forward on clear path with edge of field on right, then through gate into second field and diagonally downhill towards gate in middle of right-hand side. Cross school playing-field to further gate and road, turn left, and at road junction continue forward on road signed to Goodrich Castle, to return to start of walk.

ON THE ROUTE

[**a**] Very fine views, N to **Titterstone Clee**, W to the **Black Mountains**; nearer by is 12th-century **Goodrich Castle**, an impressive ruin built from the local red sandstone, intact until destruction by a Parliamentary siege

the Civil War.

] This bridge used to carry the **Wye Valley Railway, but has now been repaired for use as a footbridge only and is part of the Wye Valley Walk. The line ran from Chepstow to Monmouth, part of a dense network in the Forest of Dean and Wye Valley.

] English Bicknor Church Has an unexpectedly rich Norman interior, with 12th-century piers in the arcades, and fine woodwork. The church is in the outer courtyard of a Norman motte and bailey, and some remains of the castle are visible. This section of the walk also gives a view of the high plateau of the Forest of Dean.

] The path gives fine **views down through the hanging woods, and occasional stone pinnacles, to the River Wye far below.

[e] The path over the footbridge leads on to **Symonds Yat** rock itself, a spectacular 650-foot high viewpoint from which you can see the river Wye to both left and right as it curves around the deeply incised meander.

[f] As well as waterfowl on the river, this section of the walk is memorable for the **view** ahead, across the bend in the river, of Goodrich church and spire, beautifully sited and somewhat isolated. The path of the river consists of broad meanders formed when the river flowed across a level plain, but the block of land forming the Forest of Dean was subsequently slowly lifted up, forcing the river to cut down into the rock while maintaining its old path.

Ross-on-Wye and Penyard Hill

A very varied walk at the north end of the Wye gorge with good views and plenty to look at.

Length 7 miles (11km), 3¹/₂ hours
Difficulty 2–3
Start Centre of Ross-on-Wye
OS maps 1:50,000 162; 1:25,000 SO 42/52 and SO 62/72 (Pathfinder 1064 and 1065)
Refreshments Pub at Howle; full range in Ross-on-Wye

WALK DIRECTIONS

① From the Market House [a], with Broad Street sloping down to your right, take High Street towards Lloyds Bank, turning left into Church Street opposite King's Head pub. Opposite almshouses on left, go diagonally right across churchyard (you can detour along edge of churchyard to see mock-Gothic town wall [b]), past church porch and proceed around to right of church.

At end of church, keep forward (do not enter park on right through stone pillars) alongside wall on right, and where this reaches a corner continue forward through graveyard. After 75 yards turn right at T-junction, then after 30 yards take first left to reach kissing-gate, beyond which enclosed path leads to end of driveway. Cross to enclosed path opposite, to reach gate, then go down steps to path junction: turn right and fork left after 15 yards; immediately keep left (right goes down steps).

Path proceeds with hedge on left and steep wooded slope on right, then along edge of fields, at end of which ② take kissing-gate, go down steps and turn left on to track between fields. Soon join driveway, and proceed to residential road. Take surfaced path opposite. At next residential road (Roman Way) turn

left. ③ Cross main road to minor road opposite, immediately forking right into Fernbank Road. Follow this uphill, ignoring side turnings. Road becomes track climbing through wood. At top of rise, when buildings of Hill Farm appear ahead, turn sharp right and continue uphill on gravel track; you are now following the waymarked Wye Valley Walk ④. After 50 yards, pass through barrier and then immediately take the left-hand fork.

When track levels off near summit of Chase Wood, continue forward on main track, initially with field on right (but still inside woods) [c]. ⑤ 250 yards after end of field on right, continue forward at junction of tracks, ignoring cross-tracks, to take slightly concealed track going sharply downhill. Almost immediately, take right-hand fork, and after another 30 yards turn left on to path going steeply downhill, following waymark.

At cross track after 30 yards continue downhill on short flight of steps, eventually reaching corner of field at bottom of hill. Turn left, keeping edge of wood on right, and soon go through gate into field. Continue forward and downhill on track across (first) field towards farm buildings, soon with hedge on right [d]. Go through gate into second field, then after 30 yards go through right-hand of two gates into third field; then through gate into farmyard and straight ahead on to road ⑥.

Turn left along road for 100 yards, crossing small stream, then after house turn right into entrance, then immediately left over stile. Ascend field alongside hedge on left, then at top left corner of field cross pair of stiles, then over track and third stile to continue forward up second field, keeping just to left of sunken way.

Halfway up field, turn left by

marker post and cross to stile opposite. Once over stile, do not turn right as indicated by Wye Valley Walk markers, but go straight ahead, to left of cottage, on a steep concrete track between hedges. Track swings round to right at top; right of way goes straight ahead, but was blocked when we inspected, so follow track but then ⑦ turn left on to terrace in front of next cottage. Keeping to left of the cottage go through gap in hedge and turn right on to path running steeply uphill between hedges.

At T-junction of paths at top of rise, turn left on well-defined track along side of hill. Soon come to parking area in front of house; keep to right of the house, going through stone archway, then follow track, initially poorly defined, going half right uphill. At corner of field ahead, turn half right more steeply uphill on path which soon runs between hedges. Turn right in front of cottage to emerge on minor road ⑧.

Turn left on road, and left again at junction after 80 yards, ignoring unsurfaced tracks; the entrance to the Crown Inn is on the left after another 60 yards. At entrance to Woolleys' follow road around to right, but 40 yards later when road again swings right, and another track branches left, continue forward and steeply downhill on path between hedges.

At end of field on left, path merges into small wooded area; ignore field entrances to left and right, but continue downhill on clear sunken track. ⑨ At bottom of track, turn left along road for 30 yards, then right after Paddock Cottage down track between fences.

After 70 yards, go right over stile by footpath sign, then half left across field, keeping to right of Lodge Farm. Cross stile in middle of fence ahead, and continue forward for 150 yards,

rising towards stile in right-hand edge of field. Cross track running just inside wood and continue forward on sunken track uphill and curving round to left.

At top of rise, cross another track and go up bank to stile into field. Follow left-hand edge of field for 40 yards to corner, then maintain direction across field, heading for the right-hand end of group of trees on skyline. When far edge of field becomes visible, turn quarter right, making for stile by electricity pole half way between two houses ⑩.

Continue forward across end of garden, then through gap in hedge and turn left on track. After 15 yards, main track swings left towards house but continue forward on track running downhill through wood. At bottom corner of wood, turn right on to concrete access road and continue downhill. At bottom of hill, track turns left by barn. *If field ahead is passable* continue forward over stile to right of barn, to projecting corner of field and then quarter right to stile, then right on to road just in front of Parkfields (house). *If field is impassable* continue along track to join road, then right on road, passing Bill Mills [**e**] and then, after a sharp right-hand bend, passing Parkfields.

Continue along road, and *both routes* 100 yards after road junction turn left up track between hedges ⑪. At top of rise, follow track round to right in front of house, then take track between fences half right uphill, to right of double garage. Track swings round to right and rises to join track around hill merging in from left, running along just inside wood with fence and field on right. Continue along track for ¾ mile, passing Birches Barn on right, an impressive semi-ruined barn, then dropping into a slight dip and rising again. ⑫ Track then turns sharp right and descends hill for 40 yards to meet surfaced farm road.

Turn sharp left on the farm road, leading through wood; after 400 yards, follow road sharply round to left and steeply uphill, ignoring two tracks branching off on right. At top of rise, road turns right again, with hedge and field on left. At end of wood, continue forward through gate

beside stile as farm road becomes track between hedges. Pass Lawns Farm on your right, and at end of track continue forward through gate into field, keeping along right edge.

When wood begins on right, go through gate beside stile and follow path just inside right-hand edge of wood, with fence and field on right. ⑬ Field on right ends after ¹/₂ mile,

ut continue forward on track
through wood, to meet gravel
forestry track coming in from left.
Continue forward on forestry
track until just before it turns
sharply right, then drop down to a
stile to the left. Go half left across
field towards isolated tree near
projecting corner of wood (14), then
turn right and follow Wye Valley
Walk signs along sunken way with
wood on right and field initially on
left. At end of wood, go through two
gates beside stiles in succession,
then turn left and downhill across
field on grassy path [f].

At bottom left corner of field turn

left through gate on to track at
bottom edge of wood. Track curves
around to right, becoming track
between fences, then through gate to
pass entrance to Alton Court [g].
Drive becomes public road, Penyard
Road, passing entrance to industrial
estate on right, and at T-junction
turn left on to Alton Street. Take
second turning on right, into Chase
Road, to reach main road where you
turn left to return to Market House.

ON THE ROUTE

[a] **Market House** A 17th-century
arcaded structure commanding the
centre of town. Ross was granted its
first market charter by King Stephen
in the 12th century.

[b] Carry on round the right edge of
the churchyard, turn at the end left
past the Royal Hotel. The hotel and
mock-Gothic town wall were built
in the 1830s at a time when
travellers came to view the
picturesque and romantic qualities
of the Wye valley.

[c] The summit of the hill is the site
of an Iron Age **hill-fort**, the single
rampart marking the edge of the
fields on top; traces can be seen to
the right of the track.

[d] **Goodrich Castle** is now visible
half right on hill across Wye.

[e] Now a soft-drink bottling plant,
but there is still a **mill pond** between
the road and the substantial
buildings. The weir and diversion
sluice is by the road just before
Parkfields.

[f] Just to your right is an old
reservoir building disguised as a
chapel.

[g] Attractive half-timbered house,
with a 16th-century gable facing
the road.

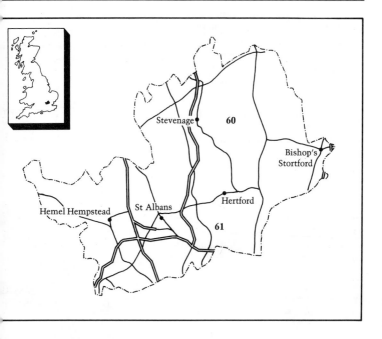

HERTFORDSHIRE

Holiday Which? Good Walks Guide

Ardeley and Benington

Characteristic East Anglian landscape at its best, sufficiently undulating to sustain interest, with the villages of Ardeley and Benington the main focal points. Most of the going is along gentle farm tracks and the route is quite easy to follow.

Length 8½ miles (13.5 km), 4 hours
Difficulty 2
Start Wood End, on minor road signposted SE from Ardeley and E of Walkern; roadside parking near small grass triangle with road signpost at junction in centre of hamlet. Grid reference 326255
OS maps 1:50,000 166; 1:25,000 TL 22/32 (Pathfinder 1073)
Refreshments Pub in Ardeley; pubs and shop in Benington

WALK DIRECTIONS

①From signpost on grass triangle, with direction for Great Munden on your left, turn right along cul-de-sac, passing post box on your right. Keep to the principal road, which becomes an unsurfaced track at end of village. Fork right at major fork of tracks (just before lone brick bungalow); 100 yards after the bungalow keep on track as it bends left.

After ⅓ mile ②, fork left (right goes towards distant white building); 250 yards later ignore sharp right turn. 500 yards later, bear right at track junction by waymarker post with blue arrow, following a track along right edge of field towards Ardeley. Emerge at housing estate, go forward to T-junction with main village road [a] where turn left, past church.

③ Where road bends right (after 400 yards) turn left (signposted Wood End) on concrete track, keeping forward after 30 yards where it bends right through gate, now on path between hedgerow trees, and

later with hedgerow on right only, along edge of field [b]. At end of field pass through strip of woodland, then ④ turn right at path T-junction.

After 80 yards, reach corner of track by signpost, turn left downhill dipping then rising, to reach farm

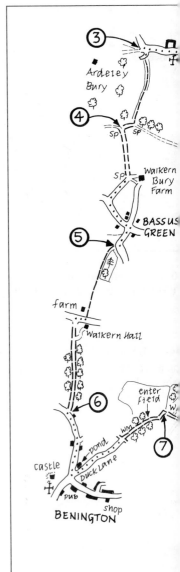

ad with farm away to left. Bear
ght along farm road to T-junction
ith lane where turn left. At houses
Bassus Green) turn right at
rossroads, towards Clay End.
5) After 150 yards, where trees
egin, fork right on to track

signposted public bridleway,
initially with woods on left, then
along left edge of field, dipping then
rising to Walkern Hall Farm. Turn
right on road, then left after 50 yards
by signpost to Benington [**c**], on
track which later merges into

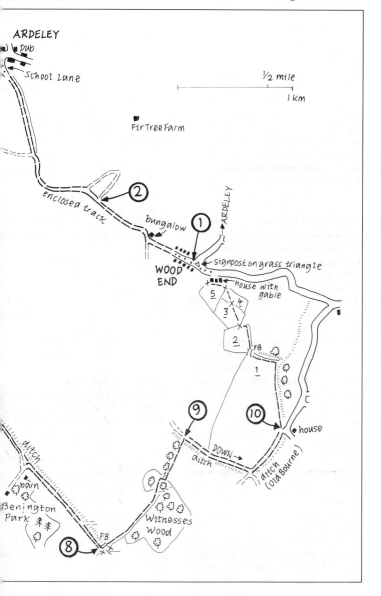

concrete track, and proceeds along avenue to reach road **(6)**. Left on road, into Benington [**d**]. At road junction in village centre, turn sharp left into Duck Lane (signposted Clay End. Where lane becomes unsurfaced track, go forward; 50 yards later, at junction, keep forward by blue waymarker post.

Track soon drops gently and bends left to enter field with ditch on right. **(7)** After 80 yards, turn right by waymark post, crossing the ditch and now on track with a ditch alongside of left, along bottom of valley. After $1/3$ mile cross track and keep forward alongside ditch, soon merging into better-defined track, still along valley floor. 200 yards before going under power-line, ignore left fork; keep ditch on left, go under power-line and **(8)** immediately cross footbridge on left and go uphill with fence on right and soon wood on right.

Enter the wood at recessed corner, keep forward inside woods (immediately ignoring minor right fork) to reach field after 100 yards. Turn right for 20 yards and then left along grassy strip (old field Boundary) which soon becomes hedgerow (walk along right-hand side of it), leading towards power-lines. **(9)** At end of hedgerow, reach waymark post and ditch, and turn right at T-junction with track.

Follow down to bottom of valley where turn left at junction, on track with ditch on right. **(10)** Where bridge and road appear on right, ignore them and keep forward (or to avoid field route you can turn left along the road, then left at next junction to return to Wood End), still with ditch on right. Soon pass another bridge on your right, ignore minor left fork, and turn left at end of field, with hedgerow and ditch on right.

At next field corner, turn right

over low brick bridge to enter second field, where go forward up right edge, turning left at top right-hand corner, then after 50 yards take gate on right into third field. Go diagonally left across to gate in line with nearest house (with dormer gables) in this and the fourth field.

Enter fifth field, proceed on right edge (past the house on your right) and soon take gate on right by open-sided barn (not through farmyard just before this) to follow concrete track to road. Turn left to centre of Wood End.

ON THE ROUTE

[**a**] **Ardeley** A semi-circle of whitewashed thatched cottages around the green; its brick well is not ancient but built in 1917 as a romantic feature. The church opposite has interesting 15th-century roof tracery, ornate roof-bosses and angels bearing musical instruments.

[**b**] **Ardeley Bury** is seen away to right. The house has a late-Tudor core, but what you see is a capricious indulgence of 1820, built for a Mr John Murray, with fanciful flint turrets, pinnacles, Gothicised windows, a baronial hall, a musicians' gallery and wedding-cake vaulting.

[**c**] **Walkern Hall** (on left) is early 19th-century with a Greek Doric porch.

[**d**] **Benington** Enchanting village green with a pond overhung by willows and surrounded by 16th-century plaster-rendered and half-timbered cottages, with the ancient Bell Inn, close by. Near the church stands The Lordship, a Georgian house incorporating a strange mock Norman folly made out of ruins of castle demolished in 1212. With gatehouse and portcullis, the effect is eye-opening.

ssendon and Stratton's Folly

**urprisingly rural despite its
roximity to suburban
.ertfordshire, and justifiably one of
ae most walked parts of the county.
he pub at Essendon is midway and
ae folly tower is seen in later
ages. Route-finding moderately
asy, but mud can be a problem.**

ength 6^1/$_2$ miles (10.5km), 3^1/$_2$
ours

ifficulty 3

tart At W end of village of
'ewgate Street (N of Cuffley),
gnposted from war memorial in
:ntre of Goff's Oak (from which
:ep left at next T-junction as
gnposted and left opposite
'ewgate Street church, by Gable
ouse Restaurant); park on roadside
.st before houses end. Grid
ference 295052

S maps 1:50,000 166; 1:25,000 TL
)/30 (Pathfinder 1120)

efreshments At Essendon; shop
pen Sunday) and pub at Little
erkhamstead; Beehive Inn at ⑬

'ALK DIRECTIONS

① Proceed on road (in opposite
rection from which you arrived),
assing New Park Farm and house,
ad then on farm track. After ^{1}/$_2$ mile
ack bends right; ② 50 yards later,
:ep straight on (ignoring minor
ack on left) to reach houses, then
> forward to road. Left on road and
nmediately right at junction
gnposted Essendon.

③ After ^{1}/$_4$ mile, where lane is
bout to bend right, fork left on to
aymarked woodland track, which
>es along inside edge of woods;
ter views open up to right as track
)w runs in narrow woodland strip.
.ventually keep forward on joining
nsurfaced driveway (at brick gate-
osts on left); finally, past houses on
ft, track soon reaches road ④.
Cross road and take signposted

driveway opposite. Follow 120 yards
to T-junction by signpost, where
bear right [**a**]; 150 yards later ignore
left turn, go forward on woodland
track to enter the open ⑤. Enter
left-hand of two fields and continue
in same direction along right edge
(in line with distant tower on
skyline), down to bottom of valley.
In bottom corner of field, find
narrow path through hedge and turn
immediately left at junction of
woodland paths (immediately past
remains of kissing-gate at time of
inspection).

The route proceeds inside woods
with stream away to right, mostly
on sunken path with edge of woods
on left. Cross a tributary coming in
from left (footbridge had disappeared
at time of inspection, and it was
necessary to cross a bridge a few
yards to the left before re-joining
path on other side), and enter field
⑥. Go forward along left edge. Just
before end of field go through break
in hedgerow on left, and
immediately turn right on to track
between hedges.

⑦ After ^{1}/$_3$ mile, after track rises,
reach signpost at junction, and 20
yards later cross stile on right, and
go down left edge of field to take
gate at bottom. Cross footbridge and
go up to stile into semi-open wood,
where path rises, close to fence on
right. Beyond the next stile there is a
strip of cypresses and coppice on
left; ⑧ 80 yards after field begins on
left, take stile on left and head
across to stile in line with Essendon
church.

In second field proceed along top
(right) edge until stiles on the right
give access to third field, where head
to gate at left-hand end of
churchyard. Pub is reached by
enclosed path – or go through
churchyard [**b**].

Either way, turn right on village
street to reach T-junction with main

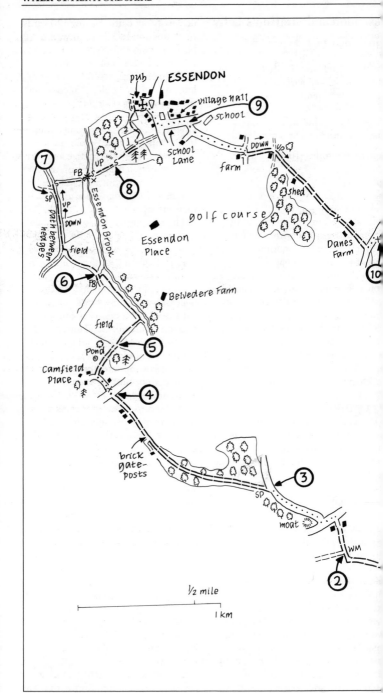

ad. Turn right and take first left
chool Lane). **(9)** 50 yards after the
illage hall on left, bear right on
ignposted farm road for Little
erkhamstead; ignore private
riveway on right after 70 yards.
his farm road drops past a barn on

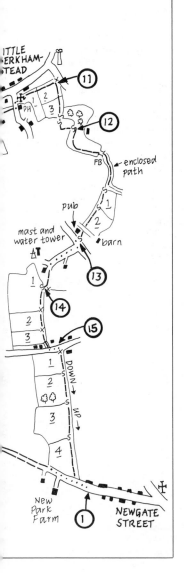

your right, then immediately after it
keep on main farm road which bends
right (left goes to house) and then
immediately turn left at cross-
junction (where right goes to
farmhouse).

Follow this track which drops
down to mock-timbered house then
rises through trees and later passes
Danes Farm to reach road. Turn left
on road. **(10)** After 100 yards, take
gates on right (by mains post marked
3 WO 10); follow left edge of field for
50 yards, then cross stile on left and
follow left edge of cricket pitch
towards houses at Little
Berkhamstead.

Turn left on road then take
signposted stile on right
immediately before church lych-
gate. Enter field, follow left edge
(with tower in view [**c**] on left),
proceed along left edge of second
field (you can detour to tower by
taking gate at end, turn left on road
and right at junction.

(11) At end of the second field, turn
right (still inside the field, with
hedge on left), and along left edge of
third field, entering trees at end of
field and crossing stile. Path
proceeds inside edge of woodland for
a short distance before entering next
field, where go forward along right
edge for 30 yards: here do not cross
stile on right, but turn left downhill
to cross stile into woodland **(12)**.
Immediately turn right by waymark
post (route 3; blue arrow) by path
junction; path leads round the
woods, eventually curving left and
later crossing footbridge to leave
the woods.

Where main path bends markedly
left, take stile ahead into field; go
forward to follow right edge of two
fields, cross track and follow right
edge of third field to reach road
(Beehive Inn is on your right) **(13)**.
Left on road and after 20 yards turn
right on to minor road (signposted as

bridleway to Little Berkhamstead).
50 yards before road ends by mast
(no access); bear left in front of
house, and proceed with brick
garden wall on the right, then water
channel on right.

⑭ At end of this field take stile
on right, and turn left to proceed
along left edge of three fields until
path by house gives access to road.
Left on road and after 100 yards turn
right by signpost, taking right-hand
of two gates (left goes to house).
Newgate Street is now visible on
rise ahead: go down left-hand side of
two fields (at bottom, a plank
crossing flooded area was rather
precarious at time of checking –
after heavy rain), then up left-hand
side of two more fields to reach
starting point.

ON THE ROUTE

[**a**] The lake on your left is part of
the grounds of **Camfield Place**,
where Beatrix Potter used to stay as
a child and where she wrote her first
rabbit story; the house, which she
described as 'the place I love best in
the world' was built by her
grandfather, Edmund Potter. More
recently it was acquired by novelist
Barbara Cartland.

[**b**] **Essendon church** contains a
shapely classical font made of black
Wedgwood basalt-ware; given to the
church in 1778 by Mary Whitbread,
who also wove the Royal Arms
hanging here. A fine cedar of
Lebanon shades the churchyard.

[**c**] **Stratton's Folly** Built 1789, by
John Stratton; 150 spiral steps lead
up to a former library.

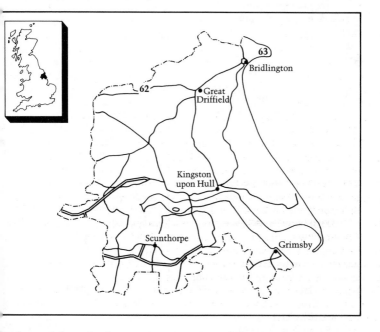

Thixendale and Wharram Percy

Extensive views over open rolling farmland, empty and sinuous dry chalk valleys and occasional woodland make up the highly distinctive Wolds landscape. A sparse path network makes some road-walking inevitable for a circular walk in the area. Good waymarking along the Wolds Way makes route-finding easy.

Length 7½ miles (12km), 3½ hours
Difficulty 2-3
Start Fridaythorpe village centre (A166, between Bridlington and York). Grid reference 874593
OS maps 1:50,000 100, 101 and 106; 1:25,000 SE 85/95 and SE 86/96 (Pathfinder 666 and 656)
Refreshments Shop at filling station, also pubs, in Fridaythorpe; tea-rooms, shop, dairy shop and pub in Thixendale

WALK DIRECTIONS

① [a] Turn off A166 by Manor House Inn, signposted Thixendale and Birdsall, passing village pond and green at end of which keep forward (signposted Thixendale). 150 yards later, at end of village, take signposted track on left; you are on the Humberside Way, well waymarked and signposted throughout.
② Reach top of dale, take stile giving on to track descending to right, to bottom of dale and go up other side with woodland on your left. ③ Keep straight on as signposted where woods on left reach a corner and head up slight side-valley (no defined path), to reach a projecting fence corner where continue half right as signposted to reach another signpost by a stile beneath power-lines. Go forward, towards trees, across two fields, through farmyard then turn

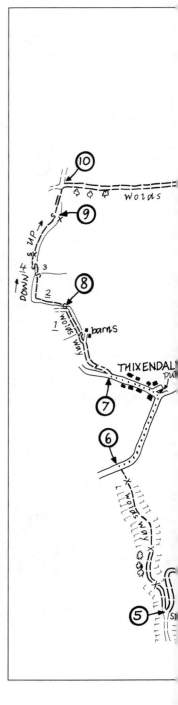

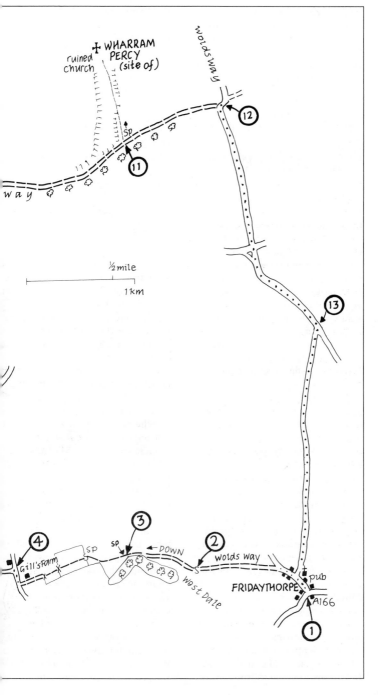

right on tarmacked lane.

④ After 100 yards turn left by signpost in front of house to follow track down into next dale. ⑤ At bottom, turn very sharp right along dale floor for ³/₄ mile [b]. ⑥ Emerge on to tarmacked lane, turn right, entering Thixendale by next left turn (signposted Malton) [c].

Go to far (west) end of village. ⑦ Just after last house on right, fork right on to rising chalky track as signposted. At top, fork left shortly before barns on to grassy track (signposted) to cross ladder-stile, then go forward along right edge of first field, soon joining track.

⑧ At end of field (where track bends left) cross stile ahead into second field and turn left as waymarked, with fence on left: skirt field perimeter by turning right in next corner. Enter third field by stile, continue downhill with fence on left; after 120 yards take stile on left [d] and turn right, down to stile beside gate; then keep right to proceed up side-valley with fence on right.

⑨ At top keep forward over stile (ignore small gate on right) along field edge, soon along grassy track lined with hedgerow trees; where track bends left, keep straight on following narrow waymarked path. ⑩ Reach corner of stony track and turn right (now along a grassy track along belt of trees).

⑪ Dale down on left bends left [e] (here you can *detour* to Wharram Percy, in view below: turn left by signpost for Wharram Percy, on path along top right-hand side of dale and gradually descending to the ruined church which can be seen ahead). Proceed along the belt of trees [f].

⑫ Emerge on to lane, turn right down to crossroads by pond; keep forward, signposted Fridaythorpe. ⑬ ¹/₂ mile later, take road on right and follow to Fridaythorpe

(25-30 minutes' walk).

ON THE ROUTE

[a] **Fridaythorpe church** Norman doorway and chancel arch, and Early English arcades.

[b] One of the finest sections of the **Wolds Way**, a 79-mile path. Starting at Hessle Haven near the Humber Bridge the path follows the River Humber, turning along the western edge of the Yorkshire Wolds to end at the rocky promontory of Filey Brigg on the North Yorkshire coast. An official Countryside Commission path, it is a welcome boon to ramblers in an area with few recognised rights of way. This section of the path follows a long empty dale with plunging slopes too steep for cultivation; a long avenue of hawthorns accompanies the path along the bottom.

[c] **Thixendale** In a secluded setting, the most striking location of any Wolds village; its name refers to the meeting of six, or possibly sixteen, valleys.

[d] At time of inspection, the stile had a verse attached, written by an appreciative rambler.

[e] **Wharram Percy** Down to the left is a deserted village of which the roofless church of St Martin and a 19th-century labourer's cottage are the only obvious remains at first sight. At its peak the population numbered 150; hard hit by the Black Death, the village nevertheless continued until the early 1500s, when farmers turned arable holdings into sheep pasture (it is now surrounded by arable land again). From the air, the outline of a 12th-century manor house, a farm, field systems and the village layout are visible. Managed by English Heritage. Until 1950 there was a small railway station at Wharram, the platform being in the valley bottom just below the

ottage. The line ran from Malton
o Driffield and was known as the
**Malton and Driffield Junction
Railway**. It was one of George
Hudson's schemes, opened in 1853.
Never a busy passenger line, it
erved the scattered farming
ommunities on the Wolds,
orming a link with the coast, and
vas principally a busy freight
route transporting stone quarried
at Wharram and nearby Burdale. In
1940 the station sign was taken
down in anticipation of a German
invasion. It has since been
reinstated (attached to the cottage
wall).

[**f**] Extensive views, N over **Vale of
Pickering** and the **North York
Moors**, S over the **Wolds**.

Flamborough Head

A level cliff path at the start, with spectacular transition at the headland to rugged coastal scenery, with changing views. Short inland link section along field edges. Easy route-finding and no difficult terrain.

Length 7 miles (11km), 3½ hours
Difficulty 2
Start Flamborough parish church (on B1255, ENE of Bridlington); parking in village. Grid reference 226702
OS maps 1:50,000 101; 1:25,000 TA 26/27 (Pathfinder 646)
Refreshments Cafés by lighthouse, at North Landing and Thornwick Bay; shops and pubs at Flamborough

WALK DIRECTIONS
(1) From B1255, take path through churchyard [**a**]; on other side take Church Lane ahead and slightly to the left; road bends right after 130 yards; 80 yards later at junction take track on left into Beacon Farm, signposted as footpath to Beacon Hill. Track goes through farmyard, along edge of fields, soon (2) with hedge on left and proceeding slightly uphill to gate: do not pass through this but take waymarked stile just to the right of it.

Proceed towards sea, where (3) turn left on coast path by signpost [**b**]. At South Landing (beach) drop to sea level via steps to road; take steps opposite, turn right at top to regain cliff-top. (4) At Flamborough Head [**c**], pass on seaward side of fog signal station (square white building). Just before lighthouse, join road for a few yards, but leave it to skirt around right side of lighthouse, on other side of which cliff path continues down steps. Descend to life-belt (ahead goes down steps to beach), where the coast path turns left up; just after small brick building (sewage

pumping station) turn right along the cliff-top path. (5) Reach big bay at shacky development of North Landing; continue through car park and pick up cliff path.

(6) At Thornwick Bay (the next cluster of shacks), join stony track

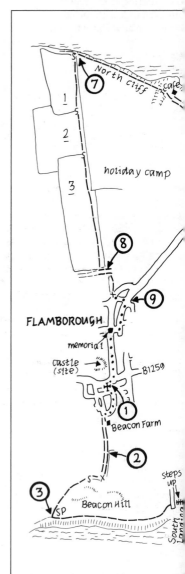

round top of cliff, then go beyond
ow café building, to resume along
coast path (which drops steeply to
bridge over inlet then ascends). ⑦
½ mile later take stile over corner of
ence on left to leave coast path:
ollow path along left edge of three
large fields.

⑧ Emerge on to track, turn left
then right after 50 yards (with fence
on right) towards houses at edge of
Flamborough, to reach stile. Cross
main road to take narrow semi-
metalled lane opposite to emerge by

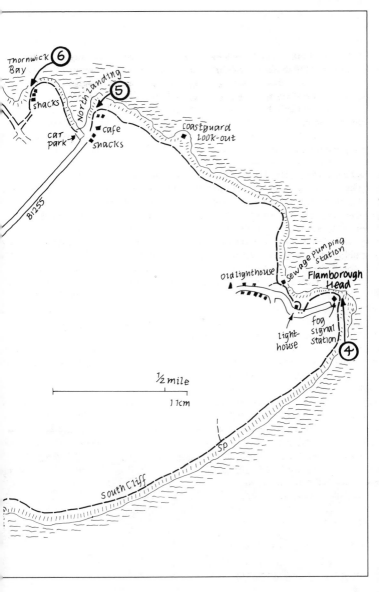

Rose and Crown pub, where ⑨ turn right along High Street; turn right by Ship Inn to memorial at village centre [d]; turn left (signposted Lighthouse and Bridlington) [e] to reach church.

ON THE ROUTE

[a] **Flamborough church** has a Norman chancel arch, a 16th-century carved rood screen, and a memorial to Sir Marmaduke Constable, who died in 1520 from eating a toad.

[b] From here until Flamborough Head there is a sweeping curve of coast to the S, from Bridlington to Spurn Head (far left: a thin spit of shingle and sand, moved inshore on a 250-year cycle).

[c] **Flamborough Head** Exposed eastern headland, the scene of many shipwrecks; at the head itself is a virtually detached promontory on to which it is possible to walk. **Views** open out dramatically to the N, and include Filey Brigg and the coast towards Scarborough. The deeply indented cliffs, precipitous inlets and ledges are rich in **birdlife**; echoing cries of kittiwakes are immediately noticeable; also here are fulmar, guillemot, gull, razorbill and puffin. The **lighthouse** was built 1806, and stands 85ft high; the nearby **fog signal station** emits a loud electronic bleep when needed, but when built in 1859 used a cannon signal. Inland, the **old lighthouse** was built in 1674.

[d] **Monument** at centre of Flamborough is dedicated to the crew of the coble (a local open-decked, flat-bottomed fishing boat) *The Two Brothers*, who were killed in 1909 while attempting to rescue another crew.

[e] On the right, after the houses end, grassy humps and a portion of masonry of the **castle** is visible; here lived the Constable family, lords of the manor for nearly 500 years until 1537.

KENT

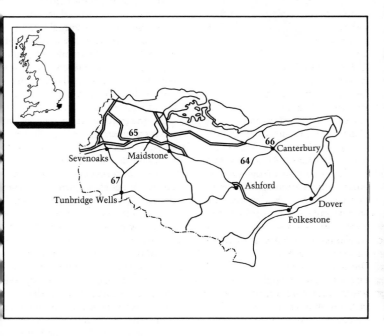

Holiday Which? Good Walks Guide

Chilham and Godmersham Park

A route joining two interesting villages mostly by downland and field paths, with changing views for much of the way. Route finding a little complicated, but helped by good waymarking.

Length 5¹/₂ miles (9km), 3 hours
Difficulty 2
Start Chilham rail station (¹/₂ mile E of Chilham and immediately E of junction of A28 and A252). Grid reference 078537. *Alternatively* start at Godmersham, on A28 6 miles NE of Ashford; park by bus shelter and phone-box on main road (near signposted turning for Crundale and Waltham) and start walk directions at ⑩. Grid reference 066507
OS maps 1:50,000 179 or 189; 1:25,000 TR 05/15 (Pathfinder 1211)
Refreshments Two pubs, shop, tea-room and castle tea-room in Chilham

WALK DIRECTIONS

① From station, walk to main road, turn left then left again on to A28 (towards Ashford). 100 yards later, by garage, turn left into cul-de-sac ②; this leads over level-crossing. Beyond bridge, keep right (left goes to mill house) [a], then after second bridge keep left on main track which soon rises to reach field: keep forward (signposted FP17), along hedgerow and soon along left edge of field, and when hedge on left ends, proceed forward to stile ③, turning right on woodland track beyond it (this section is waymarked with yellow arrows on stiles and posts).

Ignore left turn after only 20 yards; track runs between trees before field appears on right, and after field ends, ④ reach junction with main track bending right downhill and narrow path proceeding ahead. Take

signposted stile on left here, and cross field diagonally, making for entrance in woods away to your right (half-way up the field). On other side of woods, turn left in field, following its edge uphill, then in next field turn right along bottom edge for 80 yards to reach a waymark post, where ⑤ bear half left across field, uphill, to reach stile in fence ahead.

Beyond it, path continues between hedges with grassy slope up on left and field on right. ⑥ As soon as you reach woods, fork right on to waymarked path which runs along inside edge of woods, with fence on right. Soon reach field, keep forward alongside fence (with farms visible down to your right) and go forward into wood; path snakes a little, bending left at waymark post after 40 yards, then a few yards later ⑦ turn right at next waymark post, soon entering field: stiles (to left of farms) are visible ahead, marking your route, which almost immediately enters field on right, then follows its left edge down to next stiles.

⑧ Turn right on track, then just after first house (Forest Farmhouse), take signposted stile on left and bear half right in first field, heading up to stile just to left of prominent triangular bank (which is a reservoir). Beyond stile, keep forward (slightly uphill) on track along left edge of second field, turning right after 130 yards by waymark post to enter third field: turn left along top of third field for 100 yards, then at waymark post bear half right diagonally across field (in line with church in far distance) [b].

⑨ Continue same direction down across fourth field, to leave by far corner on to lane. Turn right on lane, then right again after ¹/₂ mile at junction (signposted Chilham), passing under railway and through

Godmersham. ⑩ Cross main road to turning with weight restriction sign, then keep forward after bridge where road bends left, taking estate gates to right of lodge [**c**]. Immediately take small gate on right, and cross parkland (soon almost joining wooden fence which is on left) to stile [**d**], then ⑪ left on wide track between fences which heads towards estate farm.

Soon reach track junction and turn right (signposted Footpath Only), again between fences, then soon forward along right edge of field. ⑫ Reach junction of tracks, with North Downs Way ahead and sharp left, and go forward. Soon reach corner of lane and go forward (right is signed as a private road leading to Hurst Farm). ⑬ After ¾ mile fork left at edge

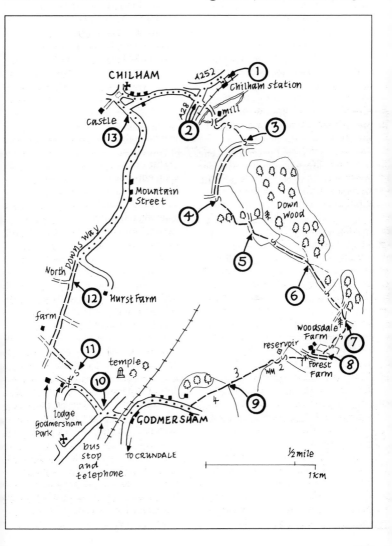

of Chilham, to reach village centre [e]. From village square, with castle gate behind you, take far right exit from square (the road to the right of the church path), keeping left at next junction (by pub). **(14)** At end of village, road almost joins A252 (on your left); however, turn right here, towards garage (where turn left to return to station; straight on, along cul-de-sac to continue walk, picking up directions at **(2)**).

ON THE ROUTE
[a] Large weather-boarded **water-mill** on the River Stour. Soon after you ascend from here, there is a view of **Great Water**, one of a number of artificial lakes in the Stour valley.
[b] View over the **Stour valley** and **North Downs**. Oast houses (for drying hops) in the distance , complete a classically Kentish scene.
[c] 18th-century landscaped parkland surrounds **Godmersham Place**, built by Thomas Brodnax in 1732, and later inherited by his cousin Edward Knight, Jane Austen's brother. Jane used to stay here and look after the house. Her letters to her sister Cassandra described in great detail the boorish men and artless women

whose company she was obliged to keep here, a society that provided some of the raw material of her novels. $1/2$ mile S, further along the road is the **church**, which has a Norman carving of a bishop, very possibly St Thomas of Canterbury; it is a rare survival of the destruction wrought on such features in churches across the country.
[d] To the right, a **Grecian temple**, erected to catch the eye, stands on a hillock.
[e] **Chilham** Perhaps the most handsome of all the Kent villages, with a central square surrounded by black and white houses, an ancient pub, the church and the castle entrance; narrow lanes slope downhill from each corner. The **castle** (open late April-Oct 14, daily 11-5) was built in 1616 for an officer of James I, but its keep is Norman. The gardens (open, as for castle, to 6pm), with yew and box hedges look out to the downs, and there are falconry displays; inside is a Kent Battle of Britain museum. Large **church**, with many monuments, and 15th-century flint chequerwork tower; to the N is the Queen Anne **rectory**.

Birling and the Coldrum Stones

An invigorating and varied walk through surprisingly remote Kentish countryside, taking in a fine archaeological monument and some good views from the top of the North Downs. It's well worth persevering with some tricky route-finding.

Length 9 miles (14.5km), 4½ hours
Difficulty 3
Start Centre of Trottiscliffe village (pronounced Trozley), 1½ miles N of Wrotham Heath (which is on A20); take A227/Gravesend exit from M20 or M26. Car parking in village is limited: it may be necessary to park a few hundred yards from centre. Grid reference 640602
OS maps 1:50,000 188; 1:25,000 TQ 66/76 (Pathfinder 1193)
Refreshments Pubs in Trottiscliffe and Birling

WALK DIRECTIONS

①[a] From crossroads in centre of Trottiscliffe village (at junction of Wrotham Water Lane, Church Lane and main street), walk uphill on main village street, soon passing village pond on your left. After 50 yards along Green Lane, and where metalled road swings left into small modern estate, continue forward on clear footpath across field, heading for church.

Pass through gate into farmyard and continue past church on road. When road bends right, turn left by post marked with a black 'G' sign. Cross stile at top of bank, and continue into field with fence on left. Cross stile at end and go forward over road on to the unmetalled track signposted Coldrum Long Barrow, soon passing car park on your left.

This track later passes through copse and re-emerges into field; at

bottom of this field turn right at T-junction of paths. Track soon becomes made up with concrete. Keeping Coldrum Stones [b] away to your right, ② continue on concrete track, and where (50 yards later) this swings away to right, fork left on grassy track.

A track later joins from your right; 40 yards later turn left on clear path into field, alongside edge of wood on your left. Continue direction after wood swings away to left to re-enter copse on far side of field. On emerging from wood, bear quarter right on clear path across field, to re-enter wood at far corner. 300 yards later emerge on road just by fork.

③ Turn right on road, and then immediately take left fork. 300 yards later, you reach a small hamlet: 20 yards beyond first house on left, turn left on gravel track (marker-post) forking immediately left to continue into first field with hedge on right. At end of first field, cross over earth bridge and turn right in second field in front of fence to continue with fence on left and ditch on right.

Cross stile into third field, and turn half left and make for projecting corner of field. On reaching this turn left, and continue with hedge on left. Cross stile into fourth field and continue quarter right to top of rise. On reaching this, turn right to find two big black posts (squeeze-stile). Turn left on road and continue into centre of Birling village, later passing pub on your right.

④ Continue forward through village, avoiding turnings to right. 50 yards beyond entrance to church, turn left on signposted path up bank. Cross stile and pass into first field. Continue with fence on left, aiming for gate beside stile just to right of farm buildings. Enter second field, again keep alongside fence and hedge on left. At end of this field go forward on grassy track with fence

239

on right and hedge on left.

⑤ [c] Cross over concrete road into third field, and proceed with fence on your right. Go forward over stile at end, ignoring cross-track, on to track between fences which soon swings right with fence on right and scrubland on left, and then climb steeply. **⑥** [d] Cross stile on to road, and go forward along Holly Hill, which you follow for ¹/₂ mile avoiding turns to left and right.

150 yards after passing entrance to Holly Lodge on your right, turn left on signposted footpath which drops steeply across two fields. At bottom of valley, ignore cross-track and continue uphill into field with hedge on left. Continue forward at top of hill on to track between fences, then when main path swings away right, go forward over stile (Weald Way marker). Go over cross-track and continue through kissing-gate into field, which you cross to stile on far side. Turn left on road.

⑦ After 300 yards, where road swings away to right, continue forward on clear path, following left edge of first field. After 50 yards turn left over stile, and turn right in second (very narrow) field. Cross this, and two further fields, still following fence on right, to pass between farm buildings to road **⑧**.

Turn right on road for 70 yards, then turn left on public path (signposted Weald Way). On entering wood, fork right and 20 yards later turn sharp right (at marker-post) to follow 'footpath 237'. 30 yards further on, where main track swings to left, continue forward on narrower path. This soon brings you to a concrete track where you turn left then immediately right ('footpath 236' marker). At T-junction of tracks beyond, turn right and then immediately left. Go over further cross-track to reach another

cross-track where turn half-right. This soon brings you to a broad cross-track marked 'public byway' with a gate beyond, and 'Trosley Country Park' sign.

(**General Note:**) This section between points **⑧** and **⑨** is a confusing warren of paths through scrubland, criss-crossed by occasional concrete tracks. If you follow the directions carefully, you shouldn't have trouble, but if things go wrong, aim for the right-hand edge of the wood, and the broad track beyond. Then follow this track down till you reach the top of the North Downs slope and the Trosley Country Park).

⑨ 30 yards later turn left on path (marker-post with a 'G' on it] which soon drops down slope on to cross-track. Turn right (marker-post) and continue forward over two cross-tracks. ¹/₂ mile later reach clear

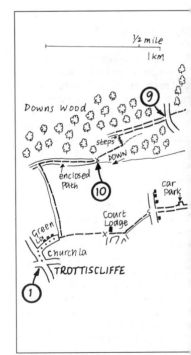

ross-roads with a gravelled, stepped
ath down to your left; ahead of you
o your right at this point is a
arker post with red and blue paint.
ere, turn left downhill on the
ravelled path which soon emerges
nto open. Bear left with wood on
ft for 20 yards, then turn sharp
ght on path heading downhill,

with the red marker-posts.

⑩ At bottom of slope, bear left to
cross stile next to gate, and turn
immediately right on path between
fences. 40 yards later, turn left on
path down bank, passing between
barriers. Cross road, go over stile and
cross two fields keeping hedge on
right. At end of second field, turn

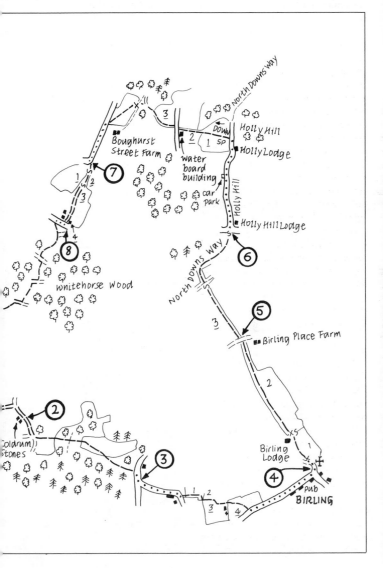

right and continue along road to
return to the starting point.

ON THE ROUTE
[a] **Trottiscliffe church**
Victorianised, but good box-pews,
fine brass, and a flint tower.
[b] **Coldrum Stones** Weathered
remains of a long barrow from the
Neanderthal period, 4000 years old.

The burial chamber, contained the
remains of 22 bodies when it was
excavated in 1910.
[c] **Birling Place** A lovely part-18th-
century, part-medieval house with
fine mullioned windows.
[d] Fine views of **Maidstone**,
Aylesford and the **Weald** from this
point. The prominent white buildin
is **Leybourne Hospital.**

:anterbury

**World famous for its cathedral and a
pilgrimage centre for many
centuries, with much to see: town
walls, the priory and a host of
historic buildings along the city's
main thoroughfare and tucked away
in back streets.**

Length 3 miles (4.5km), 2 hours
Difficulty 1
Start St Dunstan's Street, by West
Gate, Canterbury (car park in North
Lane, just outside gate). *By train*
Canterbury West (join walk
directions at beginning) or
Canterbury East (cross footbridge
opposite station entrance and join
walk directions at ③)
Refreshments Full range in city

WALK DIRECTIONS

① Follow St Dunstan's Street [a],
under West Gate and into St Peter's
Street [b], keeping straight on where
traffic is diverted right into St
Peter's Place. ② Turn right by
Lloyd's Bank into St Margaret's
Street, then detour right down Beer
Cart Lane to Poor Priests' Hospital
[c],[d] (now the Canterbury Heritage
Museum) before continuing along
Castle Street.

At end, by Norman Castle [e],
detour to right down Gas Street [f] to
St Mildred's church, then take path
opposite Gas Street, soon reaching
city wall ③ . Either walk through
Dane John Gardens [g] (to left) or
along wall [h]. After bus station, city
wall path descends to road; cross by
pedestrian subway to proceed along
city wall, then ④ cross road on right
into Church Street St Paul's.

By Cemetery Gateway [i], turn
right; road immediately bends left,
pass entrance to St Augustine's
Abbey on your left then keep
forward on joining main road
(Longport). Just after prison on left
[j], take lane on left for St Martin's

Church [k] ⑤. Return to Cemetery
Gateway, and go along Monastery
Street, then left opposite Fyndon
Gate into Lady Wootton's Green.
⑥ Cross Broad Street and take small
gateway in city wall opposite,
entering the Cathedral Precincts [l].

After visiting cathedral and
cloisters, leave by Christ Church
Gate ⑦ (the main gate into the
Cathedral Precincts), then turn right
(where Seven Stars Inn is ahead) into
Sun Street [m], then keep right,
along Palace Street. By Sir John Boys'
House (where road bends right) turn
left into King Street, then soon
⑧ right into Mill Lane [n], soon
detouring left at junction with
Blackfriars Street to Blackfriars [o],
then continue along Mill Lane to T-
junction by Miller's Arms pub,
where ⑨ go left over river and
follow Pound Lane [p] to reach
West Gate.

ON THE ROUTE

[a] **St Dunstan's Street** Traditionally
the pilgrims' entrance to the city,
proceeding up High Street and
Mercery Lane to Christ Church Gate
by the cathedral entrance. A busy,
interesting street: scarcely two
buildings are alike. Buildings to look
out for, starting from the London
Road/ Whitstable road junction at
NW end: **St Dunstan's church** (on
right as you walk SE towards West
Gate), has a 14th-century tower. A
modern ledger stone on the floor
records Sir Thomas More, whose
head lies in the vault under the
chapel; his daughter, Margaret
Roper, brought the head here after
Henry VIII executed him. **Roper
Gateway** (left), is the Tudor brick
entrance to the now-demolished
home of Margaret Roper. After the
railway, **House of Agnes** (right), a
17th-century triple-gabled, timber-
framed hotel. **Rose and Crown**
(right), and **Falstaff Hotel** (left), are

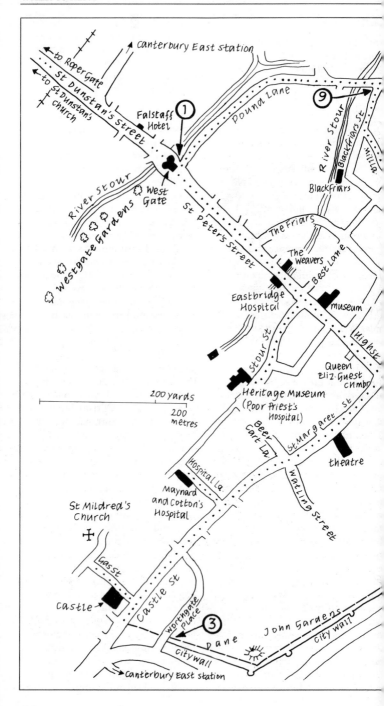

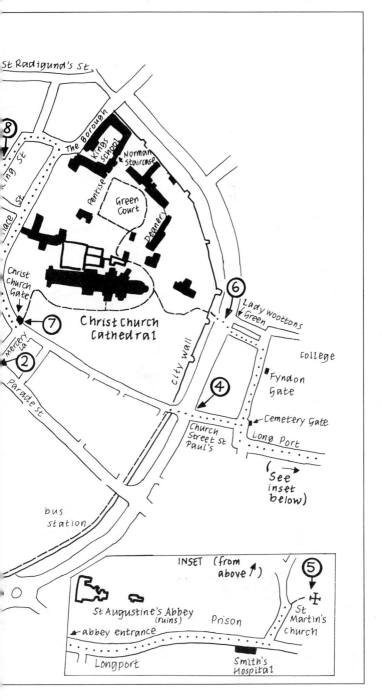

St Radigund's St

⑧

King St

The Borough

Kings School

Norman Staircase

Palace St

Pentise

Green Court

Deanery

Christ Church Gate

⑦

Mercery La

②

Parade St

Christ Church Cathedral

City wall

⑥

Lady Woottons Green

College

Fyndon Gate

④

Cemetery Gate

Church Street St Paul's

Long Port

(See inset below)

bus station

○

INSET (from above ↑)

⑤

St Augustine's Abbey (ruins)

abbey entrance

Prison

St Martin's Church

Longport

Smith's Hospital

ancient pilgrims' inns. **Westgate House**, (opposite the latter), is *c* 1725. **West Gate**, with its massive twin turrets, is the sole survivor of the city's eight medieval gates. **Westgate Gardens** (to the right of West Gate) occupy a narrow strip by the River Stour, with Tower House (now the mayor's parlour) incorporated into a 14th-century bastion of the city wall. There are remains of medieval arches among the flower-beds.

[b] St Peter's Street and High Street **Sidney Cooper Centre (Chaucer Heritage Centre)** (left), pantile-hung; formerly an art school, founded by 19th-century artist Sidney Cooper. **St Peter's church** (left), 12th-century, with Norman font and fragment of red Roman tiles in its walls. **Plaque marking site of gate of Dominican Priory** (left, on corner of The Friars). **Cogan House (No. 53)** (opposite The Friars), an unassuming building of brick appearance, concealing stone and timber structure dating from the 12th century; the house next door (No. 52) is one of the city's more obvious examples of a building with mathematical tiles, 18th-century sham bricks covering timber – the timber behind and thinness of the bricks can be seen where the fabric has deteriorated. **All Saints Lane** (left) with 15th-century half-timbered All Saints' Court. **The Weavers** (left), the much-photographed black and white former weavers' houses, occupied by Walloon and Huguenot refugees who fled here in time of religious persecution in Holland and France. It was built in the 15th and 16th centuries, but the sham half-timbering was added much later. **St Thomas' or Eastbridge Hospital** (on right), founded *c* 1180 as a hostel for poor and sick pilgrims; became a charitable boys' school in the 16th century, and was later turned into

almshouses (open daily 10 (11 Sun) 1, 2-5). **Stour Street** (right), leads to entrance (on right) to **The Grey Friars**, the oldest Franciscan priory in Britain, erected after the arrival of Franciscan friars in 1224. **Beaney Institute** (left), a florid, Victorian mock-timbered building housing the city art gallery, museum (open 9.30 5.30 Mon-Sat; free) and library. **Queen Elizabeth's Guest Chamber** (right), a former inn built *c* 1454 with 16th- and 17th-century alterations; spectacular stucco decoration, rather like confectionery. **Mercery Lane** (left), the narrow overhung lane leading to the butter-market and Christchurch Gate.

[c] **Canterbury Heritage Museum** Housed in the Poor Priests' Hospital which was founded as almshouses *c* 1220 by Alexander of Gloucester and rebuilt in stone in 1373. The museum has a display of the city through the ages, including archaeological finds from Roman times to the last war (open all year, 10.30-4 Mon-Sat, and Sun afternoon in summer).

[d] The junction of St Margaret's Street with Beer Cart Lane marks the exact centre of the site of what was the greatest **Roman theatre** in NW Europe, a semi-circular building over 250 feet across. **Castle Street** is curving, with many good 18th-century and earlier houses – brick, colour-washed and pantiled. In **Hospital Lane** (right) is Maynard and Cotton's Hospital, a row of single-storey almshouses.

[e] **Norman Castle** Built as a royal stronghold; the dungeons were used as the county gaol until the end of the 16th century. This is the fifth largest keep in the country, and one of the oldest. It originally stood 80 feet high.

[f] In Gas Street, on left is a former **water-mill**, and at the end **St**

ildred's church, one of the city's
dest churches, with Roman
asonry in its S wall.

Dane John Gardens Crossed
agonally by an avenue of limes,
d enclosed by early 19th-century
ouses on one side and the city wall
the other. The name is thought to
e a corruption of 'dungeon'. Its
rious hillock is reputedly one of
veral Roman burial mounds (1st or
d century), later called the
ongeon Hills; it now has a
iralling path up it and an obelisk
mmemorating the provision of
e gardens.

City walls The walk takes in the
ost impressive portion of the
rgely medieval walls and
mbattlements, which survived
most intact until the late 18th
ntury. Today 13 of the 21 watch-
wers remain. The area around the
us station was virtually rased to the
ound in a Baedeker raid in June
042, when 100 high-explosive and
000 incendiary bombs were
opped on the city; miraculously,
e cathedral was scarcely damaged.
he post-war rebuilding scheme for
is area was unfortunately
mewhat dreary. Two church
wers survived: St George's and
ary Magdalene.

Cemetery Gate and **Fyndon Gate**
way to the left, and passed later)
e two former entrances, built 1390
d 1300 respectively, to **St
ugustine's Abbey**. The gateways
w lead to a school and the present
bey entrance is in Longport. St
ugustine arrived here as a
issionary in AD597, establishing
e cathedral inside the city walls
d the abbey outside; the abbey in
s day was one of the greatest
onasteries in Europe. Today the
llest ruins standing are the N wall
the church nave and parts of the
oister, but the foundations of the
st have been excavated and the

outline of the original 6th-century
church is visible. The site's size is
still impressive, and there is a good
distant view of the cathedral.

[j] Opposite the prison is **Smith's
Hospital**, a row of shuttered single-
storey almshouses.

[k] **St Martin's church**, 6th-century
and documented in AD731 by Bede,
is England's oldest parish church,
which St Augustine originally made
his headquarters. The pre-Norman
font has 22 pieces of Caen stone and
is decorated with interlinking circles
and arches. The W wall, through
which you enter, is of rough stone
and blocked-off windows. The ghost
outline of a large doorway around
the present one are visible in it, as
well as red Roman bricks. Brass to
Thomas Stoughton (1591) in
the porch.

[l] **Cathedral and precincts** Enter by
Queningate (faint vestiges of red
brickwork of a Roman gateway in
the wall, just to left of existing
entrance); enter Kent War Memorial
Garden by bastion chapel; leave
garden, turn right at near end by
cathedral. Ahead and to right is
Meister Omers, built *c* 1395 as a
guest house and now part of King's
School. Continue round cathedral,
past ruined arches of 12th-century
Infirmary Chapel, built for monks
too sick to attend mass in the
cathedral. **Linacre House**, with its
oriel windows supported by breasty
female figures, is on right, with a
squarish flint-faced building (the
14th-century **Infirmarer's Hall**)
joined on to the rear of the house.
Go on past **Chequer Tower** into
Infirmary Cloister (site of the
monks' herb and kitchen garden) and
turn right along the **Dark Entry**
(corridor), under the **Gate House** into
a large courtyard known as **Green
Court**. Turn left and make a
clockwise tour of the courtyard.
Behind railings on left are the ruins

of the **monks' dormitory and necessarium** (lavatory), built *c* 1160, then in the first corner of Green Court is **Chillenden Chambers** (No. 29), a 14th-century guest-house. Behind gates the 14th-century **Pentise**, a covered walkway connecting Court Gate and the Cellarer's Hall, is visible. In the second corner, **Court Gate** leads into Mint Yard and parts of King's School, then through another gate and on to the street. Return into Green Court, past the Norman staircase, a unique feature for its date, starting at right-angles to North Hall, into which it leads. Go past the chequer-fronted brick and flint **Cromwellian house** (1659), set back from the rest, past the gate in the third corner of the courtyard (just inside the gateway some primitive early items of fire-fighting equipment are suspended from large hooks), then past the **Office of the Precentor (former prior's house)** and go back into Infirmary Court, under the rib-vaulted arches of the circular **Water Tower**, then into the 15th-century **Great Cloister**, with its chapter house. Here you can enter the cathedral by a door leading into the Martyrdom where Thomas à Becket was murdered in 1170. The **cathedral** is the premier cathedral of England and seat of the Archbishop of Canterbury, Primate of all England. Its earliest parts are 11th-century but there are 15th-century

modifications (the nave dates from then). Its central tower, known as Bell Harry soars 235 feet and dominates the city. Among the buildings greatest treasures are exceptional 12th- and 13th-century stained glass, the Black Prince's tomb, and a Norman crypt. Particularly striking are the change of level: steps lead up from the nave to the choir and from the choir to the altar. Leave Cathedral Precincts by the elaborate **Christ Church Gate**; covered with heraldry, including a Tudor Rose as the vault boss, and with fine 17th-century carved doors; this leads on to the **Butter Market**, with picturesque Mercery Lane straight ahead.

[m] **Sun Street** and **Palace Street** have a number of exceptional buildings, notably the overhanging **Sun Hotel** (left), **No. 8 Palace Street** (right), half-timbered **Conquest House** (left), with oriels and overhangs, **The Old Huguenot Weavers' House** (left), and (at the corner with King Street), **Sir John Boys' House** (now King's School shop), with its comically crooked door.

[n] **Mill Lane** is early 19th-century and smaller in scale.

[o] **Blackfriars** Like Grey Friars, built by Dominican Friars; *c* 1300.

[p] **Pound Lane** Remains of water-mill by river; Sudbury Tower on right, is a medieval flint-faced hous

eigh to Penshurst

uintessential Kentish countryside
ith village cricket greens, oast
ouses, parkland, woodland, a fine
ver and a country house. Easy
ing on field and woodland paths.

ength 6 miles (9.5km), 3 hours
ifficulty 2
S Maps 1:50,000 188;
25,000 TQ 44/54 (Pathfinder 1228)
tart Centre Leigh, 3 miles W of
onbridge. Grid reference 549466
y train Leigh (start at ⑧)
efreshments Pubs in Leigh; pub,
op and tea-rooms in Penshurst

ALK DIRECTIONS

) [a] From cricket green in centre of
eigh village take road to right of
avilion (Green View Avenue).
hen road ends continue over stile
nd go forward on marked path
P432). This soon passes under
ilway bridge, and continues
etween fences on far side. Pass
arough gate and into field, first
ith fence on right. When fence
nds, continue across open field to
netal footbridge.

Cross bridge and bear left on far
de, forking right after 10 yards to
ross further bridge 30 yards beyond.
ross stile and turn right through
mall copse, to emerge through
queeze-stile into field. Turn right
nd follow fence on your right to
ass through further stile. Follow
ght-hand edge of large field, to find
tile in corner and road beyond.

② Turn right on road, and
nmediately after bridge turn left
arough stile to follow river [b] on
our left. 100 yards after passing
edge at end of field, turn half right
find metal footbridge on far side
f field (marker sign on tree).
ontinue up bank on far side,
ollowing marker-posts. Cross over
tile, turn right on concrete track
nd then immediately left at T-
junction.

③ After ¼ mile, concrete track
swings left: continue forward at this
point, over stile and on to grassy
track with fence on left. Pass over
second stile and, in open field, bear
half left. After crossing brow of
slope, make for wooden stile in far
left corner. Cross this, go along left-
hand edge of second field and turn
left to small road.

Turn right on road, and follow for
½ mile, later passing car park for
Penshurst Place [c] on your right, to
emerge through gateway in centre of
Penshurst village. Follow road into
village [d], but after 30 yards, ④ turn
right through archway into
churchyard. Keep to left-hand side of
churchyard to pass over stile in far
corner. Continue forward in field
first with fence, then with moat and
wall on right. When moat and wall
turn away to right, bear quarter right
heading for double gate in fence
ahead. Cross stile just to right of
gate, cross road and pass over second
stile. Continue direction on far side,
soon with fence and edge of cricket
pitch on your right. Where this fence
veers round to the right, continue
forward, heading just to right of
prominent line of trees and keeping
the lake well away to your right.

Cross stile on far side of field, and
turn right to continue with fence on
right. This later swings slightly left,
with lake and trees on far side.
⑤ On reaching corner of field,
where main track veers away left,
turn right to cross stile and turn half
left on far side.

On reaching fence at far side of
field, bear left uphill, and pass over
stile in fence opposite. Continue
uphill through trees for ¼ mile.
⑥ At top of hill, at cross-track, turn
right and go through gate to follow
grassy track along ridge. Continue
direction for ¾ mile ignoring cross-
track, and passing through stiles.

(7) At end of wood turn left into field, and proceed alongside fence on left. Turn right on reaching corner of field, again alongside fence on left. Cross stile next to gate, and continue downhill on clear track. Turn left on road.

(8) After passing Leigh Station (if starting walk from this point, turn right on road on emerging from platform), turn right at T-junction in village to return to cricket green.

ON THE ROUTE

[a] **Leigh** With church and almshouses; a typical Kentish village grouped around its cricket green.

[b] **River Medway** Rises near Turners Hill in Sussex and takes a northerly course, becoming a major industrial river at its late stages near the busy Medway towns (Rochester, Gillingham and Chatham). Traditionally, Kentish men live to the W of the Medway, while any male resident to the E is a man of Kent.

[c] **Penshurst Place** A medieval manor house enlarged into a magnificent Renaissance palace in Tudor times by Sir Philip Sidney for his father, Sir Henry Sidney (Lord President of the Council of the Marches). (Open to public Apr-end Sept, Tues-Sun 1-5.30, grounds 12.30-6, bank hol Mons and Easter.)

[d] **Penshurst village** attracts hordes of visitors at weekends, but has charming corners. Monuments to the Sidneys in the family chapel in the parish church.

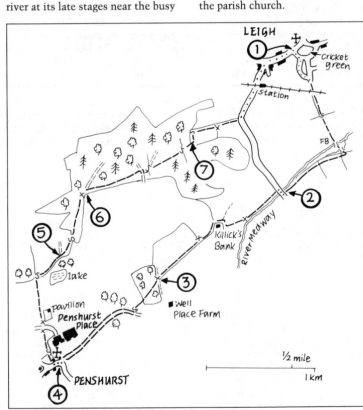

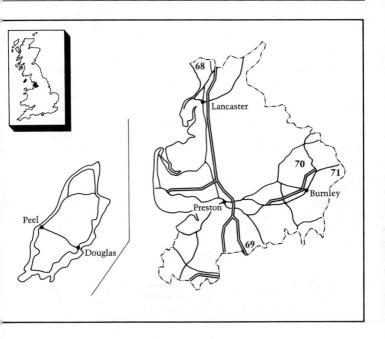

Holiday Which? Good Walks Guide

Warton Crag and Leighton Moss

The north side of Morecambe Bay, renowned for its birdlife and flora, provides a walk of great scenic variety – limestone hills, native woodlands, marshes and parkland with several splendid features of interest. Route-finding intricate at times, and field routes are not defined.

Length 7½ miles (12km), 4 hours
Difficulty 3
Start Silverdale rail station (1½ miles E of Silverdale). Grid reference 476752; if small car park by station is full, start at Silverdale Green (½

mile SE of Silverdale, by junction with Bottoms Lane and signpost for Arnside 4¼, Milnthorpe 6; railway station ³⁄₄; Carnforth 4; Silverdale ½); walk along road in Silverdale direction and start directions at **⑤**.
OS maps 1:50,000 97; 1:25,000 SD 37/47 and SD 56/57 (Pathfinder 636 and 637)
Refreshments Pub at Yealand Conyers

WALK DIRECTIONS
① With station on right, walk along road; after 100 yards, go left through signposted gate into golf course. Follow signposted path across the course (mostly a well-defined route)

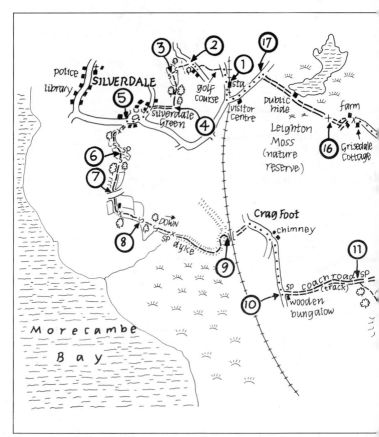

Head up to rightmost house to find signposted gate on to lane ②; turn right on lane for 100 yards, then immediately before bungalow turn left on signposted woodland path to The Green and village.

After wall on right ends, continue forward at staggered cross-junction. Descend, down steps, to ladder-stile into field; go forward, soon over footbridge, then ③ immediately turn left along edge of the field (with woods on right) until crossing stile at end of field into woods [**a**], where follow a well-defined and broad woodland path.

④ At far end of wood, path bends right to reach houses at Silverdale

Green; then proceed to road. Turn left on road; bear right at road junction by signpost (towards Silverdale).

⑤ After 150 yards, turn left in front of iron gate for Woodwell House on to signposted track between walls (for Woodwell and Gibraltar) to reach gate into field, where go forward over steps on enclosed path along right edge of field and into woods at end. Immediately turn left on path along top edge of wood, gradually dropping and crossing two stiles to enter irregularly shaped field (where path disappears): continue forward, ⑥ turning right by signpost after 100 yards (for Hollins Lane) to find stile in field corner.

Then continue forward along woodland path [**b**], soon with vertical drop on right and field on left, to reach road ⑦. Take signposted path opposite and slightly to right (for Heald Brow and Crag Foot), through gate; beyond, pick up enclosed path (to left of field-gate, and follow to end of enclosed section (don't enter field on left; at time of checking, a broken signpost confusingly pointed into it); where fields on either side end, turn left into wooded area and immediately left again through small gate into field, and turn right to follow edge of this and next field.

⑧ At end cross stile. 30 yards later, fork right as soon as woods begin (follow red paint waymarks ignoring right fork after just 15 yards) [**c**], soon over stile and steeply downhill with fence on right. At bottom, turn right through gate and immediately left (signposted Crag Foot) along raised grassy dyke [**d**].

⑨ Just before railway bridge, take gate on right to cross canalised river, then left under the bridge (gate difficult to open) on to reach road. Turn right along road, left at next

253

junction, signposted Warton. **⑩** At top of rise, turn left by wooden bungalow on to enclosed track (signposted Coach Road, Warton).

⑪ After ¹/₂ mile, turn right on to path (signposted Concessionary Path to Warton Crag), keeping right after 300 yards at next signpost and follow main path to next signpost 300 yards later – left is continuation but first detour right a few yards to viewpoint at top of Warton Crag [**e**]; return to signpost and follow path (soon forking left as waymarked where right goes through section of wall) to rejoin the enclosed track (coach road) where turn right; this eventually drops to road.

Turn left on road. **⑫** 200 yards after Manor House Farm (on left) and just before road bends right, turn right through gate: gate is not signposted but is opposite woodland track (*note* if Leighton Hall is open (times below) you can continue on road and take drive on left down to the hall to rejoin route at **⑮**).

Go forward along right edge of field. At end, exit between stone posts and follow faint track ahead, gently downhill, past old lime-kiln on your left, then corner of woods on your right; the track gets better defined. 200 yards after the lime-kiln, woodland wall begins on right; **⑬** 40 yards later, turn half left (opposite gap-stile – two stone posts and gap between, in the wall), walking along level with a wall on your right, to reach stile, then continue forward across small semi-open area to emerge on road by 20% gradient sign. Turn right.

To continue, omitting pub After 100 yards, where road bends right, take stile beside gate on left, into woods and bear left following power-lines uphill. *For pub in Yealand Conyers,* follow road to bottom, left at T-junction for pub, passing the return route on the way – look for steps and railing on left, opposite The Old Post House (house No. 28-30), into field, and bear half left up to gate at top left-hand corner of field, (passing prominent signpost on driveway then past copper beech tree). Then, in woods, follow power-lines up hill *Both routes* **⑭** At top of slope, emerge into field by small, man-made hillock (cairn), just to left of power-lines; continue forward across field, towards line of trees (with power-lines now 80 yards away to right) to find gate in wall [**f**]. Descend to Leighton Hall, picking up estate driveway before the hall itself.

⑮ At entrance to hall, keep to right fork (left goes into hall grounds), on tarmacked estate farm road. After ³/₄ mile, after second farm, take gate ahead (continuing now on stony track, and forking right across grass as signposted after 30 yards, to join track at break in fence). Continue forward, to enter nature reserve by gate **⑯** [**g**], and follow the main track ahead, past the public birdwatching hide, to reach road **⑰**. Left on road, then turn right after crossing railway, to Silverdale station.

ON THE ROUTE
[**a**] An eerily dark wood of **yews**.
[**b**] A large, natural **limestone pavement** can be seen in these woods.
[**c**] Views over **Morecambe Bay**, famous for its 200,000 wader population; tides here are among the fastest in Britain, and reveal a huge expanse of sand and mudflats at low tide. Inland are the **Forest of Bowland** and (further away) the **Pennines**.
[**d**] Chimneys on either side of this marshy bay are remains of old **lime-kilns**.
[**e**] Recent concessionary paths (not marked on current OS maps) lead

out to this viewpoint, which overlooks **Morecambe Bay**, the **Cumbrian Fells** (including Black Combe, Fairfield and High Street), **Heysham Power Station** on the coast and the **Forest of Bowland**.

f] Probably the best possible view of **Leighton Hall** (open May-Sept, 2-5), in a landscaped parkland setting with glimpses of southern Cumbria beyond. Home of the Gillow family – the furniture-makers – this Georgian house was gothicised in 1810. Gillow furniture and antique clocks inside; eagle flying display (weather permitting) at 3.30 when house is open.

[g] Leighton Moss RSPB reserve (day permits are available from visitor centre passed later in walk; this main path, a public right of way through the reserve is always open). Fenland, wetland and woodland site, a habitat for **otters**, red deer, profuse **birdlife** in its meres and reed beds and diverse **flora**. The birds, which include water rail and the only breeding colony of bitterns in northern England, can be watched from a public hide on the path.

Rivington Pike and Lever Park

The former estate of Lord Leverhulme, founder of Port Sunlight: parkland, overgrown terraced gardens and a lakeside path lend variety. Route-finding fairly straightforward.

Length *Full walk* 7¹/₂ miles (12km), 4 hours
Difficulty 3
Start Anglezarke car park by signpost for Adlington 2¹/₂, Chorley 4, near SE corner of reservoir (on right if coming from White Coppice). Grid reference 620161
Length *Short walk* 4¹/₂ miles (7km), 2¹/₂ hours
Difficulty 2–3
Start Great House Barn visitor centre; parking on drive opposite, ¹/₂ mile S of Rivington. Grid reference 628138. To join route, walk along minor road to right of Great House Barn, keeping forward where road bends left into short-stay car park, on track beyond barrier, heading towards reservoir. Continue forward at cross-junction 50 yards later, down steps then right 50 yards later in front of barrier on path closest to reservoir and with iron railing on right; pick up directions at ⑫.
OS maps 1:50,000 109; 1:25,000 SD 61/71 (Pathfinder 700)
Refreshments Café at the Great House Barn

WALK DIRECTIONS

① From car park return to road and turn right (signposted Adlington and Chorley); left at next junction (signposted Belmont); after 300 yards, at top of rise, take gate on right and follow track along right-hand side of reservoir. ② After ³/₄ mile, turn left beyond gate on stony track into wood; 100 yards later, just after crossing channelled stream,

turn right on to waymarked path which has the stream on its right. Where stream bends right, path goes forward over stile, across field, up steps, then continue forward to flag pole in Rivington village green ③ [a].

Go forward to take road signposted Horwich. ④ 150 yards later (just after last house on left) fork left on to broad stony track; (keep left after 80 yards where right goes to road), follow to reach Rivington Hall Barn, where turn right, passing to right-hand side of barn and in front of hall [b]. Pick up hall driveway for a few yards, but leave it immediately before it goes between ponds: instead, keep left across grass for 50 yards to pass between stone gateposts, then turn left on track.

⑤ At back of the hall, turn right through gate and barrier (with red waymark for Terraced Garden Trail which you now follow: trail is waymarked with red numbers and red hoops on posts). After 140 yards fork left (waymarked) to path junction at bottom of grassy slope a edge of woods, with gate ahead: kee forward on rising path up to woods.

Follow the trail markers [c] (fork left at post 2, quarter right at next junction on level path; over footbridge at post 5, then 30 yards later sharp left up steps and right at top; ignoring minor right turn 100 yards later; path rises gently and bends sharp left to reach track with gate on right and post 7 ahead) ⑥. Here, take steps opposite, bear right at next junction (just after post 8 on left), around right-hand side of pond Turn right at next fork, up rough steps and then left by post 13; pass ruins on your right.

Turn right at post 15, take steps opposite by post 18 up to arch, beyond which turn right. Turn left at top along large flattened area;

gnore sign for trail at end, which
leads down steps, but keep along top
terrace (leaving the trail), soon on
arrow path to gate near Pigeon
Tower ⑦.

Turn sharp right beyond this gate,
on hard track, heading for Rivington
Pike Tower. Fork left opposite
toilets towards the tower – a track

skirts round the base of the hillock:
detour right to the tower [**d**];
continue on the track around the
hillock, with Horwich and church in
distance ahead, descending with
fence on left. Beyond gate, reach
junction ⑧ and take gate opposite
to follow the track descending
through field.

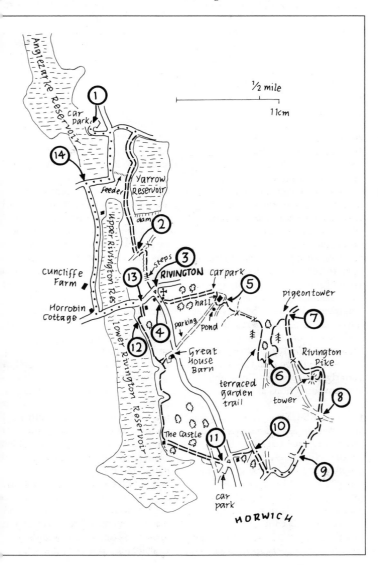

(9) At corner of farm road keep forward (still downhill). Immediately after electricity sub-station (on right) take lower of two tracks on right, into woods. **(10)** Immediately before power-lines cross over track, take narrow woodland path sharp left. After 50 yards this reaches close to corner of field: fork right, keeping close to edge of woods (later between fences) to reach road.

Cross to path opposite; **(11)** 75 yards after, turn right on broad track, follow ¹⁄₃ mile to reach castle [e], beyond which turn right on path close to water's edge of Lower Rivington reservoir. Keep as close to reservoir as path allows. Follow path close to reservoir [f] (path kinks right: 300 yards later, where metal railings appear, next right fork leads to Great House Barn for refreshments and end of short walk) until **(12)** path bends right and reaches track; turn left to road **(13)**.

For long walk turn left over road between reservoirs, then right on other side in front of house on reservoir road (no entry to traffic but open to pedestrians) along W side of Upper Rivington Reservoir; **(14)** turn right at end, on road along S end of Anglezarke Reservoir [g]; this bends left on other side, soon reaching car park entrance.

For short walk, turn right to reach Rivington village green [a], where turn right (signposted Horwich); continue directions at **(4)**.

ON THE ROUTE

[a] **Rivington** Retains stocks on the green; interesting 16th- or 17th-century **church** has double-decker pulpit with linenfold panelling and box-pews.

[b] **Hall Barn** and nearby **Great House Barn** are cruck structures dating from the early 18th century but altered by W.H. Lever (who later became Lord Leverhulme) after

acquiring the estate in 1899. The barns were then used for social functions. Lever, a Liberal MP and philanthropist with a keen interest in the arts and landscaping, had opened the Sunlight Soap works at Port Sunlight (near Birkenhead) in 1889, and built a village for the employees where there was a strong emphasis on good sanitation, clean air and landscaping; the quality of workers' living conditions was much higher than the norm. He purchased 18th-century Rivington Hall and park, and created a country park, retaining some of the estate for personal use but donating the rest to Bolton Corporation in 1902.

[c] **Terraced gardens** (trail leaflet available from Great House Barn). Began in 1905, but fell into disuse after Lord Leverhulme's death in 1925; now overgrown and many pavilions and other features have deteriorated or disappeared, but thanks to recent restoration, it is still possible to imagine what the gardens were like in their heyday. The main features are at these stages of the trail: **5** artificial ravine; **9 to 1** Japanese Garden, with bases of Tea Houses; **14** Kitchen Garden; **19** Great Lawn; **20** Tennis court; **23** Ballroom (black and white tiled floor visible); **29** Pigeon Tower, a pigeon and dovecote built 1910, used by Lady Leverhulme as a sewing room.

[d] **Rivington Pike** Nearly 1,200ft above sea level; an ancient site of a defensive beacon to warn of invasion. The **tower** was built 1733 for John Andrews of Rivington, probably to show the extent of his estate. Two annual events occur here: a **fair** is held on Good Friday; and the **Pike Race**, from Lever park entrance to here has been held since 1892 (current record 15 minutes 53 seconds). **View** SW to Wigan cooling towers and Snowdonia and the Clwydian Range; W to the

ancashire coast, including
outhport, Blackpool Tower,
eysham Power Station and
1orecambe Bay; WNW the Isle of
1an; NNW to the edge of the
ake District.

e] The **castle**, a replica of 13th-
entury Liverpool Castle as a ruin
rior to demolition in 1725, was
uilt by Lord Leverhulme in 1912 as
n addition to Lever Park.

[f] Lower Rivington reservoir
Constructed 1856, one of eight
reservoirs in this valley to supply
Liverpool. From here, water flows
downhill to a storage reservoir at
Prescot on the edge of the city.

[g] Anglezarke Reservoir Good for
watching **wildfowl** (mallard, great
crested grebe, gull, tufted duck,
whooper swan) and **waders** (coot,
curlew, moorhen, sandpiper).

Pendle Hill

**Rolling pastures meet windswept
moorland in this rural walk, despite
proximity to industrial Lancashire.
1,100ft of ascent is rewarded by a
section along the top of the hill's
escarpment. Route mostly
undefined; field boundaries aid
route-finding in lower sections but
path on to Pendle Hill is not always
clear; a compass would be useful
in mist.**

Length 5½ miles (9km), 4 hours
Difficulty 3-4
Start Barley car park and picnic site
at Barley village, NW of Nelson.
Grid reference 822404
OS maps 1:50,000 104; 1:25,000 SD
63/73, SD 64/74, SD 83/93 and SD
84/94 (Pathfinder 680, 669, 681, 670)

Refreshments Pub, restaurant and
car park kiosk in Barley

WALK DIRECTIONS
① [a] Turn right out of main car
park entrance to reach crossroads
where go forward (signposted 'to
Barley Green; bridlepath to Ogden
Clough; no unauthorised vehicles').
After 80 yards, immediately before
road goes between castellated
gateposts, fork right on to rising
track.

Where wall on right ends (and
track ends) keep forward with ditch
on left. **②** 100 yards later turn right
by isolated fragment of wall, up to
gateway in wall 100 yards ahead.
Immediately turn left on track
alongside wall on left [b]; at end of
field, proceed across two more fields

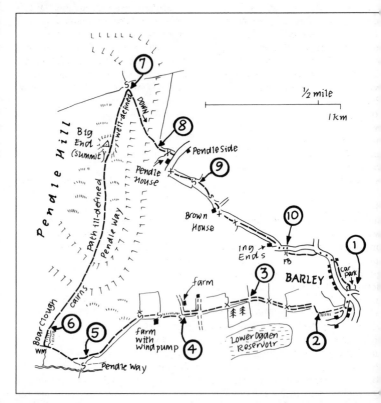

(3) Where conifer plantation appears on left, go forward with wall on left along edge of field [**c**] to gate at end (heading for leftmost of farms – with windpump when walk was checked). Maintain direction up left edge of next two fields (picking up a defined track in the second field, but leave the track as it bends right to farm).

(4) Go over stile beside gate and up towards aforementioned farm, keeping on left-hand side of hedgerow trees and ditch to cross stile just to right of the farm. Keep forward in open land, uphill, alongside wall on left. Beyond next gate beside stile, keep alongside wall as it bends left, on well-defined path (dropping slightly).

(5) Just above stream at bottom of valley (with ladder-stile at stream level crossing the wall) path bears right to join Pendle Way which heads along right-hand side of the valley [**d**]. Path crosses gully (Boar Clough) and passes wooden barrier with witch motif waymarking the Pendle Way (which you now follow to top of Pendle Hill; in the event of waymarker posts having fallen, the piles of stones into which they are embedded should be noticeable). 50 yards later, turn right uphill as waymarked.

Ascend close to left-hand side of Boar Clough. **(6)** Where the gully suddenly becomes much less deep at waymark post, cross it and continue on path on other side. 200 yards later, at next waymarker, leave the gully by bearing half right on less-defined path marked by cairns (piled-up stones). Keep forward all the while: eventually the summit is visible. Make for the big cairn on its right-hand side, then go forward up to trig point (summit pillar) on Pendle Hill (Big End) [**e**]. Keep forward, close to the steep edge until **(7)** reaching stile by a waymark: do

not cross the stile, but turn sharp right (doubling back) on steeply descending path.

(8) At bottom, go through gate, along left-hand side of field, then turn right on surfaced lane, over cattle-grid. Pass farm (Pendle House) on your right, then take waymarked gate beside stile immediately on your left to proceed along left edge of field to gate.

In next field go forward 20 yards to waymark post at corner of wall **(9)**, then go forward and slightly to right, heading for waymarked stile 150 yards away (on far side of gully). Pass to left of farmhouse, where keep forward (ignoring track on left) to take waymarked kissing-gate: a clear path now follows left edge of field, and then is enclosed.

Turn left on surfaced lane. **(10)** 130 yards later, take waymarked footbridge on right, turn left on other side, keeping close to stream, to reach stile at end of field. Emerge into Barley village. Turn right on road; take waymarked path to left of bench and bus stop, past swings, into car park.

ON THE ROUTE
[**a**] **Barley** Former hand-loom weaving village; at Barley Green, just beyond the castellated gateposts mentioned in the walk directions, a pumping-station stands on the site of a cotton-mill.
[**b**] View over **Ogden reservoirs**, constructed 1906-14 to supply the Nelson area, and **Pendle Hill**.
[**c**] Right of way is actually on enclosed path between wall and plantation, but had been deliberately wired off at time of inspection; it appears that the path unofficially now goes the way described.
[**d**] **Pendle Way** is a 45-mile waymarked circular walk around the Pendle area, which was notorious for its persecution of witches (hence the

waymark motif). In 1612, ten witches from Pendle, including Alice Nutter from Roughlee Old Hall near Barley, were executed at Lancaster and York for witchcraft. [e] **Pendle Hill** (1,831ft) A wild, treeless expanse on the upper carboniferous series of the millstone grit. Its famous **view** was a source of inspiration to George Fox in 1652 when he set up the Quaker movement. N are **Three Peaks** (Ingleborough, Whernside and Pen-y-ghent), NW the upland mass of the **Forest of Bowland**, SW to E are the S Lancashire hills and the **Pennines**, SE Burnley and E Colne, NE Wharfedale.

Foster's Leap and Wycoller

Characteristic South Pennine country – green hills, dry-stone walls, views all around – and an historic village at the end. Route is not defined all the way, and special care is needed with directions from start of walk to Foster's Leap.

Length 3½ miles (5.5km), 2 hours
Difficulty 2
Start Wycoller Country Park car park (E of Colne and ENE of Trawden).
Grid reference 927395
OS maps 1:50,000 104; 1:25,000 SD 83/93 (Pathfinder 681) or Outdoor Leisure 21
Refreshments Café at Wycoller visitor centre, near end of walk

WALK DIRECTIONS

①Turn right out of car park on to road ('no motor vehicles' sign here; you can pick up path on right-hand side of road to avoid short stretch of road-walking – path rejoins the road further down). ② At houses, immediately after road crosses brook, take track ahead as road bends right. 40 yards later take grassy track on left, immediately entering field by gate, where bear right to cross ladder-stile. Bear half right uphill (no defined path) across open pasture to take ladder-stile over old stone wall ③ [**a**].

Continue forward (following yellow marker arrows) on the level to prominent gateway in wall. In next enclosure, keep forward, slightly uphill, past waymarks by two isolated stone posts (remains of a wall), then on to waymarked stile ④. Beyond this stile, fork left, taking upper path (waymarked) and heading diagonally up to cross low wall. Proceed up in same direction towards rocks at Foster's Leap, around top side of wall, over ladder-stile and soon across hard track to reach the rocks [**b**].

From Foster's Leap, return to the hard track you have just crossed, turn left on it, downhill to reach houses ⑤. By second house, take gate into field and turn left to cross ladder-stile. Bear half right (waymark misleading at time of inspection) across enclosure to farm, in front of which cross footbridge and turn left on track (initially close to brook). ⑥ Go through gate beside stile and turn right at T-junction immediately beyond (signposted Wycoller and Pendle Way). 80 yards later, fork right on to path by signpost, keeping alongside wall on right, to reach gate, beyond which path continues with wall on left and intermittent wall on right.

⑦ 80 yards after next gate, take ladder-stile on right (signposted Wycoller) and follow left edge of large field to reach house ⑧. Go forward (keeping house on right), picking up hard track beyond, descending to brook by signpost ⑨ where keep forward (for Wycoller) and proceed past Clam Bridge [**c**], then over double-arched packhorse bridge by ruins of hall [**d**] and into village centre [**e**]. Follow road as it bends left, over brook and return to car park.

ON THE ROUTE

[**a**] Several field walls here are primitive structures of single, jagged upright slabs; this so-called **vaccary walling** was constructed between 1100 and 1400.
[**b**] **Foster's Leap** Rock outcrop, high up above Wycoller valley, with views into some of the country immortalised by the Brontës who lived over the moor at Haworth; Pendle Hill is away to the right (W). The 'leap' was a feat of daring by Foster Cunliffe of Wycoller Hall, who successfully made the jump

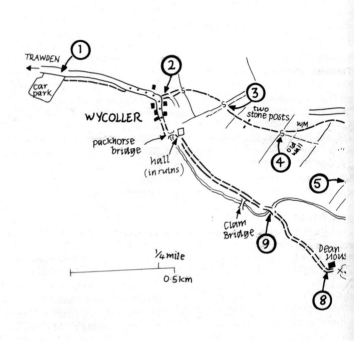

across the cleft between the rocks –
presumably for a bet.

[c] **Clam Bridge** The single gritstone
slab bridge is Iron Age, washed away
in a flood in 1989 but since
reinstated.

[d] Ruins of **Wycoller Hall** stand by a
pretty packhorse bridge. The 16th-
century hall was built for the

Hartley family and extended in
1774; abandoned in 1818. This is the
model for Ferndean Manor in *Jane
Eyre*, where Jane meets the blind Mr
Rochester. A **visitor centre** is
adjacent.

[e] **Wycoller** Typical pre-industrial
hamlet of the area, a busy weaving
village from the 17th century until

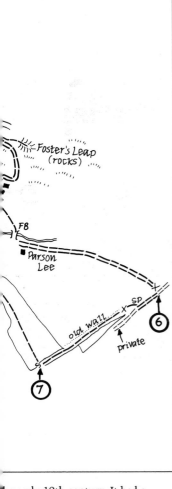

he early 19th century. It had a
opulation of 350 in 1820, but
leclined with the introduction of
ower looms into the towns. The
rillage was purchased when the
vater board planned a reservoir here
n 1890, but the project failed to
naterialise; the cottages that remain
1ave now been re-occupied.

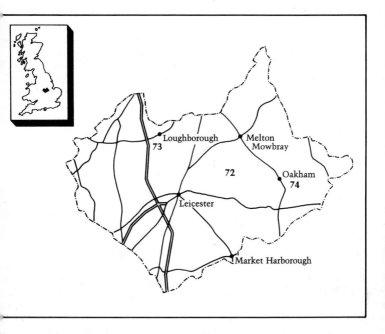

72 Lowesby, Baggrave and Quenby Halls
73 Broombriggs, Beacon Hill and Outwood
74 Rutland Water

Holiday Which? Good Walks Guide

111 Bradgate Park   112 Burrough Hill   113 Foxton Locks and Saddington
Reservoir

Lowesby, Baggrave and Quenby Halls

A trio of country houses, with Quenby Hall the grandest, are the main features of interest; the route crosses intimate and varied landscape in between, over parkland and farmland. Finding the way across fields requires some care in places, but the somewhat complicated sections ⑥ and ① can be avoided by walking along a quiet road.

Length 6 miles (9.5km), 3 hours
Difficulty 2
Start Lowesby, 9 miles E of Leicester (off B6047), limited parking by church. Grid reference 724075
OS maps 1:50,000 141; 1:25,000 SK 60/70 (Pathfinder 895)
Refreshments Pub in Hungarton

WALK DIRECTIONS

① Standing by church gate, take road with No Through Road sign (towards estate buildings of Lowesby Hall, with churchyard on your left). At end of churchyard take gateway on right with yellow waymarker and keep left over stile to proceed along left edge of fields closely parallel to the private driveway to the Hall; take gate into second field, where Lowesby Hall now appears on your left [a].

Go forward, past corner of garden wall of the hall, and then proceed ahead across semi-parkland: a well-defined track between an avenue of trees proceeds straight ahead, but keep just to left of it (aiming for distant red-roofed barn of Portels Farm). Once you are over the rise, a road with prominent signpost can be seen ahead.

② Cross the road at this signpost and take track opposite. Follow the waymarked route, close to left edge of three large fields, with stream close by on your left (in the second field you leave the track as it bends right just after disused pit). In the middle of fourth field, path joins woodland fence but does not enter woods, then drops to gate with signpost beyond ③. Turn right, over stile, signposted Baggrave.

Again proceed along edges of field with stream close by on left (but not always visible). ④ Where Bell Dip Farm is visible upon right, keep

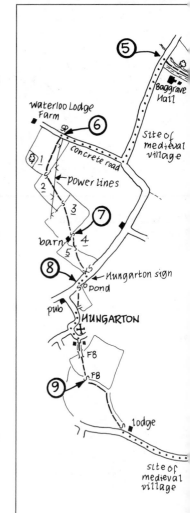

forward, now on farm track and still parallel to stream. Leave the track as it bends left into woods but at end of same field take stile on left into woods. Proceed along plantation fence on left to take footbridge over stream, and carry on a few yards to reach a long duck pond. Turn right along the pond [**b**].

(**5**) Turn left along road. After ¹/₂ mile where road bends left, turn

right on concrete farm road (or you can shorten walk by keeping along road, go forward at junction by lodge towards Hungarton for ¹/₄ mile; rejoin route at (**8**)).

(**6**) Shortly before reaching farm, where power-lines cross the farm-road, take signposted stile on left and go diagonally across field to find stile in far left hand corner. In second field, bear diagonally left to

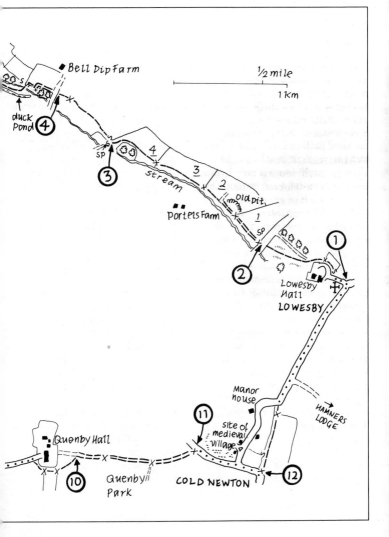

reach stile 100 yards to left of point where powerpoints leave the field. Go diagonally right across third field to take stile just to left of barn ⑦.

Turn right in fourth field, around the barn, to find stile in hedgerow, and bear diagonally left up across fifth field to reach gate beside stile at top of field on to road. Turn right on road. ⑧ Just after sign for Hungarton, take signposted stile on left (or continue along road for pub). Head towards Hungarton church to find kissing-gate on to track giving on to road, where turn left through the village towards church [c].

Fork left into Church Lane by war memorial, pass church on your left; at end of churchyard, keep forward at junction, downhill. 30 yards later (with brick house away to right and older house on left) proceed on enclosed path to enter field. Cross slab bridge, then bear half right slightly uphill: route is not obvious but exit from field can be found by keeping to left of group of trees lining right-hand side, to reach prominent yellow marker-post by stile and footbridge, which you cross ⑨. From here you can see lodge in trees up half left; reach it by turning left alongside hedgerow at bottom of field, keeping right inside field at corner by cattle-trough. Emerge by stile on to road, and turn left along it through entrance gate to Quenby Hall (*note* path is always open, even if Hall is closed). Keep to right of Hall [d], to take gate just to right of wall. ⑩ Beyond the Hall, join unsurfaced driveway coming from the Hall, and follow it 1/2 mile.

⑪ Turn right on road. Keep forward at next junction (left is signposted Lowesby) [e], then after 150 yards where road bends right,

take signposted gate on left and follow left-hand hedgerow (soon ignore stile on left) to exit at end of field, then cross grass to reach road. Turn right on road to Lowesby.

ON THE ROUTE

[a] **Lowesby Hall** Isaac Wollaston built this two-storey brick mansion in the 1700s around a 17th-century core; a later wing and stable block were added by Edwin Lutyens in 1910, who was partly responsible for laying out the garden.

[b] **Baggrave Hall** once belonged to Leicester Abbey, and was acquired by Francis Cave after the Dissolution and then by the Edwyn family in 1686. John Edwyn rebuilt the hall in the 1750s, and his work can be best seen from the road; the house retains some elegant interior features, including a Jacobean Revival drawing-room and a staircase hall with rococo stucco.

[c] **Hungarton** Much of the village was rebuilt, 1766-75, by Shukbrugh Ashby: his work is distinguishable by yellow and red brick chequer-work and date-stones. Ashby's monument is in the church.

[d] **Quenby Hall** The finest early 17th-century house in Leicestershire, built for George Ashby, and acquired by Shukbrugh Ashby in 1759; the latter was responsible for renewing the structure and decor, but its Jacobean interior was later reinstated. The house has strong similarities in design to Doddington Hall in Lincolnshire.

[e] On the left, grassy humps mark the site of the abandoned **medieval village of Cold Newton**. Lowesby and Baggrave also have medieval village sites, although far less is visible.

Broombriggs, Beacon Hill and Outwood

Some of the county's highest land, with volcanic crags peeping out from the bracken, forms the attraction of this varied walk, taking in mixed woodland and farmland. Route mostly waymarked.

Length *Short walk* 3 miles (5km), 1¹/₂ hours. *Full walk* 4¹/₂ miles (7km), 2¹/₂ hours

Difficulty 2

Start Beacon Hill Lower car park, S of Loughborough and W of Woodhouse Eaves; follow B591 E from junction with B5330 and take first turning left (signposted Nanpantan); car park is on left after ¹/₄ mile, opposite lodge for golf course. Grid reference 522148

OS maps 1:50,000 129; 1:25,000 SK 41/51 (Pathfinder 874)

WALK DIRECTIONS

① From car park entrance, with the road behind you, take track beyond barrier half left, signposted Broombriggs Farm. Where, after 200 yards, corner of wall appears on left (just before you reach cross-junction with waymarked horse track), turn left downhill alongside wall to emerge on to road ②.

Turn left on road and immediately right by Woodhouse Eaves sign, to pass into field just to left of car park. In second field, a well-defined path leads up to gate in corner of woods. Turn right, immediately leaving woods to follow right-hand side of third field, alongside wall, towards Broombriggs Farm (ignore first stile on right) [a].

③ Take stile ahead into fourth field, where turn left as waymarked along bottom of fourth, fifth and sixth fields. ④ As soon as you enter seventh field, turn right uphill (opposite gap in wall) with woodland on right, past memorial benches and

along right edge of eighth field [b], past picnic site.

Keep to left edge of ninth and tenth fields, then drop on enclosed path to farm road where ⑤ turn left to reach main road. Cross road and take gate opposite, keep left (signposted Beacon Upper car park) and left again on to well-defined hard track, soon into open land with Beacon Hill ahead. Fork right up to top of Beacon Hill [c]. Beyond view indicator, proceed, to left of trig point (summit pillar) to turn right on track, with wall on left ⑥.

For short walk follow this track to reach lower car park.

For full walk follow the track, which soon bends right. Just before woods begin on left, take path on left through gap in wall, proceeding over moorland and alongside woodland wall on your right. At edge of moorland and corner of the woodland wall, path keeps right through gateway (with woodland wall still on right).

50 yards later, take signed Jubilee Walk ahead (avoiding Rippin Memorial Walk on left). ⑦ Cross road to take gate beside stile opposite (keep dogs on lead; this is a permitted path which may be closed without warning – in the unlikely event of closure, retrace your steps to the tracks skirting Beacon Hill and turn left to follow short walk back to lower car park).

Follow the waymarked route, down through woodland strip, over stream and turning right along bottom edge of three fields, then over footbridge to follow path through woods and into rough land. ⑧ Fork right (signposted Outwoods) as soon as the woods begin on left (left fork crosses woodland wall), proceeding alongside the wall on left to reach house and then road.

Left on road and then right after 150 yards over signposted stile.

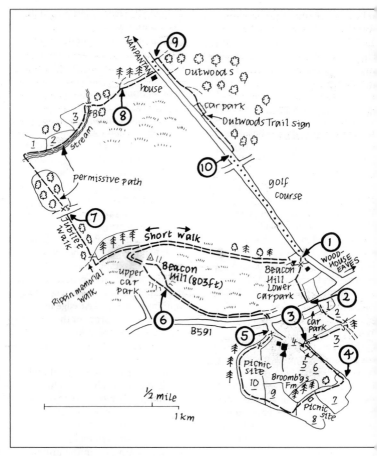

⑨ 30 yards later turn right through (intentional) break in fence to take path closely parallel to road on right (not always in view). Keep forward at cross-junction of paths where fence comes in from left.

At car park, continue closely parallel to road, taking path to right of sign for Outwoods Trail [d].

⑩ Just before road sign indicating a right turn, emerge by gate on to road. Turn left along the road and follow ½ mile to starting point.

ON THE ROUTE

[a] Broombriggs Farm Owned by Leicestershire County Council and run as a 139-acre arable and stock farm. Information boards are placed around the estate in summer months to explain the working of the farm.

[b] As you round the hill, the view opens out over **Loughborough**, the cooling towers of **Castle Donington power station** and **Charnwood Forest**. To the left, amid the heathland of Bradgate Park, stands **Old John's Folly**, commemorating a retainer who died in a bonfire accident at the Earl of Stanford's 21st birthday party in 1786.

[c] Beacon Hill (853ft) A moorland summit with small crags; a view

ndicator identifies the panorama
ver the Trent and Soar valleys, with
he Derbyshire Hills in the distance.
The rocks are volcanic, striped with
ayers of grey, cream and green
epresenting successive stages of
ava eruption laid down on the sea
ed 700 million years ago that was
ilted by movements from within
he Earth. Erosion has subsequently
created a series of parallel, broken
ridges which form the present-day
hills of Charnwood Forest. The
rocks of Charnwood harbour the
oldest known evidence of life forms
more complex than seaweeds.

[d] **Outwoods** 44-hectare site of oaks
and conifers, mostly planted but of
ancient origins; possesses rich flora.

Rutland Water

A waterside walk without rival in Central England, around the landscaped shores of the huge man-made lake of Rutland Water. Further interest is added by the waterfowl, windsurfing and sailing scene, and the varied views as you round the peninsula. Route finding entirely straight-forward.

Length 3½ miles (5.5km), 1½ hours
Difficulty 1
Start Hambleton E of Oakham, signed off A606 (Oakham-Stamford); roadside parking in village centre. Grid reference 900076
OS maps 1:50,000 141; 1:25,000 SK 80/90 (Pathfinder 896)
Refreshments Pub in Hambleton

WALK DIRECTIONS

① [a] Follow road in Oakham direction, past pub on right, out of village. 150 yards after last house, take track over cattle-grid on right, and follow it close to lakeside [b].
② Cross road and take track opposite around S side of peninsula [c].

③ Go forward on reaching road (left is private to Old Hall) [d]; at next cattle-grid, you can follow road back up to village or proceed along lakeside track and shortly **④** take stile on right. Go up to top of triangular field to find stile, and proceed a few yards to next stile and follow snaking, enclosed path to reach back of churchyard.

ON THE ROUTE

[a] **Hambleton** A pleasant village

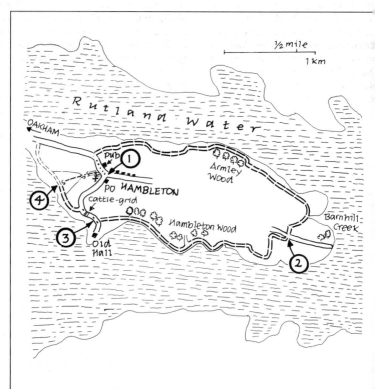

entre, with 'Arts and Crafts' style state cottages and post office (1892) opposite the restored 12th-century church; the village gives no hint of its remarkable peninsular site, all but surrounded by Rutland Water, under which its twin, Nether Hambleton, disappeared when the reservoir was constructed.

b] **Rutland Water** Covering an area of 3,500 acres, with a shoreline of 24 miles, this is the largest lowland lake in England. Its 900-million gallon capacity is an important water source for the east Midlands. After it was completed in 1977 the shore was landscaped and picnic sites laid out. Rutland Water is now a major recreational area, attracting 400,000 visitors every year. Its 350-acre nature reserve at the west end is an important site for waterfowl. Beyond the woodlands above Rutland Water you can see **Burley House** a rebuilding (1696-1700) on a grand scale, in the Palladian style, by Daniel Finch, second Earl of Nottingham, to his own design; colonnades enclose a 650 x 500-ft piazza. Its landscaped grounds were modified by Repton; a grand avenue led to fish ponds, now underwater.

[c] View of **Normanton church**, a survival of the largely underwater Normanton Estate, which belonged to Sir Gilbert Heathcote, a man of immense wealth – one-time Lord Mayor of London and in 1694 one of the founders of the Bank of England. The church, which has a baroque tower inspired by St John's, Smith Square in London (architect Thomas Cundy was surveyor of the Grosvenor Estate in Westminster), was retained as a landscape feature. It has rather ignominiously lost its proportions as its base has been lowered into rubble, but from a distance the church splendidly graces the water's edge. The church is now a museum.

[d] **Old Hall** Built 1611 in Jacobean style; an unusual design with mullions and gabled wings in an H-plan; the building has been altered over the years and now enjoys a magnificent site by the water.

LINCOLNSHIRE

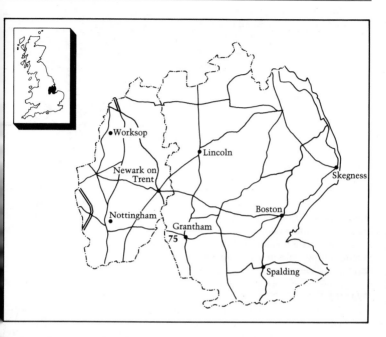

75 Grantham Canal and Denton

Holiday Which? Good Walks Guide

114 Tennyson's birthplace and the Central Wolds   115 Louth, Raithby and Hubbard's Hill

Also, in Nottinghamshire: 119 Clumber Park

The Grantham Canal and Denton

The Grantham Canal towpath, followed by green tracks and part of the Viking Way are the distinctive features of this walk, which ends on a note of considerable drama. Route-finding mostly easy.

Length 8½ miles (13.5km), 3½ hours

Difficulty 2

Start Woolsthorpe by Belvoir, E of Belvoir Castle and W of Grantham (do not confuse with Woolsthorpe S of Grantham). Roadside parking by sign for Chequers Inn. Grid reference 341837

OS maps 1:50,000 130; 1:25,000 SK 83/93 (Pathfinder 835)

Refreshments Pub and shop in Woolsthorpe; pubs at Woolsthorpe Bridge and Denton

WALK DIRECTIONS

① With pub sign on your right, follow Main Street. Go straight over at junction into Sedgebrook Road. **②** ¼ mile after end of village, fork right (by advertising sign for Rutland Arms). **③** After crossing canal, cross stile on right and join canal towpath, along which turn left (walking with canal on right) [a]. Path soon leaves canal and rises up steps over embankment of old railway line, then rejoins canal. Bridges are numbered with plaques.

④ At bridge 66 (with house up to right), leave canal and cross the bridge. On other side take signposted steps on right into field. Follow right edge of three fields, close to canal (briefly inside woods above canal at end of second field): the third field narrows to a thin strip at its far end.

⑤ Ignore gate beside stile on left and proceed forward along left edge of fourth, fifth and sixth fields to reach Denton reservoir. Turn left on waterside path. **⑥** At end of

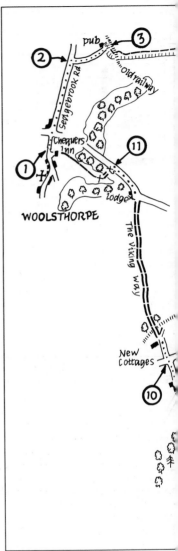

reservoir, cross water channel on right by footbridge, turn left and follow track alongside the channel to gate beside stile giving on to track (of old railway). Take gate beside stile opposite, still with channel alongside on left.

⑦ Emerge on to road, turn left into Denton village [b]. Keep forwar

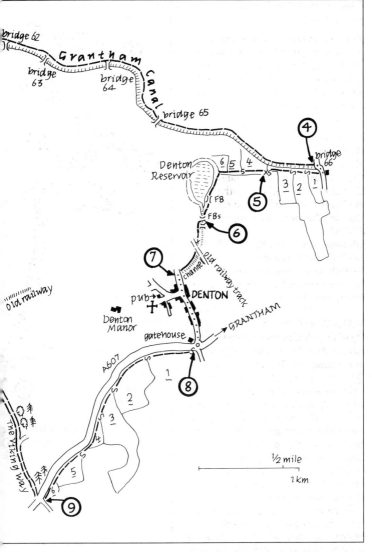

crossroads, signposted Grantham
pub is to right), through village.
8 At cross-junction with A607,
cross main road and take stile to
right of the turning opposite:
continue to the right, closely parallel
to A607 for 1¼ miles along edges of
fields.
9 Emerge by stile on to road and

track by county boundary; cross
A607 and take track opposite
(signposted Viking Way) [c]. Keep
forward as main track bends left to
farm after 50 yards, and forward just
as you enter woods (ignoring minor
right fork into field) [d].
10 Cross road and take road
opposite; go past row of houses on

left and ignore right fork; proceed 1 mile to road. Turn left on road then ⑪ after 350 yards, where road is about to descend and woodland is about to start on the right-hand side of road, take gate beside stile on left and follow woodland track to emerge by gate beside stile on to strip of pasture. Turn right along this strip; view ahead opens out [e]. Drop to stile into left-hand side of cricket field (which is the right-hand of two sports fields below) and follow left edge to emerge by pub in Woolsthorpe.

ON THE ROUTE

[a] **Grantham Canal** runs 33 miles from Nottingham to Grantham to the Vale of Belvoir; it was used commercially until 1797. Coal, limestone, coke and building materials from Nottinghamshire were transported eastwards; the return journey took agricultural products destined for market at Hull via Newark and the River Trent.

[b] **Denton** Unspoilt L-shaped village of mellow ironstone, lying beside the estate wall of the private manor (the Tudor-style gatehouse of which is passed on the walk). A minor architectural storm occurred in 1980 when 17th-century almshouses in the park, reckoned as among the most delightful in England by architectural writer Sir Nikolaus Pevsner, were demolished.

[c] A long-distance path across Lincolnshire, through many settlements with Viking origins, the **Viking Way** starts at the Humber Bridge and ends 140 miles away at Oakham in Leicester.

[d] View to right of **Harlaxton Manor**, a palatial mansion covering half the hillside. Its first owner was Gregory Gregory, a devoted collector of the arts, who commissioned 32-year-old Anthony Salvin to design it, largely to accommodate his growing collection. Not surprisingly the building work took time: Gregory, who owned the smaller 17th-century manor house, only lived here for the last 3 years of his life. It is likely that he took a large part in planning the design.

[e] Arresting view of the spectacular outline of **Belvoir Castle** (pronounced 'Beaver'), against the huge Midland plain beyond. This massive pile, with its castellations, was remodelled, 1801-30, by James Wyatt and Revd Sir John Thoroton. The site has Norman origins. The late 11th-century structure was built by Robert De Todeni, standard-bearer to William I (open Mar-Oct, exc Mon).

GREATER LONDON

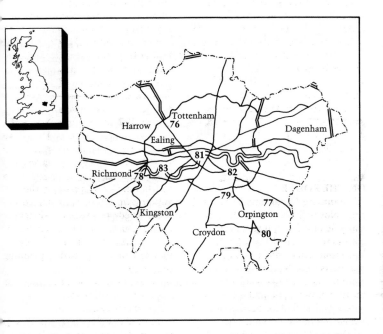

Hampstead and Kenwood House

Enjoying a blend of intricate townscape and semi-rural heathland, historic Hampstead lies on a hillside, laced with a maze of 18th- and early 19th-century streets, stepped alleys, small greens, sloping lanes, grand town mansions, luxuriant suburban villas and intimate terraces that have been homes to the famous. Route-finding across the Heath is somewhat involved, owing to a multitude of paths (should you prefer to devise your own walk, try to incorporate Kenwood House and the Parliament Hill Fields viewpoint).

Length 3 miles (5km), 2 hours
Difficulty 1
Start Car park opposite junction of East Heath Road and Downshire Hill, on SW edge of Hampstead Heath. *By train* Hampstead underground station (Northern Line) at ④ or Hampstead Heath (British Rail) just SE of start.
Refreshments Plenty in Hampstead

WALK DIRECTIONS

① Cross road from car park, into Downshire Hill [a] then first right into Willow Road (or detour to Keats House [b] by continuing along Downshire Hill and taking next left, by church, into Keats Grove; the house is on the right). Take next right fork, into Christchurch Hill, then ② when heath on right is about to end take path on right along edge of heath, soon turning left through gate into Gainsborough Gardens [c] beyond which ③ turn left into Well Walk [d].

At small green, with New End Square on right [e], fork right into Flask Walk [f]. ④ Cross High Street, take Oriel Place opposite and slightly to left, then cross Heath Street and take Church Row [g]

(opposite and slightly to left). ⑤ At church [h] turn right into Holly Walk [i], at top of which turn right at T-junction into Mount Vernon [j], then left into Holly Hill [k].

⑥ Fork right into Hampstead Grove [l] (the road to right of wrought-iron gates of Fenton House), past Fenton House, then left into Admiral Walk [m]. ⑦ At end, bear right over Lower Terrace [n] (go just to right of No.4, Fountain House), up past small triangular green and over Upper Terrace to reach edge of Hampstead Heath [o] ⑧. Turn right, skirting edge of heath to reach road junction by Whitestone Pond. Cross to far side of pond, then left on North End Way.

⑨ Just before road divides by obelisk [p] in front of Heath House, take steps on right leading to path descending heath [q] (fork right after 50 yards) and passing close to fairground site towards houses at bottom; this cluster of streets is known as the Vale of Health [r].

Path joins road by the Vale of Health: keep houses to the right, almost immediately leaving road for path ahead, and ⑩ just after houses end keep forward at path junction (right turn leads to lake), heading up past small circular brick building. Shortly after, path joins a broader one: continue forward, past toilets on your left, and ignore side-turns.

⑪ 150 yards after toilets, turn left over bridge (if you reach large bridge over end of lake, you have overshot by 50 yards), and proceed until reaching large junction of paths, with notice-board for Kenwood Woodland Area ahead. Bear half left skirting close to the railings which enclose Kenwood Woodland Area, then 80 yards later take entrance through these railings; Kenwood House can be seen ahead [s].

At Kenwood House, the route back to the car park is to the right

s seen standing with the house to
the left and ponds to the right).
outes can easily be improvised
om here; should you wish to take
the Parliament Hill Fields
ewpoint, the following is
commended: with Kenwood House
a left, go forward to other side of
ailings ahead, then ⑫ turn right on
armacked path which runs
ongside the railings, on the other
de of which are soon seen the
onds mentioned above. Soon pass
nother pond, then the Kenwood
adies' Pond, both on your right.
ust after the next pond, turn right,
hen left on other side, alongside
oating-pond. At end of boating-
ond, bear half right on ascending
ath, which leads up to cluster of
ees, then proceed a few yards to
op of hill **[t]** ⑬.

Turn right on tarmacked path,
making for distant church spire.
oon reach path junction close to
ouses on left and continue forward,
lose to these houses, to lakes and
hen on to car park.

N THE ROUTE

] Downshire Hill Early 19th-
entury, stock London-brick
erraces; some houses have good
xamples of **fire-marks** (denoting
with which insurance company the
wner had insured against fire), for
xample Nos. 16, 26 and 27. **St
ohn's Chapel** (1818) is a period
iece, with galleries and box-pews.
Nearby, **No.47** was, at different
eriods, the home of two artists –
aetano Meo, who entertained
minent pre-Raphaelites, and
tanley Spencer.

] Keats House (1816) (open 10-1, 2-
; 2-5 Sun). Keats moved into the
eft side of the house with his friend
Charles Brown. On the other side
ved Mrs Brawne and her three
aughters, including Fanny, with
whom Keats fell in love; here he
composed love letters to her and
Ode to a Nightingale, and learned
that he was dying of consumption.
On medical advice, he went abroad
but died in Italy at the age of 25.
Memorabilia of Keats and the
Brawnes is on display here.

[c] Gainsborough Gardens An
attractive circus of late 19th-century
villas encompasses lush communal
gardens.

[d] Well Walk Immediately to the
right as you emerge from
Gainsborough Gardens, and semi-
obscured by a clematis bush, a
plaque on a house records the site of
the wells which turned Hampstead
into a health spa in the 18th
century, soon bringing an often
raucous clientele; gambling- parlours
and beer-houses sprang up to satisfy
a new demand. By the early 1800s,
Hampstead's spa days had declined.
Numerous plaques record celebrated
residents: historian Henry Hyndman
(No. 13), actress Marie Stopes (14),
J.B. Priestley (27), D.H. Lawrence
(32) and John Constable (40). No. 46
has an appealing Gothic oriel
window.

[e] New End Square Flask Cottages
have a curious external bird-cage
hanging from the upper storey, and
comically shaped chimney-stacks.
Burgh House, a little further up, is a
fine three-storey house of 1703, now
housing local artists' work (open 12-
5, Wed-Sun).

[f] Flask Walk So called because this
was where spa water from Well
Walk was put into flasks for sale at
the Eagle and Child in Fleet Street.
Bottling was carried out in the
Thatch'd House Inn (on the site of
the Flask Tavern).

[g] Church Row One of Hampstead's
finest streets, a row of tall houses
built in the 1720s at the time of
Hampstead's early days as a health
resort. Handsome brown brick,
plum-coloured dressings, original

railings and one or two torch-stands by the front entrances. View over central London from the end of the Row.

[**h**] **St John's church** (1745, altered in 19th century), a gilt, barrel-vaulted interior, with whimsical pew-ends and Ionic columns; unusually, the tower is at the E end. The gates came from the Duke of Chandos' demolished mansion at Stanmore in Middlesex. Constable and his family are buried here: to find his tomb, stand with your back to the church door and turn right; the tomb is in the bottom left-hand corner of the

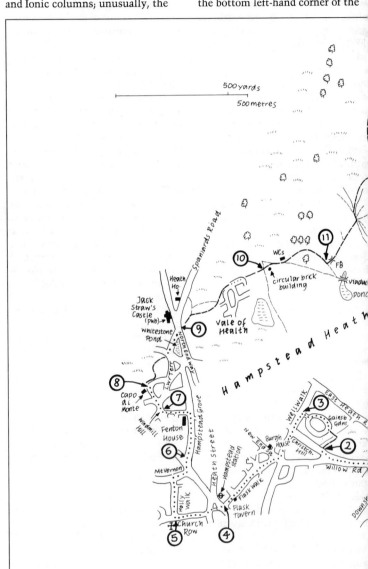

urchyard and is surrounded by
on railings. There is also a good
ar view of Church Row from here.
Holly Walk Escapees from the
ench Revolution settled here and
ie tiny terraces leading off, hence
: **Mary's Catholic Church** (1816),
l stucco and rather foreign-looking,
despite the Englishness of the
terrace into which it is incorporated.
In the 1830s **Holy Berry Lane**
(leading off right from Holly Walk)
had a watch-house for the recently-
formed Hampstead police force;
down the lane is a plaque to
composer William Walton.

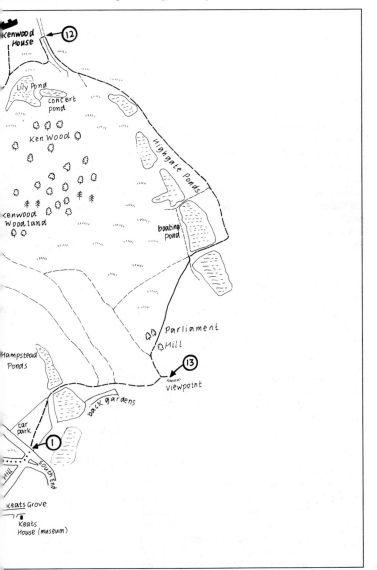

[j] **Mount Vernon** Named after George III's aide-de-campe. Abernethy House has a plaque to R.L. Stevenson.

[k] **Holly Hill** One of Hampstead's steepest streets, sloping down suddenly to join Heath Street. Holly Mount, leading off from the right, is an alley of great charm, with an improbably minute cottage (No. 14) at the end. The Holly Bush is a pub, originally a stable block for Romney's House next door (see below); here, in 1829, James Fenton (of Fenton House) organised local residents to fight the long-running but ultimately successful battle to preserve Hampstead Heath (see below).

[l] **Hampstead Grove** On the right is **Romney's House** (1797), built for George Romney, a fashionable portrait-artist of the day. Further on, on the right is **New Grove House**, with a plaque to George du Maurier, 19th-century novelist and cartoonist for Punch (the originator of the celebrated 'curate's egg' cartoon). Opposite is Fenton House (1693-95), Hampstead's oldest and finest house, an outstanding example of the William and Mary style (National Trust, open Apr-Oct; 11-6, Sat-Wed; in Mar 2-6, weekends; gardens free). Period furniture, paintings, porcelain, and a large collection of antique keyboard instruments.

[m] **Admiral Walk** Admiral's House is 18th-century, five-storey and rambling; plaque to George Gilbert Scott, 19th-century architect responsible for designing the Albert Memorial and St Pancras Station. The 'Admiral' was Admiral Matthew Benson, who was alleged to have lived here (but didn't) and who was reputed to have fired a cannon from the roof on fitting occasions. Next door is **Grove Lodge**, home of John Galsworthy, 1918-35, where he wrote much of *The Forsyte Saga.*

[n] **Lower Terrace** Plaque on No. 2 to John Constable.

[o] **Judges Walk** Allegedly named because in the 1660s High Court judges fled here to escape the plague and held court. The house on the left, Capo di Monte, has an 'S' over its door, perhaps recording a visit by actress Sarah Siddons in 1804. The view from here was painted by Constable.

[p] **Obelisk** At 442ft, this is the highest point in London.

[q] **Hampstead Heath** 800 acres of woods and parkland, joined on to Parliament Hill Fields to E, Kenwood estate to N, Golders Hill Park to W. The nearest countrified expanse to central London, it owes its survival to a fierce campaign by local residents, 1830-90, who formed the Heath Protection Committee. Sir Thomas Marylon-Wilson, Lord of the Manor, wanted to develop the heath; his private parliamentary bill to enclose the common were constantly frustrated by the committee, whose members' influence in parliament was considerable. Marylon-Wilson managed to fell many trees, and run sand-extraction operations (the former sand-pits now appear on the heath as attractive hollows), but after his death tracts of the heath were sold to public ownership.

[r] **The Vale of Health** Originally an area of malarial swamp known as Hatches Bottom, drained in the 18th century and given a more wholesome-sounding name. Development was piecemeal and sporadic, resulting in a warren of tiny lanes and more suburban-looking roads – an example of what would have happened to the rest of the heath had the campaign for its preservation not been fought and won. Celebrated residents have included James Leigh Hunt (with

hom Byron, Coleridge, Lamb and helley stayed), D.H. Lawrence, ompton Mackenzie and Edgar allace.

Kenwood House (If outdoor oncerts are in progress, detour ound the back of the house). The eat of the Earl of Mansfield in the eign of George III, rebuilt in 1767 by obert Adam, and given to the ation in 1927 (open daily mid-Mar-d Sept, 10-6; Oct-mid-Mar, 10-4; ank hols; free) and has a fine ollection of paintings and period rniture. Up on the left, just efore reaching the house, is Henry Moore's sculpture *Two-piece reclining figure No.5* (1964).

[t] **Parliament Hill Fields** This is where Guy Fawkes' fellow conspirators are alleged to have met on the evening of 5th November 1605 to watch the blowing-up of Parliament. Huge view over central London and beyond, with Highgate close to the NE, the City and West End to the S (Nat West and Telecom towers are prominent amongst the many landmarks) and the distant Crystal Palace ridge beyond (with large TV transmitters).

Chislehurst and Scadbury

Attractive Green Belt farmland and woods well within built-up suburbia, but screened from it, which creates the illusion of deep countryside.

Length 4 miles (6.5km), 2 hours
Difficulty 1
Start St Nicholas parish church (opposite Tiger's Head pub), Chislehurst; from war memorial at junction of A222 and A208 go SE along A208, then third right into Manor Park Road. Grid reference 444699

By train Chislehurst: cross footbridge over main road (Summer Hill), continue along Gosshill Road (unmade), past railway arches on your right then 150 yards later take path on left where there are No Entry signs ahead. Just before bridge over stream, turn right through barrier and start directions at ③
OS maps 1:50,000 177 ; 1:25,000 TQ 46/56 and TQ 47/57 (Pathfinder 1192 and 1176)
Refreshments Pubs and shops in Chislehurst near starting point

WALK DIRECTIONS

① [a] Take Hawkwood Lane, just to left of Tiger's Head, opposite church; pass Coopers School and Catholic church. Just after house called The Old Coach House, road surfacing ceases; bear left, along tree-lined stony track by No Through Road sign. ② After 200 yards, take signposted path on right, through barrier, to follow path between fences, with field on your left.

Beyond end of field, continue in next field along left-hand edge, eventually dropping down among trees to cross bridge over stream. (Continue ahead after bridge if starting from rail station and retrace steps along Gosshill Road to start). Immediately after, turn left through

barrier and ③ follow path along left edge of fields, with stream on your left.

In middle of third field, by footbridge with farm visible up on left, turn right on path across field and into strip of woodland ④, where path turns left alongside railway. At footbridge, do not cross railway but keep left alongside field, on enclosed path to reach edge of woodland ⑤ [b]. Immediately fork left (you will be walking close to the left inside edge of the woods in this section), then turn left again

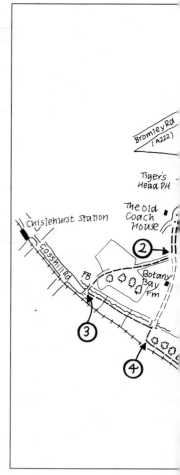

0 yards later at T-junction.

After 150 yards, path crosses small stream (may be dry in summer); fork right immediately after (left fork peters out). ⑥ 100 yards later, at four-way junction (with broad path coming up from right), turn left on to narrow path that soon runs along inside edge of woods.

At corner of woods continue forward on path across field into woods again at far side, then ⑦ immediately turn right inside woods at path junction. 30 yards later, turn left on to broad path (by

wooden railing), which is waymarked by blue and white hoops on trees; ignore minor side-turns and follow to main road.

Cross to broad (semi-metalled) track opposite, into Scadbury estate; ⑧ 100 yards later, at gate, turn right by sign for Scadbury Circular Walk. 80 yards later, enter nature reserve on left by sign and barrier, follow path ahead to reach post numbered '5' and turn right [**c**]. Follow the Circular Walk (well marked, past series of numbered posts, with waymarks encircled by white

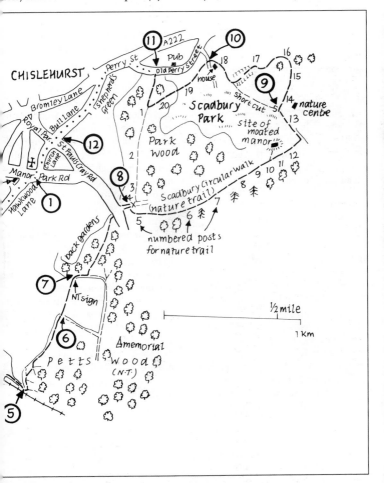

arrows), ignoring signed exits from the route (to the right). After passing signs to the left to site of moated manor [d], reach T-junction of paths in front of fence, where the Circular Walk turns left (signed for Nature Centre).

(9) Reach junction where view opens out: either turn right along the Circular Walk or take signposted path ahead to shorten route. The two routes rejoin at bottom of valley, where the path heads up to prominent house. Past house continue, over driveway (10), on the Circular Walk (ignoring signed exit to Perry Street).

Proceed through woods, to reach another driveway, where turn right (signposted Old Perry Street), to leave the Circular Walk. (11) Left on road, then left along main road. Just after Farrington's School, turn left into cul-de-sac (Shepherds Green; opposite Ashfield Lane), soon continuing along Bull Lane.
(12) Cross next main road and take Church Lane ahead (to left of Bull's Head inn), to reach church.

ON THE ROUTE

[a] **Chislehurst** Joined on to suburban London, its large Common and rustic survivals have helped its old centre to retain a village character. Near the station (off route) are the extensive **Chislehurst Caves**, where guides will tell you stories of druids and point out 'dinosaur fossils', in fact 18th- and 19th-century chalk excavations. The **parish church of St Nicholas** is mainly 15th- and 19th-century, but there are remains of an earlier building and the font is Norman. Its great shingled spire is a local landmark. Also of interest are the Scadbury chapel, and numerous monuments, including the Chantrey Monument in the South aisle, and one to Lord Thomas Bertie (1749) with carved representation of a naval battle.

[b] **Petts Wood** has given its name to a large nearby suburb, but the original woodland (predominantly silver birch), is owned by the National Trust and remains a rural oasis. In the middle of the woods (not on route) is a **memorial to William Willett**, who was inspired while riding here in the 1900s to champion the idea of British Summer Time, following his publication of a booklet titled *Waste of Daylight*. After a fraught campaign, the proposal achieved Parliamentary approval in 1916.

[c] **Scadbury Estate** 300 acres of parkland, oak and alder woods, and some open downland, municipally owned and run as a local nature reserve (trail leaflet available from London Borough of Bromley); a circular walk, most of which is incorporated into this walk, follows the nature trail with a series of numbered posts.

[d] **Moat and partly restored ruin of Scadbury Manor** Christopher Marlowe, escaping a plague, took refuge here, 1592-93, with his friend Thomas Walsingham, and completed *Dr Faustus*. In 1956, an American eccentric who was convinced that Marlowe was the author of Shakespeare's plays, managed to get Walsingham's memorial stone in Chislehurst parish church opened up in his quest for the play manuscripts; only to find sand and rubble.

Richmond and Ham

Explores Richmond's wealth of Georgian (and earlier) streets and follows the edge of Richmond Park where it slopes abruptly towards the Thames, whose towpath provides the return route. An extension further into Richmond Park is given. Easy route-finding.

Length 5 miles (8km), 2½ hours Extension adds 1½ miles (¾ hour); further extensions into the Park can easily be devised

Difficulty 1

Start Richmond station (BR and District line); car parks in town centre; or park in Richmond Hill or at Pembroke Lodge car park in Richmond Park (both are on the route)

Refreshments Full range in Richmond; café in Pembroke Lodge in Richmond Park; pubs in Ham and along the river at Richmond

WALK DIRECTIONS

① Turn left out of station, along The Quadrant; keep right at junction with The Square (ignoring left fork signposted to registry office), then soon left into Church Court by signpost to Parish Church. Keep to left of church, cross main road and take Halford Road opposite. Turn right at T-junction, along The Vineyard [**a**]; keep straight on past church where road markings indicate compulsory left turn for traffic, then turn left into Hill Rise which becomes Richmond Hill; soon walkway to right of pavement gives excellent views [**b**].

Follow up to pass through gates of Richmond Park, just beyond Star and Garter Home. ② Inside park, take path to right of traffic roundabout, along top of slope [**c**]. Soon go through deer-gate into garden, taking any of several paths leading past Pembroke Lodge on

your left [**d**], then exit by deer-gate; continue along top of slope).

③ Eventually, near road junction and signpost, pond and Ham Gate (a prominent large white lodge) are visible down on right. *For short walk* bear downhill on any path to reach these, and pick up walk directions at ⑥. *For extension further into Richmond Park* proceed to road junction, and take track opposite signposted Pen Ponds (any 'no admittance' signs refer to vehicles). Ignore side-turns (but detour right after 200 yards to the Isabella Plantation [**e**] is recommended) and follow ¾ mile to reach road by car park ④. Turn left, up to White Lodge [**f**], at which turn left on grassy track to Pen Ponds.

Take the causeway between the two ponds [**g**]; turn left on far side. Ignore side-turns, and 600 yards later ⑤ join broad horse track, which crosses tiny brick bridge over channel; immediately after, bear right and soon join track you were on earlier. Follow back to road junction, and take road opposite to Ham Gate.

⑥ Just after Ham Gate, turn left into Church Road: find path running just inside woods and parallel to road. ⑦ Where pillars for driveway to Wilmer House are visible away to left, turn right, still inside woods and parallel with road; houses are visible away to left. ⑧ When level with church, either follow road or take any of several paths leading half right through woods; both routes soon lead to a large green flanked by houses (Ham village) [**h**].

Follow right edge of green; 100 yards after Martingales Close (on right) take path on right leading towards Ham House. In front of Ham House gates [**i**], turn right, then ⑨ left at corner of wall towards river. ⑩ Join towpath (access is possible at numerous points) and

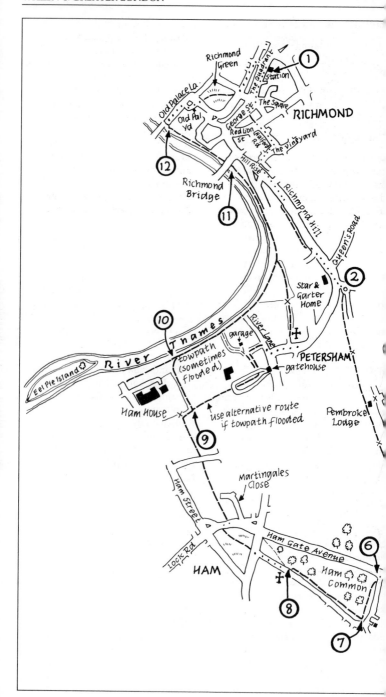

then turn right [**j**]. At high tide the towpath may be flooded, in which case see next column.

Follow towpath beyond Richmond Bridge ⑪ [**k**], then just before next bridge ⑫ turn right on road by sign for White Swan pub. Just after pub turn right into Old Palace Yard [**l**], exit via archway, then cross Richmond Green [**m**], aiming for Richmond Theatre (with prominent green copper domes). Continue past theatre, over railway, then take signposted path on right into town centre, emerging opposite station.

If river towpath is flooded return to corner of wall at ⑨, turn left on long straight path to gatehouse, 50 yards before which cross school driveway on left and take track opposite. 200 yards later, turn right on path between fences, to reach River Lane in Petersham, where turn right to join main road. Left along main road for 200 yards through Petersham village [**n**], then left on path signposted to St Peter's church. Beyond church continue forward by remains of old lamp-post, on path. After crossing field, path reaches

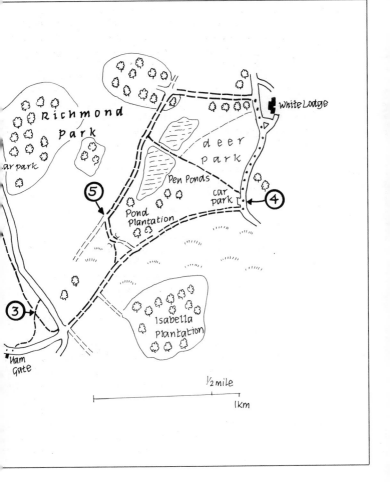

river, where turn right and resume walk directions at ⑪.

ON THE ROUTE

[a] The Vineyard Its name is probably historically accurate; now this is a quiet side street with several good 17th-, 18th- and 19th-century houses and two sets of 19th-century almshouses, one a rebuilding of an ancient foundation of Bishop Duppa.

[b] Richmond Hill The Richmond end of the Hill has a pocket-handkerchief triangular village green and some fine 18th-century houses. The Queen's Terrace is a 17th-century feature; grand prospect of Windsor, the Thames, the park, London airport and more. Numerous artists and poets including Turner, have been attracted to record the view. No 116 (Downe House) was once leased to playwright Sheridan; by the junction with Nightingale Lane is Wick House, once home of Joshua Reynolds. The Wick next door is also 18th-century, strikingly handsome.

[c] Richmond Park (note: closes before dusk). An area of 2,358 acres, enclosed in 1635 by Charles I as a hunting park, and encompassed by a 10-mile wall. Public access was gained in the 18th century after a vigorous campaign by brewer John Lewis, and remains one of London's largest semi-untamed expanses, with rough pasture, woodlands and ponds. Warning notices remind you not to approach the deer, especially in summer.

[d] Pembroke Lodge, the 18th-century former home of Bertrand Russell, is now run as a refreshment room; fine Wedgwood ceilings, extensive view from tables outside.

[e] Isabella Plantation Fine azaleas and heathers in a plantation crossed by an attractive stream.

[f] Porticoed **White Lodge**, is a splendid villa with its specially created vista down a broad park ride built 1729 as a rural retreat, birthplace of Edward VIII in 1894 and now housing the Royal Ballet School.

[g] After crossing the causeway between Pen Ponds (ducks and swans in abundance), a surprise view of the **British Telecom Tower**.

[h] Ham Remains rural in feel, with mainly 18th- and 19th-century houses scattered around its large green, and a pond at its far end. Odd vista down bridleway of Ham House which is much more impressive when you get close up.

[i] Ham House (entrance from river side; gardens open daily 10-6, free; house Tue-Sun, 11-5, fee). Built in H-plan in 1610 for Sir Thomas Vavsour; Jacobean mansion giving outstanding insight into fashionable living of the period. Gardens, laid out in 17th century, are partly restored.

[j] The Thames First is Eel Pie Island, so-called because a now demolished hotel on it used to sell eel pies to visitors. Later, **Marble Hill**, built 1729, a stucco Palladian mansion on the other side of the river.

[k] Richmond Bridge Elegant structure built 1777 of Portland Stone; now London's oldest bridge; **Heron Square** (1986), immediately after the bridge; Quinlan Terry's controversial neo-classical creation; loathed by some post-modernists as shameless pastiche, venerated by others for its amazing period detail, variety and sensitive use of materials; go through the iron gates to the centre of the courtyard to get the full effect.

[l] Old Palace The gate-house and various brickwork now incorporated into adjacent houses are remains of the palace built by Henry VII, former Duke of Richmond (the Yorkshire own giving its name to this one), on he site of the priory of Shene, which ad first been occupied by Henry I in 125. Edward III, Henry VII and Elizabeth I all died here. Much of the palace's destruction was wrought by Cromwell's men.

m] Richmond Green A former knights' jousting ground belonging o the palace, and now a handsome green tucked round the back of Richmond's main thoroughfares. It s worth taking in each side, for the quality of its predominantly 17th- and 18th-century houses (some now offices) is exceptional. Leading from the S corner, Paved Green, a 17th-century alley, is now a fashionable shopping street. The theatre (built 1899) is a capricious piece of late Victoriana, with two mock burning torches at the podium entrance.

[n] Petersham Noisy main street, but some outstanding houses, including 16th-century Montrose House (former home of Tommy Steele) with superb wrought-iron gates. St Peter's church is a Saxon foundation, rebuilt 1266 and altered every century from the 16th to this one. Internally it is very much early 19th-century in appearance, with late 18th-century box-pews. Gatehouse near school is 1898 mock-Jacobean. The village makes partial compensation for walkers who are denied the towpath section because of flooding.

Dulwich and Sydenham Hill Wood

A real surprise in the heart of the inner suburbs: Dulwich village and an unexpected survival of rural woodland side-by-side.

Length 3¹/₂ miles (5.5km), 1¹/₂ hours
Difficulty 1
Start Dulwich Wood House (pub), Crescent Wood Road, SE26 (at corner with Sydenham Hill) *By train* Sydenham Hill. Leave station on 'Down side' (Orpington-bound trains), follow walkway to reach College Road. Cross road and take woodland track opposite, beyond barrier. Turn left after 100 yards through gate and start walk directions at ②.
Refreshments Pub at start; pub and shops in Dulwich; café in Dulwich Park

WALK DIRECTIONS

① Take broad path opposite Dulwich Wood House (Crescent Wood Road side), behind picket fence and descending between woods [a]. 100 yards before reaching road at bottom ②, take gate on right into woods and follow broad path with back gardens down on left *(note:* future public access to this path is in doubt; if gate is locked, continue to College Road, turn right along it to toll-house. This is point ④). After 300 yards turn half left at big junction of paths (by seat and bin) and follow path, eventually reaching gate on to end of Grange Lane ③ [b].

Turn left down the lane to reach College Road by toll-house ④ [c]. Turn right along College Road [d], left into Dulwich Common [e], then right into Gallery Road. Pass Belair House on your left [f]; ⑤ 100 yards later turn right through kissing-gate and follow enclosed path to College Road, where turn left [g].

⑥ Opposite picture gallery and old college [h] continuation of route is to right into Dulwich Park (through Old College Gate), but first detour ahead past the roundabout along Dulwich Village [i]. Return to

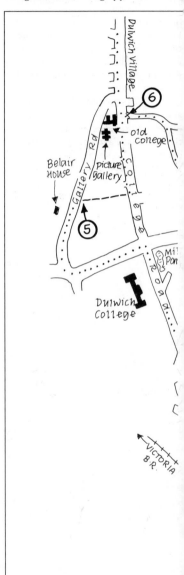

Old College Gate and cross Dulwich Park [**j**], making your own way to Rosebery Gate: easiest route to find is to keep right and follow park road until reaching the gate (by black and white lodge and near rhododendron

area) although it is pleasanter to divert slightly to left on the paths past the ponds.

Cross main road (Dulwich Common) and turn left along it. ⑦ Just before traffic lights, take gate

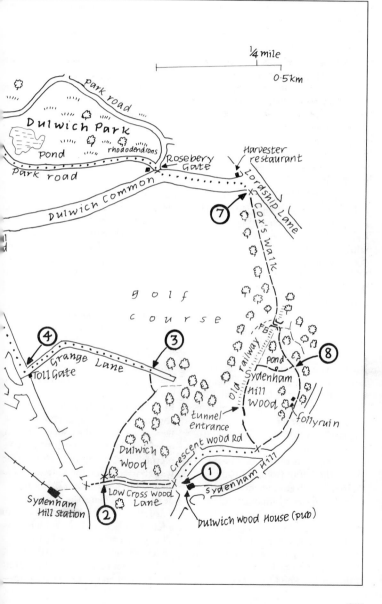

on right (opposite Harvester restaurant called The Grove) and follow broad, rising woodland path; as soon as you cross footbridge over old railway [k], fork right through barrier on to path up steps. Follow this through Sydenham Hill Wood.

8 ¹/₄ mile later reach fork with right fork leading down to fence enclosing pond: you are now on a small circular nature trail. Take either fork: left one bears left just in front of mock ruin [l]; right fork leads past pond, then turn left along old railway track, left again just before old railway tunnel. Both lead up to gate on to Crescent Wood Road, where turn right [m] to reach Dulwich Wood House.

ON THE ROUTE

[a] **Dulwich Woods** Together with neighbouring Sydenham Hill Wood forms the largest remaining fragment of the great North Wood which once covered what is now South London. The nearby suburb of Norwood takes its name from this.

[b] **Grange Lane** Retains the appearance of a rural lane, fringed with hedgerows and with allotments and golf course on either side. Big **view** ahead of central London, with Palace of Westminster and the British Telecom tower among the landmarks; the Dulwich College campanile is in the foreground. The huge Crystal Palace TV transmitter aerial is to your left.

[c] Dating from 1789, this **toll-house** is the only one in use left in London, and displays its old charges board.

[d] On the left of College Road, **Dulwich College** (a leading public school) is a richly ornamented complex in North Italian renaissance style. Its design by the younger Charles Barry in 1870 made one of the earliest uses of terracotta on such a large scale. Opposite, the 18th-century **Pond Cottages and old**

mill-pond make an attractive scene. French impressionist Camille Pissarro painted the pond and college while staying in the area in 1871.

[e] The old finger-post on the corner of Dulwich Common on your right is one of several passed on this walk Into Dulwich Common itself, you pass several fine houses on your right: **Northcroft** (early 1800s); then **Old Blew House** (rendered Georgian three-storey); then **Elm Lawn** (18th-century).

[f] **Belair House** is a small Adam-style mansion built 1785. The house and park are now municipally owned.

[g] **Pickwick Cottage**, opposite where you emerge, is a Regency house renamed after Dickens made it the fictitious retirement home for Mr Pickwick in *Pickwick Papers*. Along College Road on right are **Bell House** (No. 27, with belfry) 1767, and a boarding-house for the college, and **Bell Cottage**, weatherboarded, early 1700s with Doric door-case; Nos. **13 and 15** are ivy-clad Georgian, with fine porches.

[h] **Dulwich College Picture Gallery** (open Tue-Fri 10-1, 2-5; Sat 11-5; Sun 2-5; closed bank hols). England's oldest art gallery, opened in 1814, with noted collection including works by Rembrandt, Murillo, Gainsborough and Reynolds. In 1790 King Stanislaus of Poland commissioned art dealer Noel Desenfans to build a collection for a projected Polish National Gallery; pictures where acquired but the plan was aborted when the king was deposed five years later. After the death of Desenfans the collection was left to his wife under the care of a fellow collector, Francis Bourgeois. The paintings were added to a collection left by Edward Alleyn, and after Bourgeois' death Margaret Desenfans had the gallery built to

he design of John Soane, complete
vith a mausoleum to Bourgeois and
he Desenfans. Later extensions
vere added in 1910 in Soane
astiche; heavy bombing destroyed
nost of Soane's original building but
he gallery and mausoleum has been
ebuilt as it was. Adjacent, the **Old
College** is the original site of
Dulwich College of God's Gift, set
p by actor-manager Edward Alleyn
n 1619 as a charitable foundation of
lmshouses for twelve poor men and
school for twelve poor scholars.
ntry was gained by drawing lots;
uccessful boys drew a slip of paper
nscribed 'God's Gift'. The tower
nd cloister are 1870, and the
lmshouses have mostly been
enewed, althought part of the W
ving is original. The chapel is still
sed by the college.

] At the roundabout, the **old
Grammar School** (designed by
Charles Barry in 1842) is on your
eft. This functioned until 1858 as a
haritable free school for local boys
fter the college became fee-paying.
n **Dulwich Village**, the right side is
rander (Nos. 97-105 are particularly
ne, with 103 and 105 c.1700) and
he left more rustic and cottagey,
vith some 18th-century shop-fronts.
] **Dulwich Park** has a famous
isplay of rhododendrons, in flower
ate May to early June. Near the
ond is Barbara Hepworth's
culpture *Two Forms (Divided
Circle)*.

<] The footbridge crosses an **old
ailway track** which operated

1865-1954 from Nunhead to the
terminus at Crystal Palace. From the
bridge, Pissarro painted Lordship
Lane Station, erroneously titled
'Penge Station, Upper Norwood'
until 1972; it depicts a view to your
left, of a train approaching, with
trailing steam drifting to the left and
houses in the middle distance, but
the site is now overgrown and very
different. The path leads into
Sydenham Hill Woods, the largest
area of ancient woodland left in
inner London; its oaks and
hornbeams are direct descendants of
a 10,000 year-old post-Ice Age tree
cover. There have been 53 bird
species recorded (including all three
varieties of British wood-pecker), 52
species of tree and 40 of butterfly
and moth. Towards the top of the
wood the trees are more mixed and
contain some trees that have
survived from the gardens of large
19th-century houses once on the
site; prominent are a large cedar of
Lebanon and a monkey-puzzle tree.
[l] This mock-up of a ruined chapel
(now ruined even further) was built
in the 19th century as a romantic
garden feature.
[m] Just before the pub, on your left
is **Six Pillars**, built by Harding and
Tecton in 1935 in International
style: a rendered concrete block with
a partly revealed brick drum of the
staircase. Opposite, set back, a large
house (future threatened) with a
plaque to John Logie Baird, pioneer
of broadcasting.

Downe and High Elms

From the very edge of suburban London this walk leads straight into deep countryside: undulating farmland with pleasant views. The return from Downe is through the mature woodlands of the High Elms estate. Field-paths well defined and route is easy to find, although mud may be a problem.

Length 4 miles (6.5km), 2 hours
Difficulty 1
Start The George, Farnborough village centre, on B2158 (just off A21, 4 miles SE of Bromley). Grid reference 443643
OS maps 1:50,000 177 or 187; 1:25,000 TQ 46/56 (Pathfinder 1192)
Refreshments Pubs and shop in Farnborough, pubs and tea-room (plus teas on Sundays Easter-Oct in village hall) in Downe, golf clubhouse at High Elms

WALK DIRECTIONS

(1) From central village triangle by The George, find lane signposted 'Leaves Green 2½'; this soon becomes a path between hedges. Keep forward on entering big field, proceed into storm-damaged woodland. (2) 100 yards later, turn left (signposted) and follow right edge of field to road.

Cross carefully to signposted footpath opposite and slightly to the right, go up strip in centre of field, at top turn right on path between hedges. (3) After 100 yards, turn left at path junction, and proceed to reach T-junction with lane. Cross lane to gate opposite (signposted Downe), and bear half left across field (keeping to left of modern house ahead), to leave by stile in far left-hand corner, then turn right along edge of next field, soon leaving by path to reach road. Turn left on road, into Downe village, and proceed to church [a] (4).

For detour to Down House bear right at church, along Luxted Road, then left after 100 yards on footpath signposted to Cudham. Soon enter field, follow left edge of it until signposted stile on left gives access into second field. Turn immediately right inside second field, and follow edge to enter third field by gate. Down House [b] is ahead: reach it by stile on to road. Return either the same way or (with Down House behind you) turn left along road.
To continue route from Downe church take road signposted to Cudham and Farnborough, turning left at end of churchyard (signposted High Elms and Farnborough). Avoid left turn after ¼ mile called Mill Lane, but 100 yards later take signposted stile on right into field. Proceed up to top of field, then go diagonally across second field, at far side of which turn right along edge (with woods on your left).

(5) At bottom corner of this field, enter woods: immediately bear sharp left uphill, then 20 yards later turn right at path junction. Follow this broad path through woods, ignoring side turns [c]: after ¼ mile keep ahead at cross-junction by horse barriers, then ⅓ mile later follow this path as it bends left and rises.

At top of rise, keep ahead at cross junction, and (6) fork left 150 yards later (by bench); edge of golf course is now visible through trees to the left. Shortly, reach path junction just before terraced gardens are reached: turn right to continue (or detour through the gardens), past old stable block (nature centre) and along surfaced driveway to reach lodge (7)

Turn left on road, then right after 100 yards on path signposted to Farnborough. Proceed through woods, ignoring minor side-turns, soon enter field by wooden barrier, and follow right edge until entering Farnborough churchyard. On other the side of churchyard, proceed to village centre.

ON THE ROUTE

[a] **Downe** The village centre has a Kentish character, with a pantile-hung pub and some fine houses, which include Petley's. The church

has a plaque on its tower commemorating Charles Darwin.
[b] **Down House** An unremarkable house architecturally, but notable as the home of Charles Darwin from 1842 until his death in 1882. The interior has been carefully preserved and is full of relics, including the

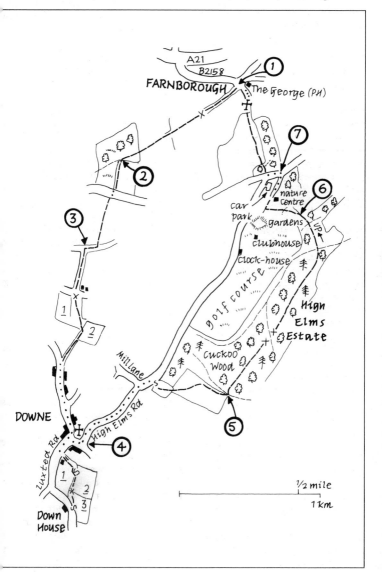

study where he wrote the seminal work on evolution *On the Origin of Species*. In the garden one can follow the 'Sand Walk' where Darwin did much of his creative thinking. (Open Mar-end Jan, Wed-Sun 1-6, bank hol Mons.)

[c] **High Elms** This was the home of Sir John Lubbock, a friend of Darwin and himself a distinguished naturalist. It was he who introduced the bill into Parliament which set up Bank Holidays. The house was destroyed by fire in the 1960s, but the grounds and golf course are maintained by the London Borough of Bromley. There are fine trees (some sadly damaged by the storms of recent years) and an exceptional flora with several varieties of orchid. The estate is designated as a Site of Special Scientific Interest.

The South Bank

The riverside path gives a superb
view of central London, first of
all looking across to Westminster,
then the City, and finally the rapidly
changing docklands – Europe's
largest development area. Tower
Bridge and a tour around the Tower
of London make a most apt
conclusion.

Length 3 miles (5km), 3 hours
Difficulty 1
Start Westminster Underground
station. Walk ends at Tower Hill
Underground station; return by
District or Circle line.

Refreshments Full range, including
some attractive waterside pubs

WALK DIRECTIONS

(1) [a] With station on left, head over
Westminster Bridge via traffic lights
or pedestrian subway. Turn left on
other side of bridge, on to riverside
esplanade [b] [c].

(2) Emerge on to road at
Blackfriars Bridge and proceed on
riverside path opposite [d]. (3) After
Anchor pub [e], route slightly leaves
river; take first left as road bends
right, now proceeding along Clink
Street [f]. Proceed to reach a boat
called *Kathleen and May*, where
route makes obligatory right turn
away from river towards Southwark
Cathedral [g]; enter churchyard by
gate and go around right-hand side of
cathedral, up steps and on to main
road just to left of railway bridge.
Turn left, towards river (crossing
road by traffic lights [h]), and just
before river, (4) turn right down
steps on to riverside walk.

(5) [i] Reach *HMS Belfast*: at time
of writing, it was not possible to
continue along river – instead, turn
right to reach main road (Tooley
Street), turn left along it, then
opposite King of Belgium Pub turn
left into gardens and head towards

Tower Bridge.

(6) [j] Before crossing Tower
Bridge, detour ahead along river path
(soon joining river by alley on left –
Maggie Blake's Cause), past Museum
of Design [k] to reach wharf. Return
to Tower Bridge, reaching it by the
West (far) side, up steps and over the
bridge. Turn left on other side on to
river esplanade via steps.

Make a circuit of the Tower of
London (after going through
gateway, turn right through gardens
above Tower moat) [l]. (7) After
passing beneath underpass, keep
right by World Trade Centre to enter
St Katherine's Dock complex (8) [m].
After visiting the docks, return
beneath underpass to remains of
postern gate where turn right for
Tower Hill Underground station.

ON THE ROUTE

[a] **Westminster** The apparently
medieval appearance of the Houses
of Parliament is misleading: it was
completed in 1860, to the design by
Charles Barry, aided by Pugin.
The South Bank Lion The imposing
lion at the eastern end of
Westminster Bridge was originally
the trademark of a brewery. For a
long time it stood outside Waterloo
Station, and was moved here only in
1966. It is made of 'Coade Stone',
an artificial stone which is
extremely durable and resistant to
weather; the secret of making it has
now been lost.
[b] **County Hall** Formerly the home
of the London County Council, and
of its successor the Greater London
Council. Ralph Knott won a
competition for its design: work
started in 1908 and the main
building was completed in 1922.
[c] **The South Bank Complex** This
owes its placing to the Festival of
Britain (1951) which was sited here
and which gave its name to the
Royal Festival Hall; it was joined by

the National Film Theatre in 1958, by the Hayward Gallery in 1968 and by the National Theatre in 1976. This rather piecemeal development has meant that the spaces between these important cultural centres are less inviting than they should be. A major scheme is now under discussion to provide sheltered walkways and a livelier ambience. Meanwhile the view across the river is a fine one. Beyond Waterloo Bridge, Somerset House can be seen on the opposite bank. Built in 1776 by Sir William Chambers, it now houses a repository for wills and part of King's College (the University of London), and the Courtauld art gallery.

[d] Just after an attractive range of buildings at Cardinal Cap Alley are the sites of the **Elizabethan Theatres of the South Bank**. In the 16th and early 17th centuries this district was a distinctly raffish area where great drama and deplorable brothels were

to be found in close company. The Rose theatre was built here by a partnership of Phillip Henslowe and Edward Alleyn, who was not only a celebrated actor but was in 1594 keeper of the bear pit which gave its name to the Bear Gardens. The Globe theatre was on the site now covered by the Courage Brewery, marked by a plaque on the wall in Park Street; a major project involving reconstruction of the original theatre is underway near Cardinal Cap Alley, and is due to be completed in 1992. Shakespeare had an interest in this theatre, and it saw the performance of many of his plays, until in July 1613 it burned down during a performance of *Henry VIII* when a cannon fired by the effects man set fire to the roof. The only casualty were the breeches of one spectator, which were doused with beer. **Bear Gardens Museum** (in Bear Gardens) is a Museum of Elizabethan theatre history, with

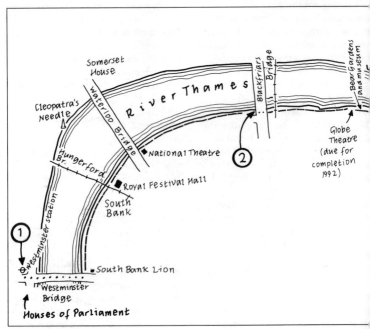

replicas of the theatres. (Open 8-5; Sun 2-5.30).

e] The Anchor This largely 18th-century pub has connections with Dr Johnson. The iron posts nearby defined the edge of the Bishop's Clink Street territory.

f] Clink Street The Bishops of Winchester had their town residence here from the 12th to 17th century. One gable wall of their palace remains, supporting the end of a warehouse. Winchester Square was the courtyard of the palace, whose park extended along Bankside to Blackfriars Road. Much of the property given over to taverns and brothels belonged to the Bishops: Shakespeare called the brothel-keepers "Winchester Geese". The 'clinks' which gave its name to the street was the prison where heretics were confined.

g] Southwark Cathedral 'A proper working cathedral', says Ian Nairn in *Nairn's London*, 'a large friendly lump of a building but no more. Just what a cockney cathedral ought to be.'

[h] London Bridge Site of the Roman's first wooden bridge across the Thames. The famous medieval bridge with its houses and shops stood 600 years until 1831. The stone bridge which replaced it was sold in 1973 to be erected in Arizona (allegedly the purchaser thought he was buying Tower Bridge until it was too late. Beyond the bridge, view across river to the **Monument** (where the great fire of 1666 started), to Billingsgate (the former fish market), and to the Custom House (a reminder that this is the Pool of London, once busy with shipping).

[i] HMS Belfast The last surviving warship of World War II.

[j] Tower Bridge Built 1886-94, it is about 800 feet long. In the heyday of the Port, the bridge was opened up to fifty times a day, now only two or three times a week. The high-level

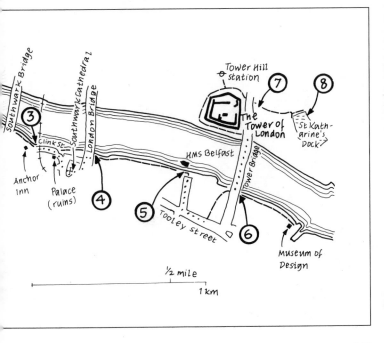

footbridge, long closed to visitors, is now open. Entrance from the Norman Tower, access by lift. The Museum explaining the structure and working of the bridge is by the south Tower exit. (Open daily Apr-end Oct, 10-5.45; Nov-end Mar, 10-4; bank hols)

[k] **Museum of Design** A museum on how consumer objects function and why they are designed as they are. (Open Tue-Sun and bank hol Mons, 11.30-6.30).

[l] **Tower of London** The wall following the river that passes Traitor's Gate, where alleged traitors were landed from the river. They included Thomas More, Anne Boleyn, Thomas Cromwell, Katherine Howard and the Earl of Essex and the Duke of Monmouth. 'Treason doth never prosper, what's the reason?/For if it prosper, none dare call it treason.'

[m] **St Katherine's Dock** Designed by Thomas Telford and closed in 1968, the dock has found a new use as a yacht haven with a Historic Ship collection. Opportunities here for rest and refreshment.

Blackheath and Greenwich

Elegant Georgian-Regency suburbs face the Heath; further on the walk drops through Greenwich Park, with central London and the revitalised docklands in view across the river. Greenwich, rich in nautical and architectural history, needs plenty of time to be explored in full.

Length 4 miles (6.5km), 4 hours
Difficulty 1–2
Start Blackheath rail station
Refreshments Full range in Blackheath and Greenwich; café in Greenwich Park

WALK DIRECTIONS

(1) With Blackheath station on your right, following main street uphill through Blackheath Village. At top of rise, fork left at mini roundabout, then take first left into Blackheath Park [a].

(2) Turn left into Norden Lane to reach the edge of the 'Heath' with the Paragon [b] to your left and the entrance to Morden College [c] to your right; keep right, alongside the houses that flank the right-hand side of St Germans Place [d]. Go past bollards and proceed (3) to cross busy A2 by traffic lights, and take road to left of filling station (Stratheden Road); take first left into Langton Way, and turn right along Angerstein Lane to emerge on to Heath.

Cross road and bear half left across this corner of the Heath; Greenwich Park is ahead and to the left. Emerge on to road by seven-foot width-restriction road sign (4). Just to left of this road sign, take gate into park [e]. Turn right along the edge of the park. Where park wall ends, Vanbrugh Castle [f] is to your right. Bear half left at this point along high ground through the park; just before reaching viewpoint by railing, head down to right end of National

Maritime Museum (the classical building with collonades at the N side of the park) [g].

(5) Emerge on to corner of road, take Park Row ahead (detouring as desired into museum grounds on left [h]). Cross main road (Romney Road) and take road opposite. (6) Just before the end, turn right in front of Trafalgar Tavern and keep close to river, soon past almshouses [i] and past Cutty Sark Inn to reach old harbour-master's office (7).

Return to Trafalgar Tavern, proceed along the river in front of Naval College to *Cutty Sark* (ship in dry dock) (8) [j], and go beyond it see *Gypsy Moth IV*. Return towards *Cutty Sark* but turn right in front of it, to pick up street past Gypsy Moth Pub on your left, heading towards St Alfege's church tower; join main street (Greenwich Church Street) and continue to the church [k], where cross the road and turn right on other side (still along the main street).

(9) Turn left in front of Ibis Hotel into Croom's Hill [l]. Take second right, into Gloucester Circus [m], exit far side, turn left into Royal Hill and turn left opposite Prince Albert Pub into Hyde Vale [n]. (10) Where houses end on left, take steps up on left. At top, cross over Chesterfield Gardens and bear half right towards the Ranger's House (the last house to your right across the road [o]). With Ranger's House behind you, turn right downhill to follow Croom Hill to the point where you left it for Gloucester Circus (11): here enter Greenwich Park by gate and make your way by any route to the Royal Observatory.

Keep to the left of the Observatory, and the 24-hour clock and meridian line [p], then pass Planetarium and either take the straight park road to the main park gates or (much more interesting)

⑫ just after café on left, head half left, passing just to right of bandstand and into gardens (with lake); proceed through the gardens to reach main gate.

Cross main road, walk along right-hand side of Duke Humphrey Road opposite, over busy A2 by traffic lights, and head over grass towards All Saints church [q] at edge of Blackheath Village ⑬. Pass around right-hand side of the church, then follow down (to right) into shopping area in village and proceed to reach Blackheath station.

ON THE ROUTE

[a] **Blackheath Park** 'The original leafy layout received another dimension . . . the exhilaration of new and old together when both are good.' (Ian Nairn in *Nairn's London*). St Michael's church (1830) has a fanciful twin spire nicknamed 'The Needle of Kent'.

[b] **The Paragon** A crescent, overlooking Blackheath, built 1794-1807 to the design of Michael Searles, a local architect/surveyor. Damaged by bombing but very carefully repaired, it has been described as 'The best of all London's surviving 18th-century schemes.' (Ian Nairn).

[c] **Morden College** (1695) (on the right) These almshouses, for 'decayed Turkey merchants', were designed by Wren. Statues above the entrance porch represent the founder and his wife. (Open by appointment only, but it is usually possible to look at the grounds.)

[d] **The Heath** Blackheath is now a bland, largely treeless expanse of grass devoted to kite-flying and dog-walking. In earlier centuries it was a place of much turbulent activity: the Roman construction of Watling Street, the gathering of Wat Tyler's rebels in 1381 prior to their march on London, and of Jack Cade's rebels

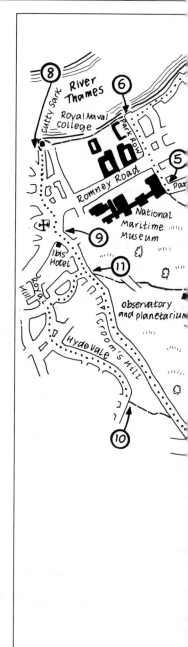

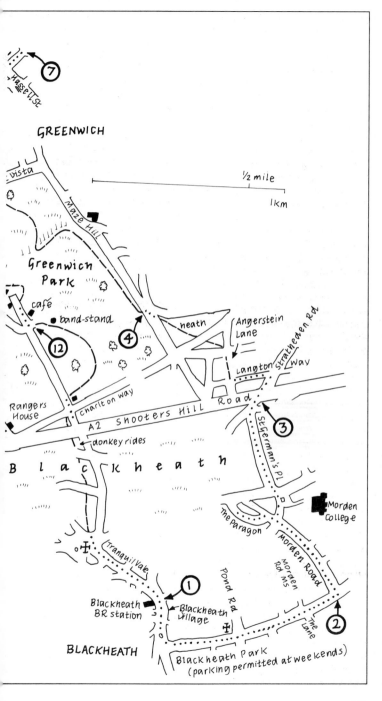

Hassell St.

⑦

GREENWICH

Vista

Maze Hill

Greenwich Park

café

band-stand

⑫

④

heath

Angerstein Lane

Langton Way

Stratheden Rd.

charlton way

Rangers House

A2 Shooters Hill Road

③

St. Germans Pl.

donkey rides

③

Black heath

Morden College

The Paragon

Morden Road

Morden Rd. Ms.

Tranquil Vale

Pond Rd

Blackheath BR station

①

Blackheath Village

②

The Lane

BLACKHEATH

Blackheath Park
(parking permitted at weekends)

½ mile

1 km

in 1450. Later it was the haunt of footpads and highwaymen. The first English golf links were established here in 1608; the Royal Blackheath golf club continued to play here until 1932.

[e] **Greenwich Park** The oldest of London's ten royal parks. It was formerly the grounds of Greenwich Palace, laid out by Le Notre in the 17th century. Fine panorama over Greenwich, the Thames, the Docklands developments on the Isle of Dogs, and Central London.

[f] **Vanbrugh Castle** This mock castle (1718-26) was designed by Sir John Vanbrugh, architect and dramatist, for his own use. Although untrained as an architect he also designed Castle Howard in Yorkshire and Blenheim Palace in Oxfordshire. In the early 19th century it became a school: once for the daughters of gentlemen, while in the 20th century it has been an orphanage and school for the sons of RAF officers. It is now converted into private houses.

[g] **The Queen's House and National Maritime Museum** The Queen's House was designed by Inigo Jones (1616) for Anne of Denmark, wife of James I. She died before it was finished, and it was later completed by Charles I (1637) for his queen, Henrietta Maria, to whom it was 'My house of delights'. It was England's first truly classically-proportioned building and is regarded as one of the most important buildings in our architectural history.

The National Maritime Museum (open 10-5 winter, 10-6 summer), the Queen's House with its centre-piece, occupies what is arguably the most beautiful museum complex in Britain. The collection, devoted to the whole breadth of the maritime history of Britain, is a very large one, not capable of being seen thoroughly

in a short visit, but the rooms in the Queen's House, with its famous Tulip Stair are well worth seeing even if there is no time to venture farther.

[h] **Royal Naval College** Originally a hospital for aged and disabled seamen, designed by Wren and completed in 1705. The Painted Hall (ceiling by Thornhill) and the chapel are open to the public (2.30-5 exc Thur); since 1873, the college for naval officers has been here.

[i] **Trinity Hospital** Almshouse founded 1613 but much altered in the 19th century. Fine Flemish glass in the chapel (appointment needed to view). The Cutty Sark Tavern dates from 1804 and has a fine original bow window.

[j] **Cutty Sark** (open 10-5 in winter, 10-6 in summer) This is the last surviving clipper ship, in service 1869-1922, dry-docked here since 1954. Just beyond it is **Gipsy Moth IV** (open 10-6; 12-6 Sun; closes 5 in winter). The ketch which Sir Francis Chichester sailed round the world single-handed in 1966-67, taking 226 days.

[k] **St Alfege's church** designed by Nicholas Hawksmoor 1711-14, on the site of an earlier church commemorating Archbishop Alfege, martyred in 1012 by the Danes. The fabric was much damaged by bombing, which destroyed fine carvings by Grinling Gibbons, but has been subsequently restored. Henry VIII was baptised here, and Thomas Tallis, Elizabethan organist and composer, is buried here. (His epitaph is worth seeking out if the church is open.)

[l] **Croom's Hill** An ancient road, once the most fashionable street in Greenwich. 'There are not many streets near London which give so good and sustained an air of the well-to-do private house from the 17th century to the early 19th

entury.' (Bridget Cherry in
'evsner's *Buildings of England*
eries.)

m] Gloucester Circus Further
>lanning by Michael Searles (1791),
vith 19th-century additions and
ebuilding after bombing.

n] Hyde Vale Hereabouts was the
Blackheath Cavern, a large cavern
liscovered in 1780, cut in the solid
halk to a depth of 160 feet. Balls
vere held here in the mid-19th
entury. In 1938 the cavern was re-
ntered to assess its possible use as
n air-raid shelter, but the project
vas dropped. In 1946 the entrance
vas finally sealed.

o] Ranger's House (open free of
harge 10-6 summer, 10-4 winter).
This fine house of 1699 was
>riginally the home of Vice-Admiral
rancis Hosier. Subsequently it
>assed to the Stanhope family and
vas occupied by Philip Stanhope,
Earl of Chesterfield, who was
elebrated for his earnest letters of
dvice to his son, and whose name
vas given to nearby Chesterfield
Walk. He was a keen gardener who
;rew pineapples, melons and other
ropical fruits, and was a
:onnoisseur of the arts, adding a
>icture gallery. The house contains
he Suffolk Collection of paintings
nd the Dolmetsch Collection of
nusical instruments.

[p] Royal Observatory The old
observatory was designed by Wren
for Flamsteed (1675-76). The
meridian line is marked nearby with
a brass strip, making it possible to
straddle the eastern and western
hemispheres. On the north-east
current is the **time ball**, dropped at
1pm each day to enable ships on the
river to set their chronometers in
the days before radio. The
observatory has now moved from
London because the glare of lights
prevents observation, but the
buildings are open (end Mar-late
Oct, 10-6 Mon-Sat, 12-6 Sun; late
Oct-end Mar, 10-5 Mon-Sat, 2-5 Sun)
and the Planetarium has
demonstrations. From near the
statue of General Wolfe, a fine
panorama of the historic buildings of
Greenwich, with the Thames and
the Isle of Dogs beyond.

[q] To the right of the church was
'Washerwomen's Bottom', an old
gravel pit where these women had
the right to hang out the village
washing, providing they avoided
Sundays, Christmas Day and Good
Friday, and cleared everything away
by one o'clock on Saturday and five
on other days. If it started to rain a
bell was rung. The pit, like others on
the Heath, was filled with bomb
rubble during the war.

Barnes Common and Chiswick

The pond and woods of Barnes Common introduce the mostly rural theme of this walk in the south-west suburbs, soon following the Thames and taking in delightful riverside streets at Chiswick before reaching Chiswick House, London's finest Palladian villa.

Length 4½ miles (7km), 3 hours
Difficulty 1
Start Pond at Barnes Green; alternatively start near Putney Bridge (parking rather easier there)
Refreshments Pubs and shops in Barnes; pubs by river in Chiswick

WALK DIRECTIONS

(1) [a] At pond with Sun Inn on left, go along Church Road. At end of pond turn right to walk along its east side, then go forward with Barnes Green on your right and residential road on left to reach footbridge. (2) Turn left on other side, on tarmacked path with lamp-post. After 200 yards fork left on to another tarmacked path (right fork goes to main road). Follow this, ignoring left fork after 60 yards, to reach main road. Cross to minor road opposite signed to bottle and can banks, in front of toilets and Rocks Lane recreation ground.

Where road ends, go forward on surfaced path, now along avenue of trees with small cemetery on left; (3) 100 yards later enter open grass area and immediately turn left on to grassy path to reach big crossing of paths after 100 yards: go forward, soon entering large flat expanse of grass with hospital buildings ahead.

Keep to left of hospital to find footbridge over Beverley Brook; turn right on other side (playing fields now on left) and follow to reach river (4) [b] where route continues to left. (5) Cross Hammersmith Bridge and turn left on other side along river (you can cross road by riverside path which goes under bridge) and follow riverside closely [c] until Church Street by Chiswick parish church (mostly directly along waterfront though you leave the river briefly at two points).

(6) Keep right as road bends right into Church Street (you can detour left into churchyard [d]) and immediately after church [e], turn left along Powell's Walk, keeping to right of cemetery, then between walls to reach main road. Turn left and cross at main road at pelican crossing [f].

Turn left then (7) immediately right into Chiswick Park and House [g]. Turn left inside park; the next gate on your left is your exit (level with villa away to right); explore park as you wish. Leave Park, cross main road carefully, take Grantham Road opposite and half left.

(8) At end, take road opposite, between brick pillars (private cul-de-sac but open to cyclists and pedestrians). At end of road, continue beyond bollards on path leading to left to river. Follow riverside to Barnes Bridge (9) which cross and go along The Terrace [h] with river on your left. Turn right by Waterman's Arms along High Street to reach Barnes Pond.

ON THE ROUTE

[a] **Barnes** The green and its pond is the original village centre, where the stocks stood until 1835; around it is a mixture of suburb and old village, notable being the 17th-century Sun Inn, timber-framed Essex Lodge and early-18th-century Nos. 66 and 68 Station Road. Church Road to the left leads past St Mary church (often locked), dating from the 12th century, with an interesting interior despite recent fire damage.

[b] **Putney Bridge** to the right is the

tart of the University Boat Race; pposite and to the right are the rounds of 16th-century **Fulham** alace, residence for 1,000 years of he Bishops of London (now nunicipally owned). Proceeding owards Chiswick the towpath asses a **memorial**, exactly one mile om Putney Bridge, to Steve airbairn, founder of the Head of the iver Race.

] **Lower Mall** Forming part of a harming riverside promenade, this roup of Georgian houses is part-ndered, part-'London Stock' brick, ith much variation in detail anlights, balconies and so on). Nos. l and 12, built in the 17th century fishermen's cottages, are the dest. After passing Furnival ardens is **The Dove** tavern, once a offee house. It claims numerous storical connections. James hompson supposedly wrote the ords for *Rule Britannia* upstairs, nest Hemingway and Graham reene were customers, and .P.Herbert used the pub as the odel for 'The Pigeons' in *The ater Gypsies*. Prince Augustus ederick, son of George III, was so nd of the view that he bought just the building as a smoking-box for anning his anti-slave trade mpaign. The bar on the right as u enter is reputedly London's hallest. Into **Upper Mall**, No. 26 s a plaque to poet and novelist eorge MacDonald, and was also me of William Morris, designer d champion of the Arts and Crafts ovement; engraving for Morris and s Kelmscott Press was carried out Emery Walker in Sussex House posite The Dove. Above the ach-house door, a plaque mmemorates the first electric ple (laid 1816). By the Black Lion, mmersmith Terrace is entered, ing sight of the river temporarily; No. 12. lived A.P. Herbert, lawyer

and author of *Misleading Cases*, who ran a passionate (but unsuccessful) campaign for the commercial use of the Thames. Continue along **Chiswick Mall** where riverside gardens belonging to the houses form a strip on the left-hand side, looking onto the island Chiswick Eyot, with its population of ducks and swans. Regency **Cedar House**, **Strawberry House** (1700) and 17th-century **Walpole House** (once the residence of Barbara Villiers, one of Charles II's mistresses, shunned by all when by the time of her death here in 1708), while **Eynham House** with its almost comically narrow windows was formerly part of Bedford House. At **Greenash** lived the parents of John Thorneycroft, who used the river to carry out underwater weaponry experiments that resulted in his invention of the torpedo.

[d] **Church of St Nicholas** is heavily restored, but the churchyard is famous for the grave of satirical artist William Hogarth, with epitaph by David Garrick (much criticised by Dr Johnson); the tomb, surrounded by railings, is easily located.

[e] **The Old Burlington** The most striking of several attractive houses ranged informally around in Church Street, this was once the Burlington tavern and has 15th century origins.

[f] **Hogarth House** (open 11-6, 2-6 Sun; closes at 4 and all day Tue, Oct-Mar; free) *Turn right on other side of the crossing over the main road, then immediately left into Paxton Road, turn right at end into Sutherland Road, then right at main road; the house is soon reached, on right.* This was Hogarth's summer country house (now hard to imagine, with the traffic thundering past) from 1749 to 1764. Hogarth used to make visits to the Foundling Hospital to sketch children: he took

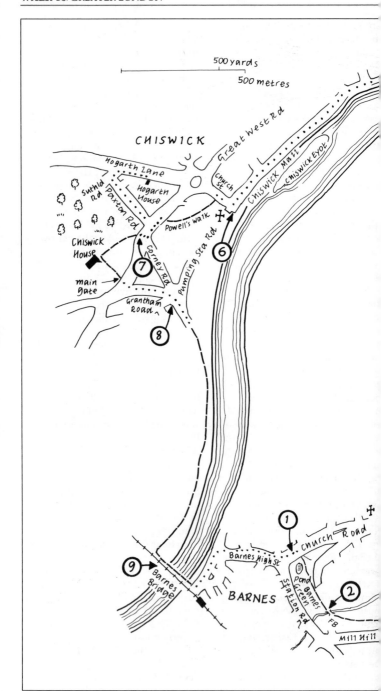

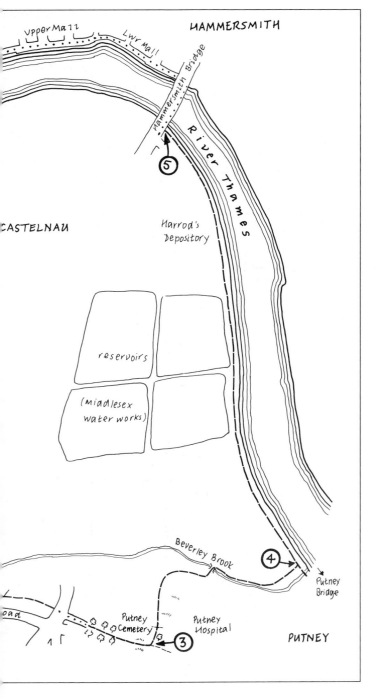

Upper Mall

Lwr Mall

HAMMERSMITH

Hammersmith Bridge

River Thames

CASTELNAU

Harrod's
Depository

reservoirs

(middlesex
water works)

Beverley Brook

Putney
Bridge

oad

Putney
Cemetery

Putney
Hospital

PUTNEY

315

with him mulberry tarts that his wife made – the tree that supplied the fruit is still here. Inside the walls are covered with his engravings, including *The Election* and *Marriage à la Mode*.

[g] **Chiswick House** (English Heritage, open 10-6; closes 4 Oct-Easter; grounds free, fee for house). Approached through lovely grounds, landscaped by Richard Boyle (the third Earl of Burlington) and William Kent in the naturalistic style that was to become the essence of English landscape gardening; the house was built more as an object of admiration than a residence. This immaculately proportioned design of 1727-29 by Burlington was modelled on Palladio's Villa Capra near Vicenza, which also had a square plan around a central dome, but also draws from elsewhere – the portico columns, for example, are copied from Palladio's drawing of the Roman Temple of Castor and Pollux in Naples, and the dome itself is derived from that on the Pantheon Rome. The interiors by Kent incorporate some designs of Inigo Jones. Burlington had it built more as an architectural essay than a residence, using it mainly for parties and as a library; it became a leading social venue. The grounds include an Inigo Jones arch, an ornamental 'River', a temple and obelisk.

[h] **The Terrace** Nos. 13 and 14 are early 18th century, No. 12 flamboyantly Regency; No. 10 has a plaque to composer Gustav Holst.

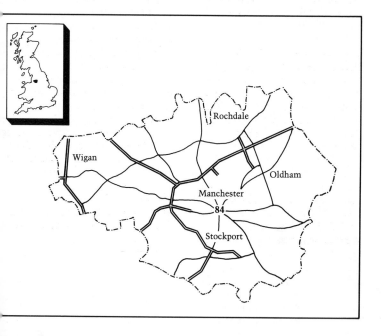

4 Manchester

Holiday Which? Good Walks Guide

Manchester

The city mushroomed in the 19th century from a modest town to a major industrial centre, where fortunes were made in the cotton trade. Many of the landmarks survive from this era. Elsewhere there are some rather uninspiring 20th-century city views, but it's possible to avoid nearly all of them on this walk which also takes in the revamped Castlefield area and an intriguing section along the Rochdale Canal.

Length 2 miles (3km), 3 hours
Difficulty 1
Start Albert Square (by town hall)
Refreshments Plenty

WALK DIRECTIONS

① [**a**] From Albert Square, by Albert Memorial and with town hall on your right, leave square by left-hand corner, along Cross Street (by Nationwide Anglia building) [**b**], which later becomes Corporation Street [**c**]. **②** Where cathedral is visible to left, go into Cathedral Street, to cathedral [**d**][**e**].

Return to Corporation Street, turn right into Market Street, **③** left into Exchange Street (pedestrianised) at corner of Royal Exchange [**f**][**g**]. Pass just to right of St Ann's church [**h**]; just behind it, turn right into small arcade called St Ann's Passage (The Old Exchange), and turn right along King Street [**i**].

④ At end of precinct area, turn left into Deansgate [**j**][**k**]. **⑤** Turn right into St John Street [**l**]; at end, take gates ahead into gardens [**m**], then left along Lower Byrom Street, past Museum of Science and Industry [**n**]. **⑥** Turn left along Liverpool Road, and then right by the White Lion pub; head towards re-created Roman Fort [**o**], through small park, under fort arches. Turn right then immediately left

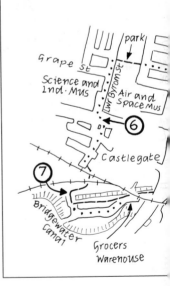

(signposted to Grocers Warehouse) before castellated brick wall; follow the road under railway bridges to canal basin **⑦** [**p**], where turn left.

70 yards later, cross Rochdale Canal, where left along canal is

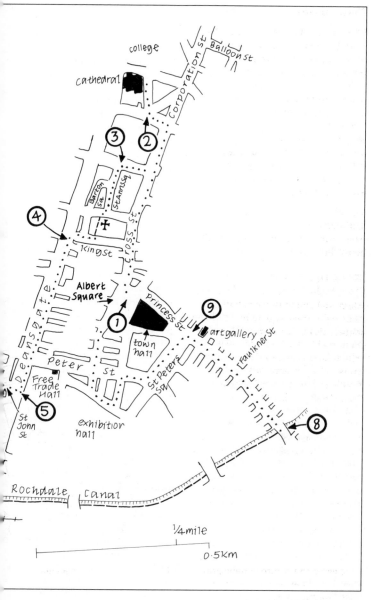

ntinuation, but first continue
rward to see Grocers Warehouse
head and round to the left - marked
reinstated metal water-wheel).
turn to Rochdale Canal and
low towpath (this goes under

tunnel), ignore steps on right to road
level just after, but continue under
two more road bridges.

(8) Go up steps into Princess
Street just after second bridge (right
is Central House, left is tall

chimney), and turn right along it [q][r]. ⑨ By art gallery [s], turn left into Mosley Street (which forms one side of St Peter's Square).

Leave square in diagonally opposite corner, beyond library (circular building with columns). Turn right into Peter Street, detour left into Mount Street to see exhibition complex [t], then return along Mount Street [u], over Peter Street and into Albert Square.

ON THE ROUTE
[a] **Town Hall** (1877) Monumental in scale, faced with carboniferous sandstone extracted from quarries near Bradford, and possessing a 286ft clock tower, Alfred Waterhouse's vast gothic building occupies a triangular site on the E side of Albert Square, one of the rare examples of 19th-century town planning in the city. The original town hall in King Street was too small for Manchester as it became a major industrial city in the 1860s, and an architectural competition was held for a new building; Waterhouse's design was selected from twelve schemes. Regular tours (Mon to Fri, at 10 and 2.30) take one round the spectacular interior of the hall, with its collection of sculptures, staircases, state rooms, council chamber and Great Hall — the latter housing a series of murals by Ford Madox Brown, showing the history of Manchester. In the centre of Albert Square, Thomas Worthington's **Albert Memorial** (1861), with its gothic canopy has a marked similarity to the more famous one in Kensington, London, which it predates.
[b] In King Street (on right), the imposing **TSB Building**, begun 1845, formerly premises of the Bank of England.
[c] Arndale Centre (on right) attracts a million shoppers every week and is Europe's largest covered shopping centre.
[d] **Manchester Cathedral** Mainly 15th-century, with the broadest medieval nave in England. It acquired cathedral status in 1847, after which embellishments were added giving it a predominantly 19th-century character. The site is the heart of pre-industrial Manchester (a town of 5,000 in 1650), which was a centre for finishing coarse woollen cloth.
[e] **Chetham's School of Music** (opposite the cathedral, across Fennel Street). Originally a manor house for the Barons of Manchester it was rebuilt by Thomas de la War in the 1400s as a college to what is now the cathedral (then the collegiate church). In 1653 it was purchased with money from a bequest of Humphrey Chetham and became a charitable residential school for boys. In the former priests' dormitories, the public **library** is the oldest such establishment in Europe. To the right (as seen from the cathedral) is the 1870 former building of **Manchester Grammar School**, founded by the Bishop of Exeter in 1515, and which moved out to the suburb of Rusholme in 1931. Further to the right (off route) and off Corporation Street, Balloon Street was the site of the world's first manned balloon flight in 1785 when James Sadler took to the air.
[f] In Shambles Square, the 16th-century **Old Wellington Inn**, another survival from the old town, was formerly the home of John Byrom (1692-1763), inventor of phonetic shorthand and poet; he composed the words for the hymn *Christians Awake*, here, as a Christmas present for his daughter.
[g] Royal Exchange (main entrance on left) In its day, the largest hall for business transactions in the world,

here up to 11,000 representatives
the textile industry and its
fshoots (including woollens,
ipping, iron and steel, and
emicals) took part in frenzied
enes of buying and selling twice a
eek. Its heavy classical marble
terior topped by glass domes is
w the foyer for a 740-seat theatre
hose lunar-module appearance
ovides an astonishing contrast.
arton Square (set back, on right) is
outstanding example of a
ictorian shopping arcade in the
rystal Palace style, a creation in
rved glass and ornate ironwork.
] **St Ann's Square** Completed by
e 1720s, this square and Exchange
reet (1777) was the first attempt at
wn planning in Manchester; trees
ere planted in an effort to emulate
e Georgian townscapes of
shionable London and Bath. St
nn's Church was the first church
be built in the city after the
llegiate church (now the
thedral). Its rectangular plan,
mplicity of design, round-headed
indows and semi-circular
nctuary are typical of the
enaissance style; the fine altar
ble was given by the founder,
dy Bland.

On left as you enter King Street,
e **National Westminster Bank** was
iginally a town house, built
1736.

On right at corner with Wood
reet, the **John Rylands University
ibrary of Manchester** (founded 1890
v the wife of a merchant who was
voted to theology) has a decorative
ndstone exterior of spectacular
chness; inside, the Althorp Library
s several volumes printed by
axton, and there are a number of
anuscripts and other early printed
orks. A research library since 1973,
is open to the public 10-5.30, Mon
Fri, 10-1 Sat.

On left, after corner with Peter

Street, the red and yellow brickwork
of the old **Great Northern Railway
depot** (1885) can be seen.

[l] **St John Street**, a Mancunian
Harley Street, is the city's most
complete Georgian street, with
Nos.8-22 particularly fine. Around
the corner into **Byrom Street**,
Nos.25-31 have delightful Gothic
porches.

[m] **St John's Gardens** The old
churchyard of St John's Church,
built 1769 by Thomas Byrom and
demolished in 1931; one tombstone
still stands in situ by a flower-bed.

[n] **Museum of Science and Industry**
(open all year, daily 10-5, except
Christmas). The world's oldest
railway station (Liverpool Road)
provided the site, and although the
station has closed the buildings have
now been restored as part of the
railway exhibits. It also includes the
world's largest collection of working
stationary steam engines and,
outside, two columns from
Ferranti's voltage generating station,
the world's first in 1889; vintage
vehicles, electricity, the story of
flight, a Victorian sewer and a
science centre are also on offer.

[o] **The Roman Fort** A mock-up of
the stone fort built in AD200 above
the confluence of the rivers Medlock
and Irwell. A wooden stockade built
by Agricola in AD79 had been
replaced in AD160 to house a unit of
1,000 soldiers. The Roman
settlement of Vicus grew up nearby,
and had a population of 2,000; after
the Romans left, the town came to
be known as Alport ('old port').
Although the fort fell into disrepair
after AD410, remains of the
structure survived until the building
of the railway.

[p] **Canal Basin** The meeting of the
Bridgewater and Rochdale Canals.
The Bridgewater Canal, constructed
for transporting coal from the Duke
of Bridgewater's mines at Worsley to

supply industrial Manchester, became the major waterway route of the early 19th century, its absence of locks and its great width making transportation easy. Whereas the coming of the railways killed off the canals financially, this one continued to be used commercially until 1974. Above are massive **railway viaducts** of the Manchester to Liverpool railway, which opened in 1830; the castellations are an acknowledgement to the Roman Fort, whose vestiges the building of the railway swept away. Coal was brought in at **Grocers Warehouse** (demolished in 1940 but partly reconstructed), hauled up by James Brindley's (reinstated) waterwheel. The Rochdale Canal was the first trans-Pennine waterway when constructed in 1804, leading to the expansion of a number of textile towns. It is no longer navigable for its entire length (restoration is underway), but this section carries leisure craft. As the towpath is followed, on left a **lock-keeper's cottage** is angled to give a view of the whole section of canal from one window; canal tolls were originally collected here. Further on, the gracefully arched cast-iron **railway bridge**, formerly of the Manchester South Junction and Altrincham Railway, is overhead. Beyond the Deansgate Tunnel (a survival of the time when most of the canal was underground) another lock-keeper's cottage stands ruined on the opposite bank. Straight ahead is the 220ft clock tower and green dome of the **Refuge Assurance Building**, designed 1891 by Alfred Waterhouse, with extension by his son, Paul.

[q] **Chinatown** On right, in Faulkner Street, a Chinese imperial arch (specially made in China) forms a flamboyant entrance to this ethnic quarter, where there are a number o Chinese shops and small businesse The dancing dragon at the Chinese New Year festivities here is a colourful event.

[r] **Atheneum**, on right, designed by Charles Barry (architect of the Houses of Parliament) in 1837, was the introduction of the Italian *palazzo* style to Manchester. Up to 1938 the building functioned as a non-political club, celebrated for literary soirées and readings.

[s] **City Art Gallery**, on right at the corner with Mosley Street, also by Barry (1824), but in Greek revival style, has a major collection of British and European art, and a reconstruction of L.S. Lowry's Lancashire home and studio.

[t] **G-Mex Centre** The exhibition centre is housed in the former Central Station, which functioned 1880-1969, and whose train shed ha a 210ft single span, similar in scale to St Pancras station in London.

[u] As you re-enter Peter Street, to the left is the classical **Theatre Royal** (1845), now a sad shadow of its former self and used as a bingo hall. Close by is the **Free Trade Hal** (rebuilt 1856), whose previous building was the headquarters of th Anti-Corn Law movement (lasting from 1830 until the repeal of the corn laws in 1846). It has a magnificent Renaissance facade wi stone carving including shields of Lancashire towns which supported the movement, plus figures representing agriculture, the arts, commerce, free trade and manufacturing.

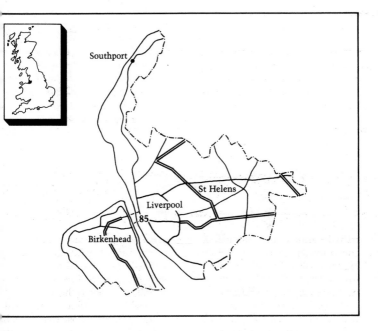

Liverpool

Liverpool

One of the great Victorian cities, which grew rich as an international port but has since hit harder times. Its centre retains much of its original character, while new life has been injected into the docks and Mersey water-front. There are more first-class (and free) museums than anyone could manage to visit in a day.

Length 3 miles (5km), 3 hours
Difficulty 1
Start Lime Street BR station
Refreshments Full range

WALK DIRECTIONS

① From station cross Lime Street to St George's Hall (large colonnaded building on corner of St George's Place) [a]. Turn right along Lime Street, heading towards Wellington Column and passing horseback statues of Prince Albert and Queen Victoria. Turn left in front of Museum of Labour History, past Walker Art Gallery and library [b].

② At bottom, cross main road by pelican crossing and take Manchester Street Kingsway (to left of road tunnel), passing statues to George V and Queen Mary, then left into Dale Street [c]. **③** Beyond town hall [d], continue forward (Water Street). Cross A561 and go forward, passing to left of Royal Liver Building (optional detour right to Large Objects Collection) [e].

④ Turn left by ferry terminals, along riverside walkway, passing through Maritime Museum and Albert Dock [f]. **⑤** Exit Albert Dock on left-hand side, at pumphouse chimney [g], where take road ahead, away from river. Cross main road to go into Canning Place (with Merseyside Police Headquarters on your right) [h]; ignore right turn signposted Birkenhead.

⑥ After traffic lights, keep forward into Hanover Street. Just before Neptune Theatre, detour left into School Lane to see Bluecoat Chambers [i]. Continue along Hanover Street, turn right at traffic lights into Bold Street (pedestrianised) towards tower of St Lukes [j], where keep forward [k], passing to left of church along Leece Street. **⑦** Take Rodney Street (second road on right) [l]. In front of Anglican cathedral [m], turn left up Upper Duke Street, **⑧** left along Hope Street [n]. **⑨** In front of Metropolitan (RC) cathedral [o], turn left down Mount Pleasant [p]. At bottom, pass Britannia Adelphi Hotel on your right [q], continue into Lime Street.

ON THE ROUTE

[a] **St George's Hall** One of the greatest examples of the 19th-century Classical revival style, designed by Harvey Lonsdale Elmes and completed after his death, in 1854. Corinthian columns encompass the outside; the Great Hall inside has a fine floor made of Minton tiles. Built as assize courts, but the future use of the hall is uncertain at time of writing.

[b] A parade of civic pride, comprising the **Wellington Column**, the **Museum of Labour History**, in the former County Sessions building (working-class life in Merseyside; open 10-5 Mon-Sat, 2-5 Sun); the **Walker Art Gallery** (huge European collection including early Italian and Flemish paintings, Pre-Raphaelite works, modern art, sculpture; open 10-5, 2-5 Sun); the circular **Picton Reading Room** (1877); and the **Liverpool Museum and Planetarium** (worldwide collections, science, natural history; open 10-5, 2-5 Sun). On left, **St John's Garden** has statuary, including Liberal Prime Minister Gladstone and a Boer War memorial.

[c] **Dale Street** Runs through the heart of the grandest part of Victorian Liverpool, showing the city's great wealth at that time. **Municipal Buildings** (1883), on left at corner of Sir Thomas Street, has an Italianate tower and lamps adorned by griffin figures. The **Prudential Insurance Building**, 1886, is a design by Alfred Waterhouse in red brick and terracotta; the tower was designed by his son Paul. On left at the corner of North John Street is **Royal Insurance Building** (1903) in white stone, with a golden dome, the earliest steel-framed building in Britain.

[d] On right, the **Town Hall**, built 1860-66 in French Renaissance style.

[e] **The Large Objects Collection** (open 10-5 daily) displays vehicles of all types, industrial and scientific artefacts, a blacksmith's, a Blue Streak rocket and much more. Ahead, the **Royal Liver Building**, a bold ten-storey design (a very early architectural use of a reinforced concrete frame, with granite facing) of 1911 by W. Aubrey Thomas, for the Royal Liver Friendly Society, has become a major landmark of Liverpool and the Mersey; the Liver birds perch high up on the towers. Adjacent is the **Cunard Building** (1913-17), another indicator of the prosperity that international shipping brought to the city. From Pierhead ferries cross the Mersey to Birkenhead, a trip worth making for excellent views of Liverpool. **The Merseyside Maritime Museum** (open daily 10.30-5.30; last admission 4.30) is housed in a restored docks complex surrounding the Canning Half-Tide Basin, and includes Harbourmaster's house, pilotage building, boat hall, exhibitions on shipbuilding and European emigrants.

Albert Dock This imaginative restoration in 1988 has rejuvenated the Mersey river-front; the docks opened in 1846 but had fallen into disuse. Now it bustles with shoppers, tourists and buskers drawn to the arcaded waterside piazza, restaurants, and shops. The northern branch of the **Tate Gallery** (open 10-5.50 Mon-Sat, 2-5.50 Sun) is devoted to modern art exhibitions.

[g] Outside the Atlantic Pavilion is a rare **Liverpool 'special' post-box**, painted gold and blue and topped with a crown; cast by Cochrane and Co. in 1863, moved here in 1987 and the only one of its kind still in use.

[h] View ahead of the **Anglican cathedral**.

[i] **Bluecoat Chambers** Built 1719 as a Bluecoat School, now an arts centre; has a cupola and delightful cobbled courtyard.

[j] On the left, the **Lyceum** (1799-1803), by Thomas Harrison in Greek Revival style, originally housed the Liverpool Library, a subscription library for gentlemen and the first of its kind in England. **St Luke's church** (1831), at the top of the street, was bombed in 1941 but its ruin has been preserved.

[k] Down to the right is the edge of **Chinatown**.

[l] **Rodney Street** The best Georgian street in the city takes its name from Admiral George Rodney, who led British victories against the French. It was laid out in the 1780s and completed over the next 40 years; all plum-red brick, with some good wrought-iron balustrades. The church was built as St Andrew's Presbyterian Church of Scotland in 1824 and has an unusual classical facade.

[m] **Anglican cathedral** The largest of its denomination in the world, standing on a rise above the Mersey, its huge tower visible from North Wales. Started in 1906 but only completed in 1980, to 21-year old Giles Gilbert Scott's design.

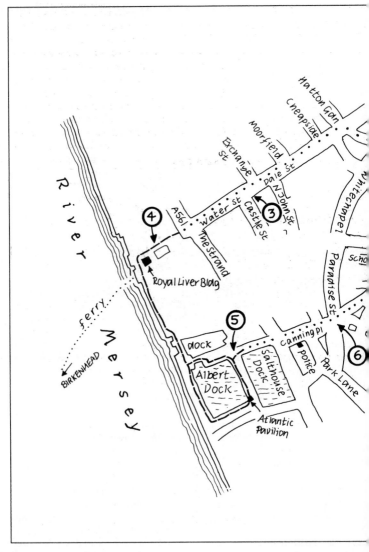

[n] **Hope Street** Mostly Georgian terraces. On left half way along, the **Philharmonic Hotel**, built 1898-1900, has art nouveau gates and an extravagant interior.

[o] **Metropolitan Cathedral (Roman Catholic)** A total contrast to the Anglican cathedral at the other end of Hope Street, Frederick Gibberd's design was consecrated in 1967 and has a circular plan with vividly coloured glass from the lantern casting light effects on to a white altar. Look for the 'Rolling Stone', monolithic circular stone door into the Archbishops' Chapel. The crypt is the only extant part of the original plan by Edwin Lutyens for a much larger cathedral (whose dome would have been larger than St Peter's,

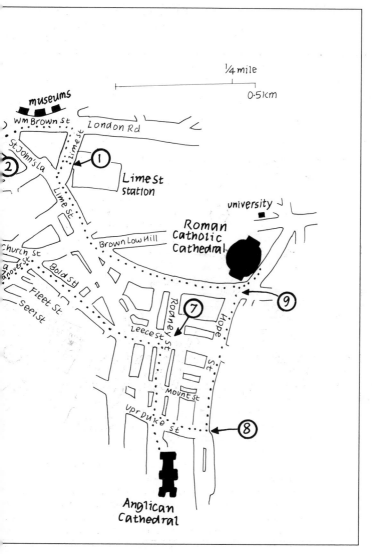

me). Straight ahead, beyond the
thedral is the pointed clock tower
the **Victoria Building, Liverpool
niversity**, designed by Alfred
aterhouse 1892 in brick and
racotta.

More fine Georgian houses in
ount Pleasant. On right, the
mer **Wellington Rooms** (now the
sh Centre) of 1816, built as

subscription assembly rooms
providing entertainment for
prosperous residents.
[q] The **Adelphi Hotel**, completed
1914 but later altered, was built at
the height of Liverpool's days as a
passenger port. Opposite, **John Lewis**
displays a huge, stone male nude at
the fore of a ship, and a relief panel,
both by Epstein.

NORFOLK

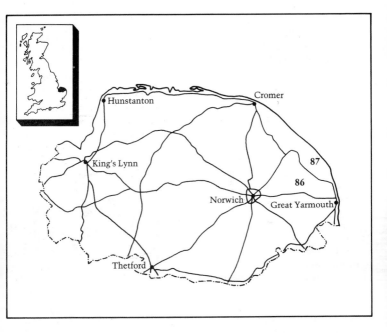

86 River Bure and Upton Fen
87 Around Horsey

Holiday Which? Good Walks Guide

116 Gore Point and Thornham   117 Sheringham and Cromer
118 Holkham Hall and Burnham Overy Staithe

River Bure and Upton Fen

A busy boating area of the Broads contrasts with the memorable empty expanses of drained fens, with windmills dominating the landscape for miles around. South Walsham Broad and the mysterious woodlands of Upton Fen are glimpsed in the final section. Easy route-finding on level paths and tracks.

Length 7 miles (11km), 3 hours
Difficulty 1-2
Start White Horse Inn, Upton; N of Acle and E of Norwich off B1140; roadside parking in village. Follow Chapel Road from post office in village centre to reach pub. Grid reference 397127
OS maps 1:50,000 134; 1:25,000 TG 21/31 and TG 41/51 (Pathfinder 883 and 884)
Refreshments Pub and shop at Upton; shop at South Walsham Broad

WALK DIRECTIONS

(1) Take Boat Dyke Road opposite White Horse Inn. Turn left at first crossroads (signposted Dyke) at the Green, and keep right at next junction (left is Back Lane).
(2) Immediately before car park on left (where road is about to end), turn left to reach Upton Dyke, a waterway. Take path on its left bank, which leads out to turn left at confluence with River Bure.

Proceed along river: path keeps left at a confluence of rivers after 1 1/2 miles, then left again at the next one, 1 1/2 miles later (3) [a]. Path later loses sight of river for short section, then bends left at beginning of South Walsham Broad, continuing as a track past boatyard, then as a surfaced lane. Ignore right fork (Kingfisher Lane), but 30 yards later (4) take signposted field-path on left. This path proceeds along left edge of field, switching to other side of

hedge midway through field. Turn left on surfaced lane, past Tiled Cottage, then (5) fork right onto waymarked enclosed path, soon with hedge on right only and then bending right to pass farm, where continue along road [b].

At staggered junction, turn left to farm (6) At end of farm buildings turn left on to path along left edge of field. Path is easily followed: it bends right at field corner to proceed

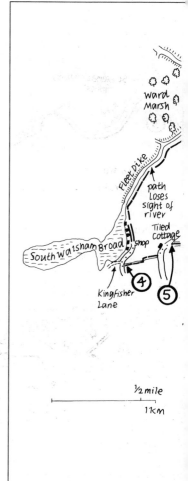

½ mile

1km

nside edge of woods of Upton Fen
nd later re-emerges into field,
ollowing edge and bending right at
next field corner over plank
ootbridge, then soon bends left to
each road and houses ⑦. Left on
oad. After ½ mile, turn right into
Marsh Road to reach pub at Upton.

ON THE ROUTE

a] St Benet's Abbey ruins on
opposite bank just before the
confluence of rivers. An 11th-
century Benedictine foundation, of
great importance in its heyday.
[b] Upton Fen Nature Reserve to left
of road, later skirted by footpath. A
50-hectare area of fen and woodland,
which is totally undisturbed and
unpolluted and contains landlocked
Upton Broad. Especially noted for
water-lilies and other aquatic plants.
Access restricted.

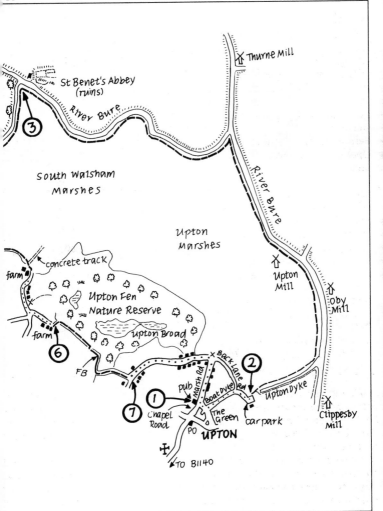

Around Horsey

Reed beds, diverse bird life, marshland plants, sand dunes and a long sandy beach are all part of this memorable walk which starts from one of the best-known pumping windmills on the Broads. Easy route-finding.

Length 4½ miles (7km), 2½ hours
Difficulty 1
Start Horsey Mill car park, on B1159 just S of Horsey village; between Mundesley and Great Yarmouth. Grid reference 457222
OS maps 1:50,000 134; 1:25,000 TG 42 (Pathfinder 863)
Refreshments Shop at Horsey Mill car park; pub at Horsey near end of walk

WALK DIRECTIONS

① [a] From car park, go to right of thatched toilet block, then turn right along waterway. After 100 yards, the path bends right as waterway is about to enter Horsey Mere [b], and has ditch on right. After 200 yards, ignore footbridge on right and keep to main path (which bends left).

② (If the following diversion no longer applies, ignore this section up to ③). When level with lakeside building away to left, the path is diverted to right and cuts diagonally across field to marker-post and footbridge, to proceed with ditch on left, then later crosses footbridge on left and rejoins dyke, keeping right along it ③.

Soon, path reaches waterway (Waxham New Cut) and turns right along it. ④ After ½ mile, turn right at Brograve Windmill [c], and follow right edge of two fields towards trees. At end of second field, path bends left in front of the trees, and immediately after the trees end take

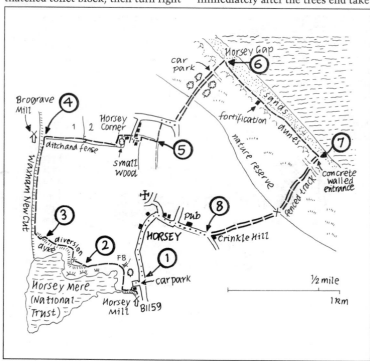

ootbridge on right (this was on a tilt
t time of inspection, but was robust
nough) and go forward alongside
rees to house.

Emerge on to surfaced lane, turn
ight then immediately left on track
which narrows to path after 30
ards, entering field. Path bends left
long field edge, then bends right at
irst corner, to reach path T-junction
t far side of field (with line of
lectricity poles going off to right)
5. Turn left here, and proceed
o road.

Turn right on road, and after 120
ards, where road bends right, take
rack on left. This leads out through
lunes and on to beach **6** [d]. Turn
ight along beach. **7** After ³/₄ mile,
ust after steps up onto sea wall, take
obvious concrete-walled entrance in
he sea wall and follow track
oetween fences leading inland
crossing over track which skirts
nland edge of dunes).

After ¹/₂ mile, by gate, track ceases
o be enclosed. **8** Keep right by lone
ed-brick houses, on road soon past
oub and on to B1159. Keep forward
n direction signed for Horsey Mill

(where road bends left, you can
detour right to church [e], keeping
left at next T-junction).

ON THE ROUTE

[a] **Horsey Mill** (National Trust,
open Apr-Oct). A windpump
constructed to drain marshes into
the waterway. Reeds from beds on
Brayden Marshes to the W have been
used for thatching for centuries.

[b] **Horsey Mere** Rich habitat for
wildfowl, including marsh harriers
and bitterns. Otters also inhabit the
1700-acre site which has been
declared a nature reserve.

[c] **Brograve Mill** 18th-century brick
tower; named after the family who
owned nearby Waxham Hall.

[d] **Horsey Gap** Highly vulnerable to
the sea which has breached the
dunes on several occasions,
including during the great floods of
1953. A concrete sea wall has now
been built to protect the dunes.

[e] **Horsey church** Thatched and
pleasingly simple, with nave and
chancel in one, and a charming
yew-shaded churchyard; octagonal
flint tower.

Northamptonshire

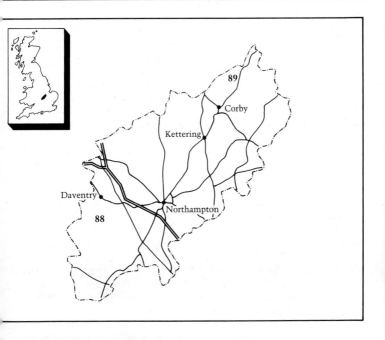

Everdon and Fawsley Park

Three attractive villages in orange-coloured stone amid rolling farmland and parkland are the high points of this route. Mostly on waymarked paths, the route is less obvious when crossing arable land between Everdon and Bullshill Farm.

Length 8 miles (13km), 4 hours
Difficulty 3
Start Preston Capes church; turn off Maidford-Charwelton Road at Preston Capes, taking N turn signposted Daventry, down High Street and turn left into Church Way. Grid reference 574548
OS maps 1:50,000 152; 1:25000 SP 45/55 (Pathfinder 999)
Refreshments Pub at Everdon; pubs and shops at Badby

WALK DIRECTIONS

① [a] Return along Church Way to High Street, and take path opposite and slightly to right, through gates of Manor Farm. Go forward (not on the track to the farm) across (first) field to where the wall meets fence to the right of the farm, and here take gate into second field. Keep forward alongside wall on left and then alongside fence on left to take gate in corner.

In third field, go forward to waymarked stile at far end, keeping just right of slight rise (stile is in line with and just to left of barn on skyline). Proceed half right across fourth field towards another barn, to reach minor road. Turn left along road; after 200 yards ignore track on left up to barn; carry on along road to **②** just where, before field on left-hand side ends, take gate on left through the hedgerow.

Go forward on track through field; in next (second field), proceed close to right edge, at end of field which is to right and beyond the hedgerow, turn right on track which leads

down through gates and up left side of the third field.

Track bends left near top of field, through break in hedge, to follow bottom side of fourth field (soon bending right at corner), past red-brick barn and along bottom of this field then, then as enclosed track, eventually reaching Snorscombe Farm **③**. Keep to left of farm buildings, on main track. Beyond the farm, track dips down to gate and bends left. Past next house on left (Snorscombe Mill), then **④** fork left.

Track crosses bridge, then immediately turn right to leave track, and cross stile; cross another field (a narrow one) to stile ahead. Emerge into next field, where go forward and slightly left (keeping well to right of church tower), passing to right of red-brick barn and just to right of projecting corner of hedge coming down from left, to take stile at corner of field, into allotments.

Proceed through the allotments or track towards Everdon church, turning right on the road to enter village [b]. Turn left on Main Street, past village green. **⑤** Near end of village, fork left, signposted Fawsley 100 yards after 30mph speed derestriction sign, take signposted stile up on right into (first) field. Turn left, alongside hedgerow fence on left, to leave by stile in top left-hand corner.

In second field, the route proceeds forward with right edge of field about 30 yards away (at time of inspection, it was easier to skirt right edge of field) to reach waymark in hedgerow ahead; in third field, go quarter right to cross right-hand hedgerow at waymark on tree which is 90 yards before far end of field **⑥**.

Go diagonally across fourth field to stile in left-hand hedgerow. Cross fifth field to prominent gate in hedge (keeping level). Follow right edge of

th field on defined track to gate in
right-hand corner; turn left in
enth field downhill, to farm in
ttom corner. Go through farmyard
d on to road.

Turn right along road. ⑦ Turn left
er ¹/₂ mile at crossroads, and
low minor road ³/₄ mile to Badby.
forward into village centre [**c**]
ning left at T-junction by green,
ng Main Street. ⑧ After 200
rds, turn left into Vicarage Hill. At
urch follow road as it bends to
ht but immediately take enclosed
th on left, signposted Knightley
ay to Fawsley.

Path drops, rises and crosses stile
o field, where bear right to
ymarked stile. Cross second field
agonally left up to stile at corner of
dby Wood [**d**]. Proceed on
odland path along inside edge of
ods ignoring all left turns.

After ¹/₄ mile, leave woods by gate
d immediately keep left over gate
side stile as waymarked, bearing
ead and slightly left across open
ea to waymarked stile into semi-
en woodland.

Follow waymarks (slightly left and
wnhill) to stile, and descend
rough three fields to waymarked
les below and slightly left. Emerge
to estate road, turn right and
after 50 yards where road bends
ht, take gate ahead and cross
rkland, passing just to left of
wsley church [**e**].

At the church, note the direction
route which proceeds down
tween the two lakes and then
eps half left towards a barn (which
sappears from view at the lakes,
d which is to left of and below
stant tower of Preston Capes
urch. Thus by keeping half left
ter the lakes, ⑪ leave (first) field
way-marked stile, at point where
wer-line leaves field and 100 yards
fore brick ruin.

Go straight uphill in second field,

initially with right edge and the barn
100 yards away; the route finally
veers right to leave field by far right-
hand corner. Ascend third field
slightly right (keeping just to left of
drinking trough on skyline) then
drop to stile. Preston Capes village is
now in view. Head straight to
waymarked stile at end of fourth
field and continue ahead, to leave
fifth field by gate beside stile in far
left-hand corner, giving on to road
⑫. Turn right on road, up to
Preston Capes.

ON THE ROUTE

[**a**] **Preston Capes** An ironstone
village, with its church on the hill
looking down towards Fawsley.
Castellated brick cottages were built
as 'eye-catchers' for Fawsley Hall.
Here between 1090 and 1107 was a
Cluniac priory comprising just four
monks. In the grounds of the large
house next to the church, peacocks
and deer may be seen. The **Knightley
Way**, which much of this walk
follows, is a twelve-mile path from
Greens Norton to Badby, taking its
name from the Knightley family of
Fawsley.

[**b**] **Everdon** A broad street flanked by
orange-coloured ironstone cottages
and broad verges with a chestnut
tree on the village green.
The defunct post office overlooking
the green retains an ancient
advertisement for Lyons tea. The
spacious church possesses a 15th-
century traceried screen, carved box-
pews, an ancient roof and a rare
musician's gallery. A plaque in the
chancel commemorates Timothy
Dods, a much loved Daventry priest
who was too fat to get into his
pulpit.

[**c**] **Badby** A large village of suburban
houses but with some considerable
charm around its central green and
in Vicarage Hill, where cottages are
ranged on the slope beneath the

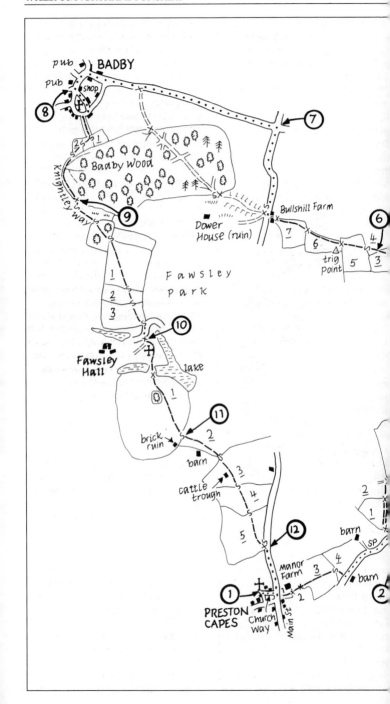

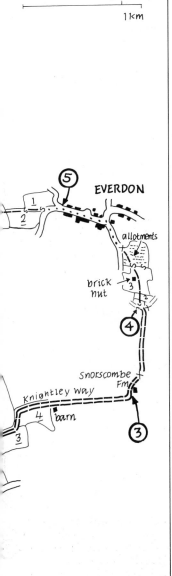

14th-century church.

[**d**] **Badby Wood** Enchanting in spring for the spectacular shows of bluebells; also a habitat for foxes. Good views from the S edge over Fawsley Park.

[**e**] **Fawsley** The house and the estate church were built for the Knightley family, and nestle amid lovely landscaped parkland with artificial lakes and ancient trees. Charles I used to come here to hunt, and the ruined Dower House NE of the hall is reputedly haunted by a phantom nocturnal hunter. The Great Hall is 16th-century with Victorian additions by Anthony Salvin, the fashionable country-house architect of the day; it is best seen after you cross the lake. The unlit church (not always open) has carved beasts on its pew-ends and monuments to the Knightleys (including a very fine one of 1539 to Sir Richard Knightley and his wife). When the Knightley family moved here in 1415, tenants on the land were evicted; grassy mounds near the church mark the site of their settlement.

King's Cliffe, Westhay Wood and Laxton Hall

A walk in Rockingham Forest - a vast hunting area in King John's time, now combining parkland, farmland and planted forest. This route passes three country-house estates and an appealing village. Field-paths not defined or waymarked so take care with directions.

Length 8 miles (13km), 4 hours
Difficulty 3
Start Laxton (W of A43 and NE of Corby), park by village green.

Grid reference 951961
OS maps 1:50,000 141; 1:25,000 SP 89/99 and TL 09/19 (Pathfinder 917 and 918)
Refreshments Pub and shops in King's Cliffe

WALK DIRECTIONS

①[a] With Laxton village green on left, follow road in Bulwick directio towards church. After 60 yards, jus before reaching path to church on right, take field-gate beside hydrant on left: with the road behind you, bear half right up to gate at top of field (just to right of where

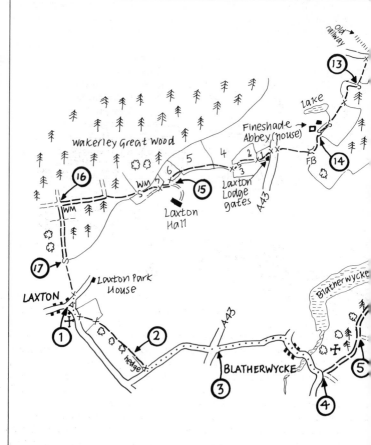

wer-lines leave the field).

Go directly forward in next field
ong row of trees marking former
eld boundary. ② Further down, a
edge begins; keep to left-hand side
f it to take gate at bottom of field to
ad, and turn left along road.
③ Cross A43 and take turn opposite
Blatherwycke, keeping right at
nction after ⅓ mile (signposted
ulwick) to pass through
latherwycke village.

④ 150 yards after river bridge, as
ad bends right, take track on left
gnposted to church (immediately
rking left), heading along left edge

of large field [**b**]. ⑤ After ⅓ mile
keep forward at four-way junction
(right goes up towards scarecrow).
Track later becomes indistinct, but
route is obvious along edge of field
close to woodland and, for a period,
beside lake.

⑥ ¼ mile after leaving the lake,
at end of field, go through the corner
of hedgerow (no stile at time of
writing, but easy to pass through as
fence and hedgerow were both
broken) and go across middle of next
field towards Alders Farm. At the
farm, pick up track through
farmyard, ignore left turn just before

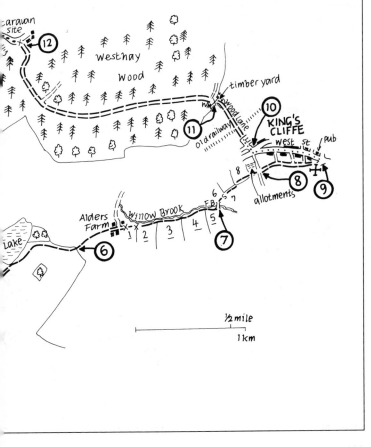

341

the brick farmhouse and keep forward to enter field by gate. Keep along left edge of five fields, close to Willow Brook on left, until ⑦ crossing footbridge over the brook in the fifth field. Go 100 yards across sixth field to stile, then go forward along left edge of seventh field and right edge of eighth field towards King's Cliffe, passing through allotment then on to track junction ⑧.

Go forward, towards church, ignoring left turns. ⑨ Just after church, bear left and left again along main street (West Street) through village [c]. ⑩ At end of village, follow on into Wood Road and immediately turn right up Wood Lane (keep forward ignoring side turnings to housing estate, soon proceeding on unmade track).

⑪ On entering timber yard, keep to track which bears left, entering Westhay Wood by gate. Follow main track ahead through the wood, ignoring two major right turns. ⑫ After 1 mile, where houses appear on right edge of wood, route continues through barrier and along road (avoid entrance on right to caravan site). As soon as you cross bridge over old railway, take signposted gate on left into field: head quarter right past leftmost power-line in field, to reach stile at top of field, 80 yards to right of recessed corner of woodland ⑬.

Beyond the stile, path continues to right through grass (may be indistinct in summer) close to fence on right for 60 yards but then bending left towards house (Fineshade Abbey) [d], into woods and dropping to gate into field. Go forward, keeping immediately to left of fence which skirts Fineshade Abbey, crossing stile at the fence corner and continuing on enclosed path just above the house.

⑭ Beyond the next stile, head

down to cross footbridge and go up towards field-gate just to right of prominent lodge gates for Laxton Hall. Cross A43 and take field-gate opposite (just to right of lodge gates). Walk towards right side of Laxton Hall [e], leaving the first field by gate ahead, and following left edge of second field to take stile on left just before end of field.

Turn right in third field (towards hall) immediately entering fourth field by gate. Follow left edge of fourth, fifth and sixth fields. ⑮ When roughly level with hall, leave sixth field by gate on left to join enclosed track and turn right along it. The track enters seventh field, where keep along the right-hand side of the field beside woodland, until taking stile on right into the woods.

Immediately turn left by waymarker post (walking initially with field fence on left), inside the woods. After 300 yards, keep forward on joining corner of forestry track. ⑯ After 350 yards turn left at crossing of tracks by waymarker post. Proceed to reach stile into field with Laxton village ahead ⑰: go across field, keeping towards left side of village to find stile beside gate. Go forward over another stile and proceed to reach driveway, where turn right to enter Laxton.

ON THE ROUTE

[a] **Laxton** Stone cottages grouped around a triangular green; mostly rebuilt in the 19th century by Lord Carbery of Laxton Hall (see below), who was an amateur stone-carver and carried out some of the work on the exterior of the church.

[b] **Blatherwycke** The partly Norman church is seen beyond overgrowing shrubberies to the left. The church was inside the old estate of the mansion (demolished 1948) which belonged to the Stafford and O'Brien families, whose monuments are in

he church. Also buried there is Thomas Coles (died 1684) whose will made provisions in perpetuity for Christmas puddings to be given to the six oldest poor men in the parish. A statue from the estate has been moved to make a most original scarecrow, seen up on the right. Blatherwycke Lake, soon passed, was a landscape creation for the hall, and is a good site for observing waterfowl.

c] **King's Cliffe** A pleasing street of grey-stone cottages of a variety of ages. The 13th-century church spire makes a distinctive landmark. Revd William Law was an 18th-century benefactor responsible for several charitable buildings in the village, including Law's Library in School Hill ('books of piety are here lent to any persons of this or ye neighbouring towns' announces a plaque over the door), two schools and almshouses.

[d] **Fineshade Abbey** A Georgian mansion built on the site of an Augustinian priory, largely demolished in 1956, but the handsome stable block (with cupola) remains.

[e] **Laxton Hall** A classical mansion completed *c* 1811 by J.A. Repton for the Evans family (Lords Carbery); altered 1868.

NORTHUMBERLAND

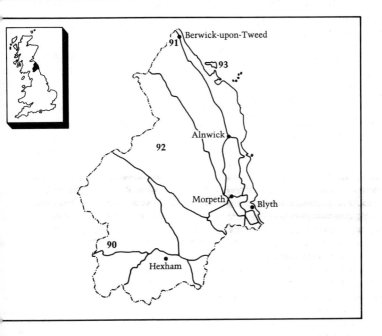

0 Hadrian's Wall: Walltown Crags and Great Chester's Fort
1 Berwick and the Tweed
2 Coquet Dale and Clennell Street
3 Holy Island

Holiday Which? Good Walks Guide

Hadrian's Wall:
Walltown Crags and
Great Chester's Fort

Takes in a host of Roman sites, both along the Wall and away from it. This is not the most walked part of Hadrian's Wall, and so a good route to escape crowds that concentrate on Housesteads fort, where there is a splendid section of Wall, but there you will do best to keep along the Wall.

Length 7 miles (11km), 3½ hours
Difficulty 2–3
Start Walltown car park; turn off B6138 just NE of junction with A69 (W of Haltwhistle) at signpost for Roman Army Museum and Walltown Crags. Turn right opposite museum; car park is ½ mile along on left shortly after cattle-grid. Grid reference 675663
Alternatively start at larger car park at Cawfields picnic site (turn off B6138 opposite Milecastle Inn, signposted Cawfields and Whiteside); begin directions at [5]. Grid reference 713666
OS maps 1:50,000 86 or 87; 1:25,000 NY 66/76 (Pathfinder 546)
Refreshments None, but there is a café at the Roman Army Museum ½ mile from start

WALK DIRECTIONS

① Walk across grass towards Hadrian's Wall, in direction of signpost for Walltown Crags (don't veer too far right, otherwise you wi miss Turret 45a) [**a**].

② Turn right at the Wall – wall itself soon ends and path is not wel defined, but route along top edge of cliff (Walltown Crags) is obvious, dropping and rising twice [**b**] and later entering woodland ③[**c**], and leaving it by stile to enter field. Proceed past farm to continue alongside wall on left, passing over series of stiles along field edges to Great Chesters Farm [**d**], where:
For short walk turn right downhill on farm track to reach junction wit farm road; this is point ⑧.
For full walk continue forward ove stile just to right of farm to continu along left edge of fields (the curiou quarried rock face you will soon reach is prominent ahead), past house on your left, then ④ over sti on left on to road. Turn right on road, over stream, then left at T-junction and immediately right int Cawfields car park where turn left.

⑤ Pick up path from inside car park, towards big quarried rock fac leading around left side of lake to reach gate by this rock face [**e**]. Tur right through another gate and turn

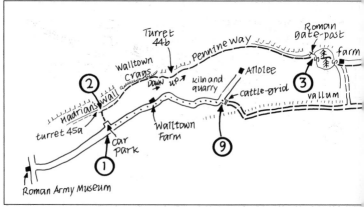

ft along Hadrian's Wall [**f**]; later
nother wall appears alongside
n right.

6 On reaching corner of right-
and wall (shortly before road), turn
ght downhill along wall for 50
rds, then **7** cross ladder-stile on
ght (thus doubling back) to
ntinue on faint grassy path with
g grassy ditches of the Vallum [**g**]
osely parallel on left to reach gate
ssed through earlier (by quarried
ck face); now proceed to Great
hester's Fort – left through second
te to retrace steps to Cawfields car
rk; left out of car park on to road,
ke first turn on right over stream,
en immediately over signposted
ile on left (Pennine Way) and turn
ght past house along field edges to
ach Great Chesters Farm again [**d**].
Turn left at farm on track
ownhill to reach surfaced farm road
). Turn right [**h**]; road becomes
nsurfaced. Follow this all the way
noring two right turns. **9** After
ttle-grid, join surfaced road and
ep forward along it [**i**], later to pass
alltown Farm [**j**] and reach car
rk.

N THE ROUTE

Hadrian's Wall The largest
oman monument in Britain.
anned by Emperor Hadrian in

AD122 (although he never saw it
completed), the Wall was a
fortification across the neck of
Northern England, from the Solway
Coast in Cumbria to the Tyne on
the east coast. Of its 73½ miles, 10
have visible remains. A 30 million-
year-old natural outcrop of hard rock
called the Great Whin Sill provided
the ideal ridge for much of its
length. To the N along this stretch
the scenery is still barren and wild,
and it is easy to imagine the Wall
when it provided protection against
barbarian raiders. Originally the
Wall was 15ft high, with a 6ft
parapet on its top, and a 9ft deep
ditch on its N side. Milecastles were
placed at intervals of one Roman
mile (1,620 yards); these, and
remains of square turrets and some
of the original 17 forts, are still in
evidence. At **Walltown Crags** is a
well-preserved portion of the Wall (it
is worth detouring a few yards to the
left) and a turret (numbered as
Turret 45b); Pike Crag to the W is
the site of a Roman signalling tower.
Quarrying has produced sheer drops
but has unfortunately obliterated the
Wall. The route dips and rises along
the Nine Nicks of Thirlwall, a series
of gaps where weaker rock has been
eroded away; the quarrying has
reduced the 'nicks' to seven.

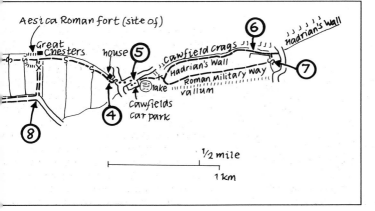

347

[b] At the first drop, a metal well cover is over **King Arthur's Well**, where according to legend Paulinus may have baptised King Egbert in AD627. Just after, the outline of turret 44b can be seen.

[c] Immediately before the woodland, look for a gate on left, whose left-hand post (rounded and holed) is a Roman **mile-post**.

[d] **Great Chester's Fort (Aesica)** There are few visible remains of this three-acre infantry fort (built about AD128), which originally had gates, a strong-room, granary, shrines, baths (fed by an elaborate aqueduct) and latrines. A vaulted entrance to the strongroom, fenced in at the centre of the field, is the most conspicuous relic, but in the SE corner (by the track at the lower end of the site) there is also a fine carved **stone gate-post**, its above-ground portion now about six feet tall.

[e] **Cawfield Crags** Quarrying has left a striking cross-section of the Whin Sill; below it are a small reservoir and picnic site.

[f] A very well-preserved part of the Wall, with **Milecastle 42** (excavated 1848).

[g] This S rampart, or **Vallum**, consisted of a 20ft wide ditch with mounds on each side: it has disappeared in many places but this is the finest remaining portion. You are now following the course of the **Roman Military Way**, which provided quick access between forts on the Wall.

[h] Another visible stretch of the **Vallum** is immediately on the right after the wall ends.

[i] A quarry and lime-kiln together, once produced agricultural fertiliser

[j] **Walltown** Once a village, now just a farm. NW of the building a grassy outline is sometimes visible of a fortified tower. Here lived John Ridley (whose brother Nicholas was a Protestant martyr burned at the stake in 1555 with Latimer).

Berwick and the Tweed

A route along both banks of the river and around the historic town walls, with the first glimpse of Berwick from its three great bridges.

Length 5 miles (8km), 3 hours
Difficulty 1
Start East Ord picnic site, by A1/A698 roundabout just S of A1 bridge over river Tweed. Grid reference 975515
OS maps 1:50,000 75; 1:25,000 NT 95/NU 05 (Pathfinder 75)
Refreshments Full range in Berwick

WALK DIRECTIONS

(1) Walk from car park and picnic site towards river Tweed, to find stile in corner of fence (50 yards to right of A1), giving access to path dropping to river. Just before reaching river level, path rises, to pass to right of ruin (path overgrown but discernible in summer when walk was inspected).

Path soon continues along edge of fields, just above river [a]. (2) Keep left on reaching corner of road and soon after, where road bends right into sewage works, keep left through gate into field. Follow track 40 yards, then fork right onto narrow path (track goes to river and ends) to follow right edge of this and next field, then along river. After passing under railway viaduct [b], (3) reach residential road at edge of Tweedmouth but leave it immediately for riverside path, passing under Royal Tweed Bridge [c] (road bridge). Cross (low-arched) Berwick Bridge [d]. (4) Turn right on other side to join level walkway, with town wall on right (here doubling as quayside wall).

Make complete circuit of town walls. [e] to [t]. (5) Immediately before Royal Tweed Bridge, take path on right down to riverside where turn right [u]. Pass under

railway viaduct. (6) Path becomes unsurfaced as it enters woods, where it rises and then levels. Turn left at T-junction with stony track.

(7) As soon as woods on left end, cross ladder-stile on left and go towards river (with woods on left), thus doubling back towards railway viaduct. Just before river, cross footbridge on right over channel and follow riverside along edge of field (this required stepping over a low fence at time of inspection, but it posed no real problem) back to A1 road bridge.

(8) At foot of the road bridge, path bends right then left up steps on to bridge itself. Cross the A1 road-bridge (there is a pavement) to return to car park by stile.

ON THE ROUTE

[a] The **River Tweed** is famous for its salmon, fished since the 9th century. Mute swans are a common sight.
[b] **Royal Border Railway Bridge** A 28-arched railway viaduct designed by Robert Stephenson and opened by Queen Victoria in 1850.
[c] **Royal Tweed Bridge** Road bridge opened 1928.
[d] **Berwick Bridge** Early 17th-century; 15 arches span the river. This was the fifth bridge, earlier structures having been washed away.
[e] to [t] *Berwick town walk* This route follows the well-preserved **town walls**, first fortified by Edward I and then Henry VIII, but what remains is the great Elizabethan Fortification, the most complete surviving example of its period in the country. This was the plan of 1558 by Sir Richard Lee, an English military engineer, who made bastions of stone, filled with earth and joined by a long curtain wall.
[e] Handsome 18th- and 19th-century houses line the **quay**. Steps lead down by No. 5, at the bottom of

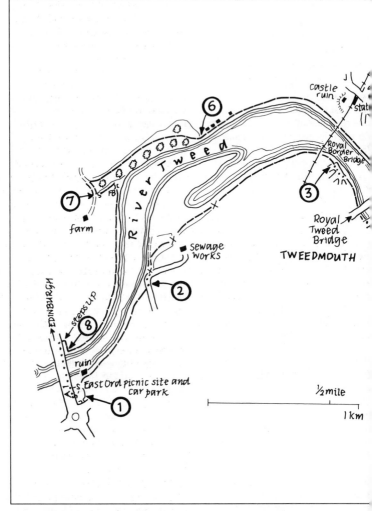

which is **Sallyport**, one of the
original passages or 'ports'
connecting Bridge Street with the
quay. Steps on left after No. 9
descend to a car park, where **Dewar
Lane**, to left, has the area's last
surviving old warehouses.

[f] View up **Hide Hill**, which was a
major route into Berwick before the
Royal Tweed Bridge was opened. In
1861 Charles Dickens stayed at the
King's Arms, one of the town's main
coaching-inns, and gave a reading of
his work to a large audience.

[g] **Customs House**, a former
dispensary, is part of an attractive
Georgian group with Nos. 19-23.

[h] **No. 1 Wellington Terrace** has
replica harpoon heads on its door
and railings, indicating the town's
connection in the early 19th century
with the whaling industry.

[i] **Palace Green**, a former bowling-
green on left at end of Quay Walls is

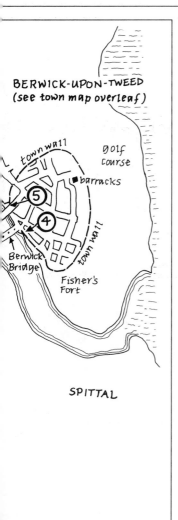

BERWICK-UPON-TWEED
(see town map overleaf)

town wall

golf course

■ barracks

⑤

④

town wall

Berwick Bridge

Fisher's Fort

SPITTAL

cannon placed here was taken in the Crimea. View of **pier** and **lighthouse** (both constructed in the 1820s) and **Holy Island** in the distance.

[**l**] **The Avenue** The grass rectangle was a rope-walk used by the rope industry in the 18th century.

[**m**] Detour left into Ness Street to see **Ravensdowne**, the finest Georgian street in town. The 18th-century former Military Hospital is being restored.

[**n**] **Windmill Mount** Across the moat are earthworks of the Great Bulwark in the Snook, part of Henry VIII's fortification.

[**o**] **Berwick Barracks** (entrance from the Parade; English Heritage, open 10-6, daily except Mon; closes at 4 Oct-Easter). Built 1717-21, Britain's first purpose-built barracks, used until 1964, housed 600 men and 36 officers. Some of the stone used in its building was taken from the castle. A fine coat of arms of George I is over the entrance; inside are a regimental museum, a museum of army life and a part of the Burrell Collection (of art, porcelain and glass).

[**p**] **Parish church of Holy Trinity** (also in the parade, opposite the far end of the barracks) A rare Commonwealth church of 1652: rectangular plan, Venetian doorways, 19th-century chancel and turrets, 16th- and 17th-century Flemish glass, and an altar-piece by Edwin Lutyens. As you return to the wall, look for **Cow Port**, the only surviving Elizabethan gate under the wall.

[**q**] At **Brass Bastion** at the wall corner, part of the original sentry walk above the west flanker has been uncovered.

[**r**] **Marygate** View down the main market street to the **town hall**, built 1750-61, with Tuscan columns beneath a portico and 150-foot high tower; guided tours are given around

hus called because of the array of overnment buildings here, ncluding the early 18th-century **overnor's House** on the E side of he green. The **guard house** (labelled) 18th-century and was moved here 1 1815 from Marygate.

Thirteen gun emplacements along **aluting Battery**. Coxon's Tower is a vo-storey **watch-tower**.

] **Fisher's Fort** Six gun-ports guard e harbour entrance. A Russian

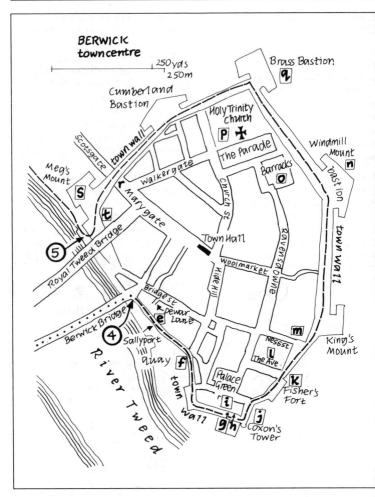

the building at 10.30 and 2, weekdays Easter to Sept, and there is a museum of local history upstairs.
[s] **Meg's Mount**, a good viewpoint, is named after a large gun placed here called Roaring Meg.
[t] On left (with clock), the old **Corporation Academy** was founded for children of Freemen. Just below the Royal Tweed Bridge, on left, is an **ice house**, which once supplied ice for the packing of Tweed salmon
[u] The **castle**, dating from at least the 12th century, is up on right. Has had a long history of attack, but the building of the railway caused most of the destruction. A tower over the river path was built 1539-42 for artillery.

Coquet Dale and Clennell Street

Typical Cheviot scenery: lonely grassy moors, a river valley and the occasional patch of planted forest, here explored along Coquet Dale and then along the top of ridges. Ascents and decents are gradual and terrain is easy-going. Route mostly defined, but needs care in a few places, especially in section ③.

Length 8 miles (13km), 5 hours
Difficulty 4
Start Alwinton car park (on minor road WNW of Rothbury). Grid reference 918063
OS maps 1:50,000 80 ; 1:25,000 NT 80/90 and NT 81/91

(Pathfinder 499 and 487)
Refreshments Pub in Alwinton

WALK DIRECTIONS

① [a] Turn right out of car park, along road for ³/₄ mile [b]. ② Take narrow gate on right (unsignposted at time of checking, but no other gates to confuse it with); keep left, along well-defined path which runs close to road initially then veers away from it.

After crossing stream, path goes through gate and has fence on right-hand side until next gate ③, where continue forward 50 yards on track to reach track junction. Here, fork right (left track descends) and 50 yards later fork left on to faint path

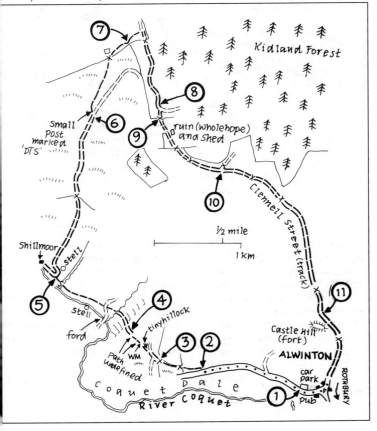

which goes around left-hand side of tiny hillock immediately in front of you.

After 150 yards, reach waymarker post embedded in pile of stones; the arrow gives the direction across moorland for 200 yards towards lowest point in skyline ahead, but path is undefined. **(4)** Reach top of steep slope (by another waymark) where well-defined broad path drops (notice the route, visible ahead to right of and just above river).

On crossing stream [c], keep left, on a roughish path, close to edge of slope. Cross well-defined track (left goes down to ford) and take path opposite, which contours above river [d]. After path crosses stream and stile, a wall starts on left.

(5) 200 yards later, and just before farm (Shillmoor), reach signpost and farm track and turn sharp right on the track, uphill. 1/2 mile later, beyond gate, track goes along centre of ridge [e]. **(6)** After a further 1/2 mile, where track makes bend to right, keep left (path faint at start, but soon well-defined), by small post marked DTS (not prominent). This path continues along top of ridge, soon to pass through gate in front of prominent walled enclosure; beyond, turn right alongside fence on right.

(7) As soon as forest begins on right, it is best to keep with the path (half left to reach hard track) although you can cut a corner by keeping alongside forest fence over boggy ground. Either way, turn right along the hard track, entering forest by gate. **(8)** After 1/4 mile, where main track bends left, continue forward on lesser track to leave forest after 130 yards by gate **(9)**.

Track leads to gate by shed and ruin (on left) [f], where continue forward; track is briefly undefined until next gate, then well-defined again, with forest away to left. Track continues along this slight ridge to reach fork **(10)** where bear right (left goes down to corner of forest) heading up to gate and over left shoulder of hill. **(11)** Track bends to left in front of hillock [g] and becomes better defined, eventually reaching houses at Alwinton. Turn right at centre of hamlet to return to car park.

ON THE ROUTE

[a] **Alwinton** Now a sleepy hamlet, but an important junction on Clennell Street in the Middle Ages. Its October sheep show is a major Cheviot event.

[b] 1/4 mile along the road, on the other side of the river to the left is **Barrow House**, a farm with remains of a peel tower (a fortified tower used as a retreat for livestock during times of attack); attacked in the 16th century by Scots.

[c] This area was notorious up to the 18th century for its border skirmishes. The house straight ahead (Linbriggs) was destroyed by Scots in 1541. Men were posted in troubled times by the stream to keep watch for Border reivers (bandits). It has now reverted to a peaceful, unspoilt dale. Dipper, gossander and grey wagtail can be seen on and around the river Coquet.

[d] On the left a dry-stone sheep enclosure, known as a **stell**, is built in the circular shape traditional to the area.

[e] Extensive views open up behind, over Coquet Dale and south Northumberland.

[f] **Clennell Street** This grassy track is an ancient route, once used by both drovers and reivers; the high route left one less vulnerable to attack. The **ruin** on the left just after you leave the forest is the former Wholehope youth hostel (supposedly haunted).

[g] On top of this hillock (Castle Hills) are traces of a hill-fort, probably Iron Age.

Holy Island

A short sea-level walk of great
historic, natural and scenic interest.
At its best in winter when the only
crowds encountered are of wildfowl
and waders.

Length 3 miles (5km), 1½ hours
Difficulty 1
Start Holy Island car park,
signposted on left as soon as you
enter village from mainland (from
which turn off A1 between Berwick
and Belford). Tide times are
displayed at mainland and in car
park; at high tide the island is cut off
for five hours. Grid reference 126422
OS maps 1:50,000 75; 1:25,000 NU
04/14 (Pathfinder 452)
Refreshments Pubs, shops, cafés in
Holy Island village

WALK DIRECTIONS

(1) Turn left out of car park main
entrance, and left again into
Sandham Lane, soon to reach farm
where keep forward (now on
unsurfaced track). (2) At nature
reserve sign [a], continue forward,
cross large area of dunes to reach
beach where turn right. Follow coast
past marker obelisk at Emanuel
Head.

(3) After next nature reserve sign,
path runs S along coast [b], to reach
castle [c] (4). After castle, pick up
road [d]; where road bends right,
keep left along coast to pick up
track, leading to low wooden
building (5), in front of which turn
right (left goes to jetty).

Soon take turnstile on right and
follow tarmac path towards priory
ruins; turn left at Crown and Anchor
Hotel to enter square (detour ahead
and to left to see priory [e]), where
(6) first street on right leads to car
park (turn right at T-junction by
Northumberland Arms and first left
into Sandham Lane).

ON THE ROUTE

[a] **Lindisfarne Nature Reserve** Tidal
mudflats attract great numbers of
waders and wildfowl in winter. This
is Britain's most important coastal
site for wigeon (whose population
here peaks at 25,000), and the only
wintering ground for pale-bellied
Brent Goose. Among the wild
flowers is a fine seasonal show of
orchids. In the dunes is a huge rabbit
colony, once an important resource
for the island. From the obelisk on
Emanuel Head is a good **view** N
along the coast towards Berwick and
St Abbs Head.
[b] View S to the mainland,
including **Ross Back Sands** and 12th-
century **Bamburgh Castle**, with the
Cheviot Hills further inland. To the
left are the **Farne Islands**, whose 15
isles are a haunt of seabirds and
seals; monastic hermits from
Lindisfarne had cells there up to
1246.
[c] **Lindisfarne Castle** was built a
year after Henry VIII's dissolution of
the monasteries, marking the
island's new role as a naval base
instead of a religious centre; stone
taken from the ruined priory was
used as building material. Edward
Hudson, founder of *Country Life*
magazine bought the ruined castle in
1903 and commissioned Edwin
Lutyens to convert it into a
comfortable home (National Trust,
open Easter-Sept; 1-4.30 except Fri;
Wed, Sat and Sun only in Oct). The
lime-kiln (labelled) just before the
castle is reached, produced fertiliser
which was transported to Scotland.
[d] Lobster and crab pots are much in
evidence, and these shellfish are on
sale locally. Notice the sheds made
out of upturned boats.
[e] **Lindisfarne Priory** The English
cradle of Christianity, where Aidan,
a missionary from Iona, arrived in
635 at the invitation of King Oswald
of Northumbria and founded a

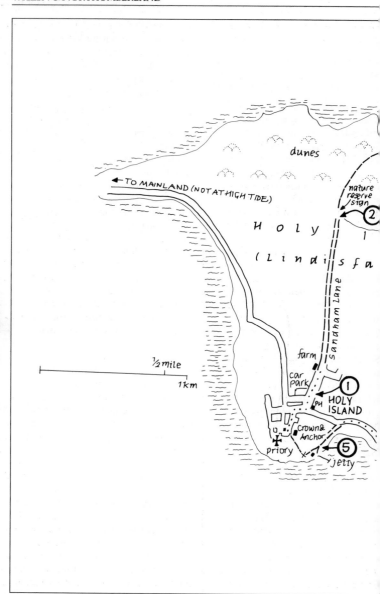

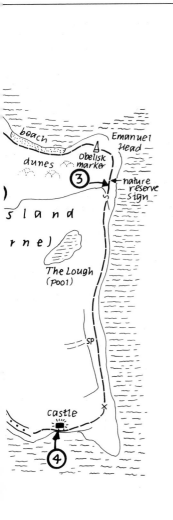

monastery (then a simple wooden structure), with the aim of spreading Christianity across northern England. It became a Benedictine monastery in 1082, and despite its exposure to the elements since its ruination in the Reformation, much of the fine stone decoration and arches survive. In the adjacent museum are inscribed stones and an historical display. (English Heritage, open Easter-Sept 10-6 daily; 10-4 Oct-Easter). The celebrated Lindisfarne Gospels, a superb illuminated manuscript made about 700, is in the British Museum.

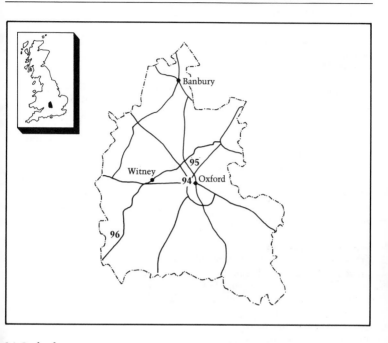

94 Oxford
95 The Cherwell Valley, Kirtlington and Bletchingdon
96 Coleshill and Badbury Hill

Holiday Which? Good Walks Guide

96 The Sinodun Hills and Dorchester-on-Thames   97 Streatley, the Ridgway
and Unhill Wood   98 Goring Heath and Mapledurham

Oxford

A busy city as well as a world-famous seat of learning, but the bustle is easily escaped, and much of the yellow-stone historic centre can be enjoyed from back lanes. Christ Church Meadow, just south of the centre, lends a semi-rural contrast to this walk, which passes many of the most famous colleges.

Length 3 miles (5km), 4 hours
Difficulty 1
Start Magdalen Street, by Martyrs' Memorial (near Randolph Hotel); parking is difficult in the centre and you may find it easy to take 'Park and Ride' from the city ring road
Refreshments Full range

WALK DIRECTIONS

(1) Standing with Randolph Hotel [a] on your right, take road to left of Martyrs' Memorial; at end turn left into Broad Street [b]. At end of this main street, cross into Holywell Street. (2) Take alley on right (Bath Place), turn left at end into yard of Turf Tavern, turning right at end (by lamp-post; left goes into pub gardens), under metal staircase and along narrow alley to reach Queen's Lane, with covered footbridge on right; turn left [c][d].

(3) At High Street turn left and proceed to Magdalen Bridge [e]; return along High Street and turn left opposite main tower of Magdalen College and find kissing-gate into Botanical Gardens [f] (if gardens are closed use Rose Lane to your right); turn right by fountain and left at Rose Lane to reach gate into Christ Church Meadow (4) [g].

Keep to left (ignore two right turns; however these can be used as a short cut if you do not wish to walk the entire loop of the Meadow). Follow path, soon along River Cherwell. Path reaches the broad River Thames where the path

continues to right for 200 yards; then turn right, leaving river, on to broad path heading towards Christ Church College.

(5) Go through paying turnstile into the college [h] (if it is closed, turn left to reach main road), past Cathedral and leave by gate in main quadrangle. Turn right on main road then (6) turn right at High Street [i]. Take second turning on right, into King Edward Street; keep to the principal street (bending left into Oriel Square) which becomes Merton Street [j].

(7) At end of Merton College on your right [k], turn left into Logic Lane (a narrow path). Turn left along High Street, then turn right just before University Church into Catte Street, to enter Radcliffe Square; keep to left of Radcliffe Camera [l] (the large circular building) and (8) just after the Camera [m] take lane on left.

At the end [n], turn right into Turl Street and first left into Ship Street. (9) Turn right at end, along pedestrianised shopping street to reach start.

ON THE ROUTE

[a] **Ashmolean Museum** (on the right) Opened 1683 to house the collection of curiosities made by Elias Ashmole and the Tradescant family. The museum now has an important collection of art, archaeology, coins and medals. Open (Tues-Sat 10-4; Sun 2-4. Closed Mons and Sept 3, 4 and 5, and a period over Christmas, New Year and Easter, but open bank hol Mons, Easter to late summer 2-5).
[b] **Balliol** (on left) A college with a high reputation for scholarship, particularly since the mastership of Benjamin Jowett from 1870-93. As a disrespectful rhyme put it: 'First come I, my name is Jowett/There's no knowledge but I know it/I am

master of this college/What I know not is not knowledge.'

c] New College In spite of its name, one of the oldest colleges in the university (founded 1379), as well as one of the finest architecturally. The cloister, the chapel and the hall all repay a visit. The celebrated Dr Spooner was warden here. He was one of the few people whose name gave rise to a dictionary word in his lifetime, though most of the famous 'spoonerisms' ('the lord is a shoving leopard' 'kinquering congs' etc) are apocryphal.

d] St Edmund Hall Small but charming, it was for a long time the sole survivor of the eighty or more medieval academical halls, the earliest type of residential society for undergraduates. Its quadrangle has the original 13th-century college well.

e] Magdalen In size and magnificence a great contrast to St Edmund Hall. On May mornings choristers greet the dawn from the Tower (built 1492-1501), a major landmark with a fine peal of bells. The grounds incorporate The Grove and Water Walks.

f] The Botanic Gardens The oldest such gardens in England, opened in 1621, with a gateway by Inigo Jones. Oxford ragwort was brought here from the cindery slopes of Vesuvius. It escaped and is now one of the commonest weeds of cultivation. Open (all year 9-5, closes 4.30 in winter).

g] Christ Church Meadow The scene of bitter controversy in the 1950s and 1960s over a proposal to construct a relief road over the Meadows. The plan was defeated and the Meadow preserved, but the trees have been ravaged by Dutch Elm Disease.

h] Christ Church (entrance fee payable). The foundation of Cardinal Wolsey in 1546, the Christ Church buildings include the cathedral, which serves also as the college chapel. Tom Quad is the largest in Oxford: it shares its name with Great Tom, the seven-ton bell in Tom Tower. From the fountain in the centre of the quad with its statue of Mercury, four paths radiate to the cardinal points of the compass. The Hall (1529) is splendid, both in its proportion and decorations. It has portraits of numerous celebrated members of 'the House' including John Locke, John Wesley, William Gladstone and Lewis Carroll.

[i] High Street This noble, curving street, lined throughout its length from Magdalen Bridge to Carfax with buildings of great distinction, has a claim to be considered one of England's finest.

[j] Oriel (on left) The college was founded in 1326, but the buildings are largely 16th- and 17th-century. Students have included Gilbert White, Thomas Hughes, author of *Tom Brown's Schooldays* (a sequel, *Tom Brown at Oxford*, is based here), Matthew Arnold and Cecil Rhodes.

[k] Merton Founded in 1264, it can claim to be the oldest university foundation in England: it was certainly the first establishment where students were lodged and supervised. In the first half of the 14th century, six out of seven Archbishops of Canterbury were Merton men. Tending to be blocked out of sight by surrounding buildings, Merton nevertheless has much of architectural excellence, having largely escaped restoration. The picturesque Mob Quad is flanked by the oldest medieval library in England. J.R.R. Tolkien, Merton Professor of English Language and Literature, completed *The Lord of the Rings* here in 1955.

[l] The Radcliffe Camera Designed 1737-49 by John Gibbs, this was

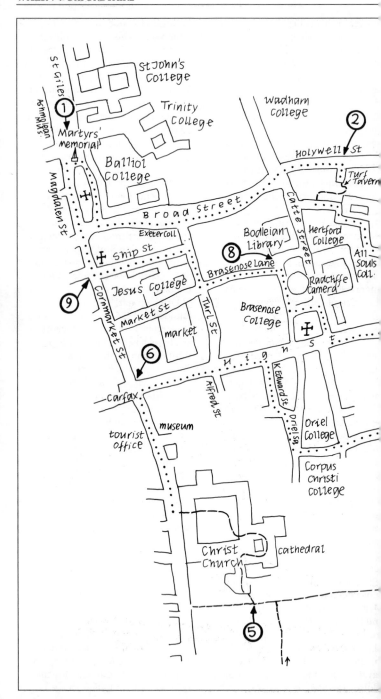

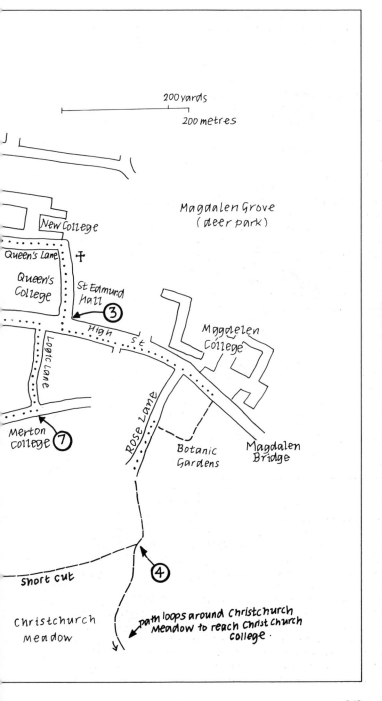

200 yards

200 metres

Magdalen Grove
(deer park)

New College

Queen's Lane

Queen's
College

St Edmund
Hall

③

High St

Logic Lane

Magdalen
College

Merton
College ⑦

Rose Lane

Botanic
Gardens

Magdalen
Bridge

Short cut

④

Christchurch
Meadow

path loops around Christchurch
Meadow to reach Christ Church
college.

originally the home of the Radcliffe Library, endowed by Dr John Radcliffe, physician to William III and Mary, and to Queen Anne. Now a reading room for the Bodleian Library.

[m] **The Bodleian Library** Originally founded in the 15th century, it was re-founded and rebuilt by Sir Thomas Bodley about 1600. It is one of the six copyright libraries entitled to receive a copy of all new publications, and can claim to be one the great libraries of the world. Connected by tunnel to the new Bodleian building in Broad Street.

[n] **The Covered Market** (opposite and just to left) This lively market is an excellent place to gather the makings of a picnic lunch, and has retained its Victorian character.

The Cherwell Valley, Kirtlington and Bletchingdon

The route features two and a half miles of the towpath of the Oxford Canal, running up the Cherwell Valley north of Oxford, followed by the attractive villages of Kirtlington and Bletchingdon and ending with the almost abandoned village of Hampton Gay. Includes three pubs at roughly equal intervals along the walk.

Length 6½ miles (10.5km), 3½ hours

Difficulty 2

Start Shipton-on-Cherwell church. Shipton-on-Cherwell is down a short cul-de-sac 2 miles N of Kidlington, off the A423 Oxford-Banbury road. From the turn-off, go down the minor road for ¼ mile and then, when the road swings round to the left, continue forward and park around the triangle of roads in front of Shipton Manor.

Grid reference 480165

OS maps 1:50,000 164; 1:25,000 SP 41/51 (Pathfinder 1092)

Refreshments Pubs at Enslow and Kirtlington; pub and shop at Bletchingdon

WALK DIRECTIONS

1) From the parking area continue forward and, when the path forks, go left and downhill towards the canal; the right-hand path leads into Shipton churchyard [a]. Cross the canal [b] and immediately turn right to join the towpath. Turn right along this and go under the bridge you have just crossed (thus proceeding with canal on your left. After ¼ mile, pass under a railway bridge which used to carry a branch line to Woodstock, and then immediately under another carrying the Oxford-Banbury line.

2) After another ¼ mile, cross the canal by a bridge over a set of locks and continue forward on the left bank [c]. **3)** After another ½ mile, and 200 yards after going under the railway again, cross the river by a foot-bridge and continue forward on towpath, keeping canal on right and passing Baker's Lock.

4) Soon pass under new road bridge at Enslow, then immediately left through gate beside stile and follow footpath just to left of old bridge, to rejoin towpath (cross old bridge if you want the Rock of Gibraltar public house on far bank of canal). Continue along towpath on left bank of canal for next mile, passing under a railway bridge just after Enslow and a minor bridge at Pinsey.

5) Pass under the next bridge just before Pigeon Lock, but immediately turn left up bank on to track, then turn left on track and cross bridge over canal. Once over bridge, turn left to resume direction of canal towpath on track between hedges. The track is parallel to the canal but climbs away from it, and after a mile reaches Kirtlington village **6)**.

At the edge of the village the track becomes a surfaced road. Keep right of a small triangle of grass with a fine sycamore tree at its centre, pass between two cottages (the one on the right thatched), then go around the right-hand side of a larger triangle of grass to go down the main village street. The Dashwood Arms is on the right as the main road swings sharply right; cross the main road and maintain previous direction on minor road running across green area, through gap between houses, then running between high wall on left and houses on right towards village church. At end of road, enter churchyard, go around right-hand end of church then follow path down side of church, passing porch, to gate at far corner of churchyard [d].

Follow short track between fences, with cricket pitch on left, to rejoin main road on bend ⑦. Continue forward along road for about 250 yards, passing lodge and drive into Kirtlington Park, then 50 yards after the lodge, opposite house No. 15, turn right into field over stile marked by yellow footpath sign on post.

Go half right across (first) field to stile 20 yards to right of gate, then cross second field to projecting corner on far side. At corner, turn right along edge of field, keeping hedge and wood on left, for 50 yards then when wood on left ends turn left over waymarked stile. Turn right along edge of third field with hedge on right, at next minor corner joining track coming in from right and continuing down side of field.

⑧ Just before track swings round to left, turn right through gate, and in fourth field turn half left to make for gate in gap between two wooded areas, just to the left of the chimneys of Bletchingdon Park

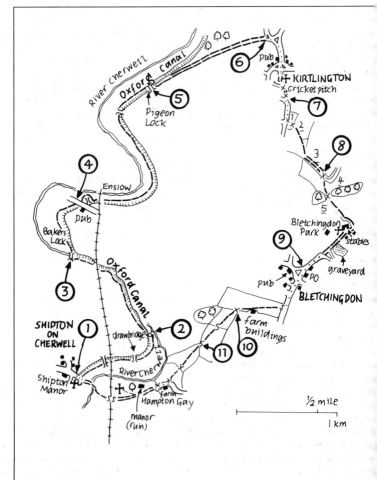

sible above trees. Enter fifth field
⸝ this gate, then continue forward
⸝d uphill [e], keeping fence on left.
At the top of the rise, bear right to
⸝n alongside belt of trees on right-
⸝nd side of field (you should be able
⸝ go into wooded enclosure about
⸝lfway down the side, but at time
⸝ inspection the path was
⸝structed). At corner of field, turn
⸝ght through gate and continue
⸝ead on concrete track between
⸝rm buildings, and passing to left of
⸝d stable block.

When track forks, keep right to
⸝ss between detached portion of
⸝aveyard and Bletchingdon church
⸝ right, then forward again at
⸝nction after church, on track
⸝eping metal fence of Bletchingdon
⸝rk on right. Continue along this
⸝r 300 yards, ignoring turns to left,
⸝til you pass through kissing-gate
⸝ join village street, and continue
⸝rward.

⑨ Unless visiting the Black's
⸝ead to the right, keep to the left-
⸝nd side of the village green and go
⸝raight over at crossroads, following
⸝gnpost to Hampton Poyle. When
⸝ouses on left end by the entrance to
⸝e village recreation ground, and
⸝st before the speed limit signs,
⸝rn right over a stile and cross field
⸝agonally, aiming just to the right
⸝ farm buildings. At the corner by
⸝e buildings, turn half left to gate
⸝ yards to right of isolated tree in
⸝nce ahead ⑩. Once through gate,
⸝oss next field to stile in middle of
⸝ fence, then maintain direction
⸝wards hedge on right [f]. Follow
⸝is hedge along until end of first
⸝·ld on right, then ⑪ go over stile
⸝to corner of second field on right.
⸝escend across this field to gate in
⸝ne with farm buildings ahead, then
⸝ake for gate just to right of nearest
⸝·ctricity pole, which leads out on
⸝ a farm road.

Turn right along the farm road,
passing between Manor Farm on the
left and some cottages. ⑫ At the
end of the road, continue forward
over stile into field and follow track
just to the left of belt of trees
directly ahead [g]. Once past the
trees, continue forward on slightly
raised track to stile, leaving
Hampton Gay church slightly to the
right. Cross stile, then the railway
line (with care) and another stile,
then go quarter right across
field ahead.

Passing thorn trees two-thirds of
the way across the field, footbridge
across Cherwell becomes visible
ahead (resembling a very small-scale
version of Sydney Harbour bridge).
Go over the bridge, and the stiles at
both ends, then forward across field
keeping to right of corrugated iron
shelter. Go through gate on to short
section of track between fences,
then over canal bridge to return
to start.

ON THE ROUTE
[a] **Shipton-on-Cherwell** church was
rebuilt in 1831 by William Turner. It
is not easy to see from close up, but
there is an interesting view of it
from Manor Farm, near the end of
the walk, when it can be seen just
beyond Hampton Gay church; the
two village churches are just
$1/4$ mile apart.
[b] **The Oxford Canal** connected the
Thames at Oxford to Leicester and
Birmingham. For a short period in
the 18th century, before the
construction of the more direct
Grand Union Canal from London to
Birmingham, it was the main inland
route for freight between London
and the north of England. Walking
along it now, it is hard to believe
that it was once the equivalent of
the M1.
[c] Immediately after these locks, the
canal joins the River Cherwell. The
canal follows the valley of the

Cherwell for about 20 miles to a point north of Banbury, and it alternates between canalised sections of the river and specially constructed cut-offs.

[d] **Kirtlington church** was rebuilt in 1877 by Giles Gilbert Scott, but includes sections dating from the early 12th century, and part of a 15th-century wall painting shows St George and the dragon, with St Christopher to the right.

[e] At this point, you have the best view of **Bletchingdon Hall**, otherwise inaccessible to the public and surrounded by trees. The Hall is a Palladian villa, created for the Earl of Anglesey in 1782 by James Lewis, who also designed the austere stable block.

[f] There are good views ahead across this third field towards **Oxford**. The John Radcliffe Hospital, a large white building off to the left on the hill at Headington, is far more conspicuous than the famous 'dreaming spires'.

[g] The ruin of **Hampton Gay manor house** is just inside this belt of trees, and the track you are following is the old village street. The village of Hampton Gay dates from Saxon times, and is well-documented in the Domesday Book; the manor house was erected in the second half of the 16th century. The village's period of greatest prosperity was in the 18th century, when the water-mill was used for paper making. The church was rebuilt in 1767, and the population rose to 86. However, in 1887, the paper-mill closed down and the manor house was gutted by fire; since then, the site of the former village is the field you see between Manor Farm and the church (church key available from Manor Farm or Manor Cottage).

oleshill and Badbury Hill

compasses two small hills
tween the Vale of White Horse
d the Thames valley with a
mber of features of interest,
cluding Coleshill village, Badbury
ll, and the great barn at Great
oxwell. Some field-paths ploughed
t at time of inspection.

ngth 5¹/₂ miles (9km), 2¹/₂ hours
art Great Coxwell post office;
eat Coxwell is just off A420,
vindon-Oxford, west of Faringdon.
id reference 270937
S maps 1:50,000 163; 1:25,000 SU
/39 (Pathfinder 1135)
freshments shop at Great
oxwell; shop and pub at Coleshill

ALK DIRECTIONS

) With your back to the post office,
rn left along road for 30 yards,
en turn left down Puddleduck
ne, marked as no through road.
ter 300 yards, road passes barns on
t and becomes track between
dges. ② After another ¹/₂ mile,
ack enters field by gate; cross to far
rner on reasonably clear track,
en go through gate to next field [a].
Continue through this second
ld, keeping hedge on right, to gate
corner. Go through gate on to
rm road; immediately to right are
ildings of Colleymore Farm, but
rn left down road, soon becoming
ack, for 200 yards. ③ Immediately
ter passing cottage on left, and just
fore track enters field ahead, turn
ght through gate into field. Keep to
ght-hand edge of field, then
rward over double stiles into
cond field, still with hedge on
ght.

Just before buildings of Ashen
opse Farm, cross stile to right then
mediately left, keeping farm
ilding on left. Before second farm
ilding, turn right up bank then
mediately left alongside building;

at end of second building, continue
forward on concrete track, and when
this meets tarmac farm road cross
this to enter field ahead by gate
beside stile ④.

Track bends half left to run
alongside wood on left; at end of first
field, track passes through gap
between wooded enclosures to
continue forward in same direction,
with wood on right. Continue on
track through third field, but
⑤ when wood on right ends do not
continue forward on obvious track
across fourth field, but follow edge
of wood around to the right.

Once around corner, make for
right-hand end of conspicuous
clump of trees about 50 yards to left
of edge of wood, and then to stile
directly ahead (at time of inspection
this field, and the next two, had
recently been ploughed, but the
stiles were well-maintained and
there were signs that the path had
been well-defined across the wheat
fields prior to ploughing).

Once over stile, continue to stile
in opposite fence; this is in fact a
double stile, with a bridge across a
ditch in between ⑥. Coleshill
village is now visible ahead [b]; cross
wide field to stile in line with right-
hand end of visible buildings, and
then forward to gate to right of
buildings. Go through this gate on to
short section of private road
alongside house, then forward
through gateway on to road at
junction ⑦.

Go straight ahead, and continue
along road for 200 yards to emerge
on main road at centre of Coleshill
village, opposite church [c]. Turn
right on main street, passing
remains of cross and then the post
office on right, followed by Radnor
Arms public house on left.
Immediately after Radnor Arms,
turn left on minor road. ⑧ At next
junction, after 150 yards, turn left on

369

road but then immediately right into field ahead, following footpath sign; ignore gravel track to right. Follow left hand edge of field over brow of hill and through gap in hedge into second field [**d**].

Descend second field, still with hedge on left, to stile at corner and then enter wood. Maintain direction on grassy track along side of wood, and ⑨ when edge of wood curves around to right, continue forward over plank bridge and stile into field. Continue up side of field, with hedge on left, then over stile on to fenced path along side of next field. Cross plank bridge between stiles, then half left across corner of field to another plank bridge between stiles 10 yards to right of telephone pole ⑩.

Bear half right across field ahead aiming for buildings of Brimstone Farm, just to left of prominent clump of trees. Go through gate from field, then immediately half right through second gate towards farmhouse, down short section of track between fences, and then cross concrete farm road to gate immediately to right of farm buildings (keep to right of all the farm buildings).

Continue forward through field, keeping hedge on left, to bridge over ditch and gate at far corner. ⑪ In next field, turn left but right after 10 yards, to stay within field, and follow left-hand edge of field. At corner, enter wood through gap in hedge marked by footpath sign and continue forward on path with hedge and field on left. When field on left ends, continue ahead on path uphill, which becomes better defined. Go directly uphill through wood, ignoring cross-tracks.

⑫ As path levels out, it runs alongside wire fence on left, but when fence curves left continue forward and slightly downhill,

keeping to right of gate into enclosure ahead. Follow enclosure around as track starts to rise again, then run alongside ramparts to left [**e**], and over stile beside gate into Badbury Hill car park.

Continue through car park, then turn left on to road for 200 yards. ⑬ Turn right over stile on to footpath signed to Great Coxwell. Descend on track across field; after 200 yards, fence comes in on left and track runs alongside, with plantation then small wood on left. 100 yards before end of field, turn left over stile into wood, then half right across corner of wood to footbridge and stile into field [**f**].

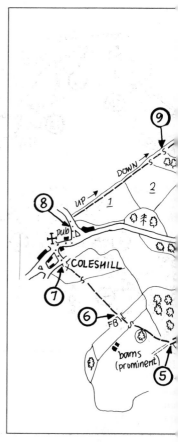

Once in field, turn left along edge
wood and follow edge of field
und until footpath sign directs you
ft over gate beside stile into
closure around Great Barn.
eping to right of the barn,
ntinue forward to road then turn
ght to return to start of walk.

N THE ROUTE

Fine **views** S over the Vale of
hite Horse towards the Wiltshire
wns.

The field ahead used to contain
oleshill House, erected *c*.1650 but
tted by fire in 1952, and
bsequently demolished. Inigo
nes contributed to its design, and

the house was once described as the
best Jonesian mid-17th-century
house in England. All that remains
are four lodges and traces of the
park. A mile due south of Coleshill
is Strattenborough Castle Farm, an
ordinary farm whose rear, facing the
great house, had two castellated
sham towers erected in 1792 to add
romance to the view.

[c] **Coleshill church** has a complex
and obscure history, but the earliest
part appears to be late Norman. The
village also contains many attractive
stone houses.

[d] Good **views** N over the Thames
valley, with the woods around
Buscot House visible in the middle

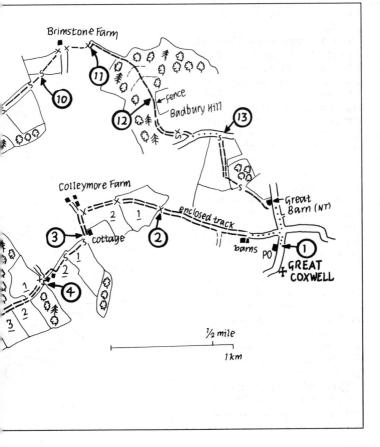

distance.

[e] The ramparts are the remains of pre-Roman **Badbury hill-fort**.

[f] From this point, Great Coxwell's **Great Barn** is clearly visible. This was built by the Cistercian monks of Beaulieu Abbey in Hampshire, proabably in the mid-13th century, and is now in the care of the National Trust (pay admission into honesty box). It is 152ft long, 44ft wide, and 48ft high, and has been described as the finest of the surviving medieval barns in England and one of the most impressive structures of its kind in the whole of Europe. William Morris, who lived nearby at Kelmscott, thought it 'as noble as a cathedral'.

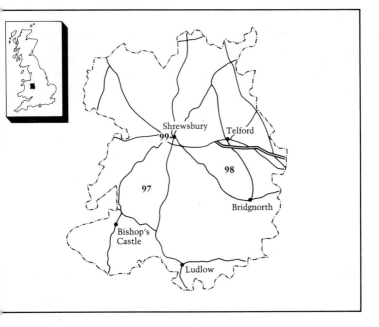

oliday Which? Good Walks Guide

Ratlinghope and the Long Mynd

A stunning round walk which takes in remote farmland on the west side of the Long Mynd and the best stretch of the ancient Portway, which straddles the summit of the moor. Mostly easy going, and fairly simple route-finding, but moorland paths could be confusing in misty weather.

Length 8½ miles (13.5km), 4 hours
Difficulty 2–3
Start Ratlinghope church, 4 miles NW of Church Stretton (take signs for Burway out of Church Stretton, forking right on top of Lond Mynd, and turning right at T-junction after descending). Grid reference 403969
OS Maps 1:50,000 137; 1:25,000 SO 29/39 and SO 49/59
(Pathfinder 909 and 910)
Refreshments Pub at Bridges

WALK DIRECTIONS

(1) With the path to St Margaret's church behind you, go forward along lane, and turn left after 50 yards on semi-metalled track. Cross footbridge and turn on far side of stream to follow clear farm track into field. This soon swings slightly to the left; when it starts to lead slightly uphill, turn right through metal gate (to Shropshire marker [a]).

Continue through two large fields on grassy track, keeping stream away to your right. Pass through gate, with farm buildings beyond – but instead of making for these, turn left just beyond footpath sign up stony track. Pass through gate into field, and fork right to cross stile in corner of field. Bear quarter right in second field to follow bank and remains of hedge.

(2) Cross footbridge, and continue in same direction for 20 yards before turning left to pass Shropshire Way marker. Bear quarter right at second marker-post to find stile. In next field, head for top of valley on faint path, which first bears quarter left and then half right across rough earth bridge. Keep left at top of field to pass through metal gate (3).

Turn right on track [b] and follow for 1½ miles, first with fence on your right, later with fence on your left. Soon after reaching small coniferous plantation on your left, pass through gate and continue for a short distance between fences, to drop down to stream. Cross stream, but immediately afterwards, where main track bears left, continue forward up grassy track.

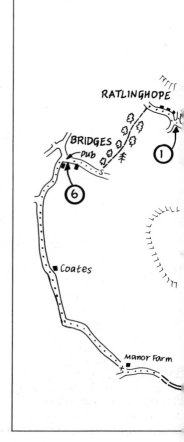

④ Turn right on road, and fork left after 150 yards on broad grassy track across moor. Continue direction for 1 mile, ignoring turnings to right and left; this track later becomes a 'triple carriageway'. Where this happens, follow middle track, aiming just to left of hut which soom becomes visible. Cross road and continue uphill on clear track, continuing forward over cross-track after ¼ mile to reach trig point and view indicator [**c**].

⑤ Retrace steps from summit to reach cross-track after 250 yards. Turn left and continue downhill for ¾ mile [**d**] later with fence on right. Pass through gate just to right of cottage, and continue on semi-metalled track for ½ mile. Fork right

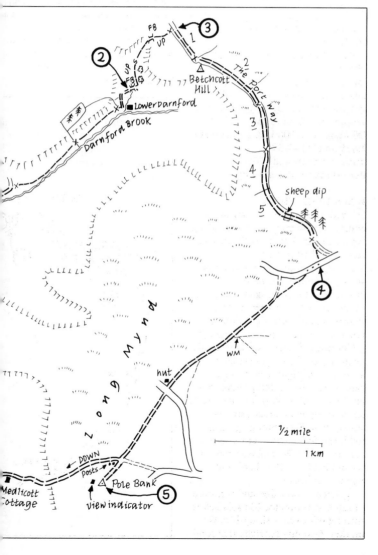

on reaching hamlet and follow gated road which drops to stream and then rises steeply. Turn left on reaching second hamlet, immediately in front of farmhouse, and follow road for a further ³/₄ mile, later passing Horseshoe Inn on your right.

⑥ Turn right at T-junction, soon passing Bridges Youth Hostel on your right. 250 yards later, just before stone bridge, cross stile Shropshire Way marker-post. Follow clear track through trees, keeping stream to your right. At end of first field, turn left up slope to cross stile.

Turn right in second field, and cross stile in bottom right-hand corner. Pass through wood crossing further stile at end. Turn right on farm track, cross footbridge and pass through gate to follow track which soon becomes metalled and bears right to return to Ratlinghope church.

ON THE ROUTE

[a] **Shropshire Way** A 125-mile rou developed by local rambling clubs, leading from Wem south over the Long Mynd to Ludlow, then returning to Wem via the Clee Hil Wenlock Edge, Ironbridge and the Wrekin.

[b] **The Portway** An ancient trackway over the Long Mynd, use by Neolithic axe traders; numerou Bronze Age burial mounds alongsi

[c] **Pole Bank** (1,696ft) The highest point on the Long Mynd, with the Arenigs, Brecon Beacons, Cader Idr and the Malvern Hills visible on a clear day.

[d] View of **Stiperstones**, Shropshir highest point (1,731ft), a ridge capped with quartzite outcrops. Th most prominent part is the Devil's Chair, whose boulders, it is said, fe from the Devil's apron when its strings broke.

onbridge and the
evern Gorge

**spectacular tour of the cradle of
e Industrial Revolution, starting
om a village and following
otpaths between most of the main
ghts. Some very fine scenery
cludes the rocky dingle between
ints ② and ③, and the Severn
orge. Route-finding intricate but
t especially difficult.**

ength 7½ miles (12km), 4 hours
ifficulty 2–3

art High Street in Broseley (on
4375 6 miles north of Bridgnorth.
rid reference 675017

S Maps 1:50,000 127; 1:25,000 SJ
/70 (Pathfinder 890)

efreshments Several pubs in
oseley, two at Coalport, several in
onbridge. Cafés in Ironbridge

ALK DIRECTIONS

) [a] From Broseley High Street
ke turning 50 yards downhill from
bion pub, immediately opposite
ctoria Hall and memorial garden.
his road appears to be unnamed,
t an obscured sign on the right
veals that it's Dark Lane.
After 300 yards, just beyond red-
ick lodge, turn right on to clear
ack. This soon opens out to follow
t-hand edge of field, then skirting
e edge of a small copse fork right
meadow at bottom, to pass
rough wooden barrier to road ②.
Turn right on the road, and left
er 30 yards just before Broseley
llage sign on to small road
gnposted to Coneybury and
oodhouse Farms. On reaching
ossroads after 200 yards, continue
rward on unmade track, avoiding
rk to right just beyond. Pass
rough wooden gate and continue
rward on track, later passing
tween barriers to drop into
ooded dingle.
Avoid a turning to right, and

continue along bottom of valley
with rocks rising to your left.
Emerge at bottom of wood by small
brick house, on your left, and
continue forward in driveway which
soon become metalled and passes
under railway bridge. Bear left at
bottom to reach the Boat pub ③.

Turn right over footbridge and
turn right again along canal towpath.
Turn left over footbridge at end, and
continue on far bank. On reaching
entrance to Coalport China Works
museum [b], turn left uphill, and
then turn immediately left on road.
Just before reaching the Shakespeare
pub turn right on path marked the
Silkin Way, first following steps
uphill and then turning left on cross-
track (marker post).

Follow for about ½ a mile [c]; 15
yards after passing through tunnel
turn right up steps, turn right again
at the top, and turn right a third
time to reach road ④ [d]. Turn left
on road, and turn immediately right
on driveway in front of The Villas.

Turn right after 20 yards on to
narrow stony path with garden wall,
later fence, on your left and
woodland on right. When fence
ends, continue forward, avoiding
path which bears away to left, and
50 yards beyond this point fork
right uphill on clear path marked
with wooden steps. Cross over
stile at top and continue in field
with fence on your left. Keep left
at fork to follow clear path
through trees.

Follow for ½ mile, avoiding all
turnings to right and keeping close
to the top of the slope, which drops
away sharply to your left. ⑤ On
reaching wooden barrier, fork left
past post bearing footprint sign, and
continue with fence on right. Path
soon passes into second field, and
into small copse just beyond. Turn
left on cross-track just inside this
copse, to drop steeply downhill, soon

joining driveway which merges from the left.

Turn right on road at bottom, and keep left just beyond pub (avoiding right turn up Jockey Bank). Continue on gravel path where road ends, to reach main road ⑥. Cross over into Belmont Road, which you follow for about 500 yards. Watch out for Belle Vue Road on your left (the third proper turning on the left); 30 yards beyond this turn right on unnamed road which climbs uphill between cottages.

Where the road ends, continue forward through metal barrier to

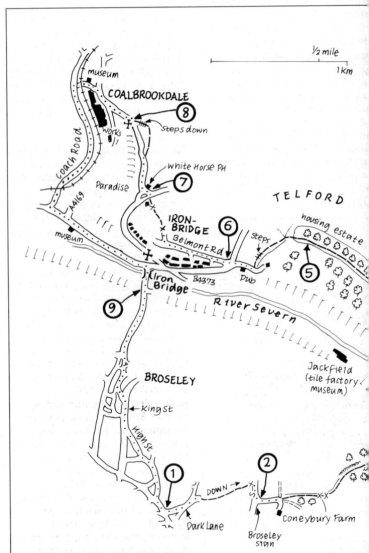

low well-defined grassy track
ross common land. Pass through
te just to right of bungalow and
ntinue down to road and T-
action ⑦. Cross road and
ntinue up on far side, passing
hite Horse pub on your right. 75
rds beyond brow of hill, fork right
path into woods, and fork left 350
rds beyond.

On reaching clear cross-track, turn
t down wooden steps to reach
rrier with road and church beyond
. Turn right on road, and on
ching main road take road
gonally opposite to pass through
albrookdale works [e].

After passing under railway bridge,
n left on Coach Road, which you
low for ½ mile, passing under
ther bridge. Turn left on main
d along the bank of the river on
ur right to reach the Iron Bridge
[f].

Turn right across bridge, cross
road on far side and climb steps to
continue up surfaced path. After ¼
mile, at top of steep rise, turn half
left (avoiding sharp left turn into
Cobwell Road) on to surfaced
driveway which continues to climb
steeply uphill.

Road later joins from left, and
after a further 70 yards fork left,
continuing uphill. Turn right in
larger road (King Street) to pass
King's Head Inn on your right.
Follow this road for ¼ mile avoiding
turnings to left and right, and at end
turn left into Broseley High Street to
return to the centre of the village.

ON THE ROUTE

NB The Ironbridge Gorge Museum is
spread over six sites, five of which
are passed on this walk; combined
entry tickets for all sites have no
expiry date (it is not possible to get
more than a superficial idea of all
the museums in a single day), or you
can buy a single site ticket
(proportionately more expensive).
The museum sites are: the Iron
Bridge, the Museum Visitor Centre,
Coalbrookdale Furnace and Museum
of Iron, Coalport China Museum,
Jackfield Tile Museum (not on this
walk), and Blists Hill Open Air
Museum. (Open daily exc
Christmas, Apr-late Oct, 10-6; late
Oct-Apr, 10-5.) Fully detailed
guidebooks are available.

[a] **Broseley** Street names such as
Foundry Street and Foundry Court
are reminders of the town's busy
past; it was the main urban centre
in Coalbrookdale in the 18th
century and the area was the
country's major coal and iron
centre. Ironmaster John Wilkinson,
who in 1787 built the first iron
barge, lived in The Lawns, an
imposing house in Church Street.
Broseley still produces drainage-
pipes and roof tiles.

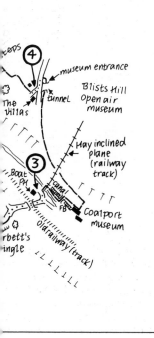

379

[b] **Coalport China Museum** The porcelain works, established in the 1790s, became world-famous; they closed 1926 when the Coalport Company moved to Stoke-on-Trent. The museum has displays of the production processes as well as much fine porcelain, and visitors can walk inside the shapely bottle-kilns.

[c] **The Hay Inclined Plane** (over the path) A remarkable engineering feat, the restored double-track railway was built to transport tub boats by gravity from the Shropshire Canal (at the top of the Blists Hill Museum site) to the River Severn at Coalport.

[d] **Blists Hill Open Air Museum** A re-created industrial community of the type found in the local coalfield about 1890, with forge, candle factory, sawmill, bank and locksmith's to be found in the high street, and a tollhouse, coal mine railway and furnaces elsewhere on the site. Most of these exhibits were transported from other parts of the country and reconstructed here.

[e] **Coalbrookdale** The true birthplace of the Industrial Revolution. It was here in 1709 that Abraham Darby first smelted iron using coke instead of the traditional charcoal, a far more efficient process. Soon the world's first cast-iron wheels, bridge and rails were made in Coalbrookdale. Antique Coalbrookdale fireplaces now fetch high prices. Numerous buildings survive from the village's heyday, including terraces of workers' cottages (Carpenters Row, overlooking the Old Furnace, was built about 1783) and the Institute, opened 1859 for educational purposes, now a youth hostel.

[f] **Iron Bridge** The world's first iron bridge, erected 1779, has become the most famous symbol of the Industrial Revolution. Designed by Thomas Pritchard under the direction of Abraham Darby; its table of tolls is still in place on the tollhouse wall.

hrewsbury

ne of England's best-preserved
udor and Georgian towns, which
serves to be better known. The
reet pattern is haphazard and it's
ite easy to miss some of the more
cked-away sights. Looping tightly
ound the town, the Severn is the
ey to Shrewsbury's early role as a
rategic Marches town in turbulent
mes; it now provides a calm
verside walk.

ength 3 miles (5km), 3 hours
ifficulty 1
art The Square, (old market hall
d tourist information)
efreshments Full range

ALK DIRECTIONS

) [a] From The Square with clock
old market hall behind you, go
st statue of Lord Clive into High
reet [b], turn right then
mediately left into alley
gnposted Toilets)[c]. At top
ntinue up Bear Steps [d] (opposite
d slightly to right), up steps and
der archway into St Alkmond's
uare [e]. Turn left just after toilets
enter Butcher Row [f].

② Turn right at end along main
destrianised street (Pridehill/
stle Street); turn left into School
ardens [g]. At end turn right (Castle
reet); detour left into castle [h];
ntinue along Castle Street and
tour left under gatehouse into
uncil House Court [i]. Continue
ong Castle Street, then ③ left into
indsor Place and immediately fork
t into St Mary's Water Lane [j], [k].
Turn right at river [l] and follow
th until English Bridge (the next
dge) ④. Turn right on to main
ad, keeping right after multi-storey
r park on your right, up Wyle Cop
]. Opposite Lion Hotel turn right
to Dogpole [n]. ⑤ Just after road
nds left, take passage on left into
Alkmond's Square.

Turn left in front of St Alkmond's
church, as path bends left again at St
Julian's church. Go down steps into
Wyle Cop. Turn right, and
⑥ immediately left into Milk Street
(leading into Belmont) [o]. At end
reach Town Walls [p]. Turn right and
immediately left into Crescent Lane.
⑦ Turn right at river, along
riverside path [q]; later join road
along river to reach Welsh Bridge
where ⑧ turn right to leave river.

Go past multi-storey car park,
then keep left [r] towards tall brick
clock tower, but before it is reached
take Claremont Hill on right. Left
along St Chads Terrace [s]. After
hospital on right, ⑨ left into Swan
Hill, right (opposite Admiral Benbow
pub) into College Hill [t], left at end
by Old St Chad's church and left at
bottom (Princess Street) to reach old
market hall, where turn right to
enter The Square.

ON THE ROUTE

[a] **The Square** The town's market-
place for 600 years, from 1269, as
Shrewsbury prospered as a centre of
the wool trade. The arcaded market
hall, built 1595, displays carved
figures taken from elsewhere in
town. Among these are a figure
(taken from the old Welsh Bridge) of
Richard Duke of York (below the
clock), who was father of Edward IV;
peg-holes on the structure were once
used for recording fleece sales. At
the back of the square is the town's
music hall (1839). The early
Victorian **pillar box** is a 'Penfold
hexagonal', named after its designer.
[b] **High Street** Two exceptionally
fine timber-framed houses stand on
the left. **Owen's Mansion**, across the
road, is dated 1592, and is decorated
with quatrefoils and cable moulding,
both typical features of the town's
houses of that period. Opposite it is
triple-gabled **Ireland's Mansion**, late
16th-century with windows replaced

381

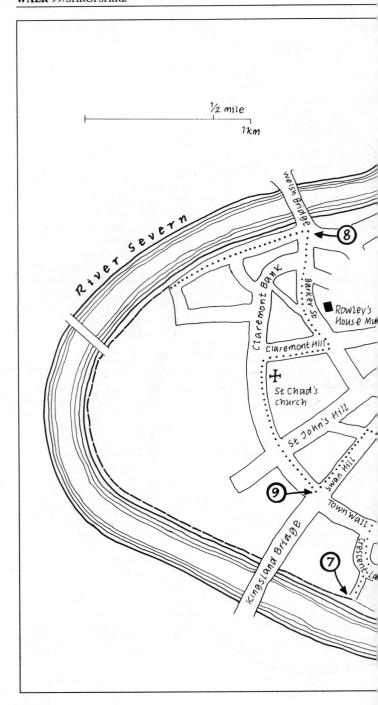

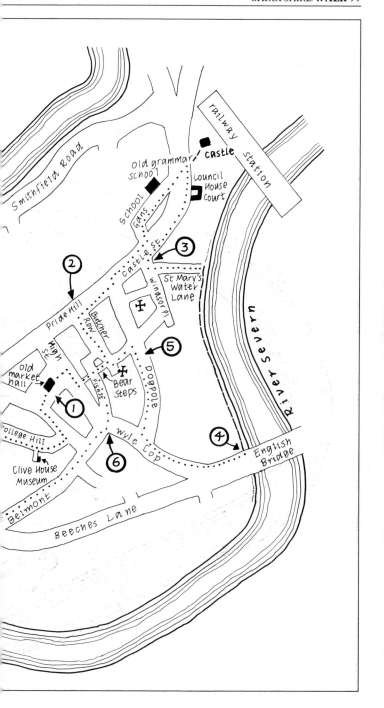

Smithfield Road

Old grammar school

School Gdns

castle

Council House Court

railway station

Castle St

③

② Pride Hill

St Mary's Water Lane

Windsor Pl

Butcher Row

High St

Old market hall

①

Bear Steps

Fish St

⑤

Dogpole

④ English Bridge

River Severn

Wyle Cop

College Hill

⑥

Clive House Museum

Belmont

Beeches Lane

in the early 18th century. In contrast, directly opposite The Square, **Halifax Building Society** (1892), with its richly detailed gable, is one of Shrewsbury's most exuberant Victorian buildings.

[c] On the right as soon as you enter this alley (Grope Lane) a small metal plate on the first building, with three animal heads and the legend 'Salop', is an old **fire-mark** (placed by the insurance company to mark an insured building). Several of various designs are passed on this walk.

[d] **Bear Steps** The picturesque alley leads up steps past an L-shaped group of buildings. On left, after the arch, Bear Steps Hall was probably originally part of property belonging to the guild of the Holy Cross, which wool merchant Thomas Pride founded in 1389. Inside the hall, which is now used by the town's civic society, a fine trussed roof is visible.

[e] **St Alkmond's Church and Square** After the nearby St Chad's church collapsed, the church authorities rebuilt this one in 1795. The square was the town's original market place.

[f] **Butcher Row** Built up as butchers' stalls, known as 'ffleshomeles' or flesh shambles, in the 13th century. In the 18th century it was known as Double Butcher Row; records show that fifteen butchers carried on trade here in 1828. **Abbots House**, on left, is c. 1500 and the best building in Shrewsbury of that date to survive in virtually its original form.

[g] **School Gardens** On left, the houses making up **Sydney Court** have in their basements the cells from the old county gaol (closed 1793). The public library and Christian Science Society are within the former buildings of **Shrewsbury School** (now on a suburban site), founded 1552 for the sons of wealthy local families. Riggs Hall, at the rear,

is the original building; the handsome facade is early 17th-century. Philamathon and Polymathone, two statues in Jacobean dress, stand by the doorway with a Greek inscription which translates 'If you love learning you will be learned.' Charles Darwin, also commemorated in statue form, was the school's most celebrated pupil. Before venturing into the castle, devotees of railway architecture may like to detour left down the main street for a view of **Shrewsbury station**, built in 1848 in a grand Perpendicular style by the Shrewsbury and Chester Railway.

[h] **The castle** (open 10-4 all year; closed Sun Oct-Easter; free entry to gardens) Built 1067, at the narrowest neck of land enclosed by the great loop of the River Severn, the castle defended the town's northern approaches. The gate is original; the rest was rebuilt by Edward II, and in 1787 Thomas Telford converted the whole into a private house for MP Sir William Poultney. It now houses a **regimental museum**, including relics and uniforms from Napoleonic times onwards, among them items once belonging to the 'grand old' Duke of York. **Laura's Tower**, named after Poultney's daughter, to the right as you enter the garden, has a wide view of the town. Beyond the divide in the railway, **Lord Hill's Column**, the world's tallest Greek Doric column (133ft) commemorates the right-hand man to Wellington at Waterloo and the Peninsular War, (later army commander-in-chief). To its right can be seen the **abbey church**, founded 1083.

[i] **Council House Court** The Council House was the meeting place for the Council of the Welsh Marches, which tried to keep law and order in the border lands. Meetings were also held at Ludlow and Bewdley until the council was

bolished during the Civil War.
Convicted criminals were
imprisoned in the **gatehouse**, a fine
timber-frame structure of 1618. The
council house (1501) fronts on to an
enchanting cobbled yard.

[j] Before descending St Mary's
Water Gate Lane, detour a few steps
left to see **St Mary's**, the only
medieval church left in the town
centre (but no longer used for
worship), with a noted 14th-century
Jesse window (one of only eight in
England) from St Chad's church at
its E end. When the 15th-century
spire collapsed at the end of the last
century, the vicar preached that it
was a divine judgement on the town
for erecting a statue of Darwin. The
W side of the tower has a memorial
to a Mr Cadman who had a fatal fall
from a tight-rope suspended from
the spire in 1739.

[k] **St Mary's Water Gate Lane**
Parliamentarian forces entered the
town up this lane in 1645 and
stormed the castle. The archway at
the bottom is a 17th-century
entrance in the town walls.

[l] **English Bridge** Built 1774 and
broadened in 1925. In both instances
the stone came from quarries at
nearby Grinshill.

[m] **Wyle Cop** The street-name
comes from the Welsh for 'hill top';
the street winds steeply up, past a
series of overhanging half-timbered
buildings dating from the 15th
century (the stepped effect is partly
diluted by the building-out of the
lower storey). On left, Nos. 66-69
and 71-73 are particularly striking;
at the latter, now Henry Tudor
House, Henry VII stayed on his way
to victory at Bosworth Field.
Paganini, Dickens and Jenny Lind
are known to have stayed at the Lion
Hotel, an important coaching inn on
what became Telford's London to
Holyhead road.

[n] **Dogpole** Another of Shrewsbury's
strange street-names, this one of
uncertain origin. One theory is that
it comes from 'ducken poll',
meaning 'stoop summit': a low gate
once at the bottom of the street
required taller people to stoop. On
right, the half-timbered **Old House**
was once the home of Anthony
Rocke, servant of Katherine of
Aragon; Mary Tudor is thought to
have stayed here in 1526. At the
corner, the red-brick **Guildhall** was
Shropshire's first classically
proportioned house when erected in
1696 as Newport House. Its fine
staircase and panelling can be seen
from the street.

[o] **Belmont** This and the
surrounding streets became the
fashionable part of town from 1700,
and is of predominantly Georgian
appearance, with some good
brickwork. On right, the remains of
St Chad's church stand on a swathe
of turf; the bulk of the church
collapsed in 1788. At the end of the
green and on left, the **Judge's
Lodging** (1701), six bays wide, used
to accommodate circuit assize
judges and still belongs to the
judiciary.

[p] **The Crescent** Directly opposite,
this shallow curve of four houses is
late 18th-century. To the left, across
the street, is a 500-yard long part of
the **town wall**. Henry III ordered the
fortification of Shrewsbury, which
by 1220 had become an important
border town; 17th-century
restoration was carried out in
preparation for the Civil War. The
wall was largely intact in the 18th
century, but this is the only
substantial remain. To the right can
be seen a 13th-century **postern
tower**. Alongside it is an old pump
with the slogan 'Waste Not, Want
Not. Turn the Handle.'

[q] **River Severn** Quarry Park looks
on to Britain's longest river, with
Shrewsbury School and leafy back

gardens on the far side. Welsh Bridge was erected 1795 and has survived unaltered.

[r] **Rowley House Museum** (open 10-5, Mon-Sat, all year; 12-5 Sun, Easter-Oct). Rowley's House, a large timber-framed late 16th-century town house, adjoins Rowley's Mansion (1618), a brick-built former vicarage (where the vicar of St Chad's once entertained Dr Johnson). Together they form the museum housing the main collection of remains from the nearby Roman town of Wroxeter (including the Forum inscription and a rare silver mirror), as well as local hoards, historic costumes and geology displays.

[s] **St Chad's (New) Church** After the collapse of the old church, this striking building, with its circular Grecian nave, was consecrated 1792.

[t] **Clive House Museum** (Open 2-5 Mon; 10-1, 2-5 Tue-Sat). On right, at the end of a narrow lane, this was once a dwelling of the dean and clergy for the college of St Chad, converted 1752 for residential use; Clive of India lived here when MP and mayor. Now run as a museum, the house has period rooms, furniture and a collection of Shropshire china.

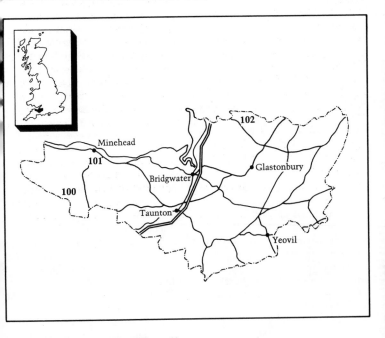

SOMERSET

100 Tarr Steps and the Barle Valley
101 Dunster Park and Grabbist Hill
102 Around Cheddar Gorge

Holiday Which! Good Walks Guide

30 Cow Castle and the Barle Valley   31 Hurlstone Point and Selworthy
Beacon   32 Horner Woods and Dunkery Beacon
33 The Northern Quantocks

Tarr Steps and the Barle Valley

Starting from the much-visited packhorse bridge, the walk leads into solitary grazing land on the west side of the Barle valley. Skirting Withypool Hill via moorland paths, the descent to Withypool village is followed by one of Devon's most attractive river walks. Take care with field directions (route partly way-marked); erosion along the river-path makes the going underfoot rough in places.

Length 8½ miles (13.5km), 4 hours
Difficulty 3
Start Tarr Steps car park, in Barle Valley SE of Withypool (well signposted). Grid reference 873324 *Alternatively* start at Withypool. Grid reference 846355; car park in village (follow road with church on left and pass pub on left and start directions at ⑪)
OS maps 1:50,000 181; 1:25,000 SS 83/93 (Pathfinder 1235)
Refreshments Lunches and teas at Tarr Farm by Tarr Steps; shop and pub in Withypool

WALK DIRECTIONS

① Turn left out of Tarr Steps car park, down to Tarr Steps (an ancient stone bridge), which you cross over the River Barle [a]. Pick up road on other side. ② Immediately fork right on rising driveway signposted Withypool Hill and by sign to Tarr Steps Hotel. After 80 yards fork right in front of hotel entrance gate, now on unmade enclosed path, leading to gate and bending right.

Path is now sunken and has field up on left. ③ At the end of this field turn left (still inside the same field; yellow waymarks here are helpful), with hedgerow on right uphill. Pass through gate into (second) field and continue on the left edge alongside

the hedgerow [b].

Proceed on left edge of third field, now on a track, but at end of field ④ turn right on track (still inside third field; do not go ahead to farm). Proceed on top (left) edge of fourth field and right edge of fifth field to stile beside gate, where path proceeds with fence on left (ignore a signposted path to left), until entering field by gate where ⑤ follow bottom edge close to stream towards gate on to road.

Turn right on road (signposted Withypool Hill). ⑥ After ½ mile cross cattle-grid at beginning of open land, and immediately fork left on to moorland track with hedgerow on left. ⑦ Where hedge away to left reaches a corner, fork right. This immediately becomes less distinct: keep forward on the level, initially close to the left fork but later diverging from it.

The route is defined, however, and in clear conditions a steep section of road ahead and slightly to right is a prominent marker in the distance. A neat enclosure of fields with hedgerow trees is seen away to left: when level with far side of it ⑧ turn right at obvious crossing of tracks, slightly downhill (soon ignore a track ascending to right, up Withypool Hill).

⑨ Just as you reach road, turn right on rising moorland path which soon levels (ignore a right fork); Withypool village comes into view. Path later becomes indistinct: head for nearest house (easiest route may be to go to two telegraph poles to the right of it). ⑪ Turn left on road and cross river to enter Withypool village [c].

Continue on main village street past church and pub on your left. After end of village, road ascends. ⑪ Cross stile on right signed as riverside path to Tarr Steps. The route is obvious all the way back, following river [d] closely (the path is not always defined however; there are one or two rough sections where erosion has occurred and you have to pick out your own way).

ON THE ROUTE

a] Tarr Steps The most famous antiquity in Exmoor, a low bridge of 17 slabs of local gritstone. It has had a chequered history of flood damage and has been washed away and rebuilt many times; its date of construction is unknown but is thought to be medieval. Local legend claims this to be the Devil's favourite sun-bathing place.

[b] The route takes in typical Exmoor scenery with moorland and higher ground surrounding a lush, unspoilt river valley. You are following the **Two Moors Way**, a long-distance path across Devon from Ivybridge (S of Dartmoor) to the N coast at Lynmouth; the river path along the Barle is an alternative route taken by the Way.

[c] Withypool A six-arched bridge at the entrance to the village, then the road continues past the church (much restored but with a Norman font), and the Royal Oak Inn, where R.D. Blackmore is thought to have written part of *Lorna Doone*.

[d] The **River Barle**, placid, clear and shallow, takes a course through one of the finest Exmoor valleys, rising in lonely country W of Simonsbath to join the Exe beyond Dulverton. Heron and kingfishers may sometimes be seen near the river.

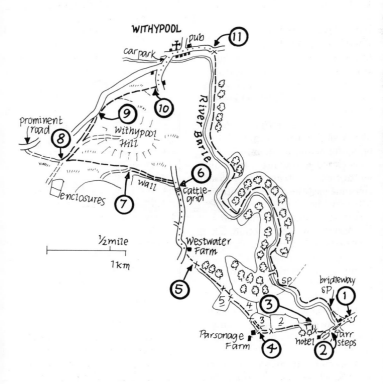

Dunster Park and Grabbist Hill

Through estate parklands looking on to Dunster Castle, then sheltered walking in the forest through the quietest of combes. A lengthy and steep haul 650 feet up is rewarded by a superb final mile along the ridge of Grabbist Hill, with views of Dunster as you descend. Route is not waymarked, but is reasonably easy to follow.

Length 6 miles (9.5km), 3 hours
Difficulty 3–4

Start Dunster town centre (on A396 SE of Minehead), by octagonal Yarn Market, facing the castle. Grid reference 992438

OS maps 1:50,000 181; 1:25,000 SS 84/94 (Pathfinder 1215)

Refreshments Pubs, cafés and shops in Dunster

WALK DIRECTIONS

① [a] Walk along the main street towards castle, before which the street bends right in the Tiverton direction. Past the church on your right, the road bends left and soon **②** turn left into Mill Lane (signposted Dunster Working Mill). Turn right by signpost for packhorse bridge (or detour to the mill first [b]), on enclosed path to reach road; turn left to cross packhorse bridge [c] and continue past the thatched cottages on the right.

③ Just after cottages turn left at signpost at four-way junction, taking direction for Carhampton, over stile by gate, then keep forward (immediately ignoring path to right signposted Withycombe) [d]. The track becomes indistinct: keep forward soon with fence close by on left to take gate into next pasture, again go forward with fence close on left.

④ At end, gate gives on to corner of track, where turn right uphill [e].

Keep to main track throughout, which sometimes has wall on its right. **⑤** After ½ mile ignore left-hand track; just after, ignore gate on right (with signpost beyond it); the main track then starts to drop and bends round gradually to right; fields briefly appear on left and **⑥** after they end ignore minor right fork (the main track here loses the wall). The track descends very gently along valley with stream close by on left with open strip of land beyond it. **⑦** After passing footbridge (do not cross), ignore an ascending right

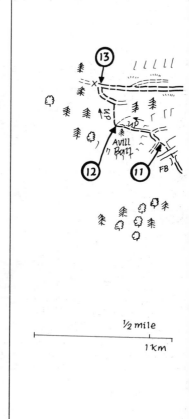

½ mile

1 km

fork. **(8)** Emerge on to surfaced lane on which turn right and keep right at next T-junction. **(9)** Turn left along main road. **(10)** 300 yards later turn right on track at Avill Farm: pass just to left of cottage, over footbridge, and proceed to surfaced lane.

Cross the lane and take path opposite, steeply uphill with field and hedgerow close by on right. **(11)** Near the top of the field on your right, reach corner of forestry track along which keep forward, but after 30 yards take narrow path ahead

where the track makes a bend to the right. This path leads steeply uphill alongside old wall with wooded slopes of Avill Ball up on your left.

(12) Where slope on left ends, turn right, still ascending, to reach open land at top. Turn left at T-junction with track, which bends right and **(13)** reaches T-junction (with gates on left into wood and view opening out on north side of ridge). Turn right on track along centre of ridge [**f**]; fork right after 200 yards.

The track enters woods, passes National Trust sign for Grabbist

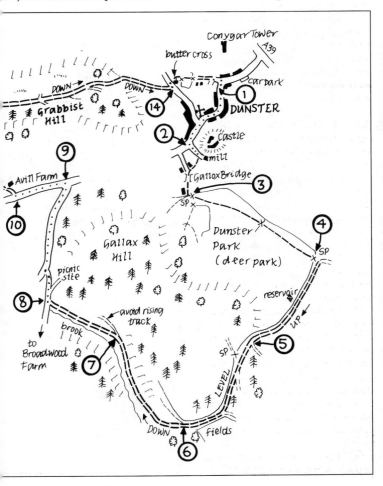

Hill: ignore side-turns, now proceeding first with fence on left and then dropping into mature woods. As you leave the woods, Dunster comes into view and the track then drops to road ⑭.

Turn left on road, past 30mph derestriction sign, then right at the Butter Cross (signposted) [g]. Beyond the cross take a kissing-gate to right of track and follow field path to kissing-gate just to left of house. Keep forward on driveway to reach road close by Yarn Market.

ON THE ROUTE

[a] **Dunster** One of England's most handsome small towns, with the 17th-century Yarn Market at the centre of a broad main street with picturesque homes and inns, looking N to the 18th-century folly tower on Conygar Hill and with Dunster Castle at the S end of the street presiding over the scene. The **castle** (National Trust open Apr-Sept, daily exc Fri and Sat, 11-5; Oct-4 Nov, 2-4; Jun-Aug garden and grounds only open on Fri and Sat) has Saxon origins, but its oldest surviving part is 13th-century. It was largely destroyed after the Civil War and most of what you see is a 19th-century rebuilding by Anthony Salvin in romanticised medieval style, to make an opulent country house for the Luttrell family, owners of the castle, 1376-1975. The walk leads past the partly 14th-century **Old Nunnery**, an ancient slate-hung timber-frame house of unusual design with overhangs, and the 15th- and 16th-century church, with its bells, whch ring out hymn tunes.

[b] You can continue a few yards to the 17th-century **water-mill**, a working flour-mill that has recently been restored. Its twin overshot wheels are unique. Open Apr-Oct exc Sat, and daily July and Aug.

[c] **Gallox Bridge** A tiny medieval packhorse bridge, in a picturesque setting by a group of thatched cottages.

[d] The **Deer Park** gives some of the best views of Dunster castle.

[e] Views of The **Glamorgan Coast** and **Severn Estuary**. The prominent island is Steep Holme, near Weston-super-Mare.

[f] **Grabbist Hill** provides one of the best ridge walks in Exmoor, with views on three sides. **Minehead** and the **Severn Estuary** are to the left with South Wales beyond the upland massif of the **Quantocks** ahead, and **eastern Exmoor** is to the right.

[g] Remains of the triple-stepped **medieval Butter Cross**, with a broken-off shaft. Views of Conygar Tower.

Around Cheddar Gorge

Britain's most famous limestone land-form is often viewed from the road which follows its floor, but the Gorge is remarkable when seen from the high-level path on this route. Earlier sections of this walk lead through the farmland of the Mendip plateau and a fine nature reserve.

Length 3 or 4 miles (5 or 6.5km) or 2½ hours

Difficulty 3

Start Cheddar (town); turn off A371 in Cheddar town centre by market cross on to B3135 signed to the Gorge. Follow road until car park on right immediately before Butchers Arms pub. Grid reference 461536

OS maps 1:50,000 182; 1:25,000 ST 45/55 (Pathfinder 1198)

Refreshments Full range in Cheddar

WALK DIRECTIONS

1 [a] Follow road towards Cheddar Gorge, passing Galleries Inn on right then take second bridge on left, signposted as path to Gorge and toilets; bear right in front of White Hart Inn, then just after the path bends left in front of waterworks gate, fork left (signposted). **2** Path rejoins road.

For 3 mile walk via Gorge follow the Gorge road to beyond end of Gorge, then take signposted stile on right for Draycott 3½ and West Mendip Way, and pick-up walk directions at **3**.

For 4 mile walk as soon as you re-join road take signposted ascending track sharp left. Initially you pass trees on your left, then a field appears down on your left. **3** At the end of the field, turn right on signposted enclosed path just before house.

The path bends left to pass behind the house and just before next house (with iron balconies) turn sharp right on to rising path, up into woodland.

4 Cross stile into open scrubby land and keep forward and slightly to right, uphill alongside dilapidated wall.

Scrubland later gives way to open grassland, where path is undefined but keep forward alongside wall; on re-entering more woodland, path is clear again and reaches solid wall at edge of farmland **5**. Cross the wall via stile and proceed along left edge of three fields to pass immediately left of Piney Sleight Farm. After the farm proceed on enclosed track.

6 Where after cattle-grid, track ceases to be enclosed, turn right by signpost for Cheddar [b] to continue with wall on right along edge of two large fields. **7** at end, pass through gate beside stile into woodland and follow track gently down, entering nature reserve at bottom by gate and proceeding forward on track along bottom of valley [c]. This leads to gate on to road. Cross road and take stile opposite and slightly to right, signposted Draycott 3½, West Mendip Way **8**.

The path leads steeply up through woods. **9** 50 yards after emerging into the open, fork right and follow the path keeping as close to edge of cliff as possible to enjoy the remarkable sequence of views to the Gorge [d].

10 At Prospect Tower, you can either take steps ('Jacob's Ladder') down on right in front of Tower or continue to left of Tower on path dropping to road at edge of Cheddar, where proceed downhill to reach starting point.

ON THE ROUTE

[a] **Cheddar** The world-renowned cheese was made in local farmhouses as early as the 12th century but has more or less disappeared as a local cottage industry. At the town centre is a famous hexagonal market

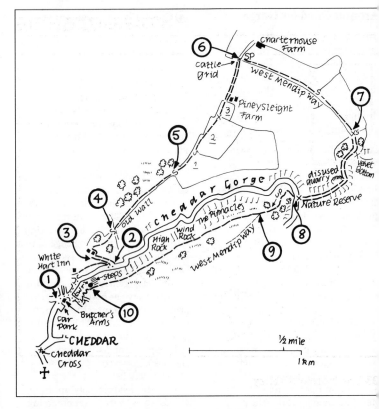

cross, of medieval origin.

[b] West Mendip Way A 30-mile long distance path developed by local Rotary Clubs, from the cathedral city of Wells, to Uphill on the Bristol Channel, passing Wookey Hole cave and Bladon Hill on the way. The scenery here gives a good idea of the Mendip plateau, with no hint of the nearby drama of Cheddar Gorge.

[c] Black Rock and Velvet Bottom Nature Reserves Limestone valley and woods, strongly resembling the Derbyshire Dales, with carboniferous limestone overlaid with glacial loess giving a rich flora; the presence until the 19th century of lead mining has meant that species have adapted to the high lead content of the soil. Trail leaflets are available at a dispenser near the road.

[d] Cheddar Gorge For one mile, gre limestone cliffs rise 450ft on either side of the road, to make one of the most enthralling landscapes in the country. A primeval river gouged ou a tunnel through the rock, and the collapse of its roof creates the canyon we see today. The high-leve path used on this section of the wal gets the most remarkable views of all - both into the Gorge, and westwards across the fenlands of th Somerset Levels and Cheddar Reservoir to the Quantock Hills. 27 steps lead up Jacob's Ladder to the Prospect Tower (opened 1908), a tinny structure which is something between a lighthouse and a helter-skelter ride.

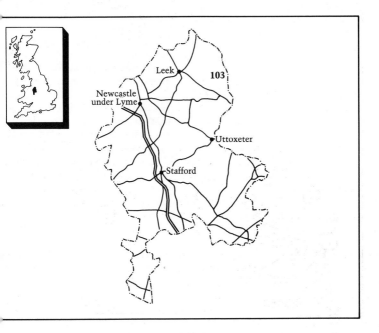

oliday Which? Good Walks Guide

The Manifold Valley

Route enters a deep limestone dale from the plateau above, follows the valley floor, then leads into remote and more open country around Wetton Hill. Route-finding easy along the dales, but field-paths are undefined.

Length 4½ miles (7km), 2½ hours
Difficulty 2–3
Start Wetton (on minor road NW of Ashbourne and ESE of Leek). Roadside parking in village or park

in car park by toilets just outside: from Old Royal Oak Inn take turn for Alstonefield and Ilam then first right. Grid reference 109554 (village) 108551 (car park)
OS maps 1:50,000 119; 1:25,000 Outdoor Leisure 24
Refreshments Pub in Wetton; café at Wetton Mill

WALK DIRECTIONS

① With pub on left, take village street uphill, signposted Wetton Mill; turn left after 80 yards by

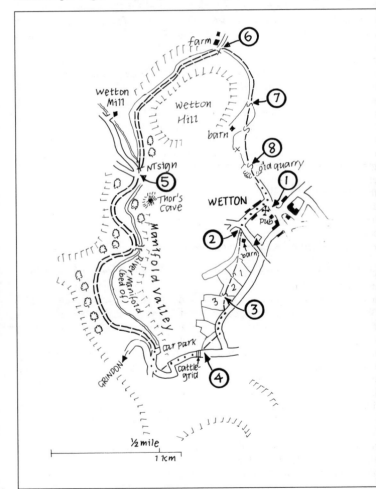

396

:lephone box. At end of village, the
)ad divides **(2)**.

o *avoid field route* into Manifold
alley (which takes a little finding;
nis alternative involves walking
own tiny lanes - generally
elightful, but can be traffic-ridden
: peak weekends) turn left, then
ght at next junction; descend to
-junction, where bear right, over
attle-grid at **(4)**.

or *field route* take stone stile
etween these two roads, to left of
)ad signpost. Pass to right of house
y keeping along wall, then beyond
ext stile go forward on track, past
arn on your left. Where track ends,
) into the left-hand of two fields:
head, in distance, is a prominent
ointed hill: go across field heading
1st to left of this, finding stile 50
ards to left of far right-hand corner.
roceed across second field in same
irection to narrow gap (functioning
s stile). **(3)** In third field, go forward
) steps in far left-hand corner, then
ght on surfaced lane. Count two
elds on your right: at beginning of
iird field, go through narrow gap-
:ile (a deliberate gap in wall); if you
iiss this, follow the lane down,
eeping right at T-junction, then
ver cattle-grid to pick up directions
t **(4)** to enter top of field). Follow
ght-hand edge of field, down to
attle-grid road sign, cross
attle-grid **(4)**.

Where lane bends sharp left, cut
ff a corner by descending steep
orsy slope and turn right at bottom,
ver bridge, then immediately right
n surfaced track (closed to motor
ehicles), alongside River Manifold
1): follow for 1¼ miles. **(5)** Reach
ridge and road junction.

)etour ahead for refreshments at
Vetton Mill, along right-hand road
with 3-ton restriction signs), then
ght over next bridge to mill [b].

o *continue*, take gate opposite and
slightly to the right, with National
Trust sign beyond for Wetton Hill.
Follow track along valley. This
bends right after ¼ mile, then ½
mile later **(6)** goes through gate at
farm. Just beyond gate cross small
bridge over stream on right, and
ascend slope, keeping along wall on
right. Follow wall (which bends
right) over brow of hill to stile **(7)**,
cross field diagonally left to
next stile.

Beyond, take rising path, in same
direction: this peters out after
ascending – keep forward, on the
level, with wall on right in view.
(8) Eventually reach gap-stile with
National Trust sign (facing other
way). Proceed through old quarry to
gate ahead, then follow lane into
Wetton.

ON THE ROUTE
[a] **Manifold Valley** Deep limestone
dale, wooded at this end, running
from Longnor S to Ilam, just after
which the Manifold joins the Dove;
the Manifold disappears
underground between Wetton Mill
and Ilam. Among the caves and crags
is **Thor's Cave** (high up and
prominent on the right at the most
dramatic part of the dale). The
Hamps valley just to the S has a cave
where an Anglo-Saxon hoard of
coins and jewellery was found in
1924. The track is the bed of an old
railway which operated from 1904-
34 for transporting milk and tourist
traffic. **Orchids** are abundant in
spring and early summer. **Dippers**
and **grey wagtails** are common along
the river, **green woodpeckers** in the
woods and **wheatears** around the
crags and pastures.
[b] **Wetton Mill** was a corn-mill until
1957. The nearby bridge, rebuilt
1807, was used by packhorses
transporting lead from the lucrative
Ecton Copper Mines (further N).

397

SUFFOLK

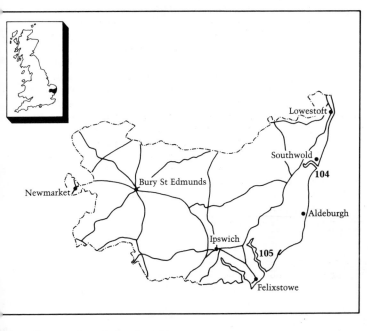

104 Walberswick and Southwold
105 Shottisham, Ramsholt and the River Deben

Holiday Which? Good Walks Guide

Walberswick and Southwold

To the west of the River Dunwich the route covers wide expanses of marshland and heath, much of it nature reserve. Continue over a breezy, open common to Southwold, whose intricate townscape and strong character make it one of the most distinguished of East Anglia's coastal towns. Easy route-finding.

Length 7½ miles (12km), 3½ hours (or can be shortened to 6 miles if the River Blyth ferry is in operation)
Difficulty 2
Start Car park at the seaward end of Walberswick village, where the B1387 terminates at the river. Grid reference 501748
OS maps 1:50,000 156, 1:25,000 TM 47/57 (Pathfinder 966)
Refreshments Pubs and tea-room in Walberswick; Harbour Inn near the footbridge at ⑥; full range in Southwold

WALK DIRECTIONS

① From the car park, walk back along the road towards Walberswick, passing the Bell Inn on the left-hand side and two tea-rooms on the right. After 300 yards the road turns sharply right: just beyond this corner, take the path going left immediately before the Plough Inn.

The path ascends past allotment gardens, then turns to right at junction with another path coming in from left. Continue to T-junction with broader track, where turn left. The path skirts the field and turns right at the far corner. ② 20 yards past this corner, take a smaller path diverging left through the bushes. This leads out through reed beds [a] with wooden duckboards underfoot to the bank of the Dunwich river.

Turn right, along the bank. At footbridge (do not cross), drop down off the bank and continue closer to the river edge. ③ When the brick

tower of a former drainage pump is reached, cross small tributary and turn right at T-junction of paths beyond.

The path heads towards woods with semi-reclaimed marshland on the right and reed beds on the left (part of Walberswick Nature Reserve) [b]. After 300 yards, path enters woodland, bearing a little left as it continues through the wood. Shortly it skirts an area of open gorsy heathland away to the left. [c] The path joins a track coming from the Reserve and continues up to a minor road ahead.

④ Cross the road to a notice-board with large scale map. The walk continues behind this board, following grassy track which can be seen curving left across heath towards woodland. [d] When the track meets the spinney ahead, it bears right following the edge of the trees. When the track forks keep right. This reaches a road: turn right along this for about 200 yards to house on the left-hand side. Just past this a signpost points left over the common ⑤.

Pass through a metal gate just behind the signpost (which reads Walberswick ¼). At junction of paths ignore tracks right and left and keep ahead. Continue for 500 yards to a second gate. Through the gate, take the path half left, going uphill on to old railway embankment [e]. This is now a sandy track between banks with gorse: follow this to reach surfaced path at a T-junction with notice forbidding horses and motor vehicles. Turn left along this and continue with marshland on the left to cross footbridge over the River Blyth ⑥.

On far side of bridge, (detour right for 300 yards for Harbour Inn). Continue straight ahead. At top of rise, path ceases to be surfaced: here take track to right (signpost

ootpath over common to town
entre), passing golf clubhouse away
o right, over the common aiming
eft of water-tower. Just short of
he tower, a cross-track is met: turn
eft here.

At a further junction of paths, take
he rather faint path half right
owards a white-painted wooden
arrier which can be seen breaking
he line of the row of houses ahead.
Do not take the better-marked path
ight leading to the road.) At time of
hecking, the correct path passed
ust to the right of a small tree.

(7) At the barrier, pass through
vooden turnstile into the unmade
oad beyond. (Spinner's Lane). [**f**]
merging on to a road ahead,
pposite a row of houses named
Station Road Villas", turn right for
00 yards to a road junction [**g**]. Turn
eft here into Victoria Street, passing
outhwold Museum [**h**] and parish
hurch [**i**]. The green here is
artholomew Green [**j**].

Note here on the right a row of
'ictorian houses with a remarkable
rray of painted sculpture heads just
elow the eaves. Further down the
treet you pass Adnam's brewery
nd reach East Green. On the left is
ne Sole Bay Inn [**k**]. Just past this is
tradbroke Road, containing
outhwold's lighthouse, a prominent
andmark. Turn right along the
ea-front.

(8) At St James's Green, which is
narked by a mast and two
rnamental cannons, detour right for
ne High Street and Market Place.
eturn to this point to resume the
valk. Continue along sea-front:
vhere the road bears right, go
etween white posts straight ahead,
nd continue along path following
ow cliff-top, passing the Sailors'
eading Room [**l**].

The path drops down to beach
evel at a concrete area just behind
ne beach: where it does, take the

path ahead going back up the slope
again, keeping railings on the left,
leading out on to Gun Hill [**m**].
(9) The path drops down again to a
crossing path: turn left to a small
refreshment kiosk and then turn
right behind a row of beach huts.
The path can be seen stretching
ahead, over loose sand at first, and
then over grass, heading for a small
group of houses in the distance.
Keep to the left of these, to meet a
wooden hut (Suffolk Wildlife Trust
information centre) (10).

Continue to the river edge and
return right. The track continues
alongside the river, reaching after
400 yards the crossing point for the
Walberswick ferry [**n**] which will
shorten the route back to the
starting-point. If, however,
inclination or the time of year
excludes the ferry, there are further
pleasures still to come. The track
leads through an area of boats, tarred
shacks (some selling fish), a ship's
chandlery offering teas, the Harbour
Inn, a pleasurable stretch for those
who appreciate a scene of busy
marine activity [**o**].

At the end of the stretch, take
footbridge you crossed earlier and
return down the opposite bank to
reach ferry crossing-point, where a
flagged path leads away from the
bank, back to the car park.

ON THE ROUTE
[**a**] The **reeds** are managed by
cutting, with a rotational harvest
which provides supplies of reed for
thatching, while keeping a suitable
habitat for the bearded tit, bittern,
reed warbler, water rail and
other birds.
[**b**] The **Walberswick Reserve**
consists of about 1300 acres of
reedbeds, mudflats, heathland and
woods. Apart from its prolific bird
life, it offers such plants as bogbean,
marsh pennywort, marsh sow-thistle

and wild celery, and has a good range of butterflies and moths (see information panels).

[c] This is a good example of the surviving **Suffolk sandlings**, the areas of sandy heathland in the Suffolk coastal region which were once far more widespread than now.

[d] The name of this heath – **East Sheep Walk** - is a reminder of the extent to which sheep farming and the wool trade created the economy of East Anglia in the Middle Ages and financed the building of many of the region's great churches.

[e] The **Southwold Railway** closed in 1929. Never a successful line, it tended to be regarded with affectionate derision locally. Its gauge was narrow (only 3 feet), which meant that all freight had to be manhandled on to Great Eastern trucks at Halesworth. Speed was limited by regulation to 16mph, while its bus competitors were allowed 20mph, and the rolling stock was antiquated and odd – some claimed that it was a job lot from a failed order for a line in China.

[f] The name **Spinner's Lane** is, of course, significant: the cottage names reflect the former presence of the wool trade.

[g] On the left here is the house where **George Orwell** (Eric Blair), the author of *Animal Farm* and *1984*, lived.

[h] **Southwold Museum** has displays on local topography and history. (Open late May-late Sept in the afternoons, plus Easter weekends and May bank hol).

[i] The **church** is not to be missed, nor can this great 15th-century building be categorised in a few lines. It's a place to savour slowly, while recalling with gratitude the wartime bomb which blew out its Victorian stained glass and left the present clear windows, admitting a great flood of light to the superb nave and chancel. Don't miss the beautiful painted screen, dating from about 1500.

[j] The **greens** of Southwold are one of its pleasures. A disastrous fire in the 17th century destroyed much of the town: when it was rebuilt, some plots were left undeveloped, and it is said that these became the present-

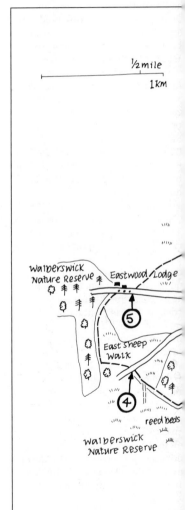

ay greens. Whatever their origin, the varied character of these green bases and the pattern of houses round each do much to give the own its delightful and individual atmosphere.

.] The name is a reminder of the **attle of Sole Bay**, fought against the **D**utch at Gun Hill.

The **Sailors' Reading Room** is a major Southwold institution: full of paintings, photographs and models of ships. There are generally fishermen playing cards or chatting, but they are good-naturedly tolerant to visitors who want to look at the exhibits.

[**m**] The **Cannon on Gun Hill** provided a pretext during the 1914-18 war to regard Southwold as a

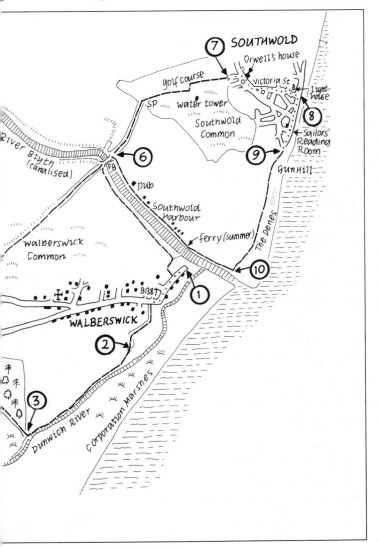

fortified place, and the town was accordingly bombarded from the sea. The octagonal building is a coastguard headquarters.

[n] The **Ferry** operates from Whitsun to September, and occasionally at weekends at other times.

[o] The artist **Wilson Steer** was very fond of this scene, and painted aspects of it many times in water-colour and oils.

hottisham, Ramsholt nd the River Deben

he heart of this walk is a stretch of st over two miles along the bank the River Deben, with wide views ver this beautiful river, abundant rd life and marsh flora. The river is proached and left by easy, pleasant acks through parkland and rmland with a short section of uiet country road.

ength 6½ miles (10.5km),
½ hours

ifficulty 2

tart Shottisham (on B1083 SE of Voodbridge), outside the Sorrel forse, the village's thatched pub. rid reference 320446

S maps 1:50,000 169; 1:25,000 TM 4/34 (Pathfinder 1031)

efreshments Pub and shop at hottisham; pub at Ramsholt

VALK DIRECTIONS

① With your back to the pub, turn ght up the by-road signposted Church Lane, no through road". his passes the track leading up to ne church on the right. [a] Where oad ends at Tower Cottage, take a rassy path on left which soon ecomes choked with undergrowth. Vhen it does, use the edge of the eld on the right to continue the ame line.

From stile in corner of field, the ath diverges half right across next ield. It crosses two shallow vatercourses by footbridges with ow brick abutments. Cross the stile eyond and fork left towards a vooden fence which can be seen reaking the line of the hedge on the ar side of the field near a cottage.

② Beyond next stile, go over a mall footbridge on to a road. Cross o the driveway of the Wood Hall fotel opposite. (A notice says "no ublic right of way for vehicles", but here is in fact a right of way for

pedestrians.) Walk up the drive to the hotel and skirt to the right of the hotel grounds along a surfaced track. A sign is reached warning against wildfowl crossing the road [b].

The track continues to Sutton Street, a small group of flint and thatched cottages. Beyond the cottages, fork left, to pass Nut Tree Farm, track bears left then slightly right to Pettistree Hall ③ [c]. Follow signposted path going left through the farmyard, then continue along a broad, sandy track. After 500 yards bear right at fork [d]. This leads down towards river: keep left at the derelict farm building, as waymarked.

Left along river, either at the foot of the bank in the field or on top of it if bushes permit. After ½ mile, where Shottisham Creek empties into the River Deben at Sluice Cottage, a notice directs the walker on to the top of the bank. ④ 400 yards later, reach conifer plantation: keep *inland* of this to where, near the far end of the wooded area, the path swings right as a clear track into the woodland [e].

Follow this, and just before wire fence ahead take a few steps up to right on to sea wall, and cross stile ahead. Path continues with marshland on right and open water on left. Cross another stile and proceed to Ramsholt, to reach which you have to drop on to the foreshore for last 50 yards [f].

⑤ From the quay and the Ramsholt Arms return over the short stretch of foreshore which you crossed to reach Ramsholt. At the point where you dropped to the beach, a sign reads "Bridleway, please keep to the path". Go up here, with Ramsholt church clearly visible on the rise above. Follow the grassy trodden track over the rough field ahead, through a gate, following curving path round to right to where in the hedge ahead a white notice points the way through. Continue over the field beyond [g], then take small path up the bank on right to reach gate of churchyard [h].

⑥ Return from the church to the path by which you reached it. Continue on from here, away from the river, for the last section of the walk back to the starting point. At the top of the field, turn right at T-junction of tracks shortly veering left past a small wooded area to reach a minor road at a point where there is a surviving wartime

fortification, now grassed over ⑦.

Turn left up this quiet road between hedges for 600 yards. At T-junction, take sandy track opposite to left of pair of cottages. This brings you alongside two fields and a paddock to Shottisham, where emerge on to the road directly opposite the Sorrel Horse public house.

ON THE ROUTE
[a] **Shottisham Church** has a fine tower and is worth a brief pause. Ke at the Sorrel Horse.

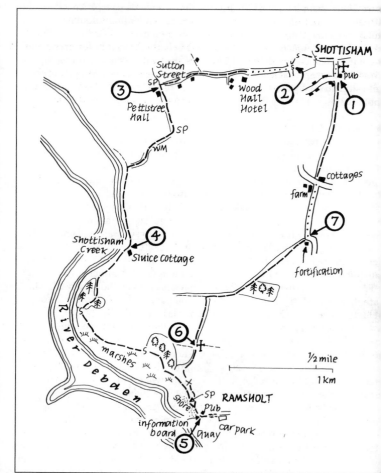

] Note the picture on the sign, of a
bandaged duck on crutches: the
wildfowl habitat can be seen in a
lake beyond the hedge to the left.
] The OS map shows a path cutting
across the field to the left and by-
passing the farm buildings. This is
now evidently impractical: the route
given works perfectly well.
] Again the OS map is misleading.
: shows a right of way going off to
the right before this fork is reached,
but this leads into nettles and
difficulty. The track shown in the
walk directions is clearly indicated
with yellow arrows as a bridle path,
although it is not marked in green
on the map.
] The map shows the path as
passing the plantation on the
riverside. There is no clear route for
this, and the used path is as
described.

[f] A Suffolk County Council Suffolk
Heritage Coast panel on the
foreshore is worth studying for its
history of **Ramsholt**, once a
flourishing village, but now much
reduced in population and size, and
for its account of the birds and
plants of the district. The Ramsholt
Arms has grown from what was a
very simple waterside pub into a
flourishing establishment with a
yachting clientele. A very pleasant
terrace with a view across the
Deben.
[g] These humpy fields look like the
site of the lost part of the village, an
impression strengthened by the
remains of a brick wall.
[h] **Ramsholt church** deserves a
detour, with its round tower, a
simple chancel and box-pews of the
early 19th century. The churchyard
offers a fine view over the Deben.

SURREY

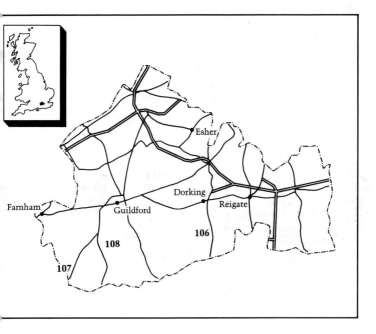

oliday Which? Good Walks Guide

Holmwood to Leith Hill

**South East England's highest point –
the only place in the region that
reaches 1,000 feet – is the key
feature of this walk. Beautiful
woodland paths make the climbing
easy, but directions need to be
followed with care. There are some
helpful signposts to Leith Hill's
summit.**

Length 7 miles (11km), 3¹/₂ hours
Difficulty 3
OS maps 1:50,000 187; 1:25,000 TQ
04/14 (Pathfinder 1226)
Start Holmwood station, just off
A24, 4 miles S of Dorking. Grid
reference 174438
Refreshments Pub at Holmwood
and Coldharbour; tea and snacks
sometimes available at Leith Hill
Tower

WALK DIRECTIONS

① With entrance to station behind
you, turn left along road. After 150
yards, just beyond end of row of
cottages, turn left through second of
two gates and continue on path
between fences. 200 yards later, pa
on to small metalled road and
continue direction.

After ¹/₄ mile, keep right at first
fork, avoiding turning to Brookwoo
and Copse Farm; 20 yards beyond,
fork left avoiding turning to
Greenstone cottage. Path then
dodges round to right of large meta
gate (yellow marker arrows) to rejo
main driveway on far side. Contin
for ¹/₂ mile, later bearing half right
when metalled driveway merges
from left.

② Continue forward across road
taking track just to left of lodge

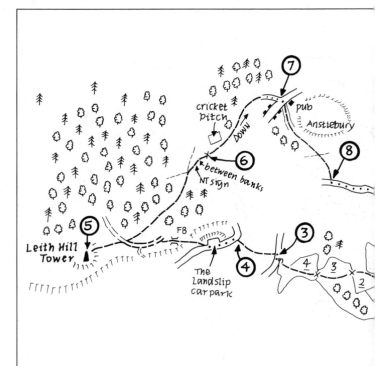

me marked 'Bearehurst – no
oroughfare'. 50 yards later,
mmediately after crossing bridge,
rn right on signposted path
tween fences. Cross stile into field
d continue with fence on your
ght for 15 yards, but then turn left
follow edge of wood with fence on
ur left.

Pass through gate at corner of
ld, and turn half right in second
ld to follow hedge on right. Pass
rough gate into third field,
oiding stiles into woodland, both
left and right. Follow left edge of
ird field to find gate just below
yline. Continue forward in fourth
ld and make for top right-hand
rner, just to right of cottage. Cross
er two stiles to road ③.
Turn right on road and after 5
rds turn immediately left to pass

to left of metal post, on to path
which rises steeply through
woodland. Continue direction on
this, ignoring cross-track, and later
passing seat on your right. ④ Turn
left on road for 50 yards, and turn
right into car park (National Trust
sign) to find sign pointing you to the
'Tower, ¾ mile'.

Bear half left at top of car park,
following signs to cross footbridge,
later descending steps. Turn right on
cross-track (further signpost, marked
with tower sign). Continue forward
at top of rise, passing between posts
with metal National Trust sign to
your right. Track later joins from
right; continue straight on, following
further signposts, later turning left
to reach tower at summit [a] ⑤.
Retrace steps from summit, first
following sign showing a car with an

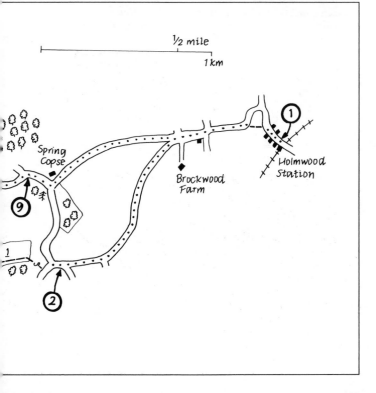

'L' inside it (for Landslip car park). On reaching cross-track after 200 yards, at bottom of rise, go forward, instead of going right for car park, soon passing green marker post and National Trust sign for Duke's Warren on your right.

Continue on clear track for about ¼ mile, with successive tracks merging from left. Immediately after second track joins from left, take right fork, ignoring left fork and green marker post. This soon emerges by further sign for Duke's Warren, and passes between earth banks, then past wooden barrier, to arrive at corner of cricket pitch with pavilion on your left ⑥. Go forward, keeping cricket pitch on your left, on clear track which is soon joined by track merging from right.

Continue on clear track with land dropping away steeply to your right to reach cottages and road at bottom ⑦. Turn sharp right in front of Plough pub, and just beyond first house turn left on signposted path, which later passes between hedges. Follow top edge of first field [b] and cross stile into remains of woodland, continuing on clear path which winds downhill. Cross over track at bottom making for high brick wall with house beyond.

⑧ Turn left on gravel drive to continue with wall on your right, later keeping left where footpath continues straight ahead. 100 yards further on, fork right to reach road 250 yards later ⑨. Turn right on road for 150 yards, and turn left on to ancient unmade lane (just beyond entrance to a house called Spring Copse).

After ½ mile, a driveway joins from right; continue forward on metalled road. ¼ mile further on, where road swings left, continue forward through kissing-gate on to path between fences. Turn right on road to return to Holmwood station.

ON THE ROUTE
[a] **Leith Hill** (965ft). The tower is over 1,000 feet above sea level. Wide views from this greensand escarpment towards the South Downs. 'Leith' actually means hill, so the name is tautological.
[b] On left is **Anstiebury**, the site of an oval-shaped hill-fort of pre-Roman origin, whose banks enclose 11 acres.

he Devil's Punch Bowl
d Gibbet Hill

**llows the rim of the Devil's
nchbowl, one of Surrey's most
riking natural features, later
merging from woods into the open,
ith charming rural views; Thursley
the halfway point and the view
m wooded Gibbet Hill the final
max. One ascent, near the end.**

ngth 6 miles (9.5km), 3 hours
fficulty 2
art National Trust car park,
ndhead, on N side of A3 at E end
village, immediately E of filling
ation and Devil's Punchbowl
otel. Grid reference 890357
maps 1:50,000 186; 1:25,000 SU
/93 (Pathfinder 1245)
freshments Hotel and cafés in
ndhead; pub in Thursley

ALK DIRECTIONS

) Take track to left of Hillcrest
fé, past toilets. Proceed on the
vel, around the top edge of the
vil's Punchbowl (with back
rdens away to left), ignoring any
scending forks to the right.
) After ½ mile, fork right by
ational Trust sign for Highcombe
ft is private to Packways),
mediately avoiding a right
scending fork; you are now
llowing power-lines. Just after
ing under power-lines, take
htmost of three paths by wooden
st with blue waymarker arrows.
This path leads out to viewpoint
d bench [a]; then take path just to
ht of memorial stone, and 50
rds later turn right on broad path.
) ⅓ mile later, keep straight on at
ss-junction by waymarker post
ere main path bends sharp right.
th gradually descends, eventually
ving woods and reaching junction
lanes. Turn right, soon passing to
ht of farm [b] and continuing on
ck between hedges, which soon

descends to cross footbridge,
immediately after which ④ take
signposted stile into field and turn
left. Follow edge of field, soon uphill
to cross stile, and follow path
between fence and hedge [c] until
tarmacked lane.

Turn left on lane, then ⑤ after
30 yards take signposted driveway
for Hedge Farm on left (or to cut
out the following section across
fields, continue along the lane to
Thursley church at ⑦). Almost
immediately fork right onto path
between fences (waymarked by
yellow arrow), soon enter field by
stile and proceed along left edge of it
and next two fields.

At end of third field, cross stile on
left and follow enclosed path, which
bends right by house and soon joins
lane. Continue forward along lane,
then ⑥ turn right after 100 yards,
opposite Smallbrook, taking
signposted gate. Cross field to stile
(which soon comes into view), then
follow path between fences to
Thursley church [d].

In churchyard, keep to right of
church, turn left on lane then 50
yards later ⑦ where lane bends left
keep forward on track, (signposted
Footpath), (or continue on lane to
centre of Thursley; turn right at T-
junction to reach pub). Where track
bends right (by Rack Close), take
gate into field ahead and bear half
right across field (blue arrow on top
of gate-post indicates the direction),
eventually joining end of hedgerow
away to your right, then beyond gate
go forward on path to reach A3.
Cross road and take lane opposite,
which soon bends right (ahead is
private, to Cosford House) [e].

⑧ ¼ mile later, where lane
bends left, take signposted track on
right. This soon passes Hole Cottage
away to your left and later reaches
staggered cross-junction by signpost:
turn left for Upper Valley Farm

(avoid a driveway on right 50 yards later). Track soon passes small pond on your right (ignore stile on left just after), then **(9)** ¼ mile later fork right towards Blackhangar Farm. Just after crossing stream, and just before farm itself, take stile on left and follow top of field, close to garden fence, to find stile into woods, beyond which emerge into field.

Follow left (bottom) edge, along power-lines, until yellow waymark arrow on post (near to end of field) points left into next field, which cross to gate beside stile into woodland **(10)**. Follow woodland path it is clear at beginning, but may be obscured later by fallen branches (but ramshackle fence on right is a useful waymarker); on reaching

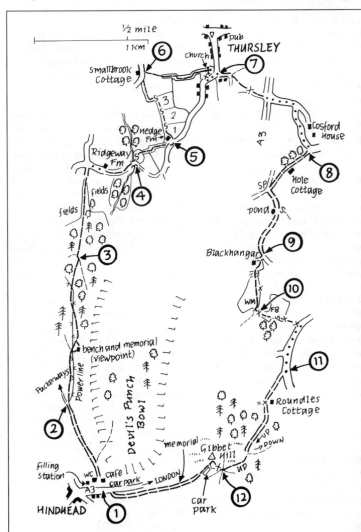

orner of fence, cross slab footbridge
n left, go over stile and follow left
dge of woods (with field on left)
ntil stile into field.

Continue in same direction along
dge of field to gate and stile in
orner, then follow woodland track
 road. Turn right on road, then
ep left at next junction, along cul-
-sac to High Button. ⑪ 120 yards
ter, fork right on to track (wooded
ibbet Hill, which you will soon
cend, is ahead). Follow to reach
orner of driveway, then go forward
st Roundles Cottage, on ascending
ack.

After ¼ mile, bear right at oblique
-junction (still ascending).
⑫ Reach 7-way path junction, bear
lf right (through barrier) and go to
ig point (summit pillar) on top of
ibbet Hill [f]. Turn left at trig
int, (in the Petersfield direction, as
arked on top of the trig point
self) towards low wooden fence
closing car park and follow broad
ack on right side of car park; ignore
inor forks. Soon A3 is audible
wn to right. Follow back to
indhead, emerging on A3 opposite
ational Trust car park.

N THE ROUTE

View over the **Devil's Punch
wl**, a huge natural amphitheatre
rrounded by mixed woods (Scots
nes, birch, oak and others) and
tches of heathland (bracken, gorse
d heather) on the elevated sandy
ound.

Ridgeway Farm, a fine example of
e vernacular style, with steeply
pping roof, and part timber
nstruction; the first of a number of
d farmhouses and cottages to look
t for on this walk; others include
nallbrook, Hole Cottage and
ackhangar Farm.

Sudden emergence from

woodland into the open is marked
by good **views** N to the Hog's
Back ridge.

[d] **Thursley** Unspoilt and rural, with
cottages scattered around the central
green and its back lane. The **church**
has an unusual wooden structure
beneath the belfry in its centre,
(installed in Henry VIII's time), a
font thought to to be of Saxon origin,
and England's only surviving
wooden Saxon windows. In the
churchyard, by the war memorial
cross, is a tombstone and epitaph to
an unknown sailor murdered in 1786
on Hindhead Common by three men
he met on his way on foot from
London to Portsmouth.

[e] **Cosford House**, with its artificial
lakes, can be seen down to the left.
There follows a particularly pleasant
section of the walk, with a mixture
of woods and views into more open
country.

[f] **Gibbet Hill** (894ft, the second
highest hill in Surrey, after Leith
Hill). Extensive **view** from the
heathy summit over a complex
landscape of rolling woodland, heath
and distant hills, N over the Devil's
Punchbowl and towards the Hog's
Back, and S over the broad, wooded
vale of the Sussex Weald. Here stood
the gibbet from which the three
murderers of the sailor buried in
Thursley churchyard (see above)
were hung; their bodies were kept
hanging for years afterwards as a
warning to others. A memorial stone
to the incident is seen on the right
between the trig point and the
return to Hindhead (with a curse
inscribed on the back against anyone
who removes the stone). The broad
track followed back to Hindhead is
the old Portsmouth road, the stage-
coach and packhorse route over the
top of Gibbet Hill towards
Petersfield.

Winkworth Arboretum and Hydon's Ball

The deepest, leafiest Surrey countryside, given an added bonus by the superb National Trust arboretum and lakes of Winkworth, and the picturesque village of Hascombe, complete with village pond. The walk finishes with a surprisingly prominent ridge with views to the south.

Length 6½ miles (10.5km), 3 hours
Difficulty 2–3
Start Hydon's Ball car park, 2½ miles S of Godalming. From A3 and A286, take turning for Milford Station, continuing for further ¾ mile to staggered crossroads, where you turn left then immediately right. Car park is ½ mile beyond this, just opposite road coming in from your left – turn right and follow rough track past National Trust sign. Grid reference 979403
OS maps 1:50,000 186; 1:25,000 SU 84/94, SU 83/93 and TQ 03/13 (Pathfinder 1225, 1245, 1246)
Refreshments Tea-room at Winkworth; pub in Hascombe

WALK DIRECTIONS

① Follow track out of car park, and back to road, where you turn right. After 50 yards, turn left on waymarked path, passing through squeeze-stile. After 10 yards, turn right on broad cross-track. After 500 yards, path emerges from right and main track swings left; 30 yards beyond, fork right on path marked 'bridleway'.

Path climbs and then falls, soon leaving wood to pass between fences with fields on either side, and later continuing between high banks. Farm driveway soon merges from left – continue forward, and turn right at T-junction to reach road ②. Cross road and go forward past barrier to corner of car park.

Continue down right-hand side of car park, and take path just to left of 'National Trust – Winkworth Arboretum' sign [a] soon passing tea room. Go forward on main path into arboretum, avoiding turnings to right. You're soon joined by a fence on your left; where this swings away left again, bear right downhill on main path, with lake soon coming into view. Avoid path branching away down to lakeshore, but keep forward on clear path which keeps edge of lake away to your left.

As you near end of lake, this path climbs a short rise, and swings right to the top. 75 yards later, turn left up steps on narrow path which passes two cross-tracks. At top of rise, with fence ahead of you, turn left to follow clear path with fence on your right. Follow top of high bank before dropping down to road ③.

Turn left on road (follow verge to avoid traffic) and follow for about ½ mile [b]. 25 yards beyond Hascombe village sign, turn left on signposted public bridleway. 150 yards later, turn right on cross-track. Follow for 500 yards, avoiding all turnings to right and later swinging slightly to the left.

④ Turn right on reaching surface lane, with cottages on your left. The lane soon passes in front of church [c], with village pond on your left, to reach the White Horse pub at centre of village ⑤.

Immediately beyond pub, turn right on signposted bridleway, passing first between posts (one marked 'pedestrians only', then continuing half-left over stile into first field. Cross into second field to continue with fence and hedge to your left. When fence on left ends, continue uphill into woodland. At top of rise, 50 yards later, turn right and 200 yards later turn sharp right on path marked with blue arrow.

15 yards further on, turn left at

marker post, again following blue arrow. Continue direction on straight track through wood for about ¾ mile, ignoring a series of crossing tracks, to drop down to road ⑥.

Turn right on road, and 10 yards later turn left on clear signposted path, which soon swings half-left uphill through trees.

Emerge at top to continue along left edge of two fields with slope dropping away to your left [**d**]. At far corner of second field, go forward into woodland to continue with fence on right. ½ mile later, path merges from left: bear half right uphill to top of rise, later dropping to pass on track between hedges ⑦.

Just after passing electricity sub-station on your left, reach five-way junction of tracks. Take left fork ahead of you, to climb slight hollow in hillside. Ignore broad sandy track branching to your right 300 yards later, and climb for a further 150 yards to reach prominent manhole cover. Turn right to arrive at summit of Hydon's Ball, marked by a large stone seat [**e**] ⑧.

Follow path immediately to the left of the seat, and bear right at first

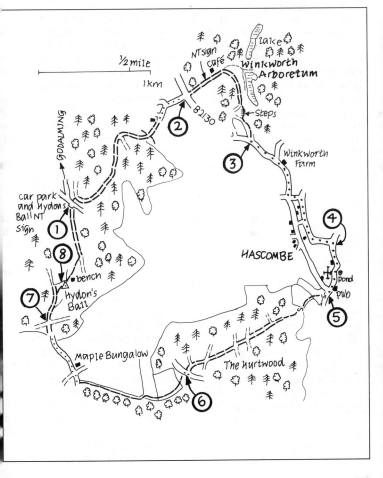

fork to reach cross-track after 200 yards. Turn left on this, and follow blue marker arrow to reach car park.

ON THE ROUTE

[a] **Winkworth Arboretum** National Trust, voluntary fee, but entry not controlled as a right of way crosses the land. 97 acres of hillside planted with over 150 species of specimen trees and shrubberies, with the 81 grass 'Azalea Steps' leaving from the boathouse by the artificial lakes up to the Main Walk. The site was acquired in 1937 by Dr Wilfrid Fox, an amateur arborist and founder of the Roads Beautifying Association (which was instrumental in planning trees along newly-built main roads). With the aid of friends who visited at week-ends he cleared the area of scrubland, started planting – beginning with several species of maple and during the war adding a now famous collection of sorbus. The arboretum has continued to expand since and has become especially well-known for its autumn colours.

[b] **Winkworth Farm** Fine medieval range grouped around a courtyard.

[c] **St Peter's Church, Hascombe** An unusual church of 1864, by Henry Woodyer, a pupil of Butterfield; finely painted chancel roof, organ case, restored 15th-century screen (from the previous church on the site) and stained glass showing the 153 fishes caught in a net drawn by the disciples and Old Testament stories.

[d] A good section of the greensand ridge, with **views** across the low-lying Weald to the South Downs.

[e] The seat commemorates **Octavia Hill**, Victorian philanthropist and pioneer of improved housing for the working classes.

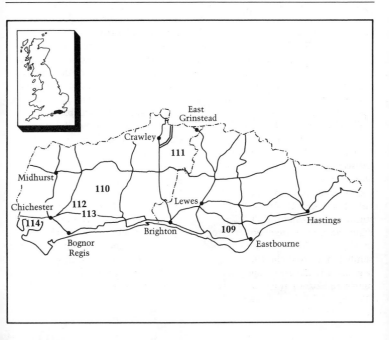

109 Lullington Heath and the Long Man of Wilmington
110 Parham Park and Amberley Wild Brooks
111 Ardingly Reservoir and the Forest Ridge Country
112 Stane Street and Slindon
113 Around Arundel
114 Nutbourne Marshes and Chidham

Holiday Which? Good Walks Guide

56 Kingley Vale   57 Older Hill and Woolbeding Common   58 The Racton Monument and Stansted Park   59 Clayton windmills and Wolstonbury Hills   60 Friston and the Seven Sisters   61 Glynde, Mount Caburn and Lewes   62 Hartfield and Pooh country   63 Fairlight Glen and Hastings Old Town   64 West Hoathly and Selsfield Common   65 Bewl Water and Scotney Castle   66 Fairwarp and the Ashdown Forest   67 Mad Jack Fuller's monument and Bateman's

Lullington Heath and the Long Man of Wilmington

One of the finest short walks in the South Downs, leading out of picturesque Alfriston, along the Cuckmere River and up on to the Downs, later skirting their base and passing an extraordinary hill-carving. Good final section, with wide views from a route descending across fields. Route-finding easy most of the way.

Length 6 miles (9.5km), 3 hours
Difficulty 2
Start Alfriston (2 miles S of A27 Lewes-Eastbourne road); car park. Grid reference 521031 *Alternatively* start at Litlington (³/₄ mile SE), which adds the pleasure of arriving in Alfriston on foot; limited roadside parking near pub; start walk at (2), heading towards church. Grid reference 524016
OS maps 1:50,000 199; 1:25,000 TV 49/59/69 (Pathfinder 1324)
Refreshments Pubs and tea-room in Alfriston and Litlington; pubs in Wilmington and Milton Street

WALK DIRECTIONS

(1) [a] Start in main street in Alfriston with George Inn on left, follow street 30 yards, then take path on left signposted to church: keep left where right goes to Clergy House, and proceed to river bridge. Cross bridge [b] and turn right, and follow path along river for ³/₄ mile.

Just before next bridge, turn left on tarmacked path, leaving river to reach Litlington (2). Turn left on road, then just after church take track on right signposted Jevington: this immediately bends left (straight on leads to house), then soon bends right, rising gently [c]. (3) After ¹/₂ mile, keep straight on, ignoring sharp left turn.

(4) ¹/₄ mile later, fork right (signposted Jevington) just before

Lullington Heath Nature Reserve sign, to pass immediately to left of this sign. Track falls gently, then rises (ignore stile on right for Charleston Bottom). (5) After ³/₄ mile, just where trees begin and track is about to descend, turn sharp left (this, and the track descending ahead, is part of the South Downs Way). Beyond next gate, path across grassland is hardly visible: keep to the higher ground (parallel to fence

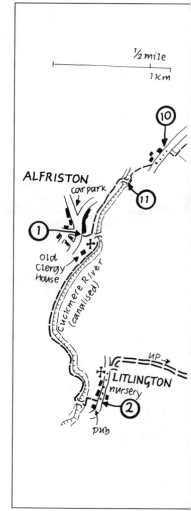

away to right), following prominent South Downs Way marker posts.

Later, route follows a track, around head of valley (which is down on left), through a gate by a sheep-pen (this is Windover Hill), then soon begins to descend. ⑥ 200 yards later (just after track is joined by fence on right), fork right (along fence). 150 yards later, take gate on right and follow path which skirts base of steep slope.

⑦ When level with the Long Man of Wilmington (the chalk carving on the hillside) [**d**] continue ahead on path skirting base of slope (*note*: part of the following section into Litlington can be very muddy; if you prefer to by-pass the mud, turn left downhill when level with the Long Man of Wilmington and take gate, leading to path down to road, where turn right to Wilmington church and enter churchyard; this is ⑧). Keep

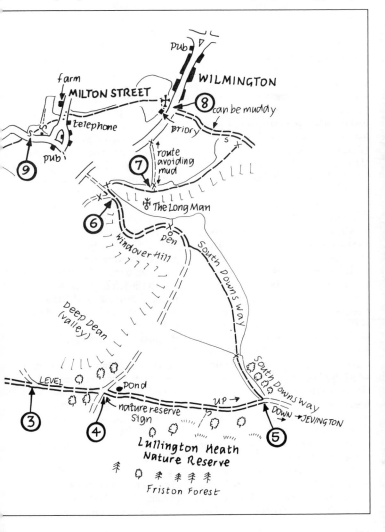

to the level; after ¹/₂ mile turn left [e] onto track between fences and follow to Wilmington. [f] Cross road and pass ⑧ through churchyard, taking gate on far side; cross track and take stile opposite. Proceed across field (along uncultivated strip), then forward along track on right edge of next field to reach road. Left on road, then right just before telephone box, over stile signposted Alfriston.

Cross field to stile, then cross second field diagonally, aiming for far left-hand corner, and emerge on lane ⑨. Cross to stile opposite, and bear half right across big field towards Alfriston, then turn right in second field to reach road. Left on road, then just after last barn of Milton Court Farm (on right) take signposted path on right and bear half left across field to reach road bridge ⑩ Turn left along river, using paths on either side. ⑪ At next bridge, a path on right leads to Alfriston.

ON THE ROUTE

[a] **Alfriston** Old-world village, its narrow, winding main street lined with tile-hung houses. The ancient timbered **Star Inn** has a heavy roof of Horsham slabs, and a front adorned with wooden carvings, including St George and the dragon; at the corner of the Inn is a figure-head taken from a Dutch ship washed ashore 300 years ago at nearby Cuckmere Haven. Opposite is the **George Inn**, which has Tudor wall paintings. Under the chestnut tree in the tiny square is the shaft of one of only two market crosses in Sussex (the other is at Chichester).

Off the main street, near the river, is the **church**, dubbed the 'cathedral of the South Downs', a spacious and regular building of c.1360, with fine tracery in its windows. Nearby is the half-timbered **Clergy House**, of the

same age as the church, built as a priest's house. In 1896 it became the first building to be bought by the National Trust (open Apr-Oct 11-6 daily or sunset if earlier).

[b] **Cuckmere River** Canalised, to prevent tidal flooding, there are often fleets of swans and ducks present. Pleasant **views** of the South Downs and the Cuckmere valley. ¹/₂ mile E of the Alfriston footbridge, and on the hillside, **Lullington church** stands isolated, reached only by trackway. Only the chancel remains of a larger building, making the 13ft-square building one of England's smallest churches.

[c] The modest ascent is soon rewarded with views disproportionate to the effort expended. First comes a deep valley immediately down to the left, the slopes of which are too steep for ploughing and have thus remained as rugged grassland. On the right is the untamed, rolling expanse of **Lullington Heath** (a nature reserve maintained by the Nature Conservancy Council), of botanical interest because of coinciding chalk and acid soils, with typical species of each co-existing, for example gorse and salad burnet. A labelled pond just to the left of the path is a restored dewpond with dragonfly population. Finally, at **Windover Hill**, an expansive view N across the Sussex Weald and the Ashdown Forest.

[d] **The Long Man of Wilmington** Seen at its best from this path, a 226ft figure cut in the chalk hillside, carefully done to avoid any distortion from foreshortening. The Man appears to have a staff in each hand but the precise origin and purpose of the figure are uncertain; one theory is that he represents Balder, Norse God of Spring. The earliest written record is 18th-century, but

he **Man** is probably much older.
e] At the top of the grassy spur to
your right is **Hunter's Burgh**, a long
barrow which is thought to be the
burial place of a Neolithic hunter.
f] Wilmington One long street runs
up from a green at the N end to the
church and priory ruins. Outside the
church is a great yew tree, reputedly
1,000 years old and Sussex's oldest
tree. **The church** itself has a 12th-
century chancel, a 14th-century

nave, and a square, Jacobean font.
The adjacent **priory** (open Mon-Sat
11-5; closed Tue, Sun 2-5) is an 11th-
century Benedictine foundation
which belonged to Grestrain Abbey
in Normandy; this was the abbey's
principal English possession. It was
seized by the Crown during the war
with France, and later became a
farmhouse (hence 14th- and 16th-
century modifications). Inside is an
agricultural display.

Parham Park and Amberley Wild Brooks

Three very different landscapes in the space of a few miles – deer park, marshy levels and the chalk ridge of the South Downs, with an exceptionally picturesque village half-way round and a finely sited castle. Easy route-finding; Amberley Wild Brooks, between ⑦ and ⑧, may be boggy.

Length 9 miles (14.5km), 4 hours
Difficulty 3
Start Crown Inn, Cootham (hamlet is not named on all road maps), on A283 1 mile W of Storrington, and ½ mile W of junction of A283 and B2139; roadside parking in nearby cul-de-sacs off main road. Grid reference 074145
By train Amberley. Walk down station approach road, turn right along B2139, then next right into High Titton (South Downs Way). ⅓ mile later turn right at junction near Highdown (house); start walk directions at ⑨
OS maps 1:50,000 197; 1:25,000 TQ 01/11 (Pathfinder 1287)
Refreshments Pub at Cootham; pub and shop at Amberley; pub and tea-room at Amberley station (off main route, but useful for those arriving by train); tea-room at Parham House (when house open)

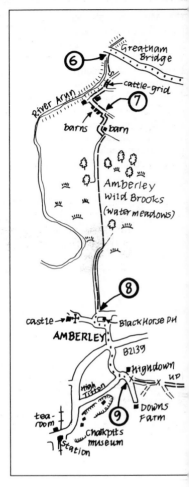

WALK DIRECTIONS

① With Crown Inn on right, follow A283 out of Cootham and away from Storrington. After 300 yards where road bends right go forward on estate drive by signs for Parham House (note you are allowed to walk on the path to Rackham even when house is closed to the public) [a].

Proceed past lodge, ignore sharp left turn shortly after, but ② 100 yards later fork right on grassy path signposted to Rackham and proceed with fence on right until reaching junction of tarmacked estate drives: keep forward, leaving estate at lodge ½ mile later. Turn left on road, and keep straight on at next road junction (signposted Amberley).

③ 100 yards later (where woods on right end), turn right by buildings, on broad track leading past Pine Cottage and skirting edge of woods [b]. Soon avoid footbridge on your left, but bear right (signposted), still along edge of woods, avoiding a right turn 100 yards later; shortly woodland appears on left of track for a while

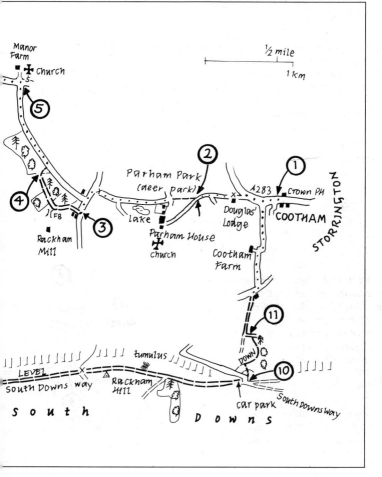

before being replaced by fields. **4)** Just as woods recommence on left, bear right by signpost (forking left after 30 yards). Join tarmacked lane, turn left along it.

5) After ½ mile reach T-junction with Greatham church [**c**] ahead and slightly to right: turn left [**d**].

6) After ¾ mile, immediately before river bridge [**e**], take stile on left and walk along raised grassy dyke alongside river. Shortly after next stile, dyke ends: bear right (signposted), soon joining farm track and keep right along it, with river

down to right. After track crosses cattle-grid, ignore sharp left turn but proceed to reach modern house, where track bends left (signposted; ahead is private), and passes barns on your right, shortly after which **7)** fork right as signposted (ahead is private) and follow snaking track to wooden barn, where signpost points left along edge of field.

In next field turn right (again signposted), with channel on right and maintain same direction (soon crossing small footbridges) over Amberley Wild Brooks [**f**] for 1 mile

until entering Amberley village.
(8) Turn right at T-junction with village street [**g**] (or left for pub), then left at next T-junction (or right for church and castle), then right at next T-junction. Soon cross B2139 and take ascending lane opposite.

¼ mile later bear left at junction by Highdown (house) [**h**] (or turn right to return to station), then **(9)** 75 yards later take rising path on left signposted South Downs Way. Follow South Downs Way signposts for 2 miles [**i**]: route ascends between fences at first, then just after a track coming in sharp right proceeds uphill with fence on left; 1 mile later a trig point (summit pillar) is seen close to the right, then 1 mile later reach car park and end of road on your left **(10)**

Turn left on the road, immediately leaving it for signposted bridleway on right, which descends through bushes (ignore left fork after 30 yards): descend steadily, soon through trees to bottom of slope where **(11)** turn left at T-junction with chalky track (signposted); track then bends right, soon reaching road [**j**]. Turn right on road, then immediately left on minor road, and follow to A283 near Cootham, where turn right to return to Crown Inn or left to continue walk if you started elsewhere.

ON THE ROUTE

[**a**] **Parham House** (open bank hols, Easter Sun to first Sun in Oct; Sun, Wed, Thur. In a fine site under the South Downs, an Elizabethan mansion set in a deer park, with lake close by. The interior contains a great hall and a long gallery running the length of the house; notable furniture and portraits. Just S of the house, the 16th-century church is worth a look: Gothicised in the 1820s, box pews and fretwork screen, and an unusual 14th-century font with the Peverell coat of arms on it.

[**b**] **Rackham Plantation** Fine woods with Scots pines, silver birch, some gorse; it suffered devastation on its eastern edge in the 1987 storm.

[**c**] **Greatham church** No road leads to the restored Norman building. Inside is simple, with harmonium and oil lamps, a 17th-century communion rail, and an early 19th-century pulpit. Adjacent is the manor house, dated 1672.

[**d**] Half right shortly after passing a telephone box, the grey-roofed farm whose farmhouse was the refectory for **Hardham Priory** (remains of an Augustinian foundation), is visible in the middle distance. Alongside it are the ruins of the chapter house.

[**e**] **Greatham Bridge** has a quaint piecemeal appearance, with ten stone arches of varying sizes and a more recent iron extension on the near side. The river Arun is canalised at this point.

[**f**] **Amberley Wild Brooks** is an area of watermeadows (probably a shallow lake in medieval times, based on the principle of flooding meadows with a system of sluices s that the organic silt from the river would enrich the soil). Outstanding for bird life: Bewick's swan, pintail, shoveler, teal and wigeon; and marsh-loving wild flowers: arrowhead, bladderwort and frogbit. Among the many who have admired the quiet beauty of this place was composer John Ireland, who named piano piece after it. 'Wild' is a corruption of 'Weald'.

[**g**] **Amberley** Remarkably unspoilt village scattered around a rough square of lanes, all half-timbered or stone and much of it under thatch. Vestiges of a wall-painting in the **church**, which is most notable for i Norman work, and a huge chancel arch with palm-tree ornamentation an iron hour-glass stand above the

lpit is a rarity. The church was obably founded by Bishop de Luffa, 91-1123, founder of Chichester thedral. In a corner of the urchyard, a peep-hole in St chard's Gate gives a view of mberley **castle**. Continue down the ne by the church to the end of the llage for close-ups of the castle's rmidable curtain wall, towering ove the watermeadows. It was ace the home of the Bishop of hichester; a licence to crenellate r to fortify) was given in 1379. uadrangular plan; large 16th-ntury house inside, half-timbered th lovely gardens.

Amberley Chalk Pits Museum pen Easter to end-Oct, 10-6 daily st admission at 5) is between ghdown and Amberley station (entrance is at the latter). Visiting this as part of the walk would make a very long day, but there is a view over most of the site from High Titton, the lane to your right. Working displays, reconstructions, railway, history of chalk extraction and much more.

[i] **South Downs Way** After the ascent, an easy ridge section with views S and N, including over all the rest of the walk. Like most of the South Downs, there are numerous prehistoric antiquities on the way; one of the more visible is a grassy **burial mound** on the left by a small group of trees, shortly before woodland ahead is reached.

[j] **Old tollhouse** (Paygate Cottage) is on your right as you reach the road.

Ardingly Reservoir and the Forest Ridge Country

Soft, unspoilt Wealden landscape of rolling pasture and deciduous woodlands, and some attractive features, including two reservoirs. Route-finding is complicated (hence the lengthy directions), but much of route is well signposted. Mud may be a problem around ⑬ and ⑭.

Length 10 miles (16km), 5 hours; can shorten to 7 miles by using road at point ⑪
Difficulty 3
Start Ardingly church, grid reference 340298 (W of main village and B2028, and 4 miles N of Haywards Heath)
By train Balcombe. Take main exit from station, left on road then immediately right on path by hurdles near telephone-box; reach residential road, turn right along it, then soon left into cul-de-sac called Jobes. This is ⑧
OS Maps 1:50,000 187; 1:25,000 TQ 22/32 and TQ 23/33 (Pathfinder 1268 and 1247)
Refreshments Café at Wakehurst Place (when house is open), pub and shops in Balcombe, fishing lodge at Ardingly Reservoir

WALK DIRECTIONS

① Take road to right of church, signposted Balcombe. Just before road crosses reservoir, take path on left, which follows close to water's edge for ¹/₂ mile [a], then cross dam.
② On other side of dam, keep straight on by signpost as road bends left: go up slope 30 yards to next signpost where bear right, over small slab bridge, leaving field by stile into woodland, where immediately bear right (signposted) then immediately left (signposted again).

Enter field, bear half left, slightly uphill to enter second field by gate; head forward to woodland ③ in front of which turn left, along edge of field. In third field, follow left edge until gate gives access to farm road, along which continue forward. In front of brick house [b], turn left (signposted), proceed to road. The continuation is over stile opposite and slightly to the left, but for close-up view of Balcombe Viaduct, detour left on road to bottom of hill, where take signposted gate on right, opposite house, to reach bottom of viaduct [c] (return same way).

To continue route, go forward beyond the stile (as signposted) across field to stile, then continue across next field to bridge over railway, immediately after which ④ turn right, along top of field, close to railway. Reach field corner, turn left (still skirting field, with woods on right); in next field continue along right edge, then soon forward on track between fences; after 30 yards keep left where fence on left veers away; ⑤ where fence reaches corner 20 yards later, maintain direction uphill to emerge by stile on to road.

Take track opposite, soon past Pilstye Farm then proceed to road junction. Turn right, then 200 yards later where road kinks right, ⑥ take signposted stile on right. Go forward, soon along intermittent line of trees (heading to right of red brick house); cross stile (50 yards to left of where two sets of power-lines cross), and cross small triangular field to find stile by signpost.

Turn left, along field edge, at first ascending, but soon descending into woods. Reach crossing of woodland tracks by signpost: take the right-hand of the two tracks, effectively ahead (signpost ambiguous at time of checking). 50 yards later, keep forward (downhill) at rough junction of tracks, soon over footbridge and ⑦ into field, where continue to gate in front of wooden barn. Turn left of

ad, then just after weather-boarded
ttage take driveway on the right to
mps House [**d**].

At end of driveway, pick up path
ead and slightly to right, over
lway, then through woods to
ach field. Follow right edge,
ading towards houses at edge of
lcombe. Find path to right of first
d-brick house, and follow to
sidential road. Cross to cul-de-sac
posite called Jobes.

8 Where cul-de-sac bends left
ep forward on path (by No Cycling
gn), soon alongside playing fields
reach road. Left on road, then
ght 30 yards later in centre of
llage. Keep straight on at next
nction, on cul-de-sac by pub. Road

bends right by private driveway to
Balcombe House, then just after last
house on right enter field on left by
kissing-gate. Follow left edge [**e**],
eventually entering woods by stile;
9 100 yards later, turn right at path
junction by signpost.

Path soon crosses plank bridge,
then goes through semi-open area.
Balcombe Lake is soon seen on left
[**f**]: path runs close to it for half the
length of the lake before entering
field by stile. Follow left edge, then
10 pass through gate on left by
signpost into second field. Proceed
to gate, turn left on road along end of
lake. ¼ mile later take signposted
stile on right, follow left edge of field
to end, then turn 90 degrees left by

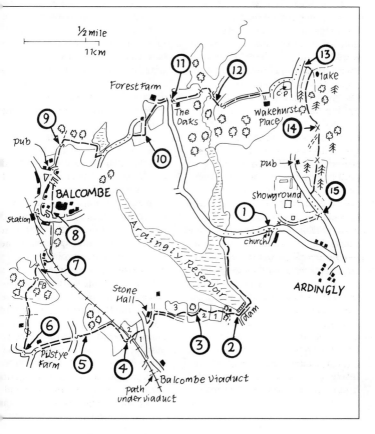

429

signpost in front of woodland into second field: head to right of barn and leave field at far right-hand corner (signposted; the left of two gates). Follow right edge of third field then forward on track where left goes to Forest Farm.

⑩ Reach road, turn right along it (*for short version of walk* follow road to Ardingly reservoir; then Ardingly church; if you started from Balcombe, turn right after crossing reservoir, on to waterside path to reach dam. Cross dam and resume walk directions at ②), then immediately left over stile to follow right edge of field until woods at bottom where keep left for 120 yards before entering woods by gate and signpost. Soon cross stream by bridges, then path soon bends right by signpost and ascends to reach parkland of Wakehurst Place ⑫ [g]: keep forward, over track, taking path ahead (signposted Public Footpath).

At end of parkland, cross stile to take path between fences, later joining track; ignore side-turns, proceed to tarmac driveway (by Sleeping Policeman sign) then forward to main road. Turn left on road then after 200 yards ⑬ take path between pair of cottages (the second one is called Oak Cottage), which descends: avoid turns marked Private (one is sharp right, then another is on left 50 yards later), and proceed to cross-junction with lake visible ahead. Here, turn right on rising path between fences. ⑭ After ¹/₂ mile, enter field by gate, follow track along field edge, then after 50 yards leave track which bends right (into field above) to keep forward along edge of field, eventually entering woods.

¹/₄ mile later, bear right at junction by signpost and near black and white house, to reach road. Left on road,

then ⑮ turn right after 300 yards by sign for agricultural showground, taking concrete track. Soon Ardingly church comes into view – track almost joins road, but bends right away from it; just after this, a gate on left gives access to the road.

ON THE ROUTE

[a] **Ardingly reservoir** Offers a rare lakeside walk in the South East; the adjacent Loder Valley reserve is owned by the Royal Botanical Gardens (permit required) and is of interest for its Wealden vegetation.

[b] **Stone Hall** A Jacobean house with fine chequer brickwork.

[c] **Balcombe Viaduct** (also visible from just before Stone Hall and in ensuing sections). One of the wonders of the railway age: 37 brick arches, 1,475ft-long, built 1841 by John Urpeth Rastrick; classical balustrade, and faced with Caen limestone imported from Normandy. Worth taking the detour described here in order to experience a spectacular perspective effect by looking through the oval arches at the base of each pier – surely the most bizarre view in this book.

[d] **Kemps House** Late 17th-century overlooks pleasant, unspoilt countryside.

[e] **Balcombe House** A brick Georgian-Gothic former rectory.

[f] **Balcombe Lake** with its reedy shores has a natural appearance, but is a man-made reservoir.

[g] **Wakehurst Place** Administered by the Royal Botanic Gardens, Kew; landscaped gardens contain exotic shrubs and trees, rhododendrons and pines, and an attractive watercourse joining a series of lakes and ponds. Suffered heavy damage in the 1987 storm (National Trust, open winter 10-4, summer 10-7).

‹ane Street and Slindon

‹ane Street, a classic Roman road
‹ow a footpath), leads across the
‹outh Downs to a viewpoint from
‹e escarpment. Slindon and its
‹earby folly add further interest to a
‹eautifully varied walk. Forest
‹acks form the route at the outset
‹nd finish.

‹ength *Full walk* 10 miles (16km),
‹ hours; *short walk* 8¹/₂ miles
‹3.5km), 4 hours

‹ifficulty 3

‹tart Eartham Wood Car Park, just
‹f A285 Petworth-Chichester road,
‹ miles S of Petworth.
‹rid reference 939107

‹S maps 1:50,000 197; 1:25,000 SU
‹0/90 and SU 81/91 (Pathfinder 1305
‹nd 1286)

‹efreshments Newburgh Arms and
‹op in Slindon

‹ALK DIRECTIONS

‹) At car park, with your back to
‹ap information board, turn left on
‹nall path, and left again when
‹ther path joins from right. Turn
‹ght on semi-metalled cross-track
‹nd then, when barrier to road is
‹bout 50 yards ahead of you, turn
‹harp left on straight track (Stane
‹treet) through woods.

‹ Follow for 1 mile [**a**], ignoring all
‹urns to right and left, to reach six-
‹ay junction with bench and
‹gnpost ②. Continue forward on
‹ath, signposted Bignor, which soon
‹aves wood. Maintain direction
‹ong this path for 1 ¹/₂ miles,
‹assing farm away to right after ³/₄
‹ile; path then rises slightly to
‹ach wide gate – do not pass
‹rough this, but turn half left up
‹ank just before it, past seat to stile
‹d signpost ③.

‹ Forward over cross-track, to follow
‹ath on top of bank; this emerges at
‹-junction of tracks after 250 yards,
‹th South Downs Way signpost ④.

Continue forward on broad track,
and turn right at T-junction towards
car park, with extensive views away
to your left ⑤.

Turn right just before car park
along track signposted Slindon, soon
on track just inside scrubby wood
with fence and field on left and
wood on right. Continue direction
downhill for 1 mile, ignoring cross-
track and later with wood on right.
400 yards after end of wood, at
bottom of rise, reach cross-track ⑥.
Turn right, and follow track with
wood on left, soon passing into
scrubby wood. Avoid tracks to either
side, to reach top of wood ⑦.

Turn right around edge of field,
and then immediately left. Continue
between fences to reach edge of
wood. After 30 yards, reach T-
junction of tracks and turn left, first
passing through scrubby woodland
and then on to gently sloping open
field. Continue forward over 3 large
fields on clear path, sometimes
walking between fences, and
ignoring a cross-track.

At end of third field, join well-
defined track, first heading slightly
uphill to follow top of ridge, then
dropping to gate and road ⑧.
For short walk continue forward to
T-junction in Slindon village [**b**], and
turn right, forward along village
street, ignoring two left turns. Road
soon rises out of top of village, and
then drops sharply, swinging away
to left. Continue downhill on
unmade track, which soon joins
surfaced road to Courthill Farm.
Turn left on track just before the
farm. Turn right over stile just
before barn. This is ⑬.
For full walk go forward on road into
Slindon village [**b**], and turn right at
T-junction (Newburgh Arms pub is a
few yards away to the left). Take
second turning on left, by tree on
island in middle of road with bench
round it, down Church Hill, passing

431

St Mary's Church on right, to reach pond at bottom of hill ⑨.

Immediately after pond, turn right on path, with hedge on right, to enter Slindon Nature Reserve by National Trust sign and wooden barrier. (NB avoid signposted Public Footpath starting on other side of hedge). Continue on main track through wood [c], avoiding turnings to right, and keeping edge of wood on left, to reach car park ⑩.

At car park, just before reaching surfaced road, take second track to right. After 500 yards, turn right on well-defined track (main road is visible ahead). Ignore cross-track after 50 yards, and two tracks merging from left, to reach large woodland clearing. 500 yards beyond this, main track bends fairly sharply to right to pass through a pronounced raised dyke on right; land falls away quite sharply to the left here ⑪.

Turn sharp left downhill on track, and after 150 yards turn right on narrow but well-defined path with conifer plantation on right. Turn right at T-junction, and continue forward avoiding track forking to right, to reach stile and road ⑫. Turn left on road for 100 yards, then turn right on bridleway between hedges uphill.

After ½ mile, turn right over stile to follow path on right edge of field. Turn right at top of field on track, which soon swings left. Just beyond flint barn on right, turn left on second of two stony tracks, over stile ⑬. Follow left-hand edge of two fields, crossing stiles, and keep left when fence on left swings left to cross stile to detour to folly ⑭ [d] and trig point (summit pillar).

Retrace steps to the stile, and turn left, following path with fence on left, and soon reaching stile at edge of wood. Cross it and turn half left into wood. At top of rise, bear right

where path merges from left, and continue along ridge for ¼ mile, ignoring side-turns. Continue forward downhill, avoiding signposted path to left.

⑮ At bottom of hill, where main track swings right (with wooden barrier ahead), turn left on well-defined track-avoiding all turnings to right, and keeping edge of wood t your left. After 1 mile, reach road by wooden Forestry Commission hut and barrier. Turn right on road to return to car park.

ON THE ROUTE

[a] **Stane Street** Once a major Roma military road which led from the E Gate of Chichester to London. Its typical form, which can be clearly seen in the well-preserved stretch o this walk, consists of a raised metalled road surface or agger made up of layers of pounded flint and chalk with a flat space on either sid bounded by small ditches. Fine **views** throughout this section over the South Downs, with a panorama northwards when you reach the car park after 2 miles.

[b] **Slindon** The village is almost entirely owned by the National Trust, who have been careful to preserve it as a community. Buildings date mainly from the late 17th century to the early 20th century, including the delightful post office; the 11th-century church has a wooden effigy of a Tudor knight. There is a fine Elizabethan house (now a school) and a thatched railway carriage – surely the only one owned by the National Trust! The poet Hilaire Belloc, author of many Sussex poems, *The Bad Child's Book of Beasts* and *Cautionary Tales*, lived for a time a a cottage by Court Hill Farm just N of the village.

[c] This is one of Europe's finest **beech woods**, dating from the early

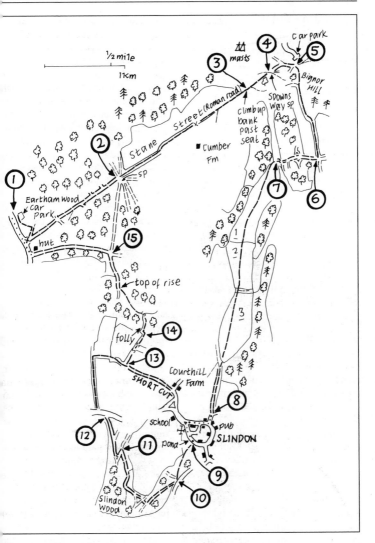

th century but sadly devastated by
e great storm of October 1987.
ow it is interesting to see the
tent to which nature is
generating the area. The National
rust has wisely decided to leave
me parts of forest to its own

process of natural healing.
[d] **The Folly** Constructed in the
early 19th century by the Newburgh
family, owners of Slindon House, as
an eye-catcher and outdoor
dining-place.

Around Arundel

A fine short walk, with river scenery, landscaped parkland and the town's steep main street offering absorbing contrasts. There is one gentle ascent through the park.

Length 3¹/₂ miles (5.5km), 2 hours
Difficulty 1
Start Town centre and Castle car park, Arundel (at bottom of town by river bridge near Maison Dieu, opposite castle entrance). Grid reference 20071 *By train* Arundel. Go up station approach road, left on main road, turn right at roundabout into town; turn right beyond river bridge.
OS Maps 1:50,000 197; 1:25,000 TQ 00/10 (Pathfinder 1306)
Refreshments Full range in Arundel, tea-room at entrance to Arundel Park at ③

WALK DIRECTIONS

① Start at car park entrance with castle gateway behind you; walk along right-hand side of car park past boat hire building, and pick up path on raised grassy dyke above River Arun [a].

② After 1 mile, cross double stile just after speed limit 5¹/₂ knot sign and turn left by signpost, leaving main river (or continue along river to Black Rabbit Inn if you prefer, then left on road until entrance lodge into Arundel Park on right). Just before footbridge in front of stone bridge, turn right on path and follow until joining road (where you can continue to right along road 200 yards to Wildfowl Reserve Centre [b]).

Cross to lodge gate opposite, entering Arundel Park ③ [c]; follow track close to the right-hand side lake. At end of lake, ignore minor left fork but keep forward over cattle-grid until reaching T-junction with track by signpost ④. Turn

sharp left, gently uphill (almost doubling back, on other side of valley). Near top, castellated Hiorn Tower comes into view away to right - ⑤ beyond gate, where wood begin on left, track soon bends righ and becomes fainter: head on (or go across grass past Hiorne Tower) to join tarmacked drive where turn lef Follow the drive to leave park by lodge gate.

⑥ Turn left on road at edge of Arundel [d], passing cathedral, paris church, priory, castle gateway [e] where road bends right and continues down centre of town as Arundel high street. At bottom of town, keep left of memorial to reac bridge, where go left past Maison Dieu to car park.

ON THE ROUTE

[a] **The Arun** Embanked as a trading route in the 16th century, it was intended as part of a through waterway from Portsmouth to London.

[b] **Wildfowl Reserve** 60 acres of open water, wet grassland and reed-bed. The breeding birds include teal lapwing and redshank, and there ar numerous passage and winter species. Ducks are fed in front of th viewing gallery at 4pm in summer and 3.30 in winter. Seven hides for close viewing of the birds are provided.

[c] **Arundel Park** Fine beeches (some storm-damaged), an attractive lake, herds of deer, and (off the route) one of the prettiest cricket grounds anywhere; above all, there is a feeling of great spaciousness.

[d] **Arundel** No town in Sussex is more finely set than Arundel. Its hill-top setting, crowned by castle, cathedral and church, has the air of an old French town. The **Catholic cathedral** was completed in 1873 by the 15th Duke of Norfolk, whose family still own the castle. The

cient Anglican **parish church** of St Nicholas is a good example of late th-century Perpendicular chitecture: unusually there is a atholic chapel under the same roof; e Fitzalan Chapel is the private apel of the Norfolk family. **Arundel Castle** has been home e Dukes of Norfolk and their cestors for over 700 years. The iginal fabric dates from the late th century. It was badly damaged in 1643 during the Civil War, and had to be extensively restored in the 18th and 19th centuries. Internally the castle has fine pictures, furniture and *objets d'art*. (Open Apr-end Oct, Sun-Fri 1-5; June, July, Aug, bank hols 12-5.)

Most of the domestic buildings of the **town centre** are 18th- or 19th-century, though often timber-framing is hidden beneath a more recent facade.

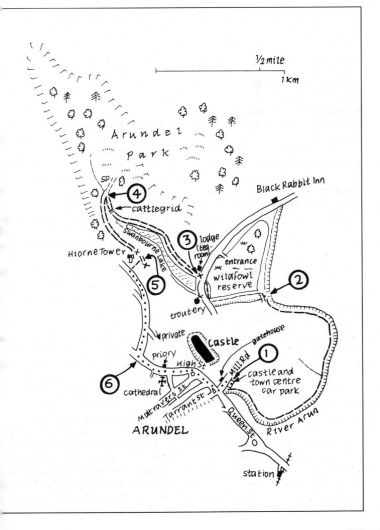

Nutbourne Marshes and Chidham

The best walk round Chichester harbour; unspoilt low-lying estuary landscape with bird life, sailing yachts and changing views across the water providing variety. Easy route-finding, all on the level.

Length 6 miles (9.5km), 3 hours
Difficulty 1

Start Nutbourne (on A27 W of Chichester, at E end of village by Barleycorn public house; parking in Cot Lane opposite side of pub)
By train Nutbourne. Turn right out of station to reach main road by Cot Lane. Grid reference 788054
OS maps 1:50,000 197; 1:25,000 SU 60/70 (Pathfinder 1304)
Refreshments Pubs at Nutbourne and Chidham

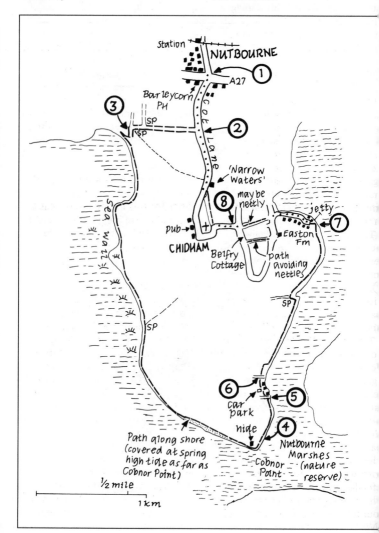

ALK DIRECTIONS

) Take Cot Lane (to left of
rleycorn pub) past houses; view on
ght soon opens out. ② 100 yards
er last house on left take
gnposted farm track on right: go
ross field, keeping forward on
sser track as signposted where
ain track bends right.

③ 100 yards later turn left at
gnpost at T-junction of paths. Soon
ach shore path and turn left along
[a]. Follow coast 2½ miles
itially along low sea wall, later
opping to shore; after Nutbourne
arshes nature reserve sign and hide
) [b], cross stile and continue along
a wall) [c].

⑤ Just before house, path diverts
land; 50 yards later path bends
ght (past Bosham Fishermen's
ub), and then follow signposted
avel path (ignoring broader one to
e left). 100 yards later, reach
gnpost by small car park and keep
raight on passing to left of low
mber buildings, over footbridge and
a to hard track ⑥.

) Take path opposite and slightly to
e right along right edge of field. In
xt field, turn right to rejoin coast
til next house (just before jetty)
), where path turns left inland,
th fence on right. Emerge on to
ad, which follow to reach T-
nction.

Turn left on road, 50 yards later
opposite second house which is
o. 2 Easton Cottages) take
gnposted path along left edge of
eld then go forward on enclosed
th to reach the road ⑧ where keep
rward (along Cot Lane).

ther follow lane all the way back
ast village pub and church) [d] *or*
here road bends left in front of red
ick wall take path on right along
ft edge, towards house, just before
hich emerge on to Cot Lane on
ur left; turn right along the lane.
NB To avoid nettles in summer

you may prefer to continue along
road to where it bends right just
after Easton Farm: here, take
signposted track on right by post-
box, keeping forward after 30 yards
where main track bends left. At
road, turn right then left at junction
with Cot Lane.

ON THE ROUTE

[a] **Chichester harbour** This area of
3,000 acres is of prime importance to
bird life. Together with Langstone
harbour, across the Hampshire
border, it forms the largest area of
estuarine mudflats on the south
coast of Britain, and is an ideal spot
for watching waders and wildfowl. It
is particularly fascinating in autumn
and winter, when thousands of birds
can be seen driven off their feeding
grounds by the incoming tide, and
roosting on Thorne Island across the
harbour.

[b] **Nutbourne Marshes** 1,000 acres
of saltings, creeks and tidal
mudflats, this nature reserve has a
range of marshland plants as well as
prolific bird life; the path maybe
covered in water at spring tide.
A nature reserve sign lists some
of the species.

[c] Views across an arm of the
harbour to **Bosham village**
(pronounced Bozzam). The church is
partly Saxon; according to legend,
the youngest daughter of King
Canute was buried here, and it is
thought that Harold prayed here
before his visit to Normandy in 1064
which led to the Norman Conquest.
Bosham church is depicted in the
Bayeux Tapestry. The village is now
a flourishing yachting centre, and is
well worth a visit after you have
completed the walk.

[d] **Chidham** Long famous for
'Chidham wheat', which was
discovered growing in a hedge by a
local farmer. It proved to be highly
productive.

WARWICKSHIRE

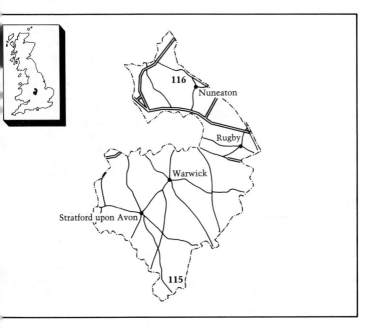

oliday Which? Good Walks Guide

Sutton-under-Brailes and Cherington

The attraction of this walk lies in the succession of stone-built villages with their fine 17th- and 18th-century houses, village greens, and churches. Good views in the country sections over rolling farmland. Most of the route is along well-defined tracks, but care is needed when the route is undefined, particularly at point ⑨.

Length 7 miles (11km), 3¹/₂ hours
Difficulty 2–3
Start Whichford (5 miles N of Chipping Norton), roadside parking by church. Grid reference 312346
OS maps 1:50,000 151; 1:25,000 SP 23/33 (Pathfinder 1044)
Refreshments Pub and shop in Whichford and Stourton

WALK DIRECTIONS

① [a] With Whichford church on left, follow road to reach village green by junction (left is signposted Cherington), at war memorial. At end of green take road between pub and shop signposted Ascott. After 200 yards, turn left just after end of village on to minor road.

② After ¹/₂ mile, near top of rise, take track on left by sign for North Leasow Farm. 100 yards short of the farm, fork right on to grass track.
③ After a gate, the track becomes enclosed and drops to Whichford Mill. On far side of the mill proceed over bridge up to road. Turn right on road.

④ After 400 yards, left on track which heads uphill; after 300 yards pass through hedgerow (fields have been extended here; there is a chance hedgerows may be further grubbed out). ⑤ Track ends in front of line of hedgerow trees; keep left through the hedgerow, to descend on grassy track in line with barn on hillside ahead; track is mostly

well defined, and soon passes a bar and eventually becomes enclosed o both sides as it heads for Sutton-under-Brailes.

Reach road, turn left along it, int village [b], and keep forward, following signposted direction for Birmington and Shipston; keep on road as bends right at end of green.
⑥ 60 yards after church, which is away to your right, take signposted stile on left, along left side of garde to enter fields by stile. Bear half right, towards left end of farm buildings ahead, to find bridge (between two power-posts in this field).

In next field turn right to reach gate; beyond it, head diagonally across field to stile in line with church tower and just to right of nearby red-brick former chapel; follow enclosed path to road at edg of village [c]. Bear right along the road, ignoring left turn (Featherbed Lane) just after shop on left.

⑦ At end of car park, take tarmacked path on left, between back gardens and soon reaching small road; turn right on the road, almost immediately reaching garages, where keep forward over signposted stile. Head for gate just left of church tower.

Go through churchyard, around right-hand side of tower, to take ga on to road. Turn left on road into Cherington village [d], turn right at next junction signposted Moreton and Long Compton. ⑧ Take first turn on left, opposite post-box in wall (just before bus shelter); this immediately becomes unsurfaced and goes through gate, along right edge of two fields and left edge of third field.

⑨ At end of third field, track ends; route is not easy to find here and care is needed (the following was the easiest route at time of checking, but follow waymarks

any have since been instated). Go
ead to enter fourth field, turn
mmediately right alongside hedge
 right, to go through gate and
ntinue up hill now with fence on
ft, and go through another gate at
p of fifth field. Proceed on well-
fined track towards farm.

Go through farm and follow track
road. Turn right on road. (10) After
0 yards, turn left on to woodland

track; track drops to reach fork after
150 yards where keep right, then
immediately bear left; track rises.
(11) At top, field appears on right and
track bends slightly left; after 130
yards, keep forward where hedge on
right ends, along edge of two large
fields alongside woods on left.

(12) At end of the second field,
woods bend to the left; leave them
for a track ahead, entering third field

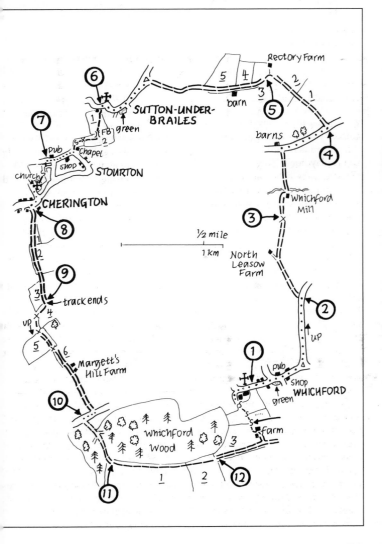

by obvious break in hedge, and now with hedge on right. When level with farm (which is in middle of field), turn left on track to the farm. Just before old stone barns, and just after open-sided barn, turn left and immediately right, pass the stone barns at end of which go forward (church is visible below), to find stile in hedgerow opposite ⑬.

Head down slope towards church to makeshift stile (this was a fixed gate at time of inspection) at bottom in fence corner. Go across field to stile to left of leftmost house (red-brick) in village. Proceed along road to junction and turn right into centre of Whichford.

ON THE ROUTE

[a] **Whichford** Occupying the level bottom of the small river valley, Whichford is recorded in the Domesday Book. The Norman church, extended about 1300, has a fine octagonal 14th-century font and delicately traceried Perpendicular clerestory. Around the village green are numbers of attractive old houses including the The Leasowes, a two storey house of mid-17th-century design, and some stone barns.

[b] **Sutton-under-Brailes** A well-preserved picture-book example of an English village: stone houses surround a large green, and the church has a 13th-century chancel and a Perpendicular window, but has been heavily restored. A hollow tree, festooned with drawing-pins at time of writing, acts as the village notice-board.

[c] **Stourton** The river here is the Stour. Village green, fine limes and thatched stone cottages, mostly of the 17th century.

[d] **Cherington** Its mill was still working until 1948. The church of John the Baptist is 13th-century though later restored: there is 16th century glass and a Jacobean altar; a compact village attractively grouped with open land between cottages and church.

artshill Hayes and ıe Coventry Canal

ne of the most impressive ewpoints in Warwickshire sets the ood for an absorbing short walk in ıd around the woodlands of artshill Hayes country park, aking use of the towpath of the oventry Canal. Nature trail leaflets ·ailable from visitor centre.

ength 3 miles (5km), 1½ hours
ifficulty 1-2
art Hartshill Hayes country park, ˙ of Hartshill, and S of Atherstone; gnposted from A5 SE of therstone. Grid reference 316944
S maps 1:50,000 140; 1:25,000 SP ›/39 (Pathfinder 914)
efreshments Café at visitor centre ·eekends only)

·ALK DIRECTIONS

) Take signposted path at back of ır park, behind warden's office and › right of fenced-off grassy bank ·eservoir). This leads to hillside, .ith reservoir fence up on left and ·oodland fence down to right. ·roceed as you like on the hillside ·eep high up to enjoy the view to ıe full) [**a**], to enter woodland at ˙gn for St Lawrence's Wood at the ıd of the grassland [**b**]. ② Just after ıtering the woods, there is a post ıarked 4, indicating a left fork (this part of the short St Lawrence's ·ood nature trail: you can either ·llow to the left, then go down ·eps, or keep on main path; the two ·utes soon rejoin).

At post 5 keep forward (leaving ıature trail, which bears right) and ·rk right 20 yards later as aymarked, to enter field. Go ·rward on path along right edge of ·eld, ③ bending left at first corner ·f the field. Mid-way along next edge ·f the field, take waymarked gate on › enclosed path on right.

At end of enclosed section, turn

right on to enclosed track leading uphill. At top, route continues along left edge of field until ④ passing through break in hedgerow on left (where field beyond the hedgerow on left has ended) to follow well-defined cart track down to farm. Keep to left of farm buildings, turn right on road and bear right at next road junction.

⑤ Cross canal, then turn right to join canal towpath; turn left along towpath, walking with canal on right [**c**]. (Bridges are numbered with plaques.) ⑥ Immediately after bridge 33, turn left up bank and cross the bridge to follow path across field (bisecting the rightmost two power-posts in the centre of the field) to gate in hedgerow ahead ⑦.

Turn right on farm track between hedges. Ignore right turn to Cherry Tree Farm, then soon after the houses on left end, fork right. ⑧ After 150 yards, just where track is about to bend right to farm, take gate on left into grassy area. Keep right, to take stile in corner of woodland and follow path leading uphill along inside edge of wood with fence on right [**d**]. After ⅓ mile, playground is visible ahead: proceed straight up to reach open hillside, where turn left into the car park.

ON THE ROUTE

[**a**] **Hartshill Hayes** View over four counties: Warwickshire, Leicestershire, Derbyshire and Staffordshire; Mancetter church, the A5, the Coventry Canal, Drakelow power station and the Peak District are all in view.

[**b**] **St Lawrence's Wood** This was a plantation created to landscape the ground of vanished Oldbury Hall, the site of which was at the top of the hillside, just off the end of the present-day reservoir; the hall was built 1770, on the site of a medieval nunnery and was demolished in the

443

1950s after bomb damage. The wood contains Scots pines and sycamores, and supports a variety of mosses.
[c] **Coventry Canal** built 1771; linking Coventry with Bedworth, Nuneaton and Tamworth it was one of the most profitable canals up to the Second World War.

[d] **Hartshill Hayes** 114 acres of mixed coppiced woodland, a fragment of the ancient Forest of Arden which once covered the area. Larch predominates, but the species also includes birch, hazel, holly, lime, rowan and oak; the site is a rich habitat for birds and insects.

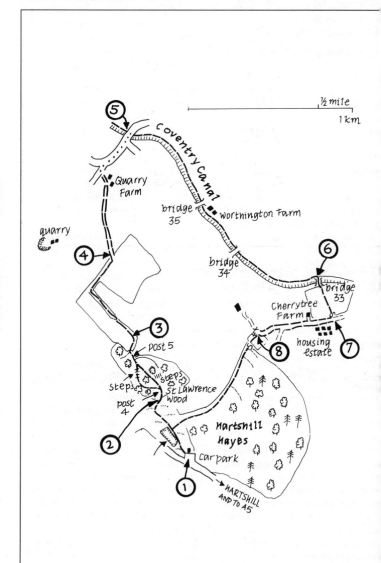

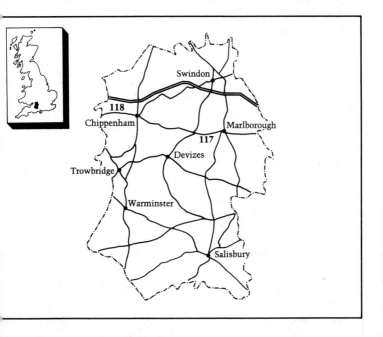

Holiday Which? Good Walks Guide

Avebury: an archaeological tour

A pleasant country walk in its own right, over cultivated chalkland, but the concentration of major archaeological sites makes this route well worth seeking out.

Length 6½ miles (10.5km), 3½ miles
Difficulty 2
Start West Overton (just off A4 W of Marlborough). Park on roadside in village centre near bus shelter and telephone box. Grid reference 132680
OS maps 1:50,000 173; 1:25,000 SU 06/16 and SU 07/17 (Pathfinder 1185 and 1169)
Refreshments Pub (just off route) and shop at West Overton; pub, shop and restaurant in Avebury

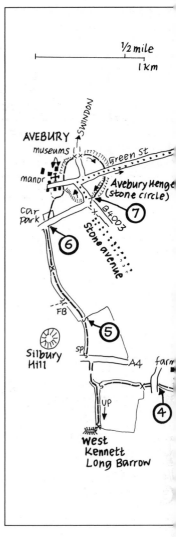

WALK DIRECTIONS

① With telephone and bus shelter on your right, follow the main village street, bear left just after shop on your left (ignoring next left turn). ② At T-junction at edge of East Kennett, turn left, then immediately take enclosed path on right. At road turn right, then take next left (just after telephone box and opposite gate to big house) into main part of village.

After church, lane becomes an unsurfaced track, bends right and just after house called Fortwitchen soon bends right again. ③ After 250 yards take track on right down to reach T-junction tracks where take stile ahead. Keep alongside left edge of three fields over a series of stiles.

④ Emerge on to surfaced lane and take track opposite soon reaching gate beside stile where keep forward, along right edge of field [a]. At far end of field cross stile on to fenced path: detour left uphill to West Kennett Long Barrow [b]. Return to the fenced path and follow it down

to A4. Turn left on A4 but after 30 yards take signposted stile on right.

Go forward away from A4 and along left edge of field ⑤ to reach stile on to path running along enclosed strip (soon ignore footbridge on left) which follow to reach road ⑥. Cross into car park opposite and slightly to right and take surfaced path in far right-hand corner (between litter bin and

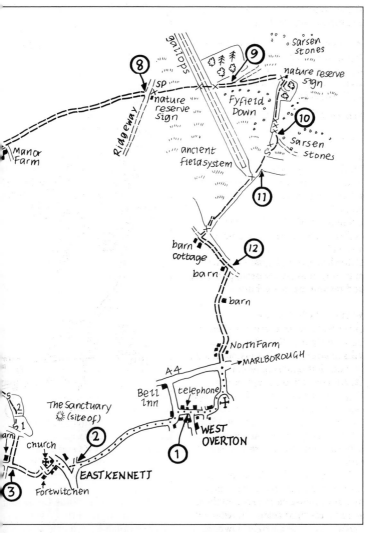

aformation board). Path soon bends ght between sports fields and through rampart of Avebury stone rcle and into road at Avebury llage [**c**].

Go forward following signs for useums but before you reach the st museum take steps up on right d turn left on the ramparts which inge the stone circle [**d**]. Soon cross ajor road and later a minor road but still continue along rampart and follow to reach road junction where the ramparts bend right [7]: here you can detour left to cross road and take gate opposite to view the Stone Avenue [**e**].

Return to ramparts, heading to village and reaching road in front of Red Lion pub. Turn right on road and immediately keep forward as main road bends left in Swindon direction: you are now on Green Street (with No Through Road sign). Keep straight on for 1 1/4 miles (road becomes track at a farm after 1/2 mile).

(8) Reach junction by signpost with ridgeway to left and right. Here take gate ahead (signposted Fyfield Down) [f] and follow faint grassy path towards right corner of woodland ahead; (shortly before reaching the wood, cross broad grassy 'gallops' by gates) [g].

(9) 200 yards after passing the woodland, fork right on to grassy track, aiming for left and end of woodland strip ahead. Take gate to enter the strip of woodland and turn right on chalky track but immediately leaving it for grassy track alongside fence on right as the chalky track bends left. Descend path through sequence of gates close together (care needed as the route is not obvious here); **(10)** by the last of the gates keep alongside right-hand fence, now walking across rough downland.

After 160 yards take stile alongside gate on right (avoiding gate just before this). Proceed up to corner of fence and hedgerow 150 yards away **(11)**, then go forward with fence on your left, eventually going through double-gate at end of gallops; then continue with fence on your left to reach gate at bottom of field where proceed down on to well-defined track to cottage and barns.

Turn left at T-junction of tracks in front of the cottage. **(12)** 400 yards later just after big barn on right, turn right at junction eventually to reach big farm where go forward, just to left of thatched barn, and continue down to A4. Take turning opposite signposted West Overton and take first right to reach village centre.

ON THE ROUTE

[a] **Silbury Hill** First seen here on the right and passed later; it has been called 'a great, green plum-pudding'. This is the largest man-made prehistoric mound in Europe, its origin and purpose a mystery. No burial has been found here, and it may have served some astronomical or religious function.

[b] **West Kennett Long Barrow** A mound of chalk 100 yards long and 8 feet high, accessible at its E end, with glass covers providing natural illumination and enabling visitors to walk right into the depth of the barrow. Excavated 1859 and 1956. At least 46 individuals are buried in the tomb; an unknown number of bodies which were removed in the 17th century. Pottery finds suggest the barrow was used for burial for a very long period, perhaps 1000 years; in the course of excavation a scatter of objects was found, which might have been funeral gifts. The great blocking stone at the entrance was placed to seal the burial chambers.

[c] **Avebury** Pleasant village street of stone and brick cottages, some under thatch. **Avebury Manor** was built on the site of a Benedictine cell; it was for sale as we went to press. Close by are two museums: the **Great Barn**, has a main collection of rustic bygones, and the adjacent English Heritage **Alexander Keiller Museum** is concerned with the archaeology of Avebury.

[d] **Avebury Henge Stone Circle** John Aubrey said in 1663 that Avebury 'does so much exceed in greatness the so renowned Stonehenge as a cathedral does a parish church.' The site probably dates from about 2600 BC and was largely lost to view until 1939 when Alexander Keiller cleared it of trees and undergrowth. The area is roughly circular and covers 11.5 hectares (4 1/2 acres), enclosed by a ditch. Within this lies an outer circle of 98 sarsen stones (from nearby Fyfield Down), with two

smaller inner circles.

[e] Stone Avenue Sited on a strip parallel to the modern road, 2000 stones, thought to predate Avebury Henge by 1000 years. The avenue led to the Sanctuary, another stone circle, destroyed by farmers in the early 18th century, as one observer put it, 'for dirty little profits'. It is worth going over the brow of the hill to get the best impression of the site.

[f] Marlborough Downs One of the foremost areas in England for race-horse training. There are numerous gallops such as this one.

[g] Fyfield Down A National Nature Reserve, famous for the surviving traces of Celtic field systems, whose divided lynchets (or banks) stand up to 10 feet high. The sarsen stones used to construct the circles at Avebury probably came from here. Many other stones are scattered through the reserve.

Castle Combe and By Brook

A route through a pleasing landscape
of soft green hills and intricate
woodlands, entering Castle Combe
through an archway. The walk
passes some of the mills which
contributed to the village's medieval
textile industry. Route-finding
somewhat complicated at the start,
but then becomes easy.

Length 4½ miles (7km), 2½ hours
Difficulty 2
Start Lay-by by telephone opposite
church in Ford, on A420 5 miles W
of Chippenham. Grid reference
841739
OS maps 1:50,000 173; 1:25,000 ST
87/97 (Pathfinder 1168)
Refreshments Pub and shop in Ford;
pubs, shop, tea-room in Castle
Combe

WALK DIRECTIONS

① With church on left, follow A420
downhill (towards Chippenham);
take first left after 100 yards by bus
shelter, and immediately fork right.
After 90 yards, just before track
reaches last house, take stile on left
into open area, turn right on well-
defined path along bottom edge.
Path soon enters woods; 100 yards
later, it goes down small slope on
right (at yellow waymarker on tree)
and continues in open area initially
alongside trees on left.

② Soon path crosses stile and
bridge together, then path ascends
slope, soon through small wood and
out again on far side where you
continue diagonally left uphill (away
from woods) on main path to
hedgerow along top of slope. Turn
left alongside the hedgerow, soon
past waymark and over stile by gate
into woods.

Path continues inside edge of
woods, with fence on right initially.
③ Reach road junction at gate and
turn left (towards West Kington)

along it. ④ After ½ mile, where road
bends left, take signposted woodland
track on right (soon between hedges
running between fields) which then
later descends to cross river at
bridge. ⑤ Turn right on other side of
bridge, on track alongside valley
close to stream and soon go over
ladder-stile by gate (ignore path on
left just before this). Reach restored
mill on right (with chimney), turn
right just after it to take metal gate
signed 'footpath only: this is a
conservation area' (gate itself is
usually locked, but there is a
concealed kissing-gate on its right).

Follow the track through woods,
with stream on left; it narrows to
become path on leaving the woods -
keep to main path which soon bends
left over stone footbridge ⑥. Turn
right on other side of bridge; on
passing ornamental gateway (to right
of, but separate from, path), path
enters woods with wall on right.

⑦ 70 yards after path and wall
bend left take steps down on right to
enter Castle Combe village [a]. Go
through centre of village past
Market Cross on left, (ignoring left
turn here) and along main street.
⑧ After end of village, take second
footbridge on left over river (the first
bridge is obviously private; the
second one is walled on one side and
has a signpost on the far side).

Go over stile to pick up well-
defined path, initially uphill, but
soon levelling out with fence and
hedgerow on right most of the way
as it goes in and out of woods and
eventually reaches houses at hamlet
of Long Dean ⑨. Here turn right at
lane T-junction, then as soon as you
cross bridge over small channel keep
right at fork, now on level track;
soon over By Brook and rising past
house on your left now on narrower
path to reach gate.

Go forward along fence on your
right to enter open downland ⑩;

ere *either* continue along top edge
alongside hedgerow to reach gate on
to road *or* cut off a corner by taking a
path halfway across the downland
bearing half left to stile in recessed
corner of wood giving on to road.
Both routes turn left on road to
reach main road at Ford; and turn
right to reach starting place.

ON THE ROUTE

a] **Castle Combe** is rightly regarded
as one of England's most beautiful

villages. It grew rich in the Middle
Ages from the wool trade, and had
the great added bonus of honey-
coloured Cotswold Stone as building
material. The church tower is 15th-
century, built 'at the expense of the
clovers of the district'. In the 1960s,
the village was temporarily
transformed into a seaport as a
setting for a film of *Dr Doolittle*,
with a jetty and harbour wall along
the brook.

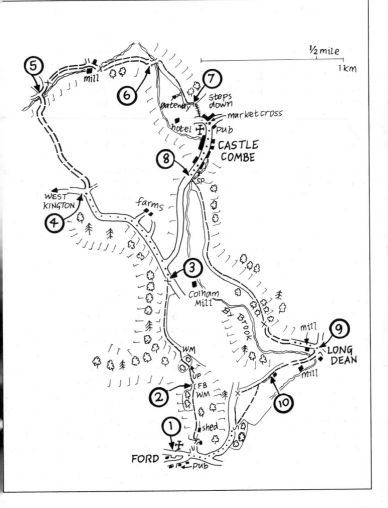

NORTH YORKSHIRE

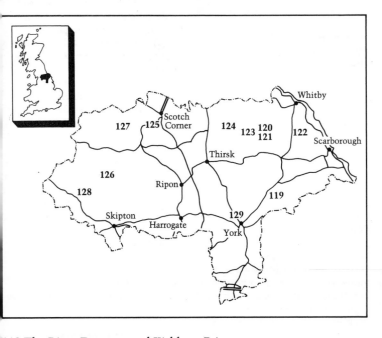

Holiday Which? Good Walks Guide

The River Derwent and Kirkham Priory

A long section along the broad River Derwent is the scenic highlight, reaching the ruins of Kirkham Priory; the rest of the route offers pleasant walking through elevated farmland and woods. Route needs care as far as Howsham, but is then easy to find.

Length 7 miles (11km), 3$\frac{1}{2}$ hours
Difficulty 2–3
Start Westow (roadside parking). Grid reference 754652
OS maps 1:50,000 100; 1:25,000 SE 66/76
Refreshments Pub and shop in Westow; pub and café near Kirkham Priory

WALK DIRECTIONS

(1) With Blacksmith's Arms on left, follow village street, past post office, keeping straight on at war memorial (signposted Leavening and Pocklington) **[a]**. Look for Westow village sign on right (facing other way, of course) – road then dips.

(2) 250 yards later take signposted track on right and keep along right edge of field as track gets less clear, to reach gate. Continue forward in next field, dropping steeply down slope with woodland fence on right. At bottom, turn left inside the field, but 100 yards later **(3)** take stile on right to join forest track: turn left along it.

(4) Fork left after 400 yards. **(5)** $\frac{1}{3}$ mile later, where track bends to right, leave track by turning left; immediately fork right on to broad path (left fork is narrower and

descends more steeply). Follow down to corner of forest: do not take gate ahead, but take gate alongside stile on left into field. Head down passing just to right of pond.

(6) 50 yards later, take gate on right into field; and turn left along field edge. At top of field, cross broad barrier, turn right along edge of fields to reach Howsham village **(7) [b]**. Turn left up village street (or detour right to see Hall). Turn right at road T-junction, descending to the river.

(8) On far side of bridge, take stile on right and follow waymarked path along river for 2 $\frac{1}{2}$ miles to Kirkham Bridge, opposite **(9)**. Cross bridge, passing priory **[c]**, following road which bends right uphill. **(10)** Keep right at next junction (by pub) and proceed to Westow.

ON THE ROUTE

[a] Westow Hall, at end of village on left, is a handsome early 18th-century house.

[b] Howsham A long row of honey-coloured stone cottages slopes down to Howsham Hall (a school), a Jacobean house remodelled in the 1720s with a stable-block, capped by a cupola, of 1725.

[c] Kirkham Priory (English Heritage: open Good Friday-Sept 30, daily 10-6; Oct 1-Maundy Thur, daily 10-4; closed Mon.) A sparse ruin of an Augustinian foundation of 1125, sited beside a loop of the Derwent. What little remains is beautiful; look for the splendid late 13th-century gatehouse ornamented with heraldic shields.

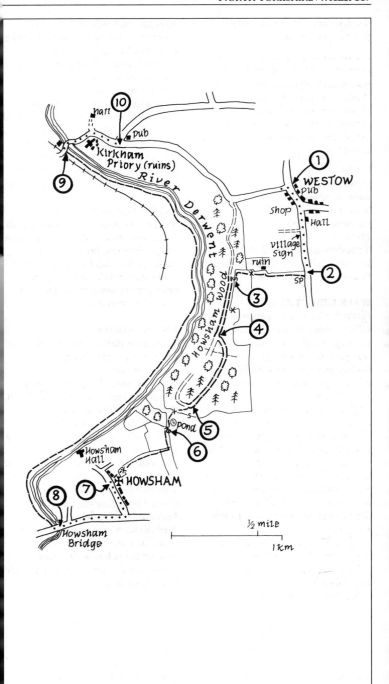

Rosedale

A traditional dale and moorland landscape, its character unspoilt despite its industrial history. A gentle rise on to moorland leads to the finale along a high moorland track. Route-finding intricate in places, as there are fields to cross and the route is not always visible.

Length 6½ miles (10.5km), 3½ hours
Difficulty 3
Start Rosedale Abbey (NE of Kirkbymoorside); two car parks in village. Grid reference 725959
OS maps 1:50,000 94 or 100; 1:25,000 Outdoor Leisure 26
Refreshments Pubs, café, shop at Rosedale Abbey

WALK DIRECTIONS

①[a] From Milburn Arms Hotel in village, take Egton turn, then turn left into car park: go through gate at rear of it and follow left edge of sports field and five subsequent fields, (soon alongside stream).

②Cross subsidiary stream by tiny slab bridge: keep straight on beyond (still close to stream) to stile just to left of power-post. In the second field after the slab bridge, continue close to stream; in third field bear half right as waymarked to reach gate by power-post; ③in fourth field go forward (farm visible ahead) to gate just to right of power-post; in fifth field turn left to skirt edge, soon along top of bank, to find gate down by stream.

Cross footbridge, take signposted bridleway ahead (not path signposted to left) to proceed with wall on right and with one field between you and the stream. ④Cross surfaced farm road, take signposted gate opposite: make for farmstead, the roof of which peeps up beneath conifer plantation ahead. Reach ladder stile at end of first field, then head uphill

towards the left-hand side of the farmstead (which disappears from view) and the fence which eventually encloses it.

Proceed towards the plantation, but ⑤just as you are about to reach it turn sharp left on track (opposite a gate), away from it; 70 yards later take gate on right on to road. Left on road. ⑥At road junction keep forward, on farm track opposite; 100 yards later take track on right into Lower Bell Farm. Go through gate at end of farm buildings and follow winding track. Keep right at fork, descending gently (left fork is level).

On crossing stream, keep to main track, close to stream; ignore right forks immediately after stream; 80 yards later, go through gate and ignore minor right fork; ⑦80 yards after, take footbridge on left to leave track. Enter farmyard by gateway, take enclosed track opposite and slightly to the left (waymarked), rising to tarmacked lane. Turn right on lane; pass Crag View Cottage on your right after 80 yards; just after, fork left on track signposted as a footpath to Farndale.

⑧50 yards later keep left (on main track) uphill; 30 yards later, fork left on to narrow path, soon to reach gate at bottom of moorland. Path bends to right, ascending diagonally up front of escarpment; there is a wall nearby down to right. Path eventually leaves wall; ⑨50 yards later, pass large boulders and continue in same direction, soon with gully on immediate right; 150 yards after the boulders, where gully crosses path, maintain direction (ignoring left fork) up to nearby hillock, which is topped by cairn (piled-up stones). From cairn, path continues to rise for 150 yards to reach level track (old railway line) ⑩: turn left along it [b].

⑪ Pass stone pillar on right side of track; 30 yards later fork left

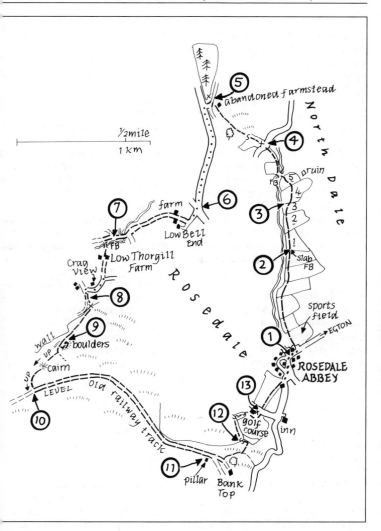

house visible ahead) on descending
track by cairn; after 50 yards, track
bends right towards house at small
group of trees: here turn left on to
descending grassy track. Your
objective is a stile over the fence on
your left (but further down slope).
Reach it by soon bearing left at a
faint track junction where right fork
goes to road; Rosedale Abbey soon
comes into view below.

Descend to cross the stile in fence
corner ⑫, turn right (with fence on
right) soon to cross another stile on
right. Proceed along edge of field to
enter small golf course by stile: path
crosses it between small fences and
turns left just after house to reach
road via stile ⑬. Cross to signposted
path opposite, follow right edge of
field down to steps beside house and
turn left on road into village.

ON THE ROUTE

[a] **Rosedale Abbey** Two buttresses and the remains of a staircase are the only vestiges of the 12th-century Cistercian foundation, that gives the village its name. It was demolished in the 19th century and stone was plundered for local building in the Rosedale mining boom. As ironstone production peaked, the valley's population increased from 500 in 1851 to almost 3,000 by the 1870s (6,000, including temporary lodgers); now fewer than 300 people live here. Kilns, slag heaps, inclines and track beds are still in evidence.

[b] This is the old railway track, which from 1861 to 1929 served the ironstone mines, and snaked 11 miles across the moors and around the heads of the valleys, from Ingleby Greenhow to Bank Top. Steep inclines were used, laden trucks descending providing haulage for empty ones coming up, and the line joined the main network at Battersby, from where ore was mostly sent to blast furnaces in County Durham. **Views** of two controversial additions to the landscape: huge conifer plantations, very much a feature of the E part of the National Park, and the Fylingdales ballistic missile early-warning system 'radomes' (three 140-foot white spheres, erected 1961-62), nicknamed 'the golf-balls'.

Hutton-le-Hole and Lastingham

Two picture-book villages linked by a route with changes in height and varied views.

Length 4 1/2 miles (7km), 2 1/2 hours
Difficulty 2
Start Village street, Spaunton (easy roadside parking), 3/4 mile SW of Lastingham, and NE of Kirkbymoorside. Grid reference 725899. (There is also a paying car park in Hutton-le-Hole, but this often is full at peak times)
OS maps 1:50,000 94 or 100; 1:25,000 Outdoor Leisure 26
Refreshments Pub, tea-room and shop in Hutton-le-Hole and Lastingham

WALK DIRECTIONS

1) Start with telephone box on right and walk W along street; keep on road as it bends right (ignoring semi-surfaced track on left), then 30 yards later take signposted farm road on left (with cattlegrid) into Grange Farm; fork right as signposted after 10 yards, in front of barn. At end of farm, track bends right, then left.
2) At end of two fields on left, track bends left. At end of field on right, turn right at track junction [a].
3) 1/3 mile later, view opens out suddenly ahead: turn left here (signposted), continuing along the enclosed track. 50 yards later, turn right by signpost where track ends, to follow enclosed path, soon descending along belt of trees. **4)** 20 yards after path crosses stile, take stile on right (leaving the enclosed path) to emerge at top of grassy slope with Hutton-le-Hole visible ahead.

Turn left downhill (leaving fence which is on your left) and soon reaching bottom of slight side-valley coming down from left (route-finding is a little tricky here; if you find yourself at the top of a steep wooded bank you are too far to the right). Turn right, soon picking up clear descending path. At bottom, stream appears on right: proceed to gate and stile, then forward to road at bottom of Hutton-le-Hole where turn right for a few yards [b].
5) Take signposted gate on right opposite post-box (30 yards before St Chad's church) and follow enclosed path past bowling green to gate (church ahead): turn right into field.

Route across fields is waymarked with yellow arrows, as it leads along the left edge of the first two fields, then keeps forward in third field to gate beside stile **6)**, and finally follows left edge of fourth field to cross footbridge and enter wood.
7) On leaving wood, continue along grassy track (with fence on right) to reach road. Turn right along road (or walk along grass just to left of it).

8) 50 yards before road junction by houses and bridge, take signposted track on left, soon through gate beside stile onto moorland: keep on track which runs close to wall on right along edge of moor. **9)** Beyond farm on right, track is no longer defined; continue along edge of moor always with wall or fence on right. Route descends, over stream by stepping stones (easy), then ascends to bench by signpost **10)**: turn right on track which soon becomes surfaced lane, dropping into Lastingham.

At bottom [c], turn left in centre of village (signposted Pickering), then **11)** take the first right turn (with No Through Road sign). Just after road metalling ends, turn right in front of barns as signposted uphill, on broad enclosed path which soon narrows to ascend through a wood, then reaches road junction **12)**. Detour right (on level grassy path above Lastingham road) to see Victoria Cross viewpoint [d]. Continue route along road signposted to Spaunton.

ON THE ROUTE

[a] View to the S, of the **Howardian Hills** and the **Vale of Pickering**.

[b] **Hutton-le-Hole** A sheep-nibbled green runs the length of its broad main street, with a stream down the middle crossed by a series of footbridges, lined by characteristic cottages of local yellow stone and red roofs. Became a refuge for persecuted Quakers in the 17th and 18th centuries; Quaker Cottage (1695) is the oldest surviving building. **Ryedale Folk Museum**

records rural and village life over 400 years, and includes a smithy, a medieval glass furnace from Rosedale, tools, furniture and a gypsy caravan.

[c] **Lastingham** On a hillock on the edge of this compact village, stands the **church**. The Norman crypt, and Norman and Early English building was part of an abbey founded by Abbot Stephen of Whitby in 1078, but never completed. This in turn was built on the site of a monastery founded by Cedd (whose remains are

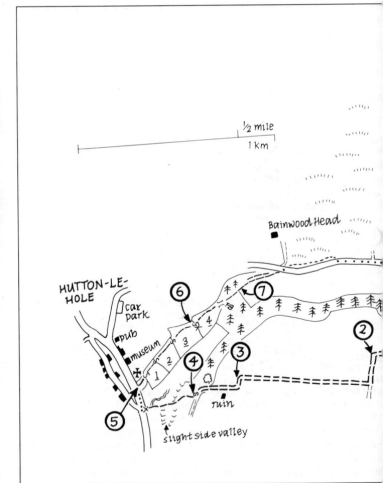

aid to be in the crypt) in 655, but
estroyed by the Danes. Repeated
ttacks caused the abbot to move to
ork, where he founded St Mary's
bbey. The partly completed abbey

became a church about 1230.
[**d**] Bench by 19th-century stone
cross is a good **viewpoint** over the
Lastingham area.

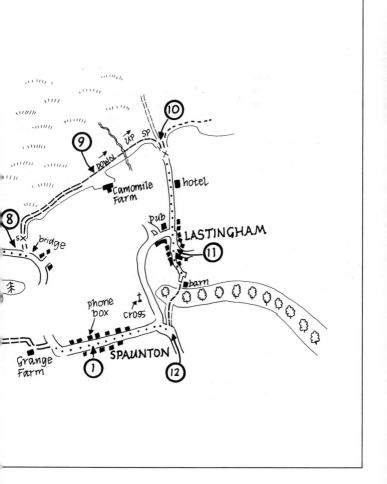

Hole of Horcum and Levisham

Wide open moorland expanses as far as Levisham, seen from the easiest of level tracks, followed by a path along a deeply incised valley which gives contrast. Easy route-finding.

Length 4½ miles (7km), 2 hours
Difficulty 1–2
Start Car park at AA box above Hole of Horcum, S of Saltergate Inn and on A169 (Whitby–Pickering). Grid reference 853937
OS maps 1:50,000 94 or 100; 1:25,000 Outdoor Leisure 27
Refreshments Pub and shop at Levisham

WALK DIRECTIONS

① From car park, cross main road, turn right on path that runs closely parallel to the road in Whitby direction, along top of the Hole of Horcum [a]. Where road is about to bend sharply right, take gate beside stile on left onto moorland track (not ladder-stile on left just before this, which leads to descending path)[b].

② Pass pond (on right) after 1 mile. ③ 1 mile later, track dips down to reach Dundale Pond [c] at track junction: take the ascending track to left, leading up to gate to continue as enclosed track (which becomes a lane) to Levisham ④ [d]. Proceed along village street to far end of village, then ⑤ turn left (where road is about to bend right) on to signposted path by bench, immediately forking left.

Path drops a little, then rises up steps and continues along top left edge of dale (ignore minor right descending fork soon after steps) gradually curving round left. Path then descends gradually to reach gate just above level of stream.

⑥ 100 yards later, step over subsidiary stream and ignore path to left up side-valley of Dundale Griff: go forward to footbridge, after which do not go through gate ahead but follow the path which keeps left along the valley, now with stream on left and wall on right.

⑦ Beyond next stile, path continues along valley in same direction. ⑧ Reach Low Horcum (abandoned farmstead), pass to left of it: proceed alongside hawthorn hedgerow on right down to gate, then head up to prominent path ascending slope (to left of barn on skyline). Emerge on to road; turn right to reach car park, or take gate beside stile on left if you started from Levisham.

ON THE ROUTE

[a] To the left, the **Hole of Horcum** is a great hollow, with an extensive view beyond over the Howardian Hills, and the E area of the North York Moors; moorland and commercial forestry dominate the landscape. Below, steam and diesel trains run along the bottom of the valley along the private North York Moors Railway.

[b] Two dykes here are prehistoric **earthworks** (one is by a sign for Levisham Moor; the other is along the right of the track), probably boundary markers marking the extent of farmland.

[c] **Dundale Pond** Probably artificially created for cattle to drink from; in medieval times this was part of a grazing pasture belonging to Malton Priory.

[d] **Levisham** A broad green runs the length of its street, with the Horseshoe Inn at its top end. The church has two fragments of an Anglo-Danish gravestone c.1000, marked with a dragon.

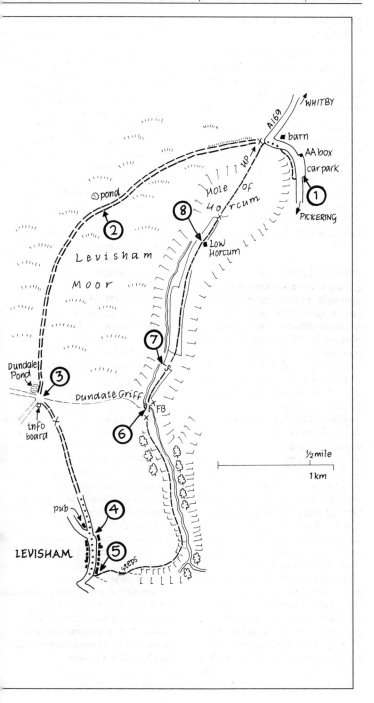

Farndale

**A streamside walk as far as High
Mill, then a gentle climb on to the
moor of Rudland Rigg, leading back
into Farndale by a quiet side valley.
Route-finding quite easy until ⑥,
then care required.**

Length 6 miles (9.5km), 3¹/₂ hours
Difficulty 3
Start Hamlet of Low Mill, Farndale
(N of Kirkbymoorside); car park
opposite post office.
Grid reference 673953
OS maps 1:50,000 94 or 100;
1:25,000 Outdoor Leisure 26
Refreshments Pub at Church
Houses

WALK DIRECTIONS

① [a] Take path by car park,
signposted High Mill, through gate.
Path crosses field to gate and
footbridge, then turns left alongside
river. Follow river (path later only
partly defined but the route is
obvious).

② After 1 mile, reach house (High
Mill); beyond it follow track for 30
yards, then cross stile on left (or
continue along track ¹/₄ mile to
Church Houses for the pub) and bear
half right in field, in direction of
waymark arrow. On far side, cross
footbridge and turn right (signposted
Cow Bank) ascending along right
edge of two fields to reach road
③ [b], along which turn right.

At next junction, keep left (no
through road signposted 'Dale End
West only'); 100 yards later pass
Monket House on your right; ④ 20
yards later take gate on left giving on
to moorland track (*not* the gate just
before this, which leads into
enclosed pasture). Beyond next gate,
track passes through old mine
workings [c]; soon after, ignore left
fork (where there is a small section
of concrete-posted railing on your
right). Track levels, eventually bends

slightly left by stone shelter [d].

⑤ Turn left at cross-junction of
tracks to proceed along top of broad
ridge (Rudland Rigg). ⑥ Just where
track is about to ascend there are a
blue waymarker post (pointing
ahead) and metal post together; 100
yards later take path on left, soon
past signpost and bearing to right,
along top right-hand side of small
side-valley. Path later passes stone
shelters [d] and view of Farndale
opens out ahead.

⑦ Where a wall appears 50 yards
down to left (at head of valley) do
not join it - your objective is High
Barn (the nearest building, ¹/₂ mile
distant, with prominent red roof).
Reach it by bearing half right to the
rightmost of two small trees 100
yards away, and following a well-
defined moorland path that heads
along the right-hand side of the
valley. Soon, a small gully appears
on the right-hand side of the path;
where the path crosses it, fork left
downhill (right fork peters out).

⑧ Pass through gate in corner of
wall: your objective is stile beside
gate near bottom of wall on your left
– reach it by following waymarks, at
first bearing half right down grassy
track then turn left after 50 yards by
signpost. ⑨ Beyond gate beside stile
turn right, alongside wall, to
footbridge, and turn right on other
side, through gate. Continue past
High Barn and pick up track. ⑩ At
farm (Horn End), ignore another
track to left but keep forward to
road. Turn right to Low Mill.

ON THE ROUTE

[a] **Farndale** A spectacular show of
wild daffodils throughout the valley
in spring attracts large numbers of
visitors (there may be crowds in the
first part of this walk as far as High
Mill). In 1955 Farndale Nature
Reserve was designated to prevent
people from picking the flowers (the

tuation had reached a crisis, with
sitors filling car boots and market
aders picking daffodils by the
nful). A minor literary storm raged
the 1980s when claims were made
at Wordsworth's 'host of golden
ffodils' were here, not in the Lake
istrict.

A strategically sited bench
erlooks a characteristic North
ork Moors **view**: above is the bleak
oorland plateau, while in the dale

below are red-roofed farmsteads and
hamlets in lush sheep-farming
country with dry-stone walls,
hedgerows and patches of deciduous
woodland.
[c] These moors were once
intensively worked for ironstone,
and coal was mined here during the
1926 General Strike.
[d] The shelters are used in the
grouse-shooting season.

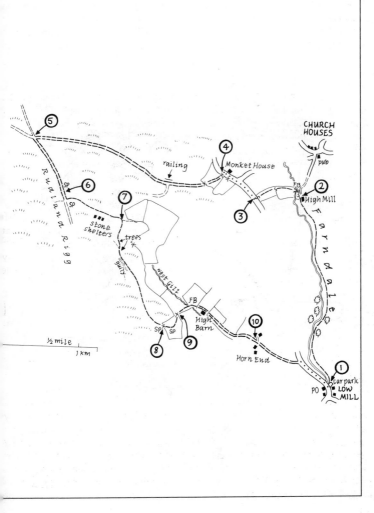

Cold Moor and White Hill

A horseshoe-shaped arrangement of moorland ridges, making easy but exhilarating walking once the modest haul on to them has been achieved. The best of the views occurs in the Cleveland Way section, 1½ miles along the top of a steep escarpment. Easy route-finding; boggy at ⑧.

Length 6½ miles (10.5km), 3½ hours
Difficulty 3 (3-4 after rain, when moorland may be a little boggy)
Start Chop Gate (on B1257 NNW of Helmsley and S of Stokesley and Middlesbrough; car park at S end of hamlet). Grid reference 559994. *Alternatively* start at Clay Bank Forestry Commission car park by turn-off from B1257 signposted Ingleby Greenhow; turn left out of car park and walk along B1257 towards Helmsley, then after 200 yards turn left through gate with signpost for Cleveland Way; start walk directions at ⑤.
Grid reference 573035
OS maps 1:50,000 93; 1:25,000 Outdoor Leisure 26
Refreshments Pub at Chop Gate

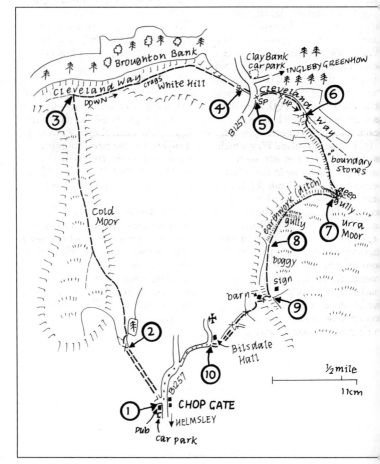

WALK DIRECTIONS

1 With Buck Inn pub on left, follow main road but soon turn left by signpost for Carlton (opposite war memorial), immediately forking right on to rising enclosed track (signposted Bridleway).

2 After ¹/₂ mile, reach gate on to moorland: keep right on path close to right-hand wall. As soon as path reaches small conifer plantation on your right it leaves the wall, climbing steadily up on to Cold Moor ridge; path is well-defined all the way and soon heads along centre of ridge with big views opening ahead.

3 Reach end of ridge [**a**], turn right by cairn (piled-up stones) at T-junction with broad path (Cleveland Way), walking close to top of edge and dropping to gate before climbing up to top of craggy hill (White Hill). Path levels and then drops to cross stile at edge of forest **4**: keep right as signposted alongside wall, to reach road. Cross to gate opposite.

5 Follow Cleveland Way which ascends with wall on left, soon passing through gate in fence just before forest on left ends [**b**]. Beyond next gate (in wall, at end of steepest section of ascent) continue up main path for 30 yards then **6** fork right (leaving Cleveland Way) on to path that initially runs parallel to wall on your right but soon bends left away from it. Path is well defined and marked by slight ditch (ancient earthwork) on right side [**c**]; it contours the moors (with mast in far distance roughly ahead for much of the way).

7 After ¹/₂ mile, cross deep gully (with stream), bear sharp right on other side on the path (still marked by the ditch). **8** Where wall appears on right, path is less well defined: keep alongside wall (boggy in places after rain). After wall ends, path is well defined again; **9** 200 yards later turn right downhill at path junction (when walk was researched this was at point level with large, rather old, sign on left about behaviour on moorland).

Very soon, gate in wall comes into view; beyond it, follow obvious snaking path down to further gate then proceed down track to tarmacked lane by Bilsdale Hall (farm) **10**. Left on lane, then left at main road to return to Chop Gate.

ON THE ROUTE

[**a**] Wide view suddenly appears to N; to the left is **Teesside** (including the Tees Transporter Bridge) and the right is the hook-shaped **Roseberry Topping**; the **Durham Pennines** stretch out in the far distance.

[**b**] Ahead is **Urra Moor**, the highest point in the North York Moors at 1,491ft.

[**c**] The **Bilsdale West Moor TV transmitter** is directly ahead in the distance; views over nearby **Bilsdale**. The **earthwork** you are following is an ancient boundary marker; **standing stones** seen close by are more recent boundary stones erected to show the limit of landowners' estates.

Richmond and the Swale

**A town and country walk, first
making a tour of Richmond – a
medieval-planned, fortified town
whose castle, square and street
layout betray a strong Continental
influence – then along the River
Swale, in one direction to the abbey,
and in the other out into rural
Swaledale, finishing with an exciting
high-level section. For town walk**

only, finish directions at ⑦. Take
care with directions after ⑩.

Length 7½ miles (12km), 4½ hours;
can shorten by 1½ miles (2.5km) by
omitting detour to abbey, or can be
restricted to a short stroll around
the town
Difficulty 3 (rather boggy underfoot
in one field; one climb)
Start Main square, Richmond. Grid
reference 171009

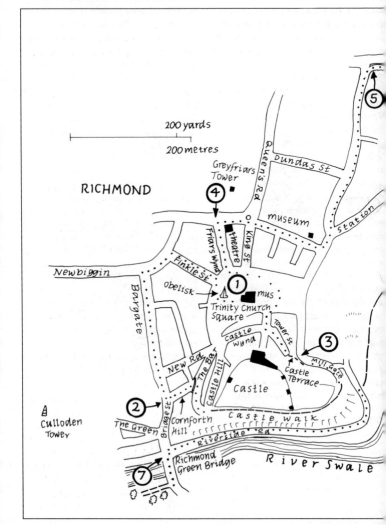

OS maps 1:50,000 92; 1:25,000 NZ 10/10

Refreshments Full range in Richmond

WALK DIRECTIONS

1 [a] From main square (Trinity Church Square), by church tower, take Finkle Street (just to right of National Westminster Bank). Left at T-junction by The Unicorn Inn into Newbiggin [b], then left again down Bargate. **2** Turn left opposite the Oak Tree pub, up Cornforth Hill [c] to archway, just after which bear right (left is The Bar), then right again along Castle Walk which skirts curtain wall of castle [d]. **3** Just as you are about to join street, take steps on left (by sign for Castle Terrace), proceed along cobbled street passing entrance to castle keep to reach main square again.

Go to other side of square, taking narrow lane called Friars Wynd just to right of Finkle Street [e]. **4** At end [f] turn right along Victoria Road and go forward at roundabout, along Ryders Wynd [g]. At end, turn left into Frenchgate, follow uphill [h], and at top **5** turn right into a narrow alley called Lombards Wynd, descending.

Near bottom, pass end of churchyard where keep straight on (ignoring right turn); **6** 50 yards later, path on right to river is continuation, *but first detour ahead* on track ³/₄ mile to Easby Abbey (at boathouse sign, fork right on to riverside path) [i]. Retrace steps from Abbey to **6** and turn right along the riverside path, under bridge, past school on your right, just after which bear left over grass to continue along river [j]. Later, join road and reach Richmond Green Bridge **7**. *Detour right*: immediately on left is The Green, with the Culloden Tower behind [k]. *To finish walk* continue up Bridge Street into town centre. *To continue* return to bridge and cross it, turn right on riverside path [l]. Soon fork left, uphill: keep to main path (edged with narrow logs), ignoring side-turns; by footbridge in woods, ignore right descending path. Main path soon descends, leaving woods by stile **8** at National Trust sign for Hudswell, then proceed through

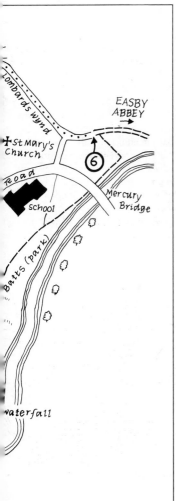

469

meadow alongside river Swale. Just after passing Hurgill on the outskirts of Richmond) on other bank, cross footbridge over river. Continue forward, past toilet block, bearing left up road to join main road, where turn left.

⑨ Take enclosed track on right (after 130 yards), before 'road liable to subsidence' sign. This goes along level; just before farm take gate on right (waymarked with yellow arrow), turn left, to by-pass the farm, through gate and stile to follow left edge of field, then over stile; keep forward beyond on path (soon track) into woods.

⑩ 100 yards after River Swale comes into view, turn right (waymarked) on to woodland path, to reach stile into field. Turn left, to join river (this involves careful stepping over a channel - various makeshift bridges across it at time of inspection; avoid temptation to strike out further to right, as it is very boggy in middle of field), past section of dilapidated wall. ⑪ In second field continue along river,

then into third field by gate beside stile: keep to left of tree-lined water channel. Enter fourth field, continu up close to right edge, past a barn then through a gateway.

⑫ In fifth field there is a farm, Applegarth, on right: bear half right to field corner, finding waymarked track, which proceeds through a gate. Just after, leave track as it bends round in front of Applegarth; and, go forward, uphill, following scant remains of wall, which immediately bends right, above the track. Where track below emerges on to a tarmacked lane, turn left, now with solid wall on right, up to stile on to lane by cattlegrid.

⑬ Turn left uphill on the lane, up Deep Dale. ⑭ Just before cattlegrid on to road at top, turn very sharp right (doubling back) on to grassy path heading to wall.

Path proceeds on level along top edge [m], with dramatic views on right, past monument and later just above top of woods. Soon after, path switches to other side of fence, to proceed just inside field with fence

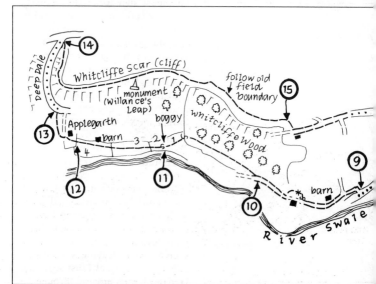

n right: at end of field, keep to left
f gorse area finding gateway a short
istance to left of edge of slope. In
ext field, path runs along
rominent grassy hump with
itermittent line of trees along it
ld field boundary) with Richmond
irectly ahead. ⑮ Reach waymarker
ost, turn right to farm, where turn
ft along stony track (later becomes
irfaced lane) and follow to
ichmond.

N THE ROUTE

] **Trinity Church Square** England's
irgest market place, a clear
idication of Richmond's prosperity
i the 15th and 16th centuries as a
ading place, and in the 18th
intury as a wool centre. The
iurch of Holy Trinity (founded
135) is a rarity in having shops
uilt into it; the building has also
en a prison, courthouse and
ranary, and is now the Regimental
luseum of the Green Howards
pen Easter-Oct, 11-5 daily). Above
ie modern shop fronts are an
iteresting range of upper facades,

curving around the square.
[b] **Newbiggin Broad** Cobbled street,
outside the line of the old town
walls; mostly 18th-century.
[c] **Cornforth Hill** One of a number
of alleys or 'wynds' in the town,
leading steeply up through one of
the two surviving town wall
gateways (there were originally five).
[d] The path skirts the huge curtain
wall of the **castle** (entrance on far
side, soon reached; English Heritage,
open Easter-Sept, 10-6 daily),
occupying a natural defensive
position with precipitous drops to
the Swale. The building was begun
in 1071, by Alan Rufus (one of
William I's men) as the Normans
strengthened their hold on northern
England. Its 12th-century keep soars
to 100 feet, and has 11-foot thick
walls; the herring-bone masonry is a
characteristic Norman feature.
[e] In Friars Wynd, the **gateway** in
the town wall gave access to the
Franciscan friary (see [f]). At the end
of the Wynd on the right, **Richmond
Theatre** looks barn-like and
unassuming but conceals the oldest

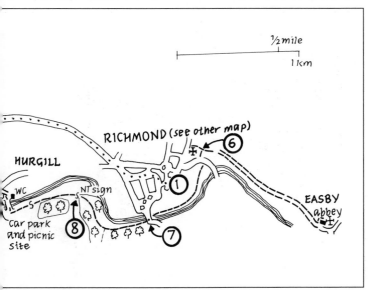

471

theatrical interior in its original form in Britain. Built by actor-manager Samuel Butler in 1788, it was reopened after restoration in 1963; open Easter-Oct, 11-4.45 Mon-Sat, 2.30-4.45 Sun).

[f] **Greyfriars Tower** (opposite). One of only three Franciscan bell-towers left in England; the foundation dates from 1258 but the Perpendicular tower is 15th-century.

[g] **Richmondshire Museum** (on left in Ryders Wynd; Easter-Oct open 11-5 daily) has exhibits on the history of Richmond and Swaledale.

[h] **Frenchgate** French followers of the first Earl of Richmond were originally housed here. There is a striking vista down the street from the top end.

[i] **Easby Abbey** (English Heritage; open 9.30-4 or 6.30 daily; closed Sun am). A foundation of about 1152 which belonged to the Premonstratensians (or 'white canons', because of the colour of their habits). It suffered from Scottish incursions and at the hands of English soldiers who were supposed to defend it. The bell and stalls were removed to the church of St Mary in the town at the time of Dissolution.

[j] Waterfalls and a weir along this fast-flowing stretch of the **Swale**. Richmond Green bridge was built in 1789 after its predecessor was destroyed in a flood.

[k] The Green has a view of **Culloden Tower**, a Georgian Gothic folly (not open), also known as the Cumberland Temple, built to commemorate the Battle of Culloden.

[l] **Hudswell Woods** Best in spring and autumn, covering steep slopes on the S side of the Swale. Worth a detour if you are confining yourself to the town section of this walk.

[m] **Whitcliffe Scar**, a limestone feature, provides a level walk high above Swaledale, looking towards the Vale of York and the North York Moors. For the rest of the walk, the long-distance **Coast to Coast** route followed, which runs from St Bees Head in Cumbria to Robin Hood's Bay in North Yorkshire. The monument passed at **Willance's Leap** commemorates an incident when a hunter fell in the fog: the horse was killed but Willance survived. He later gave a silver chalice to Richmond and built the monument to express thanks for his deliverance.

Northern Wharfedale

Route follows the side of the dale before joining the valley floor at Hubberholme and ending along the Wharfe. Route-finding mostly easy, but care is needed just before and after Cray.

Length 4½ miles (7km), 2 hours
Difficulty 2
Start Buckden (car park next to post office). Grid reference 942774
OS maps 1:50,000 98; 1:25,000 Outdoor Leisure 10
Refreshments Shop, tea-rooms and pub in Buckden; pub in Wray and in Hubberholme

WALK DIRECTIONS

① [a] From B6160 by post office, take signposted bridleway for Blackstone Edge, at entrance to car park, passing toilets, then through gate at far end of car park by signpost for Buckden Pike and Cray High Bridge. Follow track that rises gently, soon through trees. Beyond trees, track is joined by wall on left and now levels out (ignore right turn up to Buckden Pike by next gate).
② Where wall ends, proceed along level grassy track. After next gate, wall on left begins.

③ 50 yards later turn left through gate signposted Cray, heading down towards pub at right end of village and crossing ford. Cross road and take track to right of pub; behind pub keep to right (upper) fork, passing through farmyard by barns,

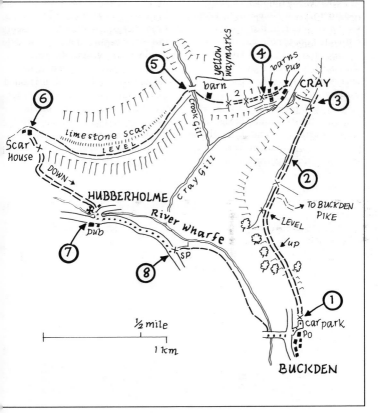

then keep forward through gate, passing further barns and picking up stony track.

④ 100 yards later, keep to right of last barn, through signposted gate for Yockenthwaite (avoiding lower track signposted Stubbing Bridge). Stony track crosses first field; (yellow paint waymarks in the following section made route-finding simple at time of inspection; these directions are given in case of problems). In second field (where track ends) keep forward to gate. In third field, continue slightly right, aiming just to left of barn, then continue along the level, with wall up on right, and cross footbridge over Crook Gill ⑤.

On other side, bear slightly left still along level, with wall (later fence) on left ⑥ [b]. After 1 mile, reach farm (Scar House) on left, by signpost. Turn left, through farmyard, and follow track down to emerge on road by Hubberholme church ⑦ [c]. Turn right on road, over river bridge, then left on other side, by pub.

⑧ ⅓ mile later, take gate on left by signpost for Buckden Bridge. Keep left, alongside wall and turn right on reaching river; follow river to Buckden Bridge. Cross the bridge and follow road up to the post office and the car park.

ON THE ROUTE

[a] **Buckden** Named after deer, a herd of which survived until recent times; the antlers from the last to be shot hangs at the White Lion in Cray (on this route). Buckden housed foresters in Norman times, when Langstrothdale Chase was a hunting forest.

[b] Large **limestone pavement**, with long limestone scar on the right; this natural terrace provides a magnificent viewing platform for admiring Wharfedale.

[c] **Hubberholme** The **church** is 12th and 16th-century and contains a rare rood loft of 1558, used as a musicians' gallery before the organ was installed. Pews and stalls have a carved trademark in the form of a mouse, signifying the maker, Thompson of Kilburn, who died in 1955. Across the Wharfe, the **George Inn** is the venue for an ancient dale 'land letting' custom, in which the tenancy of the 'poor field', which belongs to the church, is auctioned to local farmers on New Year's Eve; the vicar places a candle on the bar and waits in the other room while the auction is under way. The ensuing sing-song includes the *Song of Wharfedale*.

waledale and
Arkengarthdale

**Moorland tracks over high ground
for the most part, but low-level
sections in lush river valleys make
this a richly varied walk, not to be
hurried.**

Length 10 miles (16km), 4$\frac{1}{2}$ hours
Difficulty 4
Start Village green, Reeth (on B6270
W of Richmond); roadside parking.
Grid reference 038993
OS maps 1:50,000 92 and 98;
1:25,000 Outdoor Leisure 30
Refreshments Full range in Reeth;
pub and shop in Langthwaite

WALK DIRECTIONS

1 [a] Start at bottom end of green
and take lane just to right of
Congregational church. At T-
junction after 60 yards, turn right.
After 100 yards keep straight on at
junction taking lane with 'No
Through Road' sign. Reach gate at
end of lane. **2** Turn left (note this
section can get flooded; if so, use
directions given at end to reach **3**),
signposted Grinton, down between
walls to gate, then over footbridge;
bear right in direction of signpost to
gate, then proceed to suspension
bridge. Do not cross the bridge but
turn right along riverside path [b].

Soon path passes big flat meadow
on your right; Healaugh village
comes into view ahead and to right.
3 Turn right (signposted; this is $\frac{1}{2}$
mile after the suspension bridge),
alongside wall on right to reach gate
at right-hand end of Healaugh [c].
Turn left on road through the
village. Take second road turn on
right, by telephone box, immediately
bear left at junction. 50 yards later,
turn left on grassy track between
walls (by power-post).

4 At end of walled track, take
stone steps on left and turn right in
field, alongside wall on your right,

passing barn and going through gap-
stile (a deliberate gap in the wall). In
second field, go half right heading for
another barn, and taking gap-stile 40
yards away. In third field turn left to
find stile just to left of (same) barn.
Emerge on unmade track and turn
right along it; in front of next house
(Thiernswoood Hall), ignore right
turn but continue on into woods;
track contours around the top of the
woods, soon bending right to gate
out of woods **5**.

Beyond this gate keep left (no path
defined), alongside wall, up to stile.
Follow this wall as it bends right and
then left, uphill. At point level with
house on left (Nova Scotia), route
picks up defined track, leaving wall
on left and heading up immediately
to left of old enclosure.

6 100 yards after the old
enclosure, turn left at T-junction
with track (100 yards before an
enclosure which is still in use
ahead). Reach stone wall on left
around another enclosure. **7** 100
yards later, track ends: turn right
(opposite gate in the wall) heading
up over pathless moor to moorland
ridge 200 yards away to pick up
prominent grassy path gently
rising to the left over the shoulder
of the ridge.

8 After $\frac{1}{2}$ mile, just before gate
giving on to road, reach corner of
wall on left; turn sharp right on
well-defined track (almost doubling
back; small valley on left and
Arkengarthdale visible ahead in
distance); follow 1 $\frac{1}{4}$ miles.

9 Shortly before reaching road,
fork left. Left on road. 250 yards
after cattlegrid, turn right opposite
post box, along cul-de-sac. After 200
yards, just as road is about to bend
left, keep straight on through
signposted small gate, crossing field
(old graveyard) [d] to stile in corner,
then bear right on path dropping to
footbridge over river.

10 On other side, right is continuation, but first detour left to reach Langthwaite village [**e**]. Return to point **10** and proceed along track (which leaves river), into wood where soon fork left; track crosses field then bends right (signposted Fremington to cross footbridge **11**). Pass farm (Strothwaite Hall) on your left then, immediately after, turn left uphill between walls (signposte Hurst). Where wall on right ends, continue up alongside wall on left (blue paint waymarks here) to gate; then bear right, heading up to obvious breach in the top of Fremington Edge (old lead workings with prominent cairn (piled-up stones) on top **12**.

Turn right along the top of the

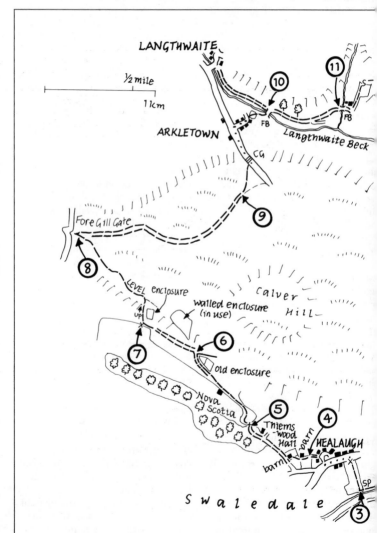

dge: there is no defined path nitially, but there is a small cairn hortly – keep slightly away from he very edge [**f**]. **⑬** Reach traversing vall, cross via gateway (if you reach ladder-stile you are 200 yards too ar to the right), and proceed now rith wall on right for 1¼ miles. **⑭** t gate beside stile in wall at right ngles to the path, with track coming in from left: take gate on right and follow the well-defined track downhill. Reeth is in view, but track heads to left of it; track later becomes surfaced.

⑮ After ¾ mile, ignore track on right signposted Arkengarthdale, but 50 yards later take grassy track on right to reach T-junction with lane. Turn right then after 30 yards, where lane bends left, fork right through gate. Follow left edge of three fields, alongside wall. **⑯** Halfway through third field, take gate on left and cross fourth field towards 30mph signs by bridge [**g**]. Cross bridge and follow road into Reeth.

Flood avoidance route: continue forward (as approaching from Reeth), signposted Healaugh, through gate, and proceed with wall on left in (first) field; in second field go forward (along grassy hump marking former field boundary) to leave by gate; proceed across three small fields heading for stile or gate ahead; in sixth field, river is close by on left. Go forward 50 yards then drop down to stile by river; turn right along riverside path. Resume directions at ③.

ON THE ROUTE

[a] **Reeth** Large village at junction of Swaledale and Arkengarthdale, with large, irregular green as its focal point. This was a flourishing lead-mining area in the 18th and 19th centuries; in the 1880s decline set in with the availability of cheap lead from overseas.

[b] The **Swale** is reputedly England's swiftest-flowing river; floods are frequent, and it has been canalised in places. Swaledale's stone barns are very much a landscape feature.

[c] **Healaugh** A one-street hamlet, which grew in the 19th-century lead-mining boom.

[d] A few tombstones are all that remains of **Arkle Town's old church** built 1145 and demolished 1818.

[e] The bridge at Langthwaite is featured in the opening sequence of *All Creatures Great and Small*, the TV series based on James Herriot's books.

[f] **Fremington Edge** is littered with evidence of lead-mining, but offers splendid walk along the top of its escarpment, high above Arkengarthdale. Halfway along, views open out E to the North York Moors.

[g] **Reeth Bridge** Built 1773 by John Carr, architect of Harewood House.

Catrigg Force and Langcliffe

A varied walk encompassing two villages in Ribblesdale, with two waterfalls, dry-stone walled pasture and an easy section along the River Ribble from Langcliffe.

Length 4 miles (6.5km), 2 hours

Difficulty 2–3

Start Stainforth, on B6479 N of Settle; car park signed off main road. Grid reference 821672

OS maps 1:50,000 98; 1:25,000 Outdoor Leisure 10

Refreshments Pub in Stainforth; shop in Langcliffe

WALK DIRECTIONS

1 Turn right out of car park, then left at next turn [a] (signposted Halton Gill and Arncliffe); road immediately bends right; 50 yards later, cross small green on right (with bench) and go over stepping stones (very easy) over river. Keep left on other side, past a second green, and take unsurfaced lane ahead which goes steeply uphill and is signed Unsuitable for Motors.

2 After ½ mile, reach gate across end of lane: detour left over ladder-stile (signposted Catrigg) entering woods on left by stile to see waterfall [b].

Return up to lane, take stile to right of the gate [c] and turn right up to gate on skyline **3**, where bear half right as signposted (for Winskill). There is no defined path here: your objective is a ladder-stile with gate alongside, 300 yards to left of nearby barn; shortly before you reach them, a clearly marked track is picked up. At cross-junction of tracks, take track ahead (towards Lower Winskill and signposted Langcliffe and Stainforth).

4 After 100 yards, take stile on left, signposted Langcliffe. Head across field to stile just beyond nearest power-post. Turn right in

next field, downhill (with Langcliffe now visible ahead); where walls on both sides end, you are at top of semi-wooded slope – there is no defined path here. Head down slope to next power-post, to find small gate and emerge into large field **5**. Make for distant (but prominent) track between walls that leads into Langcliffe village [d].

In village centre, turn right on road, then **6** take road between fountain and tree with bench around. Turn right at main road and follow it over railway, then **7** immediately take lane on left with 'no through road' sign. Reach river, cross by footbridge [e] and turn right to follow riverside path 1¼ miles [f] to reach Stainforth Force near bridge [g]. Cross the bridge and follow lane up to main road, where turn right; car park is second turn on left.

ON THE ROUTE

[a] **Stainforth** Takes its name from a 'stony ford', now crossed by a packhorse bridge; the village centre has 17th- to 19th-century cottages.

[b] **Catrigg Force** Makes a double leap of 55ft, this fine waterfall is in a secluded woodland setting.

[c] View of the **Three Peaks**: NW Ingleborough (2,373ft; with distinctive flat top, beyond quarries), Whernside (2,414ft), N is Pen-y-Ghent (2,273ft). NE is Fountains Fell (2,191ft).

[d] **Langcliffe** The village green and its 17th- and 18th-century houses make it one of the most attractive of the Dales villages; it was a cotton-spinning community from the late 18th century. Opposite the telephone box, is a stone figure in a house wall: this is a 17th-century inn-sign for the Naked Woman Inn (which lost its licence in the 1800s after a brawl involving navvies constructing the Carlisle to Settle

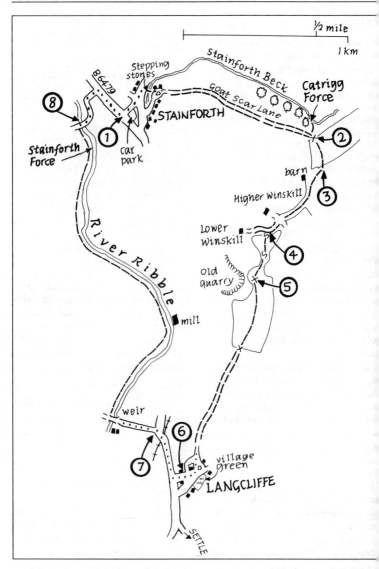

railway line; the pub was never re-opened).

[e] The **weir** on the river Ribble originally powered a watermill, which produced corn in the 18th century and cotton in the 19th century. A fish pass on the near side allows salmon and trout to bypass the weir.

[f] On the other bank is a **paper-mill**, mostly involved in recycling.

[g] **Stainforth Force** Not a large waterfall, but prettily sited, by a 17th-century packhorse bridge. The water rushes over flat rocks, making it a popular bathing place in summer.

York

A walk around the longest city wall in Britain – first encompassing Victorian suburbs, then into the historic centre – is the opening for an exploration of one of Britain's showpiece cities. If you are only visting for a day, do not attempt to see all the sights in one go.

Length 3¹/₂ miles (5.5km), 4 hours
Difficulty 1
Start Castle Museum car park, by Clifford's Tower
Refreshments Full range

WALK DIRECTIONS

① Start by oval green (the Eye of York) with Castle Museum away to left and steps to Clifford's Tower (castle) immediately on your right [**a**]: take road ahead, cross main road (Tower Street) and go into small park. Take path diagonally through park to Skeldergate Bridge, which cross.

② On other side, take steps up on to city wall (ahead and to right)[**b**]. Follow walls around, later passing over Micklegate Bar (medieval gateway). ③ Walls end at Lendal Bridge [**c**]: cross river. Take gates on left (50 yards after bridge and opposite Lendal) into the Museum Gardens. Pass on your right St Leonard's Hospital, the Multangular Tower, and the Yorkshire Museum (with classical portico) [**d**] before reaching ruins of St Mary's Abbey [**e**]: here turn left, then immediately right through gateway.

④ Turn right along Marygate [**f**], turn right into Bootham [**g**] towards Bootham Bar (gateway). ⑤ Take steps in Bootham Bar [**h**] on to city wall and walk along until Monk Bar, where turn right into Goodramgate, then ⑥ first right into Ogleforth [**i**]: street bends left into Chapter House Street and leads to York Minster.

Turn left in front of the Minster,

immediately fork right (left is College Street) [**j**], pass between bollards and go around the far side of the Minster (Deangate) [**k**] to the entrance at its west end ⑦ [**l**]. Leave Minster by west end, turn sharp left into High Petergate [**m**], which after passing Stonegate (on the right) becomes Low Petergate.

⑧ Reach Kings Square (with Goodramgate at bottom left of square: *detour* along it to see Holy Trinity church [**n**]). Leave Kings Square by far right-hand corner, immediately keeping left into the Shambles [**o**].

At end [**p**], turn left along Pavement, then ⑨ right into Fossgate: go through gateway on right-hand side for No. 40, the Merchant Adventurers Hall [**q**]; continue up steps at back, turn right along Piccadilly, left by traffic lights into Coppergate [**r**]. ⑩ Turn left into Castlegate [**s**]. At end proceed to Clifford's Tower (castle mound) by Castle Museum car park.

ON THE ROUTE

[**a**] **York Castle Museum** (open 9.30-5.30, 10-5.30 Sun; last admission at 4 Nov-Mar). Contains reconstructed streets with shop fronts from demolished buildings; also here are farm equipment, toys, costumes and a 1940s kitchen. **Clifford's Tower** (English Heritage, open 9.30-6.30; closes at 4 in winter). Built by Henry III on the site of a wooden keep, in an unusual quatrefoil plan upon a grassy motte. When in 1322 local opponents of Edward II were defeated, Roger de Clifford and other leaders were hanged in chains from the walls.

[**b**] **City Walls** Originally surrounded by a moat, with entrances through the gates or 'bars'; the medieval wall is intact to a remarkable degree, and can be followed for most of its 2³/₄ miles and over four original

gateways. Immediately to the right
as the wall is joined is Baile Hill, a
mound surrounded by trees, which
was the site of a castle built by
William I. Later are Victoria Bar
(built 1838) and Micklegate Bar,
where during the Wars of the Roses
heads of criminals and enemies were
displayed on spikes. **Bar Convent**,
outside Micklegate Bar and on left in
Blossom Street is the earliest
surviving post-Reformation convent
in England (open 10-5; Sun 2-5).
Later, on left, is **York Station**, noted
for its curved 800ft-long engine shed.
After the station and Royal York
Hotel, a **burial ground** is just to the
left below the wall. Twenty
gravestones mark the resting places
of victims of a cholera epidemic in
1832 in which 185 died.

[c] **Lendal Bridge** is adorned with
heraldic motifs, including the White
Rose of York (best seen from the
riverside walk). The Lendal tower on
the nearside was a river fortification
which was used as a waterworks
from the time of Charles II
until 1846.

[d] Seen here are the ruins of **St
Leonard's Hospital**, a Norman
foundation associated with the
Minster - 13th-century remains of
the vaulted undercroft and chapel
are seen; the **Multangular Tower**, or
West Angle Tower, a sizable 4th-
century remain of the Roman city,
part of the original fortification with
a 100ft section of Roman wall
standing to its original 17ft height;
the **Yorkshire Museum** (open 10-5;
Sun 1-5) has displays of Roman,
Saxon and Viking treasures, statuary
and domestic relics.

[e] **St Mary's Abbey** 13th-century
ruins of a Benedictine abbey founded
by William Rufus in 1088-89,
enough remaining to give an idea of
its beauty; more fragments are
preserved in the museum.

[f] **Marygate** Towards the far end of

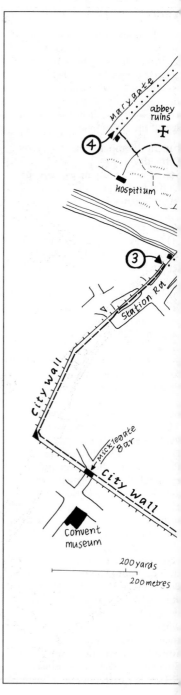

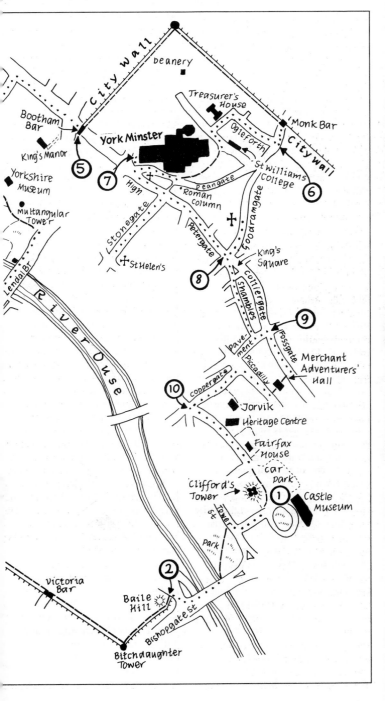

the street, look out for the city wall with shutters (a rare feature) in the castellations, installed for protecting bowmen.

[g] **Bootham** Opposite and to left, No. 49 has a plaque to Joseph Rowntree, of confectionary fame. On the corner with Marygate is **Marygate Tower**, a 13th-century fortification, restored after damage by Cromwell's men. Just before Bootham Bar on right the **City Art Gallery** (open 10-5, Sun 2.30-5; free) exhibits European art, and paintings by York-born artist William Etty; beyond this is the **King's Manor**, (courts and main rooms open to public) begun in 1280 and enlarged in brick from 1483 it was formerly the house of the Abbot of St Mary's Abbey, and after the Dissolution became headquarters of the Lord President of the King's Council of the North.

[h] **Bootham Bar** This is the only 'bar' to be on the site of a Roman gateway. Some of the best views of the city can be seen from this section of the wall, notably the Minster but also some attractive gardens of 17th- and 18th-century houses. **Monk Bar** is the tallest bar, guarding the NE entrance to the city and the main route from the coast.

[i] At the end of the delightful street of Ogleforth, a gateway leads into Gray's Court; continuing into Chapter House Street, on right is the **Treasurer's House** (National Trust, open Easter-Oct) 10.30-5. This was once home of the treasurer of the Minster; the (mostly 17th-century) building is now charmingly furnished with period pieces. Just after, on right, are the **Minster Precincts**, from which the facade of the Treasurer's House can be best seen.

[j] **St William's College** The half-timbered building on left functioned as a communal living place for the

Minster's chantry priests from 1461 up to the Reformation (open 10-5; Sun 12-5).

[k] A re-erected Roman column is on left, discovered 1969, from the fortress of the sixth legion.

[l] **York Minster** Britain's largest medieval cathedral, soaring above the city, took 250 years to complete up to 1475: its design is predominantly in the gothic style. Many features of interest include magnificent stained glass dating from 1150, the painted roof of the nave and elaborately carved rood screen. In the undercroft and treasury, you can get an underground view of the cathedral's foundations from Roman masonry up to 20th-century concrete.

[m] **High Petergate** Young's Hotel was the birthplace of Guy Fawkes, who was baptised in St Michael-le-Belfrey church opposite (which contains fine stained glass of the 14th and 16th centuries). **Stonegate** on right was a street in Roman times and is full of curiosities: look for No. 49 (on corner), a fine shopfront; the Printer's Red Devil on left above the door, just before the Star Inn sign which spans the street; just before the Devil, an entrance on the right leads to the remains of a 12th-century house; on left further along, is half-timbered Mulberry Hall (1434). Where High Petergate meets Low Petergate is the colourful figure of Minerva (1801), Goddess of Wisdom at the centre of the Roman fortress where Constantine the Great was proclaimed emperor on the death of his father Constantius Chlorus.

[n] On left, after the Old White Swan, a narrow gateway leads into **Holy Trinity church**, a 13th- and 14th-century structure with inward-facing box-pews, and late 15th-century stained glass.

[o] **Shambles** York's most famous

street, a narrow alley with overhanging buildings virtually touching in the middle. The 'shambles' was originally a set of butchers' stalls.

p] Pavement Opposite is Sir Thomas Herbet's House, a striking timber-framed mansion with two gables and overhangs.

q] Merchant Adventurers Hall (if this is closed, turn right along Pavement instead of walking along Fossgate; at traffic lights keep to left of church into Coppergate). The 14th-century great hall of the York Merchant's Guild has a spectacular timber interior; it is still used by the Guild as an assembly and banquet hall (open 8.30-5; closes at 3 and all day Sun in winter)

[r] On left, the **York Story** (open all year, 10-5; 1-5 Sun) gives an overview if the city's heritage. Alongside is the hugely (and deservedly) popular **Jorvik Viking Centre** (open daily 9-7), a time-journey back through the city's Viking past, recreating life at the time - complete with sounds and smells: well worthwhile, despite the queues - best to visit in the early morning or late afternoon.

[s] On left, **Fairfax House**, an 18th-century aristocrat's town house of considerable elegance is now a museum of 18th-century English furniture, carpets and clocks (open Mon-Sat 11-5, Sun 1.30-5; closed Fri, Nov and Dec).

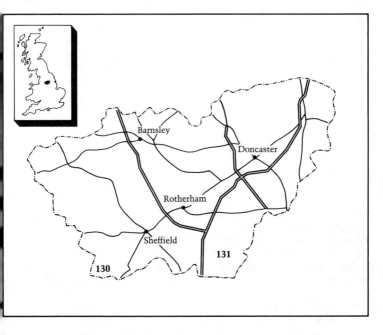

130 Burbage Rocks and Carl Wark
131 Anston Brook and Chesterfield Canal

Burbage Rocks and Carl Wark

The walk skirts a deep moorland basin, an impressive boulder-strewn expanse fringed by Burbage Rocks on one side and the summits of Higger Tor and Carl Wark on the other. Easy going, despite the harshness of the scenery, and in clear weather the route is obvious.

Length 4½ miles (7km), 2½ hours
Difficulty 2
Start Woodcroft National Trust car park, Longshaw Estate, off B6055 and 200 yards S of junction with A625 (Hathersage-Sheffield) at Fox House Inn. Entrance on W of road; not very prominently signed. Grid reference 267801
OS maps 1:50,000 110; 1:25,000 SK 28/38 (Pathfinder 743)
Refreshments Fox House Inn (near start; not on route)

WALK DIRECTIONS

(1) [a] Start by National Trust sign, facing into car park with its road entrance behind you; away to the right is a wall. Take path ahead, which reaches stone bridge just visible from car park. Beyond bridge, turn right at T-junction with track near house and (2) turn right on tarmacked driveway. Cross main road and take gate opposite and slightly to right. Follow track through semi-wooded area, forking right after 300 yards towards bus stop and Road Bends sign.

(3) [b] Cross road and take right-hand of two signposted paths, over stile and rising. Shape of walk is now apparent. You will skirt the rim of the massive natural hollow you see before you in an anti-clockwise direction; the summits of Carl Wark and Higger Tor (beyond) are half left. Keep to higher ground, avoiding left forks, soon past prominently rectangular stone trough on to well-defined path along the top of the edge.

(4) Where edge ends, path bends left, initially along line of stones (former wall), then along top of another rocky edge until reaching road (5). Left on road, then left on broad track. (6) Immediately take signposted stile on left and take right-hand of two signposted paths, which goes along top of edge before proceeding to the summit of Higger Tor [c].

After this proceed down to Carl Wark (7) [d], where path turns left past remains of stone wall: the easiest route is to keep immediately right after it does this, finding path leading directly towards road. Stream away to left can be forded at boulders, but it is easier to follow path on near side (skirting raised slope on your right). Left on road, then right through gate by bus stop and retrace steps (follow track to next road; cross to drive by lodge; turn left just before house, then left after 30 yards, over bridge, into car park).

ON THE ROUTE

[a] **Longshaw Estate** Parkland and woodland, once belonging to the Duke of Rutland, but purchased by subscription in 1927 and donated to the National Trust. Longshaw Lodge, a former shooting lodge, is soon passed on the walk. Major venue for sheepdog trials, held in September.

[b] A boulder by the road at the sharp bend is know as the **Toad's Mouth**, because of its appearance (further enhanced by a man-made addition resembling an eye).

[c] **Higger Tor** (1,261ft). Wide view of the Hope Valley (including the chimney of the Bradwell cement works), and the bleak moors W of Sheffield.

[d] **Carl Wark** (1,250ft). A hill-fort of

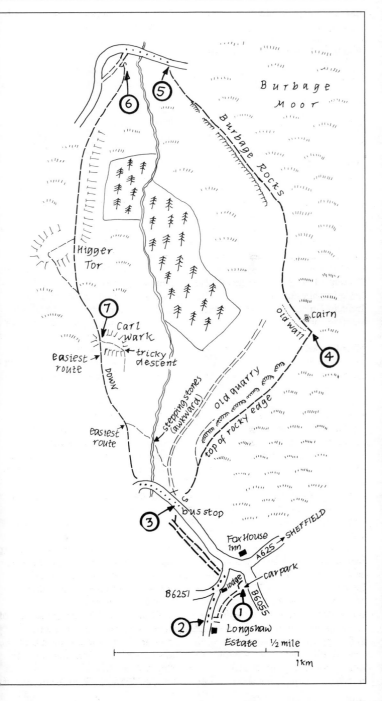

Burbage Moor

Burbage Rocks

Higger Tor

Carl Wark

⑥ ⑤

⑦

easiest route

DOWN

tricky descent

cairn

old wall

④

old quarry

top of rocky edge

stepping stones (awkward)

easiest route

bus stop

③

Fox House Inn → SHEFFIELD

A625

car park

lodge

B6251

① B6055

② Longshaw Estate

½ mile

1km

unknown date, originally thought to be Bronze Age, but a more recent theory has put it around AD500-600. A splendid natural site, with cliffs on three sides and a gritstone wall along its E side (still standing to a height of 11ft).

Anston Brook and Chesterfield Canal

A wooded valley and the tranquil towpath of the disused canal constitute something of an oasis amid agricultural landscape; the walk is pleasant throughout and the going underfoot is easy. Field-paths are well-defined.

Length 5 miles (8km), 2½ hours
Difficulty 2
Start South Anston parish church (do not confuse with Methodist church) at E side of village, at junction with B6060 and Sheffield Road, off A57/M1 junction. Roadside parking in village. Grid reference 519837
OS maps 1:50,000 111 or 120, 1:25,000 SK 48/58 (Pathfinder 744)
Refreshments Shop, chip shop and pubs in South Anston; pub in Thorpe Salvin

WALK DIRECTIONS

1 With church on right and B6060 to Dinnington on left follow Sheffield Road. Where road bends right, take unmade lane straight ahead, soon cross A57 and take track opposite (to left of filling station). At the rear of the building, bear slightly left (avoid hard-standing area) across field, go over railway and soon over footbridge.

2 Turn right on other side of the footbridge, keeping close by stream and ignoring left forks [**a**]. Path leads under railway, keeping stream on right (ignore next crossing under the bridge 150 yards later). **3** After ½ mile, path crosses under railway and has stream on left briefly before leaving it and rising to A57 **4**. Turn left along the road, then after 200 yards take road turning on right signposted Lindrick Dale.

5 After ⅓ mile fork left at footpath signpost in front of The Cottage (a house with old-fashioned

lamp-post). Track rises to reach sign for Lindrick Golf Club; go forward, entering golf course and keep right along right edge of it. The path runs through short patch of woodland and re-emerges onto golf course: keep to right edge, avoiding metal bridge on right, but **6** cross next bridge (a stone one), leading into woods.

Ignore gates on both sides just after crossing a water channel and follow track up out of woods and across field to Brancliffe Grange Farm [**b**]. Turn right in farmyard, cross stile beside gate and go slightly right to next stile beside gate, then follow path beside water channel (canal feeder).

After ¼ mile, take stile on left, and cross railway carefully, continuing on path beside canal feeder. Just before house garden, turn right to leave the feeder and reach Turnerwood Bridge, on near side of which turn right on to canal towpath (walking with the canal on your left) [**c**].

For detour to Thorpe Salvin **7** cross the next bridge but one (after ¾ mile; it is just after crossing boards over channel draining from the canal); keep left on other side (initially doubling back) on main track; after 80 yards take waymarked steps leading to enclosed path, passing to right of sewage works, then along right edge of two fields, keeping beside woodland to reach stile on to road. Village is to right [**d**]; return the same way.

To continue follow towpath from Turnerwood Bridge for 1½ miles: the third bridge you pass under is stone; **8** leave the canal immediately before the fourth bridge (a patched-up brick bridge), taking stile on right. Follow path over railway and through wooded area, then up middle of field (path was well-defined at time of inspection: if it is obscured by crops, the route runs parallel to and 150 yards from left edge of field, then continues along narrow strip, passing between stone posts at end); **⑨** continue on track along left edge of field, soon with houses on left. At road at edge of village, turn left to return to start.

ON THE ROUTE

[a] Anston Stones Wood Cowslips and bee orchids are among the flora; the woods are deep and secretive, with landstone crags here and there, and red squirrels are sometimes seen. A cave to the left, just after

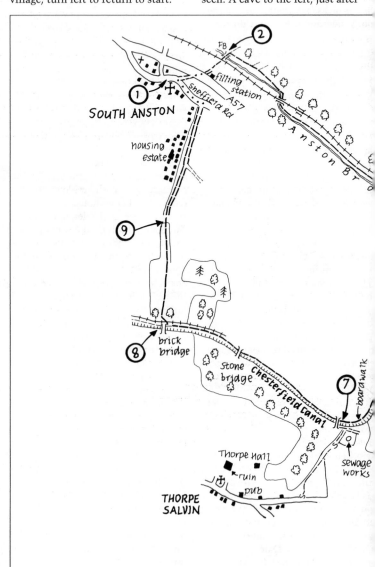

ou join the valley, has yielded
vidence of pre-historic man: flints,
cindeer and brown bear bones have
een found.

] Brancliffe Grange Until the
ssolution of Roche Abbey in 1538,
his was a monastic grange for
istercian monks.

] Chesterfield Canal Now derelict,
s locks ruined and bed choked with
eeds, the canal was surveyed by
ames Brindley, pioneer of the canal
etwork, in 1769 and completed
fter his death in 1777. It led from
hesterfield to Worksop and

Retford, linking up with the River
Trent at Stockwith; lead and coal
here carried this way. In 1908, the
half-mile long Norwood Tunnel (to
the W) collapsed and the canal never
reopened in its entirety.

[d] Thorpe Salvin If detouring to the
pub here, you may like also to visit
the **church** which has some good
Norman work, including a fine font,
and the 16th-century **hall**, built for
the Sandfords and later owned by the
Osbournes until 1697 when they
moved to Kiveton Park, abandoning
this structure to fall into ruin.

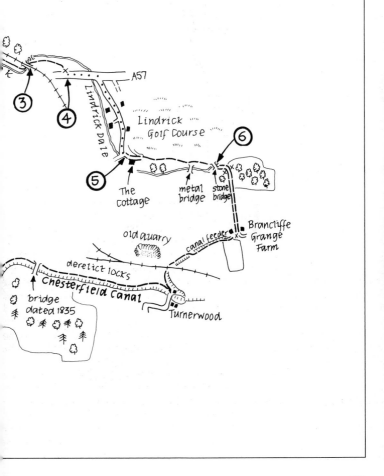

West Yorkshire

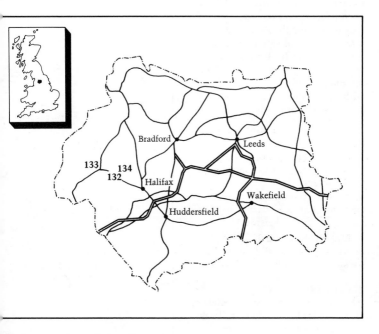

32 Cragg Vale and Stoodley Pike
33 Heptonstall and the Colden Clough
34 Luddenden Dean

Holiday Which? Good Walks Guide

Cragg Vale and Stoodley Pike

**Changes of level and the marked
transition from a partly wooded dale
up 900 feet to an exposed moorland
edge (following the Pennine Way)
provide plenty of variety. The route
is not particularly obvious, hence
the elaborate directions. Moorland
section just after ⑬ is tricky
without a compass in mist, but
fairly obvious otherwise.**

Length 7¹/₂ miles (12km), 4¹/₂ hours
Difficulty 4
Start Mytholmroyd (on A646
between Hebden Bridge and Halifax).
Grid reference 013260.
By train Mytholmroyd
OS maps 1:50,000 103 and 104;
1:25,000 Outdoor Leisure 21
Refreshments Pubs and shops in
Mytholmroyd, pub and shop in
Cragg Vale, pub just after ⑦

WALK DIRECTIONS

① Take B6138 signposted Rochdale,
over river bridge and under railway.
Fork left just after Shoulder of
Mutton pub, signposted Sowerby,
then fork right just before Methodist
chapel, up cul-de-sac (Hall Bank
Lane). Ignore side-turns and follow
uphill. ② After ¹/₃ mile, road ahead
ceases to be surfaced: turn right over
cattlegrid (opposite gas main cover
marked 'CP 29.10'), fork left 30
yards later (right goes downhill)
towards houses. At houses (Hollin
Hey), track bends left: just as it is
about to bend right (proceeding
between walls) take gateway ahead
to enter field.

Head straight uphill, along nearest
power-lines, towards stone hut,
immediately behind which turn
right on well-defined grassy path
along top of slope. ③ On reaching
woods at end of field, keep right
along top edge of woods. At next
stile, enter semi-wooded area where
path still follows top edge of slope

until level with house away to left:
here fork right, downhill, by water
mains post marked 'MCWW 15"
main'.

④ 150 yards later, path becomes
rather less defined at a fork – keep
right downhill (left fork is level),
into woods and descend to fence.
Here path turns left to enter field:
proceed a few yards to gate, picking
up track between walls towards row
of cottages. As soon as you pass

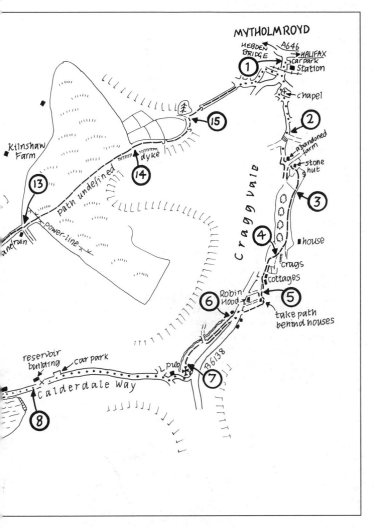

ttages, turn left (path goes directly
 front of cottage windows); beyond
st (detached) house, take small
te and follow bottom of field
ongside wall. ⑤ Emerge at corner
track, turn left up towards houses.

Find narrow waymarked path up
steps passing just to left of and
behind the houses and proceeding
between walls down to main road
(avoid driveway to right of this path).
Turn left on to road.

(6) Fork right after 50 yards by bus stop on to unmade lane. Keep left after 40 yards by first house on right. At stone bridge, take kissing-gate ahead, proceeding on riverside path with river on right [a]. **(7)** By houses, emerge on to end of lane via narrow gate and follow lane towards church. Just before church turn right over bridge, past pub; ignore right turn after 150 yards (by gatehouse) and follow the road ³/₄ mile.

(8) Beyond water works building and gate, go forward on track alongside reservoir.** **(9)** Just before end of reservoir, where wall on right ends, fork right past stone post, (heading to right of prominent farmhouse): fork right 80 yards later. Shortly you are joined by remains of stone wall on your right.

(10) On reaching solid wall of farm (with path between walls ahead), turn right, uphill, with wall on left [b]. Enter open land by gate – the route ahead is marked by stone bollards (ignore left fork by the third of these). **(11)** Reach cross-junction of paths 100 yards later [c], and turn right on Pennine Way, past stone pillar, heading along top of edge towards prominent monument on Stoodley Pike [d]. Turn right at monument on broad path, still along top of edge.

(12) ¹/₄ mile later, cross wall by stile; ignore stile on left (Pennine Way goes off here) but proceed to end of enclosure where turn left on broad track between stone walls. **(13)** On reaching open land keep forward, with wall on right. At corner of wall, by power-line, go forward (no path defined) following small stone posts. At third post, view opens up over a side-valley of Cragg Vale, with Mytholmroyd below. Head to left-hand side of valley, keeping to high ground and heading towards prominent projecting corner of wall that marks the limit of cultivated land **(14)**.

At this wall corner, keep forward, with wall on left and the side-valley down on your right, picking up well defined path. Just after stile and power-lines, where wall bends left, keep alongside it. Cross next stile to proceed along track between walls, heading towards conifer plantation. **(15)** 40 yards later cross another stile, turn right steeply downhill on enclosed path with plantation on left, and follow down to reach residential road at edge of Mytholmroyd. Turn right, then soon right again to reach main road. Turn left into centre of Mytholmroyd.

Calderdale Way Alternative Route: ¹/₄ mile after 'The Pastures' turn right to leave reservoir (signposted Calderdale Way Alternative Route). Head up toward wall, with gully on right; wall begins on left with enclosure behind it. At top of enclosure, turn left as waymarked to follow top of enclosure, along flagstoned path. 20 yards into fourth enclosure, take deliberate gap (waymarked) on right to continue along other side of wall. 50 yards later, by two stone posts, keep forward 100 yards to another stone post (keeping enclosures down to your left), heading well to right of prominent farm and now with remains of stone wall on left. In front of solid wall of farm turn right.

ON THE ROUTE

[a] **Cragg Vale** Deep and lush valley, whose secretive character clearly appealed to David Hartley, 'king' of the notorious 18th-century Yorkshire coiners. Counterfeiting was carried out on a large scale, involving clipping the edges of gold coins to add to molten base metal which was then stamped with the forger's dies. Hartley was hanged at York and buried at Heptonstall.

[b] Soon on right is a **stone** inscribed 'Te Deum Laudamus' ('We praise

ee O Lord'), placed on what was
obably a route for coffin-bearers
nking Withens with Mankinholes.
] The junction with the long-
stance Pennine Way is at **Withens
ate**; straight ahead, an old
ackhorse route goes down over
agstones to Mankinholes. The
one pillar mentioned in the walk
rections is an old **guide-post**,

known as the Long Stoop.
[**d**] **Stoodley Pike**, at the edge of the
moorland scarp, the top of its tower
is almost 1,400 feet above sea level.
The tower was built as a memorial
in 1815 to commemorate victory
over Napoleon. It later collapsed but
was rebuilt in 1856. The Pike offers
an extensive **view** over Todmorden
and the surrounding hills.

Heptonstall and Colden Clough

Distinctive Pennine landscape characterises this walk, with its numerous reminders of Calderdale's textile industry. A steep 650-foot ascent out of Hebden Bridge to Heptonstall is followed by astonishing views on the descent into Colden Clough, ending with a walk along the canal towpath. An intricate route, but for the most part visible on the ground.

Length 4½ miles (7km), 3 hours
Difficulty 2-3
Start Hebden Bridge town centre (on A646 between Burnley and Halifax), Calderdale. Grid reference 992272.
By train Hebden Bridge
OS maps 1:50,000 103; 1:25,000 Outdoor Leisure 21
Refreshments Full range in Hebden Bridge; pubs and shop in Heptonstall; pub at Jack Bridge (off route)

WALK DIRECTIONS

① [a] From A646 take turning by Tourist information centre and Yorkshire Bank, called Bridgegate. 80 yards later, opposite the White Swan, cross stone packhorse bridge on your left [b]. On the other side, take the steep cobbled lane opposite, which is signposted Footpath to Heptonstall [c].

② At top turn left on road [d] then 30 yards later half right on lane signed as private driveway to Breeze Mount and Delph House (avoiding road sharper right). 130 yards later, just past last house on right, lane ends near power-post: take path very sharp right rising between walls, passing house and reaching road where ③ turn left up into Heptonstall. Follow cobbled street up through village [e]-[r].

(If you do not follow the detour described in On The Route, turn left

off the main street just after the Cross Inn, signposted to the museum; just past museum, do not go through gates into churchyard but turn left down a few steps, then right along lane called West Laithe, which skirts churchyard on your right).

At end of churchyard keep left ④ go over at cross-junction 50 yards later then immediately fork right by Calderdale Way signpost. Follow track between walls to reach top of precipice ⑤ [s]: turn right on path which follows top of rim of Colden Clough. ⑥ Emerge on lane, turn left, downhill on it, then 80 yards later fork right on to track (with wa on right; there are yellow arrow waymarks in the next few stages).

⑦ After 200 yards, ignore right fork but take path just to right of seat: the stone flagged path leads along top of field to stile, then past barn. 60 yards past the barn, fork le

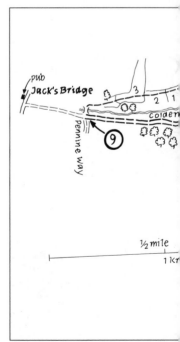

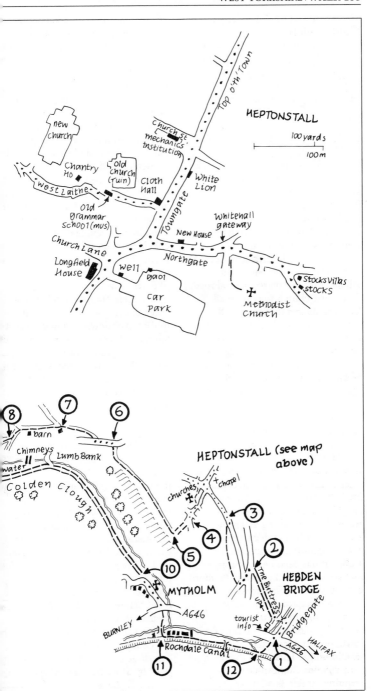

(descending on track between walls).
(8) 100 yards later fork right (still
between walls) to enter field – path
follows top edge of two fields, then
continues on flagstoned path along
edge of third field, at end of which
turn left to gap in wall by metal post
and follow flagstoned path
diagonally across field into woods,
where turn right. Path soon leaves
woods and drops to cross stone
bridge: take steps up to reach track
(9), where turn left (ignoring path
ahead ascending between walls; *note
for pub at Jack Bridge detour right
here*). Follow the track for 1 mile,
along the level and ignoring minor
side turns (ignore sharp left
signposted Lumb Bank after ½ mile).

(10) Reach edge of Mytholm
village, turn left on residential road,
down past church to main road.
Cross to deliberate gap in wall
opposite (with railings beyond) just
to left of bus stop. Follow streamside path, to cross river bridge then
continue forward up a few steps to
reach canal after 50 yards **(11)**.

Left on canal towpath [t]. ½ mile
later, canal crosses river; **(12)** turn
left just after (at bridge) and follow
road to centre of Hebden Bridge.

ON THE ROUTE
[a] **Hebden Bridge** Mill town which
grew in the 18th and 19th centuries,
finely situated at the confluence of
two deep valleys, with terraces
stacked up the slopes and mill
chimneys below giving a precarious
and intriguing appearance to the
whole. It has become a commuter
satellite town for Leeds and Bradford
but much has been carefully
preserved; a good town trail is
available locally. Britain's last
remaining clog-mill is on the edge of
town, near the station.
[b] **Old bridge** This gives the town its
name. James Grenewode of
Heptonstall left 3s 4d 'to the fabric

of Hebden Bridge' in 1508, replacin[g]
a wooden bridge. The bridge has
stone inscriptions detailing repairs
from 1602.
[c] **The Buttress** This very steep
cobbled lane is the original
packhorse road from the bridge to
Heptonstall and is part of an old
route from Halifax to Burnley.
[d] Old **milestone** by the road to
Slack Colden and Blackshaw Head.
[e] **Heptonstall** Hill-top village
predating Hebden Bridge and a
remarkable survival. It began as an
agricultural village but expanded an[d]
prospered in the 18th century as a
hand-loom weaving centre. Its
cobbled streets and side lanes are
particularly interesting (see the ins[et]
map):
[f] to [r]: *A walk around the village*
[f] **Longfield House** (on left as you
enter the village) is *c.* 1730, with
mullion windows, a typical wealth[y]
family residence of the period.
Go into car park opposite.
[g] On the left is the **old well** (under
low arch); towards the back of the
car park, on left, is the **village
lock-up.**
*Continue up into Towngate, take
first right; this is Northgate.*
[h] On left, **New House**, with its
lintel dated 1736, may have been a
Quaker house.
[i] On left, the decorative **gateway t[o]
Whitehall** is dated 1578 and bears
the initials of owner John Bentley.
[j] On right, the eight-sided
Methodist church is the oldest in
the world to be in continuous use.
Built 1764 as a preaching house afte[r]
John Wesley's preaching had
attracted large crowds to the village[.]
It deliberately avoided the
traditional church shape in an
attempt to avoid confrontation with
the church authorities.
*Continue along Northgate, fork
right by Stocks Villas; this is
Northwell Lane.*

] On left, a **milestone** to Haworth
as once also part of the village
ocks.

*o back into Towngate and turn
ght.*

After the Cross Inn on right, the
loth Hall on left was where
oollen cloth produced by villagers
as sold to dealers.

n] After White Lion pub on right,
ie **Mechanics Institution** in Church
treet on left was set up as an
ducational establishment in 1868;
ie building itself is much older.

] At Top o th' Town, on left, the
illage pump (1891) was originally
ne of four.

*eturn past Cloth Hall, then turn
ght.*

] On right, the ruin of the **old
hurch**, first built 1260, but most of
ie remains are 15th-century;
amaged in a storm in 1847 it was
ever repaired. Cragg Vale coin
orger 'King David' Hartley, hanged
t York in 1770, is buried here. John
Vesley preached here and
ronounced it 'the ugliest church I
now'.

] On left, the **Grammar School
useum** (open Easter-Aug, 11-4
4on-Fri, 11-5 Sat, 12-5 Sun, week-
nd afternoons in Mar, Apr, Sept and
)ct). The school was founded by the
ord of the Manor of Heptonstall in

1642 and rebuilt 1771; after closure
in 1889 the building was occupied
by the Yorkshire Penny Bank, which
preserved its interior (including
desks and flagged floor, which can
still be seen).

*Immediately turn left down steps
into West Laithe, where turn right.*

[q] **Chantry House**, between here and
the churchyard, is the former
charnel house, where human bones
were stored.

[r] The **new church**, consecrated
1854 contains relics from the old
church, including a table, settle and
chair, and the coats of arms of
George III.

*Keep to left of the new church and
resume walk directions at ④*

[s] Spectacular views into **Colden
Clough**, with a dizzy 500-foot drop.

[t] **Rochdale Canal** An absorbing
section of the 33-mile, 92-lock canal,
through a slice of early industrial
landscape. When the canal opened in
1804, it was the catalyst for the
expansion of Hebden Bridge (and
hastened the decline of fortunes of
Heptonstall). The canal is a cross-
Pennine route, climbing 521ft from
Lancashire, and 358ft from
Yorkshire; restoration is under
way to make it navigable for
pleasure-craft.

Luddenden Dean

Traditional Pennine landscape at its best, the reminders of a great industrial legacy set among quiet pastoral scenery fringed by the moors. Route-finding intricate (especially from ① to ④) and route is partly undefined, but an abundance of man-made and distinctive natural features make it reasonably easy to find.

Length 4 miles (6.5km), 2 hours
Difficulty 3
Start Midgley, on minor road N of A646, between Hebden Bridge and Halifax. Parking on road near Sportsman Inn. Grid reference 031264
OS maps 1:50,000 104; 1:25,000 Outdoor Leisure 21
Refreshments Pub and shop in Midgley and Luddenden; Cat i'th' Well (pub) just before ⑧

WALK DIRECTIONS

① With pub behind you, follow village street 30 yards, then right on track signposted as Link to Calderdale Way. Immediately fork left: this leads up to house [**a**]. Immediately behind house, track bends right, but take steps on left up into field: follow paved path, heading to left end of terrace of houses, where find small gate ②. Continue forward, uphill, with wall on right in small field, then wall on left in second (larger) field. Go through narrow gate into third field, where ③ turn right along bottom edge with wall on right [**b**].

At end of this field, join track coming down from left, but leave it 30 yards later (in fourth field) as it bends right downhill through gate – instead, keep along edge of fourth field a few yards then take next gate on right, by house, on to lane. Turn left, uphill. Beyond next house, lane becomes an unsurfaced track and moorland appears on left. ④ Pass through gate, turn right on track along the level, now with wall on right and moors on left.

¼ mile later, near barn (on right), wall is replaced by fence; 50 yards later, track goes through gate, leaving moorland, and becomes a surfaced lane, descending. 100 yards later, keep right at oblique T-junction, then ⑤ left at next T-junction (50 yards after; by sign for Dry Carr Lane). Ignore farm track after 200 yards (leading sharp right) but 50 yards later turn sharp right down next farm track, leading to derelict house by footpath signpost. Take the signposted path (on left immediately after this house), follow bottom edge of two fields down towards house. Just before house, cross stile on right (rather steep on far side of stile: care needed) to reach lane ⑥.

Turn right on lane, then after 140 yards, where woods start, take steps on left to follow path cutting diagonally down through woods and over footbridge. On other side of river, go uphill to nearby corner of wall (enclosing field) and follow path up, with wall on left. ⑦ At top, turn left (alongside top of field, but still in woods, then soon on enclosed path).

At house (The Hullet), take gate on right and follow lane up to T-junction with road: turn right. After pub, road crosses Caty Well Brook. ⑧ 60 yards later, turn right on track; keep just left of houses, to enter steeply sloping field, where go forward to follow bottom edge of field along low stone wall with track parallel away to your right. Reach road and turn right downhill on it [**c**]. ⑨ ⅓ mile later, road reaches stream: fork left (principal road goes uphill), past terraced cottages, 100 yards after which (by houses) keep forward (ignoring a right turn uphill)

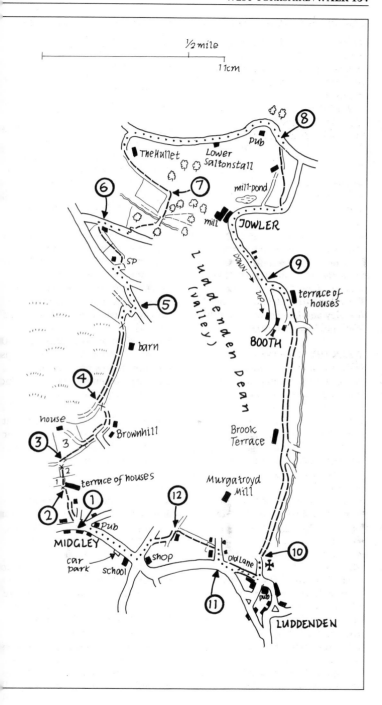

½ mile

11cm

⑧

pub

The Hullet

Lower Saltonstall

mill-pond

⑦

⑥

mill

JOWLER

SP

DOWN

⑨

UP

terrace of houses

⑤

BOOTH

L u d d e n d e n   D e a n   (valley)

barn

④

house

Brownhill

Brook Terrace

③

3

2

1

terrace of houses

Murgatroyd Mill

②

①

⑫

Pub

MIDGLEY

car park

school

shop

Old Lane

⑩

⑪

pub

LUDDENDEN

505

then a left turn to other side of valley); follow the track (intermittently cobbled) along bottom of valley with stream close by on left. Beyond Brook Terrace ignore left turn [d].

¹/₃ mile later ⑩ reach Luddenden church and emerge on road at village by Lord Nelson pub [e]. Turn right then immediately right again up Old Lane (cobbled). ⑪ At top *either* go forward on road signposted Midgley *or avoid some road walking* by turning right, then after 50 yards turn left just after first terrace of houses, finding small gate in right-hand corner at back of covered hard-standing area belonging to house No.8 (it looks private, but there is a Public Footpath signpost here). Continue along right-hand side of back garden, then into field where take gate a few yards ahead to continue up right-hand edge of field, on paved path.

⑫ At top, take left-hand of two gates, to turn left to house, where ignore left turn: follow driveway to T-junction, turn left down to school, where turn right along road to Midgley.

ON THE ROUTE

[a] Tray Royd is an attractive old Pennine house; 'royd' is Yorkshire dialect for 'clearing', and occurs in many local place names.

[b] Good **views** S over hills around Mytholmroyd, including the monument on Stoodley Pike.

[c] **Mill pond** down to right, the typical terrace of former mill-workers' cottages at Jowler. The mill is still run by a textile company.

[d] From this unmade lane, view to right of the six-storey tower of **Murgatroyd Mill** (now a glass-works).

[e] **Luddenden** The vale's major village, given much charm by its steep site and terraced houses clinging to the sides and squeezed into the hollow. Branwell Brontë became clerk at Luddenden Foot station in 1841 and was a regular at the Lord Nelson inn, where he was a paid-up member of the pub's library.

Scotland

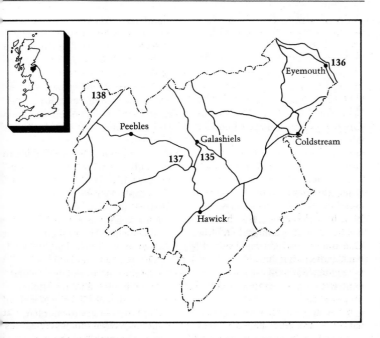

35 Melrose and the Eildon Hills
36 Eyemouth to St Abbs Head
37 Brown Knowe
38 Bore Stane and East Cairn Hill

Holiday Which? Good Walks Guide

62 Scott's View, the Wallace statue and Dryburgh Abbey

Melrose and the Eildon Hills

The landscape beloved of Walter Scott is explored from Melrose and by the banks of the Tweed before a 900ft ascent on to the Eildons, one of the best-known natural features of the Borders and an outstanding viewpoint. On defined tracks and paths, the route is waymarked some of the way.

Length 4½ miles (7km), 3 hours
Difficulty 3
Start Melrose; car park in St Dunstan's Park (road name), on W side of town opposite rugby ground.
Grid reference 546342
OS maps 1:50,000 73; 1:25,000 NT 43/53 (Pathfinder 461)
Refreshments Full range in Melrose

WALK DIRECTIONS

(1) [a] From car park, turn left along main road, then turn right into St Mary's Road; immediately take tarmacked path to pass to right-hand side of church (keeping left at next junction, by lamp-post) to reach river (2) where turn right on tarmacked path [b]. Pass suspension bridge (do not cross), then along riverside road 60 yards before picking up path on left which goes along top of broad wall (3) [c].

Follow this path, soon alongside river and later into large field (4) where continue alongside river; beyond end of field, path becomes well-defined as it crosses footbridge and leads away from river, past swings on your right and then a house on left, and becomes a surfaced lane leading into village of Newstead [d].

Turn right on main village street, and immediately left into Claymires Lane and turn right at T-junction with Back Road (unsurfaced) (5). 50 yards later, turn left under old railway bridge [e], and follow track up to main road. Turn right on main

road, then after 100 yards, turn left on rising track.

(6) Reach gate on to open moorland at foot of North Hill, where continue forward, initially alongside woods on left and picking up yellow arrow waymarks to ascend Eildon Hill North by well-defined path. (7) [f] At summit, continue down (keeping slightly to right) to reach saddle between Eildon Hill North and Eildon Mid Hill (8) (where you can continue up obvious path for detour to Eildon to Mid Hill and along ridge to Eildon Wester Hill).

To continue route back to Melrose, take care to pick up the waymarked route (*not* the path marked by prominent red and white marker-posts): find Eildon Walk marker-post on the saddle and follow the path to the right which drops slightly and then contours round the lower slopes of North Hill with Melrose away to your left.

(9) Reach path junction with waymarker (pointing the way you have come) and turn left down past MOD sign (facing other way) and towards abbey in distance, crossing stile, following right-hand side of field to reach stile onto enclosed track (10); cross the track and take stile opposite, go down left-hand side of stile to find waymarked stile in bottom corner and beyond it take path down steps to reach road. Turn right on road to reach town square [g]; left to reach car park.

ON THE ROUTE

[a] **Melrose** Perhaps the most attractive of the small towns in the Borders, nestling at the foot of the Eildon Hills. The **abbey** (open Mon-Sat 9.30-7; Sun 2-7), founded 1136 by David I for Cistercian monks from Rievaulx Abbey in Yorkshire and in its time probably the wealthiest abbey in Scotland, suffered

estruction from English incursions
n the 14th century; most of what
emains is post 1385 – nave,
ransepts, tower, chancel, S nave.
Noted for its outstanding stone
arving. Adjacent is Priorwood
Gardens (National Trust for
cotland), which has ancient apple

varieties and where flowers are
cultivated for drying. The **rugby
ground** is the birthplace of Rugby
'sevens', first played here in 1883.
[**b**] The fertile farmland by the River
Tweed was a prime attraction for the
Cistercians at Melrose, who were
renowned for their farming skills.

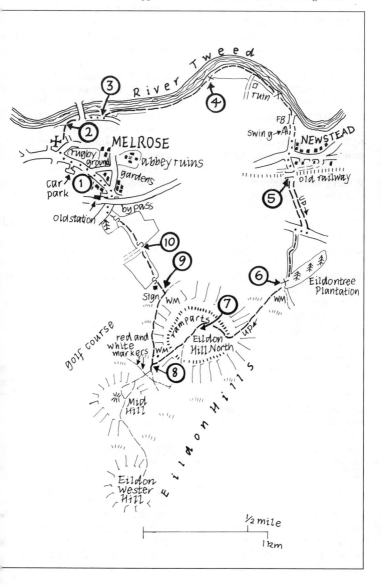

The long-distance Southern Upland Way branches off here and crosses the bouncy suspension bridge.

[c] Overhanging branches were a slight problem here when walk was inspected; the alternative is to continue along the road a further 50 yards, until a broad gate on left gives access to the wall.

[d] Near Newstead, the Romans set up **Trimontium** ('the camp of the three hills').

[e] Part of the much-lamented **Waverley Line** which used to run from Edinburgh to Carlisle, scenically comparable to the Settle to Carlisle line. It operated 1849-1969.

[f] The three-peaked ridge of the **Eildon Hills** is volcanic, but legend has it that it was the work of 13th-century wizard Michael Scott (a real person, who features in Dante's *Inferno* as Michele Scoto). North Hill is ringed with ancient ramparts here up to 2,000 years ago the Segolvae tribe kept an Iron Age hill-fort; from the 1st century the hill was used as a Roman signal station. A view indicator on Mid Hill (10 minutes' walk up from this route) identifies Melrose, Cheviots and Peniel Heugh Monument to SE; E Smailholm Tower; NE the Moorfoots and Lammermuir Hills.

[g] Just before reaching the town square, a signposted turn on the left leads to the handsome **Melrose station** (open daily, free), built in Jacobean style with Dutch gables; although the line has closed (see above) the station was restored in 1986 and now contains a railway museum, craft shop and restaurant.

Eyemouth to St Abb's Head

A coastal walk with several variants:
do the whole coastal stretch, looping
round inland and finishing at the
visitor centre for the bus back, or
start a shorter walk from
Coldingham (walking back along the
road or taking the bus). Try the
shortest route from St Abb's visitor
centre, or split the full walk into
two separate excursions. The scenic
highlight is St Abb's Head, but there
are also good beaches (popular in
summer) at ② and ④. Frequent bus
service on weekdays, less frequent
on Sundays (when you are advised to
park by the visitor centre and take
the bus to Eyemouth before starting
the walk)

Length *Eyemouth to St Abb's Head
visitor centre* 6½ miles (10.5km),
3½ hours; Coldingham to St Abb's
Head visitor centre 4½ miles (7km),
2½ hours; round walk from St Abb's
Head visitor centre 3 miles (5km),
1½ hours;

Difficulty *Full walk* 3,
shorter walks 2

Start *6½-mile walk* Sea-front,
Eyemouth, grid reference 946645;
4½ mile walk Coldingham (car park
in village centre opposite war
memorial, grid reference 902659;
take B6438 signposted St Abb's,
turning right at end of village on
road signposted 'Sands ¾'; opposite
'unsuitable for motors' sign take
path parallel on left-hand side of
road and follow to beach where turn
left to start walk directions at ④);
3-mile walk St Abb's nature reserve
visitor centre (turn off by sign for St
Abb's Head; to start walk, go to right
of coffee shop to reach road, and take
waymarked path opposite, on left-
hand side of road and parallel to it to
reach 30mph road-sign, where turn
left on path signposted St Abb's
Head); grid reference 913675

OS maps 1:50,000 67; 1:25,000 NT
86/96 (Pathfinder 423)
Refreshments Full range in
Eyemouth; pubs and shops at
Coldingham; café and hotel at
Coldingham Bay; shop at St Abb's;
coffee shop at the St Abb's Head
visitor centre.

WALK DIRECTIONS

① [a] Facing Eyemouth sea-front,
turn left along esplanade, joining
beach at Dolphin Hotel (which is to
left); leave beach by prominent path
up on to cliff-top, and then keep
along top of cliffs (ignoring left
forks), with caravan site on left and
soon diverting out to headland (with
cannons) [b].

② After going around edge of
large bay (ignoring path descending
to beach), path keeps to edge of
fields on seaward side and crosses
three stiles; ③ just after the third
stile, path goes over footbridge and
drops down on to shore, where turn
left. 250 yards later, pick up path on
left (rather overgrown when walk
inspected in summer, but easily
followed once you have found it)
which climbs up to regain cliff-top.
Path soon descends into small bay
and climbs hillock to reach
Coldingham Bay (with beach huts
and café).

For Coldingham [c] turn left inland
on tarmacked track between café
and lifeguard hut and follow road
(signposted path runs parallel to it
on right-hand side for a distance to
avoid road-walking).

④ *To continue main walk* After
beach huts, take steps up on to cliff
and follow path to St Abb's village
[d], where keep as close as possible
to coast, to drop down into harbour;
take steps between last two cottages
in harbour (with red-tiled roofs) and
ascend path to road where turn right,
past church to end of village.

⑤ Turn right by 30mph speed
derestriction sign, on enclosed path

signposted St Abb's Head, soon along cliff-top [e]. By fence corner on left, sea briefly disappears from view; soon after, cross stile: path goes ahead up valley floor (becoming less defined towards top), but there are much better views by ascending steep slope on right ⑥ and walking along cliff-top; meanwhile the main path route goes up the valley until sea reappears (where these two routes merge).

Continue along the coast soon keeping to left of lighthouse buildings at St Abb's Head; briefly join lighthouse road, but it is best almost immediately to divert off it and rejoin cliff top for more sea views [f].

Eventually drop steeply to reach corner of the road ⑦. *Either* retrace steps to St Abb's *or* (easier) keep right along road, over cattle-grid to reach visitor centre [g] (which is on left just before road junction). At B6438, you can get the bus back to Eyemouth via Coldingham; to the latter it's an easy, though unexciting, 15-minute walk along the road to the right.

ON THE ROUTE
[a] **Eyemouth** is a busy fishing port specialising in shellfish; lobster

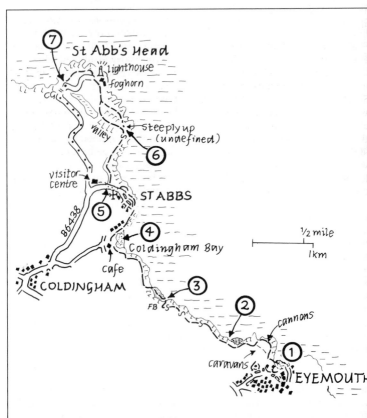

tanks and fish-smoking sheds can be seen in town, and a fish market operates Monday to Thursday when catches are landed. A tight cluster of terraces and yards adjoins the quay; the town's museum (fishing, local history and rural life) is housed in the Auld Kirk, close by. In the 18th century smuggling was rife, and the town was riddled with underground passages for the purpose (some reputedly still exist).

[b] The **cannons** are 32-pounders cast about 1830, probably placed as a defence against a possible French invasion in the 1850s. They are on the site of a fort which existed 1547-60 and was built by the Duke of Somerset, protector to the boy king Edward.

[c] **Coldingham** (off route); site of an 11th-century Benedictine **priory**, largely destroyed by Cromwell's men in 1648, but foundations and a S aisle arch are visible, and N and E walls of the 12th- and 13th-century choir have been incorporated into the adjacent parish church.

[d] **St Abb's** Quiet fishing village with picturesque harbour; crabs and lobsters are often unloaded. At Castle Rock (the house on the cliff)

lived 19th-century landscape artist Gemmel Hutchison.

[e] **St Abb's Head** Some of the best cliff scenery on the Scottish E coast; stacks, deep inlets and precipitously sited ledges provide nesting places for some 50,000 birds, including guillemots, razorbills, fulmars, herring gulls, kittiwakes, shags and a few puffins; offshore are sooty and Manx shearwater. The greatest concentrations of birds are near the lighthouse. Varied soils (acid and mineral rich) result in rich flora and insect life, including the Camberwell Beauty butterfly and death's head hawkmoth. St Abb's is a corruption of Ebba, a Northumbrian princess who was shipwrecked here and founded a nunnery.

[f] Just beyond St Abb's itself, a rugged coastline is revealed to the N; you are now looking towards **Fast Castle**, a shattered cliff-top ruin used by Walter Scott as the model for Wolf Crags in *The Bride of Lammermoor*. Close to the lighthouse road is **Mire Loch**, a haunt of waders.

[g] **Visitor centre** for St Abb's has a small exhibition and a café.

Brown Knowe

The route follows a section of the Southern Upland Way, taking in high grassy ridges that typify the remote beauty of the Borders. Mostly on defined tracks; boggy in places after rain. Ascent 1,000ft.

Length 5½ miles (9km), 3½ hours
Difficulty 3–4
Start Broadmeadows, on A708 W of Selkirk (hamlet is not signed as such on main road; look for sign indicating Yarrow Water when it is crossed); park in lay-by near telephone box and opposite post-box, to W of bridge over Yarrow Water and near path signpost for Innerleithen by Minchmoor. Grid reference 407300
OS maps 1:50,000 73; 1:25,000 NT 23/33 and NT 43/53 (Pathfinder 460 and 462)

WALK DIRECTIONS

(1) [a] With telephone box on right, go E along road. Just before bridge over Yarrow Water turn left on minor road signposted as footpath to youth hostel; after 50 yards, take signposted path on right for youth hostel. Path enters woods and goes up left side of glen; keep to right of hostel, on track which soon narrows to path width.

(2) Leave woods by gate and turn right alongside woods on right (waymarked with Southern Upland Way motif, although you are not yet on the Way itself) immediately through another gate; continue until end of woods on right, then turn left on well-defined grassy track by waymark post; later a wall joins on left but route soon leaves the wall near small enclosure (just after, keep straight on at minor path crossing).

Path rises and becomes less well defined, but wall rejoins on left and is followed up to ladder-stile, at top of ridge (3); beyond the stile turn left

on the Southern Upland Way, a well-defined route along top of ridge with wall on left [b]. (4) After wall on left reaches a corner (just after wood on left ends), cross ladder-stile beside gate and beyond it fork right on to well-defined waymarked path, heading up with fence on right to Brown Knowe (the highest point on this walk), which is marked by a large cairn (piled-up stones).

After the summit, continue forward on the Southern Upland Way along top of ridge until forest begins on right, where (5) leave the Way 40 yards after waymarker post)

and turn sharp left on well-defined track (known as Minchmoor Road) which gently drops along side of grassy ridge. ⓖ Eventually track bends left on reaching forest wall and proceeds along field edges until bending right to enter forest; reach T-junction, turn right and follow into Broadmeadows.

ON THE ROUTE

[a] Yarrow valley was once part of Ettrick Forest, a hunting ground for game and a notorious hiding place for thieves on the run; in 1528 James V of Scotland and 12,000 men hunted here. Now predominantly sheep country, but still remote in character.

[b] The **Southern Upland Way** is a tough W to E route over S Scotland, running 212 miles coast to coast from Portpatrick in Dumfries and Galloway to Cockburnspath in the Borders; in difficulty it is comparable to the Pennine Way. This is a relatively undemanding section, but there are fine views over Lauderdale, the Eildon Hills (to your right) and later on over the Cheviots (to the left, from Brown Knowe).

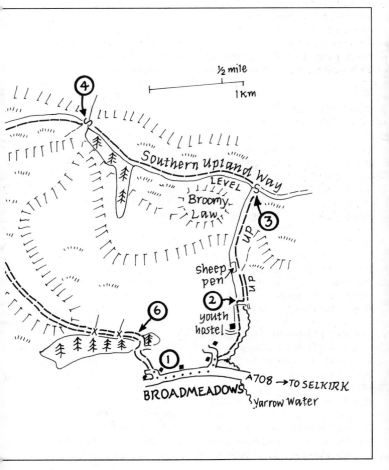

Bore Stane and East Cairn Hill

An upland walk in the Pentland Hills, which, despite their proximity to Edinburgh, offer peace and quiet; the best of the views are from Bore Stane to East Cairn Hill, and beyond Baddinsgill. Access may be restricted in shooting seasons. Route-finding generally quite easy, but pathless route between ② and ③ requires some care.

Length 9 miles (14.5 km), 5½ hours
Difficulty 3–4
Start Carlops, on A702 SSW of Edinburgh (small car park by village hall at S end of village).
Grid reference 161558
OS maps 1:50,000 65 or 72; 1:25,000 NT 05/15 (Pathfinder 433)
Refreshments Pub at Carlops

WALK DIRECTIONS

① Take track 20 yards to left of village hall, signposted Balerno by the Bore Stane (soon ignore left turn to farm); this winds up past trees near Fairliehope Farm and nears reservoir [a].

② Where track bends right to houses by dam, keep half left by signpost over stile beside gate, and carefully follow the signposted direction; path is ill-defined, as it heads for stile beside gate at right-hand corner of conifer plantation (if in doubt, follow fence on your right, stepping over stream and then reaching woodland wall where there is a stile beside a gate); keep to the right of the plantation ③, to pick up well-defined path, passing a signpost and then proceeding with fence on right before crossing the fence at the next stile beside gate and going over stream by slab footbridge towards prominent signpost.

Path continues up valley to top of pass at Bore Stane (where there is gate and prominent post) ④[b]. Turn left and ascend East Cairn Hill by walking alongside wall on left. ⑤ For final 200 yards of the ascent, leave wall-cum-fence and follow cairned path to summit [c]. *For easy route-finding descent* return to the fence and follow it down to bottom of next pass (Cauldstane Slap); *for more interesting fair-weather route* (better views) make your way SW downhill from summit, with West Cairn Hill, the next summit, straight ahead.

⑥[d] *Both routes* turn left along bottom of pass (Cauldstane Slap), crossing the fence by a signpost at a gate, where there is a well-defined path. Path later broadens to become track. ⑦ Reach houses near S end of Baddinsgill Reservoir and proceed, now on road. After road crosses stream, ignore minor left turn; soon cross cattle-grid, and 80 yards later ⑧ turn left at signpost for Carlops via Stonypath. Path immediately drops to footbridge and continues along left-hand side of stream with fence and wall on left: keep alongside fence where it leaves stream, to reach wall corner by signpost ⑨ where turn right on well-defined level track.

Reach Stonypath Farm, where continue forward on surfaced farm road. ⑩ Where the road bends right, continue forward on unmade track (signposted Carlops). ⑪ Where there are houses on both sides ignore right turn but continue forward through gate into open land; 40 yards later continue forward (as main track bends right to house), on the level and through another gate to follow well-defined grassy track , later past succession of shacks, to reach road at Carlops.

ON THE ROUTE

[a] **North Esk Reservoir** was constructed in 1846 to provide water supply for mills on the banks of the

River Esk (to the S).

[b] Bore Stane Name of the 1,200-foot high pass, marked by a small group of rocks and trees; at the northernmost point of Borders region and of the old county of Peeblesshire. Impressive view N over the Firth of Forth.

[c] East Cairn Hill Capped with an ancient cairn (piled-up stones); extensive view over the Firth of Forth, and beyond to the Ochils (the start of the Highlands) and the Lomond Hills in Fife. Quarried stone from neighbouring West Cairn Hill was used in 1830 for building the National Monument on Calton Hill in Edinburgh.

[d] Cauldstane Slap ('slap' meaning pass) is mentioned on early maps and was a natural N-S route through the Pentland Hills; it was much used as a drove road for cattle bought at trysts at Crieff and Falkirk, and for droving sheep between Linton and pastures in the Highlands.

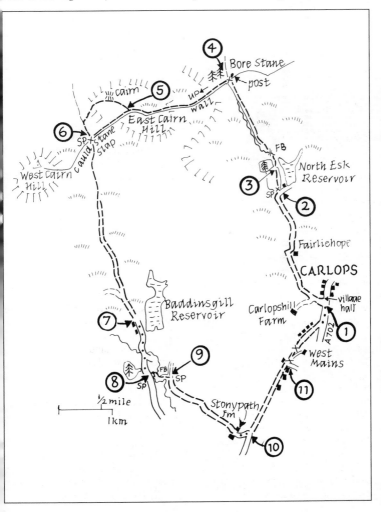

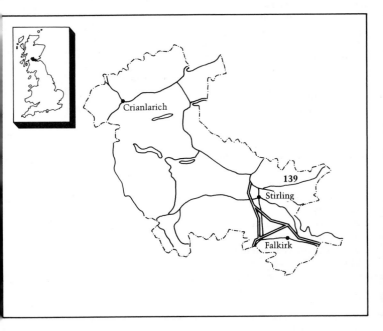

139 The Burn of Sorrow and Castle Campbell

Holiday Which? Good Walks Guide

163 Achray Forest and Loch Drunkie   164 Bracklinn Falls and Callander
Crags

The Burn of Sorrow and Castle Campbell

Deep glens make a natural route around the Ochils, with an opportunity to make your way over grassland to a superb viewpoint over S Scotland; the castle provides the other focal point. Return by old railway track. Ascent 1,900ft, gently graded. Route-finding rather complex at outset.

Length 7½ miles (12km), 4½ hours; can shorten by using bus service between Tillicoultry and Dollar
Difficulty 4
Start Clock Mill (tourist information centre) on NW side of Tillicoultry (between Stirling and Kinross); turn off A91 in town by Royal Arms (signposted Clock Mill and Mill Glen). Grid reference 914974
OS maps 1:50,000 58; 1:25,000 NN 80/90 and NS 89/99 (Pathfinder 371 and 383)
Refreshments Pubs, shops, cafés in Tillicoultry and Dollar

WALK DIRECTIONS

① Go to top of road, past Clock Mill [a] on left then immediately right on signposted path to Blackford, past WCs on your left; path then bends left up steps (ignore sharper left, passing ruin) to reach gate into open moorland [b]. Carry on up zigzagging path until a small fork is reached ②: fork right, leaving main path which is part of nature trail [c]; immediately there is a metal bench on left-hand side of path (placed in rock outcrop). Carry on a short distance to another bench: keep ascending (path not very clear at first, but soon well-defined – avoid dropping to nearby lower path (nature trail). From here, path is easy to follow, as it leads up right-hand side of valley.

③ At head of valley, step over low

fence: route continues forward, down bottom of valley of Burn of Sorrow: but first it is worth the 15-minute climb up King's Seat Hill to your half right [d].

Return to Burn of Sorrow, where path is soon well-defined; later cross a fence; ④ take second footbridge on left (by green-hooped waymarker post), on entering woods by

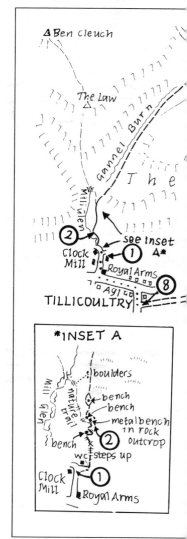

waterfall. As soon as you reach road leading into Castle Campbell [**e**], note continuation of route before you visit the castle: to take path on right immediately before road enters castle grounds by gate, and follow descending path into wooded gorge and around right-hand side of castle itself, dropping to footbridges and descending the gorge via a series of catwalks and bridges through spectacular clefts and chasms [**f**].

⑤ Just as path begins to climb, turn sharp right on path (left goes up back to castle; no more natural wonders in that section), to continue down glen, always with stream on right (ignore left forks). ⑥ Reach residential road at edge of Dollar and continue forward down to the main

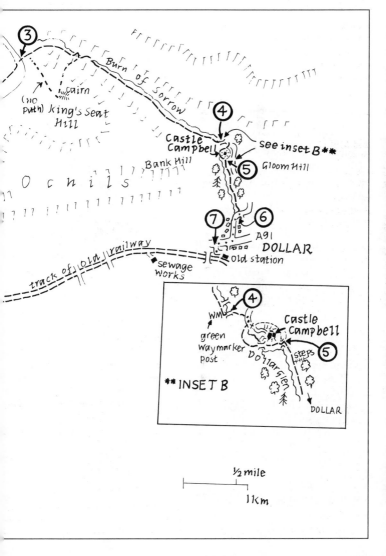

½ mile

1 km

road, at which point turn right.

⑦ Soon turn left into Station Road; where road bends left, continue forward to reach old railway track [g], where turn right. Ignore all side turns and follow 2¼ miles to road at Tillicoultry.

⑧ Turn right, left at junction, then right at end of town just after Royal Arms (signposted Clock Mill and Mill Glen).

ON THE ROUTE

[a] **Clock Mill**, built in 1824 for the Walker family, is one of a large number of local woollen mills in the towns S of the Ochils; it is now a visitor centre with craft workshop and displays. Also in Tillicoultry are the still-operational Paton's and Sterling mills. Local handwoven woollen cloth is known as 'Tillicoultry serge'.

[b] Expansive **views** open up behind over the Firth of Forth and Pentlands;the nearby Tillicoultry quarry produces whinstone, mainly used for road building.

[c] Both routes go up the side of Mill Glen, but this higher one is the one to take, as the nature trail (lower route) loops back round on itself. If accidentally on the lower route, follow it until it is about to drop to footbridge and bear half right (leaving path) to ascend grassy slope, soon picking up a path leading up to join the upper path at two large boulders; turn left to continue. The path from the footbridge is the main route up **Ben Cleuch**, the highest peak in the Ochils; an easily managed path, with grand views on the way back down.

[d] If you haven't time to go up Ben Cleuch (see above), this is an excellent substitute, with an extensive **panorama**: W and NW are the SW Highlands including Ben Chonzie (3,048 ft); S the Firth of Forth and the Pentland Hills; E the Lomond Hills. On the very edge of the Highlands; the abrupt change in level is the result of the Highland Fault which led to a 10,000ft upheaval of the ground 280 to 340 million years ago. The route up is over grassland; be sure to follow the same way back. Although it's tempting to cut a corner, the valley soon deepens and the slope down into it becomes rather tricky; experienced compass-users may like to keep to the high ground and bear ESE until Bank Hill then drop NE into the Burn of Sorrow before it enters the woods.

[e] **Castle Campbell** (National Trust for Scotland; open to public Mon-Sat 9.30-7, 2-7 Sun). First sighted on this walk from a superb vantage point where the woods suddenly open out, revealing the fairy-tale castle (also known as Castle Gloom; above are the Burn of Sorrow and Glen of Care), improbably perched on a huge rock set against the backdrop of Dollar Glen and the SE Lowlands. Former home of the Clan Campbell; John Knox is said to have preached here in the 16th century. It was built about 1481; and came into the Clan Campbell by marriage; but was burned by Cromwell's men.

[f] Precipitous rock slopes, the cascading stream, breathtaking overhangs and luxuriant ferns and broad-leafed woodland oak, sycamore, wych elm and ash) make **Dollar Glen** one of the most memorable half-miles in Scotland.

[g] Remains of platform of **Dollar station**, on the old Alloa-Kinross line, are visible to the left.

DUMFRIES AND GALLOWAY

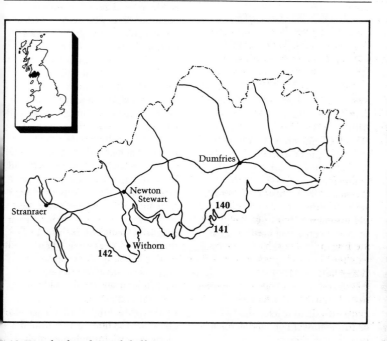

Kippford and Castle Hill Point

Forest plantations and Barean Loch provide the prelude for a bracing coastal walk taking in two pleasant resort villages, followed by a more rugged section along cliff-tops. All on defined paths and tracks, with some road-walking at end.

Length 8½ miles (13.5km), 4 hours
Difficulty 3
Start Colvend, on A710 SSE of Dalbeattie; park in front of village hall (by filling station and shop). Grid reference 868545
OS maps 1:50,000 84; 1:25,000 NX 85/95 (Pathfinder 555)
Refreshments Shop at Colvend; shop and pub at Kippford; hotel at Rockcliffe

WALK DIRECTIONS

(1) Take enclosed track immediately right of village hall, soon into forest and continue to reach barrier; continue forward on well-defined path, which soon widens to become track. (2) 130 yards after passing Barean Loch on your left, a track merges sharply from the right; 250 yards later, avoid sharp left turn, but 120 yards after (3) turn left (50 yards before the next right turn).

Follow track, to reach gate after 150 yards; continue forward with fence and wall on left along edge of two rough fields to reach gate into yard at house. Take gate ahead, in front of house, and follow lane (soon ignoring right turn signed to Loch House Bank) to reach road (4). Cross the road and take track opposite and slightly to left, soon into forest; 300 yards into the forest, avoid sharp left turn; (5) 200 yards later fork left; 300 yards after avoid sharp left (uphill) and continue forward.

Soon a house appears close on left, and reach Forestry Commission sign for Mark Hill (6): here take gate on

left then immediately turn right (ignoring paths signposted Mote of Mark), passing between wooden posts to follow well-defined path immediately to left of the Mark Hill sign, initially with wall on left [a]. Proceed, ignoring minor left turns to reach road at edge of village of Kippford [b](7).

Go into centre of village to reach quay and turn left along coastal road; continue forward until a signpost points left to Rockcliffe, which follow. The path bends right after 80 yards, alongside wall on right (avoid left turns just after) and 30 yards later, path ascends gently to leave wall and enter open land (ignore minor left fork after 80 yards). Path roughly follows power-lines for a distance, then (8) passing house and following track, past shore and then cottages on left (with three gables) [c], just after which the track enters field. After 30 yards, fork right over footbridge and follow right edge of small field to reach gate; turn left along driveway and immediately right through gate to reach shore at Rockcliffe [d].

Turn left on road skirting the bay; (9) 40 yards after concrete bin on right, take right turn (private road and signposted path to Castle Point). At last bungalow ('Clifton'), continue forward as road bends left, now on coast path [e]; soon, you can detour beyond kissing-gate on to headland Castle Hill Point [f].

Path continues along top of cliffs, sometimes just inside edges of fields; route is obvious. (10) At White Hill (where path ascends steeply), it is worth detouring left to trig point (summit pillar); but although it is tempting to descend across fields to Colvend, there is no recognised path. Instead, continue along cliff path and drop to road. Left on road, left again on main road (11) and follow ¾ mile to Colvend.

ON THE ROUTE

a] Good **coastal views** from the so-called Jubilee Path. Across the river lies a section of coast previously a haunt of Solway smugglers who had a brisk trade in lace, brandy and wine; caves and thickets were ideal for the purpose.

b] Kippford Former fishing village and boat-building centre which has become a popular sailing resort, at mouth of Urr Water. Nearby **Rough Island** can be reached on foot via a causeway known as the Rack, when tide is at ebb (enquire locally for tidal conditions). Owned by National Trust for Scotland as a bird sanctuary; no access May and June when terns and oystercatchers are nesting here.

c] Just above the cottages is a hill called **Mote of Mark**, a Celtic hill-fort dating from the 5th to 7th century; excavations have revealed evidence of metal- and glass-working, thought to have been fired in the 7th century by Angle invaders.

[d] Rockliffe has a pleasant rock and sand beach. **Bird life** along the coast includes curlew, dunlin, greenshank, godwit, knot, oystercatcher, shelduck and whimbrel.

[e] Tombstone, by the path, to Joseph Nelson of Whitehaven, drowned at sea in 1791; he may well have been a smuggler.

[f] Castle Hill Site of a 12th-century fort overlooking Solway Firth, the Lake District, St Bees Head and the Isle of Man; the Antrim coast in Northern Ireland is visible on a really clear day. There is access nearby to a nicely secluded beach.

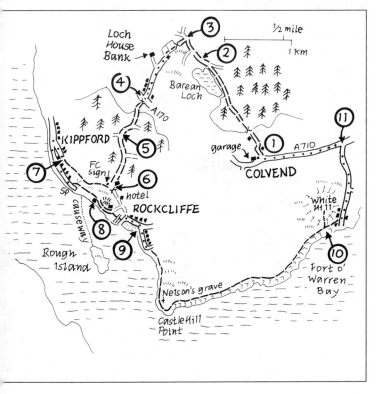

Balcary Point

Beyond Loch Mackie a track leads down to the shore to pick up a coast path which rises gently on to cliffs and around Balcary Point, the finest part of this short walk. Easy route-finding.

Length 3½ miles (5.5km), 2 hours
Difficulty 2
Start Balcary Bay Hotel. Turn off A711 at E end of Auchencairn (signposted Balcary); just past hotel entrance, park on right-hand side of road by pine trees and just beyond

signpost on right for 'Right of way past Loch Mackie to Rascarrel Bay'. Grid reference 821495
OS maps 1:50,000 84; 1:25,000 NX 85/95 (Pathfinder 555)
Refreshments Balcary Bay Hotel

WALK DIRECTIONS

① [a] Take signposted track for Loch Mackie and Rascarrel Bay. Just before house, continue forward (ignoring left turn), to pass house on your left, then derelict cottage on right ②. Track then goes along edge of two fields to reach Loch Mackie

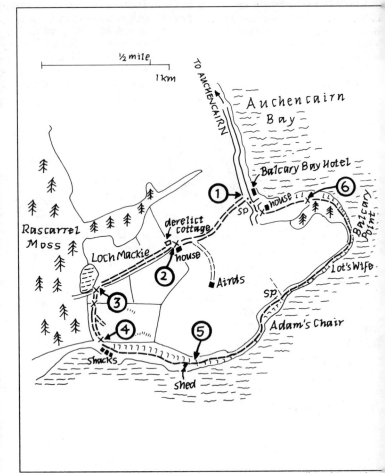

[b]. ③ As soon as you reach the loch, take gate on left (do not carry along loch edge) and follow grassy track along right edge of field. After next gate, enter rough land and fork right after 120 yards to gate by coast ④.

Beyond it, path leads to left to reach shore by shacks. ⑤ Later the path ascends to reach cliff-top. Continue along the cliff path all the way, past Balcary Point [c], then later into woods, eventually reaching gate into field ⑥, where follow right (bottom) edge, past house. Then go right, through gate and continue forward on enclosed path to reach road, where continue forward to reach starting-point.

ON THE ROUTE

[a] The **hotel** was built by the notorious Solway smugglers for their headquarters.

[b] In summer, the loch is the haunt of colourful **dragonflies**.

[c] Good cliffs for watching **sea birds**, whose cries echo on the sheer cliffs far below. Charming view across **Auchencairn Bay**, which appears almost land-locked, hemmed in to the east by Hestan Island (site of an ancient manor house).

White Loch and Kirkmaiden

The walk takes in the fine woodlands of the Monreith estate and historic sites, dating from prehistoric to medieval times. Ends with a coastal section to a remote and tiny hermit's chapel. Easy route-finding most of the way.

Length 6½ miles (10.5km), 3 hours
Difficulty 1-2
Start Monreith.
Grid reference 359410
OS maps 1:50,000 83; 1:25,000 NX 34/44 (Pathfinder 564)
Refreshments Bar with restaurant in Monreith; caravan site shop on main road E of village (off route)

WALK DIRECTIONS

① Start at W end of village by signpost for Wigtown. With the long terrace of houses making up Monreith on your right, take minor turn on right immediately before signpost for Wigtown; pass a telephone box and enter small housing estate, where keep left (by post box), taking track to left of chapel-like hall. Soon houses end and you are now walking between hedges.

Reach tarmac lane, turn left for 30 yards, then ② turn right on track past Bridge Lodge, then after barn on right, proceed on grassy track. This follows right edge of field to gate, then is fainter as it crosses next field diagonally (if in doubt, keep to lowest ground) to gate into woods.

③ Immediately reach T-junction with track that skirts edge of woods (make a mental note of this point). Turn left, to reach tarmac drive, where go right. After 200 yards, ignore a right fork which goes to private house [a]. ④ 50 yards later, fork left on to track; soon lake on right appears.

Halfway along lake, track bends left to leave the lochside; ⑤ 50 yards

later turn right on track which soon rejoins lochside. At end of loch, by house on left, keep forward on path which soon broadens to track, following power-lines. ⑥ Reach tarmac drive. Detour left, to Drumtroddan Standing Stones [b]: on reaching the road by a lodge, turn right; 100 yards later, the stones are visible from a gate on left. Return to the the lodge and re-enter estate by the tarmacked drive.

Fork right after ⅓ mile where left goes up to estate office; a high wall appears on left, followed by the castle tower [c]. Continue 250 yards further to reach crossing of track and drive ⑦. Turn left. ⑧ 130 yards later turn sharp right on to descending track, immediately with edge of woods on left. Just after track curves right, turn left on the track by which you entered woods earlier, and retrace steps across fields, past Bridge Lodge to tarmacked lane, where turn left.

Continuation is to turn right after Burnside Cottage, but first detour ahead along the lane, past modern house on left, to enter field on left by gate near farm ⑨. Head to centre of the field to see standing stones [d], then retrace steps to start.
Extension to shore On reaching Monreith, turn left on road, then right on semi-metalled track opposite the middle of the terrace of houses which line the road (soon ignore a minor left fork) to reach shore ⑩, where turn left (unless the tide is very high).

Some way before the grassy headland which is capped by huts, take steps on left up into old churchyard (Kirkmaiden) [e], turn right at top of steps (detour left into church), then ⑪ left on road. 50 yards after a cattle-grid road-sign, take steps on left to see Gavin Maxwell memorial [f]. From here retrace steps along shore to start.

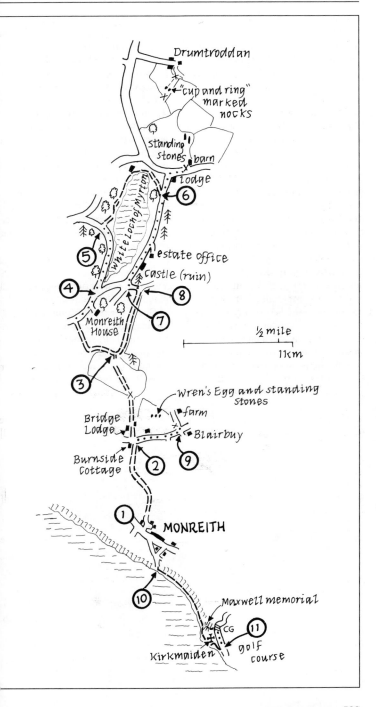

Drumtroddan

"cup and ring" marked rocks

standing stones   barn

Lodge

⑥

White Loch of Myrton

⑤

estate office

castle (ruin)

④   ⑧

⑦

Monreith House

½ mile

1km

③

Wren's Egg and standing stones

farm

Bridge Lodge

Blairbuy

Burnside Cottage

②   ⑨

①   **MONREITH**

Maxwell memorial

⑩

CG   ⑪

Kirkmaiden   golf course

ON THE ROUTE

[a] Monreith House The former home of Gavin Maxwell, writer and naturalist (1914-69); the house is in landscaped grounds containing fine specimen trees adjacent to an attractive loch.

[b] Drumtroddan Stones Visible from the road, towards the top of the field. Two 10ft standing stones and a fallen one, *c.* 2,000-1,500 B.C. Two fields further north are cup and ring-marked slabs, whose precision-carved motifs are an enigma – possibly to do with sun worship or used as reference maps. To see the latter stones requires a 1$\frac{1}{2}$ mile detour to Drumtroddan Farm (not an interesting walk).

[c] Myrton Castle Only the tower survives of the 15th century castle built by the McCulloch, master falconers to the Scottish crown, on the site of a 12th-century timber castle. Myrton was adapted for residential use in the 17th century, when a house was added on on the side. It was gutted by fire and the tower later became a dovecot.

[d] Wren's Egg and **Standing Stones** The 'egg', ironically nicknamed, is a large glacial erratic boulder, forming a group with two others. Little is known of their purpose but they are thought to date from prehistoric times.

[e] Kirkmaiden (church of St Medana). Former hermit's retreat, which attracted pilgrims because of a nearby well with alleged miraculous healing powers. Blank gravestones of the 16th and 17th century are uncommon survivals; the graveyard also has remains of 10th-century crosses, indicating its importance as a place of pilgrimage from early times. The church (usually locked) dates from the 12th century, partly ruined, partly with Victorian restoration; used as a mausoleum by the Maxwell family.

[f] Gavin Maxwell Memorial A bronze otter commemorates one of the naturalist's favourite views over the coast. Nearby among the hills inland is the Fell of Barhullion, topped by a prominent hill-fort.

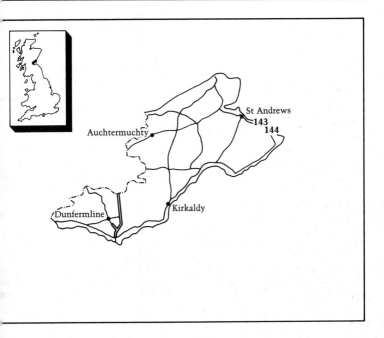

43 Boarhills to St Andrews
44 Kingsbarns to Crail

Holiday Which? Good Walks Guide

65 Falkland and the Lomond Hills

Boarhills to St Andrews

A low-level seashore walk over quite rough ground in places, with changing views of the distant coastline. Ends with a comprehensive tour of one of Britain's most remarkable and historic coastal towns. Return by bus; hourly services every day.

Length 5 miles (8km), 3½ hours
Difficulty 3
Start Boarhills, just off A917 between St Andrews and Crail; parking limited in village, though usually possible (easier to park in St Andrews, and take the bus before starting the walk; bus station is off City Road). Grid reference 565137

OS maps 1:50,000 59; 1:25,000 NO 41/51 and NO 60/61 (Pathfinder 363 and 364)
Refreshments Shop in Boarhills; full range in St Andrews

WALK DIRECTIONS

(1) Walk through Boarhills village away from main road, past school and post office (just after, ignore minor left turn). (2) Beyond end of village fork left on farm track in front of large barn. After end of first field on right, take field track on right, heading towards sea; this track runs along field edge, bends left and goes through gate, beyond which path leads along shore (with sea on right).

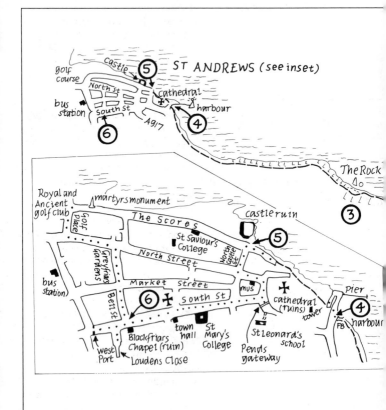

From here follow shore all the way, soon past Buddo Rock [a]; path is sometimes easy, but sometimes rough, passing over rocky and uneven ground. ③ Pass unmistakable land form called the Rock and Spindle [b] (path forks here, take either one; they later rejoin). Eventually path passes caravan site and then leisure centre at edge of St Andrews [c].

④ At harbour, cross footbridge to enter town [d], where immediately keep right close to sea [e]. Pass entrance for cathedral ruins and St Rule's Tower [f]; then continue on coastal road to castle [g] where ⑤ left into North Castle Street; left in North Street, heading towards cathedral [h]; turn right into Gregory Lane [i], where next right (South Street) is continuation after detour through The Pends archway [j].

Go along South Street [k], and before turning right into Bell Street detour ahead, past Loudens Close on left, to West Port. ⑥ Go into Bell Street, continue forward at Market Street into Greyfriars Gardens; go left into North Street, then ⑦ turn right into Golf Place to reach Royal and Ancient Golf Clubhouse [l] and first tee of old course. If desired, you can turn right along the coast road (The Scores) to make a circuit and reach castle.

ON THE ROUTE

[a] **Buddo Rock**, with its narrow natural arch, is a remnant of resistant sandstone where the weaker surrounding rock has been weathered away. **Views** N towards the Sidlaw Hills in Angus and Tentsmuir forest; S towards Fife Ness.

[b] **Rock and Spindle** The prominent rock column is the 'spindle' – a volcanic plug that has risen through calciferous sandstone.

[c] **St Andrews** Of three-fold importance as a religious city, a seat of learning and an international golf centre. Pilgrims came here to worship St Andrew, Scotland's patron saint, whose bones were brought here. A Celtic church was superseded by St Regulus church, then the priory and cathedral were founded. The first university in Scotland was subsequently established here in 1410. Early St Andrews developed around the harbour; the **pier** was constructed in 1668 from stones taken from the castle and cathedral.

[d] Straight ahead is part of the **priory wall**, built in the early 16th century.

[e] Foundations of the **Celtic church**

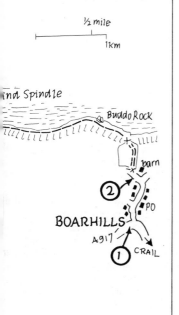

533

of the **Culdees** are visible on left; in the 12th century there was a Celtic settlement here.

[f] Ruins of **cathedral** (founded 1160 by Arnold, abbot of Kelso), which has the largest nave in Britain after Norwich cathedral; the adjacent Augustinian priory ruins are 13th-century. Look for covered portions of preserved floors, which can be lifted to reveal tiles. **St Rules tower** has 151 steps leading up to an excellent viewpoint over the city. There is also a **museum** (open April-Sept, Mon-Sat 9.30-7, Sun 2-7; Oct-Mar, Mon-Sat 9.30-4, Sun 2-4) containing early Christian sculptured stones, cross shafts and sarcophagus.

[g] St Andrew's **Castle** (opening hours are the same as for St Rules museum above).

Originally a bishop's palace, built around 1200. It has had a bloodier history than most castles and was the scene of many attacks over 400 years, notably during the Reformation. John Knox fled here before the French took the castle in 1547, and was then sold into slavery. No one succeeded in escaping from its famous **Bottle Dungeon**, named after its shape. The initials of George Wishart can be seen on the pavement in front of the castle; Wishart, a Reformer, was burned at the stake on this spot in 1546.

[h] On right, just before the end of North Street, a small **museum** displays antiques and bygones.

[i] **Dean's Court** (on right), now a post-graduate hall of residence, is 16th-century.

[j] **Pends archway** A 14th-century vaulted gatehouse, forming the main entrance through the priory wall. Beyond it, to the right is the entrance to **St Leonard's College** (part of the university) a pilgrim's hospice from the 12th century until 1512; St Leonard's chapel is in the courtyard.

[k] **South Street** contains much of interest (all listed are on the left-hand side, in order). **Queen Mary's House** late 1500s, now St Leonard's library but sometimes open; Mary Queen of Scots reputedly stayed here. **South Court** is a survivor of the narrow alleys called 'rigs' which developed between the main streets; it leads to the modern Byre Theatre (originally housed in a cowshed); one former town house still displays a family coat of arms. **St Mary's College**, founded 1537, has a delightfully spacious courtyard with a **holm oak** planted in 1728; Mary Queen of Scots is said to have planted the thorn tree by the tower entrance. Also here are the university library and senate room. **Town Hall**, (tourist information), built 1858 in baronial style; opposite is 15th-century **Town Kirk**. **Blackfriars Chapel** (1525) is a remnant of a church of a Dominican monastery founded in the 1270s. **Loudens Close** is another picturesque example of the 'rig development'. At the far end of the street is **West Port**, the main entrance to the old city; formerly 'Southgait Port', it was rebuilt 1589 in imitation of Netherbow Port in Edinburgh.

[l] The **Royal and Ancient Golf Club** or the 'R and A' for short, founded in 1754, one of the earliest golf clubs to be formed. Since 1897 it has been the world headquarters of and ruling authority on golf. British open championships are held on the Old Course. The word 'royal' was prefixed to the name when William IV was nominated as patron. Just N of the clubhouse is **Bow Butts**, where townsmen were made to practice archery. Nearby, the **Martyrs' Monument** is dedicated to martyrs burned at the stake before the Reformation.

Kingsbarns to Crail

A coastal ramble along expansive
sandy beaches and rocky shores,
rounding the promontory of Fife
Ness for a sudden change of view,
and ending at a pretty fishing town.
Terrain rough at times. Return by
bus (hourly, every day).

Length 6 miles (9.5km), 3 hours
Difficulty 3
Start Kingsbarns, on A917 between
St Andrews and Crail; plenty of
parking in central square near
church. Grid reference 593120
OS maps 1:50,000 59; 1:25,000 NO
51/51 and NO 60/61 (Pathfinder 363
and 364)
Refreshments Pubs, cafés, shops
in Crail

WALK DIRECTIONS

(1) [a] With church and square on
left, follow main road southwards.
At end of village turn left on road
signposted to car park and sea. (2)
At coast (Cambo Sands) turn right
[b]: there is a path between fences, or
you can walk across sands.

Path later goes through tiny
section of woodland and over
footbridge [c]. Keep along shore
(mixture of small rocks and sand),
soon with golf course and huts on
right (don't enter the course)[d]. (3)
At Fife Ness (coastguard look-out,
mast and houses) join tarmac track
briefly, but leave it just before it
reaches the mast, keeping by the
coast on a narrowing path to left of
coastguard look-out: take care to

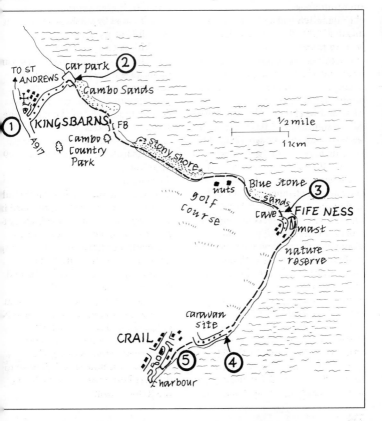

keep to defined path, which runs close to coast [e].

④ Reach caravan site and follow tarmac track through it: at the end of the site, after gate, continue forward on coast path as the track bends right; soon houses at edge of Crail appear.

⑤ [f] Just before prominent castellated building up on right, path turns right inland. Keep left at junction with lane to pass castellated building (where there is a view indicator) [g], to reach harbour [h]. Buses leave from main street.

ON THE ROUTE

[a] **Kingsbarns** Once a site of royal grain stores; the fertile Fife farmland supplied royal residences at Crail and Falkland.

[b] The **beach** had a small harbour until about 1920. **Views** N towards the Angus coast.

[c] **Cambo Park**, a country park, can be entered here; there are woodland walks, rare farm breeds, a nature trail and tea-room (open May-Sept, 10-6 and week-ends Mar and Apr).

[d] **Balcomie Golf Club** is the world's seventh oldest (founded 1786). After passing huts on the golf course, and where the rocky beach gives way to sand, there is a smooth crystalline blue-grey rock (about three feet high) called the **Blue Stone**, probably transported by an iceberg. After you pass the old lifeboat house (RNLI emblem still on it), you pick up a path which immediately passes

Constantine's Cave, where according to legend King Constantine was killed by the Danes in 847.

[e] **Views** open up over the Firth of Forth; the towering islet of Bass Rock (famous for gannets) is visible and the conical hill of Berwick Law is beyond.

[f] At the point you leave the coast the 16th-century **Old Priory Doocot** (dovecot), painted white as a marker for sailors.

[g] The **look-out tower** is on the site of Crail Castle, built in the 12th century as a defence for Crail harbour, and a hunting-lodge for Scots kings. Only part of a turret staircase remains, and the present house dates from the 1800s. At this corner is a 17th-century sun-dial which stood by the harbour until 1853.

[h] **Crail** A narrow street, lined with stone-built cottages slopes abruptly down to the lively **harbour**, still an important lobster-catching centre. The present **church of St Mary** was founded in 1517, but there are remains of a 12th-century church and there is an 8th-century Pictish cross-shaft here; Knox preached in the church at the start of the Reformation. Grooves on a stone by the door were made by archers who sharpened their arrows here. Also in Crail are the 9th-century **standing stone of Sauchope** (in Victoria Gardens) and a **folk museum**.

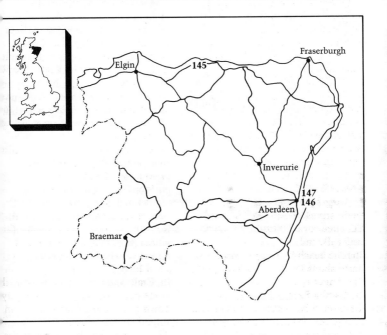

Holiday Which? Good Walks Guide

Cullen to Portsoy

A coastal route, first at shore
level then along cliff-tops, linking
three particularly appealing fishing
ports and two sandy beaches.
Well-defined path (up and down)
as far as Sandend, then undefined
but mostly level route along cliff-
tops to Portsoy. Return by bus
(frequent service Mon to Sat; about
five a day on Sun).

Length *Full walk* 7 miles (11km),
3½ hours. *Cullen to Sandend* 4
miles (6.5km), 2 hours
Difficulty 2-3
Start Cullen harbour, on A98
between Banff and Elgin. Grid
reference 511673
OS maps 1:50,000 29; 1:25,000 NJ
56/66 (Pathfinder 148)
Refreshments Full range in Cullen
and Portsoy

WALK DIRECTIONS

① [a] With harbour on left, follow
shoreside road which soon becomes
unsurfaced track and later narrows
to path, which is well defined as it
runs along shore below cliffs, [b].
② At Logie Head, path goes up and
then down steps at rock buttress.
③ Cross stile on entering Sunnysid
Bay [c]: path then leads to right (now
as a broader track) up to top of cliff,
where it turns left with fence on
right: ignore track leading to right
inland, and keep along cliff-top [d],
soon past Findlater Castle (on
promontory) [e] and continue along
cliff-tops over series of stiles (path
not defined, but route is obvious).
④ Enter Sandend Bay (stiles still
mark the route) to reach Sandend
village [f]; path goes to right of
highest-placed house in village to
reach road. *To finish walk here, tur*
right and proceed to main road for

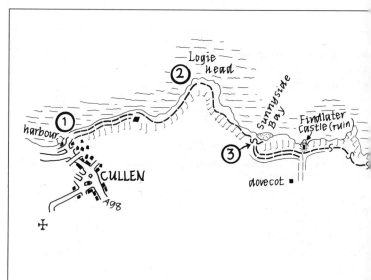

e bus service back to Cullen.
To continue walk across beach,
eside dunes, to climb steps at far
de of bay **⑤**, on to cliff-top, and
on through kissing-gate: from
ere, proceed on level cliff-top
ongside fence on right (path
ndefined but route obvious).
⑥ After you round Redhythe Point,
ass concrete wartime bunker on
our right; fence on right ends soon
'ter, then pick up well-defined
ack which bends inland after 100
ards to reach T-junction with farm
ack after 300 yards, where **⑦** turn
ft.
Proceed to reach road, turn left on
; after 100 yards, where road bends
ft (dropping to shore) continue
orward on tarmac path. **⑧** On
aching road at edge of Portsoy,
eep left on grassy path around cliff-
p, soon reaching harbour [g].
Turn right into North High Street,

cross a square into South High Street
to reach main street in town; bus-
stop for Cullen is to left (just beyond
Bank of Scotland).

ON THE ROUTE
[a] **Cullen** gives its name to a local
haddock broth called 'Cullen skink'.
The upper town has a broad main
street with a market cross at the
centre and a disused railway viaduct
at the bottom end; below is the
harbour. Off the route, ¹/₂ mile S, the
Auld Kirk has a sculptured tomb to
Alexander Ogilvie, carved panels and
a 16th-century sacrament house.
[b] **Views** N to the peninsula of the
Black Isle.
[c] **Sunnyside Bay** has a secluded
sandy beach set beneath rugged
cliffs; at its W side is a recess known
as 'Charlie the Rock's Cave',
inhabited by a Frenchman until the
1930s.

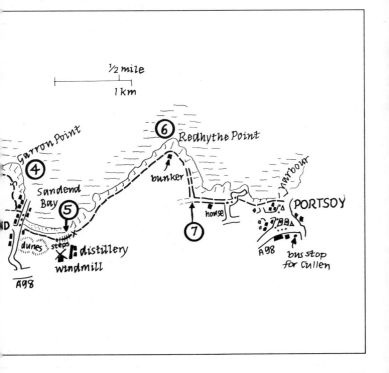

[d] Inland is a prominent 19th-century **dovecot** ('doocot').

[e] Scant remains of **Findlater Castle,** a three-storey stucture built by the Ogilvies in 1455 and abandoned in the 1600s (take great care – sheer drops).

[f] The fishing village of **Sandend** lies huddled beneath the slope on the W side of the bay; its quaint cottages and lanes are on toytown scale. Fresh fish are often on sale. The large and popular beach has attracted holiday development. Inland are a distillery and the tower of sailless Glasslaugh Windmill (built 1761), nicknamed the 'cup and saucer' and built on the site of a prehistoric burial mound.

[g] **Portsoy** has a wealth of fine 17th and 18th-century buildings, particularly around its harbour, which prospered in the 1700s as a major port trading with the Low Countries and Scandinavia. The old harbour dates from 1692, the 'new' one from 1839. Portsoy marble is still produced (there's a workshop a you enter the harbour). A famous product of green and red serpentine colour. It was used in many European palaces, including Versailles.

Central Aberdeen

An exploration of the heart of the city: its early 19th-century plan, and extensive use of local granite are distinctive features. The city is endowed with a good range of free museums.

Length 1½ miles (2.5km), 2 hours
Difficulty 1
Start Mercat Cross, at NE end of Union Street
Refreshments Full range

WALK DIRECTIONS

① [a] By Mercat Cross with Salvation Citadel behind you, walk past Tilted Wig pub to fork left into Exchequer Row (to left of Union Street), which bends left by cinema, past Provost Ross's House [b].

Cross over Market Street and into Trinity Lane opposite, then right into Exchange Street, **②** first left into Imperial Place and first right into Stirling Street. Turn left at market building and immediately right under bridge under road, to follow Correction Wynd. **③** Turn left through gates and up steps into churchyard [c]; keep close to church and on its far side go through gates and turn right into Back Wynd, then left at junction with Upper Kirkgate which becomes Schoolhill [d], the Rosemount Viaduct [e].

④ Turn left in front of Wallace statue to enter Union Terrace Gardens [f]; keep along top edge to far end, then **⑤** turn left into Union Street. Follow Union Street (can divert to left into old quarter: left into Belmont Street, right into Little Belmont Street and turn right again in Back Wynd to rejoin Union Street) [g].

⑥ Just before Town House, turn left into Broad Street: Queen Street on right is the continuation after detouring ahead to Marischal College [h] and left by tourist information office signposted to Provost Skene's House [i]. Follow Queen Street, between bollards at end to Arts Centre **⑦** where turn right along King Street.

ON THE ROUTE

[a] **Castlegate** No traces remain of the castle, which was on site of the present-day tower blocks behind the Salvation Citadel, but this is still the city's focal point, two main streets meeting at this market square. The **Mercat Cross** (1686) has a hexagonal base topped with an arcaded structure and crowned with a unicorn; on it is a frieze of Stuart portraits from James I to James VII, and the royal and city coats of arms.
[b] **Provost Ross's House** (open 10-5, Mon-Sat). One of the oldest houses in Aberdeen (built 1593), now a maritime museum with displays on the city's changing fortunes as fishing port, ship-building centre and boom city in the 1970s with the advent of North Sea oil and gas. From the street is a view over the **harbour**.
[c] **St Nicholas Kirk** A re-building of a 12th- and 15th-century structure, divided into two churches at the time of the Reformation. The **vestibule** was once the transepts, and contains reclining figures of the Irvines of Drum Castle. The **West Church**, rebuilt 1752 by James Gibbs (architect of St Martin in the Fields in London), has a galleried Council Loft. There are medieval transepts in the East Church, whose crypt was used as a witches' prison in the 17th century (the shackles are still there).
[d] On left, **James Dunn's House**, named after a rector of the nearby old grammar school (demolished) which Byron attended; now municipally owned for special exhibitions (open 10-5, Mon-Sat). On right, the **Art Gallery** (open 10-5, 10-8 Thur and 2-5 Sun) of 19th- and

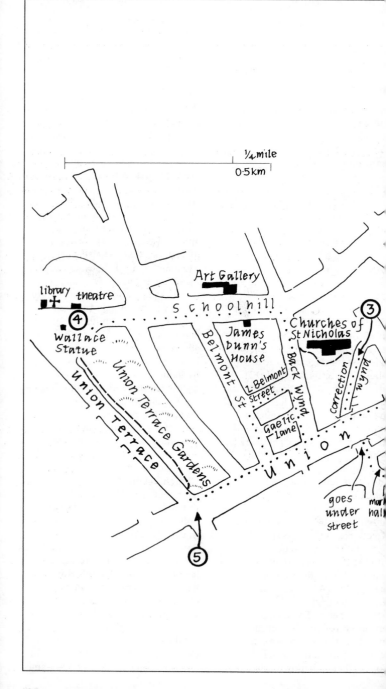

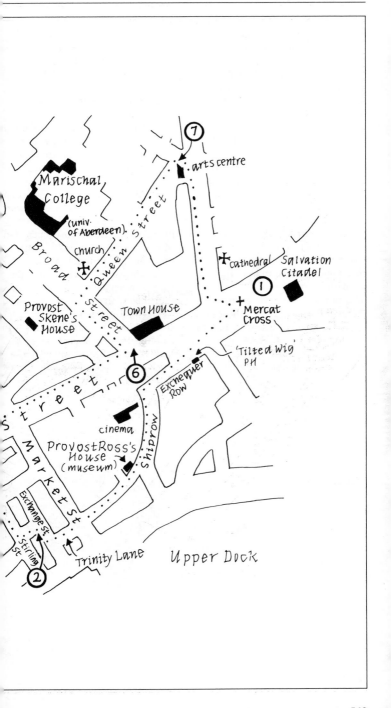

20th-century art, including sculpture by Rodin and Moore, a Scottish collection (notably William McTaggart, a Scots impressionist) and the MacDonald collection of 92 portraits of British artists (mostly self-portraits); Toulouse-Lautrec, Monet and Reynolds are also represented.

[e] The **library**, **St Mark's Church** (both 1892) and **His Majesty's Theatre** (1906) form a trio known locally as 'Education, Salvation and Damnation'. The patriot William Wallace is celebrated by a massive statue.

[f] **Union Terrace Gardens** Careful arrangement of a narrow site on two levels, with floral gardens below and good views of the city from the top path.

[g] **Union Street** The broad, main thoroughfare of the city, whose light-grey granite presents a uniform and dignified effect. Archibald Simpson (1790-1847) was the architect responsible for much of Union Street and King Street

although the layout was planned in 1801. The **Town House** (1886) incorporates a tower of the 17th-century tolbooth, outside which public executions took place up to 1867.

[h] **Marischal College** Founded 1593 this building was built in 1906, a quirky design with innovative use of granite in its pinnacled facade, and a 235-ft tower; its hall, portrait gallery and anthropological museum are open to the public. In 1860 the college joined with King's College (in Old Aberdeen) to form Aberdeen University.

[i] Provost Skene's House (open 10-5 Mon-Sat). House of a 17th-century merchant and former provost, fine 16th-century painted ceiling in the chapel, much panelling and rooms furnished with period antiques in Georgian, Regency and Victorian styles. From the far side of this building, looking along Flourmill Lane to the right, is a gabled house above a shop, one of the oldest buildings in the city.

Old Aberdeen

A tour of the cathedral city, a separate burgh from the present-day city centre, dating from 1498 to 1891; it retains a remarkably unspoilt and old-fashioned village atmosphere, dominated by the university.

Length 2 miles (3km), 2 hours
Difficulty 1
Start University Road (N of city centre; turn off King Street by signpost for Johnston Hall and Crombie Hall); roadside parking

WALK DIRECTIONS

① Walk along University Road away from King Street, turn right into College Bounds [a] (becomes High Street) to reach town house ② [b]: take Chanonry, opposite and slightly to left [c].

Past cathedral [d], ③ enter Seaton Park by gate [e], turn left on path around top edge of park, past Wallace Tower, to emerge on road; turn right and ④ immediately right again on enclosed path to right of house, to re-enter park and drop to river where keep right and follow riverside, initially along park road and then across area of grass, at end of which ⑤ it is necessary to fork right on to higher path (as path at river level soon reaches dead end).

⑥ Emerge on road (Don Street): right is continuation, but first detour left to see Brig o'Balgownie [f]. Return along Don Street (opposite entrance to Hillhead Halls of Residence, you can use path on left of road to avoid road-walking: this rejoins road by tennis court and then leaves it again) until reaching the near end of Bon Accord Football Club ground [g], opposite which ⑦ turn right on park road between gateposts, past row of modern houses on left and then continue forward into Seaton Park.

⑧ At bottom of slope, turn left past ornamental fountain, taking path across park and aiming for cathedral (leaving park by gate entered through earlier). Just after cathedral, turn left along Chanonry [h] and ⑨ turn right at Don Street (keeping with one-way sign). Cross St Machar Drive and retrace steps along High Street to reach starting point.

ON THE ROUTE

[a] **College Bounds and High Street** The main street of the old town. As you proceed, on the left is the **gateway to Powis Lodge**, built in 1834 for John Leslie of Powis, who had connections with the Middle East, and is in a flamboyant exotic style with minarets and pinnacles. On right, **King's College**, founded 1500-05 by Bishop Elphinstone, has a great lantern-tower as its central feature; in the college chapel are canopied stalls, misericords, and superb 16th-century wood-carving. Further along, on right, **Grant's Place** and **Wrights' and Coopers' Place** are restored single-storey cottages, once belonging to the incorporated trades of the burgh. Notable among many good 17th-, 18th- and early 19th-century houses are **No.70** (right), double-fronted with bow window, and **No.81** (on left, set back).

[b] **Town House** Town hall for the burgh. Handsome building of 1790 looking down the High Street, displaying the coat of arms above the door.

[c] **Chanonry** So called because canons to the cathedral formerly had manses here. Now a pleasant residential district of houses occupied by university professors. **Cruickshank Botanic Garden** (on left; open May-Sept, 9-4.30 Mon-Fri, 2-5 Sat and Sun), covers 8 acres, with rock and water gardens.

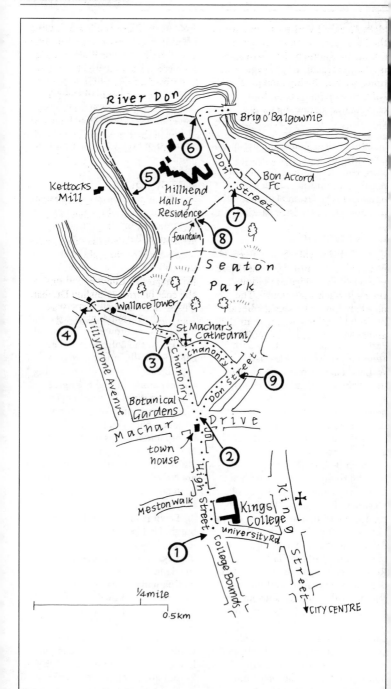

River Don

Brig o'Balgownie

Don Street

Bon Accord FC

⑥

⑤

Kettocks Mill

Hillhead Halls of Residence

⑦

fountain

⑧

Seaton

Park

Wallace Tower

④

Tillydrone Avenue

St Machar's Cathedral

Chanonry

③

chanonry

Don Street

⑨

Botanical Gardens

Machar   Drive

town house

②

Meston walk

High Street

Kings College

King Street

university Rd

①

College Bounds

¼ mile

0.5km

CITY CENTRE

[d] **St Machar's Cathedral** Founded in the 12th century, on the site of a 6th-century church. The twin spire is a famous landmark, but the west front, with its highly individual and boldly austere design, is the outstanding feature. Inside is a notable 16th-century heraldic ceiling adorned with 48 coats of arms, attributed to Bishop Gavin Dunbar.

[e] **Seaton Park** Retains a certain rural character, situated by the River Don. Previously the grounds of Seaton House (which burned down in 1963). The Wallace Tower is a reconstruction of a 16th-century tower.

[f] **Brig o'Balgownie** (best viewed from the river: turn right just before you reach the bridge and follow riverside track a few yards). The oldest and most famous medieval bridge in Scotland, dating from 1329 and repaired in the early 1600s; the kink at its south end is a defensive feature. A prophecy was made when it was built that the bridge would collapse were it crossed by an only son riding a mare's only foal.

[g] **Bon Accord Football Club** A famous name in soccer history as the club that suffered the heaviest defeat in the British game when they lost 36-0 to Arbroath on 5 September 1885. The score may have been greater if the goals had had nets, as time was presumably wasted retrieving the ball after a goal had been scored; seven further goals were disqualified for offside. The Arbroath goalkeeper is said to have smoked a pipe throughout the match.

[h] **Chaplain's Court** on left diplays the coat of arms of Bishop Dunbar. The house was built in 1519 as accommodation for cathedral chaplains.

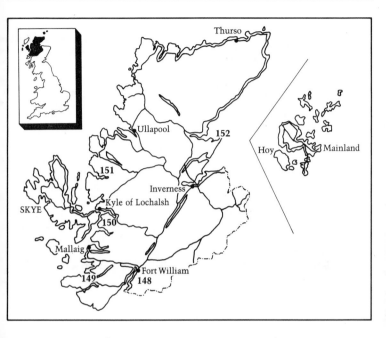

148 River Leven Glen
149 Loch Moidart and Castle Tioram
150 Loch Alsh and Kyle Rhea
151 Diabaig Bay and Loch Torridon
152 Tarbat Ness

Holiday Which? Good Walks Guide

169 Loch na Creitheach and the Eastern Cuillins   170 Southern Skye shores and Loch Slapin   171 Rogie Falls   172 The Quiraing   173 Glen Coe and Glen Etive   176 The Old Man of Hoy (Orkney)

The River Leven Glen

The route rises gently up a majestic valley, broad and sinuous, loosely dotted with broad-leaved trees mingled with rushing waterfalls. Beyond two lochans you reach the valley head and vast bleak expanses of moorland surrounding the Blackwater Reservoir; return same way. Terrain may be boggy briefly after ③, but otherwise this is a good path.

Length 8 miles (13km), 4¹/₂ hours there and back
Difficulty 3
Start Kinlochmore on (B863 at E end of Loch Leven, SE of Fort William). Turn off at signpost for Grey Mare's Waterfall, turn right at T-junction in front of St Paul's church to follow long road with housing estate on left and woods on right; park on roadside

at far end. Grid reference 192619
OS maps 1:50,000 41; 1:25,000 NN 06/16 and NN 26/36 (Pathfinder 290 and 291)
Refreshments Pubs and shops in Kinlochleven (¹/₄ mile from start, but not on route); shop in Kinlochmore

WALK DIRECTIONS

(Make a mental note of the outward route, as you will return the same way)

① [a] With houses on left, follow the road to end. 100 yards after last house, road becomes an unsurfaced track (by shed); immediately after, turn left at track junction. Soon pass electricity sub-station on your right; just 20 yards after, take rising path on right and 35 yards later ② turn right (along level) at oblique cross-junction of paths [b].

Path leads through semi-wooded

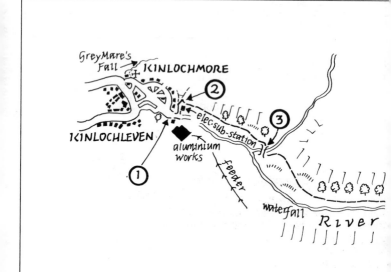

area, eventually crossing footbridge ③, beyond which path keeps left, initially with river on left (but soon river bends away to left). Path leads up semi-wooded valley – boggy for a short section, but soon gets easier and very well defined as it climbs gently.

④ Path crosses small stream at waterfall (care needed). ⑤ After footbridge, path emerges into open, and finally heads towards Blackwater Dam, following reservoir pipeline for final stage [c]. ⑥ From reservoir, retrace steps to starting point [d].

ON THE ROUTE

[a] **Feeder** for water supplying hydro-electric power from Blackwater Reservoir for the aluminium works at Kinlochleven is visible across the valley.

[b] For much of the following sections there are fine **views** of major peaks: WSW is shapely Garbh Bheinn (2,835ft); N Mamore Forest, including (left to right) Am Bodach (13,382ft), Binnein Mor (3,700ft), Sgurr Eilde Mor (3,279ft) and Glas Bheinn (2,587ft); S are the northern Glencoe group. OS maps show a path leading NE towards Loch Eilde Mor (which would make a round walk), but we could see no sign of it.

[c] **Blackwater Reservoir** 8 miles long, constructed 1905-09 in a bleak setting – a total contrast from the valley from which you have just emerged.

[d] On the return to Kinlochmore, it is worth taking in the **Grey Mare's Waterfall**. Signposted from the car park by St Paul's church, there is a path leading 200 yards to viewing point.

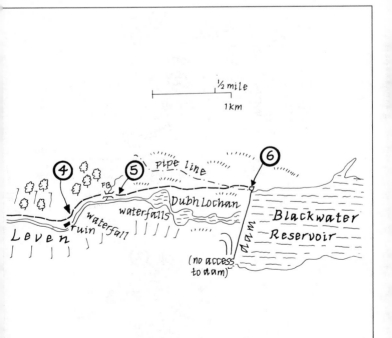

Loch Moidart and Castle Tioram

A moorland route using a reasonably well-defined path (often boggy, so good footwear essential) past two small lochs, before dropping towards Loch Moidart; route then follows low-level coastal path, with a classic highland view near Castle Tioram. Dogs must be on a lead. No access to moorland part of walk in stalking season (1 Sept to 21 Oct).

Length 6 miles (9.5km), 3 hours
Difficulty 3
Start By turning off A861 sign-posted Dorlin, 18 miles SW of Lochailort (where the A861 joins the A830 Fort William to Mallaig road) and 3 miles N of Salen; roadside parking nearby. Grid reference 675692
OS maps 1:50,000 40; 1:25,000 NM 66/76 and NM 67/77 (Pathfinder 288 and 275)

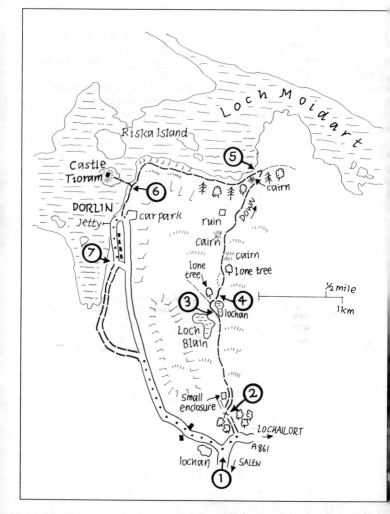

WALK DIRECTIONS

(1) From road junction, with Dorlin road to left, walk along A861 in signposted Lochailort direction. After 250 yards, where road bends right, take stony track on left which rises gently through woods until reaching gate into moorland (2): here keep to the main track which first bends right and then narrows to path width.

Pass lochan (small lake) on your left. (3) Path continues around left side of second lochan, just after end of which turn sharp right at path junction (continuing around the lochan) – there was a lone tree at this junction when walk was inspected. (4) Path soon bends left away from lochan (initially with stream on right).

Where path begins to level out, it very briefly becomes ill-defined (at time of inspection, there was another small lone tree near this point) – bear slightly left, soon picking up clear path again, which later passes two cairns (piled-up stones) [a] and drops steadily towards Loch Moidart, veering right as it does so, and entering semi-wooded area. (5) A short distance above the coast, turn sharp left at path junction by cairn and follow this coast path to reach Castle Tioram [b] (6). Continue along coast, joining road and follow back to starting point. (7) Just after car park and bollards on road, you can take 'private road' on right for better coastal views; this rejoins the principal road later.

ON THE ROUTE

[a] Good **view** from highest cairn over Loch Moidart and its islands.
[b] **Castle Tioram** (always open), stands on a tidal promontory watching over the sea loch. This five-sided 14th-century keep, standing to its original height, was the seat of the Macdonalds of Clan Ranald. It was burned by its chief in 1715 when he feared the Campbells would take the castle. The castle's lack of seaward windows was probably intended as a defensive measure against sea attacks.

Loch Alsh and Kyle Rhea

**Offers sweeping panoramas over
Loch Alsh, after a mild inland start
along a forestry track. Early
sections along the shore are easily
managed, but be prepared for steep
and uneven terrain at ⑦ as the
path leads through forest above
the coast.**

Length 7½ miles (12km),
3½ hours
Difficulty 3
Start Car park on mainland near car

ferry from point N of Glenelg to
Kyle Rhea (Skye; ferries operate Mon
to Sat in summer only). From A87
turn off at Shiel Bridge (signposted
Glenelg and ferry), and turn right
after 9 miles, ½ mile before Glenelg
(signposted ferry). 80 yards before
road makes sharp left bend down to
ferry slipway, turn right into
unsigned car park. Grid reference
795213
OS maps 1:50,000 33; 1:25,000 NG
62/72 and NG 82/92 (Pathfinder 204
and 205)

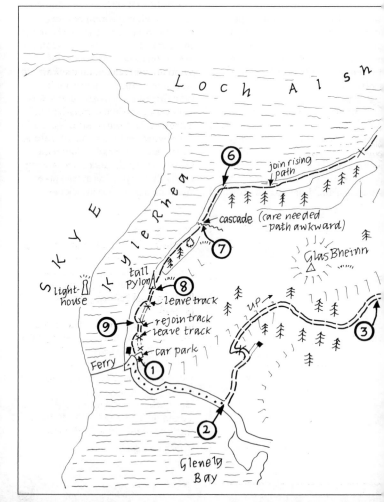

WALK DIRECTIONS

① Turn left out of car park, along road [a]. Valley later appears on left, with conifer plantation; ② at end of the plantation, take hard track on left. This passes houses and leads up to enter forest via gate. ③ Track continues through more recently planted area [b] (there are no side-turns).

④ [c] Track drops, eventually to reach shore, where track bends left. ⑤ 100 yards later, reach track junction (by boat-winching apparatus). Here, avoid both tracks, and walk along the shore, which is easy-going along grass at first, and is later joined by forest on left.

⑥ Just before coast bends left, pick up rising woodland path (between fence-posts), parallel to coast, soon step over low fence (no stile, but easily managed at time of inspection) at the point where coast actually bends left. The well-defined path continues with fence on left and coast close down to right for some way.

⑦ Take care where path crosses stream by waterfall as the ground is steep and uneven; path becomes easier as it continues through woods and semi-open area, until reaching open ground ⑧. Go under tall pylon [d], where pick up track which reaches gate (marked 'private'): immediately before this gate, turn right on narrow path, initially with fence on left, to cross stile ⑨.

The path later rejoins track, along which turn right and follow 60 yards, but fork right in front of next gate (again marked 'private') on to signposted path. Follow to reach road just below car park.

ON THE ROUTE

[a] **Views** of Skye, close up, and Eigg and the Ardnamurchan peninsula (the most westerly point on the British mainland) in the distance.
[b] **View** S of Beinn Sgritheall (3,194ft).
[c] Extensive **views** over Loch Alsh, the isle of Glas Eilean, distant peaks on E Skye, Castle Moal to W at Kyleakin; upland ranges to N include Killilan and Applecross forests.
[d] Try the bizarre perspective effect gained by looking straight up from the base of this abnormally tall pylon.

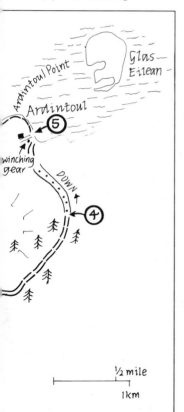

½ mile

1km

Diabaig Bay and Loch Torridon

A sequence of magnificent coastal and mountain panoramas, in some of the finest Highland landscape. Suitable footwear essential for rough (but well-defined) undulating moorland path that runs above the shore of Loch Torridon (towel helpful for drying feet after wading across stream at ②, and a stick may aid balance; there is a longer road alternative).

Length 8 miles (13km), 4½ hours
Difficulty 4
Start Road by Loch Diabaigs Airde:
turn off A896 by National Trust information centre, signposted Torridon, and follow road around N side of Loch Torridon, ignoring left turns. Road goes steeply uphill; at top, park in small unsigned car park on left by bench overlooking Loch Diabaigs Airde, or use space further on. Grid reference 824595
OS maps 1:50,000 24; 1:25,000 Outdoor Leisure 8

WALK DIRECTIONS

① Walk W along road (away from Torridon); there are two lochs down to left, joined by neck of water. At end of the lochs, turn left to walk

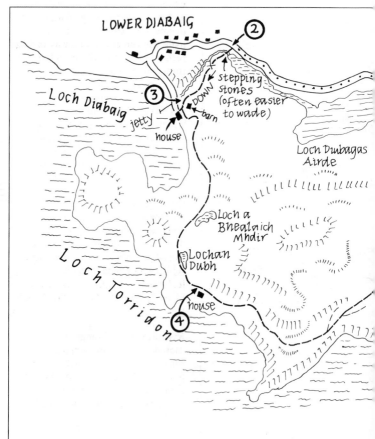

etween fence (on right) and loch,
oon to reach fast-flowing shallow
cream draining from the loch ②:
ross it [a] by rough stepping-stones
t time of inspection, after heavy
ain, stones were just submerged,
ut wading across not difficult) and
ick up clear path on other side.
ath soon reaches gate, and
ontinues along the level for a short
istance before dropping steadily
owards Diabaig Bay [b]. Shortly
efore house at bottom, and opposite
arn on right, turn left (signposted)
o pick up coast path ③. Follow this
ath, which is waymarked by
aint-marks and piled-up stones

and is relatively well defined.

After a short and steep ascent, the
path undulates, later passing lochs
on left [c] and a house on right ④;
soon after, view opens up over Loch
Torridon [d] (soon, there are forks to
avoid on left and then right, but no
waymark cairns at these junctions
when walk inspected). Keep roughly
level; hamlet of Wester Alligin
comes into view).

⑤ Very soon after crossing
stream, take gate in fence on right
and follow cairns down towards
Wester Alligin; path peters out near
the houses. Continue just below
highest house to reach road, on
which ⑥ turn left uphill. Turn left
again at T-junction. ⑦ Where
telegraph wires on right leave the
road, you can cut a corner by taking
path which follow them up to rejoin
road; proceed along it to the
starting point.

ON THE ROUTE
[a] **To avoid crossing stream**,
continue along the road, take the
next left, (just after post box); road
descends into Lower Diabaig to
shore. Go past jetty, then take gate
at last house, where a signposted
path leads to left to nearby barn
where turn right by signpost to pick
up coast path at ③.
[b] **View** over Diabaig Bay and its
complex of isles and headlands, with
Applecross Forest beyond.
[c] From the second lochan, Beinn
Bhan (2,938 ft) in Applecross Forest
is visible.
[d] The **view** is one of the finest in
this book, and includes many of
Torridon's most famous peaks. The
main ones are, left to right, Beinn
Alligin (3,232ft), Liathach (3,456ft),
Benn Eighe (3,188ft), the Sgurr Dubh
(2,566ft) and Ben Damph (2,957ft).

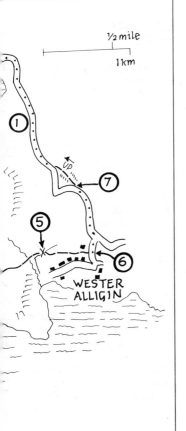

Tarbat Ness

A peninsula that lends itself to one of the best round walks on the Scottish east coast: attractions include contrasting views on N and S sides, rich bird life, and a castle near the end. Mostly along grassy or stony shores, with some rough sections and diversions on to top of low cliffs.

Length 7 miles (11km), 3½ hours
Difficulty 3
Start Portmahomack sea-front (car parks), off B9165 on S side of Dornoch Firth. Grid reference 915846
OS maps 1:50,000 21; 1:25,000 NH 88/98 (Pathfinder 124)
Refreshments Pubs, shops and cafés in Portmahomack

WALK DIRECTIONS

① [a] With sea on left, follow road along sea-front; where road ends, continue forward on track and then proceed along turf by shore [b] where track leads to bungalow. Keep close to shore and along edge of field [c].

② At shed on right it is best to divert right, through the gorse, and continue along top of low cliff (as there is a tricky rock and gorse area by the shore). Keep to edge of cliff, soon through narrow gate and later along shore again, heading towards lighthouse at Tarbat Ness.

③ Before lighthouse, keep to seaward side of fish-pools (do not enter fenced area around them) and proceed through field gates where necessary to reach lighthouse. Lighthouse grounds are bounded by stone wall (no entry via gate), immediately in front of which turn right to proceed alongside the wall (now on your left) to reach corner of road [d]**④**. Left on road (avoid next

left, to lighthouse) to reach jetty where turn right through gate by hut and proceed along grassy shore [e].

Follow shore all the way to Rockfield. It is best to divert up to cliff-top after ⅓ mile **⑤** where shore is too rocky to be easily managed, but 100 yards after passing through gate take track down to rejoin shore. **⑥** Path diverts up to castle [f], beyond which it is easy to rejoin shore. **⑦** At village of Rockfield [g], go beyond first cottage and turn right on road uphill (but soon level). **⑧** At edge of Portmahomack, turn left by war-memorial then immediately right to reach sea-front.

ON THE ROUTE

[a] **Portmahomack** Small port turned resort, with harbour improved by Thomas Telford, a Reformation period church and a funny black and gold cast-iron fountain on the esplanade recording the introduction of gravitation water in 1887.
[b] **Views**, until Tarbat Ness, N to Sutherland and Caithness.
[c] The first stile displays an old 'beware of the bull' sign; local people we met said that the bull died 'a long time ago'.
[d] **Tarbat Ness** protrudes at the S side of the mouth of the Dornoch Firth. Good for watching migrating birds. A sandbank nearby, called Gizzen Briggs, attracts colonies of **seals**.
[e] **Views** S until Rockfield across the Moray Firth to Burghead Bay.
[f] **Ballone Castle**, now a precarious and dangerous ruin (do not venture in), was built for the Earl of Ross in the 15th and 16th centuries, and was later owned by the Mackenzies. Inhabited until the early 1800s.
[g] **Rockfield** is a typical fishing hamlet of single-storey cottages.

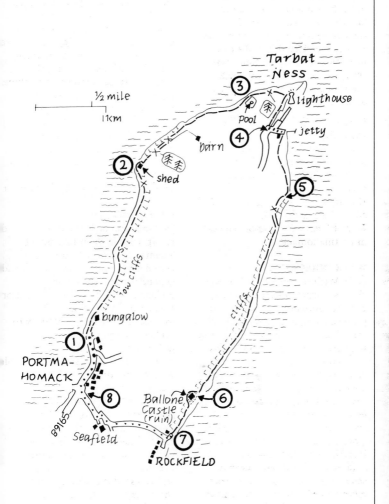

Tarbat Ness

③

lighthouse

Pool

④ jetty

barn

② shed

⑤

low cliffs

cliffs

bungalow

①

PORTMA-
HOMACK

⑧

Ballone
Castle
(ruin)

⑥

B9165

Seafield

⑦

ROCKFIELD

½ mile
1 km

LOTHIAN

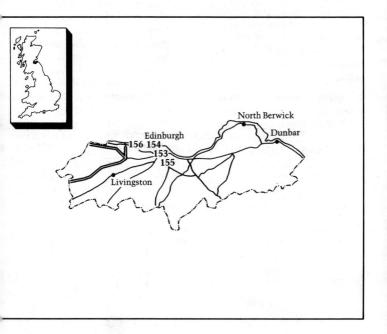

Edinburgh Old Town

A tour of the historic heart of Scotland's capital, including the Royal Mile and less touristy areas to the south, finishing with superb views from Calton Hill. Note that this is quite a tiring walk.

Length 3 miles (5km), 4 hours
Difficulty 1
Start Scott Monument, Princes Street
Refreshments Full range

WALK DIRECTIONS

① From Scott Monument [**a**], walk W along Princes Street (best to walk along promenade along top of Princes Street Gardens [**b**], with Princes Street parallel on right), to reach Royal Scottish Academy [**c**]. Cross The Mound by traffic lights near junction with Princes Street and turn left up The Mound [**d**], over railway, then ② first right into Mound Place, leading into Castlehil (which is part of a long street that changes its name but is known in it

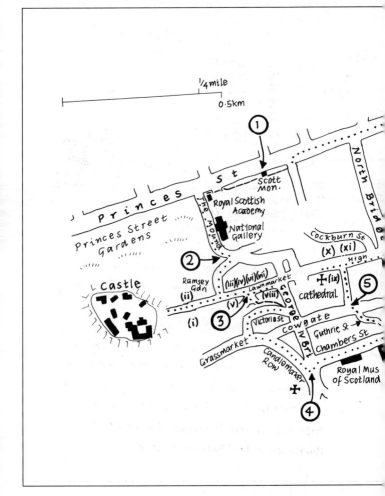

ntirety as the Royal Mile).
etour right for Castle Esplanade [e];
therwise *continue* left, heading E
wn Royal Mile [f]. ③ Just after
olbooth Church, note the
ontinuation of route, which is to
ght into narrow street called Upper
w: however, first continue a few
ards to see Gladstone's Land and
ady Stairs House (both on left); now
roceed into Upper Bow (leaving the
oyal Mile for the present), at end of
hich turn left on raised walkway
ove Victoria Street [g]: continue

until the walkway drops down to
street level, then turn right along
Victoria Street itself. At the end,
Grassmarket opens out to your right
[h], but continue half left up
Candlemaker Row.

④ At top [i], cross road and
continue along Chambers Street
opposite and slightly to the left, past
Royal Scottish Museum [j] then left
into Guthrie Street (or first *detour
ahead* to see Old College [k]); at
bottom reach Cowgate and ⑤ take
alley called Old Fishmarket Close

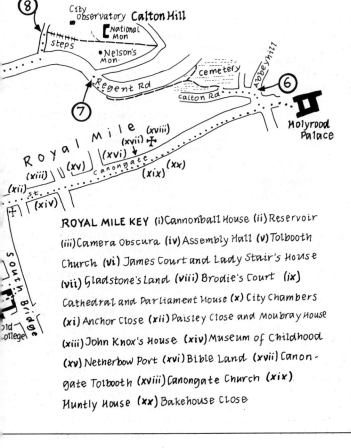

ROYAL MILE KEY (i) Cannonball House (ii) Reservoir
(iii) Camera Obscura (iv) Assembly Hall (v) Tolbooth
Church (vi) James Court and Lady Stair's House
(vii) Gladstone's Land (viii) Brodie's Court (ix)
Cathedral and Parliament House (x) City Chambers
(xi) Anchor Close (xii) Paisley Close and Moubray House
(xiii) John Knox's House (xiv) Museum of Childhood
(xv) Netherbow Port (xvi) Bible Land (xvii) Canongate Tolbooth (xviii) Canongate Church (xix)
Huntly House (xx) Bakehouse Close

opposite and slightly to the left, leading up to rejoin Royal Mile, along which turn right (or first *detour left* to St Giles Cathedral) [l].

Follow to Holyrood Palace [m]; after visiting Palace, return to roundabout at the foot of the Royal Mile and turn right into Abbeyhill and then ⑥ first left (Calton Road). Pass arched entrance to old Craigwell brewery on your right, then take rising path on right, keeping left at next path T-junction in front of high wall, to join Regent Road along which turn left.

⑦ Take first right (open park gates) on to park road and follow until it is possible to short cut left across grass to monuments on Calton Hill [n]. Continue on path between (mock Grecian) National Monument on right and Nelson's Monument (tall tower) on path, past cannon. At next junction by Stewart Dugald Monument continue forward to descend on paths with railing. ⑧ Turn left at bottom, then rejoin main road, where turn right and follow back to Scott Monument.

ON THE ROUTE

[a] **Scott Monument** The huge monument to the author of the *Waverley* novels was built by George Kemp (1844), a joiner and self-taught architect who, against all odds, won a competition for this design submitting his architectural plans under a pseudonym. The statue is by Sir John Steell.

[b] The area between Princes Street and the Old Town (with castle) was formerly the **Nor'Loch**, drained in the 19th century for the building of the railway. North Bridge, built in the 1700s, was the first link to the area N of the loch which became the fashionable New Town. **Princes Street Gardens**, a major landscape feature, occupy part of the basin of the old loch; the floral clock is

the world's oldest.

[c] **The National Gallery of Scotland** is one of Britain's major art collections, with paintings, drawings and prints from the Renaissance to Post-Impressionism. Raphael, Titian, Tintoretto, Velazquez, Rubens, Vermeer, Rembrandt, Gainsborough and French Impressionists are represented as well as Scottish artists (open 10-5, Mon-Sat, 2-5 Sun). The **Royal Scottish Academy** has special summer and Festival exhibitions.

[d] View of the **Old Town**, showing its magnificent site, up on a volcanic ridge. The route leads up through **Ramsay Garden**, the turreted block of which was romanticised in the 1890s as part of a scheme to draw university professors back into the Old Town, which had suffered a serious decline.

[e] **Edinburgh Castle** From early times a strategic place of refuge, atop the precipitous rock. An early fortress was called Dun Eadain, and later Edwin, a 6th-century Northumbrian king, rebuilt it: the city's name probably derives from one of these names. Much of the building can be appreciated from the outside, and its outlook can be enjoyed from the Castle Esplanade. The complex of buildings includes 12th-century Margaret's Chapel, the Great Hall (its timber roof dating from the 1500s), a fine 18th-century barrack block, various museums and the King's lodging (birthplace of James VI).

[f] **The Royal Mile** The mile-long central axis of the Old Town, ranged along a gently sloping ridge, began in medieval times as a religious centre fortified in 1450 by the town wall. By the 18th century the area had become a slum. Writing in 1847, Hans Christian Andersen observed, 'poverty and misery seem to peep out of the open hatches which

ormally serve as windows'.
espite some renewal, much of
istoric and architectural interest in
ie street and in its steep side-alleys
ading off has survived.

A full exploration from the castle
• the Palace of Holyroodhouse at
ie far end could take a day; the
iain features are listed here and
nder [l]. From the castle, walking
own the Royal Mile:

•n right **Cannonball House** (1630)
as a cannon-ball embedded in the
•all on the Castle North Wynd side;
•rmerly thought to have been a shot
red during the 1745 siege, but is in
ict a marker for the gravitation
•eight of the city's first piped water-
upply from Comiston Springs to
astlehill reservoir (1681).

•n left the building just before
amsay Lane housed **Ramsay**
•arden Reservoir the first reservoir
1 Edinburgh (1720; rebuilt 1849).

he Outlook Tower was built by
•ew Town planner Sir Patrick
•eddes, in order to enjoy the view
•ver the city and the Firth of Forth.
1 the 1850s an optician added two
toreys and devised the **Camera**
•bscura, a revolving device
•eflecting views of the city on to a
•hite surface. Open daily, but best
isited on a sunny day when details
•f the panorama can be clearly
icked out.

Assembly Hall (1850), built on site
•f the 16th-century Palace of Guise.
•n right, **Tolbooth Church** (1844)
•as originally the General Assembly
Iall of the Church of Scotland.
•n left, in **James' Court**, historian
•avid Hume lodged, 1762-70, and
•hnson visited Boswell in 1773.
•he courtyard leads to **Lady Stair's**
Iouse (1622) named after the widow
•f the first Earl of Stair, who was
•ady Primrose by her first marriage,
•nd was the model for Walter Scott's
:ory *My Aunt Margaret's Mirror*.
•he house is now a museum with

relics and manuscripts of three of
Scotland's great literary men; Scott,
Stevenson and Burns (open 10-5,
Mon-Sat, June-Sept; 10-6 plus Sun 2-
5 in Festival week). **Gladstone's
Land** Built by merchant Thomas
Gledstones in 1617, is the only
example left of an arcaded shop front
of the tenements once found
throughout the Old Town. Owned
and restored by the National Trust
for Scotland; painted ceilings and
walls, period furnishings (open
Easter to Oct 10-5 Mon to Sat, 2-5
Sun). *On right* in **Brodie's Court**
lived William Brodie, a respectable
town councillor by day and burglar
by night; he was hanged at the
Tolbooth in 1788. Brodie's career
gave R.L. Stevenson the inspiration
for *The Strange Case of Dr Jekyll
and Mr Hyde* published in 1886.
[g] **Victoria Street** (completed 1846).
An unusual street design with a
pedestrian terrace high above the
road. Among the specialist shops
below is an old-fashioned brush
store.

[h] **Grassmarket** Public executions
were once held here. In 1736, a riot
broke out during an unpopular
execution. Captain Porteous,
commander of the city guard,
ordered his men to fire into the
crowd, killing several people. The
angry mob hanged Porteous from the
gallows; a cobbled cross within a
railed enclosure marks the site.

[i] **Greyfriars Church** (1612), on
right, stands on the site of a 15th-
century Franciscan Friary. In 1638
the National Covenant was signed
here (some signed their names in
blood), for 14 years from 1848 a
Skye terrier watched over his master
John Gray's grave; a special licensed
collar was given by the city provost
so that the dog would not be
destroyed as a stray. 'Greyfriars
Bobby' as the dog has come to be
known, is immortalised in the form

of a statue on a pedestal at the top of Candlemaker Row.

[**j**] **Chambers Street** Broad dignified street with university buildings (including Heriot Watt University, founded 1821). On right, the **Royal Scottish Museum** is a full-day visit (natural history, transport, power, evolution, fine arts, oriental arts, geology and more), but it is worth looking into the inside of the Venetian-style building to glimpse its spectacular soaring design of cast-iron and plate-glass.

[**k**] Detour to end of Chambers Street, turning right into the main road; immediately on right is the entrance to the **Old College**, founded 1581, rebuilt 1789 to a design of Robert Adam; his plan of two courtyards was modifed to one in 1834. The upper library has an impressive arched ceiling; there are free guided tours arond the site (daily), and it is always possible to look into the courtyard from the main gate.

[**l**] **Royal Mile** (second part). The lower part of **Old Fishmarket Close** was a fishmarket in the 1700s, described by one visitor as a 'stinking ravine'. Home of the town hangman, the last one being John High, who died in 1817. Daniel Defoe also lived here while a secret agent for the English government at the time of the Union.

Entering the Royal Mile: detour left **St Giles Cathedral**, with its beautiful crown spire, is probably the third church on the site; the first was 9th-century, this building is mostly 15th-century but has been much restored. John Knox was minister in 1560 and was buried in the churchyard which has now been covered over by the street (the approximate site of his grave is marked by his statue at the back of the cathedral). The Cathedral was formerly used as a meeting hall by the Parliament and General Assembly. Royal proclamations are read from the **Mercat Cross**. On the far side of the building. **The Heart o Midlothian** is a heart-shaped arrangement of cobbles marking the site of the 16th-century tolbooth, where tolls were collected and where later the Scots Parliament met and the Town Hall functioned; from 1640 it became a prison until its demolition in 1817. It is a city tradition to spit on the spot. Behind the cathedral **Parliament House** has a fine hammerbeam roof and staind glass in the Great Hall; Scottish Parliament met here until the Unio of 1707, and it now houses law courts. By the junction with George IV Bridge, brass plates in the road mark the site of the last public execution in 1864. *Continue down the Royal Mile towards Palace of Holyroodhouse.*

On left, **City Chambers**, by John Adam (1761), built at the beginning of the classical revival in Edinburgh Originally the Royal Exchange; later expanded. In **Anchor Close**, William Smellie had his printing works where he produced the first edition of Encyclopaedia Brittanica in 1768 and Robert Burns' works. After North Bridge, *on left* Paisley Close witnessed the collapse of a tenemen in 1861-35 people were killed. The inscription above the entrance ('Heave awa' lads, I'm no' dead yet') immortalises the words of a boy found trapped in the rubble.

Moubray House has an outside stair once typical of the older houses but now a rarity. Here, Defoe edited the *Edinburgh Courant* from 1710. **John Knox's House** (1490) is an excellent example of an Old Town house, with its overhanging wooden upper floors and crow step gable-end surviving many alterations. Knox reputedly lived here 1561-72.

On right, the **Museum of childhood**

splays toys of all ages (open 10-5,
on-Sat Jun to Sept, 10-6 plus Sun
5 in Festival week).

n *left* Brass plates in the street
ark the site of **Netherlow Port**
513-1764), one of six gates in the
ty wall. Heads of criminals were
aced on spikes above the gate as a
arning to others. Beyond the gate,
u would have been out of the city
d into the burgh of Canongate.

ble Land, a restored 17th-century
nement, has a turreted outside
airway and a sculptured shield
er its door inscribed with the first
rse of Psalm 135. **Canongate**
olbooth is now a museum about
e people of Edinburgh (open 10-5
on to Sat, Jun to Sept, 10-6 plus
5 in Festival week). **Canongate**
hurch was built 1688 for the
ngregation which attend Holyrood
bbey but were ousted by James VII.
ree graves to look out for are
onomist Adam Smith, Robert
rns' 'Clarinda' and poet Robert
rguson (whose epitaph Burns
mposed).

n *right*, **Huntly House** dates from
17; its plasterd timber upper floor
neath three gables would once
ve been characteristic of Old
wn architecture. **Bakehouse**
lose is best seen from its rear,
here there is a yard full of old-
orld charm; previously owned by
e Incorporation of Bakers of the
anongate.

] Abbey and Palace of
olyroodhouse According to legend,
avid I, while hunting in Holyrood
rk, was attacked by a stag, and on
izing the beast's antlers found
mself holding a crucifix. As a
sult of the miracle he founded the
ugustinian Abbey of the Holy Rood
1128; the 12th- and 13th-century
ofless nave still stands. The
lace was originally a guest house

of the Abbey, enlarged into a royal
residence by James IV and rebuilt by
Charles II in Palladian style to the
design of Sir William Bruce of
Balcaskie. Queen Victoria and later
monarchs have used the palace
regularly as the official Scottish
residence of the Royal Family.
Visits are by guided party, but it is
possible to enjoy much of the
building from the front courtyard.
(open all year except when Queen is
in residence).

[n] **Calton Hill** Another of the city's
volcanic summits, never
incorporated into the development
of the New Town. In the late 18th
to early 19th century it acquired its
wonderful medley of monuments.
First on the scene was the **Old
Observatory** (1776) by James Craig,
the original planner of the New
Town – one of the few buildings of
his to survive. **Nelson's Monument**,
106ft high, is the tallest item on
show, a circular tower built in tiers,
supposedly shaped like a telescope;
143 steps lead up to a viewing
gallery (open Apr-Sept, 10-6 Mon-
Sat, 1-6 Sun.

The **National Monument** was
built as a replica of the Parthenon, to
honour the dead of the Napoleonic
Wars, but funds ran out and only
twelve columns and a portico were
completed. Playfair's monument to
Dugald Stewart, a Professor of Moral
Philosophy, is an imitation of
Lysicrates' Lantern of Demosthenes
in Athens. Outstanding **view** over
the city, with Arthur's Seat the large
hill close to the SE, the Pentland
Hills in the distance to the S, while
N are the Firth of Forth (with the
Forth Bridges to left and Bass Rock
near North Berwick to right) and the
Ochils beyond (marking the
beginning of the Highlands) and the
Lomond Hills in Fife.

Edinburgh New Town

A tour of the city's Georgian quarter,
one of the great examples of early
town planning. A surprisingly
countrified return route, via the
Royal Botanic Garden and the
wooded gorge of the Water of Leith.

Length 4 miles (6.5km), 3 hours
Difficulty 1
Start Scott Monument, Princes
Street
Refreshments Plenty at start; tea-
room at entrance to Botanic Garden
from Easter to autumn

WALK DIRECTIONS

①[a] Cross Princes Street by traffic
lights and take St David Street
opposite, follow to George Street
where turn left [b]. ② At end, turn
right into Charlotte Square [c] and
leave by far right-hand corner into
Glenfinlas Street, and continue
forward into Ainslie Place (with oval
green in centre) where turn right [d].
Take first turning on right (Moray
Place), then ③ second right into
Darnaway Street, soon proceeding
along Heriot Row [e].

Turn left at traffic lights into
Dundas Street, which eventually
curves round to T-junction by clock-
tower ④; turn left over bridge into
Inverleith Row.

Turn left near pedestrian traffic
lights into Royal Botanic Garden
(signposted) [f]. Make your way
across the garden via any route (past
the rockery is recommended) to
West Gate ⑤, where turn left along
Arboretum Place. Keep forward at
next junction, soon with river on
left. Just before lodge-house, turn
left at T-junction with St Bernard's
Row, then ⑥ turn right just before
river bridge on to riverside path.

Take steps up at next bridge, cross
main road and continue opposite
along Dean Terrace; cross next river
bridge and turn right to continue

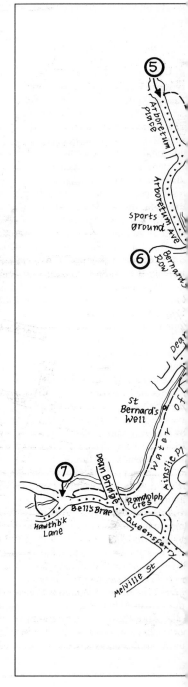

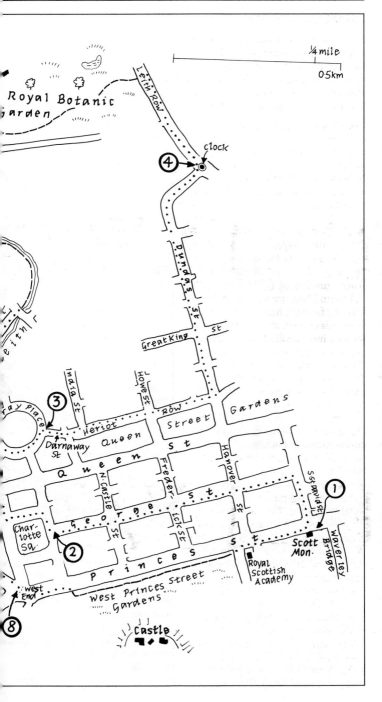

¼ mile

0·5km

Royal Botanic Garden

Leith Row

clock

④

Dundas St

Great King St

India St

Howe St

③

ray place

Heriot Row

Street Gardens

Darnaway St

Queen

St

Q u e e n

N. Castle St

Frederick St

Hanover St

St David St

①

G e o r g e St

Charlotte Sq

②

Waverley Bridge

P r i n c e s St

Scott Mon.

Royal Scottish Academy

West End

West Princes Street Gardens

⑧

Castle

along riverside path, later passing St Bernard's Well [**g**] and going under Dean Bridge to reach road at Bell's Brae at Dean village ⑦.

You can turn left up Bell's Brae here, but a detour around Dean village is recommended [**h**]. Proceed up Bell's Brae to reach busy Queensferry Street; detour left on to Dean Bridge [**i**], then return to junction with Bell's Brae where cross to NE side of Queensferry Street and turn right along it [**j**] passing around Randolph crescent on left and rejoining main road.

⑧ At West End where Queensferry Street bends very sharp left to form Hope Street cross at pedestrian lights and take half left into Princes Street. Cross and take third gate on right into Princes Street Gardens, and turn left along terraced walkway along top of the gardens [**k**] to reach starting point.

ON THE ROUTE

[**a**] **Scott Monument** Sir Walter Scott and his dog are represented in this famous 200ft-high Gothic memorial; 64 niches contain statuettes of characters from his novels, and 16 poets' heads can be seen on the capitals. 287 steps inside lead up to a viewing platform looking out over the city centre.

[**b**] George Street is the central axis of Edinburgh's **New Town**. In 1767 it was decided that Edinburgh should expand to the north; the building of the North Bridge over the Nor' Loch (now occupied by Waverley Station and Princes Street Gardens) gave access to this area. The architectural competition for a new town was won by James Craig, a 23-year old architect. In plan the idea was a simple one: George Street would run along the length of a natural ridge, and a grid-iron pattern ᶠ terraced streets leading from it, ᴜounded by Queen Street to the N and Princes

Street to S, provided vistas. Craig's layout stipulated the line of house-fronts, but new regulations were added in 1782 to ensure uniformity of width, height, window design, an facades. The earliest surviving grou of houses is on the N side of St Andrews Square. Further phases of New Town development quickly followed as the area became increasingly fashionable. Its uniformity of design is still very striking. **George Street**, 115ft wide, has a parade of fine buildings (many now banks and shops). **St Andrew's and St George's Church** (on right as you proceed towards Charlotte Square), the first church to be built in the New Town (1785), it was the scene of the 1843 Disruption, when Dr Chalmers and a number of ministers walked out of the church in a dispute over patronage, and formed the Free Church of Scotland From the junction with **Hanover Street** and **Frederick Street** there is ɑ view over the Firth of Forth to the Lomond Hills in Fife. In the **Assembly Rooms** (on left, after crossing Hanover Street) Walter Scott announced his authorship of the *Waverley Novels* which he originally published anonymously. A statue of Chalmers stands at the junction with **Castle Street**, looking along at a vista of the castle. On th other side, No.39 North Castle Street was Walter Scott's home from 1802-26; here he wrote the *Waverle Novels* (begun 1805 and published 1814).

[**c**] **Charlotte Square** The highlight o the New Town is the carefully balanced composition of its N side, designed by Robert Adam, and reckoned to be one of the finest domestic facades in Europe. No.7, on that side, known as the **Georgian House**, has been restored by the National Trust for Scotland and furnished throughout as it might

ave looked around 1790-1810; an udio-visual display in the basement hows the lifestyle of an early New 'own resident (open Easter to Oct, 0-5, 2-5 Sun). **West Register House**, ith its high green dome, (Robert eid, 1814) was built as West St eorge's Church but is now an nnex of the Scottish Record Office. harlotte Square residents have ncluded Lord Lister (founder of ntiseptic surgery) at No.9, Henry ockburn and his son Lord ockburn (advocate and Senator of he College of Justic respectively) at Jo.14, Douglas Haig (leader of the ritish Army in the First World War nd founder of the Earl Haig Fund or the care of ex-servicemen) at Jo.24, and Alexander Graham Bell nventor of the telephone) at 6 outh Charlotte Street just off he square.

|] Ainslie Place, Moray Place and een later on walk) Randolph rescent constitute the **Moray state**, begun 1822 by J G Graham or the Earl of Moray (who later lived t 28 Moray Place). This handsome evelopment of circuses and rescents represented the start of the econd phase of development of the Jew Town.

|] **No.17 Heriot Row** (just after raffic lights) was the childhood ome of Robert Louis Stevenson. here is an information board ttached to the railings opposite.

] **Royal Botanic Gardens** has its rigins as a physic garden near Iolyrood Abbey; it later moved to a ite now occupied by Waverley tation; the plant and tree species vere transplanted into the present 0-acre site in the 1820s. In the elightful, landscaped park are a heath garden, rockery, rhododendron walk, tropical and temperate glass-houses, arboretum and peat garden. From the view-indicator by 18th-century Inverleith House is a panorama over the Pentland Hills, the Old and New Towns and Arthur's Seat. Since 1889 the garden, renowned for its plants from China and the Himalayas, has been Crown property, establishing Edinburgh as a major centre for taxonomic research.

[g] **St Bernard' Well** A Doric rotunda of 1780, once popular for its waters. Forsyth remarked in 1805 that 'this spring has a slight resemblance in flavour to the washings of a foul gun barrel'.

[h] **Dean Village** For 800 years grain-mills were busy here: now a residential district, but retains its village atmosphere to a surprising extent, a jumble of buildings ranged on a steep site. Baxter's tolbooth, dated 1675, is in Bell's Brae. A short circuit of the village can be made by turning right down Bell's Brae, past arch on left, then left over footbridge and left on other side to take Hawthornbank (cobbled, by prominent mock-timbered houses) up to Bell's Brae.

[i] **Dean Bridge** (Thomas Telford, 1832) takes the road 100ft above the wooded gorge of the Water of Leith.

[j] View to right along Melville Street of **St Mary's Cathedral** (G.G. Scott, 1870s) whose huge three spires dominate this side of the city.

[k] **Princes Street** The S side of the New Town was originally residential, but became commercial from the mid 19th century and is now the city's main shopping street.

Edinburgh: Holyrood Park and Arthur's Seat

Edinburgh's own mountain dominates the city skyline and draws even the most diffident walker to its craggy summit. Much easier to climb than it looks, it still makes for a wonderful short circular walk with views all around.

Length 2½ miles (4km), 1 hour
Difficulty 2
Start Holyrood House Palace car park. Grid reference 270748
OS maps 1:50,000 66; 1:25,000 NT 27/37 (Pathfinder 407)

WALK DIRECTIONS

① Start on Queen's Drive facing the hill with Holyrood Palace behind you, go to the far left end of the car park, cross Queen's Drive and follow a short tarmacked path to St Margaret's Well. The hill in front has the diagonal line of Salisbury Crags rising from the left – your objective is to pick up the path leading along the top of them.

② Immediately after the well, turn half right on unmade path, crossing the main tarmacked path and continuing up on the unsurfaced one. After 50 yards, near a two-foot boulder, the path swings sharp right and climbs to join the top edge of the crags [**a**]. Continue along the crags until they end, and drop down to the road just to your right ③.

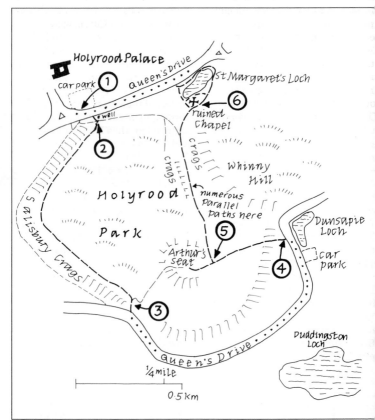

urn left along it [b] and follow it to ar park ④. Here, take one of the road paths on the left, which all ead up to summit, Arthur's Seat [c].

Retrace route down to a small flat rea where the path changes from xposed rock to grass and turn sharp eft down an unsurfaced path. ⑤ A hort distance before path passes ver some small crags, it divides: ork right, on path leading down owards ruined chapel. Turn right nce past the chapel [d] and follow ath and steps down to St Margaret's och. ⑤ Turn left at loch on path hat rejoins Queen's Drive near tarting point.

)N THE ROUTE
a] **Holyrood Park** Hilly moorland rea (of volcanic rock) with crags, oughly four miles in circumference.)avid I was reputedly attacked by a tag here: when he grasped its ntlers he found himself holding a rucifix and was then inspired to ound Holy Rood Abbey in 1128. he area later became a hunting reserve for Holyrood Palace. Fine **views** from the top of Salisbury Crags of the city and the Pentland Hills.

[b] Views down to right of **Duddingston Loch** (a bird sanctuary) and **Duddingston village**, with its Norman church.

[c] **Arthur's Seat** (823ft). It is not clear who or what Arthur was: it certainly was not the English king - more likely are the theories that it was a 6th-century Prince Arthur of Strathclyde, or that it is a corruption of 'archer', or that it comes from the Gaelic 'Ard Thor' ('Thor's height'). Impressive **view** over most of the city, the Pentland Hills to S, and the Ochils (marking beginning of the Highlands) and the Firth of Forth to N.

[d] **St Anthony's Chapel** above St Margaret's Loch, is probably 15th-century. This and the nearby St Margaret's Well seem both to have been connected with curing the eye disorder called St Anthony's Fire; James I founded a hospital at Leith in 1430 for combating the disorder.

Firth of Forth: Dalmeny and the Forth Bridges

A consistently interesting coastal walk on level tracks from the edge of Edinburgh, through woods and parkland and ending at the spectacular Forth Bridges. No dogs allowed. Return from South Queensferry by bus (frequent services; half-hourly service on Sun). Ferry operates 9-7 Apr to Sept; 10-4, Oct to Mar; closed for lunch 1-2. Queensferry Gate closes at 9pm in summer and 6pm in winter.

Length 5¹/₂ miles (9km), 2¹/₂ hours
Difficulty 1–2
Start Cramond Brig Hotel, on A90 on W edge of Edinburgh; follow signs for Firth of Forth Bridge from city centre, and hotel is on right at edge of built-up area (walkers may use hotel car park). Grid reference 178756
OS maps 1:50,000 65; 1:25,000 NT 07/17 (Pathfinder 406)
Refreshments Cramond Brig Hotel at start; pub at Cramond; tea-room at Dalmeny House for house visitors; pubs and shops in Queensferry

WALK DIRECTIONS

(1) Take road called Cramond Brig Toll (just to left of hotel as seen from main road) to cross bridge [**a**], then immediately left into Dowie's Mill Lane to follow river until reaching ferry stage near estuary at Cramond (2) [**b**].

Cross river by ferry. On other side, go through turnstile at cottage and pick up path close to shore; this soon enters woods [**c**]. (3) Path later passes houses on your right; after them cross tarmacked driveway and take grassy woodland path opposite.

Soon emerge from woods, go over footbridge and go around right-hand (seaward) side of golf course [**d**], at end of which (4) turn left as

signposted (sea wall ahead to castle is private) to join tarmacked driveway which turn right (or left if you want to visit Dalmeny House).

(5) After ¹/₄ mile, where woods on left end, fork right as signposted on to track (left fork, the continuation of the tarmacked driveway, goes over cattle-grid and is signed

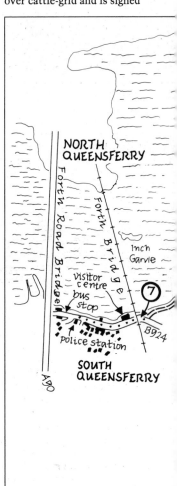

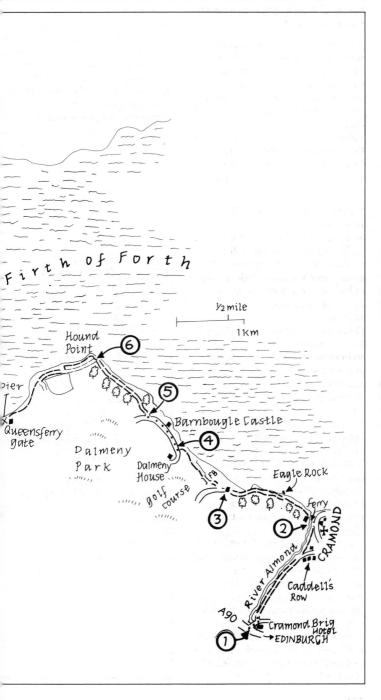

Firth of Forth

½ mile

1 km

Hound Point

⑥

Queensferry gate

⑤

Barnbougle Castle

④

Dalmeny Park

Dalmeny House

Eagle Rock

golf course

FB

③

Ferry

②

CRAMOND

River Almond

Caddell's Row

A90

①

Cramond Brig Hotel

EDINBURGH

'private'). **⑥** Where track bends left (in woods) it is worth detouring to right out to Hound Point for view of bridges [e]; there is a well-defined path leading back on to the track from here.

Continue along the track, close to coast; eventually join road **⑦** and go under rail bridge, past visitor centre and into centre of South Queensferry [f]; the bus stop for buses back to Cramond and Edinburgh is on the right just after police station.

ON THE ROUTE

[a] The **bridge** (Cramond Brig) is triple-arched, in a lovely situation on the River Almond; remains of a water-mill are seen later by the river.

[b] The old maltings, whitewashed cottages and the boat scene contribute to the strong local colour of **Cramond**. The road rising from here leads past the church, next to which are the foundations of a Roman fort, built AD142 to guard the harbour and thought to have been used by Septimus Severus in AD208 when mounting his expedition in NE Scotland; the site has been used for Christian worship since the 6th century. From the esplanade you can detour East, or venture on to a causeway leading out to Cramond Island.

[c] **Eagle Rock** is on the shore (just visible from path); a plaque records that it might (or might not) be a Roman carving, depicting what could be an eagle.

[d] Dalmeny House comes into view close by on your left built in 1815 for the Earls of Rosebery (who married into the Rothschilds), and the first house in Scotland in Tudor-Gothic revival style. The Rothschild and Rosebery collections include fine 17th- and 18th-century furniture, porcelain and portraits an the hall has a noted hammerbeam roof. Open May-Sept, Sun-Thur, 2-5 Nearby Barnbougle Castle is part of the estate (private).

[e] The **Forth Railway Bridge** (1882-89) was the engineering wonder of its age, with a total span of 1 mile 1,005 yards, 135 acres of painted surface (requiring continuous repainting on a four-year cycle) and carrying the railway 157ft above the water. The cantilever design was by John Fowler and Benjamin Baker. Below it is the islet of **Inchgarvie**, with its fort (defended against Cromwell and rebuilt 1779). When the **Forth Road Bridge** opened in 1964 its 512-ft towers, 3,300ft central span, 39,000 tons of steel an 150,000 cubic yards of concrete made it the world's largest suspension bridge. In the foreground the **Forth Tanker** is a loading stage for oil from the BP Forties Field.

[f] By the rail bridge the **Forth Bridges visitor centre** has an informative display; open 9-7 daily. Boat trips from here operate in summer to **Inchcolm Island**, which has a well-preserved abbey and a grey seal colony; for bookings telephone 031-331 1454. The attractive village of South Queensferry lost its 900-year old status as a ferry stage when the road bridge was built; the 'queen' was Queen Margaret (Malcolm Canmore's wife) who used to pass this way around 1070 to and from Edinburgh and her palace and abbey near Dunfermline.

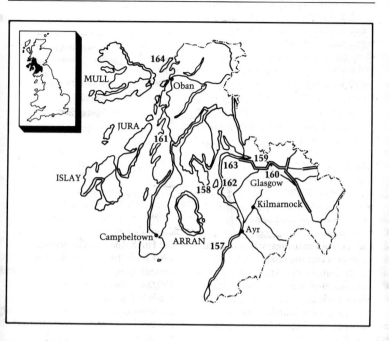

157 Culzean
158 South Bute and St Blane's Chapel
159 Glasgow's West End
160 Central Glasgow
161 Dunardry and the Crinan Canal
162 Kelburn and Fairlie Glens
163 Greenock Cut
164 Lismore

Holiday Which? Good Walks Guide

177 Falls of Clyde and New Lanark   178 A tour of the Craignish
Peninsula   179 A Scottish Stonehenge: Nether Largie Linear Cemetery
180 Inveraray and Dunchuach Tower   181 Isle of Kerrera   182 Craigend and
Mugdock Castles

Culzean

A great castle estate (now a country park), with much to see and many quiet tracks in delightful mixed woodland with occasional patches of more open parkland. Walk begins and ends with a stroll along a big sandy beach. Park facilities are closed in winter, but there is free pedestrian access all year round.

Length *Full walk* 4½ miles (7km), 2½ hours. *Short walk* (omitting old railway track) 3½ miles (5.5km), 2 hours

Difficulty 1

Start Maidens village, SW of Ayr. Turn off A77 NE into Ardlochan Road (which runs along sea-front) and start from unsigned car park on left just before 'no through road' sign, after speed derestriction sign and opposite house No 99. Grid reference 216083
Alternatively start in Culzean Country Park and park at Swan Pond car park at ③ (fee for cars, free for pedestrians; start walk with car park on your left). Grid reference 225095

OS maps 1:50,000 70; 1:25,000 NS 20/30 and NS 21/31 (Pathfinder 491 and 479)

Refreshments Restaurant at visitor centre and snack bar by main car park in Culzean Country Park

WALK DIRECTIONS

① Take path from car park past toilets to beach where turn right [**a**].

② Just after last house visible (by caravan site) turn right inland and immediately left on track to reach gate by lodge where continue forward to enter estate on track.

Soon pass cottage, then 100 yards later go through barrier where continue forward. Track becomes surfaced park road, passing Swan Pond car park on your left ③ (with pavilion-like gothic building close by); 150 yards after the track has

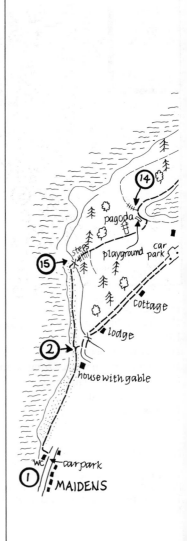

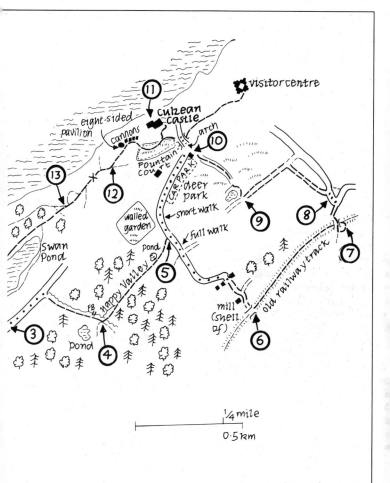

1/4 mile
0.5 km

become surfaced park road, turn right on broad path with pond and channelised stream on left.

Avoid footbridge on left after 250 yards, but 50 yards later ④ turn left at cross-junction. Follow path through semi-exotic woodland [**b**] to reach T-junction with surfaced driveway ⑤.

For short walk turn left, then turn right at gateway of walled garden on left, and follow driveway past Camellia House and main car park (tourist information) at ⑩ then turn left through archway into Culzean Castle. Pick up directions at ⑪.

For full walk turn right to follow signs for disused railway; driveway bends left at estate house then immediately bends right (now unsurfaced). Ignore left turn after 100 yards (remains of mill are seen to right of track [**c**]), and proceed to reach old railway bridge over the track ⑥.

Go up rough path on to the old railway and turn left along it [**d**]. ⑦ Just after bridge overhead, take steps on right and turn right again to cross the bridge. After 100 yards, reach surfaced drive where keep left [**e**]; ⑧ 100 yards after, turn left on surfaced track down edge of field to T-junction, where turn left on level track.

⑨ Immediately on reaching woods take path on right, down right edge of the woods and around right-hand side of Fire Pond [**f**]. After 50 yards, just after path bends left (continuing to encircle pond) take steps on right to stile, then descend on path between high fences enclosing deer park.

Emerge by tourist information and main car park ⑩. Detour left past Camellia House (right) to walled garden [**g**]; but route continues to right, then left through archway into Culzean Castle. As you go over the bridge beyond the archway, notice

track underneath: the detour to the right along the track to the visitor centre is recommended [**h**].

⑪ From castle [**i**], with castle main door behind you, take gateway on right to join top of terrace, with Fountain Court (gardens) [**j**] down on your left and the castle on your right. Pass cannons, then take steps down on left into Fountain Court and turn right at the bottom past a conservatory. Just after, take small gate on right and cross the grass towards the sea to find row of cannons [**k**] ranged along a gravel path; turn left along this path which bends left by octagonal pavilion, then ⑫ soon bends right into woods, with sea away to right.

Avoid minor side-turns and reach barrier; ⑬ 350 yards later reach major fork (*right fork*, which you might like to try as a variant, descends and continues along cliffs before dropping down steps to T-junction by lake, where keep right at ⑭).

Keep forward and ignore minor side-turns but soon fork right on broad path marked by log border along its left-hand side and pass around right-hand side of lake [**l**], turning left at end ⑭. Follow lakeside path round to reach adventure playground.

If you started from Swan Pond car park, carry on; otherwise turn right on track, past ruined pagoda [**m**] and continue forward to reach view over beach ⑮, then go down steps on to beach where turn left. At toilet block turn inland to reach car park.

ON THE ROUTE

[**a**] View of two islands: **Arran** and **Ailsa Craig**; the latter is 1,114ft high and just 2 miles round, with a sheer fall on its W side; once occupied by a monastic community and now a bird sanctuary. Quarried ailsite, a kind of granite from Ailsa, has been used for

making stones used in the sport of curling.

[**b**] Part of Culzean's magnificent **woodlands**, which are home to 155 **bird species**. Many trees near this path and around Happy Valley Pond are exotic specimens, including palm trees and bamboo. Britain's oldest and largest sitka spruces are also here.

[**c**] Shell of **Sunnyside Mill**, used until 1900; its wheel was removed for scrap in the last war.

[**d**] The **old railway** ran from Maidens to Dunure; opened 1906 and carried passenger traffic until 1930. View on right of **old castle**, a sandstone block adjoining a farm.

[**e**] Good view of **Culzean Castle** and the isle of **Arran**

[**f**] **Fire Pond** was created to supply water for fire-fighting, and now feeds the castle fountain. Just below, the **deer park** contains red deer which have been re-introduced.

[**g**] **Walled garden** includes kitchen and pleasure gardens; its corners are at the points of the compass.

[**h**] The **park visitor centre** is within the well-restored Home Farm, a design of Robert Adam (1777); four arched ornate entrances lead into an arcaded courtyard.

[**i**] **Culzean Castle** (National Trust for Scotland; open Apr-Oct 10-5 daily). One of Robert Adam's greatest designs, built in three phases, 1777-92, for the 10th Earl of Cassillis on the site of 16th-century Scots Tower House. Among the internal masterpieces are the oval staircase and round drawing-room. Culzean was given to Eisenhower for his lifetime.

[**j**] **Fountain Court** Two parallel terraces, ornamental fountain and herbaceous borders; at its best in July and August.

[**k**] The **battery** was placed here against a possible Napoleonic invasion.

[**l**] **Swan Pond** (13 acres), set in woods, has 700 ducks in winter, moorhens, herons and coots as well as mute swans; water lilies in summer.

[**m**] The **pagoda** was built as a romantic landscape feature.

South Bute shores and St Blane's chapel

Route takes a grand sequence of island views, following the coast before rising past the remote ruins of a monastery. Final sections, including modest summit of Suidhe Hill (but steep descent at end), can be avoided in poor visibility by using road. Ground generally firm, with patches of uneven terrain; route not always defined.

Length 5½ miles (9km), 3½ hours
Difficulty 4
Start S end of Kilchattan, on Isle of Bute at end of road; roadside parking. Grid reference 105546
OS maps 1:50,000 63; 1:25,000 NS 05/15 (Pathfinder 428)
Refreshments Hotel and shop at Kilchattan

WALK DIRECTIONS

① [a] Continue to end of shoreside

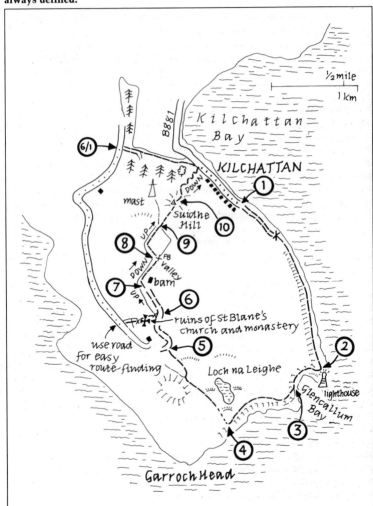

road and pick up track ahead; beyond gate, this narrows to path, leading along grass just above shore level [b]. ② At lighthouse keep close to shore (path scarcely defined), around Glancallum Bay [c]; on far side of there are two paths ③: take the upper one, rising and soon round the slope above the shore. Later this becomes less well defined, and lake (Loch na Leighe), close on right, comes into view [d].

④ Immediately after passing the loch, turn right to proceed close to its left side. The easiest route loses sight of loch; beyond the loch do not go too far left but soon pick up track heading towards Plan Farm. Do not go as far as the farm – instead, ⑤ pick up well-defined stony track 100 yards to right, which can be seen curving round along a valley to right of, and a short distance before, the farm, then heading up towards trees. ⑥ As soon as fence begins on left-hand side of track, make a detour left through gate to see St Blane's Chapel [e].

Route back to Kilchattan via road, avoiding hill walk. Descend hill from the chapel to reach kissing-gate, then follow path down edge of fields until gate gives access on to road; turn right along road. After 2 miles, woodland begins on right. 150 yards later, soon after milestone on left, turn right on woodland track, initially following power-lines. Track narrows to path width and continues along left edge of wood to reach road at Kilchattan. Turn right to reach starting point.

Route back via Suidhe Hill (steep descent at end; route-finding quite easy in good visibility). Return to track, turn left along it to continue uphill. ⑦ At top of slope, track ends (barn visible close by to right): here, continue forward, alongside fence on left, soon bending right as

fence does the same, and drop into slight valley ⑧ .

Here continue to keep alongside fence, which now bends left; soon cross footbridge and go through gate. 100 yards later, at end of enclosure turn right uphill (alongside fence on left); a mast soon comes into view. ⑨ At top of enclosure enter open land at fence corner and head for top of Suidhe Hill (the obvious hill to right of mast). It is easiest to ascend by keeping to right. At top, cross stile to reach trig point (summit pillar) ⑩ [f].

Pick up narrow path on other side leading steeply down to Kilchattan, skirting woods and dropping to road and house. Turn right to starting point.

ON THE ROUTE
[a] **Kilchattan** was named after Cattan, a 6th-century saint .
[b] This grassy strip is one of the many examples of a Scottish west coast **raised beach**, now just above sea level. Excellent **views** of Great Cumbrae Island close up, Little Cumbrae Island to the right; to the S, the lone granite island of Ailsa Craig towers 1,114ft; later the Isle of Arran should be visible, with Goat Fell (2,866ft) its highest point.
[c] A striking **sill** of hard, grey rock protrudes across the bay, overgrown ruins remain here of an **old inn**.
[d] The loch is rich in wildlife, including **teal** and **tufted duck**.
[e] Remains of the splendidly sited **St Blane's chapel and monastery** in a sheltered glade looking down to the coast. Founded in the 6th century, its last church minister was ordained in the 1700s. The ruined Norman chapel with its archway is the most prominent feature.
[f] Spectacular **view** over Arran, Kintyre, the Cumbraes, Bute and the mainland.

583

Glasgow's West End

The university area: leafy parks and a charming river walk add rural touches to a route that includes some fine 19th-century streets and a number of free museums of national importance.

Length 3 miles (5.5km), 3 hours
Difficulty 1
Start Royal Botanic Gardens main gate, Great Western Road (A82); frequent buses from city centre
By underground start from Kelvin Bridge station at ⑦
Refreshments Plenty around Great Western Road; café in Kelvingrove Museum

WALK DIRECTIONS

① Cross Queen Margaret Drive by pelican crossing and walk along Buckingham Terrace [**a**] (lining N side of Great Western Road, heading towards city centre). Cross Great Western Road by second set of traffic lights, (just after Ruskin Place on left) to take steps opposite into Hillhead Street. At end continue forward past university library and Hunterian Gallery [**b**] to reach University Avenue [**c**] where ② turn left [**d**].

After passing university, turn right on unsigned road (Kelvin Way; parking on both sides). ③ Take second turn on right into park (at statue of Kelvin) and continue forward initially towards big 19th-century building (Kelvingrove Museum) and proceed along river path [**e**].

Follow to reach main road where turn left. Immediately after crossing bridge, fork left to Kelvingrove Museum [**f**]. Go round to left of the museum to reach river bridge (do not cross) and ④ enter Kelvingrove Park opposite: follow main park road, which immediately bends left.

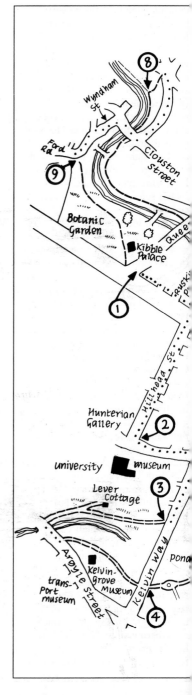

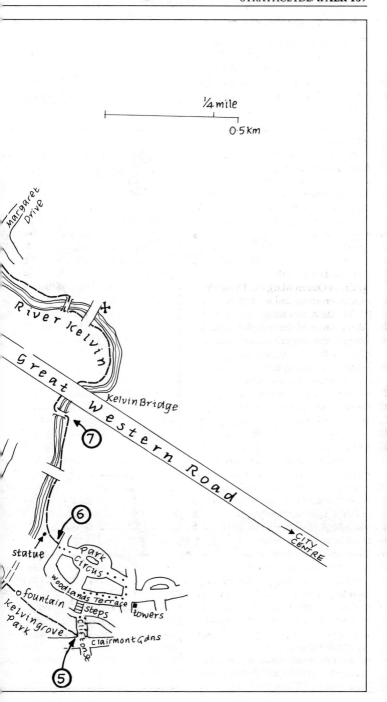

¼ mile

0·5 km

Margaret Drive

River Kelvin

X

Great Western Road

Kelvin Bridge

⑦

⑥

statue

Park Circus

Woodlands Terrace

fountain

steps

towers

Kelvingrove Park

Cliff Ons

Clairmont Gdns

⑤

CITY CENTRE

As soon as you reach pond on left, take path on right past ornate fountain and pick up straight path beyond, reaching road at prominent classical church ⑤. Turn left up Clifton Street and at end of street continue up steps and turn right along Woodlands Terrace [g] to reach tall towers where turn left and left again into Park Circus Place. Go around either side of Park Circus to leave by Park Gate opposite.

⑥ Cross road at T-junction, to re-enter Kelvingrove Park. At equestrian statue of Earl Roberts, bear half right on descending path, to pick up riverside path [h], soon under road bridge. ⑦ Just before next road bridge (Kelvin Bridge), cross footbridge and continue now with river on right.

After next bridge (with church on top), path crosses river by footbridge, then goes under Queen Margaret Bridge (here you can cut off a section of the walk by crossing next footbridge, taking steps up on left to reach Kibble Palace and leaving Botanic Gardens by main gate to finish walk). Carry on under next major bridge (with marble columns).

⑧ 200 yards later fork right to leave riverside and go up to road. Turn right on road and right again opposite Clouston Street to cross the marble topped bridge you have just passed under. Take the first left on other side (Wyndham Street, unsigned), which soon bends right to reach junction with Ford Road ⑨. Here turn left into Botanic Gardens [i] (do not confuse with stretches of riverside passed earlier which also have Botanic Gardens signs). Make your way across to glasshouses (Kibble Palace); leave by main gate.

ON THE ROUTE

[a] **Buckingham Terrace** Typical of the dignified West End terraces, this was built by J.T.Rochead in 1852

and has balconies at either end to make it a formal composition. Grosvenor Terrace (now Grosvenor Hotel) behind and on the other side of the road, by the same architect but recently rebuilt after a fire, has Venetian influence in its rounded window-heads.

[b] On the right, the **Hunterian Art Gallery** (open 9.30-5 Mon-Fri, 9.30-1 Sat; closed Sun) is famed for its **Mackintosh Wing**, a reconstruction of the house of Charles Rennie Mackintosh (1868-1928), the foremost architect and designer of the art nouveau movement in Glasgow, who lived nearby. As well as his highly individual interior designs, there are over 600 of his sketches and water-colours. The gallery also has a noted Whistler collection, and Scottish and European art are represented.

[c] **Gilmorehill Building** A major part of Glasgow University, a grandiose design in Gothic revival style, with vaulted undercrofts and a huge turreted tower, by George Gilbert Scott. The university was founded by Papal Bull in 1451 (making it the fourth oldest British university); its 17th-century buildings were in the High Street until the university moved to this site in 1872. One survival from the old building is the **Lion and Unicorn Staircase**, which was rebuilt by the large green (called the Square; the staircase is unmistakable).

On the S side is a view over the city from the building's façade; the terrestrial stone globe is thought to have been made by Lord Kelvin or his father, James Thompson (Professor of Mathematics, 1832-49). Attached to the building is the **Hunterian Museum**, Scotland's first museum when it opened in 1807, built to house the collection of coins, manuscripts, paintings, South Seas curios, zoological specimens and more, gathered by William Hunter (1718-83) who was Doctor of Medicine, Professor of Anatomy and Physician Extraordinary to Queen Charlotte (open 9.30-5 Mon-Fri, 9.30-1 Sat; closed Sun).

d] On left, **Wellington Church** was built in 1883 to the classical design of T.L.Watson, a pupil of Waterhouse.

e] A sharp right turn just before the road leads to a pair of mock-Tudor cottages, sole survivors of the 1901 exhibition: these are replicas of workers' cottages at Port Sunlight, a Cheshire garden village designed by Lord Leverhulme (of Sunlight Soap fame).

f] **Kelvingrove Museum** (open 10-5; 2-5 Sun). Palatial sandstone building, opened 1902 with bequests from local industrialists. Worth a look into the main hall, with its organ and bas-reliefs of the great composers all round. The museum covers a broad range of subjects, including fine arts, archaeology, science and natural history. Opposite is the **Museum of Transport** (open 10-5; 2-5 Sun).

[g] **Park Conservation Area** The grandest townscape in the West End, and perhaps the finest mid-19th-century development of its kind in the country, on a hill-top site with glimpses of the Campsie Fells N of the city; an oval 'circus' forms the central feature. The three Lombard towers are part of the former Trinity College (now antique showrooms), first built as the Free Church College; the church was later converted into a library.

[h] **River Kelvin Walkway** This green corridor can be walked from central Glasgow to the edge of the city. Here it passes along a wooded gorge, below a series of imposing 19th-century bridges.

[i] **Botanic Gardens** (open in daylight hours). World-famous for its orchids and ferns. The Chronological Border groups plants according to when they were introduced to Britain. The **Kibble Palace**, an outstanding example of a 19th-century iron conservatory, has white statues amid its exotic tree ferns (open 10-4.45; closes 4.15 in winter).

Central Glasgow

A look at the architecture of the city centre, perhaps the finest concentration of Victorian buildings in Britain. The route takes in a stretch of the river and the length of Glasgow Green for a tranquil contrast.

Length 2¹⁄₂ miles (4km), 3 hours
Difficulty 1
Start George Square, by column and City Chambers
Refreshments Plenty in centre; café in People's Palace

WALK DIRECTIONS

(1) [a] With City Chambers behind you, leave George Square by St Vincent Place (ahead and to left) [b], take first right (Buchanan Street, left by St George's Tron church into Nelson Mandela Place [c] and continue along West George Street [d]. (2) Left into Hope Street [e], left into Gordon Street, past Glasgow Central rail station [f] then turn right into Union Street [g][h] (which becomes Jamaica Street) [i]. (3) At end cross by traffic lights and turn left on river Clyde walkway, past suspension bridge [j] and continuing alongside river along Clyde Street to enter Glasgow Green via main park gates (by green statue) (4) [k]. Take path across the green, past ornate fountain [l] and obelisk to reach People's Palace (annexed to glass building of Winter Palace) [m][n].

Return same way across green, past obelisk again. Just before main gate by which you entered park, and immediately after children's playground on right, turn right to continue into Turnbull Street (5). Turn left opposite St Andrew's church [o], into St Andrew's Street. Turn right at main road (Saltmarket) and left at traffic lights at major junction [p], into Trongate [q].

(6) Turn right into Candleriggs,

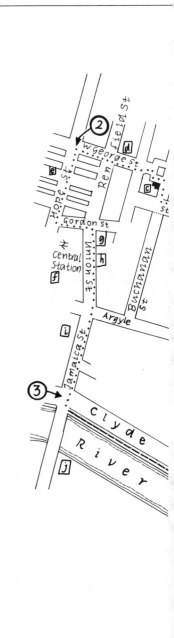

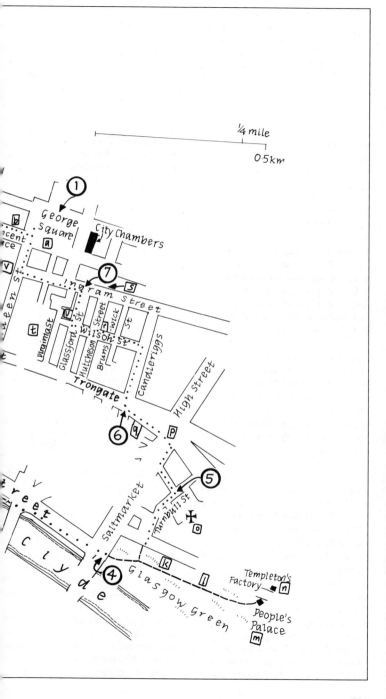

¼ mile

0·5 km

① George Square

City Chambers

ⓑ

ncent ce

ⓥ

ⓐ

⑦ Ⓢ

Ingram Street

en St

ⓣ

ⓥ Virginia St.

Glassford St.

Wilson Street

Hutcheson St.

Brunswick St.

Candleriggs

High Street

Trongate

⑥ ⓠ

ⓟ

ⓥ

Saltmarket

⑤

Turnbull St

✝ ⓞ

reet

ⓥ

Clyde

④ Glasgow Green

ⓚ

ⓛ

Templeton's Factory ■ ⓝ

◆ People's Palace

ⓜ

left into Wilson Street [r][s][t] then right into Glassford Street [u].
⑦ Turn left into Ingram Street towards Royal Exchange [v], where turn right along Queen Street to enter George Square.

ON THE ROUTE

[a] **George Square** Marks the present-day centre of Glasgow. The square was laid out in 1781, and later became the hotel centre; the hotel on the NW side is the only original building left. Occupying the E side, the Italian renaissance-style **City Chambers** has opulent interiors with much show of marble and ornament, while outside its tower soars to 216ft; guided tours are available. **Merchant House** on the other side is the headquarters of the oldest chamber of commerce in Britain. The representation of **Sir Walter Scott** is the centre-piece of the statuary in the middle of the square, but the 80ft column was originally intended for a statue of George III.

[b] Two fine bank buildings, the **Bank of Scotland and Clydesdale Bank** (both on right) are typical of the confident 19th-century commercial architecture of the city centre as Glasgow prospered with the advent of ship-building and heavy industry. The grid-shaped street pattern, noticeable straight away, is an important feature of the city's plan.

[c] **Stock Exchange House** (on left). Venetian Gothic, with massive arcades, by John Burnet (1877), with extension by J.J. Burnet junior (1895, 1904).

[d] **Royal Faculty of Procurators** (on right), by Charles Wilson, 1854; has a splendid Venetian interior.

[e] **No. 142-44 Vincent Street** (on right at junction with Hope Street) Known as the 'Hatrack' because of its appearance: a ten-storey building squeezed into a 29ft frontage. Its

design by James Salmon (1899) makes ingenious use of windows, maximising the light and minimising stonework. There are art nouveau flourishes in the details.

[f] **Central Station and Hotel** (1884). Grand design, with ornate cast-iron entrance, signalling the advent of the Caledonian Railway which bridged the Clyde in the 1870s.

[g] **Ca d'Oro** At the corner of Union Street and Gordon Street, and now a bookshop; 1872 by John Honeyman, recently rebuilt after a fire. An innovative use of iron and glass, with unusual window tracery. The original was built as a furniture warehouse.

[h] On left, **Nos. 84-100 (Egyptian Halls)**; 1873 by James Thompson, who designed a number of city warehouses, this being the last to survive. On the top floor a detached glass curtain wall stands beyond the façade of Grecian columns.

[i] **Gardner's Warehouse**, on right; John Baird, 1856. A very early use of the iron frame which revolutionised architecture in the late 19th century and 20th century, ending the need for thick load-bearing walls and allowing for much more glass on the outside. Here the rounded windows produce a particularly pleasing effect.

[j] **The Clyde** The riverside walkway passes under the **suspension bridge**, with its Grecian triumphal arches at either end; a detour on to the centre of this footbridge is recommended for river views. On the other side, **Carlton Place** (1802, recently restored) is the city's earliest street with a symmetrical plan, although it is incomplete. Beyond are the 1960s high-rise tower blocks of the Gorbals, replacing a notorious slum area. Just after the railway bridge, a daily second-hand market known as **Paddy's Market** operating in a cramped site by the bridge's arches,

...as 19th-century origins. At the far end, bizarrely exposed, is the gleaming **St Enoch's Shopping Centre**, the world's largest 'glass tent' with its 17-pyramid roof structures over a 6½ hectare (16 acre) site.

k] Glasgow Green The city's common was previously used for grazing, executions and free speech. A stone commemorates the place where James Watt was inspired, while out on a Sunday walk, to improve the steam engine.

l] Doulton Fountain (1888), in the middle of the Green. Queen Victoria atop, her peoples underneath, including panels to Canada, India, South Africa and Australia. A most fetching piece of Victoriana, sadly vandalised. A few yards on, to the left, is **McGlennan Arch**, removed from the demolished Assembly Rooms, designed by R and Adam (1796).

m] People's Palace (open 10-5; Sun 2-5). Opened in 1898 as a cultural centre for the east end, now a museum outlining the social history of Glasgow. The adjacent **Winter Gardens** is a glasshouse in high-Victorian spirit, containing exotic plants and shrubs.

n] Across the road from the People's Palace is the astonishing front of the former **Templeton's Carpet Factory**, a dazzling composition in multi-coloured brick and tile, modelled on the Doge's Palace in Venice. The architect was William Leiper (1889).

o] St Andrew's Church (1756) A handsome, slender steeple in the local style; splendid interior Rococo plasterwork by Thomas Clyton who also worked on Drum and Blair castles.

p] The crossroads, known as **Glasgow Cross**, marks the heart of Glasgow up to the 19th century. The **Tolbooth Steeple** (1626) is all that survives of the New Tolbooth (town hall).

[q] Tron Steeple, on left, projecting over the pavement, is the remains of a 1636 church burned down by the Hellfire Club in 1793.

[r] Court Houses and County Buildings, by Clarke and Bell (1844), a neo-classical building erected when the commercial city started growing rapidly.

[s] View to right, along Hutcheson Street, of **Hutcheson's Hall**. Built 1805 as a charitable institution to provide accommodation for poor elderly men and orphan boys. Now a National Trust for Scotland visitor centre.

[t] Virginia Street, straight ahead, is the best surviving early 19th-century street in the merchant city. **No.33** is an old tobacco or sugar exchange; the window over its entrance is believed to have been an auctioneer's box.

[u] Trades House, on left, (1774) by Robert Adam. Much re-done inside, but the façade is original; the architrave around the main door and the end bays are later additions.

[v] Former Royal Exchange (now lending library). Originally the mansion of William Cunningham, a tobacco lord. Fine coffered ceiling, window mouldings and panelled pilasters inside.

Note Since the city centre is tiring to walk around, we have deliberately omitted two further-flung sites of great interest. If you are trying to see all of the centre in one go, don't miss Charles Rennie Mackintosh's art nouveau masterpiece, **The Glasgow School of Art**, signposted off Sauchiehall Street. **Cathedral Square**, at the top of High Street, is the heart of pre-Reformation Glasgow; here is the cathedral and Provand's Lordship (1471; a prebendal manse, and the oldest house in the city).

Dunardry and the Crinan Canal

A short exploration of the northern fringe of Knapdale Forest, using easily followed tracks (partly waymarked): the canal towpath provides the return route.

Length 5 miles (8km), 2½ hours
with extension to Crinan 9 miles
(14.5km) 4½ hours
Difficulty 1–2
Start Bellanoch (signed on road), by junction of B841 and B8025, NW of Lochgilphead; limited roadside parking near garage, or park on other side of B8025 bridge; (you can also start from car park for signed Dunardry Forest Walk, ½ mile W of

Cairnbaan, and follow the canal section at the start of the walk; return to road to begin directions at ⑧). Grid reference 804924
OS maps 1:50,000 55; 1:25,000 NR 79/89 (Pathfinder 377)
Refreshments Shop at Bellanoch; hotel at Crinan

WALK DIRECTIONS

① With canal on left, follow B841 towards Lochgilphead. ② After ¼ mile, where road bends slightly left, take forest track on right, which winds up to reach junction after 200 yards: turn left (through gate) [a].
③ 300 yards later turn left at next junction (soon joined by power-lines on left).

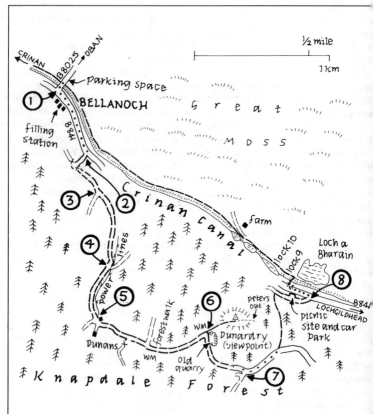

(4) After 600 yards, turn right at
xt junction (oblique T-junction),
ill with power-lines on left.
) Emerge between barn (on left)
d house (Dunans) and continue
rward on hard forestry track.
1ore later side-turns to right and
en to left (at the latter there is a
:llow footprint waymarker
dicating Dunardry Forest Walk
hich you now follow until
ain road).
(6) Track bends right in front of
1arry: here detour left up
aymarked path to reach viewpoint
]. Return to track, which becomes
rmacked. **(7)** Keep left at next
nction (keeping to main track;
ere is now a stream on your right.
ok for yellow waymarker on left
ter 150 yards (just before track
osses the stream), and take path
rough woods, soon dropping to
ack where turn right to reach car
urk and go down to road **(8)**.
Turn left on road, then just after
rst house on right, cross footbridge
vay to right and go over canal lock.
:ft on canal towpath (avoid a track
hich goes closely parallel initially,
it soon veers to right, away from
nal) [c]. Reach road bridge, and
rn left to cross it and return to

starting point (*or* continue along
canal 2 miles to Crinan [d]; return
same way).

ON THE ROUTE
[a] **Knapdale Forest** One of the
Forestry Commission's vast Argyll
plantations, at N end of the Kintyre
peninsula; occasional views of lochs
within the forest.
[b] Extensive view N over **Moine
Mhor** (or Great Moss), a fen-like
plain of fertile green fields, densely
strewn with prehistoric burial sites,
forts and other antiquities. NNE is
the great rock of **Dunadd**, where
Fergus landed in AD498; the hillock
was the site of the first recorded
British coronation in AD574;
Dunadd was the capital of the
ancient kingdom of Dalriada until
around AD900.
[c] The 9-mile **Crinan Canal**, opened
1801, avoids an 80-mile trip around
the Mull of Kintyre, and connects
Loch Gilp at Ardrishaig to the sea at
Crinan. There are 15 locks on it; the
Dunardry Rolling Bridge at lock 11,
installed in 1900, is wound by hand
and something of a rarity.
[d] At **Crinan** there is a pleasant
boating scene with yachts and
fishing craft.

Kelburn and Fairlie Glens

A nicely varied route taking in two glens, each with a waterfall and castle linked by a high-level section along the edge of the moors looking down over the coast and islands. Moorland section may be boggy in places, but paths up and down glens are well-maintained.

The Kelburn grounds are open all year (11 to 5 winter, 10 to 6 Easter to Oct) except Christmas, and Saturday, November to January. The Kelburn Country Centre, which organises pony-trekking, trails and has a 'pets' corner', is closed in winter months, when entrance fee is reduced.

Length 4½ miles (7km), 2½ hours
Difficulty 3
Start Kelburn Country Centre car park (admission fee), just E of A78 and S of Largs.
Grid reference 215564
By train Fairlie. Leave station, turn right by station sign on to enclosed tarmacked path, soon over stream (Fairlie Burn) then immediately turn right (at cottage), to cross over railway. Carry on up path close to stream to reach Fairlie Castle; continue up track to left of castle to reach gate on left with stone gateposts (one of which has fallen). This is point ⑩.
OS maps 1:50,000 63; 1:25,000 NS 25/35 (Pathfinder 429); path map of Kelburn estate from Country Centre
Refreshments Café at Country Centre

WALK DIRECTIONS

① Turn right out of car park, take first track on right, to pass Country Centre and then saw-mill on your right, and 100 yards after take steps down on left signposted Gardens and Monument. Path crosses stream by footbridge; bear right on other side (signposted Glen and Monument;

left goes into the Plaisance [a]) soon passing castle [b] and continuing along N side of the glen.

Just after castle, fork right (signposted Kelburn Bridge) for view of waterfall from above [c]. Immediately before the footbridge, fork left on to path to rejoin N glen path, and 20 yards later, fork right (left goes up steps) to pass monument [d].

② 200 yards later, fork right down steps down to footbridge; do not cross it but turn right downstream to another footbridge. After 100 yards, by wooden railing, turn left a path junction to follow path along S side of glen with view of glen down on left; keep left at T-junction 250 yards later, and 100 yards further on ③ fork right up steps.

④ Reach broad track at top of glen and stone bridge; turn right (signposted Upper Estate Road South). At cross-junction out of woods with house visible ahead, turn sharp left, through gate and proceed alongside fence on left to reach double gate ⑤. Turn sharp right on well-defined track alongside fence and wall on right [e].

Track eventually leaves the wall, and goes under power-lines; then ⑥ forks right. Track narrows to path, rejoins the wall and power-lines and later disappears (it can be boggy here), but wall is your guide. Later ⑦, step across stream (deeply incised into hillside). ⑧ Soon after forest on right ends, cross fixed gate (Fairlie Glen is immediately ahead) and immediately turn right through gate to follow well-defined path down right-hand side of Fairlie Glen initially with wall on left.

⑨ Just before power-lines, path enters woods: here it is worth detouring left a few yards, on streamside path up glen, to reach waterfall [f]. Proceed on path down, soon past bench then past gateway

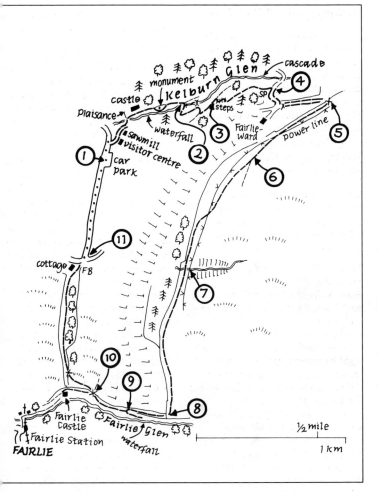

n right with stone gate-posts (one
as fallen). After detouring ahead to
ee Fairlie Castle [**g**], go through
his gateway.

⑩ Immediately turn left
ownhill alongside wall on left until
evel with the castle to reach strip of
rees at bottom of this field. Turn
ight, with strip of trees on left, soon
iving access to path within this
trip. Pass cottage close on your left:
ontinue forward to reach
ootbridge, then **⑪** continue
orward again at three-way road

junction (along the level) and follow
to reach car park.

ON THE ROUTE
[**a**] **The Plaisance**, a formal part-
walled garden, contains two 1,000-
year-old yews. Just before entering,
look on the left for the 100-ft tall
Monterey Pine, the oldest and tallest
of its kind in Scotland, and the
weeping larch, a unique mutant
whose branches touch the ground
and reseed, sprawling across half
an acre.

[b] **Kelburn Castle**, home of the Earls of Glasgow, was originally a Norman keep but has been adapted; the door was moved to the south side in 1581 (date-stone is visible from the path, with the initials of the then baird John Boyle). Open on afternoons in spring.

[c] The **waterfall** drops 20ft into a chasm with sandstone overhangs.

[d] **Monument** of 1775 to the third Earl of Glasgow, placed at his favourite spot and designed by Robert Adam.

[e] Wide **views** in this section, of Great and Little Cumbrae (islands), Toward Point, Bute, Arran, Kintyre and Ailsa Craig.

[f] Fine **waterfall** in wooded Fairlie Glen.

[g] **Fairlie Castle**, a small 16th-century keep, stands over 30ft high. There is no way over the wall from the castle, hence the need to retrace steps back to the stone gateposts.

reenock Cut

**level walk along an historic water-
course, with extensive views most of
e way, after an opening section
st reservoirs. Easy route-finding.**

ngth 7 miles (11km), 3 hours
ifficulty 1
art Clyde Muirshiel Regional Park
entre car park at Cornalees Bridge,
of Greenock; take signposted road
Loch Thom from A78.
rid reference 247722
S maps 1:50,000 63; 1:25,000 NS
/37 (Pathfinder 402)
efreshments Snack van in car park
start at most summer weekends

ALK DIRECTIONS

*you plan to follow the nature trail
r final section of walk, you may
ke to get the free leaflet from Park*
*Centre in car park before starting
the walk.*

(1) Turn left out of car park, on to
reservoir road ('no entry' sign refers
to vehicles only); pass
Compensation Reservoir then Loch
Thom (2) [a] (where road becomes an
unsurfaced track) on your right;
ignore minor side-turns [b]. (3) Reach
gate and house by water channel
(Greenock Cut); cross channel [c].
On other side, turn left on path
along Greenock Cut. (4) After 3
miles cross road and continue
alongside the Cut opposite.
Either follow path all the way back
to Cornalees Bridge by car park.
Or soon fork right at nature trail
signpost on to path leading along
bottom of valley [d]; the trail then
(5) turns left along duckboards, to
reach Kelly Cut (6), along which

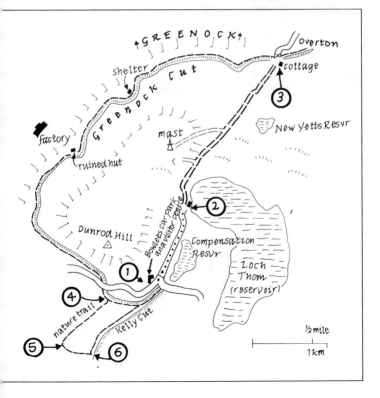

turn left to reach road at Cornalees Bridge by car park.

ON THE ROUTE

[a] These **reservoirs** fed the Greenock Cut (see below). After them, a track on the left leads to a fine **viewpoint** by a large mast.

[b] The first views open up, and are with you for most of the walk. **Greenock**, a port and ship-building centre, sprawls below – one of Britain's most dramatically sited industrial towns, looking over the Clyde to the SW Highlands; Gare Loch is to N, Loch Long and Holy Loch to NW; the many peaks in sight include Ben Lomond (3,192ft) to NNE and Beinn Chaorach (2,338ft) to N. Greenock's most prominent older building is the 245ft municipal Victoria Tower of 1886. James Watt, inventor of the steam engine, was born in the town in 1736.

[c] **Greenock Cut** An aqueduct system encircling the hill, built in 1827 by Robert Thom. Following Thom's successful scheme for creating a water supply for his Ayrshire factory, the local MP asked him to engineer a similar scheme to solve Greenock's water shortage. Water was let down to the town by sluices and contained falls of varying power tailored to the needs of its users. The opening ceremony was marked by the firing of a cannon, cheering crowds and decorated boats; soon the Cut served 31 mills (the only fall to survive is about 50 yards to the right as you reach the Cut; the cottage here was built at the time of the Cut for the sluice-keeper). As the town's fringes crept uphill, risk of contamination increased and since maintenance was becoming costly, the Cut was abandoned in 1968 and a tunnel was built from Loch Thom to Overton. The Cut is now designated an Ancient Monument.

[d] **Nature trail** takes in a **hardwood glen** of ash, birch, oak and rowan, and **Kelly Cut**, which carried water from Kellie Reservoir near Skelmorlie to Compensation Reservoir.

ismore

**n exploration of the north end of
his island, unsurpassed for views of
och Linnhe and many of the
estern isles and peninsulas; two
astle ruins add interest. This is one
f the very finest low-level walks
cotland has to offer, but requires
areful timing to avoid missing the
st ferry, and good boots are
ssential to cope with rocky shore.**

ength 8 miles (13km), 5 hours
minimum); can shorten to 6 miles
.5km), 4 hours by following road
ack from ⑨

ifficulty 4

tart Ferry jetty at NE tip of isle of
ismore, reached by passenger ferry
om Port Appin (N of Oban; NB
ban ferries for Lismore do not go to
his jetty). Make a note of ferry
mes and time walk carefully (times
displayed at jetties, also available
from Oban tourist office); about
seven services each day; crossing
takes 10 minutes. Grid reference
894462

OS maps 1:50,000 49; 1:25,000 NM
84/94 (Pathfinder 318)

Refreshments Pub with restaurant
on mainland at Port Appin; snacks
and meals sometimes at Isle of
Lismore Guest House at ⑨

WALK DIRECTIONS

① [a] From jetty, turn right along
turf, just above low cliffs and shore.
Follow coast in this way (no path
but easy going), later past small cave
to reach disused lime-kiln on your
right [b], just after which ② take
gate on right.

Continue now along track along
shore to cottages (Port Ramsay). At
end of main row of cottages, turn

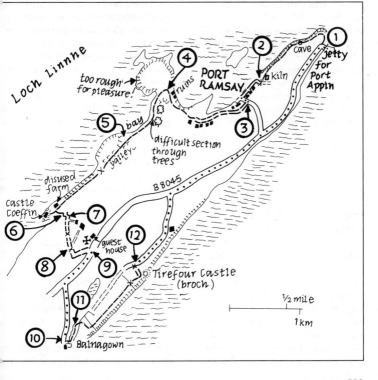

left (inland) on surfaced lane by telephone box. ③ After 50 yards turn right on gravel track, later passing houses, to reach end of track where continue forward (no path) along turf just above shore.

Pass two ruined cottages; ④ immediately after, turn left away from shore (this avoids a tricky scramble on rocks around headland), head up across grass keeping craggy hill immediately on left. Soon view opens W over bay: locate big cliff on opposite side – your objective is to follow grassy valley just to left of this.

Head across bay, crossing wall and low fence on the way. It is rough-going initially but manageable, and gets easier. ⑤ Leave the bay by ruin to enter the grassy valley; soon it is easy to divert up to higher ground on your right, and walk along the grass.

Castle Coeffin comes into view; just before you reach it, pass abandoned farm, where detour ahead to see castle [c]. Continuation of route is 50 yards after passing the abandoned farm, ⑥ turn left inland, on path leading towards prominent zigzagging (rising) track.

Follow the track up to reach gate: track then bends left, by power-post, but 50 yards later ⑦ turn sharp right on faint grassy track (as main track continues to go through wall and heads for hut where it peters out), immediately crossing stream. Keep high ground (a grassy and craggy slope) immediately on left, soon reaching gate, then continue forward along right edge of field. ⑧ At end of field, join well-defined track (go through gate) and follow it ahead. Beyond next gate, the track bends left, soon reaching farm then onto road ⑨ [d].

Easy way back Turn left along the road: an hour's brisk walking along this road will bring you to the ferry jetty. Road turning on right after ¹/₂

mile signposted for Broch avoids somewhat complex route-finding given below – follow road another ³/₄ mile then take gate on right up to the Broch; return same way and follow road back to ferry jetty.

Route avoiding (some) road-walking (route-finding less easy) Turn right on road; after ¹/₂ mile turn left, signposted Balnagown. ⑩ One field before reaching farm, take gate on left signposted to Broch and walk with fence on right. After 50 yards turn left and walk between wall on right and water channel on left; soon cross channel via plank bridge.

⑪ 20 yards before loch, take stile over wall on right to emerge on to open land, and continue uphill towards coast (or keep down just to right of loch and pass pens to pick up track, which soon becomes a surfaced farm road, until detouring through gate on right once near Broch; return to road and proceed to junction where turn right to reach ferry jetty; this is easier but misses sea views), then turn left towards the Broch (prominent circular walled structure on hillock).

To reach this, it is necessary to cross a wall (easiest to go down slope towards sea, where wall is lower and not topped with barbed wire). At Broch [e], turn left on track down to gate to farm road, where ⑫ turn right to reach T- junction with principal island road. Turn right and follow back to ferry jetty.

ON THE ROUTE

[a] **Lismore** 'Ieis More' translates from Gaelic as 'great garden'. The 9-mile long island is green and fertile, with scattered farmsteads, and its highest point only 416ft. Vertical tilting of rock strata has formed a series of valleys parallel to the sea; on a smaller scale, much of the razor-edged rock above the shore is tilted the same way. Legend has it

hat there was a boat race between
t Moluaig and St Mulhac in the 6th
entury for the possession of
ismore. The former, seeing that he
vas trailing, cut off his finger and
hrew it ashore, thus winning the
ace; he later founded a monastery
ere. **Views** are complex and ever-
hanging as the walk progresses: N
re the mountains of Kingairloch,
JE **Ben Nevis** 4,408ft and nearby
huna Island, S and W the islands of
he Firth of Lorn and Mull,
mmediately W is Morvern (with
rominent quarry); in view later to E
re Loch Creran and Benderloch.
>] The **lime kiln** is a survival of the
ismore lime trade; there, from Port
amsay, lime used for agricultural

fertiliser was shipped out. The main
quarry was at An Sailean, further S.
[**c**] **Castle Coeffin** 13th-century
Viking stronghold, looking over to
Mull and Morvern; still a substantial
ruin, and possible to get close to.
[**d**] To the left by the road is
Lismore's tiny **church** which
incorporates parts of the choir of a
medieval cathedral, the seat of the
diocese of Argyll from the 13th
century until 1507. Most of the
foundations lie to the W of the
present building.
[**e**] **Broch (Tirefour Castle)** Neatly
walled circular fort guarding the sea
approach about 25ft across. View to
the mainland.

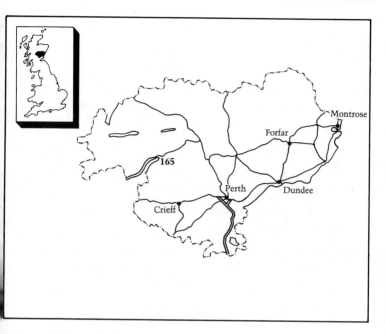

165 Acharn Falls

Holiday Which? Good Walks Guide

Acharn Falls

A gentle climb up a wooded glen, past a fine waterfall, precedes one of the easiest high-level walks above Loch Tay. Route-finding relatively easy.

Length 5 miles (8km), 2½ hours
Difficulty 2
Start Kenmore, on A827 at E end of Loch Tay; at layby opposite toilets just S of village; grid reference 775454. *Alternatively* start at Acharn village (roadside parking). This leaves road walking, the dullest part of the route, to the end instead of the start. Begin walk with lake on right and village (shop and telephone box) on left and pick up directions at ② ; grid reference 755437
OS maps 1:50,000 51 or 52; 1:25,000

NN 64/74 (Pathfinder 322)
Refreshments Bar and restaurant opposite Watersport Centre; shop at Acharn; shop, pub and tea-room at Kenmore (off route)

WALK DIRECTIONS

① With toilets on left, follow road away from Kenmore (in Aberfeldy direction); take first turning on right (signposted Watersport Centre), along S side of Loch Tay. After 1¼ miles, reach Acharn village ② . Continue along principal road then immediately after crossing stream turn left by bus shelter on rising track up right-hand side of Acharn Glen [**a**].

③ Shortly before track bends left, go through artificial cave by signpost on left to reach viewpoint over

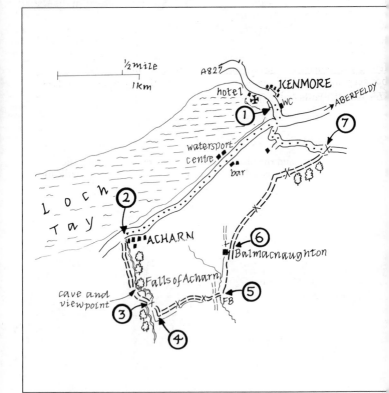

Acharn Falls. Return to track and continue along it: it bends left to cross the stream (Acharn Burn). Immediately after, route continues ahead through field gate into the open (but first *detour left* through another gate, signed 'Acharn Walk', on to descending woodland path leading to viewpoint from footbridge, where if desired you can loop round to rejoin the track near the artificial cave [b]).

Beyond the above-mentioned field gate, track enters open and bends right alongside woodland fence above the glen on right but then soon bends left ④ to leave the glen. Woods appear on right; ⑤ soon after they end, continue forward at track T-junction to cross stream by footbridge, then continue left on level grassy path which soon crosses channel by slab bridge, to continue with fence on left. Path later broadens to track.

⑥ After house and barn [c], avoid left fork (through gate, descending) but keep on main (level) track.

⑦ Turn left on road, downhill, and return to starting point (turn left at bottom if you started the walk from Acharn) [d].

ON THE ROUTE

[a] Wooded glen, rising to a 'hermitage cave' (a 19th-century landscaping feature) overlooking **Acharn Falls**, strikingly pretty and an impressive drop, set among fine mature trees.

[b] This short path leads to the **upper waterfall**, much smaller than the main one, but also attractive.

[c] From here to the road: good views over **Loch Tay** (14$\frac{1}{2}$ miles long and up to 500ft deep), with Ben Lawers (3,984ft) towering above it to the W; E is the Tay valley, and Taymouth Castle, built 1801-42, by the Earl of Breadalbane, and used as a hosptial for Polish army officers in the last war.

[d] It is worth the short detour past the lay-by into Kenmore, a well-preserved model estate village started by landowner Colin Campbell and completed in 1760.

Wales

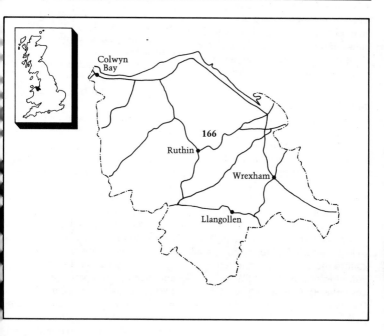

166 Foel Fennli and Moel Fammau

Holiday Which? Good Walks Guide

187 Vale of Llangollen and Castell Dinas Bran   188 Gop Hill, Graig Fawr and Dyserth Falls

Foel Fennli and Moel Famau

A walk around both sides of the Clwydian Range, a rounded upland of grass and moor giving a marvellous panorama of Snowdonia. Route-finding quite easy (some care needed in early stages); the way is clearly marked once the Offa's Dyke Path has been joined.

Length 6¹/₂ miles (10.5km), 3¹/₂ hours
Difficulty 3–4
Start Car park and picnic site by toilets on minor road ¹/₂ mile NE of Moel Famau car park. From A494 (Ruthin-Mold) turn off NE at Llanbedr-Dyffryn-Clwyd, immediately E of church, on to road called Lôn-cae-glâs, signposted Llandyrnog; this goes up steeply on to hills; ¹/₂ mile E of top point of road go into the car park on your left. From Mold turn off just SW of Loggerheads. Grid reference 172611
OS maps 1:50,000 116; 1:25,000 SJ 05/15 and SJ 06/16 (Pathfinder 788 and 772)

WALK DIRECTIONS

① Start on road with car park on left, walk along road (in NE direction). Take first right after ¹/₂ mile; this bends left in front of farmhouse. ② Immediately after next house (Fyn y groessord) on your right, take rising track on right, initially between walls and then into the open, then later with fence on left only [a].

③ After ¹/₂ mile, where wall recommences, with wood close by down to left, ignore left (descending) fork, but carry on along the main track (with wall now on left).
④ After ³/₄ mile, reach farm on left of track, where the track goes through two sets of gates.

70 yards later, bear left through third gate, proceeding on track on left edge of field, alongside wall,

under power-lines and dipping down to trees, then continue up and slightly to the right for 50 yards to reach gate beside stile with acorn waymarker denoting Offa's Dyke Path (which you now follow to Moel Famau) ⑤.

Turn right beyond this gate and stile, alongside fence on right and pass small plantation on your right and go over stile; the waymarked route continues forward, with fence on left, (bending right alongside fence at fence corner) to take waymark stile and continues along plantation down to stile at foot of hill (Foel Fennli) ⑥.

The path leads up towards the top of the hill: halfway up, the Offa's Dyke Path is waymarked to the left (skirting hill) but the best views are had by keeping forward to the summit [b] on a 'permissive path' and then taking a path ahead (there are several, but they rejoin); whichever way you go, paths rejoin and head towards the prominent tower on Moel Famau, first dropping on to road by prominent signpost and cattle-grid ⑦.

Cross road into small car park and take gate opposite, following waymarked main track which leads half left and gradually ascends (avoid right fork after 50 yards). ⑧ [c] At summit of Moel Famau at the Jubilee Tower, turn right to take stile 70 yards right of trig point (summit pillar), as it is seen from the tower.

On the other side of stile is the first of a series of red-hooped waymark posts, which you follow all the way back to the main car park: the route drops into forest [d], later is briefly joined by a blue route too, but keep straight on all the way down to reach car park).

ON THE ROUTE

[a] Good views E from this little-

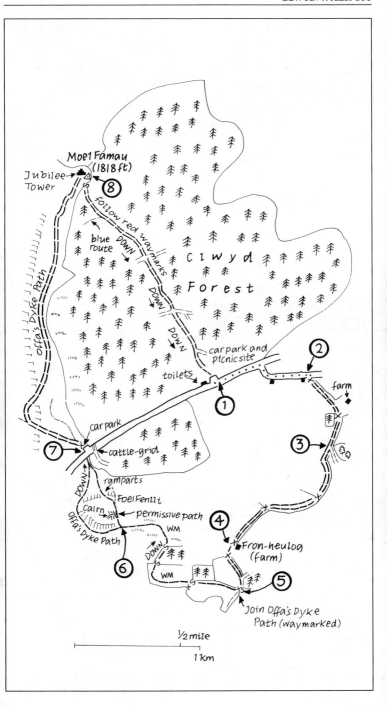

Moel Famau (1818 ft)
Jubilee Tower
⑧
follow red waymarks
blue route
DOWN
DOWN
DOWN
DOWN
Offa's Dyke Path
Clwyd Forest
car park and picnic site
②
farm
toilets
①
③
car park
⑦
cattle-grid
ramparts
DOWN
④
Foel Fenlli
cairn
permissive path
Offa's Dyke Path
WM
⑥
DOWN
Fron-heulog (farm)
WM
⑤
Join Offa's Dyke Path (waymarked)

½ mile

1 km

frequented track, with BBC mast on Cyrn y Brain (1,844ft) SE.

[b] **Foel Fennli** (1,676ft). Ramparts of an Iron Age hill-fort still encircle this hill.

[c] **Moel Famau** A view-indicator at the summit details one of the grandest views on the Offa's Dyke Path, with Snowdonia to the W (including Snowdon and Tryfan), Denbigh and Liverpool Bay N, Alyn valley and Stanlow Oil Refinery E, Cader Idris and the Berwyn uplands SW. The tower was built as a mock-Egyptian memorial to George III's golden jubillee in 1810 by a Thomas Harrison of Chester, who submitted grandiose schemes for triumphal arches and Grecian follies; this selected design was relatively simple, but its sheer bulk caused its downfall, for it collapsed in 1862. It was partly restored, and the viewing platform added, during European Conservation Year (1970).

[d] **Clwyd Forest** A mixed conifer plantation, started in the 1950s, covering 500 hectares.

DYFED

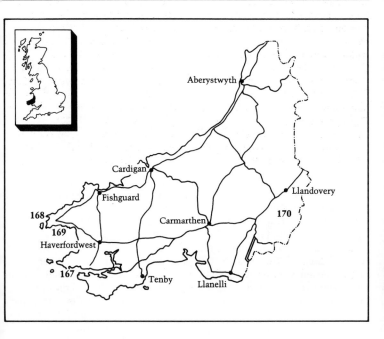

167 The Dale Peninsula
168 St David's Head and Carn Llidi
169 Solva and Dinas Fawr
170 The Carmarthen Fan

Holiday Which? Good Walks Guide

189 Devil's Bridge, the Rheidol Valley and Parson's Bridge   190 Bosherston lily ponds and St Govan's Chapel   191 Wooltack Point and Marloes Sands 192 Garn Fawr and Strumble Head   193 A tour of the Gwaun Valley

The Dale Peninsula

An unusual round walk with six and a half of its seven miles being coastal. Changing views from a level cliff are the main feature. Easy route-finding.

Length 7 miles (11 km), 3^1/$_2$ hours
Difficulty 2
Start Dale village, W of Milford Haven. Grid reference 811058
OS maps 1:50,000 157; 1:25,000 SM 70 and SM 80/90 (Pathfinder 1102 and 1103)
Refreshments Pub, café and shop in Dale

WALK DIRECTIONS

①[a] Take road signposted Dale Fort, passing Griffin Inn on right (ignore minor right fork after ^{1}/$_4$ mile through gate). ② 70 yards after trees on left end and view opens out [b], take signposted coast path on right, over stile, with fence on right to next stile, then following along field edge and along obvious route on cliff-top path; (towards the end of this field the path drops to the stile and then to shore level where you cross stile 179; soon path rejoins cliff-top).

The path leads past the prominent tower on (Watwick Beacon, and then after stile 184 passes above beach at Watwick Bay [c] (if you don't want to detour to the beach, avoid a descending fork). ③ Cross a track and keep immediately to right of Three Beacon Towers at West Blockhouse Point [d].

④ At houses at S end of peninsula, path passes to left to first group of buildings, with walled enclosure on left, and turns right in front of private gate, in front of coastguard cottages. Join road at the next signpost and turn right along it, passing coastguard tower on left, then ⑤ crossing stile on left to follow cliff-top path [e].

⑥ [f] Leave the coastpath at Westdale Bay (with big sandy beach) and cross stile on right, following bottom of valley and keeping just to right of prominent Dale Castle [g], to reach gate on to corner of road; turn right then take first left to reach starting point.

ON THE ROUTE

[a] **Dale** A popular sailing and surfing centre, the westmost village in Milford Haven and the sunniest place in Wales. 17th- and 18th-century buildings by the quay are reminders of its day as a flourishing port, when it had a brewery and 18 inns.

[b] View of **Milford Haven**, a huge natural harbour where tankers can often be seen on their way to and from its numerous oil refineries. The flatness of the cliff-tops and adjacent farmland that characterises the S Pembrokeshire coast is an example of a **wave-cut platform**: the land you see was originally the sea-bed, planed flat by the action of the sea, and part of the land mass since the sea-level has fallen. **Dale Fort** (private, but can be seen from the entrance gate), now a field studies centre, was built in 1856 as part of the fortification of Milford Haven against possible invasion; nine forts were built as Pembroke naval dockyard grew in importance in the 19th century. Because of advances in gun technology the defences were already outdated by the time they were completed, and they were never used except in the last war. Of other surviving Haven forts, **Thorn Island** (across the harbour) is a hotel, **Stack Fort** is the circular structure in the middle of the Haven, and **Popton Fort** is used as BP refinery offices.

[c] **Watwick Bay** Path access to the shore, at the foot of sandstone cliffs.

[d] At **Mill Bay** Henry VII landed in 1485 and set off on a march through

Wales that was to lead to the battle and victory at Bosworth Field.
[e] Views of the islands of **Skokholm** and **Skomer**, which together harbour 14,000 pairs of Manx shearwater and 6,000 of storm petrel; Britain's first bird observatory was set up on Skokholm, where studies are made into the dynamics of bird populations. Between the two islands, in the far distance, **Grassholm** has the largest gannet population (20,000) in England and Wales. In the foreground is **Gateholm**, which has the remains of a monastery.

[f] Path access to **Westdale Bay**, a fine sandy beach. The valley between this and Dale was caused by geological faulting: this is the Rictec Fault, which runs the length of Milford Haven. The sea once covered this valley, making the S end of the peninsula an island.
[g] **Dale Castle** has a castellated Georgian appearance (the present family have been there since 1800), but its site is Norman. It was first mentioned in a market charter granted in 1293 to Robertus de Vale, allowing a Wednesday market to be held at his manor.

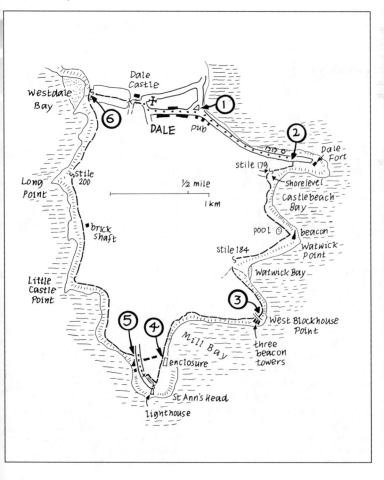

St David's Head and Carn Llidi

An impressively rugged coastal walk with perhaps the finest seaboard hill in Pembrokeshire for the climax; the changes of direction provide an interesting sequence of views. Easy route-finding.

Length 3¹/₂ or 4¹/₂ miles (5.5km or 7km), 2–2¹/₂ hours
Difficulty 2
Start Whitesand Bay car park, NW of St David's. Grid reference 735272
OS maps 1:50,000 157; 1:25,000 SM 62/72 (Pathfinder 1055)
Refreshments Snack kiosk in Whitesand Bay car park

WALK DIRECTIONS

① [a] Take signposted coast path to right of telephone box. Proceed between fences; after 150 yards fork right (left goes to promontory [b]). Follow coast path along top of rugged cliffs [c], past National Trust sign, over footbridge (left is optional detour to sandy beach), past promontory of St David's Head [d].

Keep close to cliff-top. **②** 200 yards after St David's Head, look for burial chamber [e] 30 yards off path to right but easily missed; it is just before big crags begin); inland to your right is the big hill of Carn Llidi. Continue along the coast path. **③** When you have almost passed Carn Llidi, fork right inland, heading uphill and immediately to right of prominent stone-walled enclosure to go up on to left-hand shoulder of Carn Llidi.

④ At top of shoulder, where view ahead opens, wall joins on left: you can turn right up to summit of Carn Llidi [f], but path is not defined near top. (If you want to continue along ridge make your way slightly along right-hand side of ridge until reaching concrete and brick foundation of old radar hut, where

you turn right on concrete path, down steps, and soon between iron posts and along track; rejoin directions at **⑤**). *To continue* descend from the shoulder, on well-defined path with wall on left; where wall bends right, keep right alongside it, and soon ignore a stile on left. Turn left on reaching junction with hard track **⑤**. Follow the track to farm, keeping forward as signposted in centre of farm (ignoring left fork), and descend gently to main road. Turn right on road to reach car park.

ON THE ROUTE

[a] **Whitesand Bay** The mile-long beach is one of Pembrokeshire's most popular bathing places. At very low tide, remains of a forest are revealed, consisting of stumps of birch, fir, hazel and oak trees. The Bay was on a Bronze Age trade route from Stonehenge to the Wicklow mountains in Ireland.

[b] The small **promontory** on the left is the site of St Patrick's Chapel (no ruin survives), built 6th to 10th century on the spot from where St Patrick is thought to have sailed for Ireland. Here sea voyagers used to pray for a safe journey and to offer thanks for their arrival.

[c] Views SW of **Ramsey Island**, Wales' major breeding ground for Atlantic grey seals.

[d] **St David's Head** (Penmaen Dewi). Described in a Roman survey of the known world in AD140 as the 'Promontory of the Eight Perils', this low but rugged headland looks W to the Bishop's and Clerk's Rocks.

[e] **Coetan Arthur** A 5,000-year old burial chamber with an 8ft capstone and supports. Despite its proximity to the path, it can be easily missed, as it is well-camouflaged among the rocks.

[f] **Carn Llidi** (595ft). A rough path leads to the summit of this

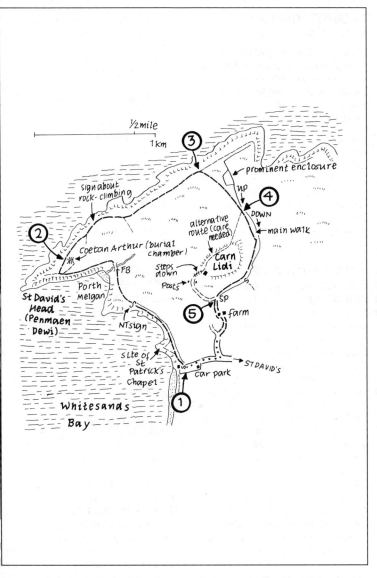

½ mile
1 km

③

prominent enclosure

sign about
rock-climbing

up

④

DOWN

alternative
route (care
needed)

②

main walk

Coetan Arthur (burial
chamber)

**Carn
Lidi**

steps
down

FB

Posts

Porth
Melgan

sp

St David's
Head
(Penmaen
Dewi)

⑤ farm

NT sign

Site of
St
Patrick's
Chapel

ST DAVID'S

Car park

①

Whitesands
Bay

miniature mountain, whose lower slopes have discernible traces of enclosures made by Iron Age farmers. Stirring **view**, even in poorish visibility, of the nearby coast; in clear conditions the Waterford and Wicklow mountains in Ireland are visible. From the top you can continue along the seaward side (care needed on the rocks), instead of rejoining the main route; it is rough going until joining concrete steps, near foundations of a building (old radar station in the last war), which later becomes a track, which you descend to ⑤.

Solva and Dinas Fawr

A cliff-top walk of a switchback nature, with splendid close-up views of the cliffs and distant vista over islands. Return route is via easy, level farm tracks and field-paths past an ancient burial chamber before rejoining the coast path. Route-finding reasonably easy.

Length 4½ miles (7km), 2½ hours

Difficulty 2

Start Solva, on A487 E of St David's (large car park by Harbour House Hotel, at bottom of village). Grid reference 806243

OS maps 1:50,000 157; 1:25,000 SM 62/72 or SM 82/92(Pathfinder 1055 or 1056)

Refreshments Cafés, pubs and shops in Solva

WALK DIRECTIONS

① [a] Cross footbridge at back of car park, turn left on other side then immediately right on signposted coast path. Fork left after 150 yards on to upper path going along ridge towards sea [b]. ② 40 yards before end of ridge take path to left, dropping steeply to cross footbridge then going across pebbly beach to regain cliff-top via sequence of signposts.

Keep close to cliff edge; path eventually becomes well defined [c]. After 1 mile, pass big promontory (Dinas Fawr), which you can detour along for views [d]. Thereafter, coast becomes less dramatic. ③ After ½ mile go over stile numbered 249 by signpost; there is a big drop suddenly on the right. At this point bear half

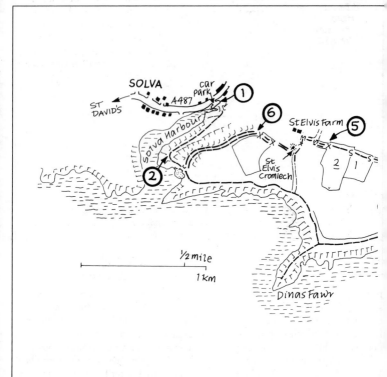

left to leave coast path, in signposted direction, along left edge of field [**e**] to cross stile at end by signpost where turn left on to path between hedges and follow path to reach farm road ④.

Turn left on road to Lochvane Farm, immediately after which keep straight on at junction, now on track between hedges (where main track enters field on right keep forward between hedges, on narrow path), to reach stile into field where go forward alongside right edge of this and next field [**f**].

⑤ At end of second field continue now on enclosed track and after 80 yards cross stile on right at signpost and then turn left along farm road. Immediately before St Elvis Farm [**g**] take stile by signpost on left; beyond it pick up gate with fenced path beyond it.

At next stile, there is St Elvis cromlech (Neolithic burial chamber) [**h**] on your right: turn right (signposted Public Footpath) to pass to left of the cromlech and pick up enclosed track which eventually enters field by gate beside stile. Here, the track bends right along right edge of field to go through another gate ⑥ and drops with valley down on your right to reach the footbridge you crossed near the start of the walk. Beyond the footbridge, retrace your steps up on to the ridge and then later fork left down to Solva.

ON THE ROUTE

[**a**] **Solva** lies at the end of a ria, or drowned river valley, with steeply rising slopes on both sides. From the 16th to 18th centuries it prospered as a small port, with a population of 1,200 at its peak, small ships calling on their way around Britain; an important link in trading of cloth and timber with Ireland. In 1848 you could have taken a direct sailing on the packet *Cradle* to New York for £3 (no food supplied, and the journey might take four months). But the harbour was not deep enough for big ships, and Solva declined from the mid-19th century; it now functions as a boating centre and resort village of considerable charm. Look for the old lime-kilns on the left side of the harbour.

[**b**] **Cribyn ridge**, ablaze with wild flowers and yellow gorse in spring and summer, is the site of several Iron Age forts. View ahead of St Elvis islands and Wooltack Point at the end of Marloes Peninsula.

[**c**] On the seaward side from this fine cliff section, **St David's Head** and **Ramsey Island** appear away to right; the sea appears almost land-locked by isles and promontories. W

Lochvane Farm ④
Pointz Castle
motte / farm
③ stile 249
SP
SP
FB
Dinas Fach

of Wooltack Point are the bird sanctuary islands of **Skomer** and **Skokholm**.

[d] **Dinas Fawr**, like a sinuous finger pointing out to sea, gives a bracing ridge walk along its top; Milford Haven, and perhaps the odd oil tanker, can be seen away to the left.

[e] **Pointz Castle**, the nearest farm ahead, takes its name from the 18ft mound visible to the right of a silo. The castle, now a National Trust-owned mass of brambles, may have belonged to Poncius, a Norman knight who was a tenant of the bishop of St David's in the 12th century. In the 19th century a stone cross was unearthed here.

[f] **Carn Llidi**, a hill close to St David's Head, is glimpsed half right.

[g] **St Elvis Farm** stands on the site of St Teilo's church. St Teilo may have accompanied St David on his pilgrimage to Jerusalem. Nothing can be seen of the church today, but the cross and font are now installed in St Aiden's at Solva.

[h] **St Elvis cromlech** An excellent example of a Neolithic burial chamber, dating back 5,000 years, and consisting of two chambers and a cap-stone some 8ft across.

The Carmarthen Fan

The mountain of Carmarthen Fan provides rugged walking and exciting views from the top of its precipitous northern face. Route defined all the way, and although landmarks help navigation in good visibility, the walk would be difficult in mist without a compass. Ascent 2,100ft.

Length 6 miles (10km), 5 hours
Difficulty 4–5
Start End of access road to Llyn y Fan Fawr reservoir, 1½ miles E of Llanddeusant church, (S of Llandovery and E of A4069). Grid reference 798239. *Directions to the start.* At T-junction at Llanddeusant, with church on right and pottery shop on left, turn left and continue for 1 mile to where road forks. Take left hand and uphill fork, signed to Llyn y Fan; road now becomes unsurfaced but has good gravel top. Continue for ⅓ mile, passing Blaenau Farm on right, then come to fork where road ahead blocked by gate marked 'Vehicle access to authorised users only'; take fork to right, signed to 'Llyn y Fan Fach reservoir', dropping steeply down to cattle-grid then turning left to run alongside stream. Park anywhere after the cattle-grid on large grass parking area between road and stream (cars must not be left beyond cattle-grid after 9pm or sunset, whichever is earlier; it may be safer to park just before the cattle-grid)
OS maps 1:50,000 160; 1:25,000 Outdoor Leisure Map 12

WALK DIRECTIONS

If you cannot see the summit ridge the walk should only be attempted if you are confident about navigating with map and compass. Before starting out, check whether it is possible to cross the stream by the parking area using stepping stones, as this will affect the last stage of the return. **①** From cattle-grid walk forward (away from Llanddeusant) with stream to right. Continue on road when wall on left ends, but 150 yards after end of wall, and 30 yards before Welsh Water Authority signs on either side of road, turn left and climb steeply up bank at side of road. At top of bank, turn right and follow well-marked path ascending side of valley, along Nant Melyn side stream on right.

After 100 yards, track crosses slight depression running down hillside, and immediately after keep uphill when path divides; after another 300 yards, again take left-hand and uphill fork, climbing up alongside Sychant stream on right.

② Shortly before reaching skyline, turn right across stream (no path defined) and make your own way up grassy ridge [a]. **③** After 1 mile, reach and turn right on to better defined path running up the left end of Fan Bryreiniog ahead just as the peaks of the main Brecon Beacons become visible over the ridge [b]. The path, marked by very occasional cairns (piled-up stones), goes up the 'brow' of the mountain but just before the top of the steep slope bears off slightly to right.

At the top of the steep slope, turn half left by a small cairn and go directly uphill, until you come to large cairn marking subsidiary summit. Continue forward for 200 yards then turn left around top of steep gully to left, then at next cairn turn right, with steep drop to left, to trig point marking summit of Fan Brycheiniog [c] **④**.

From the summit walk directly down the slope making straight for the path clearly visible, to the left of the way you have come, running up the side of the next summit to the W, Picws Du. There is no defined path but the descent to the pass

619

between the two summits is straightforward. From the pass, follow clear path ahead up Picws Du, where ⑤ continue along summit ridge for a mile with steep drop on right, until path turns N above western end of Llyn y Fan Fach reservoir and ⑥ starts to descend [**d**].

When parallel with the northern end of the reservoir, there is a path running down to the right to join the access road by the dam; if the river by the car park was impossible to cross, turn right down this and then go down the road to return to start [**e**]. Otherwise, continue down ridge

on clear path which after another 200 yards turns half left away from ridge across the open moor. Follow this down for 1 mile, keeping just to the right of the Garwnant stream, and when stream valley becomes a small ravine turn quarter right, continuing downhill in the direction of the largest area of woodland on the far side of the main valley.

Slope becomes steeper and ⑦ you soon drop on to path running along side of hill, just above fence separating moor from field below. Turn right along this path and descend gently to stream, to cross by stepping stones to return to start.

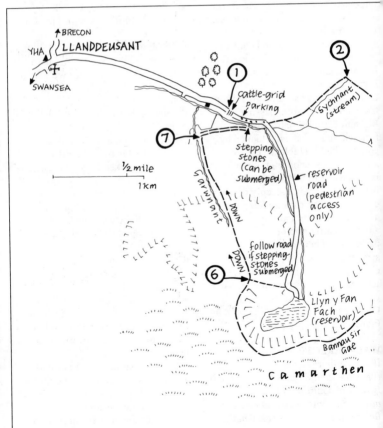

ON THE ROUTE

[**a**] View of the **Usk reservoir** in the middle distance and the **Cambrian Mountains** and the **Mynydd Eppynt** beyond. You are now within a couple of hundred yards of the **source of the Usk**, which flows down through Brecon to reach the sea at Newport.

[**b**] The main summit of the Brecon Beacons is **Pen-y-Fan** (2,906ft). Much closer and to the right can be seen the lake of **Llyn y Fan Fawr**, just below the summit of **Fan Brycheiniog**.

[**c**] From here on a clear day there is a particularly fine view to the S, over the main part of the **Black Mountain** to **Swansea Bay** and the **Gower coast**, the **Bristol Channel**, and the **coast of Devon** beyond. Slightly to the left is the escarpment marking the northern edge of the **South Wales coalfield**; the mining valleys run down to the sea on the far side of this, but surprisingly little evidence of industrial activity can be seen.

[**d**] As you go along the summit ridge, note the bright red weathered outcrops of the **old red sandstone** of which the mountains are made. From the western end of the summit ridge, there is a fine **view** to the left along the northern edge of the Black Mountain, and in the distance (8 miles away) you may be able to make out **Carreg Cennen Castle** magically sited on a prominent hill above the Afon Cennen. This was built by John Giffard after Edward I defeated the Welsh in 1283. It was used by the English lord to dominate the surrounding area, but was seized temporarily by the Welsh patriot Owen Glendower in 1403, and finally demolished in 1462 to stop it being used as a base by local bandits. It remains one of the most imposing inland castles in Wales, perched 400 feet above the river, with caves to be explored underneath, and is open to the public (daily 9.30-6.30).

[**e**] There is a fine **view** from where the paths divide back across the reservoir to the main ridge. Note the prominent banding in the rock. These rocky walls were cut by the action of glaciers during the last Ice Age.

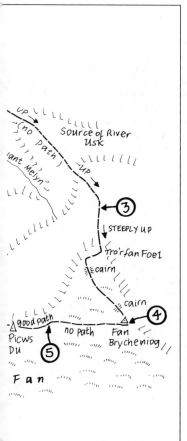

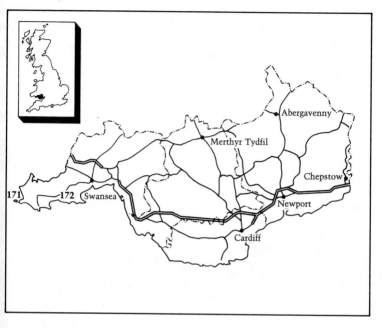

171 Rhossili Down and Mewslade Bay
172 Brandy Cove

Holiday Which? Good Walks Guide

Rhossili Down and Mewslade Bay

A breezy moorland top, pale grey limestone cliffs and huge beaches of fine sand are packed into this astonishingly varied short walk. No problems of route-finding once you have found the turn-off point at ③.

Length 4¹/₂ miles (7km), 2¹/₂ hours
Difficulty 3
Start Rhossili car park, at W end of Gower peninsula (off B4247). Grid reference 414881
OS maps 1:50,000 159; 1:25,000 SS 48/58/68 (Pathfinder 1145)
Refreshments Pub, tea-room and shop in Rhossili; tea-room and shop in Middleton

WALK DIRECTIONS

① Turn right out of car park, into Rhossili village centre, towards church [a]. Turn left at bus shelter and telephone box, on to enclosed path which turns left to skirt the churchyard.

② Reach track (on near side of road) and turn left to reach gate and National Trust sign at foot of Rhossili Down [b]. Take the path to the right of the sign, steeply up the top (keeping seaward slope close on your left) towards trig point at summit.

③ 40 yards before the trig point, find a very sharp right turn (keeping straight on at minor cross-junction after 30 yards): this is a broad grassy path which becomes a well-defined track as it descends.

④ The track turns right in front of corner of wall, (close to houses) and 80 yards later merges into better defined track which immediately bends left downhill to T-junction where you turn right along surfaced lane.

⑤ Turn left at lane road at Middleton, and after 100 yards take track on right signposted Mewslade

Bay 0.76km. This soon narrows to path enclosed between hedges.

⑥ Near end of enclosed section reach gate into open area and by nature reserve sign. Just after this, hedges end: keep right, initially with wall and fence up on right, and after 80 yards fork left on to lower path which heads along right-hand side of prominent wall along valley bottom (Mew Slade), towards the sea.

⑦ After the wall ends, the path bends right and gently climbs the cliff (beware of sudden drop by overhang) and proceed along cliff-top with wall on right [c]. ⑧ In the next bay the path divides: take either the lower or upper path (lower path gets better views and upper path continues alongside wall and then leaves it to join lower path). Continue around the cliff-top, past Worms Head [d] to reach Rhossili.

ON THE ROUTE

[a] **Rhossili** Windswept village above a superb 5-mile arc of beach from Burry Holm S to Worms Head. The **church** has a 12th-century doorway, perhaps transplanted from an older church which was in the warren below the down; there is a lepers' window into the chancel, so that lepers could watch services without risk of spreading infection. On fields near the church a farming practice known as the 'viel', by which the benefit of fertile land is shared out over the years, is a survival from the medieval open-strip field system.
[b] **Rhossili Down** Formerly a vertical cliff, but erosion has degraded the slope into a hillside, giving a most unusual juxtaposition of coast and upland. From the 632ft summit, the highest point on Gower, a magnificent view extends over the peninsula, while Lundy Island, Devon, Carmarthenshire and Pembrokeshire may also be in sight.
[c] **Mewslade Bay** Part of the South

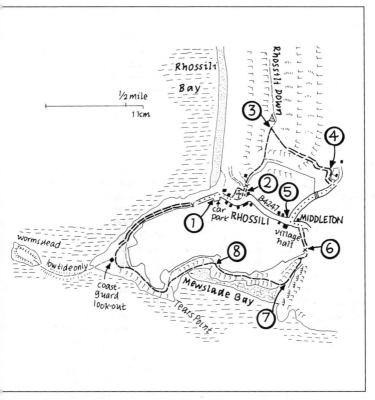

Gower Nature Reserve, these splendid carboniferous limestone cliffs, which have been tilted, folded and faulted by the earth's movements, are Gower's most striking coastal landforms. Below, the bay itself has another lovely sand beach, less frequented than that at Rhossili. This coast is a noted site both for wild flowers and insect life. It is the only British habitat for yellow whitlow grass, and spring cinquefoil, spiked speedwell, clary, and thoary rock rose may also be found; the coastal site also supports populations of marbled white butterflies and the rare great green bush cricket.

[d] **Worm's Head** 'Worm' comes from the Welsh for 'dragon': the serpentine, slender mile-long western tip of Gower is well-named. It is the most important bird sanctuary on the W side of the Bristol Channel: kittiwakes, razorbills, guillemots, cormorants, fulmars and shags are abundant, and there are occasional puffins. A slipway between the mainland and Inner Head is exposed at ebb tide, when you can walk across over rocks: rough but fun (but take care not to get cut off by the tide: only venture on to it $2^{1}/_{2}$ hours either side of low tide).

Brandy Cove

**Woodland paths along a scenic
valley precede a cliff and shore-level
route, ending at a sandy beach.
Plenty of up and down, and be
prepared for slippery woodland paths
after rain. Route-finding a little
complex in places, but
straightforward in the short
version of the walk.**

Length 4¹/₂ or 6 miles (7 or 9.5km),
2 or 3 hours
Difficulty 3
Start Car park just N of Bishopston.
From Kittle on B4436, go E and take
first turning on right (Bishopston
Road). Car park is on left after 300
yards, opposite signposted path to
Kittle 0.7km (which goes down
Middlecroft Lane). Grid reference
579893
OS maps 1:50,000 159; 1:25,000 SS
48/58/68 (Pathfinder 1145)
Refreshments Shops and pubs in
Bishopston; shop at Pyle

WALK DIRECTIONS

① Cross road from car park, go
down Middlecroft Lane opposite.
After 100 yards turn right at
junction, on semi-paved track; after
50 yards, just before gate-posts for
house called Bryn Llan, fork left on
to tarmacked path and immediately
fork left again on to unsurfaced path
which descends (churchyard soon
visible on right).

② At bottom, reach driveway
(stone gate-posts on left), turn right
to reach road, where turn left, but
immediately leave road as it bends
right, to take path beyond metal
barrier on left. Continue along stony
area which soon narrows to become
path [a].

After 170 yards, the path enters
the open: take path immediately
parallel on left (the right-hand path
soon ends at old quarry workings).
Path enters woods; on leaving them

(into semi-open area) keep to main
path (the left and upper path): there
is a cave with underground stream
close by to right. The path bends
right at next cave and follows
bottom of valley, soon with stream
on left.

③ Do not cross footbridge over
stream but continue along valley
with stream on left. ¹/₂ mile later,
pass but do not cross second
footbridge. 100 yards after, ignore
path to right (which goes into side
valley); keep alongside stream,
which bends left, for another 80
yards ④.
For short walk continue along valley
to Pwlldu Bay, where you cross stile
by National Trust sign and pick up
shore-level track along right side of
bay. Resume directions at ⑨.
For full walk turn right on to broad
path into another side valley, to
leave stream. After 250 yards, go
over stile beside gate and turn left
(immediately ignoring another stile
beside gate on right) on to path
between fences, bending left and
rising to enter field ⑤.

Cross field to take right-most of
three field entrances in opposite
hedgerow (at time of inspection this
was not obvious: the gate was rather
ramshackle, and is found 70 yards to
right of far left-hand field corner). In
second and third fields, keep forward
alongside hedgerow on left. Turn left
in far left-hand corner of third field,
just before house, go through
farmyard where turn right to emerge
on to road ⑥.

Left on road; after 80 yards fork
right on to coastpath, which initially
keeps to inward edge of rough land.
Path begins to drop at Pwlldu Head
[b] (view opens out ahead): make
sure to note Pwlldu Point from here
(beyond which the coastline makes a
major left turn) which is 350 yards
ahead and marked by a small
hillock.

7 Turn left at Pwlldu Point at (not very prominent) cross-junction of narrow paths (right goes to the edge of Point; ahead ends at edge of low cliffs from where it is a tough scramble along the coast into the bay). Once you have found this path, it is easily followed as it ascends through rough ground to reach corner of first field and keeps right, re-entering rough ground to reach wooden posts and enters next (second) field.

Follow waymark arrows (across field to waymarker 50 yards to left of shed), then go alongside edge of third field to pass farm on left. Go through gates with signpost (pointing back to Pwlldu Head); 30 yards later, turn right at track T-junction (ignore very sharp right immediately before this), where left goes towards farm.

8 After 100 yards, take signposted bridleway on right, dropping, soon down steps, then fork right to reach track at sea level, where turn right. **9** Go past houses then immediately turn left across beach. At far side of beach, take lower of two paths, running just

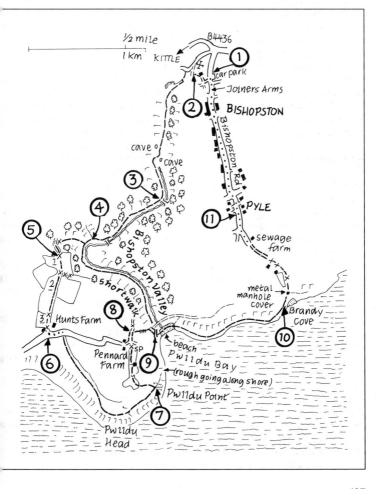

above shore level (the upper path climbs to cliff-top and omits Brandy Cove).

⑩ [c] At Brandy Cove (a tiny sandy beach, with field and house on left), turn left inland on well-defined path, soon through kissing-gate: ignore all side-turns. The path broadens to track and eventually becomes a surfaced lane. **⑪** Go forward at edge of Pyle village, and at shops keep forward on Bishopston Road for ¹/₂ mile to reach starting point.

ON THE ROUTE
[a] **Bishopston Valley** Twisting, deep, deciduously-wooded 2¹/₂-mile-long valley of both botanic and geological interest, with limestone caverns and the Bishopston stream disappearing underground and re-emerging to reach the sea at Pwlldu, where there is a beach of shingle, owned by the National Trust.
[b] **Pwlldu Head** 300ft high, and the highest coastal headland in Gower. Views S in clear weather to the Exmoor coast (Devon and Somerset).
[c] **Brandy Cove** It seems a fair guess that such a secluded beach owes its

GWYNEDD

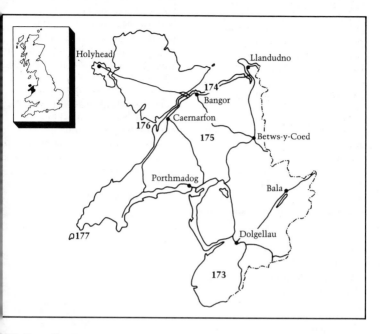

Holiday Which? Good Walks Guide

Castell y Bere

Level paths and tracks lead along an unspoilt river valley and past a ruined castle, then along the river with high hills all around. There is a slightly more ambitious finale up a narrow valley with a descent through woods; a couple of very quiet stretches of lane-walking are included. Route-finding fairly straightforward.

Length 7½ miles (12km), 3½ hours
Difficulty 2–3
Start Abergynolwyn, on B4405 SW of Dolgellau. Grid reference 070678
OS maps 1:50,000 124; 1:25,000 Outdoor Leisure 23
Refreshments Pub, cafés and shops in Abergynolwyn

WALK DIRECTIONS

① [a] With Railway Inn on your right, walk along main road through village (towards Tywyn) for 50 yards, but immediately before road crosses river, turn right on to lane (with river on left and playground and terrace of houses on right). Soon cross footbridge over river, pick up path leading to house, in front of which path bends right (it is soon briefly undefined: ignore a faint right fork). Path soon becomes well-defined as it follows left side of valley, on the level, with river down to right.

② 50 yards after waymark post, fork right (left ascends), dropping to river level and going through gate by house (Rhiwlas), where you pick up a track and follow it to road ③. Turn right on road, over river, and turn right at staggered junction (signposted Abergynolwyn).

④ After 150 yards, turn left through double gates into Caerbeyllan Farm [b]. Go through the farmyard and take right-hand of two gates, leading on to track (the left-hand gate goes to barns), which

contours below craggy slope. Soon the hill on which stands Castell y Bere is visible a short distance to your left; as soon as you are level with the beginning of it ⑤ take metal kissing-gate on left (not the small gate just before this), and with your back to the track bear half-right diagonally across field to reach signposted stile on to road.

Turn right if you want to reach Castell y Bere (100 yards away) [c], but turn left to continue the route. ⑥ After 300 yards, just after the hill on right ends, take signposted stile on right into field, and follow left edge, soon past the foot of the hill on your right, and then cross ladder-

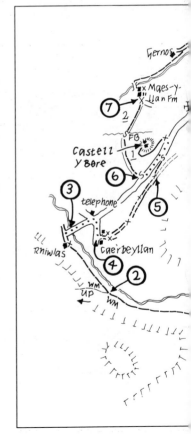

stile beside gate at end of field. Turn right in the next field, alongside right edge and towards farm.

(7) Immediately before first barn, turn right through gate and then left, past farmhouse to reach vehicle turning-circle (where track ends). Take gate ahead and go over bridge over river, turning right on other side alongside river and soon crossing a stile. Later you join a track close to house, and eventually reach lane junction (8) [d]. Turn right.

(9) At hamlet of Llanfihangel-y-pennant, turn left opposite church [e] on signposted track to left of post-box, to reach gate beside stile next to partly ruined cottage. Proceed along path by stream for 50 yards, then veer left to leave it as waymarked for a short distance; the path goes up and soon rejoins stream by a waterfall (where path forks, take either as forks rejoin).

After waterfall, fence soon begins on right: follow it as it bends left away from the stream where go over stile (50 yards to left of stream) (10). Turn right on other side of this stile on to path which rejoins stream, and continues up valley, merging into stony track. The track soon ends: head forward to gate beside stile to right of prominent ruin (no path) (11), then continue up the valley. At the

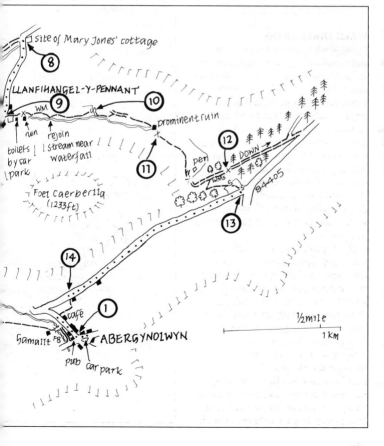

631

head of valley [f], reach solid wall with fence beyond, and cross it by gate beside stile at its right end. Follow well-defined track beyond, immediately bending left and descending gently.

(12) 100 yards after trees begin on both sides, look out for low path sharp right (at time of inspection the waymark post had fallen over, and this turn-off was not easily seen; if in doubt continue on the main track down to road, where turn right, and fork right at next junction after ½ mile in Llanegryn direction – this is (13)).

Look for yellow waymark posts as you descend through woods: after 60 yards bend sharp left, soon reaching end of woods where you keep left and follow ill-defined route steeply down towards road junction at bottom. Soon go over rough ground and cross stile, then down left edge of field to emerge on to road by stile beside gate.

Turn right on the minor road (13) and follow for nearly 1 mile. (14) Just after house on left, cut off a corner by taking signposted steps on left (or you can continue on road to next junction where turn left to descend to Abergynolwyn), dropping down to stile, then down sunken path with fence on left, bending right at fence corner. Soon go over another stile and drop to river, proceeding to bridge at Abergynolwyn. Turn left on road, back to start.

ON THE ROUTE

[a] **Abergynolwyn** A 19th-century village of sturdy terraces, which grew up to house workers from the Bryneglwys Slate Quarry (closed 1947), which was served by the still-functioning private Talyllyn Railway.

[b] **Caerbeyllan Farm** Handsome farmhouse built 1755, replacing an older structure.

[c] **Castell y Bere** The path winds round to the top of the rock and into the shattered 13th-century castle ruins. Llewelyn the Great founded it in 1221, but after the Earl of Pembroke took it in 1283 it was rebuilt by Edward I before the Welsh recapture in 1295. Finely sited above a flat-bottomed dale under the shadow of the outliers of Cader Idris (2,927ft).

[d] Straight ahead as you emerge on to the road, immediately on your right, is the labelled site of **Mary Jones' Cottage**. In 1800, 16-year-old Mary took her six years of careful savings and walked barefoot 28 miles over the hills to Bala, where she hoped to buy a Welsh bible from Revd Thomas Charles, only to find he had no such bible for sale. Touched by her efforts, he gave her his own copy, and her determination inspired him to set up the British and Foreign Bible Society, which now keeps Mary's bible at its London headquarters.

[e] **Llanfihangel church** A long, low building, typical of the area, with a solid stone lych-gate and carved slate gravestones.

[f] View ahead of the deep valley of **Glen Iago**, with the plunging slopes of **Graig Goch** to the left.

Aber and Lavan Sands

The initial 700ft ascent is by grassy tracks on to the hillside, followed by a long section along the level, and finishing off with a descent towards Penrhyn Castle. The return route along the shore gives total contrast. Route is a little intricate out of Aber, but then is easy to find.

Length 7½ miles (12km), 3½ hours
Difficulty 3
Start Aber village (also called Abergwyngregyn; E of Bangor) turn off A55 at Aber Falls Hotel; roadside parking. Grid reference 656727
OS maps 1:50,000 115; 1:25,000 Outdoor Leisure 17
Refreshments Hotel (open to non-residents) and shop in Aber

WALK DIRECTIONS

1 From Aber by shop and filling station, walk away from A55 to village [a] and take first right opposite back entrance to hotel, and marked 'unsuitable for coaches'), then after 150 yards turn right on to track by footpath signpost (in Welsh, and opposite post-box in wall).

Track leads up towards house and just before it bends into house take ladder-stile a few yards left of the house to follow rising path over rough ground, leading half right with fence close down to right. **2** Reach kissing-gate into field, and go forward along right edge of field towards house) to reach kissing-gate into second field where continue to gate just to right of the house; beyond the gate, take rising track half right (just to right of bungalow; not sharper right downhill).

3 After 170 yards turn sharp left at track junction, rising. Later this passes through narrow belt of trees; **4** immediately before next gate (where ascent ends), turn sharp right on to grassy track for the continuation - but fist detour ahead,

continuing on main track, through gate (with sheds immediately on right), to reach another belt of trees for view of Aber Falls [b].

Return to the above-mentioned grassy track and follow it, along level, through series of gates and ladder-stiles [c]; **5** where main track bends right downhill, keep forward over ladder-stile (with fence on right); soon merge into well-defined track, which goes under triple power-lines twice, and then drops gently to reach surfaced lane **6**.

Turn left on lane; turn right after 100 yards at junction to follow lane down to cross A55 at road bridge, and **7** 150 yards later (just before junction at edge of hamlet of Tan-y-Lôn), take signposted concrete track sharp right which bends round to left, becomes unsurfaced and goes into wood under railway; soon track ends at gate beside stile into field, which cross.

Turn left inside (first) field, along left edge [d]; at end of field, take gate into second field and head across to gate (in line with farm, which you soon reach) **8**. In third field go forward along right edge to reach gate on to track, and proceed to farm: right of way continues through gate ahead and slightly to left, just to left of power-post and farmhouse, reaching lane via gate 20 yards later.

Turn right [e] along the lane (soon ignore track on right), to reach car park at shore **9**. Turn along shore, initially along grassy track but later along shore itself [f]; soon after the coast bends round to the right [g], grassy track begins again but later you are diverted on to shore.

10 Past ruin on the right you soon pick up a cinder track by a house which continues close to shore (but slightly diverting from it) to reach junction after 350 yards by nature reserve sign and signpost **11**. Turn right on tarmacked lane under railway. Turn right at T-junction to reach main road (A55); Aber is a short distance to left.

ON THE ROUTE

[a] **Aber** A mound in the village is the site of a 13th-century palace of the Princes of Gwynedd.

[b] View ahead of the **Aber Falls** at the far end of the valley; Rhaeadr Fawr (the Big Fall), also called the Mare's Tail, tumbles down 170 feet.

[c] Grandstand panorama of **Anglesey**, the largest Welsh island, flat and fertile. It was settled by man from early times: evidence of Stone Age occupation (7000 BC) has been found and later it became a major centre for the Druids.

[d] **Penrhyn Castle** is straight ahead (but its entrance is well off this route). Huge mock-Norman castle of 1827-47, incorporating an earlier building. Designed by Thomas Hopper for George Pennant, Baron of Penrhyn, who made his fortune from the Penrhyn slate quarries above Bethesda. Inside and out, great show is made of the use of slate, including a slate bedstead made for the visit of Queen Victoria; she refused to sleep in it and opted for something more conventional.

[e] **Spinnies nature reserve** Entered by a gate opposite the farm, where you emerge on to the road, but there are views from the road itself; a lagoon site, where the River Ogwen took its course before being canalised.

[f] **Lavan Sands** (Traeth Lafan) Ten bird species, plus numbers of duck,

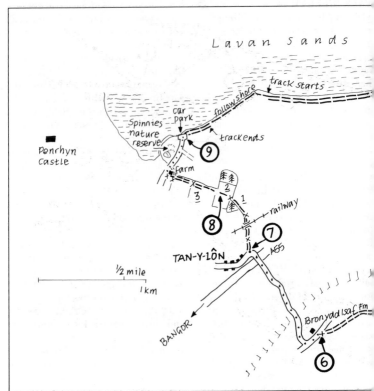

great-crested grebes, red-breasted mergansers, shelducks, curlews and oystercatchers gather to moult on the 2,000-hectare expanse of sands and mudflats. The route across the sands was once a route from London, and Anglesey was joined by dry land until a flood in the 6th century. Across the water, **Beaumaris Castle** is in view. The elaborately fortified stronghold, with symmetrical plan and moat was the last of Edward I's Welsh castles, begun 1295 but never completed and its defences hardly used. It was taken by Owen Glendower in 1403 but recaptured two years later; in the Civil War it was held by the Royalists. On **Puffin Island**, away to the right, there was a Christian community from the 6th century, and remains of a 12th-

century church survive. Its population of puffins dwindled when, in the early 19th century, pickled puffin became a fashionable delicacy.

[g] **Great Orme Head**, near Llandudno, is in view along the coast ahead.

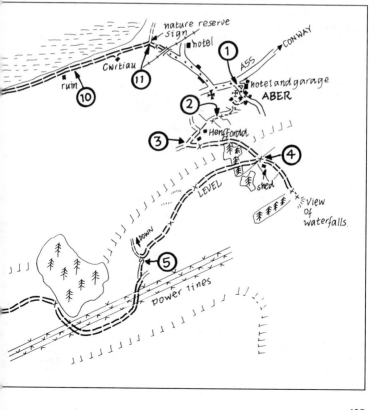

Below Snowdon

This low-level, there-and-back route to the foot of Snowdon, the highest mountain in England and Wales, demonstrates how scenery of awesome grandeur and true wildness can sometimes be experienced without special equipment or risk of losing the way. The route follows a gently rising track up 800ft, past a series of lakes.

Length 5¹/₂ miles (9km), 3¹/₂ hours
Difficulty 2
Start Pen-y-pass car park, at top of A4086, SE of Llanberis. Grid reference 647556
OS maps 1:50,000 115; 1:25,000 Outdoor Leisure 17
Refreshments Café at start

WALK DIRECTIONS

①With your back to the road, take track in far left-hand corner of car park (by board about Miner's Track, which you now follow) [a]. Proceed on well-defined track. Soon Llyn Teyrn (lake) appears down to left, then ② where next lake comes into view, fork right (left goes to shed) [b], soon crossing causeway across lake; then track turns left to follow shore before ③ bending right uphill.

At third lake Glaslyn [c] you can continue to group of ruined buildings where ④ track ends (the continuation up to the summit of Snowdon is by a very steep and rough path marked with cairns and should not be attempted without suitable footwear and clothing). Return the same way.

ON THE ROUTE

[a] **The Miner's Track** One of the spectacular routes up Snowdon, starting at 1,169ft and passing ruins of copper mine buildings before making a steep ascent to the top.
[b] Classic views of **Snowdon** (3,560ft) from the lake, Llyn Llydaw.

The peak's Welsh name, Y Wyddfa Fawr, or Great Tomb, refers to the legend of King Arthur killing the giant Rhita, who was buried on the summit. It may have been into this lake that the sword Excalibur was hurled. The water's striking blueness is caused by the presence of copper.
[c] Mining was carried out at Glaslyn from the latter half of the 18th

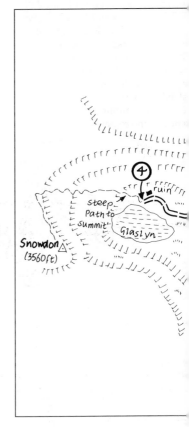

century until 1916. The remoteness of the site necessitated miners to live on site during the week, then walk home over the mountains to Bethesda for the weekend. The lake, 1,971ft above sea level, nestles at the foot of a deep glacial cirque amid the wildest of Welsh mountain scenery. On either side, the famous Snowdon Horseshoe has a wall-like appearance; the walk along its knife-edge top, including buttressed and pinnacled Crib Goch up to your right, is one of Britain's finest high-level routes.

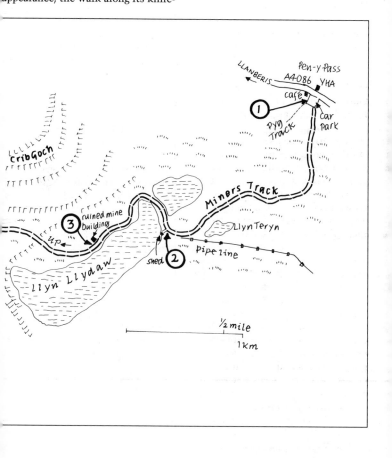

Newborough Warren

The start is tame, through forest plantation, but what follows is highly distinguished: a great expanse of fine sand and sky, looking across the sea to distant outlines of steel-grey mountains. There should be no problems route-finding.

Length 3 miles (5km), 1½ hours
Difficulty 1
Start Newborough Warren Forestry Commission car park; from White Lion in Newborough take signposted road to beach, Traeth and Llanddwyn, passing car park ticket machine and parking beyond roundabout in large car park. Grid reference 405634
OS maps 1:50,000 114; 1:25,000 SH 36/46 (Pathfinder 768)

WALK DIRECTIONS

① Go back to roundabout at car park entrance, and take untarmacked track with barrier and No Entry road sign. Ignore minor side-turns [a].
② After ¾ mile turn left at track T-junction. ③ 200 yards later, reach turning area (with bench on left and take sandy track half right to reach beach. The promontory of Llanddwyn Island begins 200 yards to your right [b] (a broken causeway leads to it): pick up the track along it, which starts by prominent shelter, later passing ruined church and cottages to reach lighthouse at point ④.

Return to the beach, turn right along it. ⑤ After ¾ mile, turn left between wooden posts to enter the car park (or detour ahead along the beach).

ON THE ROUTE

[a] **Newborough Forest** Corsican pines have been planted on part of a vast area of sand dunes. Up to the 14th century this was agricultural land, but floods covered it with sand

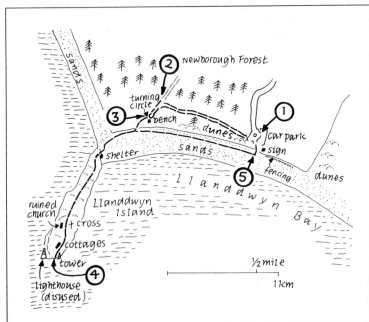

which has developed into dunes.
[b] **Llanddwyn Island** Accessible
except at the highest tides, the
narrow promontory of pre-Cambrian
rock is managed by the Nature
Conservancy Council; walkers are
asked to keep to the paths. The **Soay
sheep** here are survivors of a
prehistoric breed, later cross-bred
with white-faced species to produce
the common Welsh Mountain
Sheep. St Dwynen, patron saint of
lovers, made this place her retreat in
the 5th century, and a **church** was
founded; the ruin you see is a later
(16th-century) structure, with a
modern cross nearby

commemorating the graves of the
old churchyard. By the **cottages**,
once homes of pilots who guided
boats into harbour via Caernarfon
Bay, stands a **cannon** which was
fired as a signal to the townsfolk of
Newborough to help with the lifeboat. At the point, the **beacon tower**
(1800) was superseded by the
lighthouse in 1845. Splendid **views**
from here and the beach of the
Rivals on the Lleyn Peninsula and
the W side of Snowdonia. **Dunlin,
oystercatcher** and **redshank** are
among the bird species found along
these shores.

Pen y Cil and St Mary's Well

The tip of the Lleyn Peninsula, at
the Western extremity of North
Wales, merits a special pilgrimage
for its magnificent coastline; in parts
this is a rough cliff-top route, but
there are remarkable views all
round. Route-finding mostly obvious
but there are some undefined
sections across fields.

Length *Full walk* 7 miles (11 km),
3¹/₂ hours
Difficulty 4
Length *Short walk* 5¹/₂ miles (9km),
2¹/₂ hours
Start Aberdaron, near W end of
Lleyn Peninsula; car park in village
centre. Grid reference 173264
OS maps 1:50,000 123; 1:25,000 SH
12/22/32 (Pathfinder 843)
Refreshments Pubs shops and cafés
in Aberdaron; café at Pen Bryn Bach
Guest House at ⑧

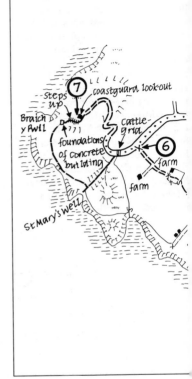

WALK DIRECTIONS

① [a] Make your way to the beach at
Aberdaron and turn right along it. At
end of beach, go up steps, bear left at
signpost (for Porth Meudwy), along
cliff-top. ② After ³/₄ mile go through
kissing-gate, descend to cove at
Porth Meudwy, and go straight up
steps again to cliff-top; take care, as
path has fallen away a little in
places.

After ¹/₂ mile, past two waymark
posts (remains of harbour visible
down to left), path then goes round
inlet of Hen Borth ③: here bear half
right (leaving the cliff-top for the
moment) past waymark post to
prominent National Trust sign on
skyline for Pen y Cil; at the sign
continue on track (still following
coast, but now higher up). Track
soon ends, but make your way
around craggy cliff-top to reach
summit cairn (piled-up stones) on
Pen y Cil [b], and proceed past
the memorial plaque to cross

ladder-stile beside gate ④.

Immediately turn left for 30 yards
to take gate (signposted Mynydd
Mawr) and follow right edge of field
alongside fence. At end, cross ladder-
stile on to rough land, where go
forward on path alongside fence/wall
on right; this reaches gate, and
continues as enclosed track 100
yards to T-junction ⑤. Turn right.
For short walk follow this lane
passing house after ¹/₄ mile and reach
junction. Bear left along road; after ¹/₄
mile take signposted path on right,
up steps and on to raised path
between fields; this is ⑨.
For full walk follow the lane and
turn left after 200 yards on to
enclosed track by waymark post.
After 120 yards, at end of enclosed
section, emerge by gate into field

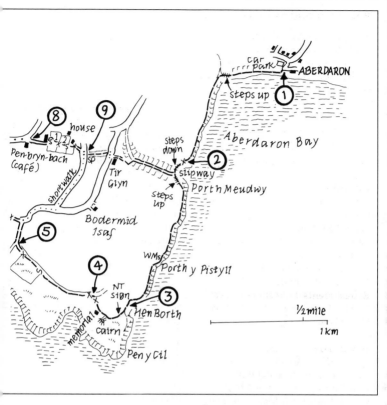

and take ladder-stile beside gate and waymarker ahead, then go half right to gate (with farm beyond).

After the gate turn left alongside fence to take waymarked gate ahead at end of field (not gate in fence on left by cattle-trough): a clear track leads alongside fence and old wall on left. Soon keep forward at corner of farm track (with farm down to left) and take gate on to surfaced lane ⑥.

Detour left along lane. After cattle-grid, immediately take grassy path on left by National Trust sign for Braich-y-Pwll, initially alongside wall on left, then down valley down to sea at St Mary's Well [c] (or you can divert on path on left to summit of Mynydd y Gwyddel). Turn right on reaching the sea and make your way around the grassy cliffs (no path

defined), ascending Mynydd Mawr.

Near the top look to right to find concrete steps up, which lead up to coastguard look-out at summit ⑦ [d]. Proceed on winding concrete track, downhill, which becomes a lane and bends left over the cattle-grid crossed earlier. ⑧ 200 yards after passing a left turn (which you avoid – it is signed as a No Through Road), take track ahead where road bends left, by Pen Bryn Bach Guest House.

Follow the track to the next farm, take gate to right of farmhouse and follow track which bends round to left behind farmhouse, but immediately cross rough steps on right, over wall and into field. Follow left edge of first field to gate, go forward in second field to ladder-stile just to right of right-hand

641

house; continue along left edge of third field to small gate, then turn right on enclosed track which reaches lane. Turn right on lane for 20 yards, then left by signpost up steps on to raised path between fields ⑨.

Soon emerge on lane and turn right (if you are tired you can turn left on the lane, and keep right at the next junctions to follow roads all the way back to the start); after 50 yards take track on left immediately before Tir Glyn.

Track leads to gate into field, where continue alongside left edge. At end of field you are above a valley: take path half right, descending gently towards valley bottom, where path goes through kissing-gate and joins a track. Turn right along the track to reach Porth Meudwy; turn left up steps and retrace route along cliff-top and on to beach into Aberdaron.

ON THE ROUTE

[a] **Aberdaron** Fishing and resort village huddled beside a sandy beach. Y Gegin Fawr Café stands on the site of an ancient pilgrim's kitchen used on route for Bardsey Island. High tide laps against the seaward wall of the 12th-century church, which was founded as a refuge for pilgrims waiting for favourable weather before crossing Bardsey Sound.

[b] View of **Bardsey Island**, a pilgrimage centre from the 5th or 6th century; its earliest monastery was probably founded by St Cadfan of Brittany. A legend that 20,000 saints are buried on Bardsey is perhaps explained by a priest's tomb inscribed *Cum Multitudinem Fratrum* ('with multitude of brethren'), where 'multitudinem' became weathered and could have been misread as 20,000 in Roman numerals. The island has remains of a 13th-century Augustinian abbey, and is now an important area for bird-watching.

[c] **St Mary's Well** This inlet was used for the taking of holy water in the Middle Ages by pilgrims who did not want to chance the treacherous sea crossing of Bardsey Sound.

[d] **View** over the Lleyn Peninsula, described on a view-indicator, including the Rivals (the highest hills on the peninsula); the Harlech area in Snowdonia and, in exceptional conditions, the Wicklow Mountains in Ireland may be seen.

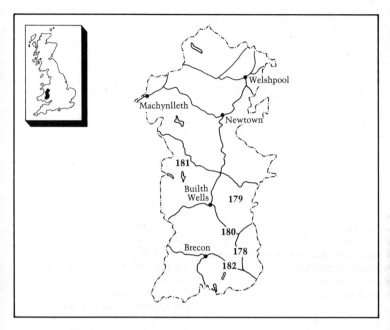

Holiday Which? Good Walks Guide

Waun Fach and Castell Dinas

A round walk taking in the highest
point of the Black Mountains, and a
historic site combining an Iron Age
hill-fort and a Norman castle. Route
is mostly obvious and direction
chosen gives the easier ascent. Other
approaches to Waun Fach involve a
long there-and-back ridge walk from
Hay Bluff or a hard-to-find starting
point in a side valley. Note that
there may be route-finding problems
in bad weather as the descent from
Pen y Manllwyn to Y Grib at ⑦ is
undefined and you need to be able to
see the lower ridge below. Compass
recommended in case of mist.
Ascent 2,000ft.

Length 7 miles (11km), 5¹/₂ hours
Difficulty 5
Start Castle Inn, Pengenffordd, 4
miles S of Talgarth on the A479.
Plenty of parking in large pub car
park (customers only), or more
limited parking on verges.
OS maps 1:50,000 161; 1:25,000
Outdoor Leisure 13
Refreshments Castle Inn at start

WALK DIRECTIONS

① With your back to the Castle Inn,
turn right and uphill along the main
road for 100 yards, then just after
'Pengenffordd' sign turn very sharply
right on to a track between hedges,
initially parallel with road then
running downhill behind pub.
Continue along this track ignoring
side-turns.

② After a ¹/₄ mile, immediately
after entrance to farm on left,
remain on track between hedges as
it bends half left and ignore minor
track going ahead through gate and
uphill. Soon cross stream at ford by
stepping stones, then almost
immediately join farm road coming
in from right. Continue forward and
uphill on this farm road, over rise,
down into valley and sharply right

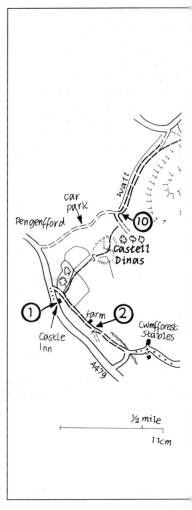

by Cwmfforest stables, then uphill
to road T-junction ③.

Turn right along road for 40 yards,
then left up sunken track between
hedges. Follow up this track through
series of gates until reaching open
moorland ④. Continue uphill and
to right on well-defined path,
initially with fence on right but soon
leaving it. Maintain this direction
for 1 mile to ascend to top of the
ridge by cairn (piled-up stones) ⑤.

At this top, turn sharply left on to

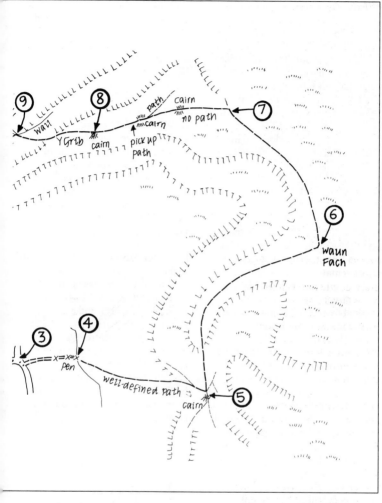

grassy path running along ridge, and follow this as it slowly swings around to the right, running just to right of crest of the ridge with drop into valley on right. As path swings around to right, it rises onto the crest of the ridge and then continues straight ahead to the summit of Waun Fach - the top is rounded and the summit not precisely marked, but the path leads you to a concrete plinth ⑥ [**a**].

At the plinth, turn 90 degrees to left of your previous direction and descend from summit mound on clear path. Follow this for a mile, skirting around the top of the valley of the Rhiangoll to the left, and then ⑦ turn half left off the path to descend diagonally down hillside onto the projecting ridge of Y Grib. Path is initially undefined, but as you descend hillside try to make for a cairn (piled-up stones) halfway down, and then for another cairn on the ridge below you.

This way you should join path running along right-hand side of top of ridge [b] and follow this when it drops diagonally down side of ridge ⑧, starting about 100 yards before large cairn marking end of flat top of ridge. Do not follow main path all the way down to the road, but ⑨ when level with corner of wall on right continue forward on minor path running across slope, to meet and keep left on track with wall on right. Follow track for ½ mile along side of ridge, rising slightly.

⑩ When track turns right and downhill through gate, leave it to turn half left and uphill for 60 yards to brow of ridge. Then cross track and take gate beside stile ahead to ascend hill of Castell Dinas [c]. Cross remains of castle on summit, and exit on ramp across old ditch to reach projecting corner of fence marked by tall ash tree, then turn right and downhill, initially alongside fence on left.

⑪ After 100 yards, by waymark arrow, turn left and downhill towards stile. Go over the stile and turn right, keeping close to fence on right, downhill. At end of this field, go over stile and continue downhill with fence and wood on right; at bottom of valley, cross stream and stile at right-hand corner of field, then half right, with fence on right, to stile near far corner. Once over stile, turn right up track between hedges to main road, then left to return to start.

ON THE ROUTE
[a] **Waun Fach** (2,660ft) The highest summit of the Black Mountains, giving a good view of the plateau-like summits of the area.

[b] Fine **view** N over Talgarth. You may be able to see gliders, which fly from a field just below you, soaring in the updraft created by the steep northern edge of the Black Mountains.

[c] **Castell Dinas**, at 1,476 feet, is the highest castle site in Wales or England. The site was occupied by both an Iron Age hill-fort, with multiple ramparts, and a 12th-century castle with two courts or 'wards'. At the centre of the upper, northern, ward is the site of the collapsed keep, 65 by 40 feet. The castle is believed to have been used by Welsh patriot Owen Glendower as the base for his operations c.1400.

Glascwm and the Forest Inn

An exhilarating tour of some of the most remote country in central Wales, including some bracing hill-top moorland, lonely farmsteads and an eerie deserted valley of abandoned cottages and crooked hawthorn trees. Some tricky route-finding, especially between points ⑨ and ⑩.

Length 9 miles (14.5km), 4¹/₂ hours
Difficulty 3
Start Glascwm village, on unclassified road between Hundred House (A481) and Gladestry (B4594). Grid reference 159532.
Alternatively start from Forest Inn, at junction of A44 and A481. Grid reference 170585 – pick up walk directions from ⑥; no pub on the way if you do it this way round
OS map 1:50,000 148; 1:25,000 SO 05/15 (Pathfinder 992)
Refreshments Forest Inn at ⑥

WALK DIRECTIONS

① [a] Take road opposite the Youth Hostel, and at bottom of hill fork right over stream to follow lane, which is metalled at first but soon becomes a rougher track. After passing through gate, reach cross-track and immediately turn right through first of two metal gates to continue uphill with fence and hedge on left.

Pass through two more gates, and in third field turn half left to follow faint but identifiable track, soon passing old quarry workings on your right. Beyond these bear half right uphill to gate on skyline. Keep half left in fourth field to reach metal gate on far side which soon comes into view ②.

Pass through the gate and turn immediately half right on clear path across moor. Follow for ³/₄ mile, avoiding minor side-tracks to reach cross-track with pool and coniferous forest beyond ③ [b]. Turn right and continue alongside fence on left. When fence on left ends, turn left to follow clear grassy track, again alongside fence on left.

On reaching first gate in fence on left, turn quarter right on clear path which soon drops downhill. Fork right just before fence and pass through metal gate. ④ Soon after passing through gate, ignore all semi-metalled cross-tracks at complex junction, and continue direction on grassy track which soon heads uphill. This track is indistinct in places; when in doubt head for clear dip in the horizon ahead of you.

A clearer track then merges from right. Pass through gate and continue forward with fence on left [c] then pass through a further gate and continue with fence on right. After ¹/₂ mile reach lake ⑤, and turn left on track to reach road (A481). Turn right on road and follow for 300 yards to Forest Inn [d].

⑥ Pass through metal gate immediately to right of pub (as you look at it from the road) and in to field. Continue through gap in fence ahead, and bear half left in second field. Pass through gate in opposite corner of field, and turn right in third field to reach gate and metalled road ⑦. Turn left on road and follow for 1 mile.

On reaching farmstead (Foyce Farm) on your left, metalled road ends: pass through gate on to unmetalled track and continue direction alongside hedge on your left. After 300 yards, on reaching gate to your left, turn right uphill following line of gully in hillside. Path is undefined at this point, but at the top of the rise a small pool becomes visible ahead of you: aim for the left-hand side of this and pass through gate beyond.

Turn left through gate and

647

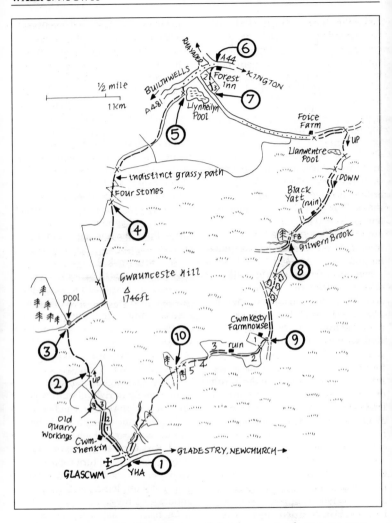

continue on stony track. After 25
yards, where fence on left ends, bear
half left to gate in fence opposite.
Continue on clear track downhill,
soon passing ruined cottage to your
right. 300 yards beyond cottage, pass
through gate at left-hand edge of
woodland.

⑧ Cross stream over plank-bridge
and continue alongside fence on
right. Main track and fence soon
swing away to right – at this point
continue forward uphill on less well-

defined grassy track. You are soon
joined by a fence to your right; pass
through two gates [**e**] and continue
on sunken lane for ¹/₂ mile ignoring
side-turnings.

⑨ Sunken lane emerges just by
farmhouse to your right. Turn right
towards the farmhouse, and then
turn immediately left through the
second of two gates. Follow left-
hand edge of first field, and after 100
yards turn left through gate into
second field. Turn immediately right

and follow fence on right. Pass through gate into top right-hand corner of field, and continue on track between fences, later emerging by ruined cottage on your right. At end of third field, on reaching corner with four gates, take second gate from the right and continue in fourth field with fence on right. Continue through fifth field to emerge through gate on to open moor **(10)**. Continue straight ahead on indistinct path, bisecting the angle between the fence on your right and the main track which bears half left. Ignore two cross-tracks and continue direction on path which later improves, soon passing just to left of fence.

Pass through field-gate at bottom of slope and continue steeply downhill to pass through two more gates to emerge on surfaced track merging from right **(11)**. Ignore gate across track immediately ahead of you and instead turn right through field-gate, continuing with hedge on left and stream on right. Path soon crosses stream and makes for stile in fence opposite. Continue forward along narrow field, later on path between hedges to return to village and starting point.

ON THE ROUTE

[a] **Glascwm** Tiny, remote village in a pretty valley, known nowadays for its small Youth Hostel, which was once the village school. The village was important in the Middle Ages, as a 'clas' settlement – a type of pre-13th-century Welsh monastery and centre of learning. St David's church, which is unusually large for such a small village, has some fine Perpendicular windows and an intricate roof structure.

[b] **Llyn-y-Waun** This is a typical 'Mawn Pool', a tarn formed from the peat (mawn is Welsh for peat). Some of them are man-made and are useful watering-holes for animals, sometimes harbouring colonies of black-headed gulls.

[c] **Llandegley Rocks** Clearly visible from this point on the path, a long craggy ridge a few miles away to your left. These are one of the few outcrops of volcanic rocks in this part of mid-Wales, most of which possess a distinctive wild flora of a kind usually associated with Snowdonia.

[d] **Forest Inn** Wayside inn which was the title and setting of a novel by H.L.V. Fletcher. The big grassy mound across the valley from the pub is the ruin of **Tomen Castle**, a 13th-century ditched motte.

[e] **River Arrow** The little stream to your left here is a source of the River Arrow, one of the prettiest rivers of the Welsh border, which flows E through Kington and Leominster before joining the Lugg and the Wye.

Brechfa Common and the River Wye

A little-known part of the Upper Wye Valley, yielding an easily followed walk with lovely views, skirting moorland in early stages then dropping to follow the River Wye.

Length 7 miles (11km), 3½ hours
Difficulty 3
Start Llyswen on A470 SE of Builth Wells and NE of Brecon; parking easiest near church (in cul-de-sac opposite Griffin Inn and A470 to Brecon). Grid reference 133380
OS maps 1:50,000 161; 1:25,000 SO 03/13 and SO 04/14 (Pathfinder 1038 and 1015)
Refreshments Tea-shop and three pubs in Llyswen

WALK DIRECTIONS

①Follow A470 in signposted Brecon direction to end of village: ②250 yards later, and after last house on right (by speed restriction sign), turn right on track, which leads to gate after only 30 yards; do not take gate which leads into field, but pick up path between hedges to left of this.

Path rises steadily (it can be rather overgrown in summer) to reach junction with lane ③, where continue forward on surfaced lane, over cattle-grid. Just after cattle-grid *either* continue along the lane *or* divert from it by forking left on to common land alongside left-hand hedge, following edge of common until reaching track in front of Brechfa Pool [a] along which turn right to rejoin lane and turn left along the lane.

④ At T-junction, turn right: open land briefly appears on both sides of road, but then it is enclosed. Notice farm (Whitehall) on right of road; just after, road re-emerges on to common land – immediately ⑤ bear left to leave road for fence on your left making for left-hand side of nearby conifer plantation, where pick up well-defined path which runs alongside edge of common with woodland wall close by on your right.

⑥ After passing through gate, field is on right; soon after, wall bends right and the view opens up over a large valley with scattered farmsteads below. Keep right alongside wall or fence on right (now with woods on right again).

⑦ Where (after 200 yards) woods on right end, fork left on to well-defined track down to reach surfaced lane. Turn right on lane and after 100 yards turn right on to level track (or continue along road for easier walking - keep right at next junction, and follow to A470 at ⑧), which soon rejoins woodland fence and later narrows to path. Keep close by the woodland fence all the way until it finally drops to road. There is some bracken to contend with, but it is generally easy to find the way. Turn right on road.

⑧ Turn left along A470 and after 100 yards, just before road crosses stream, take signposted gate on right. Follow left edge of field: soon river Wye is visible immediately down to left. Follow left edge of succession of fields. ⑨ [b] After 1 mile pick up track close to river (i.e. no longer inside field), which later becomes surfaced and then reaches road at edge of Llyswen. Turn right on road and left on main road to centre of village.

ON THE ROUTE

[a] Splendid **views** of the Brecon Beacons and Black Mountains made **Brechfa Pool** a favourite haunt of 19th-century rector Francis Kilvert, whose diary of rural life in this area has become a minor classic. The pool is now a nature reserve.

[b] To the right, **Llangoed Castle** is a large mansion in 17th-century style, mostly rebuilt in 1912 by Clough Williams-Ellis, architect of the Italianate village of Portmeirion in North Wales. This castle is regarded as his best work.

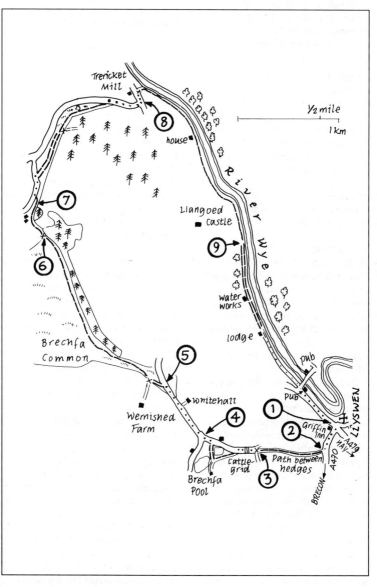

Moelfryn and the Upper Wye

This rugged upland walk takes in moorland tracks and high-level routes above plunging slopes. There is one 700ft ascent. The route is not defined all the way and although there are guiding landmarks, a compass is needed in mist.

Length 5½ miles (9km), 4 hours
Difficulty 4
Start Large layby at top of hill on old Aberystwyth mountain road, 4 miles NW of Rhayader. Take B4518 from Rhayader towards Elan Valley but turn right at end of town at signpost for Aberystwyth mountain road; layby is on left, at the top. Grid reference 921707
OS maps 1:50,000 136 or 147; 1:25,000 SN 86/96 and SN 87/97 (Pathfinder 969 and 948)

WALK DIRECTIONS

① Turn left out of layby, along road (away from Rhayader); after 50 yards, turn sharp right on grassy track (doubling back), and keeping right at next fork. This track runs parallel to road for a distance before losing sight of it; eventually a big view opens out ahead.

② Where another track joins sharply from right (¼ mile before track reaches a prominent standing stone [a]), turn left across the grass (no path defined) to reach head of large valley after 200 yards. Drop down into the valley [b], to pick up prominent path which descends the right-hand side of it; soon ③ this is joined by fence and then woods on left (path later becomes less clear, but fence is a good guide).

④ When farm appears just down to your left, cross stile beside fixed gate, and go over low fence to drop down to farm, reaching it via gate. Go through farmyard and follow track to surfaced lane, turn left along the lane.

⑤ After ¾ mile, immediately after barn and house on right, fork half left on to rising stony track (signposted Bridleway). This winds up to reach gate into open grassland, where the track ends ⑥: continue forward (gently uphill) across the grassland, to fence ahead which soon comes into view. Find a gate in the fence (at time of inspection, this gate was just to right of lone and prominent hawthorn tree). Beyond the gate, turn right on moorland track, initially alongside fence on right, ascending steadily over left-hand shoulder of large hill (Moelfryn).

⑦ [c] At end of ascent, where view opens out ahead, fork left. The track drops, soon going over stream (as track ends) then, ⑧ pass immediately to right of prominent ruined enclosure, and cross a second stream. Thereafter, route is ill defined: bottom of valley is always about 300 yards to your left.

⑨ Immediately after crossing big crags on your left (effectively at the head of the valley, which flattens out beyond this) turn left to cross the valley's main stream and pick up prominent rising stony track beyond. The track ends after only a few yards, but maintain direction uphill to reach main road. Turn left on road to reach layby at starting point.

ON THE ROUTE

[a] **Standing stone** This stone, called **Maen Serth** stands over 7ft high and is probably of Bronze Age origin. It is traditionally said to be on the site where a Welsh chieftain was slain by the English after Roger Mortimer was unhorsed in a 12th-century tournament.
[b] View ahead over the **Wye and Marteg valleys**. By the confluence of the two valleys, a motorist stopped in 1980 and spotted a puma-like

creature lying on a nearby rock. Several sightings, including one by the county surveyor, have been made. Despite much injury to livestock the 'Powys beast' has never been found.

In the Marteg valley lies Gilfach nature reserve. Here an abandoned farm, where no modern agricultural practices had been used and a rich

and diverse flora was supported, a holiday development was threatened but happily the local nature trust managed to find the funds to purchase the estate.

[c] View over the wilderness of the **Cambrian Mountains**, a large and unpopulated area which supports some rare bird life, including the red kite and peregrine falcon.

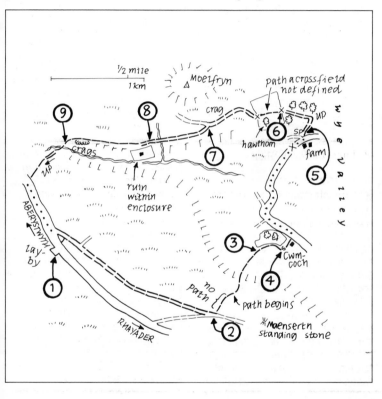

Tretower Castle and Cefn Moel

A mostly low-level walk in the Black Mountains along field-paths, tracks and quiet lanes, but rising on to the moorland ridge of Cefn Moel for a total change of mood. Field-paths not waymarked, and a few sections require care.

Length 7¹/₂ miles (12km), 4 hours
Difficulty 3–4
Start Bwlch village, on A40 between Brecon and Crickhowell. Limited roadside parking by bus shelter beside New Inn.
Grid reference 149220
OS maps 1:50,000 161; 1:25,000 Outdoor Leisure 13
Refreshments Pubs and shops at Bwlch; pub at Tretower; pub and filling station (with small shop) at Cwmdu

WALK DIRECTIONS

① With New Inn on right, follow A40 downhill out of village. Soon the road bends to right; in the middle of the bend take left turn called Tregraig Road: ignore right forks to housing estates. After ¹/₂ mile this lane rises, and ends by stone house **②**.

Turn right, through waymarked gate and enter field, descending via right edge. Midway down field this edge becomes a sunken path: join it, bending left at bottom right-hand corner of field on path now between hedges, soon over stile and continuing to drop between hedges.

③ At end of enclosed section of path, take gate on right into field containing barn on its far side and immediately turn left (continuing previous direction) alongside fence on left to join surfaced lane junction via stile. Take the lane ahead, and turn left at next junction by farms.

Where lane ends by Pont Gaer house on your right, go forward and slightly right (not into field), initially alongside garden fence, on enclosed track. **④** On crossing stream at bridge, keep right (avoid enclosed path ahead) through gate, along right edge of three fields. Just before end of third field, take gate on right and go forward diagonally, to

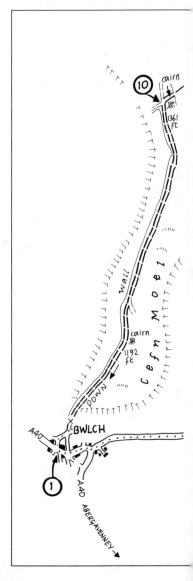

xt gate a few yards away, giving
to concrete bridge over stream.
oceed on farm track towards
etower Castle.

⑤ Emerge on to road in front of
apel. Go forward to reach castle
trance [**a**], forking left by church
r continuation of walk to reach

main road. Left on road. **⑥** 300
yards after end of village, fork right
on to enclosed track: ignore gates
into fields and proceed ¾ mile to
reach corner of road. Go forward,
ignoring turns to left and right on
road which later swings left to reach
T-junction by Cwmdu church **⑦**.

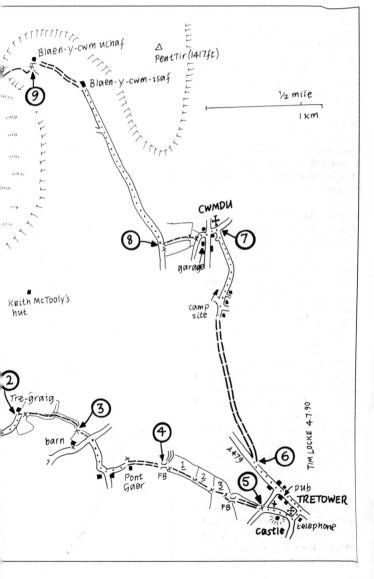

Turn left, cross main road and take minor road opposite – after 50 yards, this passes entrance to Neuadd on right; 30 yards after, take field-gate on right (as road is about to bend left) and go forward past telegraph post to prominent gate ahead. Proceed along left edge of next field (note: right of way actually goes along other side of hedge on your left but the way was obstructed at time of inspection).

(8) Emerge by gate on to surfaced lane and turn right. Ignore left turn after 1/2 mile, and 1/4 mile later keep to left of farm (Blaen-y-cwm-isaf) to follow hard track up to next farm, immediately before which take broad gate in the fence up slope on your left, to reach edge of rough land (9). Go straight up (no path) 50 yards to find beginning of broad grassy path leading diagonally right up to top of ridge of Cefn Moel.

At top, go forward at minor cross junction, then 30 yards later (10) turn left at crossing of tracks by cairn (piled-up stones) and fence corner [▶ Proceed on the track alongside fence or wall on right for entire length of the ridge, ignoring all left forks. Eventually track drops to gate on to end of lane by house. Keep right at T-junction, left at next junction to reach Bwlch.

ON THE ROUTE
[a] **Tretower Castle** (open 26 Mar–24 Oct 9.30–6.30; 27 Oct–24 Mar 9.30–4) 13th-century tower adjacent to a well-preserved 14th- and 15th-century house (Tretower Court).
[b] Fine views, to the right of **Brecon Beacons** (2,906ft), the highest point in South Wales, and **Llangorse Lake** to the left, **Crickhowell** can be seen in the valley.